The American Revolution Reborn

THE AMERICAN REVOLUTION REBORN

Edited by

Patrick Spero

and

Michael Zuckerman

UNIVERSITY OF PENNSYLVANIA PRESS

PHILADELPHIA

Copyright © 2016 University of Pennsylvania Press

All rights reserved. Except for brief quotations used for purposes of review or scholarly citation, none of this book may be reproduced in any form by any means without written permission from the publisher.

Published by
University of Pennsylvania Press
Philadelphia, Pennsylvania 19104-4112
www.upenn.edu/pennpress

Printed in the United States of America on acid-free paper
10 9 8 7 6 5 4 3 2 1

Library of Congress Cataloging-in-Publication Data
ISBN 978-0-8122-4846-3

To Frank Fox, who inspired us

And to the American Philosophical Society, Boston Beer, the David Library of the American Revolution, HISTORY, the Library Company of Philadelphia, the McNeil Center for Early American Studies, and the Museum of the American Revolution, who helped make it happen

CONTENTS

Introduction. Origins 1
Patrick Spero

PART I. CIVIL WARS: CHALLENGING THE PATRIOTIC NARRATIVE

Chapter 1. War Stories: Remembering and Forgetting
the American Revolution 9
Michael A. McDonnell

Chapter 2. The Intimacies of Occupation: Loyalties,
Compromise, and Betrayal in Revolutionary-Era Newport 29
Travis Glasson

Chapter 3. Uncommon Cause: The Challenges of
Disaffection in Revolutionary Pennsylvania 48
Aaron Sullivan

Chapter 4. Loyalism, Citizenship, American Identity:
The Shoemaker Family 68
Kimberly Nath

Chapter 5. "Executioners of Their Friends and Brethren":
Naval Impressment as an Atlantic Civil War 82
Denver Brunsman

PART II. WIDER HORIZONS: DECENTERING THE NATIONALISTIC NARRATIVE

Chapter 6. British Union and American Revolution:
Imperial Authority and the Multinational State 107
Ned C. Landsman

Chapter 7. Revisiting the Bishop Controversy 132
Katherine Carté Engel

Chapter 8. Empire's Vital Extremities: British Africa
and the Coming of the American Revolution 150
Bryan Rosenblithe

Chapter 9. The Great Awakening, Presbyterian Education,
and the Mobilization of Power in the Revolutionary Mid-Atlantic 168
Mark Boonshoft

PART III. NEW DIRECTIONS

Chapter 10. "This Is the Skin of a Whit[e] Man":
Material Memories of Violence in Sullivan's Campaign 187
Zara Anishanslin

Chapter 11. Environmental History and the War of Independence:
Saltpeter and the Continental Army's Shortage of Gunpowder 205
David C. Hsiung

Chapter 12. The Problem of Order and the Transfer of
Slave Property in the Revolutionary South 231
Matthew Spooner

PART IV. LEGACIES: THE AFTERLIFE OF
THE AMERICAN REVOLUTION

Chapter 13. The United States and the Transformation of
Transatlantic Migration During the Age of Revolution
and Emancipation 251
Aaron Spencer Fogleman

Chapter 14. First Partition: The Troubled Origins of
the Mason-Dixon Line 270
Edward G. Gray

Chapter 15. The Power to Be Reborn 289
David S. Shields

Conclusion. Beyond the Rebirth of the Revolution: Coming to
Terms with Coming of Age   300
Michael Zuckerman

Notes   319

List of Contributors   397

Index   401

Acknowledgments   409

Introduction

Origins

PATRICK SPERO

The ground strewed with the dead and the dying; the impetuous charge; the steady and successful repulse; the loud call to repeated assault; the summoning of all that is manly to repeated resistance; a thousand bosoms freely and fearlessly bared in an instant to whatever of terror there may be in war and death . . .

VETERANS! you are the remnant of many a well-fought field. You bring with you marks of honor from Trenton and Monmouth, from Yorktown, Camden, Bennington, and Saratoga. VETERANS OF HALF A CENTURY! when in your youthful days you put everything at hazard in your country's cause . . .
—Daniel Webster, Bunker Hill Monument,
dedication address, June 17, 1825

When Americans in the nineteenth century remembered the Revolutionary War, as Daniel Webster did at the Bunker Hill dedication in 1825, they painted images with their words of defiant patriots facing off with British redcoats. They told of valiant soldiers fighting for the cause of democracy and of a populace rallying around them and the cause for which they fought. "The principle of free government adheres to the American soil," Webster declared in the same speech. "It is bedded in it, immovable as its mountains." Such a rendering of the Revolution was intended to instill democratic ideals and nationalistic feeling in a generation born after the war. As Webster noted with no small a hint of concern, "Those who established our liberty and our government are daily dropping from among us. The great trust now descends to new hands." The idealism imbedded in Webster's speech represents the very first popular interpretation of the American Revolution. Its influence still lingers in the American psyche today.

But, as *The American Revolution Reborn* shows, the experience of living through the American Revolution, rather than its romantic memory, was a far more complicated affair than Webster's glorified depiction. This perspective can get lost as time makes the American victory at Yorktown in 1781 appear a mere fait accompli and the eventual prosperity of the nation that the war secured an inevitable result of a democratic revolution. The historians in this volume avoid this trap. The authors themselves embody the promise of the present generation, and their work hints at a future of renewed interest in the struggle for independence. They recover the uncertainty, fears, and discord in American society during a war that did eventually succeed and give rise to a new nation. But that eventuality is of little concern to them. Rather, they want to treat the Revolution as a historic event divorced from the interpretative pressures the present can sometimes place on historians. For our authors, the American Revolution was a lived experience filled with many contingencies and alternative paths. As one of them asks, "What did this divisive and bloody wartime experience *mean* to its many participants?"

Consider some of the things the authors of the following chapters observe. They present strong evidence to suggest that a majority of the American populace were neutrals. Indeed, a set of our authors challenge us to rethink loyalty and allegiance during the war. Seaports, they show, were torn apart by warring armies, with many residents simply swearing allegiance to whatever power prevailed at a given moment. Other urban denizens seized the opportunity British occupation presented to declare their continued loyalty to the British Crown. The American countryside was no different. Disillusioned with the tactics of both sides, many farmers simply tried to stay out of the fray. On the high seas, impressment, one of the reasons Thomas Jefferson cited in justifying American independence in the Declaration, was, in fact, a tool both sides used, and sometimes imprisoned sailors switched sides as a means to find their way back home.

Meanwhile, other contributors provide new insights on the way the war for American independence altered the status quo in many colonies turned states. War measures in the South, for instance, strengthened the institution of slavery, as patriots' use of slave labor to serve their political and military ends also rechanneled the distribution of wealth and power in their favor. The production of saltpeter, an ingredient necessary for conducting war in the eighteenth century, spurred a race to manufacture it on the home front that challenged Americans' knowledge of science and the environment.

Finally, other essayists take a more global perspective on the Revolution to demonstrate that the coming of the American Revolution and the war itself tested the limits of an expanding British Empire. The fracture of the British Atlantic community raised questions about the best ways to hold an empire together politically, while upsetting the social institutions that once bound colonists and Britons together.

While these perspectives aim to cast the American Revolution anew, they also aim to do something more. They mean to reinvigorate a field. Collectively, the essays reflect both the past successes of and current frustrations with a previous generation of scholars who once dominated the scholarly landscape. For the past several decades, scholarship on the Revolution has generally fallen into one of three competing schools. There is the neo-whig school that emphasizes the power of ideas as the catalyst for the Revolution. Then there is the neo-progressive school, which pays more attention to the economic discontent and social discord in the colonies that propelled common people to rebellion. And then there is the neo-imperial school, which focuses on the breakdown of imperial politics and the function (and dysfunction) of institutions of empire. These historiographical schools have expanded our understanding of the cause and course of the American Revolution, and they have all influenced the contributors to this volume, sometimes explicitly, more often implicitly. But none of our authors attempt to conform to one school or another. Rather, they seek to upset the patterns of historical inquiry that have defined scholarship for the past generation.

Our authors also disconnect their scholarly interpretations of the Revolution from the nation-building project to which it has so often been tied. Americans have always linked the American Revolution and the founding of the United States to the political efforts they undertake in the present, as Webster's speech reminds us. The Revolution, in other words, has persisted in the present. Its principles—real or imagined—have animated our society. It has been alive in our popular imagination, in the best-seller lists, in dramatic miniseries, in the inaugural addresses of presidents, in the protests that have filled our streets and parks, and in the built environment of our oldest cities.

The present has always influenced historians' interpretations as well. The nineteenth-century historians who vaunted the rise of a democratic nation were self-consciously trying to inculcate certain values in a populace still learning about itself. In the early twentieth century, historians concerned about the rise of big business and corruption in politics in their own time took a more jaundiced view of elite leaders at the founding, with many arguing that economic interest rather than political principles drove revolutionary fervor. The major schools of interpretation in the late twentieth century likewise tracked contemporary events. The neo-whigs' emphasis on the power of ideas to explain the cause of the Revolution and lay the foundation for the Constitution coincided with the heightening of the Cold War clash of ideologies. The neo-progressives' insistence on the power of ordinary people and the importance of class rose alongside the New Left and its critique of American power and capitalism. And the neo-imperial scholars' stress on political institutions and other processes that stretched across the Atlantic tracked the growth of international organizations and the greater integration of economies around the world in the 1980s and 1990s.

By examining the Revolution as a lived experience shadowed by an unknown future, our contributors avoid the implicit teleology of the scholars who preceded them. Their depictions of this moment may not lead to the clear interpretative frameworks that once defined studies in the field, but they may, ironically, provide a more accurate picture of an event that was, after all, a very messy one. Indeed, the great schools of thought that have dominated the history of the era, each with its own established line of interpretation, may have obscured more than clarified the true nature of the American Revolution. Instead of trying to fit the past into one of these schools, our authors embrace the diversity of experience and reject straightforward narratives to explain the course of history.

In this volume the Revolution appears as a civil war as much as a fight for independence, as the product of a failed imperial project as much as a moment of nation building, and as influenced by the environment as much as by ideology. This impetus to complicate the interpretation of the Revolution might seem to run counter to what is often taken to be the historian's obligation to clarify the past. But the willful quest for messiness is also part of a cycle that defines the development of most historiographies. When entrenched paradigms loom over a field in an almost stifling way, as seems to have been the case with the three interpretative schools of the previous generation, new scholars aim to unsettle the established narratives and approaches. While still influenced by the historians who came before them, the scholars contributing to this volume nonetheless refuse to be bound by their predecessors. Individually, they hope that their new perspectives on the Revolution will produce new interpretations of the past that move our understanding forward in new directions. Indeed, the geographic, methodological, and thematic range of these papers suggests that the new paradigm, at least for now, may be that there is no single paradigm that can do justice to an event as multifaceted as the American Revolution.

Although almost all our authors share this common impetus, their convergence did not arise by design. Each essay began as a separate study undertaken by an individual scholar, and most of them are parts of large book-length projects currently under way. In themselves, the chapters range widely. Geographically, they span a considerable swath of the globe, covering events in Europe, Africa, and America. Topically, they touch matters as diverse as the integration of Scotland with England, British policies toward West Africa during the 1760s, and the political economy of southern slave plantations. Methodologically, they run the gamut as well, with the environment, material culture, high and low politics, religion, demography, and economy as the foci of their analyses. Their diversity reflects the very nature of an event of global proportions.

Yet, despite their differences, some common themes help tie certain sets of these essays together. We have therefore arranged the essays into four parts, each of which elaborates a common concern that unites the group.

The first is "Civil Wars: Challenging the Patriotic Narrative." This cluster of essays investigates the disparate loyalties of men and women living through the American Revolution in conditions of constant flux. Rather than depict the war as one fought by a doggedly determined people bent on overthrowing a monarchy, they reveal the fears, anxieties, and mixed loyalties of a populace caught in the midst of a destructive and violent conflict. For example, one of our authors finds that in 1777, as Philadelphia fell to the British and Washington hunkered down at Valley Forge, most Americans were unsure of what the fighting was really about, what its outcome would be, and what thirteen independent yet united states would become. Another brings the turmoil of Newport, Rhode Island, to life by showing the trials and tribulations of people battered by war and torn apart by competing allegiances. Similar uncertainty is peppered throughout the essays of this volume. Whether looking at the internal battles of families torn apart by the war or at people trying to survive in an occupied city, these authors show that the experience of war was traumatic for most Americans and that the convictions and commitments of those caught in the midst of the violence were anything but unequivocal.

The second is "Wider Horizons: Decentering the Nationalistic Narrative." These pieces shift our focus from North America to consider the way other forces and parts of the world either affected or were affected by the American Revolution. Here we have historians examining the way institutions functioned in the era of the Revolution. One author contrasts the success of the Anglo-Scottish union in 1707 with the failure of the British Empire after 1763. Another shows the fissures emerging in the Anglican communion in the years preceding the Revolution. Another looks at the growth of dissenting academies in the eighteenth century and reveals that these institutions in North America educated a crop of leaders who challenged the established authority of the British Empire in 1776. Yet another shifts our gaze to West Africa to show that the divisiveness of the Revolution reverberated throughout the British Empire. Whether examining attempts to grow transatlantic denominations or comparing the politics of the Scottish Union of 1707 to the failed attempt to integrate North America into the empire in the 1760s, they show that, in the years before American independence, most British people on both sides of the ocean were more concerned with strengthening the empire than with dividing it and building anew.

The third is "New Directions." These investigations advance innovative methodological approaches to the age of the Revolution. A southern scholar analyzes the hidden economy of slave labor. A student of material culture explores the strange history of a preserved piece of skin. An environmental historian canvasses the technical and economic factors that limited American production of the saltpeter the rebels had to have to sustain their war effort.

The fourth and final part is "Legacies: The Afterlife of the American Revolution." These essays call into question our assumptions about the Revolution as a founding moment for the nation. They variously argue that it had a massively potent and positive effect on the new nation and the New World, that it had no real effect, and that its outcome remained unresolved long after the constitutional settlement. While the authors of these studies appear to agree on very little, together they force us to confront the significance of the American Revolution to the history of the United States. Indeed, their very disparities capture the spirit of this book.

The Conclusion tries to do the one thing many of these essays avoided: put their collective work in the context of the present. We hope that the range and diversity of viewpoints contained in these pages will spur scholars and students to think on the Revolution anew.

PART I

Civil Wars: Challenging the Patriotic Narrative

CHAPTER 1

War Stories

Remembering and Forgetting the American Revolution

MICHAEL A. MCDONNELL

We all love a good story. And the best stories usually pit good against bad, heroes against villains. Such stories become more compelling when they take on larger meaning than the plot itself. When a battle between good guys and bad guys becomes a battle between the forces of liberty and tyranny. When the fate of humankind hangs in the balance. When David takes on Goliath and, against all the odds, triumphs in the face of adversity, in a glorious cause.

Such stories are irresistible, especially when they are founding stories. The story of the American war for independence is one such tale. As William Huntting Howell has recently written, "the American Revolution narrates beautifully in the popular imagination." There is a clear beginning, at Lexington and Concord, and a series of "progressive middles, unfolding against now-hallowed spaces." Epic battles at Bunker Hill, Trenton, Saratoga, and Cowpens. Trials and tribulations at New York, Valley Forge, Morristown, and Charleston. Clear lines drawn between the patriots and the monarchical forces of the British and their loyalist minions. And the stakes are high and obvious: independence or dependence; democracy or monarchy; liberty or tyranny. The choices are simple and the denouement is almost inevitable: victory at Yorktown and the creation of a new nation.[1]

Historians are equally wedded to this tale. We frame our books and the courses that we teach around the story. We follow the same plot from resistance to independence, from Lexington to Yorktown, and from the Continental Congress to the federal constitution. To be sure, we tell the story in different ways and with different emphases. Some of us focus on patriot leaders, others highlight the role of popular action. We differ over the motives of patriots and the relative importance of particular groups and people. We disagree over whether rights and liberties were fought for or ought to have been extended to different communities within that new nation. We puzzle over the seeming contradictions inherent in a war fought for liberty that also entrenched slavery and legitimated the conquest of Native Americans. Sometimes we pause and consider those who opposed the unfolding story. But rarely do we question the story itself.[2]

The trouble is, far too many people—and far too many messy details—end up left out of this simple tale. When the story of the Revolution becomes a contest between freedom-seeking patriots and the despotic British, what are we to do with Native Americans who sought their own independence in this era? How do we explain the many different choices made by African Americans in bondage? How can "Tories," or loyalists, be anything other than shadowy or stuffy figures who dared oppose "liberty"? What are we to make of women who sought to keep their husbands and sons at home? And what can we make of the tens of thousands of people who were disaffected or alienated from both sides or tried to tack between them to make the best of a bad situation. At best, we compartmentalize these "others." We have separate lectures or chapters on women or African Americans in the Revolution or on the war in the West. Sometimes we make room for familial divisions and the civil war in the South, and every now and again we pause to consider "neutrals" or the "disaffected." But we all know they are not the main story. That one belongs solely to patriots who pursued liberty and independence and founded a nation. These "others" do not—cannot—fit in easily to that more important narrative, despite the fact that they made up far more than a majority of the population at the time.[3]

We tell the story this way in part because it was the tale that at least some of the participants at the time desperately wanted us to believe. Beginning in 1783 and continuing through to 1815, some sixty or so histories were written by at least forty-three different writers. Though these authors differed in their politics, they were all of the same class and they were remarkably uniform in their interpretation of events. They wrote with a clear agenda. They "self-consciously set out," as Arthur Shaffer observed some time ago, "to form the entire American past into a pattern that contradicted the reality of American life." Though "local loyalties and internal dissensions were the persistent facts, . . . national unity became the interpretive credo." As one of those early historians, David Ramsay, described it, "a sense of common danger extinguished selfish passions" during the conflict, and "local attachments and partialities were sacrificed on the altar of patriotism." These writers were all nationalists. They were all committed to the new nation and to promoting the unity they thought vital to it. So they rewrote colonial and Revolutionary history to promote an idea of a gradual, inevitable, and orderly evolution of a new nation based on a common set of ideals. They wrote to give meaning to a confusing past and what seemed like a senseless war to many. Without this idea of history, Shaffer noted, the birth of the United States would have appeared as a "parochial event born of chance circumstances."[4]

Civic- and nationalist-minded compatriots of these early historians joined them in their early efforts to orate, commemorate, and remember the Revolution in the same way. In the 1780s and 1790s, memories of the war were used in intensely partisan ways, but the metaphors of both sides almost invariably returned to shared images of battle and of a justifiable conflict that was forced upon them by the British. Though a few of these commentators occasionally acknowledged the divisive civil war that it was, most tried to remember selectively and so emphasized that the war was also humane and reasonable. As one orator asserted: "Other revolutions have been conducted with sanguinary violence; ours with a spirit of dignified moderation, worthy of the cause, and characteristic of the nation. The patriots of the revolution were as humane as they were brave." These early celebrants made sense of the Revolution by sanitizing it and creating a clear narrative of a righteous cause that required and justified a response. As several observers have noted, the public memory of the war was carefully controlled by elites in the generation or two after the event. And the interpretive framework laid down by those founding generations—the story they told—"predominated for decades and remains influential even today."[5]

But what we seem to have forgotten is that this story was told almost exclusively by the "winners" themselves, using the same language and labels they employed at the time to justify and legitimate a costly, divisive, bloody, and perhaps unnecessary war. Those who survived the war and came out on top consciously and unconsciously forgot the details of that messy war and instead wrote a story about the triumph of liberty and the birth of a nation. And because a new nation did indeed emerge from that war and survive till today, people believed that story. We continue to believe it.[6]

After almost 230 years, can we tell a different story? Where can we start? If we had the will, how could we break this impasse? How could we write a more comprehensive and more inclusive story of the Revolutionary War? The first step would have to be to uncouple the war from the founding of a nation. To undo what those first historians and nationalists tied together. To forget what came next and dwell instead on the war itself. To take the war seriously as a historical phenomenon and not merely as a waymark on the route to the founding of a nation. To tell a story that gives as much weight to the murderous riots and reckless plundering and privateering that occurred as to the deliberations of the Continental Congress; to the vicious rapes and bloody cruelties perpetrated by both sides as to the suffering of the Continental Army; to the deliberate burning and looting of houses, farms, and whole towns as to the Declaration of Independence; to the painful separations and thousands of lost lives as to the victory at Yorktown; to the destructive economic effects of the war leading to what one historian has called the "First Great Depression" as to the political machinations that led to the Constitutional Convention.[7]

We might also abandon—or at least nuance—the labels that the winners themselves used first to appropriate the moral high ground in the developing contest and then to cast the conflagration in historically favorable terms. Some colonists, reeling from accusations of treasonable rebellion, quickly emphasized their patriotism and later wrote as if all "Americans" were with them. The British preferred to call them rebels, and many other colonists regarded them as dangerous, designing agitators. As Timothy Breen has recently reminded us, in another context militant patriots might also be considered insurgents. Nor were the many who were not patriots easily lumped under the label "Tories," or its later counterpart, "loyalists." Thousands made decisions about the developing conflict that had little to do with the pejorative political term used by patriots. Thousands more were labeled as neutrals or the disaffected by patriots. Historians still struggle to comprehend an extraordinarily wide array of peoples using such simple and ultimately opaque terms. Finally, we might abandon the term "liberty" as the driving force of patriots. There were too many different kinds of liberty at stake during the war, often conflicting with each other, and equally often invoked to trample someone else's liberty. When both the British and the patriots claimed the mantle of "torchbearers of liberty," we should surely suspect the conceptual usefulness of the term, no matter how important it might seem to the rhetoric of the age.[8]

Another possible way to start writing a more inclusive and comprehensive history would be to consider a counterfactual: what if the British had put down the rebellion and won the war? It is not hard to envision. Patriots thought they were about to lose everything at several critical moments during the war. Conservative historians today emphasize the role of luck, chance, and even divine providence in the winning of independence. Most military historians acknowledge that had the French not entered the war when they did, the British would have retained most if not all the colonies. Part of the wonder of the more familiar story is knowing the patriots had to overcome great obstacles to achieve their ends and almost failed—after the evacuation of New York in 1776, following the occupation of Philadelphia in 1777, or in the wake of the fall of Charleston in 1780 and the successful British invasion of Virginia in early 1781.

If we could just imagine this, our story might change dramatically. We would have to look much harder at those "great obstacles" instead. Rather than a tale that showed how a nation conceived in liberty came to be, we would have to tell a story that emphasized the diversity inherent across and within thirteen colonies with different histories, cultures, and economies—a diversity that continued to undermine efforts at unity. We would have to comprehend how clashing interests, militant action, and terror played a role in driving a coalition of often unlike-minded people into a premature declaration of independence. Our histories would have to give at least equal weight to the role and motives of the thousands of colonists who did not support independence. We would also have to explain why both patriots and loyalists failed to capture the imagination of so many of their neighbors in making their arguments for or against independence. We might then be forced to acknowledge and understand why almost every state turned to conscription to raise its quota of Continental soldiers, most within a year of the Declaration of Independence. Ultimately we would be compelled to frame our histories of the war for independence not just as a nation-making event but also as a complicated and divisive civil war, one in which more Americans fought against each other than in any other war except the nineteenth-century Civil War. Only then might we be able to understand how a supposedly popular war for independence became one of the longest wars in America's history.[9]

We would also have to acknowledge that the Revolutionary War was one of the bloodiest in America's history. We know that at least 25,000 and perhaps as many as 36,000 people died during active military service on the patriot side. Most did not die a "glorious" death in battle like General Montgomery at the gates of Quebec. Many were conscripts and died for a cause they may not have understood or in which they did not believe. They usually died far from home, often hungry, and in the midst of deprivation. Seventeen thousand of them died from starvation or disease. They suffered on British prison ships as much as they did at patriot winter encampments. Perhaps most shocking, we still have no reliable statistics for the number of dead among loyalists, Native Americans, and civilians. For over two centuries now, no one has bothered to try counting them up. The patriot story has left the war dead in its shadow.[10]

Even if we leave this worrisome fact aside for a moment, we surely still have to tell a war story that can comprehend the staggering numbers of people enmeshed and uprooted in this conflict. The per capita equivalents of the number of deaths, refugees, and combatants in this civil war should alone make us rethink the narrative we spin around it. What would we call a civil conflict today that saw some millions of Americans take up arms against each other? What would we call a war that produced an exodus of seven million refugees and the deaths of at least three million more people? A "Glorious Cause"? A patriotic war for liberty? There can only be one answer: we would call it a human tragedy.[11]

The point is that we need to create a history that makes sense of the experiences of the many rather than the few—of the losers as well as the winners, and of the hundreds of thousands who sometimes won little, lost a lot, and most certainly suffered much. We have to refrain from using terms such as "*the* colonists" or "Americans." And we have to stop trying to shoehorn so many different stories and complicated events into a linear narrative of the rise and triumph of something so vague as "liberty." In short, we still need to examine the war on its own terms and create a body of scholarship as rich as the literature on the American Civil War, or the First World War, or just about any other war that was not also a founding moment. As we do this, we also need to start measuring the impact of this civil war and its meaning(s) among its very diverse participants. We have much work to do yet to understand fully the social, cultural, economic, ideological, religious, and political consequences of this cataclysmic event. What did this divisive and bloody wartime experience *mean* to its many participants?[12]

* * *

For now, one thing we can do is to listen to other kinds of war stories. Though there are relatively few of them, at least several dozen ordinary participants wrote their own personal accounts of the war, sometimes years afterward. In style, substance, and tone, they often contrasted markedly with the celebratory public histories being written at the time and even those written today. Some historians have struggled to use them. But even such exceptional ones have generally ended up including them more for illustrative purposes as subjects in their own right. These divergent accounts have rarely occasioned reflection on the conflict from a different perspective.

Consider John Greenwood. He seemed to embody the patriotic spirit of ordinary people. David McCullough certainly thought so. Reading Greenwood's memoir, McCullough noted that when Greenwood got news of the bloodshed at Lexington and Concord, the sixteen-year-old "set off on foot with little more than the clothes on his back" and walked 150 miles to join the patriot forces. McCullough quotes Greenwood announcing to astonished listeners that even at his tender age, he was "going to fight for my country." McCullough then draws details from Greenwood's memoir to add color and detail to his story of the travails of the Continental Army through 1776.[13]

Yet Greenwood, even after thirty-five years, could not gloss the reality so easily. He told a different story. He had been sent away from the family home in Boston in 1773, most likely to serve an apprenticeship with his uncle, who was a cabinetmaker. When word came of bloodshed to the south in the spring of 1775, Greenwood had not seen his family for over two years. He saw his chance and slipped away in the confusion. He was very clear about his motives: "My reason for going was I wished to see my parents, who, I was afraid, would all be killed by the British, for, as I observed before, nothing was talked of but murder and war." On the road back to Boston, he quickly learned that if he played his fife and told people he was going to join the army—"to fight for my country"—he was almost guaranteed "free quarters nearly upon the entire route." People were, he said, "astonished such a little boy, and alone, should have such courage." Only when he arrived at Boston and was refused entry to the besieged city did he finally enlist—but only because he found himself completely alone and desperate for the food and clothing new volunteers were promised. "There I stood alone," he wrote, "without a friend or a house to shelter me for the night, surrounded by women and children, some crying and others in different situations of distress." He thought the army he was enlisting in at the time was no better than "a mob," but he felt he had no choice.[14]

Greenwood almost deserted after three weeks with the army but ended up returning and reenlisting for one more year. Again he made it clear that he did so because he was determined not to go back to his uncle's care and equally committed to finding his family. He served in the unsuccessful invasion of Canada and a little later in the surprise attack at Trenton. But a few days after the battle, his enlistment expired, and despite being offered almost double his pay for the past three months to stay on another six weeks, Greenwood refused. "I did not enlist for the purpose of remaining in the army, but only through necessity, as I could not get to my parents in Boston, I was determined to quit as soon as my time was out." Greenwood had no mystical conversion to the patriot cause in the course of serving in the army. Though there is some anecdotal evidence that he served again in the militia in 1777 and may have done time in an independent company near White Plains in 1778, Greenwood himself never mentioned it in his memoir. He had had enough of army life. Instead, he did what many young New Englanders did during the war. He joined a privateer, bent on finding a fortune plundering vulnerable ships along the eastern seaboard and down into the Caribbean. Though Greenwood took note of the ships he served on that were officially commissioned privateers by Congress, not all carried letters of marque. In other words, he turned to pirating. And even so long after the war, he could not bring himself to omit mention of the fact that he also joined a British ship in order to escape captivity in Jamaica. Greenwood the patriot ended his Revolutionary War career by plundering a ship that flew the flag of his country's Spanish ally.[15]

Even if we overlook Greenwood's initial motivation for enlisting, he was at best a "patriot" for a year or two. At the time, he would have been cursed and sworn at and labeled the "the worst of all creatures" by patriot officers for refusing to reenlist when the army was so desperate for soldiers. Yet Greenwood did not seem to care at the time or when he wrote his memoir. And not long before he became a privateer, John Paul Jones raged against the "common Class of mankind" for doing just that. Jones thought men such as Greenwood were "Actuated by no nobler principle than that of Self-Interest—this and this Only determines all Adventures in Privateers." Robert Morris, too, just before he invested in his own privateering venture, worried about the "irregular Conduct" of the privateers that "savours more of Moorish Piracy." While members of Congress were torn about the relative merits of privateering, Continental Army and navy officers, desperate for men, were not. Privateers were mere "Moorish Pirates." They were as far from being "noble" patriots as you could get.[16]

Greenwood's unwillingness—or inability—to tilt his recollections toward the more familiar story already being told in the history books—the story of a providential fight between good and evil—was echoed by many other Revolutionary War veterans. Recalling their experiences years later, few could assign clear reasons for joining patriot forces. Historians studying the 88,000 pension applications of war veterans have been hard-pressed to find more than a few claims to have "enlisted in the cause of my country." Most men offered no explanation for joining or admitted that they did it to pick up the bounty money or clothes on offer, to escape bondage of another sort, or simply to make a living.

Daniel Trabue and his brother set off to enlist in the army in 1776, but only because they could see no other way to make money. Finding no market for their goods—"at this time no sail [sic] for produce"—they "concluded we would Join a company that was a going to the North under General Washington" and pick up the generous bounty offered for doing so. Daniel then fell ill, so he did not enlist, but his brother did. A little later, Daniel volunteered under George Rogers Clark for a special expedition westward to claim and conquer the Ohio Valley and Illinois country. Though it is not clear what Clark promised potential recruits for his secretive expedition, Trabue "astonished" his Virginia neighbors with the plunder he brought back from conflict with the Indians. He subsequently used his time in service to prospect for good western lands to settle once the war in the West was over.[17]

More generally, few veterans made any effort to relate their own experiences during the war to the stories circulating in the press and the history books at the time, unless to try to correct popular misconceptions about the conflict. Veterans wrote of friendships and family and emphasized hardships and toil. Joseph Plumb Martin, in his memoir, wrote persistently about his acute hunger. Another veteran of the Quebec campaign, John Joseph Henry, spent the first eighty pages of his memoir writing in gripping detail about the harrowing deprivations he suffered on a scouting trip across Maine ahead of the expedition. Details about his experiences on the battlefield paled in comparison. Others veterans, even when they were present at significant battles, remembered such events only because of the friends they met, the dead they buried, or the relations they missed. Even in their pension applications, they used publicly memorable events merely to situate their own, more important, memories. Contrasting civic orations and celebrations with private recollections, historian Caroline Cox concluded that "the grizzled veterans told a different story of the Revolution, one more haphazard and uncertain," even decades after the war.[18]

While veterans were often coaxed to tell their stories by courts assessing their pension claims, or by curious neighbors, many thousands who did not serve in the Continental or state forces never told their stories. No one seemed to want to listen. A very few, however, specifically wrote their memoirs because they felt the story they remembered best had been forgotten. John P. Becker of Schoharie, New York, was one of those. He opened his narrative, written around 1831, by expressing regret that there were not more recollections like his published about the Revolution, as there were "thousands, like my own father and his family, [who] suffered and lamented, rejoiced and exulted, unknown to any beyond their immediate neighborhood." Born the year of the repeal of the Stamp Act, in 1765, Becker—likely echoing his father—said that the whole province was aroused by the legislation but added "what I believe is now little known, that many of our most wealthy and influential Whigs were at the bottom of these disorders." At several points in his narrative, Becker zeroed in on Boston as the center of the troubles. Even after relating the alarm following news of Lexington and Concord, he wrote that "among the unenlightened and uneducated portion of the public, an undoubted apathy in relation to the contest prevailed." And he and his family were as apathetic as their neighbors. The Beckers were a reasonably well-to-do farming family, so John spent most of the war with his family. He worked as a wagoner when his father needed his services, and he refused to join the army because he considered his family's circumstances "rather above that which furnished the usual recruits for the regular army." His hostility to the army was evident in his aspersions on the "total incapacity, moral and intellectual," of those who served in the military. His father also declined to serve and turned down his election as a militia officer to continue wagoning. Both he and his father felt this kind of support was enough. Becker's more patriotic contemporaries might have labeled him disaffected or more generously looked upon him as a neutral in the war. But Becker was not interested in labels.[19]

His memoir was full of details and anecdotes about the roads and passages that he and his father had to cross, the amounts they were paid, their hunger and deprivations, and the accidents they had. Becker's was a local view of the war. The people he remembered and discussed were mostly local officials and officers, some of whom had achieved a degree of national fame by 1831. But his travels only reinforced his parochialism. Inhabitants of Westfield, Massachusetts, for example, amused the Schoharie native with their "quaintness and honest simplicity." The Pennsylvania troops he met were "the most quarrelsome, and I regret to say, profligate set of men I had ever seen together."

Becker also detailed the escapes he and his father made from efforts to impress them into military service. He constantly criticized Congress and its officials, too. His father was supposed to get certificates for impressed grain and supplies but never received them. "This is one of the thousand instances of the petty tyranny and injustice of public agents in the days of the revolution, and is given to corroborate the facts sets forth in our most authentic histories." Nor was his father paid when in the service of Congress. Echoing the complaints of Joseph Plumb Martin, Becker wrote that it was "one thing to be *employed* by congress, and another to be *paid* by them. It was our fortune on this occasion, as on former ones, to know the difference: we *drew* the *boards* but never *drew* our pay." Becker grew so weary of the demands for his service and supplies that for a joke he taught his horse to rear up when he was commanded to do anything in the name of "congress."[20]

For Becker, the war was mostly something to be endured. He claimed he and his family saw little "of the display, [and] much of the inconvenience of war." Nor was the war a unifying experience. Recounting the streams of refugees fleeing from General John Burgoyne's advancing army, he could only remember the selfishness that prevailed: "Every one for himself was the constant cry." Though his travails were made worse by the "Rank toryism and infamous venality" of the "disaffected inhabitants," Becker also had to defend himself and his family from the predations of patriot soldiers. Indeed, he noted that Burgoyne's troops had cut his family's wheat in order to seize it but that Continental forces then took it after the British surrendered. It was a dispiriting experience. There was only coolness among Becker's countrymen and much "suspicion which seemed to color every transaction." Everyone "seemed to imagine his own danger and difficulty as great as it was possible to encounter; and under this impression ties the most natural and affecting were like ropes of sand, broken at the very touch." He lamented the divisions between "kith and kin" almost everywhere.[21]

Becker's first sight of the bloody reality of war was no better. When he and his family began their journey back to their farm after Burgoyne surrendered, they came across some of the wounded from both sides. Becker recoiled at the "sight of these wretched people, pale and lifeless, with countenances of an expression peculiar to gunshot wounds, as the surgeons have truly informed us, and the sound of groaning voices as each motion of the litter renewed the anguish of their wounds, filled me with horror and sickness of heart." He also remembered with horror the hanging of seven "disaffected" men by a "mob" after a public brawl and queried the point of it all: "Is much public happiness then bought at the price of individual wretchedness? Must blood and sorrow be the result of even the most just and righteous controversies? . . . We were much affected with what we saw . . . and the remembrance cannot be effaced."[22]

In the end, and even after fifty-five years living in the new republic, Becker was not sure it was worth it. His memoirs were tinged with regret and bitterness. Though he had spent most of the war helping his family tend the farm and fulfill contracts for wagoning, he believed his family had sacrificed much and done more than its fair share to support the war effort. The army had seized provisions from them, and they had been impressed into service for the Continentals to ferry supplies. Becker felt they had lost much during the war and never been repaid for the services they performed or the goods that were taken from them: "My father died a creditor to the government in more than this one instance. His posterity have never gained any thing by his devotion to the cause." Before he died, his father said the unsettled state of affairs would injure his son's prospects, and Becker concluded that it had. Though he wrote that he had originally looked forward to a good future at war's end, the opportunities melted away. Investments never made their promised returns, loans went unpaid, and his brother took most of his savings. Even hope deserted him. He wrote his memoir, he said, with death and "consolation" only a few days away.[23]

Others whose voices are lost must also have wondered whether the conflict was worth the suffering. What did the inhabitants of Falmouth, Norfolk, and New York remember about their experiences of the war? Militant patriots in northeastern Massachusetts suspected that the residents of Falmouth were too cozy with the British ships lying at anchor in the harbor. So they kidnapped a British officer and stole food and liquor from the townspeople, threatening to burn the town if the inhabitants did not declare their allegiance to the patriots. But the militants did not have to burn it. The British were so angry at the kidnapping of the officer that they bombed and burned the town in retaliation. In New York in 1776, even so prominent a patriot as Nathanael Greene wanted to evacuate and burn the town because he speculated that two-thirds of the residents were Tories. Washington agreed with him but hesitated to issue the order to do so. And then, just days after the British occupied the town, a fire raged out of control and hundreds of buildings burned—up to a quarter of the town. It was a hellish event. One man wrote that it was "almost impossible to conceive a scene of more horror and distress." "The sick, the aged, women, and children, half naked, were seen going they knew not where." Amid the "shrieks and cries of the women and children," there were still more grisly scenes. British troops caught a woman in the act of starting a fire and, "without Ceremony, she was tossed into the Flames." So too was a suspected rebel with a "fire brand" in his hand. Another man was hanged from a signpost by British sailors and then hung up by the heels like an animal. Though most of the evidence suggests that rebel arsonists began the conflagration, patriot leaders denied it. Still, they were pleased with the destruction. George Washington, who had desperately wanted to burn the city, publicly called it an accident but privately concluded that "Providence— or some good honest fellow, has done more for us than we were disposed to do for ourselves."[24]

In Norfolk, Virginia, patriots most certainly did put a thriving town to the torch because they suspected the loyalties of many in it. Under the very noses of Continental officers, soldiers "with fire-brands in their hands" reduced the town "to Ashes." Over the course of three days, they burned the property of suspected loyalists and plundered and burned the houses of patriots, too. "Damn them, we'el burn them all," they cried. And they very nearly did. A total of 1,331 buildings were burned, or almost 90 percent of the town. Colonel Robert Howe of North Carolina described its "ruinous condition" yet thought the devastation "greatly beneficial to the Public." He reveled in the destruction because the patriots quickly blamed it on the shocked British. Newspapers up and down the eastern seaboard carried reports that the British had started the fire. George Washington thought the burning of both Falmouth and Norfolk would provide "flaming Arguments" for independence. Meanwhile, the General Assembly in Virginia, knowing that patriot forces were probably responsible, held off an inquiry for another year and then buried the report that clearly placed the blame on patriots. They did not make it public for another sixty years. It took another forty years for historians to notice. The inhabitants, of course, never forgot it.[25]

Though few of those who suffered in the war confided their stories to writing, many spoke with their feet. Seventy-five thousand people fled the colonies and new states, including some fifteen thousand slaves—more than those who left France during its revolution. Some of the desperate refugees told their stories to the Loyalist Claims Commission in a bid to recover a fraction of their many losses. Sometimes the commissioners listened. Their former friends, neighbors, and kin who remained in the new United States rarely did. And historians have followed suit. With few exceptions, these valuable sources have remained untapped by scholars of American history.[26]

The records of the Loyalist Claims Commission help confirm, of course, that zealous patriots were right to be concerned about the number of people in their midst who disagreed with them. Thousands of "Americans" felt strongly enough about the imperial crisis to join or support British forces in their conflict with the rebels. Historians now estimate that somewhere between 20 and 33 percent of colonists were "active" loyalists. Indeed, at least nineteen thousand loyalists served in a formal capacity in forty-two different provincial regiments and militias. Like those in the patriot armed forces, some were temporarily impressed into service and others were pressured to join by friends or family. But unlike the patriots, the British or loyalist leaders never resorted to formal conscription to raise colonists to fight for them. Surely this is one of the great ironies of the so-called war for liberty that should alert us to the need for a different kind of story.[27]

If historians have done little with the memoirs of those who stayed in the United States, they have virtually ignored the memoirs written by those who left. Like the papers of the Loyalist Claims Commission, these memoirs also tell us a very different story of the war from what we are accustomed to hearing. Elizabeth Lichtenstein wrote one of these retrospective accounts. Her war story was of a young girl coming of age amid an uncivil conflagration. Though she met her husband, William Martin Johnston, because of the conflict, hers were not the happy recollections of a newlywed. Her memory of those years was dominated by painful separations, first from her father and then from her husband, followed by months of anxiety and uncertainty about their safety as she received reports of other deaths in the extended family. Betrayal was a key theme. Mobs tarred and feathered anyone who did not declare in favor of the rebels. An old family friend whom her father had known since he was an infant headed a gang that came looking for him. "His turning against my father served to show the spirit of the times and the violence with which civil wars are entered upon." Her own teachers were among those who joined the persecutors. Yet she also recalled the betrayal of the British. Eliza was at Portsmouth, Virginia, when the British decided to decamp from that town in November 1780. She remembered in vivid detail the shock that many of the inhabitants felt at the decision, taken "just as the poor people came forward to show their loyalty, in the hope that the British would remain permanently there." Her landlady, a Mrs. Elliott, was speechless at the news, "scarce in her senses from the shock," until she could finally lament that this was the third time they had been left by the British troops "to the rage and persecution of the Americans." The peace treaty, Eliza noted, was also "shameful" to the British:

"The war never occasioned half the distress which this peace has done, to the unfortunate Loyalists." By doing nothing more than recommending clemency for the allies they abandoned, the British were "in fact casting them off altogether."[28]

The metaphor was apt. Eliza and her growing family had spent much of the war years as refugees from the conflict. She moved from place to place, taking shelter in barns, on board ships, and in the homes of strangers, even with infants in tow. Peace only cast her farther adrift. From her childhood home outside Savannah, Eliza sojourned in St. Augustine, Charleston, New York, Portsmouth, Edinburgh, and Kingston in Jamaica before finally settling in Nova Scotia. Many of these movements were taken alone or involved long separations from her husband while she struggled to raise a large family amid continuing grief. Six of her ten children died before she did, including three who died in infancy, her eldest son who died of yellow fever in Jamaica in 1805, and her eldest daughter who died in a Boston madhouse in 1819. Eliza Lichtenstein Johnston, born in Little Ogeechee, ten miles outside of Savannah, in May 1764, was also once one of those "Americans" who lived in the colonies. But her story has been compartmentalized and marginalized. She has been cast off by historians, too. We have yet to comprehend these tales within an expansive and inclusive history of the war of American independence.[29]

Among the tens of thousands of Americans who fled the colonies during the war were also many who had simply given up on the idea of living in the new states. The Loyalist Claims Commission records are dominated by those who claimed they had actively taken up arms or supported the British. The commissioners were, after all, most interested in compensating losses sustained while supporting Britain. Still, many claimants admitted that they had taken a patriot oath or served in the patriot forces and later joined the British. Many others could not prove either their loyalty or their losses, and of course thousands of exiles did not apply at all to the commission. These refugees warn us that we should be cautious in applying the label of loyalist to everyone who fled the newly independent states. Certainly, many formerly enslaved black Americans who used the chaos of war to flee their bondage might have questioned the label. Others who fled may simply have been shocked at the destruction of the war, caught up in its violence, unfairly chased out by neighbors with grudges, and/or insufficiently convinced that the newly independent states were a safe or promising place to live.[30]

At the same time, the exiled may also have been the tip of a larger iceberg. Those who left had to have the means to flee or nothing left to lose. How many thousands more across the states simply tried to weather the storm where they were and stayed put? The evidence would suggest that there was a very large group of colonists who found themselves caught between the two warring camps of patriots and loyalists. Patriots at the time often dismissed them as Tories or the disaffected, or sometimes more generously as neutrals. To understand this critical category of people, we need to take them seriously and listen far more carefully to them without trying to label them or the issues for which they stood in the same way their contemporaries did.[31]

Patriot leaders in Virginia, for example, called Edward Wright a Tory and sent an armed troop of cavalry to round him and others up at bayonet point. They accused Wright of leading a "conspiracy" to stop a militia call-out in northern Virginia in 1781. He and another "Leading" man in the county reputedly gathered together a "party of Torys" who pledged "sooner to die than perform their tour of duty." Yet even county militia officers later had to admit that Wright had done service in the militia on several important occasions. Now he was suffering and wanted some relief. He wanted to free up grain stock to feed his own family. He said he would turn out for militia duty in the fall once he had put his farm in order. Wright also claimed he was sick and tired of the many call-outs he and his neighbors had suffered. They had lost too many days away from their small farms while many of their wealthier neighbors with slaves had been exempted from any service at all. Wright was angry, too, that the laws allowed people to avoid military service if they turned in deserters from the army. As one observer conceded, the ringleaders of the alleged conspiracy resented that "the Rich wanted the Poor to fight for them, to defend there [sic] property, whilst they refused to fight for themselves." Such arguments carried no weight. Patriot officials labeled the ringleaders "disaffected to the Independence of the United States and attached to their enemies" and jailed Wright for the duration of the war. Historians need to do better.[32]

In addition to taking war memoirs more seriously, then, we also need to reexamine on their own terms the experience and meaning of the war for its many different participants. For example, we have to consider more carefully the reasons why Pennsylvania riflemen mutinied as early as September 1775. We have to try harder to fathom the thinking of the Connecticut militia who marched home when their contracts were out in early December 1775, along with a staggering 10,000 of the 11,000 troops who had gathered around Cambridge earlier in the year. We believe we know a lot about why they mobilized in the first place, but we are at loss when trying to explain why most went home and why many never showed up again. We also need to take seriously the sentiments of volunteers from northern Virginia who were happy to serve locally but refused to march out of the colony to join Washington. What did the conflict mean to them? Or to the thousands of white Virginians who rose up in armed revolt against their militia officers in the very midst of the British invasions of 1780 and 1781, despite threats of slave insurrections. Patriot officials claimed that these men were at best disaffected and at worst led by designing Tories. Yet most were heartily sick of the demands on them for taxes and the recurrent efforts to draft them into the army. One of them, John Heavin, said he just wanted to be left alone. He had "never meddled with war from the first moment and Cant think of Intangling myselfe with it now." Another, John McDonald, on trial for treason in 1780, complained of the onerous wartime impositions on him and his neighbors. He said he joined the insurrection because "he thought We had been fighting for Liberty but slavery was a consequence."[33] How many more were there like John Heavin or John McDonald who could not or did not speak up as they kept their heads down and their mouths shut during a war that brought much misery and not a lot of liberty to many of its participants.

* * *

Once we come to terms with these other stories and develop a different framework to interpret them, we can start to appreciate the historical consequences and meaning of the Revolutionary War for the people involved. There is much still to do. But for those who yet need to yoke this story to the birth of a nation, there is a way to do so in the meantime. Of course, John Greenwood's memoir does not make for a seamless or soothing story of a patriotic war for independence that culminated in the creation of the federal constitution. The range of stories and motives and interests that diverged from the stories and motives and interests of the most militant patriots obviously makes for a more incoherent central story. But the central story could yet be that very incoherence. It was critical to making the conflict a civil war. It also prolonged the war immeasurably. It made the war for independence a great deal more bloody, messy, and divisive than anyone envisioned at the outset. But collectively, Greenwood's and others' stories make for a more powerful and compelling story of how a divisive and destructive war for independence turned into a revolutionary war.

Consider a second counterfactual: had all "Americans" risen up against the tyranny of the British, the birth of the nation would have looked markedly different. Had "Americans" responded as they seemed to do at Lexington and Concord and had the British pulled out after testing the waters a few times, the wildest dreams of the most militant patriots would have been fulfilled. But there would have been no reason to appoint a commander like George Washington to unite the states. There might have been no movement toward independence, since a negotiated peace would have been more likely. And without the pressure of the British army over the course of a long war, the unity between the new states—already tenuous—would have dissolved more quickly. There would have been few innovations made in the new state governments, since colonial leaders would not have seen it necessary to make concessions to the people "out of doors" in return for their military aid. Without resistance from the "disaffected," the loyalists, the "sunshine patriots," and the lukewarm, Washington and other Continental officials would not have been so frustrated by state governments and their neighbors. Few people would have considered the Continental Congress "weak" for its inability to raise money and men during the war. The economy would not have been so badly affected by wartime disruptions, and new leaders like Daniel Shays would have had no military service to use as a platform for making troublesome demands. Indeed, the causes of later uprisings—high taxes to pay war debts—would have been lacking. There are many possibilities, of course, but few of them would have led to the movement to create a stronger federal government in 1787. In other words, paying attention to the stories of the many in the war for independence helps better explain the political developments of the era. They compel us to tie the "destructive" war for independence more closely to the so-called "constructive" political innovations of the day.

On one hand, the conflict reinforced the pervasive localism that had prevailed before the war. "Exhausted," "debilitated," and "almost desolate," most Americans wanted little to do with any further intrusions in their lives. As Sung Bok Kim has noted of war-torn Westchester County in New York, even "good Whigs" were "determined" to do nothing more for the cause.[34] Like John Becker, they were angry about the requisitions on their time and property, and they often saw the Continental Congress and its officers as worse than the British in their demands and broken promises. Many of those who lived through these terrible years yearned to be left alone. Marauding armies and onerous wartime demands had created bitter memories of intrusive Continental and even state officials interfering in their lives. In response, people wanted greater control over local affairs and cared little for fellow citizens in other provinces whom they had mistrusted before the war and mistrusted more than ever afterward.³⁵

On the other hand, the upheaval of the war led some to believe in a stronger federal government. And from the chaos of the conflict and its aftermath there arose a small group of committed nationalists. Alfred F. Young noted the presence of the "ghost" of Shays at the Constitutional Convention, as most of the so-called founding fathers looked back with a shudder on a decade or more of popular unrest. This unrest included not just the radical action taken by the followers of Shays but also the defiance of slaves and servants, the antipathy of neighbors to impressment and to joining the army, and the resistance of draft dodgers. It included those who refused to turn out for the militia, those who aided and joined the British, and those who put their families first and bid defiance to all who came to their doors. The new constitution—ratified by the smallest of margins and only after the Federalists engineered some now-well-known deceits—gave those jittery founders some newfound power over the many who had made the past so problematic and who dared to dream of a different future.³⁶

The long and complicated war, followed by the divisive contests of the 1780s, also helps explain the war story that soon arose and still animates us today. That new story reflected the desperate efforts of many to *forget* the past. Those early national historians shaped their narratives of unity in *response* to the chaos, uncertainty, and disunity that they despaired of during the war and abhorred in the politics of the 1780s and 1790s. As they embarked on the republican experiment, they were fearful about the fate of a large republic, the development of political parties, the excesses of the French Revolution, and their own divisive past that had given no salve to these concerns. They wrote with an urgency that betrayed their anxiety. At the same time, they desperately sought out new symbols of unity, looked for fresh sources of legitimacy, and toasted the future rather than recalling the past. They wrapped that troublesome past within a larger—and largely fabricated—story about the triumph of liberty. They did so even while creating a federal constitution that was decidedly less democratic than the state constitutions it was designed to curb. They did so while entrenching slavery and continuing to support a war to dispossess Native Americans of their land. They tried hard to forget a complicated war and remembered instead a simple tale of the rise and triumph of freedom.³⁷

Of course, thousands of Americans at the time remembered something different. And because of this, orators, historians, and political leaders of the founding generation would struggle mightily to control the memory of the Revolution and instill loyalty among citizens of the new nation in its first decades. No wonder, then, that securing and enshrining a more stable story of the Revolution was a slow, halting, and often uncertain process, as people like John Becker and even Eliza Johnston vied to contest and claim the memory of the Revolutionary War. No wonder, then, that in a more general sense, the Revolution may have laid the seeds of the nation's own destruction at the moment of its founding. The prolonged war gave rise to new divisions between states that each believed had given more than its fair share to the war effort, between Continental authorities and state officials, and between state and Continental officials and new citizens in the states. In their fervent desire to forget, the founding fathers were left unable to resolve these tensions. They passed an unstable polity on to their heirs, together with a story about the making of that polity that was a fabrication. Subsequent generations struggled to reconcile that story with the realities of the new nation. It might have helped prove their undoing. Finally unable to agree on a coherent version of the past, Americans once again went to war with each other in a cataclysmic conflict a mere four generations later.[38] The stories told about war mattered. They matter still.

CHAPTER 2

The Intimacies of Occupation

Loyalties, Compromise, and Betrayal in Revolutionary-Era Newport

TRAVIS GLASSON

On an overcast night in early July 1777, so the story goes, a small group of Rhode Island patriot soldiers quietly rowed five whaleboats across Narragansett Bay. Led by the young officer William Barton, their journey from the rebel-held mainland to Aquidneck Island was a dangerous one. The British had occupied the island since their seizure of Newport and its hinterland in December 1776 and three powerful Royal Navy frigates actively patrolled the bay. Barton and the forty or so men under him were engaged in a bold mission: a raid to capture the commander of Newport's British garrison, General Richard Prescott. Barton, from nearby Warren and an energetic figure in skirmishing around the bay since the British arrival, had learned that Prescott had left Newport proper for a country retreat. The general was now residing in the more pleasant but less secure confines of the rural Middletown home of Henry Overing, a prosperous merchant and distiller. Barton and his men escaped detection by British sailors and soldiers, overpowered a challenging sentry after tricking him into believing they were a British patrol searching for deserters, and successfully captured Prescott's aide-de-camp and the general himself, who was found in a bedroom in his nightshirt. Prescott's final seizure may have been thanks to the efforts of a black volunteer among Barton's troops, a man named Jack Sisson, who in some accounts of the event is said to have broken through the locked door of the room in which the general was found with a timely, powerful head butt. The general, his aide, and the hapless sentry were ignominiously hustled to the waiting boats before the alarm could be raised. According to the report of a British officer, the raiders spent all of seven minutes in the house before triumphantly carrying their prisoners back across the bay.[1]

The swashbuckling exploit was a career maker for Barton, an ardent Whig who had been a hatter until the war afforded him a wider scope for his talents. He had conceived of taking Prescott, he later said, as a response to the December 1776 British capture of the American general Charles Lee, and the officers were subsequently exchanged. The feat earned Barton promotion, Congress thanked him with a sword of honor, and he won a reputation that carried him into public office, including a seat in the Rhode Island legislature. Barton continued participating in the fighting around Narragansett Bay until May 1778, when he was shot in the hip while defending the town of Bristol from a British raid. While Barton's postwar career was checkered—its most notable feature was a long-running legal battle over land dealings in Vermont—his reputation as a Rhode Island hero was secure.

For Prescott, the event was a personal and professional humiliation. He had already been captured once by the rebels, taken in November 1775 during the American invasion of Quebec. His capture for a second time and in such unheroic circumstances made him a rather ridiculous figure. The acid judgment of Ambrose Serle, Admiral Lord Richard Howe's secretary, seems indicative of the British response. "News came, that Genl. Prescot was taken Prisoner at Rhode Island in a very idle way. He is not much regretted."[2] After his exchange for Lee, Prescott resumed his command in Newport, but he was quickly replaced by Sir Robert Pigot. As London's *Public Advertiser* noted, "taking one of our General officers, and first in Command upon his Station, must contribute to support the Spirit of the Rebels equal to a Defeat of our Troops. It shews them the shameful Indolence of our Officers, and their own superior Activity."[3]

If the *Public Advertiser* saw a morality tale in Prescott's capture, it is probably easier for us to read it as either stirring adventure story or, with its head butts and nightshirts, as farce. However, the capture of Prescott and the parts played in it by the Overing family, Jack Sisson, Barton, and others also provide a window onto a wider phenomenon that might be conceptualized as the "intimacies of occupation" in Revolutionary-era Newport. A close examination of the Prescott incident underlines the extent to which the Revolution was experienced as a civil war. It reveals the connections, complexities, and contradictions inherent in the experiences of people living in British-controlled Newport, a town that was simultaneously regarded by some as occupied, by others as liberated, and by still others as simply unfortunate in becoming a site of contestation. Like people living in other localities that were home to large numbers of American or British forces, Newporters—whatever their political inclination, social status, gender, or race—had to carefully navigate their way through the war years. For them, the war simply could not be ignored. Social bonds were strained, not just by the political issues at stake but also by the arrival of war on Rhode Island's streets and farms.

Take, for example the collective experiences of the extended Coggeshall family, which was descended from one of Rhode Island's seventeenth-century founders. Revolutionary Newport was home to three Coggeshalls identifiable as "Tory," three as likely "Whig," and one whose loyalties are uncertain.[4] Such family divisions were not unique to the Coggeshalls, and people's ties to friends, neighbors, business partners, churches, and others were also stretched, sometimes to the breaking point, by the conflict. In such environments the experience of the war was an intimate affair: new friends, loves, and enemies were found, compromises were made, and betrayals were frequent.

Thanks to recent work by Maya Jasanoff and others there is increasing awareness of the nature, scope, and impact of loyalism around the British Empire. Recent scholarship has also made clear that black people were engaged on both sides of the Revolutionary conflict, making choices about if and how to participate in it based primarily on their assessments of what doing so would mean for their own lives and freedom.[5] The Prescott capture highlights how many who lived through the conflict were motivated neither by passionate commitment to loyalism nor to the American cause, and instead found themselves pulled in multiple directions as the war affected their own families, households, and communities. Despite the fact that the "neutral" or the "disaffected" certainly formed a large proportion, and perhaps a majority, of the population of the future United States, historians have given them little consideration.[6] Paying attention to those "stuck in the middle" in Revolutionary Newport helps create a richer picture of what living through a civil war meant for a broad swath of "Britons" and "Americans" alike.

* * *

Barton's capture of Prescott occurred within the context of a bitter, frequently small-scale struggle that occurred around Narragansett Bay over the course of several years. While community change and the process of political mobilization in the buildup to the conflict have been closely considered for Newport, the local experience of the war and occupation itself have been less intensively studied.[7] For Newporters, as for others in the British Empire, the operative question during the war years was often whether one sympathized with the patriot or loyalist side at a particular moment and in relation to particular circumstances rather than whether one consistently favored the Crown or independence as political abstractions.[8] The war arrived in Narragansett Bay quite soon after the first shots were fired at Lexington and Concord, and it quickly began forcing hard choices on Rhode Islanders.[9] After the more radical Rhode Island General Assembly deposed the colony's insufficiently zealous governor Joseph Wanton in June 1775, a small British naval squadron that had been working to suppress smuggling began even more active operations against local shipping.[10] Narragansett Bay had helped the colony to prosper by giving the towns that hugged its inlets direct access to maritime trade. Rhode Islanders were soon made to realize that the bay also put their communities within easy reach of the war. Newport experienced this early on, when Captain James Wallace, the head of the local Royal Navy squadron, had the HMS *Rose* fire on Newport in late July 1775 in an attempt to compel its townspeople to supply his force with provisions. The firing understandably terrified Newport's inhabitants. Other communities were even less fortunate. Piloted by slaves loaned by the strongly pro-British son of the ex-governor Wanton, Wallace's ships and men launched raids on the island homes, property, and persons of rebel sympathizers who lived in the particularly exposed communities of Jamestown and Prudence Island. Coastal Rhode Islanders were given the most powerful object lesson in their vulnerability when Wallace ordered his squadron to bombard the recalcitrant town of Bristol in October 1775.

Bristol was heavily damaged and its fate was much on the minds of Newporters as they sought a way forward. Later that month, the General Assembly gave Newport permission to supply Wallace's squadron "with beef, beer, etc." in the hopes of preventing further destruction, but the town's attempts to negotiate a rapprochement angered patriot leaders elsewhere. Even though "a majority of the townspeople were in favor of a truce" at that moment, tensions remained high on all sides.[11] British forces under Wallace's command raided Newport in December 1775, and newspaper reports claimed that they engaged in plundering and burning while ashore. The clampdown on local shipping hurt the town's trade. With the sense of pressure and uncertainty strong, some townspeople began to leave. A 1774 census recorded the prewar population at 9,209; a 1782 census, taken after years of military occupation and the successive departures of the British and then French armies, recorded a population of 5,530.[12]

Wallace's activities continued until April 1776, when the recent British evacuation of Boston resulted in his ships being ordered to new stations. Rhode Island's rebel leaders declared the colony's formal independence in early May and began fortifying points around the bay against future British assaults, marking the beginning of a period of patriot ascendancy in Newport and other nearby towns. In June 1776 the Rhode Island General Assembly passed a Test Act empowering any assembly member to require any person to subscribe to a declaration asserting the justness of the cause of the "United American Colonies" and pledging not to aid "the Fleets and Armies of Great Britain" but rather to "assist in the defense of the United Colonies." At least five Newporters, including those holding customs offices and the postmaster and local vice-admiralty court officer, Thomas Vernon, refused to subscribe when put to the test. They were summarily banished for several months to rural northern Rhode Island.[13] Like many others, Henry Overing, whose home would later be commandeered by Prescott, was less resolute. Named in a list prepared by Rhode Island patriot military officers of those "Inimical to the United Colonies in America & the Arduous Struggle in Which they are Engaged Against the Forces of Great Britain," Overing signed when presented with the new oath in July 1776.[14]

The patriots' local dominance proved short-lived however. Soon, and not for the last time, the people of Newport were forced to respond to a sharply different political reality. On December 7, 1776, a British fleet of some seventy ships sailed from New York into Narragansett Bay and dropped anchor a few miles off Newport. The rebels' hastily constructed coastal defenses were wholly inadequate in the face of such a force and the next day British and German advance troops began coming ashore. They quickly pushed the Rhode Island militiamen on Aquidneck Island to the north, forcing them to retreat via ferries to the mainland. Other British troops soon landed and occupied Newport itself with ease. In little more than a day the town and the island were under British control without having offered any real resistance. According to Continental Army surgeon James Thacher, "many of the inhabitants being friendly to the royal cause," the British troops "were received as friends."[15] A few days later, an expedition from Newport captured Jamestown, the largest other island in the bay. To make their victory complete, the British fleet trapped Esek Hopkins's squadron of patriot warships, forcing it to take refuge up the Providence River.

Whereas the period of clear rebel dominance in Newport had been relatively brief, the British proved a more enduring presence, with more than 6,500 British and German troops soon coming ashore. A German officer noted that the troops initially occupied many houses, both those still inhabited and others abandoned by locals who had fled because of their political sympathies or simple fear.[16] Later, most enlisted men were quartered in camps spread about the island, but large numbers of officers continued to live in private homes. Having recently been put to loyalty oaths by Rhode Island's revolutionary government, Newporters now faced the prospect of similar treatment at the hands of the British army. Several previously vocal patriots were rounded up—presumably on the information of pro-British townspeople—and jailed; some were immediately released after signing loyalty oaths.[17]

Alarmed that the British troops now established on Aquidneck Island might rapidly launch attacks on Providence, towns in Connecticut, or even Boston, the New England states and Congress hurriedly assembled a force capable of opposing them. The patriots initially hoped that these men, placed under the command of Connecticut general Joseph Spencer, would be able to launch a quick counterattack and retake the island. In this atmosphere, the British arrested over sixty Newport civilians who it was thought might aid such an invasion, with several again gaining their release by signing an oath of allegiance.[18] However, the decisive battle for which the two sides prepared themselves in 1777 never occurred. What ensued, although this was clearer in hindsight than it was at the time, was a period of prolonged local stalemate. The British remained in firm control of Newport and Aquidneck Island and the strongest force in Narragansett Bay, but they were unwilling or unable to attempt to break through the patriot force facing them on the mainland.

For the opposing armies, the conflict became one of tedious, watchful waiting, punctuated by jarringly violent small raids mounted by both sides across the waterways that separated them. It was in this context that Barton captured Prescott in July 1777. While the loss of Prescott was a major embarrassment for the British, they remained masters of Newport. Pro-British local people were in the ascendancy, and the town's British garrison drew significant numbers of loyalist refugees from elsewhere. Newport also came to hold prisoners captured by the British, with sailors, soldiers, and suspect civilians held in terrible, sometimes deadly conditions aboard prison ships anchored in its harbor.[19] Raiding on both sides continued. On May 25, 1778, five hundred British and Hessian troops launched a surprise attack that inflicted serious damage on Bristol and Warren and captured several patriots; it was in this skirmish that Barton was seriously wounded.

The French entry into the conflict in the spring of 1778 introduced a new element of complexity to the local scene. After initial attempts to launch a coordinated Franco-American attack on New York failed to materialize in July 1778, the French fleet sent to aid the patriots was redirected to Narragansett Bay. There, it and the troops that it carried were to cooperate with a reinforced American army and expel the British from Aquidneck Island. It was not to be. While the French fleet briefly dominated Narragansett Bay, the new allies were beset by delays and difficulties, including a hurricane. They proved unable to mount the envisioned joint land and sea attack, and French warships withdrew to Boston Harbor. The Americans soon attempted to push the British off the island alone, but at the Battle of Rhode Island, fought on August 29, 1778, Newport's British garrison held its ground. These were particularly uncertain times for townspeople as rumors and predictions of clear victory for one side or the other circulated rapidly. Mary Almy was a loyalist whose family was split by the war. She had elected to remain in British Newport with her children even though her husband had joined the patriot army assembled on the Rhode Island mainland. Almy wrote that when the French fleet appeared off Narragansett Bay on July 29, 1778, in Newport "all was confusion in a moment" and that "the merchant looks upon his full store as nothing worth. The shopkeeper, with a distressed countenance, locks and bars his shop, not knowing what is for the best."[20]

Ultimately, the British and their German allies left Newport, but it was largely on their own terms. In October 1779, as British strategists looked to take the war to the southern states, General Sir William Howe ordered the garrison withdrawn from Newport. In scenes that presaged the large-scale evacuations of loyalists from Savannah, Charleston, and New York at the end of the war, the British fleet carried large numbers of civilian refugees with it when it sailed out of Narragansett Bay.[21] Whether motivated by political principle or more visceral fears of retribution, these pro-British townspeople and loyalist transplants preferred to leave Newport rather than remain there under patriot control. For Whigs, neutrals, and Tories alike this was a period of dramatic change. The long-term presence of British troops had affected daily life for the town's people, regardless of their political sympathies. Some people, of course, had found ways to profit from the garrison's large-scale demands for food, shelter, fuel, and other goods, but the army's presence had created many fears, hardships, and inconveniences for even the most pro-British residents. The withdrawal of the British afforded a brief respite from such demands, but there was to be no easy return to normalcy. On July 10, 1780, the war again became impossible for locals to ignore as another large fleet—this time a French one—anchored in the town's harbor. Some seven thousand French troops fanned out in search of accommodation and sustenance, and French officers occupied many of the same homes previously inhabited by Britons and Germans. This French army remained in Newport, and elsewhere in Rhode Island, for a year, as Washington and Rochambeau mulled how best to coordinate their forces.[22] When the French finally marched into Connecticut in July 1781, beginning a campaign that culminated in victory at Yorktown, it marked the end of Newport's successive experiences of occupation.

This deliberately parochial chronology of conflict puts into clear relief the challenges faced by Newporters, who experienced the war most directly as a period of dislocation and danger. Each inflection point in this chronology put new strains on individuals and communities and compelled reflection on one's previous choices and future options. Likewise, one can envision distinct and equally salient, albeit perhaps rarely so dramatically variable, locally focused timelines for other communities. If we pay attention to what we might call the "microchronologies" of the Revolution, the frequently intimate and intensely local nature of the conflict becomes inescapable and it appears as a defining feature of many people's wartime experiences.[23] For the most politically committed, a devotion to loyalism or patriotism may have served as a guide through these trying times. William Barton, for example, signaled the depth of his politicization early on, leaving Rhode Island on his own initiative to join the rebel army as it formed outside Boston in the aftermath of Lexington and Concord. When his third son was born in December 1775, the boy was christened George Washington Barton.[24] But, for many other people, personal relationships, varying understandings of self-interest, fear, and changing assessments of what the future might hold could be equally powerful determinants of action.

These less polarized people, who probably tried to minimize their contact with either nascent American or British officialdom, rarely left an imprint in the historical record comparable to that of ardent patriots like Barton or committed Tories. Nevertheless, traces of *their* war can be found, often when they failed in their efforts to keep the conflict at arm's length. Take for example the rather pathetic story related by a Newport silversmith named Tosh Sisson in an undated petition to the Rhode Island Board of War. Although the Royal Navy was for several years the strongest force in Narragansett Bay, both patriot and loyalist crews regularly conducted privateering expeditions out of Rhode Island's ports and inlets. When he wrote his petition, Sisson was evidently languishing in a patriot jail on account of his participation in a loyalist privateering voyage out of Newport. Once the British gained control of Newport, it became a place of refuge for other New England loyalists who were unable or afraid to remain in their own communities. Sisson claimed that "being accidentally at Mr. Lawton's Tavern in Newport he there fell in Company with certain Persons who had joined the Refugees and were then going on an Expedition." He was, he said, "young, inexperienced" and "pressed with continual Solicitations and moreover (to his great Grief and Shame he acknowledgeth it,) intoxicated." In this susceptible state he "gave his Word to accompany them in their refugeeing Voyage as they expressed it." By the next day, he claimed, he had "become conscious of his Imprudence." Despite his efforts to avoid them, his erstwhile drinking companions found him and threatened to have him confined by the town's British provost marshal if he did not keep his promise. Sisson confessed that, "whereby intimidated, he was compelled submissively to yield to their Request, and attended them one Trip only." He claimed "with the deepest contrition of Heart" that this was "his only Transgression," and therefore he prayed "your Honours will please to liberate him upon his giving Security to appear & answer at such Time and Place as Your Honours in your Wisdom shall think fit."[25] Sisson's pleading may have been self-serving revisionism, but it also reflects the pressures created by the intimacies of occupation in Revolutionary Newport.

* * *

Barton's raid occurred against this backdrop of continuous *petite guerre* interspersed with moments when Newport was closer to the center of significant continental and international developments.[26] While it was an extraordinary event, the capture of General Prescott provides an excellent window on the more quotidian experiences of the war for the people of British-occupied Newport. Because it was comparatively well documented, it allows for at least the partial recovery of the experiences of women, enslaved people, and other civilians, many of whom were only reluctantly drawn in to the conflict.

One of the most striking aspects of the Prescott capture is the light it sheds on the complex and varied relations that existed between Newport women and British occupiers. Elaine Forman Crane has observed that pre-Revolutionary Newport, as a maritime community with many working men either frequently away or lost to the dangers of the sea, featured an usually large number of households headed by women.[27] The multiyear presence of thousands of British and German soldiers in the town and nearby countryside upset established local gender dynamics and sexual norms. Patriot sources frequently stressed the occupying soldiery's capacity for sexual violence. The Congregational minister Ezra Stiles, for example, recorded in his diary for December 14, 1776, within a week of the British occupation, that reports had come out of the town that "the soldiers ravished two lying-in women."[28] Ten days later, the British officer Frederick Mackenzie confirmed the dangers of the period, recording in his diary that a soldier of the British Twenty-Second Regiment had been sentenced to death "for committing a Rape since our landing on this Island." He had just been pardoned, Mackenzie also claimed, "at the intercession of the injured party, and in consequence of his former good Character."[29] Sexual violence and the fear and insecurity that it spawned were part of the dark side of the military occupation of the island.[30]

Yet not all interactions between townspeople and the occupying forces were violent. As one historian of the German role in the occupation of the town has noted, "social events and socializing in general were part of the life of the British and Hessian garrison in Newport."[31] Both men and women participated in these events. A good example is the June 1777 "entertainment" that naval commander Sir Peter Parker held aboard his flagship, which was attended by "above 50 Ladies and Gentlemen."[32] Newport's social life was clearly an appealing aspect of the post to some officers. A German officer noted on the eve of landing in Newport that "it is claimed that the most beautiful women in all North America are in Newport and on Rhode Island."[33] Ezra Stiles, a refugee because of his rebel sympathies, was probably dejected by reports that British soldiers intended to turn his shuttered Newport church into an "Assembly Room for Balls &c. after taking down the Pews," but some townspeople appear to have embraced the new possibilities.[34]

It is clear from a variety of sources that, patriot disapproval notwithstanding, some Newport women chose to socialize with and form varied relationships with soldiers of the occupying British and German regiments. This could extend to marriage. Two daughters of the merchant Francis Malbone, although he "was not a tory," married British officers.[35] Three Quaker sisters, the Engs, married officers attached to the occupying forces, ultimately journeying with their husbands to novel lives in London, Hesse, and Nova Scotia after the war. Like many other "loyalists," these émigré women turned "so much loss" into "something new" in a reconfigured postwar world.[36] Henry Overing's own teenaged daughter, Henrietta, married an officer in the British garrison, Lieutenant Colonel Andrew Bruce, in August 1778. Their marriage ended acrimoniously: Bruce abandoned Henrietta when the British evacuated Newport and he subsequently requested a divorce.[37] While such relationships were relatively traditional, legally recognized, and theoretically permanent, many others formed between local people and soldiers were not.

Writing about Revolutionary-era Philadelphia, Clare Lyons has observed that "the social disruptions and physical mobility of the war years led to intimate relationships." The city, Lyons argues, also saw the creation of a new, more permissive sexual culture in the 1760s and 1770s. During the war itself, Philadelphia "witnessed the libertine sexual practices of the British military, and some had joined in."[38] Similar dynamics seem to have operated in occupied Rhode Island. Prostitution also seems to have been widespread during the occupation. As a worldly port town, and one in which women both outnumbered men and were, as a whole, comparatively poorer, pre-Revolutionary Newport was a place where "brothels flourished." This continued during the war.[39] After encountering the madam of one such establishment, British lieutenant John Peebles observed that "this place must have arrived to a tolerable degree of modern luxury when houses of that kind were publickly allowed of, and the Manners of the People by no means rigid when subjects of that sort become family conversation."[40]

Newport women's motives for entering into relationships with British and German soldiers were certainly varied and complex. Some may have found them congenial because of their personal or familial political commitments. Other women may have seen in such relationships opportunities for economic mobility or enhanced social status. Still other women may have been motivated less by hope than fear, pressured by the economic and personal insecurity created by the war. Whatever their causes, the wide array of relationships formed between local women and the occupying troops also suggest that many Newporters expected, for better or worse, the American rebellion to fail and ties between the town and the rest of the British Empire to endure.

It was this aspect of life in occupied Newport that seems to have provided a key piece of context for the capture of General Prescott, or at least public perceptions of the event. Prescott evidently shared many of his younger officers' interests in local women. Barton's biographer, while harshly critical of Prescott's behavior as commander at Newport, noted that "this man could enjoy festivity," and that, irrespective of the sufferings of townspeople during the occupation, he continued attempting to "dance the ladies to allegiance."[41] Almost from the moment of his capture, the story appears to have gained currency that Prescott took up lightly guarded quarters in rural Middletown, rather than stay in more secure lodgings in Newport proper, in order to carry on an affair or just have a more private site for trysts. Neither Barton's own account of the event nor the records of a British military Board of Enquiry into Prescott's conduct mention this, but neither side had much to gain from airing any such details. Prescott claimed to have chosen to reside at the Overings' house because it put him in "a centrical Situation" on the island, giving him easy access to the various camps of the units under his command.[42]

But other, slightly differing, versions of the story also appear to have come quickly into existence. Ezra Stiles, at this time resident in Portsmouth, New Hampshire, noted Prescott's capture in his diary entry for July 17, 1777, meaning he had learned of it within a week of its occurrence. He had no doubts why Prescott was in Middletown, recording that Barton and his volunteers had captured him "about 4 or 5 Miles out of Newp[or]t" after "hav[in]g had Informa[tion] that the Gen. was to lodge there that night with some of his Whores." Stiles sometimes added subsequent comments to entries that he made in his diary as he learned more information, and at some later point he marked this entry with the word "True."[43] Other accounts indicate that Prescott had only one companion and that she may have been more respectable than Stiles suggested. Nicholas Cresswell, who was aboard a British ship anchored in Long Island Sound when he learned the news, recorded in his journal for July 17, 1777, that Prescott "was taken by the Rebels, in bed with a Farmer's Daughter near Newport."[44] Most accounts of the capture record only the men who were in the house. It seems this was done with a wink by some nineteenth-century authors who were aware of more salacious details but considered them unfit for print. According to Barton's biographer Catherine Williams, before returning to Middletown for the night Prescott had spent the evening preceding his capture at the house of a Newport Tory, where "a jolly carouse" was held to celebrate the capture of a rebel ship by drinking wine taken from it. In a rather odd turn of phrase, Williams wrote that when the raiders arrived, Henry Overing, his son, Prescott, his aide-de-camp, and the servants "constituted the household, or the male part of it at least."[45]

In another version of the story, which may date from much later, Prescott was not using Henry Overing's Middletown house as a private site for trysts but rather quartering himself there because he was carrying on an affair with Overing's wife, Mary.[46] There appears little contemporary evidence for this suggestion, although a soldier who claimed to be one of Barton's volunteers did record, contrary to other reports, that at least one of the Overing women was in the house when the raiders seized Prescott. Abel Potter, according to his successful pension application, was one of Barton's men. So too was his brother, Lieutenant James Potter, whom various sources record as one of the officers who participated in the raid. In Abel's account, when Barton's men burst into the Overing house they were met by "the Widow Oberin" who recognized his brother, a sea captain in peacetime, and said "Capt. Potter what's the matter?" James Potter also knew the woman and replied, "We are not going to hurt you. Where is the General?"[47] It seems possible that Potter, recounting the events of 1777 some fifty years later, was referring here to Mary Overing. Although she was *not* a widow in 1777, she was widowed in 1783, she owned the Middletown house long after the Revolution, and she died in Newport in 1816.[48] Mary Overing may have been known locally as the "widow Overing" for decades after the Revolution. It also seems possible that Potter meant someone else. Given these varying accounts, it seems impossible to be sure of the identity of the woman with Prescott at the time of his capture, but it seems most likely that she was a local person and one whose life was dramatically affected by the experience of occupation.

Whether Mary Overing or another Newport woman was the object of Prescott's attentions, it is clear that reports that the general's capture was due to his sexual indiscretions quickly reached London. The humiliating detail that the general was captured in his nightshirt and propelled down to the waiting whaleboats in this state of undress, when combined with the story that he had been in the company of a woman, made good material for London wits and led to several pieces and poems lampooning him. The punning *Public Advertiser* attributed Prescott's capture to "a *sinical Indulgence* unbecoming the Character of a Soldier."[49] A September 1777 foray, "On General Prescott being carried off naked 'unanointed, unanealed,'" published in the *London Chronicle*, ran:

> What various lures there are to ruin man;
> Woman, the first and foremost all bewitches!
> A nymph thus spoil'd a General's mighty plan,
> And gave him to the foe—without his breeches.

It has been claimed that "Prescott's story so dominated the popular poetry of the time that his "britches" became a cause célèbre in their own right."[50] Such humor reflected English anxieties about the course of the war in America. It also hints at the experiences of Newporters who lived for several years on intensely personal terms with thousands of sailors and soldiers. Whatever the identity of Prescott's paramour, her war entailed making hard choices about loyalty, danger, opportunity, and the future. In this way Prescott's capture provides a window on the ways that the rather mundane, human realities of war affected women and men, whatever their political preferences, far from the battlefield.

Another striking feature to emerge from examining the Prescott capture is the substantial part African Americans played in the conflict around Narragansett Bay. People of color were key conduits of information for both sides. Because many were servants, they were frequently privy to sensitive conversations and often able to move between the armies. Barton was well aware of this. In January 1776 he concocted a scheme to "put an end to the communication by Negroes" and lured a boat crew from the HMS *Rose* into a patriot trap. Barton had a black man hail one of the *Rose*'s boats from the shore and yell that he wanted to escape from his master and turn "papers" over to the British. When the boat landed, Barton's concealed men sprang up and seized its midshipman and two sailors.[51] According to his own account of Prescott's capture, Barton learned of the general's sleeping habits through the report of a recent civilian refugee from Newport, Mr. Coffin, which was later confirmed by two "deserters" from Aquidneck Island.[52] According to some other accounts, one of these deserters, or an additional informant on Prescott's movements, was an enslaved man named Quaco Honeyman. Some later histories recorded that Quaco personally accompanied Barton's party and that he was the black man who broke down Prescott's door, but in most versions of the story this action is attributed to another enslaved man, variously identified as Jack (or Tack) Sisson or as Prince.[53]

For Quaco, as for other enslaved people in Newport during these tumultuous years, the war brought both risks and opportunities in its train. When the British first occupied Newport, Quaco was the property of James Honeyman, a locally born, pro-British Newport lawyer and longtime colonial official.[54] At the time of Prescott's capture Quaco appears to have been employed outside of Honeyman's home, perhaps as a servant in Prescott's or Overing's household or in a Newport tavern that the general frequented. In Catherine Williams's 1839 biography of Barton, based on her access to his papers and the memories of elderly Rhode Islanders, she noted in what seems to have been a reference to Quaco, that "Quam [Quaco?], the negro who had been employed in the kitchen of Mr. Overing, had carried a very perfect account of the situation of the General in the house" to Barton.⁵⁵ What these various sources also suggest is that immediately prior to Prescott's capture in July 1777, Quaco fled from British-occupied Aquidneck Island to the rebel-held mainland, bringing with him valuable intelligence on Prescott's habits that aided Barton and his men in planning their raid.

In December 1781, Quaco made a representation to the Rhode Island General Assembly that provides the most compelling explanation for why he may have left Aquidneck Island in 1777. The context for Quaco's 1781 representation testifies to the complexities of enslaved people's wartime decision making. Since escaping British-occupied territory in the summer of 1777, Quaco had lived in de facto freedom on the Rhode Island mainland. His erstwhile master James Honeyman had died in British-controlled Newport in February 1778, and Honeyman's children sailed with the British fleet that evacuated the city in 1779. Both factors probably helped Quaco preserve his precarious freedom for several years.⁵⁶ By 1781, however, his liberty was under threat. With the British now gone from Rhode Island, an executor of James Honeyman's estate, his son-in-law William Tweedy, was trying to reenslave Quaco.

Understandably "disagreeably alarmed" at the prospect, Quaco petitioned the General Assembly to recognize him as legally free. In this context, Quaco reported to the General Assembly that during the British occupation his master, James Honeyman, had agreed to sell him to a British officer, Colonel Campbell. Quaco said that "service in a British regiment being extremely distasteful to him, he fled from the island of Rhode Island at peril of his life, and placed himself under the protection of the authorities of this state." It was then, Quaco's petition related, that Rhode Island's council of war had "permitted him to go at large, and have his liberty" in recognition of his relaying to patriot leaders "the state of the [British-occupied] island of Rhode Island, and all matters of fact which came to his knowledge." This seems to have been information on Prescott; Quaco clearly provided significant intelligence of some sort to the rebel cause despite his master's British sympathies and his own ties to the occupying army. In January 1782, in recognition of his 1777 actions, the Rhode Island legislature passed a resolution guaranteeing Quaco's freedom and noting that he had rendered "great and essential service to this state and the public in general."⁵⁷

For Quaco, then, as much as for Barton or Prescott, the capture of the British general was a life-changing event. The war had threatened to destroy his life as he knew it, not by transforming the imperial relationship between Newport and London, but because in the context of the occupation Quaco's loyalist master had decided to sell him to a British officer who might have taken him anywhere without his consent. Quaco seems to have responded by taking extraordinary risks. According to one account, "the British were so incensed against him that, if they could have caught him, he would have been hung, drawn, and quartered." It was a risk that paid off. Having allied himself with the winning side in the Revolution, Quaco ultimately earned his freedom.[58] Other enslaved people made different choices. According to some sources, as Barton's patriots propelled their befuddled captives down to the shoreline, the alarm was finally raised by one of the Overings' slaves, who ran out of the house to alert the general's slumbering troop of escorts.

As the widespread knowledge of Prescott's peccadilloes and Quaco's wartime experiences suggest, the war around Narragansett Bay became an intensely personal one, a struggle in which opponents knew each other as individuals, the line between combatant and noncombatant was permeable, and civilians had ties to both camps. Quaco Honeyman obviously knew rebels, Tories, and British soldiers alike. Several accounts note that Barton knew the Overing house well, and probably the Overing family, having been quartered nearby as a member of the Rhode Island militia before the British occupation. Abel Potter's account of the exchange between "Widow Oberin" and his brother suggests the way this intimacy could inject itself into even the most intense moments. Such familiarity also could make the struggle a particularly bitter one. Thomas Austin, one of the members of Barton's raiding party, was said to have been keen to volunteer because of a personal grievance. He had previously received three hundred lashes on Prescott's orders for refusing to use his oxen to shift British artillery on the island.[59] The conflict in Newport would leave Tories embittered too. In 1782 Barton was awarded the confiscated Newport home of a prominent loyalist, Thomas Bannister, as compensation for back salary and other debts owed him by the state's wartime government. The house may have been the very one in which Prescott had a "jolly carouse" the evening before his capture.[60]

Yet, the intimacy of the conflict could also produce surprising outcomes. The sentry that Barton's men quietly captured on their way in to the Overing house was a Scots-born private named Walter Graham, who had joined the Twenty-Second Regiment in 1772. He seems to have been a rather reluctant soldier, having twice tried to desert the army even before the American war began. According to Abel Potter, who claimed to have personally taken Graham prisoner, Graham was so terrified that he trembled and could barely respond when hurriedly questioned at gunpoint about his general's precise whereabouts. Barton's men took Graham with them back across Narragansett Bay alongside their more illustrious prisoners. In May 1778 Graham was placed aboard a ship so that he could be exchanged for an American sergeant in British hands. He had apparently decided, though, that he was through with army life and the war. He escaped from the ship and disappeared.[61] Perhaps he had the help of some of his recent enemies. In either a remarkable coincidence or an intimation of collusion, Abel Potter reported decades later that he knew Graham after the war in the town of Pownal, Vermont, where Graham had become a schoolmaster and taught one of Potter's own children. For Graham too, then, it appears that Prescott's capture was a transformative event, taking him rather improbably from reluctant service as a private in the British army to life as a small-town schoolteacher on the New England frontier.

* * *

In a well-known list that he included in his diary on March 1, 1777, Ezra Stiles compiled the "names of some of the inhabitants left in the Town of Newport when it was taken 8 Dec. 1776." This list included 310 names of those living in the town under British occupation, mostly men but also a few widows and women who stayed behind though their husbands had left. Stiles also identified those still in Newport whom he believed to be loyalists and recorded the "Degrees of Toryism" he thought they each held. Seventy-six of the 310 names had between one and five stars next to them to reflect what Stiles took to be their commitment to the loyalist cause. Quaco Honeyman's master, James Honeyman, was a four-star Tory. Thomas Vernon, the postmaster who had been exiled to the mainland for refusing to take a patriot oath, was rated a two-star man. There is one Sisson on the list, with no first name given. Sissons had long lived in Rhode Island, which probably explains how the black man Jack Sisson who participated in the Prescott raid came by his name. If Tosh Sisson, the privateering silversmith who pleaded for clemency from a patriot jail, was this man, he received no stars even though he remained living in occupied Newport.

Stiles rated Henry Overing just a one-star Tory. Overing died intestate in Bermuda in 1783, but he seems to have traveled there due to ill health rather than as a loyalist refugee.[62] In either case, Mary Overing and some of their younger children stayed behind. Mary and their older son, a British army officer since 1779, would go on after the war to file claims with the American and British governments, respectively, for losses Henry had sustained during the conflict.[63] In appealing for compensation from Britain, his son claimed, despite his father's signing a patriot loyalty oath in 1776, that Henry had never aided the rebellion nor subjected himself to the American states. However, when George Wightman, commander of a Newport loyalist unit during the occupation, was asked to give evidence on the matter, he said "Henry John Overing was not a violent man on either side, but was not, in his opinion, a loyalist, and remained in R.I. after the evacuation."[64] Neither side, it appears, had too much sympathy for the Overings' ordeal.

Ezra Stiles's compilations are worth attention because the "gentle Puritan," as Edmund Morgan called him, was a sensitive and thoughtful diarist.[65] It is characteristic that his ranking system of Newport's loyalists revealed his awareness of the shades of attachment to the Crown present among his former neighbors. Nevertheless, Stiles himself was highly politicized and a strong partisan of the patriot cause. He wanted to separate friend from foe: naming the enemy was part of winning the war. Yet, many of the people on Stiles's list, whether designated as Tories or not, almost certainly had varying responses to the conflict that were highly dependent on the local course of the war. For example, Stiles marked down George Sears as a one-star Tory. At some point subsequently Stiles revised his assessment, amending his diary to record that Sears was, after all, a Whig. If Stiles was initially wrong, his error provides a warning about the difficulty of making such assessments. If Sears changed his mind as the war went on, he was certainly not alone.

Even more important, the few hundred names that Stiles recorded were but a small fraction of those who lived in British-occupied Newport. Thousands of less visible people in the town—women, the poor, servants, slaves, children, and others—were impacted by the war even though they remained unnamed and uncategorized. We know very little about what they thought of the conflict. It is especially suggestive that Stiles immediately followed this list of 310 names in his diary with two even shorter listings of occupied Newport's "Principal & Active Tories" and "Whigs." Together the two lists amounted to just forty-two names. In identifying these tiny cadres of highly politicized people in Newport, Stiles also revealed the scope of the ambivalence, disaffection, and uncertainty present in his community.

Traditional accounts of the Prescott capture put William Barton at the center of the story, with supporting roles given to his trusty band of patriot soldiers and the British general, who often appears as a rather stock villain.

Like Stiles's lists and many histories of the Revolution, they put the focus on some of the most committed and active participants in the struggle. However, if we put the focus on the stories of people like Mary Overing, Quaco Honeyman, or the reluctant warrior Walter Graham, it is possible to get a glimpse of a far more conflicted, frequently less heroic, and ultimately more human Revolutionary era. For each of these people, the war dramatically altered the course of their lives. With this in mind, we might take the scene of Barton's raiders beating in the Overings' door as a metaphor for the wider conflict. In the period between 1775 and 1783, whether they wanted it or not, the war came home to the people of Rhode Island.

CHAPTER 3

Uncommon Cause

The Challenges of Disaffection in Revolutionary Pennsylvania

AARON SULLIVAN

> The friends of the revolution excuse this tyranny by saying that liberty for all must be forced on a few by despotism.
> —Captain Johann Ewald, March 21, 1778

In 1818 John Adams wrote a letter to Hezekiah Niles famously asking, "What do we mean by the American Revolution?" He went on to claim that the answer lay, not on the battlefield, but "in the minds and hearts of the people" and that a "radical change in the principles, opinions, sentiments, and affections of the people, was the real American Revolution." This was a revolution that Adams declared "was effected before the [Revolutionary] war commenced" or, as he put it elsewhere, which took place "from 1760 to 1775, in the course of fifteen years before a drop of blood was shed at Lexington." It was a revolution in which "the people," whom Adams repeatedly invokes, were miraculously united; as he tells Niles, the alteration of heart and mind "was common to all. . . . Thirteen clocks were made to strike together—a perfection of mechanism, which no artist had ever before effected." Memorable as such quotations are, Adams's recounting of the Revolution was deeply flawed, potentially deceptive, and more than a little self-serving.[1]

It should not surprise us that Adams, ever the statesman but never a soldier, should downplay the importance of the war in his account of the Revolution, or that he, as a key player in bringing that war about, should prefer to imagine that all of "the people" who experienced it were united behind the revolutionary cause before they were made to bleed and die for it. Yet no real investigation of the period can long sustain that hopeful narrative. Adams may have heard thirteen clocks chime together in Philadelphia, but that note was only one of many contributing to the ongoing cacophony that echoed back and forth across the American colonies in the 1760s, 1770s, and 1780s. The radical changes in the "principles, opinions, sentiments, and affections" that took place in some of "the people" failed to take place in others. Even if we seek to find it in the minds of the people rather than on the colonial battlefields, the "real American Revolution" was still a war; the people's minds, no less than the battlefields, had to be won. In many cases, they had to be conquered.

It behooves us, then, to consider thoughtfully the human terrain over which this war was waged and the means by which the revolutionaries hoped to achieve their conquest. There has never been a shortage of historical works on the lives of American revolutionaries, and there now exists a growing body of historical writing on the American loyalists.[2] Yet outside these warring camps there dwelt a large and ever-shifting mass of people strongly aligned with neither that we still struggle to understand and that the revolutionaries preferred to overlook. Some of these were pacifists, but many more disengaged as a matter of pragmatism, not principle. These were the people, quite likely in the majority, whom John Shy has called "the great middle group of Americans . . . who were dubious, afraid, uncertain, indecisive, many of whom felt that there was nothing at stake that could justify involving themselves and their families in extreme hazard and suffering."[3] Persistently disinterested in or opposed to involvement with imperial politics and committed to separate goals, they quietly pursued their own livelihoods to the best of their ability amid the turmoil, helping or hurting either side more incidentally than intentionally, and hoping to come through the revolutionary storm with as little harm and as much profit as possible, whichever side eventually proved triumphant. Both the revolutionaries and the British referred to this diverse group as "the disaffected," perceiving correctly that their defining feature was less *loyalty to* than a *lack of support or affection for* either party in the imperial dispute. If we assume that all Americans must be classified either as "patriots" or "loyalists," we risk mischaracterizing these people as fickle, opportunistic, apathetic, or even treasonous. Only by recognizing them as the disaffected, without any strong attachments to betray, do their actions appear to be at all rational and consistent.[4]

Disaffection existed in a variety of forms and arose from numerous causes. Among Americans who were aware of and engaged with colonial politics, a group that expanded rapidly in the third quarter of the eighteenth century, there was nearly universal disapproval of the new taxes and regulations imposed by Britain in the 1760s and early 1770s. Differences of opinion existed as to the severity of the threat and the proper colonial response to it, but in general Americans of various stripes began to look across the Atlantic with a more wary and less trusting gaze.[5]

Yet as the resistance to parliamentary overreach expanded and developed in unanticipated ways after 1774, an increasingly large number of Americans found it unpalatable. Driven by negative personal experiences with radical revolutionaries, economic conflicts with the revolutionary program, political and ideological disagreements with the ever-evolving revolutionary agenda, or some combination of these, they distanced themselves from the movement and disengaged. In the end, some would conclude that the face of the opposition was no more desirable, or just as terrible, as that of their oppressive monarch. "I love the cause of liberty," wrote James Allen in 1776, "but cannot heartily join in the prosecution of measures totally foreign to the original plan of Resistance. The madness of the multitude is but one degree better than submission to the Tea-Act."[6] Such pressures were only rarely in direct opposition to those that moved individuals into the resistance in the first place. Rather than pushing men and women *back* toward a greater affection for the empire, they pushed them *out*, away from both loyalism and rebellion, and *down*, into a seclusion and silence that came naturally to those who could find no cause to rally around. Though much of his family embraced the loyalist cause and sought protection from the British military, Allen retreated to his country home where he and his acquaintances endeavored to "banish Politics" from their lives and conversations.[7]

Though we have often regarded this group as the "neutrals" in the conflict, that categorization is problematic for several reasons, and the revolutionaries rarely recognized them as such. For a variety of reasons, the disaffected represented a significant threat to the Revolution. Throughout the struggle, they found themselves the objects of an unwavering and, at times, brutally coercive campaign to secure their consent for and involvement in the opposition to British legislation and the fight for independence. The following review of that campaign and its consequences focuses primarily, though not exclusively, on Pennsylvania, where the most radical and democratic elements of revolutionary change confronted a widespread and well-established disaffection.

In the years prior to the war, the nonimportation and nonconsumption movements helped to unite colonists across divides of class, gender, culture, and geography, spurring the creation of a new *American* identity and granting politically marginalized elements of society a means of declaring their dissatisfaction with Britain and solidarity with their fellow colonists. Through these visible, sacrificial acts of protest, those engaged in the resistance against British taxation were able to identify one another; the use of material goods became, in the words of historian T. H. Breen, "the litmus test of commitment."[8]

Soon enough, the patriots came to see these movements not just as a means of discerning fellow travelers but also as tools for recognizing enemies. James Madison declared the Continental Association to be "the method used among us to distinguish friends from foes," and, as time passed, that binary distinction, which failed to recognize or acknowledge neutrality and disengagement, increasingly became a defining feature of the Revolution's ideology.[9] This self-imposed blindness made the Revolution a dangerous thing, not only for individuals who actively opposed it but also for Americans who simply hoped to avoid it. Those who merely continued past commercial practices could be marked, on that basis alone, as "foes to the rights of British America" and "enemies of American Liberty." They could face public denunciation, interrogation, and the threat, or even the reality, of violence against their person and possessions.[10] The ubiquity of British imports and the common language of material goods throughout the colonies, factors that made movements like nonconsumption such powerful tools for uniting the people, also meant that almost everyone could theoretically be forced into the "for us"/ "against us" dichotomy imagined by the revolutionary committees.

In addition to, and eventually alongside, the boycott movement, the creation, expansion, and regulation of colonial militias broadened the scope of involvement in the resistance to include hitherto relatively unpoliticized segments of society and allowed individuals to express their dissatisfaction through actions as well as words. John Shy has argued that the revolutionaries quickly came to see participation in the militia as a "test of loyalty" with which they could separate virtuous, supportive patriots from self-serving, antagonistic loyalists. This was particularly true in colonies like Pennsylvania, where the militia tradition was weak prior to the emergence of revolutionary tensions.

The nature of militia service and the fact that the British military eventually touched almost all parts of colonial America meant that, like nonconsumption, this was a test that could potentially be applied to nearly all white, male Americans.[11]

Attempts to remain neutral or uninvolved were increasingly deemed intolerable by the revolutionary leadership. Envisioning the militia as the embodiment of "the people" whose freedom was at stake in the Revolution, those leaders tended to look upon nonparticipants as, at best, timorous or selfish and, at worst, Tories and traitors. Alexander Graydon was shocked to encounter this mentality when he settled in Reading, Pennsylvania, where his lack of participation in the militia made his loyalty suspect. His service as a captain in the Continental Army and imprisonment by the British in New York was taken as a poor excuse for this failure. "My having risked myself in the field was nothing," he reflected some years later, "I should have staid at home, talked big, been a militia-man and hunted Tories."[12] Though Pennsylvania's militia companies were originally wholly voluntary organizations, participation in them became mandatory in 1775, and a series of ever-increasing fines were levied on those who persisted in their disengagement. By 1777, failure to participate could result in a crippling fine of £25 per annum on top of a special 25 percent tax on the value of one's estate. Those who refused to pay risked having their personal property seized and sold at auction.[13]

Once the Revolution had fully transitioned from an effort to preserve the British constitutional liberties of subjects living in America to an attempt to create a new nation ostensibly founded on the will of the people, the revolutionary leadership of Pennsylvania became far more explicit in its attempts to forcibly incorporate those who seemed to be insufficiently patriotic in their speech or conduct. Less than three months after the Declaration of Independence, the new revolutionary regime in Pennsylvania outlawed speech or writing that, in the opinion of a justice of the peace, threatened to "impede the present virtuous opposition." Violators faced potentially unlimited fines and imprisonment, not upon conviction by a jury, but simply upon the agreement of two justices.[14]

The Pennsylvania Council of Safety, established in 1777 in the face of British invasion and occupation, was given almost unlimited punitive authority, up to and including the power to carry out summary executions, over those who, in the council's view, "from their general conduct or conversation may be deemed inimical to the common cause of liberty, and the United States of North America."[15] Furthermore, the council was authorized "to take and seize, where it may be needful, provisions and other necessaries, for the army or the inhabitants" and to "regulate the prices of such articles as they may think necessary, and compel a sale thereof where the same shall be wanted." The people's supposed constitutional rights to "public trial, by an impartial jury of the country," to "hold themselves . . . and possessions free from search and seizure" except by warrant, and "to freedom of speech" were all disregarded. More so than perhaps any other moment in the history of the Revolution, the door was opened for an official and authorized "reign of terror" against those who would not support the cause. That very few loyalists and dissenters were in fact executed speaks to both the weakness of the state government and its hesitancy to fully deploy the coercive powers at its disposal.[16] Despite their claims to represent a unified "People," the patriots lacked the committed manpower to carry out a true purge of the opposition. The populace was never neatly divided into "friends and foes." Many Americans remained uncertain of their neighbor's actual allegiance. Many remained uncertain of their own.

Alongside these laws targeting perceived dissent, the same revolutionary bodies issued edicts aimed squarely at the ranks of the disaffected; silence on the question of independence would itself become an offense. In what became known as the "Test Act," Pennsylvania's revolutionaries moved against those who dared to "*withhold* their service and allegiance." All white male citizens would be required to take an oath renouncing any allegiance to Britain, pledging "true allegiance to the Commonwealth of Pennsylvania as a free and independent State," and promising to serve the cause by uncovering any and all "treasons or traitorous conspiracies" they should discover against the United States.[17] Previous oaths imposed by the revolutionary government were theoretically avoidable if one was willing to forego the privileges of voting or holding office, but now simple disengagement and isolation would provide no protection. In creating the Test Act, the Pennsylvania General Assembly declared that "allegiance and protection are reciprocal, and those who will not bear the former are not nor ought to be entitled to the benefits of the latter" and so it moved to strip the protections and privileges of citizenship from those who refused to swear allegiance. As the Reverend Henry Muhlenberg observed, anyone who failed to "swear an oath of allegiance and acknowledge the new government as the lawful authority . . . within the appointed time is to forfeit all rights and privileges and protection in the *Republic*."[18] In addition to being stripped of the franchise, those who refused the oath were forbidden to serve on juries or sue to recover debts; they could not purchase, sell, or otherwise transfer real estate; and any weapons they possessed were subject to confiscation. Like the nonconsumption movements and the militias, the Test Act was intended to cleanly divide the populace in two: "the People," who willingly declared their commitment to the patriot cause, and the others, who refused to do so and, in so refusing, negated their own existence as members of society in matters of politics, law, commerce, and defense.[19] Bringing such intentions to fruition, however, proved extremely difficult. The oath was so unpopular initially that, had they truly taken it was a measure of the people's stance on the Revolution, the patriots must have concluded that almost everyone was against them.[20]

Similar principles guided the patriots' response to violations of the revolutionary boycotts. While such transgressions could occasionally result in violence against the perpetrator, more often what Breen has called "the rituals of consumer enforcement" were designed not to destroy or even simply silence dissenters but to extract a public confession from the accused and to secure (at least the appearance of) their consent for the committees and their resolutions.[21] In extracting these confessions, the patriots were often less interested in confirming a true change of heart in the accused than in sending a message to the public. In some cases the words of the confession were penned in advance by the committee; the confessor merely had to sign and publicly read the paper he was handed. Select confessions received an even wider audience when they were published in newspapers or as pamphlets. It was crucial in these performances that the subject not only confess his guilt as a violator of congressional and committee resolutions but also make it clear that he accepted his condemnation as just by expressing great personal shame for his misconduct and/or lauding the rules he had violated as legitimate and desirable. Thus did Alexander Robertson of New York, when apprehended for violations of the Townshend boycotts, confess "To the Publick" that "I have justly incurred the Resentment of my Fellow Citizens, from my Behaviour . . . I beg Leave to implore the Pardon of the Publick, assuring them that I am truly sorry . . . I never will again attempt an Act contrary to the true Interest and Resolutions of a People zealous in the Cause of *Virtue* and *Liberty*."[22] So too did Solomon Cowles and his wife come to "voluntarily, in this public manner, utterly disapprove of and condemn" their own conduct in daring to secretly sip tea as being "to the manifest injury of the public interest of British America."[23] Such statements signaled that even those who violated the boycott were actually in agreement with the committees about the "true Interest and Resolutions of the People." They might, for a time, put their own greedy desires above the good of their country, but they did so with shame and full knowledge of their selfishness. The notion that there might have been honest disagreement about the legitimacy or utility of the revolutionaries' edicts was not to be considered.

Individuals who steadfastly persisted in commercial choices that weakened the apparent unity of the American people had to be dealt with differently. Revolutionary reasoning held that, if an individual was so lacking in virtue that he steadfastly refused to join with the community in defending its liberty, then it followed that he could not truly be part of the community at all. The Articles of Association issued by Congress called for Americans to "break off all dealings" with "such foes to the rights of British-America."[24] Commercial and social interactions between the violators and their community were to be entirely severed; they were to be made strangers in their own lands. A committee in North Carolina memorably referred to this penalty as "civil excommunication," succinctly capturing its gravity and intent.[25] The intended message was clear: true Americans were united in their love of liberty and consented to the revolutionary platform; those who did otherwise were thus not internal dissenters but, necessarily, outsiders and enemies. As with the Test Act, the very ambivalence of the people checked the extent to which ambivalence could be effectively punished. It was simply not possible to wholly cut off or "excommunicate" the thousands of men and women who violated the patriots' ideal of virtuous commerce, at least not in Pennsylvania, and certainly not while the British held the city of Philadelphia.

A similar process of excommunication and "othering" was also intended for those who persisted in verbally questioning the legitimacy of the revolutionary governments or visibly refused to declare their allegiance and consent to the new state. In what may be the most notorious example of such a punishment, in the summer of 1777, as the British army approached Philadelphia, Congress and the Pennsylvania Council of Safety joined forces to arrest forty-one Philadelphians, mostly Quakers, who supposedly "evidenced a disposition inimical to the cause of America."[26] What followed was predictable in light of the revolutionaries' earlier efforts to forcibly secure unanimous consent. As always, the preferred outcome was to have accused dissenters publicly express their support for the Revolution. The prisoners were first offered the opportunity to swear loyalty in accordance with the Test Act.[27] Those who would not join "the people" in unified consent were to be cast out from among them. In this case, the severance was not merely social and commercial. It became a physical banishment from the state. On September 11, those who refused the oath were carried out of Philadelphia to be deposited in Winchester, Virginia; two of them would die before their banishment was finally lifted.[28]

The revolutionaries' need for (the appearance of) universal consent and their consequent assault upon the disaffected in their midst also lay behind the penalties imposed on those who refused to serve in the militia. The justifying assumption for these fines in Pennsylvania was that all Pennsylvanians, whether they had voluntarily joined the militia or not, were united in the beliefs that armed resistance was desirable and that a firm opposition to Britain would bring about an end devoutly to be wished. Because "the Cause is common," declared the committee initially charged with organizing Pennsylvania's defense, "and the Benefits derived from an Opposition are universal, it is not consonant to Justice or Equity that the Burdens should be partial."[29] The militiamen themselves were adamant that all men, whether they served or not, would "reap equal advantages" and "be equally benefited" by the militiamen's service and therefore, whether they wanted to or not, should equally contribute.[30] Those who attempted to remain uninvolved had selfishly "pursued their business to advantage," while more virtuous men fought what had now become a war for independence, "which," the revolutionary leadership declared, conferred "a common benefit."[31] By explaining their actions in terms of common cause and universal benefits, the patriots furthered assumptions of universal consent and implicitly denied the existence of Shy's "great middle group of Americans," who might have shunned the militia because they questioned whether there truly were "advantages" and "benefits" in the pursuit of war and independence.

The revolutionaries' tendency to treat the disaffected as threats rather than as neutrals invites thoughtful consideration of the relationship between tolerance, consent, and representative government and should prompt us to reevaluate the meaning of loyalty and neutrality in the context of the American Revolution. Despite the fact that they held no strong attachments, declared no loyalties, and generally avoided service on the battlefield, in states like Pennsylvania, the ranks of the disaffected fundamentally challenged Adams's "real," internal revolution for the simple reason that they were unlikely to voluntarily participate in or actively affirm the legitimacy of it. The republican ideology from which the Revolution derived its justification based the legitimacy of the movement on its securing and holding popular consent. The patriots had criticized the British government for not representing the American colonists. They were therefore particularly vulnerable to accusations that their own governments were likewise being imposed on the people against their will.

Disaffection, a simple withholding of consent, even if not coupled with active support for the empire, was a profound threat to the legitimacy of the whole revolutionary enterprise, possibly a greater threat than outright loyalism, which was easier to demonize and disregard. Hence the patriots' periodic attempts to stamp it out and their tendency to rhetorically conflate disaffection with treason.

Future generations of Americans, bolstered by an expanding national mythology, a canon of established civic texts, and the weight of history, would find it easier to justify their systems of government on the basis of the *tacit* consent of the people. In time, the republic would benefit from its position as the status quo, a place in which the disengaged and disinterested members of the population supported the continuation of the existing regime by default.[32] Yet in the days of the Revolution, those advantages still lay with the British and the old colonial governments. Consequently, in order to create a nation built, as backers of Pennsylvania's revolutionary constitution put it, "on the authority of the People only," the revolutionary governments believed that they had first to create a "People" who would speak with a unified voice and direct their authority toward specific and identifiable ends, and particularly toward the end of legitimizing the revolutionary governments themselves.[33] To form such a "People" out of the fractured mass of disparate colonists residing in Pennsylvania, the revolutionaries planned and set forth the legal foundation for a campaign of enforced conformity that would target not only defiant members of the opposition but also those who expressed reluctance to support the patriot cause.

It was, of course, more than just ideology that made disaffection dangerous to the rebellion. As the patriot leaders were well aware, the strength of the revolutionary cause was proportional to the level of support it received from the populace. While their foe could call upon an army of thousands of trained regulars and hire thousands more from other nations, the American patriots depended entirely on a civilian populace willing to leave their homes, families, and economic pursuits in order to enforce and maintain the new revolutionary governments and defend independence. Anything, or anyone, that called into question the desirability or utility of such endeavors necessarily robbed the movement of its most valuable resource and left it enervated. The patriots were plagued throughout the war by their inability to consistently turn their rhetoric into reality and effectively eliminate disaffection.

Furthermore, economic imbalances, tradition, and self-interest often made the disaffected a threat to the material survival, as well as the legitimacy, of the Revolution. This tendency is difficult to recognize in settings where the revolutionaries faced no significant military threat or competition for resources. However, where the revolutionary forces lost their monopolies on coercive force and where the civilian population, caught between the lines, was allowed (or forced) to choose which side would receive the benefits of their commerce, the disaffected among them tended to pursue engagement with British rather than Continental forces. Supported by the wealth and power of the empire, the British military was simply able to offer better prices and to pay in a more valuable currency than its revolutionary opponent. Such was the case during the British occupation of Philadelphia between September 1777 and June 1778.

As early as mid-December, Major John Clark, Washington's spymaster in the region, had issued repeated warnings that the people were supplying the British army. On December 19, 1777, he wrote Washington to "again tell your Excellency that the country people carry in provisions constantly."[34] In Whitemarsh, Major John Jameson estimated that "not less than two hundred [inhabitants] a day" left the city with empty sacks and returned loaded down with meal and flour while those in the countryside made the reverse trip in order to buy salt.[35] During the first week of January, Christopher Marshall, having evacuated Philadelphia before the occupation began, recorded that there was "a great concourse of market folks from Bucks County, who attend the markets constantly; that this day week [sic] fifty or sixty men went inside of their [British] works at Kensington, and after some time returned back."[36] Less than a week later, Brigadier General James Potter confirmed that "there is a smart trade carried on between the country and the city" and that wagons loaded with flour and other provisions were safely reaching British lines.[37] Relative to the needs of the city, the quantities carried by each individual were small, but as the number of inhabitants doing business with the city grew, their combined impact became increasingly significant. In late January, Colonel Walter Stewart wrote Washington from Smithfield, not far from British lines, and tried to impress upon him the extent of the problem: "I can assure your Excellency not less flour than is sufficient to maintain eight or ten thousand men goes daily to Philadelphia, carried in by single persons, wagons, horses &c. The quantities of other provisions are great. . . . Were these articles taken in for the use of the poor inhabitants I should think nothing of it, but from all I can learn, tis a traffick, and make no doubt that the British Army receive the greatest Benefits of any persons therefrom."[38] With commerce came information, and British intelligence on the state of the countryside and the position of revolutionary forces was greatly enhanced through conversations with local farmers who were selling their produce for hard currency. Like the material goods they received, the British put this information to good use. General Sir William Howe, the British Army's commander-in-chief in America, had previously turned superior knowledge into victory at Brandywine and Paoli. During the occupation, incoming civilian intelligence allowed him to capture isolated Continental officers such as Major Francis Murray at Newtown, very nearly capture Lafayette at Barren Hill, and deliver a fatal blow to the state militia at Crooked Billet.[39]

The army's inability to isolate and starve Philadelphia deeply distressed the revolutionary leadership, both civil and military, as did the population's obstinate commitment to trading with the city in spite of all orders to the contrary. The flow of goods toward British lines not only sustained the occupying forces and contributed to the crippling shortages experienced at Valley Forge but also undermined claims that the people of Pennsylvania were responsible and consenting citizens of the new republic. As the occupation continued, the state and Continental authorities' attempts to end trade with the city and secure provisions for the revolutionary military became increasingly desperate and brutal.

In mid-December, the Continental Congress began urging Washington to set aside his "delicacy" when it came to dealing with civilians, to strip the country around Philadelphia of anything that might be of use to the British, to take "from all persons without distinction," and to leave behind only what was "necessary for the maintenance of their families." What he lacked the manpower or equipment to confiscate, he was to simply destroy.[40] Taking up Congress's recommendation, Washington informed his officers that in order to prevent "a Continuation of Intercourse between the City & Country" the troops were "hereby instructed to take the most immediate & Coercive Measures . . . I must repeat my desire that you will adopt the most rigorous Means (if nothing less will do) to put a Stop to this practice."[41] The parenthetical qualifier expressed a lingering hesitation that would not last.

As it became apparent that the Continentals lacked the manpower necessary to fully isolate Philadelphia, the army began to try out alternative strategies for controlling the populace. Having admitted that arresting all, or even most, of those who did business with the city was a goal that even "with the utmost vigilance cannot be totally effected," Washington hoped that, by inflicting particularly severe punishments on the few who were captured, the soldiers would be able to frighten the rest of the people into obedience.[42] In letter after letter he called for "proper objects to make examples of" in order "that the rest may be sensible of a like Fate should they persist." A "proper object" would be a man, caught in the act, against whom witnesses could be found. In such a case, and given a guilty verdict from the court-martial, the condemned would be subject to confinement, confiscation, and, in some cases, execution.[43]

Continental soldiers and militiamen also took upon themselves the task of carrying out harsher punishments while patrolling the roads. Circumventing the challenge of winning a court-martial conviction, officers increasingly rendered their own verdicts in the field and issued sentences for lashes and, occasionally, death.[44] Rumors that revolutionary forces were summarily shooting civilians caught carrying goods to Philadelphia began early in the occupation, but it was not until the desperate months of February and March of 1778 that such practices were given official approval.[45] A severely vexed Washington wrote to Brigadier General John Lacey, Jr., commander of the state militia, that "the communication between the City and country, in spite of every thing hitherto done still continuing, and threatening the most pernicious consequences," the militia patrols were henceforth empowered to determine for themselves whether or not those they intercepted with provisions intended to trade with the occupied city. If so, and the patrols deemed it necessary, they were now authorized "to fire upon those gangs of mercenary wretches who make a practice of resorting [to] the city, with marketing."[46] The young general quickly acted on his new authority. In orders to his scouting parties, Lacey vividly described the message he wanted his men to send to the local populace: "If your parties should meet with any people going to market, or any persons whatever going to the city, and they endeavor to make their escape, you will order your men to fire upon the villains. You will leave such on the roads, their bodies and their marketing lying together. This I wish you to execute on the first offenders you meet; that they may be a warning to others."[47] Fortunately for those carrying goods to Philadelphia, popular disaffection and a widespread refusal to turn out for militia service prevented Lacey from ever commanding a sizable force. The scarcity and fragility of revolutionary sentiment in the region around Philadelphia may have made such brutal strategies all the more necessary, at least from the patriots' perspective, but it also made them almost impossible to carry out with any consistency or regularity. Nonetheless, it is worth recognizing that, though generally limited to words rather than deeds, both Washington's persistent desire to "make an example" out of a handful of individuals and Lacey's willingness to leave bodies piled in the road as a "warning" speak to a continuing evolution in the nature and methods of the Revolution. In the face of an enemy they could not beat militarily or compete with economically and in the midst of a population that was largely indifferent to their cause, the revolutionary army, like many militant forces before and after, found itself increasingly drawn to terror as a means of controlling the countryside and the people who lived there.

Lacey's and Washington's plans to terrify the people into submission were among the many patriot strategies severely hampered by the precipitous collapse of the Pennsylvania state militia during the British invasion and occupation. Many of the measures taken to push hesitant and disaffected citizens into militia service backfired horribly when the British army swept in from the south. While self-interest and prudence prompted many individuals to accept service in the patriotic militias in order to avoid fines or other forms of persecution, when the revolutionary governments lost the power to enforce those fines and militia service meant risking life and limb in battle against British regulars, self-interest and prudence quickly sent many of them back home. The British invasion of Pennsylvania was met not by an outpouring of militia but by the lowest militia turnouts of the war and a sharp spike in desertion rates.[48]

On August 22, 1777, Congress had called upon Pennsylvania to place a force of at least four thousand militiamen under Washington's command to aid him in the defense of the capital.[49] By mid-September, the state had only about two thousand fit for duty.[50] In October, the number slipped to approximately twelve hundred, prompting the commander in chief to write the state government and express his "astonishment" that the turnout was so feeble "at a time, when the Enemy are endeavouring to make themselves compleatly masters of, and to fix their winter Quarters in [Pennsylvania's] Capital."[51] By the year's end, a discouraged Washington had revised his expectations of Pennsylvania's commitment to the cause and agreed to settle for a force of one thousand men.[52] He would not get them. Despite an earnest attempt by the revolutionary leadership to raise more troops, January saw the numbers tumble to 450. On February 15 General Lacey reported to Washington that his "force is at last reduced to almost a cipher. Only sixty remain fit for duty in camp."[53] The suddenness and totality of the collapse infuriated some patriots and wreaked havoc on Washington's attempts to isolate occupied Philadelphia.[54] Direct intervention by the commander in chief succeeded in briefly raising Lacey's numbers to several hundred, but by late April the militia forces had once again "dwindled away to nothing."[55]

The lack of manpower thwarted the Continentals' attempts to procure supplies for their own use as well as their efforts to keep them from the British, and here too the patriots increasingly came to embrace extreme and violent action against the civilian population. In February several factors, including local disaffection, poor management, bad weather, and insufficient transportation conspired to plunge the Continental Army into one of the worst logistical crises it would ever experience. Washington wrote that what had once been "occasional deficiencies in the Article of provisions . . . seem now on the point of resolving themselves into this fatal crisis—total want and a dissolution of the Army."[56] The times had become exceedingly desperate and the revolutionaries' response would be no less so.

Washington drafted orders for Nathanael Greene to carry out a massive and unprecedentedly merciless foraging expedition. He wanted the area between the Schuylkill and Brandywine rivers, stretching as far as twenty miles inland from the Delaware, entirely stripped of livestock and provisions. No distinction was to be made between friends and enemies of the cause. As historian Wayne Bodle notes, this was the first time Washington's orders "omitted his customary injunctions to leave friendly residents with at least enough resources to sustain their families."[57] What Greene could not safely carry off, he was to destroy. Those who lost goods to the army because of this expedition were to be given special certificates that could one day be used to apply for payment, but the specifics of when that day would be, where the certificates could be turned in, and to whom, were still to be determined as Greene and his men began their mission. Given the Continental Army's poor reputation for honoring its debts in the region, these mysterious pieces of paper were likely of little solace to those who watched as the last of their horses, cattle, sheep, and provender were taken from them.[58]

Over the course of the following weeks, Greene's expedition drained the countryside of the few supplies and little goodwill that remained in it. The Continental officers themselves struggled with the severity of the duty set before them. "The inhabitants cry out and beset me from all quarters," Greene wrote to Washington, "but like Pharoh I harden my heart . . . I [am] determin[ed] to forage the Country very bare. Nothing shall be left unattempted."[59] Though he took all that he found, Greene found that there was little left to take from these people who had for some months been trapped between the lines of two hungry armies. "The face of the Country is strongly marked with poverty and distress," he reported, and "has been so gleaned that there is but little left in it."[60]

As word of the foraging expedition and its methods spread, the people's pleading gave way to desperation and subterfuge. Those who could rushed to get their goods to markets in Philadelphia before all was lost to the Continentals. Others carted their provisions and drove their livestock and wagons off into the wilderness to conceal them. Greene followed, sending his men "to search all the Woods and swamps after them."[61] Farmers who tried to hide their property from the Continentals were to be arrested, while those caught trying to make it to British lines were severely whipped. Aware that dire circumstances at Valley Forge required that Greene maintain his "hardened heart," Washington did what he could to steel his resolve along the way, urging him to "make severe examples" of anyone who tried to reach the occupied city and assuring him that "our present wants will justify any measures you can take." Greene assured his commander that "examples shall not be wanting to facilitate the business I [am] out upon."[62]

In the end the provision crisis proved to be fatal, not to the army itself, but to the army's ability to actively project the revolutionaries' vision of a cleanly divided society, friends and foes, a unified "People" against a treasonous minority. Over the long months of the occupation, more and more local inhabitants forsook revolutionary rhetoric and made their own private, economic peace with the occupied city. The percentage of inhabitants who fit the model of the virtuous, committed patriot, who legitimated the Revolution and deserved its protections and privileges, diminished until, in the dark days of Greene's grand foraging expedition, the Continental soldiers went forth treating everyone they encountered with the cold brutality once reserved only for alleged enemies to the cause.

Though it never succeeded in isolating Philadelphia from the surrounding countryside, much less in forcing the British to choose between starvation and retreat, the Continental crackdown in 1778 did have a profound, if unintended, effect on the local populace. The confiscations, destruction, arrests, imprisonment, whippings, and executions carried out by the Continental Army and the Pennsylvania militia began to slowly but steadily alienate more and more civilians in the Delaware Valley. Though perhaps no more firmly attached to Great Britain than they had been previously, the disaffected grew increasingly wary of and hostile toward the revolutionaries who strove to control them. More alarming still, previously committed revolutionaries began to abandon the cause, unable to reconcile their prior devotion with the coercive acts carried out by their fellow patriots and the commercial benefits of reengaging with the British Atlantic trade via the occupied city.

Observers on both sides took note of these shifting political affections, though few patriots captured the effect so clearly as did Joseph Reed. "The intercourse between the Country & the Town has produced all the consequences foreseen by many in the beginning of the Winter," he fretted. Yet it was not the supply of provisions to the enemy that so concerned him; indeed, he counted such material losses to be "the least pernicious" of those the cause was suffering. It was not simply the war for independence but the Revolution itself, John Adams's "real American Revolution" of hearts and minds, that Reed saw collapsing in the face of a persistent British presence and the people's ability to take advantage of it. He despaired that "the Minds of the Inhabitants are seduced, their Principles tainted & opposition enfeebled—a familiarity with the Enemy lessens their abhorrence of them & their Measures. Even good Whigs," he worried, "begin to think Peace at some Expense desirable."[63] While Reed blamed the ongoing trade with the city, others recognized dangerous consequences arising from the actions of the revolutionaries themselves. In the eyes of J. B. Smith, it was "the conduct of the different departments" and "the impositions & irregularities of some of the agents" that were responsible for "the body of the people, especially of this state losing their confidence in the Commander in Chief." Yet more was at stake than the popular perception of Washington, and it was more than "irregularities" that drove the people away. Smith suggested to Reed that "if it were possible avoid *seizures* & except in particular cases acts of force, many disaffected persons, more of the indetermined [*sic*], & all real Whigs would be with us." Whether they held that trade itself or the revolutionaries' harsh and ineffective attempts to stop it were responsible, both agreed that "by the present system of conduct, we suffer a fearful increase of disaffection."[64]

The British too registered the change. Even Major General James Grant, who had at first decried Pennsylvania as "more inimical than any [province] we have yet been in," came to believe that, had it not been for Burgoyne's defeat at Saratoga, events surrounding the occupation of Philadelphia "must have put an end to the Contest, for tho' factious leaders may be unwilling to part with the power they have got into their hands, individuals are tired of the business, & tho' they have no attachment to Great Britain they would be glad to rescind Independency if they knew what terms they are to expect. They see their interests but dare not declare their opinions."[65] The British commander in chief also took note of the changing sentiments and, like Grant, came to believe that by the spring of 1778 whatever revolutionary fires had once burned in the Delaware Valley were now all but extinguished. Howe wrote that "the difficulties of the Congress in raising supplies and in recruiting Mr. Washington's army, then indeed became real, and had the appearance of being insurmountable." All this he "could not but attribute . . . to the possession of Philadelphia."[66]

It would be a mistake to assume that the people's refusal to serve in the militia, their hesitancy to trade with the Continentals, or their proclivity for defying revolutionary edicts by selling goods to the occupied city were evidence of widespread pro-British sentiment in Pennsylvania. As other scholars have noted, "loyalism was weak in Pennsylvania." The colony was instead "a stronghold of moderates, pacifists, and neutralists."[67] Though the revolutionary governments were sometimes quick to condemn civilians who traded with the British as traitors and enemies, the military officers who dealt with and tried to stop such individuals rarely attributed their actions to political motivations or allegiance. Far more often they concluded that the root causes of this illicit traffic were economic.[68] Moreover, few of those who refused to turn out for militia service or deserted before their term expired went on to cast their lot with the British army. Howe had anticipated raising several thousand provincial soldiers in Pennsylvania, a force sufficient to defend the capital while his main army carried the offensive to fresh soil. Yet he was unable, despite repeated calls for recruits, the offering of land bounties, and "the most indefatigable exertions, during eight months," to secure even one thousand new soldiers.[69] The overwhelming majority of inhabitants in occupied Philadelphia obstinately refused to commit themselves to the British cause, either by service with the military or even by taking the oath of allegiance to the king.[70]

There were many, then, at least in the Delaware Valley, who were neither loyalists nor revolutionaries in any meaningful sense of those terms. Precisely how many remains unclear, but certainly enough to sustain the British occupation of the American capital through the winter of 1777–78, to rob Washington of a considerable part of his military strength, and to constantly bedevil patriot attempts to realize their vision of a united, consenting American "people." The internal, or "real," Revolution of hearts and minds that John Adams described in 1818 was not, as he then liked to imagine, "common to all." The rhetoric of some revolutionaries to the contrary notwithstanding, the British were not uniformly perceived as foreign invaders attempting to conquer a sovereign American nation; the war for American independence was, as others have noted, a civil war. And yet there *was* an element of conquest in it. Because so many disaffected Americans abandoned or never joined the revolutionary cause, the patriots felt compelled by their own republican logic to conquer the hearts and minds of the people who refused to consent to their regime. By drawing a clean and uncompromising line between "friends and foes" and then declaring those on the other side of it traitors or "enemies of American Liberty," they hoped to cajole, prod, or simply force the hesitant and disengaged into the revolutionary fold. Yet this proved more difficult than they had imagined. Disaffection was threatening because it was so widespread, but the very prevalence of such ambivalent sentiments constantly thwarted patriot efforts to stamp it out. The revolutionaries could demand oaths of loyalty, condemn opposition, forbid trade with the British-occupied cities, and mandate universal militia service, but without widespread and energetic popular support, their rhetoric was often impotent. Around occupied Philadelphia, the Continentals found themselves wholly unable to prevent trade with the city, secure the countryside around Philadelphia, or consistently enforce revolutionary edicts. Instead, their limited manpower and supply base proved sufficient for carrying out only sporadic, though at times terrifying, acts of punishment, confiscation, and destruction, acts that appeared all the more terrible and extreme for their irregularity.

Ironically, the degree of uniformity that the patriots so dearly desired, that their acts of coercion were meant to create, and that Adams would later fondly, if falsely, imagine to have existed, proved to be wholly unnecessary in the end. The success of the Revolution and the longevity of the nation that eventually arose from it demonstrate that new nations, even new republics, can in fact be secured and established without the unified, expressed consent of the people. Loyalism and disaffection can be overcome, or at least overlooked. Some hearts and minds were altered of their own accord in the fifteen years before Lexington and Concord; others were made to yield, were conquered, through social pressure, fines, threats, or outright coercion; and still others were simply forgotten, their discordant notes and suspicious silences lost amid the historic echoes of Adams's thirteen perfectly synchronized clocks.

We would do well to restore that disharmony to our memory of the Revolution. Just as the patriotic narrative of a revolutionary people fighting solely to preserve liberty has been complicated and challenged by the addition of black and Native American perspectives, the same seems to be true if we incorporate the plight of the disaffected.[71] To a surprising extent, the revolutionaries proved to be intolerant of disaffection, and they were often willing to use coercive power to forcibly extract the expressions of consent that ostensibly legitimated their new regime. This need not be taken as a claim that they were paranoid or needlessly oppressive. The economic disequilibrium of the war meant that the disaffected's pursuit of individual self-interest over political allegiance occasionally *was* a threat to the material survival of the Continental Army. More intriguingly, the ideological underpinnings of the Revolution, and perhaps the very notion of government by "the People," evinced a tendency toward the oppression of those people who merely wished to be left alone. In many ways, it was the patriots' very aspirations to government by consent of the governed that led them to embrace such desperate and often coercive measures in the quest to secure that consent.

CHAPTER 4

Loyalism, Citizenship, American Identity

The Shoemaker Family

KIMBERLY NATH

In November 1781, ardent Quaker loyalist Rebecca Shoemaker wrote from New York to her daughters in Philadelphia about the impact of the American Revolution. She declared, "greatly as our country has changed from the once most peaceful and happy spot in the world to a land of confusion and tumult, yet I do not wish to leave it."[1] Despite being a loyalist and considering herself a subject of Great Britain and the Crown, Rebecca Shoemaker deemed Philadelphia home. Equally problematic, Rebecca, her husband Samuel, and their children learned early during the American Revolution that their long-term residence and eminent social standing in Philadelphia would be no guarantee of their continued stay in the rebellious colonies. As revolutionaries forced residents of the city to choose sides, and the British occupation of Philadelphia in 1777 as well as the evacuation in 1778 created social chaos, the Shoemakers became one of many families suspended between the colonial condition of British subjects and emerging conceptualizations of citizenship in the new polities of North America.[2]

Samuel and Rebecca Shoemaker found themselves at the epicenter of the conflict between loyalty, property ownership, rights of citizenship, and identity in Revolutionary Philadelphia. Despite being an established commercial family, belonging to the Society of Friends, and possessing a significant presence in local politics, the Shoemakers found themselves stripped of their livelihood by the Pennsylvania government's confiscation order to seize their property. As unwavering British subjects, Samuel and Rebecca were identified as loyalists early during the Revolution, punished because of their loyalty through confiscation, and driven from their home in Philadelphia when the rebels recaptured the city.

At the outbreak of the American Revolution, the Shoemaker family was part of Philadelphia's wealthy Quaker community, which was a prominent part of what Sarah Fatherly has called the London-style elite in the city. Extensive property holding was essential to membership in that elite. Major merchant families owned substantial landed estates and large inventories of merchandise, and their real estate and stocks of goods spoke to their status in the community. They forged networks among themselves and held the lion's share of political offices besides.[3]

Samuel Shoemaker, a member of that elite, was born to Pennsylvania Quaker parents, Benjamin Shoemaker, a merchant, and Sarah Coates Shoemaker. He established his own career as a merchant in Philadelphia and in 1746 married Hannah Carpenter, daughter of merchant Samuel Carpenter. They were married for nearly twenty years, until her death in 1766, and had nine children, though four died in infancy. Their children Benjamin, Sarah, Hannah, Mary, and Edward survived past childhood. In 1767, eighteen months after Hannah died, Samuel Shoemaker married widow Rebecca Warner Rawle. Rebecca had previously been married to Francis Rawle, a well-known and successful Philadelphia merchant, and together she and Francis had three children, Anna, William, and Margaret (Peggy). The marriage of Samuel and Rebecca was both socially and economically advantageous. Samuel and Rebecca merged their two families and enjoyed a position of prominence among Philadelphia's Quaker elite.[4]

Samuel and Rebecca Shoemaker's social status did not protect them during the American Revolution because they were loyalists. By siding with the Crown during the war, Samuel and Rebecca subjected themselves to harsh treatment by the patriot-controlled legislature in Pennsylvania, and this is particularly evident in regard to property confiscation. The patriots' process of identifying, seizing, and selling property was not unique to Samuel and Rebecca, but their example illustrates the significance of loyalty and the rights granted to Philadelphia residents during this time. Significantly, although the term American "citizen" was vague during these years, only just arising in Revolutionary discussions, one of its first tentative definitions included setting aside loyalists such as the Shoemakers as members of the new polity. As self-identified British subjects fought for the Crown against the patriots, the

Pennsylvania government essentially defined its citizens against British subjects. Pennsylvanians confiscated extensive loyalist property as an adjunct of this new definition, and together the policies related to citizenship and confiscation helped Pennsylvanians create an identity focused on the idea of allegiance to the patriot cause.[5]

Beginning in 1777, the governing bodies of Pennsylvania and Philadelphia passed laws that both punished the newly defined noncitizens and empowered those deemed citizens because of their patriot allegiance. The inability to own property became a crucial feature of punitive and exclusionary measures directed at loyalists. At the same time, the ability to maintain property ownership during the Revolution became a significant marker of citizenship.[6] By forming a patriot identity firmly opposed to loyalist sympathies, the patriots were also able to lay a foundation for an American identity, and its basis in property ownership, in later years.

The Shoemaker family's subjection to these laws, and especially its loss of its extensive property, illustrates these processes. "Citizen" was a vague and undefined term during the Revolutionary generation, one that drew racial, gendered, and property lines with increasing efficiency, and one that easily excluded inhabitants such as the Shoemakers and all others with professed (or suspected) loyalist allegiances. Douglas Bradburn refers to a "citizenship revolution" that began in the crisis of independence, one he defines as "the transformation in the status of persons, the potential of rights, and the meaning of sovereignty that opened when a miscellaneous collection of colonials rejected their British subjecthood and began calling themselves American citizens."[7] Yet through the narratives of particular individuals, it becomes abundantly clear that the emergence of a coherent body of "citizens" was far from easily achieved, if at all.

In transitioning to a body of American citizens, the former colonists had to determine what exactly being a "citizen" entailed and, perhaps more important, how to reconcile their past British identity with their new independent status. As Bradburn aptly notes, rejecting British identity was "difficult, shocking, and never universal." It required individuals to evaluate their local identities, histories, and regional cultures.[8] Building a body of American citizens required more than a rejection of British imperial authority. The colonists had to determine more than the legal rights of the citizen. They had to determine what being an American citizen meant and how this would play out in their given locale. The dividing line between patriot and loyalist effectively forced many individuals to turn on their former neighbors when differences of conviction arose. While there were certainly "non-associators" during the American Revolution, some individuals very clearly aligned as either loyalist or patriot.[9] In these cases of loyalist versus patriot, the patriots had to determine what the consequences of loyalty to the Crown entailed. Open declarations, written statements, and widely known public sympathies favoring the Crown made it easier to exclude loyalists from the burgeoning body of American citizens, although even then, such exclusions risked placing the patriots on the side of intolerance regarding free speech and personal opinions.

Part of this process of citizen building, then, included the practical exclusion of individuals somehow defined as outside the newly forming nation. Patriots were forced to transition from British subjects to American citizens. They essentially engaged in a process of "unbecoming" what had made them British subjects before independence and "becoming" citizens of a new country."[10] Race and gender became definitive markers of noncitizenship during early debates, but the divisiveness among white males presented further considerations for exclusion in need of resolution. Early exclusion of loyalists from rights of citizenship included the prohibition of office holding and rights in the courts, and it further forbade property ownership during the Revolutionary struggle. Like other identified and known loyalists, the Shoemakers were stripped of these rights of American citizenship because they wanted to maintain their British identity. In choosing to retain their status as British subjects, the Shoemakers found themselves denied rights and privileges they had enjoyed prior to the American Revolution.

Though the Shoemakers wanted to maintain their status as British subjects and continue to reside in Philadelphia, they found themselves forced from their home and stripped of their property. Yet they never joined the loyalist diaspora. They always sought to return to the country they had always loved. Other loyalists fled to Britain and to far-flung outposts of the British Empire such as Canada, the Bahamas, the West Indies, and India.[11] It is estimated that around sixty-two thousand loyalists abandoned the United States in and after the American Revolution. Approximately thirty-eight thousand went to the Canadian colonies, three thousand to Jamaica, twenty-five hundred to the Bahamas, and five thousand to Florida.[12] The overwhelming majority of loyalists scattered along these pathways of the British Empire. But some, such as the Shoemakers, did return. After hostilities were concluded and independence was achieved, patriots came to feel that most of those who had chosen to remain loyal British subjects no longer threatened the republic and indeed that some were worth welcoming back. In 1786, the Shoemakers took up residence in Burlington, New Jersey.[13]

Despite being Quakers, the Shoemakers had discovered that they could not avoid choosing a side in the Revolutionary conflict as war came to Philadelphia. In the summer of 1777 General Howe invaded by sea from New York, and in September British troops defeated the patriots at Brandywine and seized the city. Once there, Howe and his soldiers, aided by loyalist regiments from Pennsylvania, New Jersey, and Maryland, took control of the city and its government. During the period of British occupation, Philadelphia loyalist Joseph Galloway advised Howe and served as the "virtual" governor of Pennsylvania. An estimated two thousand deserters came in from the Continental Army and joined the loyalist cause. Fugitives from Virginia, Maryland, and New Jersey also flocked to the city for protection. But British sanctuary in Philadelphia was brief. In the spring of 1778, the patriots began to encroach, and Howe knew that his ascendancy was nearing its end.[14]

In May, Howe relinquished his command of the army to Sir Henry Clinton and set sail for England. Within a month, loyalists evacuated Philadelphia. Some left by ship for New York, some marched to New Jersey, and some removed to the countryside as prisoners of the patriots. On June 18, the British formally gave up their occupation of the city, leaving behind a trail of destruction. When the patriots returned to the city, they found that loyalists had set fire to a number of homes. An estimated twenty homes were deliberately burned, and in 1782 the General Assembly estimated the damages at £187,280.[15]

But not all loyalists left in 1778, and Pennsylvanians continued to contend with the problem of British subjects within their borders. Already in 1776 the Pennsylvania legislature identified "high treason" as "the offense of any person owing allegiance to Pennsylvania who should levy war against the state or to be adherent to the King of Great Britain or . . . others of the enemies of the United States." The punishments it provided for persons convicted of high treason included forfeiture of real and personal estates and imprisonment.[16] The legislature continued to grapple with the issue of treason and loyalty in additional ordinances in 1776 and 1777, though enforcement of those efforts to specify enemies of the state were always selective.[17]

The Test Act, passed on June 13, 1777, prior to the occupation, denied citizenship to those refusing to take oaths of allegiance to the new state. The act, which required men to renounce fidelity to King George and pledge allegiance to Pennsylvania, aimed to identify and punish loyalist traitors. It also served to punish non-jurors, those Quakers who were opposed to oaths of any kind. Samuel Shoemaker, a moderate Quaker who had originally signed a nonimportation agreement in 1765, drew the line at signing an oath of allegiance. His refusal meant that he relinquished the right to vote or hold office, serve on juries, sue for debts, and buy or transfer property. Despite decades of officeholding, in positions of high public trust, he was stripped of all political rights for his refusal to swear his loyalty to the independent state of Pennsylvania. With the Test Act, the state effectively began to define its citizens through such denials of rights to the disloyal.[18]

During the occupation in 1777 and 1778, the Pennsylvania legislature passed additional legislative acts that elaborated its definition of loyalty and citizenship rights. Moving to Lancaster during the occupation of Philadelphia, legislators immediately began punishing those who did not support the new state laws. The Council of Safety, also meeting in Lancaster, denounced those who "wickedly joined" unnatural enemies and further prohibited any aid to the British. On October 21, 1777, the commonwealth declared that "all personal estates and effects belonging to those who supported the King of Great Britain and gone within the British lines" were to be seized.[19] The legislature appointed commissioners to confiscate, record, and oversee the sale and auction of loyalist property. The commissioners oversaw confiscated goods prior to auction and collected the revenue from sales of property and personal effects. Most counties were assigned commissioners at once. Philadelphia had its commissioners appointed after the end of the occupation and the return of the city to patriot control.[20]

In early 1778, the Pennsylvania legislature passed "An act for the attainder of diverse traitors," amending its previous legislation and strengthening its resolve to single out loyalists who had "most traitorously and wickedly, and contrary to the allegiance they owe to the said state, joined and adhered to, and still do adhere to, and knowingly and willingly aid and assist the army of the King of Great-Britain, now enemies at open war against this state and the United States of America, and yet remained with the said enemies in the City and County of Philadelphia, where they daily commit diverse treasonable acts without any sense of honor, virtue, liberty, or fidelity to this state."[21] The treasonous individuals subsequently identified by the legislature's appointed agents varied greatly in profession and community status, and they were found throughout Pennsylvania. All were accused of aiding the British in some manner, especially those who resided within the enemy lines and gave intelligence to the British army or served as provisioners.[22]

A second act in 1778 clarified the process of confiscation. Goods would be inventoried and collected by a state-appointed commissioner. The sale of the goods would be done publicly at auction, following the issuance of a public notice at least ten days prior to the sale. Individuals could come forth and make claims about debts owed by the loyalists whose property was being sold at auction. Commissioners would examine debts owed by loyalists and, after verifying the debts, pay the debts from the confiscated estate. The remainder would go to the state. In a gesture of charity, the final section of the legislation outlined provisions for the wives and children of the named loyalists. The Pennsylvania Supreme Court could "order and appropriate parts of the said forfeited estates for the support of such traitor's children, or wife."[23] The Pennsylvania legislators' primary concern lay in punishing and identifying those who fervently supported the British cause, but individual creditors and loyalists' families would be spared the worst economic deprivations.

The confiscation of loyalist property helped Pennsylvanians to attach "citizenship" to adherence to independence from the British Empire.[24] Incapacity to own and transfer property became a crucial feature in excluding some former colonists from the new (albeit still inchoate) body of citizens, first as free Pennsylvanians and in time as those who would lay claim to a far broader American identity.[25] But outside of these formal legal constraints, Samuel Shoemaker also found himself at odds with his neighbors and business associates on a daily basis as interpersonal suspicions festered.[26] His outspoken loyalist intransigence angered the Pennsylvania legislature especially because he had been such a prominent figure in business and politics. He had served his colonial community in a variety of capacities, holding public offices from 1755 to 1776. In 1755 he was elected to the Philadelphia Common Council, and over the next eleven years he served as a councilman, alderman, and treasurer. Between 1769 and 1771 he served two consecutive one-year terms as mayor of Philadelphia. After his tenure as mayor, he served on a joint Assembly–Common Council committee in Philadelphia.[27] Shoemaker also belonged to the American Philosophical Society and was a founder of the Pennsylvania Hospital. His neighbors' outrage with Shoemaker's decision to declare loyalty to the Crown became palpable by 1777, when he publicly aided fellow loyalists in the city, and that anger deepened when he actively led the loyalist cause during the British occupation in 1777 and 1778.[28]

As a result of his role in the occupation of Philadelphia, Shoemaker jumped onto one of the first ships to New York during the British evacuation in June 1778. His stepson William Rawle, nineteen at the time, joined him in his flight to New York.[29] The rest of the family remained behind in Philadelphia in hopes of protecting the family's many pieces of property. By August 1778, the Pennsylvania legislature singled out Samuel as a traitor and seized his property in a first wave of confiscations. The commissioners seized his lands lying outside Philadelphia and then the family's city home and personal effects.[30] Rebecca was ordered out of her house on August 21, 1778. She initially refused, but three days later she left her home and moved in with her mother, Anna Coleman Warner. By the end of August she was separated from her husband and son William and had lost her home and the goods in it.[31]

The commissioners worked quickly to sell the confiscated property. They seized and provided an inventory for everything in the home, no matter how insignificant or worthless the item, in order to make a statement about the consequences of disloyalty. A ten-page, room-by-room inventory of the Shoemakers' Arch Street household belongings illustrates the family's high social standing as well as the detailed nature of the confiscation process. Mahogany furniture, feather beds, crystal decanters, books galore, velvet wingback chairs, and many more items were removed from the Shoemaker home and placed in storage to await auction sale. Commissioners seized "broken hewers of glass" of no value, damaged baskets worth a shilling, and "poor quality" curtains as well. These items likely brought little, if any, money at the auction sales. The commissioners also seized perishable commodities that they listed as "assorted food and goods" in the kitchen and a quarter pound of "middling quality" tea. Items such as these did not generate great income at auction, but they did emphasize the totality of the confiscation process. Their sequestering by the commissioners reveals the extent of animosity developing in the city.[32] The Shoemaker household confiscation also demonstrated the authority of the new government and its ability to drive the family from its home.

The confiscation of the Shoemakers' personal effects and properties was punitive, but it and others like it also served as a way for the Pennsylvania legislature to finance the state's share of the Revolution. The commissioners, Charles Peale, William Will, and Robert Smith, announced the auction of Shoemaker household furnishings in the local newspapers almost immediately after confiscation in August 1778.[33] Various tracts of lands, estates, and houses were sold between 1779 and 1782, revealing in the process the Shoemakers' intimate connections to other merchant families and especially to other Quaker families in the city.[34] In all, Samuel and Rebecca Shoemaker's property sold for £106,739, but not all the money was collected at the time of sale. Some money was owed to local creditors, and many payments were never made.[35]

The auctions that stripped Samuel and Rebecca of their homes and material comforts typically began at the courthouse at ten o'clock and continued until all advertised goods or property had been sold. Some auctions were held at the London Coffee House, others in the loyalist merchant stores in Philadelphia or on the land being sold. While items like household furnishings had to be paid for in full on the day of sale, acreage and houses in Philadelphia were paid for in two stages. The buyer had first to present the commissioners with one quarter of the money up front and then pay the remainder at a stipulated time.[36] The sales themselves served to publicize patriotic acts by the newly defined citizens of the city, thereby making it clear that Samuel and Rebecca Shoemaker had no place, quite literally, in Pennsylvania during the American Revolution.

The Shoemaker family suffered prolonged separations as the Revolution continued. Rebecca left Philadelphia for New York, where she arrived on June 20, 1780, and reunited with Samuel, William, and Edward.[37] She had been separated from Samuel for nearly two years, but in rejoining her husband she parted from her daughters Anna and Peggy, who stayed behind in Philadelphia to protect family land, houses, and goods to the best of their ability.[38] This hardship pervades the letters she exchanged with her daughters. Rebecca wrote extensively to Anna and Peggy Rawle from 1780 to 1783, revealing much about the consequences of loyalty for refugees.[39] The separation was painful for the Rawle sisters and their mother. Anna wrote to Rebecca on June 7, 1780, begging for her return. "I have ever day for this fortnight been expecting to hear from my dear mother, and yet three have elapsed since she left us and I have not yet had that pleasure." The pain of the separation was almost immediate for the family. Anna described the one-month separation from her mother as a "disagreeable and painful circumstance" though it was "not an hundred miles asunder."[40] The letters Anna wrote to her mother were a source of comfort and represented her ability to maintain her relationship with her mother in a time of chaos. Amid the separation, the war, and the uncertainty of everything, Anna, Peggy, and Rebecca relied on letters as their only means of contact.

Rebecca and her daughters used their correspondence to describe the day-to-day events of their lives and also the events of the war. Rebecca reflected on her comforts and security behind British military lines. For example, in June 1780, she wrote that living in New York was "pleasant, lively . . . everyone is well and in spirits." However, she also lamented that returning to Philadelphia was no longer an option, as "nothing [was] left" of family belongings or estates, despite the efforts of her children and friends to recover her property. By contrast, Anna and Peggy found their status far more directly and immediately problematic and worrisome after the British evacuation. Anna Rawle wrote about her lack of belonging and fears for her personal security in the city once the British had left. She noted how patriot soldiers often entered dwellings in Philadelphia, searching for goods and guns. The soldiers "rummaged through [her] trunks and found nothing."[41] Peggy also wrote to her mother about the entrance of soldiers into her home and the homes of other loyalists. French soldiers, ostensibly serving the patriot cause, were "plundering the Tories homes" because they wanted wages for service.[42]

As the Revolution dragged on, the letters took on radically different tones, and questions of citizenship emerged as central concerns. Anna worried that her mother's safety and comfort would be compromised in New York once the patriot victory became virtually certain, and she frequently asked whether Rebecca would consider moving to England. In March 1781, Anna wrote to her mother that "Tho' I should be distressed at your staying in New York a moment longer than it was safe to do so, yet the thought of being at a greater distance, and for how long a time we know not, is most afflicting. Could we be together, all country's would be alike to me, but such is our unfortunate situation." Although her deepest concerns may have been about dividing the family permanently, Anna remained restrained about her personal feelings and focused on the more public, political, and economic effects of loyalism and confiscation on the family.[43] As a professed British subject and an increasingly targeted loyalist, she acknowledged her vulnerable place in Philadelphia, but she was resolutely loyal to the Crown. As she stated, "I have read of people who called themselves citizens [of the] world, but in reality conceal their indifference for friends, country, kindred." In war-torn Philadelphia, she was uncertain how to reconcile her loyalty with the enticements of being a "world citizen," as she struggled with the challenges of displacement, property loss, and separation from family members. Too many of her former friends seemed to be disingenuous about their patriotic fervor and the new parameters of citizenship.[44]

The separation of Rebecca and her daughters burdened the family, and indeed the strain was felt in their correspondence. Rebecca wanted her daughters to join her in New York, although she knew their staying in Philadelphia was wise during the war. In April 1781 she believed she and her daughters would remain separate, writing "I hope you did not please yourselves with the expectation of permission to come . . . we must try to see each other in the fall." But greater separation was to come for other members of the Shoemaker family. William Rawle, who had been residing in New York, left for England on June 15, 1781. The family was now divided between Philadelphia, New York, and Britain, with fear of greater separation palpable in the correspondence. In October 1781, Anna confided her concern that her mother would be "obliged to leave New York." If that were to happen, she begged that "Peggy and myself [would] be permitted to accompany you." Anna knew this plan was premature, but she reassured her mother they would work out a plan to dispose of their property and asked her mother "if we may take some steps towards" ridding themselves of property in Philadelphia. By the fall of 1781 Anna Rawle urged her mother to allow the family to be reunited even if it meant disposing of family property.[45]

Rebecca felt the pain of separation, but she feared what would become of her family if they were all forced to leave America. The idea of exile "distressed" her, and she "pray[ed] we may not be under a necessity of leaving America. I cannot bear to think it." She could only hope for a "general peace" and the reunification of the family with its property.[46] But in 1783 Rebecca realized that the New York occupation was rapidly coming to an end. Further, her daughter Anna wrote of the worsening situation in Philadelphia when, in April, some four thousand loyalists fled from that city to New York. For weeks Anna "fear[ed] the destruction of property in Philadelphia," but she did not mention any immediate plans to leave the city.[47] Rebecca reported that she "did not know that there will be any time fixed for evacuation" from New York City, but loyalists were heading for Nova Scotia and Great Britain in "droves."[48] Samuel and their son Edward left for England on November 18, 1783, in one of the final ships; Rebecca stayed behind, alone in New York, and her daughters remained in Philadelphia.[49]

Rebecca yearned to return to Philadelphia with her husband. "I have no doubt," she wrote, that "we can live in some little rural retreat, where we could see our children and friends." Her postwar letters were filled with the idea that North America was home and that Philadelphia or its countryside was where she belonged.[50] But she demanded two things before her return to Philadelphia would be possible: the restoration of her husband's seized property and the maintenance of her status as a British subject. Rebecca recognized the difficulties that she and Samuel would face if they returned. As she wrote in 1784, "the present state of affairs may be a great disadvantage for Loyalists . . . there is a need for compensation, to be sure, to make up for what we have suffered in property." The repayment, she thought, should be "equal to what we think just and right, and thee can but return to American with safety." Remarkably, although they suffered greatly because of their allegiance to the Crown, she and Samuel contemplated resuming life in America following the war, although under the assumption that they might retain their British citizenship.[51]

In June 1785, Rebecca wrote to her husband expressing the need to determine if they could return to Philadelphia as British subjects before receiving payment for their seized property. She feared that returning too soon would hurt their claims for compensation. As she said to Samuel, "the danger is thee will not be considered [for compensation] once in America as a British subject." She clearly wanted to return as soon as possible to her beloved Philadelphia and her daughters, despite "the injury and injustice done to us by Pennsylvania," but the lack of legal clarity about compensation made it impossible for Samuel to recross the ocean. Without the return of their Pennsylvania home and lands, they would have lived more impoverished in North America than in their already-poor conditions in English exile.[52]

Samuel expressed similar sentiments. He too missed his old life and his family. He kept a diary "for the entertainment of his wife" while he was a loyalist refugee. He recorded his daily interactions and his efforts with the Royal Claims Commission, which investigated the losses of loyalists during the American Revolution. He recorded an interview with King George III in October 1784, during which the king asked him about his family and where they resided. Samuel replied that he had been "blessed with numerous family" but that they were all "removed from me except a wife and two sons."[53] Meanwhile, he petitioned the officers of the Royal Claims Commission, to whom he mentioned the threats he had received prior to leaving Philadelphia. As he noted, "the Rebel Assembly . . . attainted him by name and confiscated his property." He had left Philadelphia at the conclusion of occupation as "he was repeatedly threatened with being tarred and feathered."[54] He still worried that, if he returned to Philadelphia, his life might be further "threatened."[55] The king had earlier remarked, "Mr. S. you are well known here, every body knows you."[56] The Royal Claims Commissioners commented, in the summer of 1785, more than a year later, that Shoemaker was "a man well attached to this Country, believes no man more so." His service during the Philadelphia occupation was noted, as was his resulting loss of property. In time, he received some payment for some of his confiscated estate, though nowhere near the full value of his claim. Perhaps more important, he and Rebecca did not thereafter have to forfeit or compromise their British identity.[57]

During the early 1780s, the Pennsylvania legislature revisited the laws addressing confiscation and treason, gradually decreasing the severity of punishments.[58] While many loyalists spread out across the British Empire, some loyalists returned to North America at the close of the war and reintegrated into society.[59] Samuel and Rebecca Shoemaker reunited in 1786 and took up residence in Burlington, New Jersey, where they assiduously rebuilt commercial and cultural connections to various parts of the British Empire and never once considered shedding their British identity. Samuel reported that he "might reside there [in Burlington] in peace as a British subject," which he and Rebecca did for a few years. In 1790, twelve years after its members had gone their various ways, the family reunited in Philadelphia. While the Shoemakers had lost a great deal of their property and belongings, they were able to reside together in the city they had always considered home. In Philadelphia, they lived among family and friends and reported they lived a peaceful life. The jarring separation finally came to an end for them. When Samuel passed away in 1800, he was remembered fondly in his death notice as a man who remained unwavering in his faithfulness to his king. His legacy was that of an "affable, courageous" man who possessed an "amiable character."[60] By the time of his death, the new North American states were actively defining citizenship— excluding and including North Americans on such grounds as race, gender, and property—but with a newfound toleration for certain old enemies who had economic ambitions and cultural attributes that could easily be accommodated in a white, propertied citizenry.[61]

The Shoemakers are only one example of the loyalist experience in Philadelphia. But in many ways it was like the experience of many others. Their loyalty to the British Empire proved to be exceptionally costly during the Revolutionary years, in material terms and in terms of their identities as British subjects within the shifting discourse of citizenship in America. The confiscation of their property, both land and personal belongings, stripped them of their wealth and isolated them from the body of emergent American citizens. The legislative acts and the actions by which patriots seized loyalist wealth became crucial for rebels trying to understand citizenship—how not to be British—in the time of the Revolution. By identifying *who was not* a citizen, the Pennsylvania legislature effectively moved toward defining *who was* part of the new state and the new American nation, and it did so initially, although not completely, during the years of wrenching wartime conflict when the violence of confiscation and civil discord were at their peak. Ironically, the Shoemakers experienced a degree of reconciliation in the postwar years, not as officially integrated citizens of the new republic but as individuals determined to reside freely where they chose and to restore the business and personal connections that they had before the Revolution.

CHAPTER 5

"Executioners of Their Friends and Brethren"

Naval Impressment as an Atlantic Civil War

DENVER BRUNSMAN

On May 9, 1781, the *New-Jersey Gazette* printed two reports of naval impressment, or forced service, from the American Revolutionary War. The first, postdated "Trenton, May 9," told of what by then had become a familiar story in the war: Desperate for manpower, British navy press gangs took men indiscriminately in New York City, including 309 American prisoners on a prison ship, mostly likely the infamous *Jersey*, anchored in Wallabout Bay off Brooklyn. The report editorialized: "Such is the unexampled barbarity of the piratical nation against which we have to contend! They revere neither the laws of GOD nor of nations."[1]

The second report of impressment, also from New York, took place two weeks earlier. Yet, in this case, the roles of captors and captives reversed. The British captured an American naval vessel, the frigate *Confederacy*, Seth Harding commander, only to discover that it carried "a number of British seamen, who had been forced into the enemy's service," among its crew of three hundred. Harding had taken the British sailors from American jails. Now free in British New York, the men immediately entered into Royal Navy service.[2]

We learn no more from the second report, which included no commentary and certainly no description of the United States as a "piratical nation" because of Harding's action. Still, the mere mention of American naval impressment, in a patriot newspaper no less, complicates the standard place of Atlantic seafarers in narratives of the American Revolution.³ Rather than victims solely of British tyranny, seamen faced the threat of capture and impressment by both British and American navies. As the first report in the *New-Jersey Gazette* suggests, the British remained the supreme captive-takers in the Atlantic during the Revolutionary War. But American ship captains, such as Harding, did not hesitate to compensate for their manpower shortages by impressing American and British mariners. The result was a civil war at sea. With both sides capturing any available sailor, the loyalty of individual seamen was often impossible to detect and literally "up for grabs." Some crossed sides by choice, others by necessity. One seaman, the Massachusetts native Joseph Bartlett, was captured and recaptured twelve times during the war.⁴

I am hardly the first to describe the Revolution as an Atlantic civil war because of naval impressment. That distinction belongs to Thomas Jefferson and the Second Continental Congress in their indictment of George III in the Declaration of Independence: "He has constrained our fellow Citizens taken Captive on the high Seas to bear Arms against their Country, to become the executioners of their friends and Brethren, or to fall themselves by their Hands." If anything, their powerful statement suffered from too narrow a focus. Rather than cite the series of disturbances caused by British navy press gangs in American seaports in the 1760s or the longer history of impressment in the colonies stretching to the 1690s, the grievance referred only to the American Prohibitory Act of December 1775. The act escalated the war by putting American colonists outside the king's protection and forfeiting all American vessels to the Crown. The British navy used press gangs under the law's authority to disable America's merchant marine and claim conscripts in the process.⁵

The Declaration's grievance about impressment ultimately proved more prescient than historical. The war on seamen and civilians authorized by the American Prohibitory Act persisted through the Revolution, and the Americans as well as the British waged it. This murky situation challenges the traditional view of Jack Tar as a stalwart American nationalist.

Jack's story in fact fits better with the growing number of works on divided loyalties in the Revolution, but that literature has mostly neglected the sea.⁶ The oversight is unfortunate. If the experiences of loyalists and the disaffected made the war on land messy, the war at sea was a plain mess. The traditional categories of patriots and loyalists and of British and Americans, which have been used to define the civil war on land, do not fully capture the rich dynamics of forced partisanship at sea. The British captured native-born British subjects and colonial subjects, particularly in Canada, as well as newly independent American citizens. At the same time, Americans captured British sailors and other loyal subjects and forced them into service while also impressing fellow Americans. At sea, the American Revolution was not so much a war for hearts and minds as a war on hearts and minds.

* * *

The Royal Navy's capture of British seafaring subjects was by far the largest category of impressment in the war. Between 1776 and 1783, the navy impressed seamen on an unprecedented scale. Whereas the navy carried 18,540 men a year on its payroll between 1773 and 1775, that average rose to 67,747 between 1776 and 1783 and peaked at 105,500 in December 1782. Taking into account death, disease, and desertion, the navy had to recruit more than two men for each one who lasted in the service. The government's Impress Service, with stations concentrated mostly in England but also in Scotland and Ireland, raised about half the men used during the war; the remainder volunteered at ships or were pressed by gangs at sea. Of the approximately 116,300 men raised by the Impress Service from 1776 through 1783, about 72,600 were paid the bounty as volunteers, leaving about 43,700 who were impressed. The best estimate of the number of seamen impressed outside the Impress Service is around 40,000. A conservative estimate, then, for the entire number of men impressed during the American Revolutionary War is about 80,000, or just over a third of all the men raised by the Royal Navy.[7]

Scholars do not usually question the loyalty of the tens of thousands of British subjects impressed to fight on the British side in the war. Yet, by several measures, the American Revolution marked the height of opposition to British naval impressment in the long eighteenth century (1688–1815).[8] The climate of protest began in 1770, just as America's cycle of impressment riots slowed, when the Royal Navy mobilized for a possible war against Spain over the Falkland Islands. In the winter of 1770–71, the navy raised about 33,000 men, including more than a thousand from vessels on the River Thames in one night.[9] Sailors resisted the press across Britain by rioting, while others fled the country. A report from France in early 1771 noted that English seamen "had come over in great numbers to Calais to avoid being pressed."[10]

The Falklands crisis also established a precedent for radical political opposition to impressment. Supporters of the British radical John Wilkes adopted the issue in their movement against the central government. After the first wave of pressing in September 1770, Wilkes, then a London alderman, called the practice "a suspension of Magna Charta" and maintained the absolute immunity of the city's inhabitants from arbitrary arrest. By January 1771, London magistrates refused to back the press warrants used by navy press gangs to seize men.[11]

Although the Anglo-Spanish crisis ended peaceably in spring 1771, the politicization of impressment carried into the American Revolutionary War. In July 1775, William Lee, an American supporter of Wilkes, reported to his family from London that "the American War is really so odious & disgusting to the Common people in England that no Soldiers or Sailors will inlist, for without pressing they cannot in two months man two twenty gun ships."[12] The following March, Temple Luttrell, a leading impressment reformer in Parliament, predicted dire consequences if the navy resorted to the practice. "For next to the compelling Americans to serve against Americans," he warned, "nothing could be worse than to force Britons to fight against them."[13]

Events bore out Luttrell's concerns. After an Order in Council in October 1776 approved large numbers of press warrants, London newspapers reported that the city's sailors walked together armed in confederation, "having resolved to oppose any Violence which may be done to them, and rather die than assist the Royalists in shedding the Blood of their American Brethren."[14] In Parliament, the Earl of Shelburne cited the protests as evidence "of the unpopularity of the present barbarous war."[15] Sailors had always resisted press gangs, but the civil nature of the Revolutionary War—the prospect of warring against "American Brethren"—contributed to the especially spirited resistance in the first years of the conflict. Until 1780, the amount of violent opposition, as measured by the number of affrays between seamen and press gangs, exceeded the pace of actual naval recruitment for the first time in the century.[16]

Only France's entry in the war in early 1778 began to slow public opposition to impressment by making resistance seem unpatriotic. At the same time, sailors continued to vote with their feet. The best available evidence suggests that the British navy lost about 7 percent of its men annually to desertion during the Seven Years' War (1756–63) and in the French Revolutionary and Napoleonic Wars (1793–1815). The American Revolutionary War was an aberration. During most years of the war, the British navy lost between 13 and 14 percent of its seamen to desertion, or about 79,000 in total. The large number of British ships stationed in the Western Hemisphere partly explains the higher desertion rate. Almost two out of every five deserters ran in North America and the West Indies, the Atlantic world's safest havens from impressment.[17]

There is some evidence that not all deserters fully left naval service; some seem to have rather abandoned one warship for another. Still, it is hard to imagine that politics and the civil nature of the American Revolutionary War played no role in seamen's behavior. The American Revolutionary War was Britain's most unpopular conflict of the long eighteenth century and the only war in which Britain surrendered naval superiority for an extended period. Desertion was both a cause and an effect of Britain's diminished naval strength.[18]

The continual losses caused the Royal Navy recruiting challenges and political problems in the Western Hemisphere. By pressing men into service, the navy risked alienating Britain's remaining loyal colonies and subjects. Colonists in North America and the West Indies had contested the legality of forced naval service throughout the eighteenth century. In 1708, the Act for the Encouragement of Trade to America, better known as the "Sixth of Anne," banned impressment in the Western Hemisphere except to recover deserters. The act did not indicate whether the ban would end with the next peace or was indefinite. Although most legal authorities in Britain held that the Peace of Utrecht in 1713 ended the ban, colonists continued to hold out hope that their territories were exempt from impressment. A statute in 1746 renewed the ban on pressing, but only for the West Indies. While the navy could not press men in the sugar islands without permission from colonial governments, it faced no such restrictions in North America.[19]

In 1775, Parliament ended any lingering doubts about the legality of impressment in North America by formally repealing the ban in the Sixth of Anne. The repeal, known popularly as "Palliser's Act," had nothing to do with the imperial crisis between Britain and its American colonies. Rather, the act attempted to resurrect Newfoundland's migratory ship fishery by limiting settlement in the Western Hemisphere and securing the annual return of fishermen to the British Isles. In that spirit, the law sanctioned impressment in North America to take away any temptation for fishermen to desert or avoid naval service. During the American Revolutionary War, the navy began pressing heavily in Newfoundland at the close of the annual summer fishing season and brought surplus recruits home to Britain or sent them to the nearby fleet at Halifax.[20]

The surplus men were not enough to solve the navy's recruiting problems at its North American base in Halifax. The convergence of three events, the repeal of the Sixth of Anne, the loss of the thirteen colonies as a reliable source of seamen, and the arrival of the largest fleet of British warships ever stationed in North American waters, placed unsustainable pressure on the port's seafaring labor market. Complaints from Halifax about impressment, which began in the first months of the war, grew urgent by the end. In January 1781, a grand jury in Halifax condemned press gangs for disrupting the local coasting trade and violating the liberties of resident seamen. Sir Richard Hughes, lieutenant governor of Nova Scotia and the future commander in chief of the North American squadron, sympathized with the jury's findings, proclaiming that "impressing Men for the King's Service without the Permission of the civil Authority is contrary to, and an outrageous Breach of Law." Only the end of the war stopped the emerging crisis over the issue between the province and London.[21]

As the empire's most lucrative colonial territories, the West Indian sugar islands posed even greater risks for the British navy. The 1746 ban on impressment in the Caribbean responded in part to fears that press gangs imperiled the region's slave societies by reducing the already shrinking white population. An ironic consequence of the law, therefore, was the navy's increased use of Africans—enslaved, free, and runaways—to help compensate for its labor shortages. While colonial governments generally approved requests for limited presses by navy officers, white residents objected to the service accepting free blacks and slaves as recruits. In 1777, Vice Admiral James Young, the navy's commander in chief at the Leeward Islands, encouraged his commanders to recruit blacks "to do laborious duty, that might prove hurtful to white men in this climate." So many Africans wanted to enlist that Young gave orders to limit the slaves to four to a ship.[22]

No British colonial territory was immune from impressment. Colonial authorities in West Florida responded to the threat in a particularly creative way. In March 1777, West Florida's council cited both the 1746 law and the Sixth of Anne in rejecting the navy's request to press men in the colony. According to the council, it could not approve the request because the 1746 act, which permitted Caribbean colonies to approve impressment, did not apply to the mainland colonies. Moreover, even if it wanted to help, the West Florida government could not act under the terms of the Sixth of Anne. Of course, by 1777 the repeal of the Sixth of Anne had removed any legal obstacle to pressing men in British North America, but West Florida followed in a long tradition of colonial governments using any available argument to resist impressment.[23]

The recruitment of loyalist seamen in the thirteen rebelling colonies proved equally difficult. Broadsides in American seaports occupied by the British promised loyal volunteers preferential treatment. In December 1777, the captain of the HMS *Vigilant* pledged to potential volunteers in Philadelphia that they "shall not be carried out of America without their consent."[24] In December 1778, Governor William Tryon of New York issued a proclamation encouraging American seamen to enlist on British privateers in New York City. The proclamation promised that the seamen would "not be liable to be impressed" while in privateer service.[25] In July 1780, the navy advertised for recruits in New York, "having promised that all such shall be returned to their respective Ships, as soon as the present Emergency is answered."[26] Unfortunately for the service, such appeals rarely netted the number of sailors needed to replace those lost to death, disease, and desertion, much less approximate the nineteen thousand or so loyalists who volunteered to serve in provincial units within the British army between 1775 and 1783. The most common solution was to impress crew members from various supply and transport vessels, usually associated with the British army, which added to Britain's already considerable logistic difficulties of maintaining supply lines across the Atlantic.[27]

The Royal Navy also could not resist taking men in British-occupied areas, particularly New York City. In June 1778, reports emerged from New York of "an exceeding hot press" in the city. The navy continued to impress men, breaking only during winters, until spring 1782.[28] The Royal Navy even seized British army recruits waiting at Fort Brooklyn to be distributed to regiments. In spring 1781, a Hessian officer described soldiers who "were silently and swiftly forced to become sailors, put in sloops, and taken on board ships, where they were much needed."[29]

The Royal Navy did not breed affection for British rule by taking men from loyal populations. During the war, Stephen Allen and his brother William were apprenticed to the loyalist New York sail maker James Leonard, who profited from outfitting British privateers and providing supplies for the British army. Press gangs captured the Allen brothers on multiple occasions, each time forcing Leonard to lobby for their release. The frequent harassment by the British navy ultimately helped to turn the Allens into staunch American patriots. When Leonard sailed with other loyalists for Nova Scotia at the end of the war, the two brothers stayed behind to build their lives in the new United States. The outcome represented in miniature one of Britain's fundamental problems during the Revolutionary War: mobilizing effectively without alienating its subjects at home and in the colonies.[30]

* * *

While the Royal Navy challenged the loyalty of British subjects across the empire, the service also disrupted allegiances among American citizens. On the one hand, Britain compounded its political difficulties by its harsh treatment of American captives. As Jesse Lemisch and other scholars have shown, naval impressment and the British prison experience had the net effect of politicizing, indeed Americanizing, the majority of Britain's former colonial seamen. They responded to horrific conditions on prison ships and at Forton and Mill prisons in England with impressive unity and national pride. The defection rate of the more than twenty thousand American captives in British prisons never climbed far above 10 percent. Moreover, of those defecting, so-called "old countrymen" (recent migrants from Britain and Ireland) usually represented the largest percentage.[31]

And yet that still leaves well more than a thousand American citizens who served in the British navy during the war. We will never have an exact number because the prison defection rate does not include sailors who entered the British service at sea. Many had no choice. Through 1776, the British impressed American sailors under the Prohibitory Act. In June, the Admiralty informed Vice Admiral Lord Richard Howe that the law provided for "putting the Crews of Prizes on board His Majestys Ships where they are to be considered as much in the Service of His Majesty as if they had enter'd into it voluntarily." At the same time, the Admiralty expressed "a preference to be given to those Men who are Natives of Great Britain or Ireland," lest American rebels overwhelm loyal British subjects in the navy.[32]

Starting in 1777, the British reduced the amount of outright impressment (forced naval service) of American seamen in favor of imprisonment (captivity in jails at sea or on land). The experiences often became blurred for mariners. According to official procedure, British officers were to offer crew members on captured enemy state and private vessels the option of serving in the Royal Navy or entering a British prison. The British routinely used violence and other forms of pressure, including the threat of imprisonment, to influence the decisions of captives. In November 1777, a report out of South

Carolina claimed that a high percentage of men serving on British warships "were Americans, compelled either by hard usage, confinement, or seduction, into the service."[33] It was not uncommon for up to a quarter of crew members on captured American ships to enter the British navy. The service's stronghanded tactics make it impossible to determine with certainty the national loyalty of these sailors.[34]

Parliament gave legal backing to this confusing state of affairs by defining the American Revolution as a civil conflict rather than a foreign war. North's Act of 1777 (also known as the "Pirate Act") classified American captives as rebels, not foreign prisoners of war. The act suspended habeas corpus for those charged with treason in the American colonies or with treason or piracy on the high seas and allowed them to be detained at the king's pleasure. In spring 1777, the passage of North's Act coincided with the opening of Mill Prison at Plymouth, England, and Forton Prison at Portsmouth, England, to Americans. By then, a handful of prison ships, including the *Jersey*, had started operating in American waters. Although defined as rebels, few American captives received trials for treason as had Scottish rebels in the Jacobite uprising of 1745. Nor were Americans exchanged as regularly as they might have been as prisoners of war. Instead, they festered in prison in a state of legal limbo between domestic rebels and foreign enemies. Unlike the French and Spanish, American captives could serve in the Royal Navy, but only with a king's pardon. In spring 1782, Parliament finally designated American captives as foreign prisoners of war, in effect acknowledging American independence and removing the possibility, legally at least, of the captives serving in the British navy.[35]

Until then, American seamen had their loyalties tested continually by their British captors. A handful of surviving maritime journals and narratives suggest that Americans negotiated their captivity in different ways. The Massachusetts seaman Christopher Prince cooperated with the British when necessary while still identifying with the American cause. After the Coercive Acts of 1774 closed Boston, he worked for the British, ferrying supplies in Massachusetts Bay. In 1775, on a voyage to Quebec, Prince's ship was captured, and he faced the choice of working on a British guard ship on the St. Lawrence River or becoming a prisoner. Prince agreed to work on the British vessel, but he refused to take an oath as a British subject or to fight against Americans. "I could not consent to lift a finger against my country," Prince later wrote. The British accepted this compromise because of their need for skilled seafarers. During his service, Prince came to admire his British captors and forged friendships with several officers. He remained on the St. Lawrence until the fall of Montreal in November 1775, when the British released him amid their retreat. Prince joined the American forces laying siege to Quebec but had to work to win their trust in light of his British service—a common problem for released or escaped captives. The confidence paid off. Prince went on to serve in the Connecticut Navy and as an officer for various privateers in New England.[36]

Other Americans traded more fully on their loyalty to the Revolution to survive. During the war, the New York seaman Christopher Vail served on a number of American vessels before being captured at Antigua in early 1779. He spent more than eleven months on the island before he and dozens of other Americans were put aboard British warships. When the Americans refused to serve, the British beat them into compliance. Vail described a comrade who only "consented after being cut into a jelly." Given the violence, Vail and a shipmate, J. Foster of Boston, jumped at the opportunity to sail in a transport vessel bound for England. Once there, the men volunteered for a British privateer. The captain interrogated Foster after discovering that he was an American. "I suppose that you are a Rebel?" asked the captain. Foster answered no. The captain then asked if Foster was "willing to fight the French and Spaniards?" Foster answered yes. "Well," the captain asked, "are you willing to fight the Americans?" Foster again said yes. "You will do," replied the captain. As the exchange illustrated, patriotism proved a luxury that many American seamen could not afford.[37]

For the seaman Jacob Nagle, self-interest also trumped strict fidelity to the American cause. During the war, he served in the Continental Army, in the Continental navy, and on several American privateers. In November 1781, Nagle's privateer, the *Trojan*, fell prey to British warships while attempting to sail from Virginia to the West Indies. He was taken to a prison in St. Christopher. There his greatest regret was turning down the opportunity to join a British privateer out of Liverpool that was looking for volunteers in the winter of 1781–82. As Nagle recounted, "the *Stag* privateer of Liverpool of 26 guns came in, wanted hands, and six or eight went with him. He wanted me verry much to go, but I could not think of fighting against my country, though I learnt afterwards they [the privateersmen] fared better than we did." While Nagle languished in jail, the prisoners who accepted the offer enjoyed the best of both sides in the war. They helped the British to take several American prizes after which they were released and returned home to Philadelphia.[38]

It was the last time Nagle allowed national allegiance to determine his actions. After the French captured St. Christopher in February 1782, Nagle went free and worked on a French schooner that docked in Fort Royal. There he was arrested by the French for abetting the escape of an American who had been impressed by the British and then captured by the French, who identified him as British and held him as a prisoner. The French now also identified Nagle as British and kept him as a prisoner until the end of the war. After being exchanged, he landed in England. Rather than hold out for a voyage back to America, Nagle volunteered for the Royal Navy.[39]

The decision set in motion a remarkable British naval career. Despite being impressed twice, Nagle expressed pride in his time in the Royal Navy, which included service on the flagship of the First Fleet that settled Australia and service under Admiral Horatio Nelson in the Mediterranean. Nagle's experience fits with the general pattern of impressed seamen in the Royal Navy, what I have elsewhere termed the "impressment paradox": Although most sailors tried every measure possible to elude capture by press gangs, once in the British navy they served admirably, like the true professionals that they were. One reason is that the navy did not discriminate between impressed seamen and volunteers aboard warships. Indeed, a higher percentage of forced men than volunteers received the highest rating of able seaman. The experiences of Nagle and other impressed Americans suggest that the Royal Navy extended its meritocratic customs to rebels who submitted to the British Crown.[40]

Like Nagle, the Bostonian Joshua Davis was impressed while privateering during the Revolution. After the war, Davis also claimed difficulty finding transport back to America and thus volunteered for the Royal Navy. Davis remained in the service for several years until deserting in 1787, when Britain armed for a possible war against Holland. Davis's narrative, published in 1811 in the run-up to the War of 1812, put the best face on his British naval service by emphasizing his resistance. The work included an appendix devoted to educating his countrymen who might become impressed by the British. Davis advised buying time until the opportunity for escape presented itself. He did not explain why he "bought" an extraordinary amount of time, about four years, before leaving the Royal Navy—something that he could have done with ease during the postwar peace. Davis likely discovered the same benefits of British naval service as did Nagle, although his commitment stopped short of wartime service.[41]

In some cases, sailors escaped from British captivity without compromising their American identity. The Bostonian John Greenwood served on a privateer captured by HMS *Pomona* off the coast of Barbados in January 1779. Jailed on the island, where British navy officers routinely selected prisoners to join their ships, Greenwood found an ingenious way to avoid naval service: He borrowed an emetic from his former ship's doctor to make himself too sick to serve. The tactic worked, almost too well. "I thought I should have thrown up my entrails and shall never forget how sick I was," recalled Greenwood. Within several weeks, he was traded in a prisoner exchange and returned to Boston. After the war, he learned dentistry from his father and became George Washington's favorite dentist.[42]

Most American prison stories did not end so happily. British prisons became one of the war's fiercest battlegrounds of loyalty, as American prisoners continued to face the threat of impressment and pressure to join the Royal Navy. Scholars disagree on the exact number of American prisoners, especially aboard British prison ships off the coast of New York. Although estimates for the number of men on prison ships range as high as 22,000, the most widely accepted figure is 18,000, which includes sailors and soldiers. Newspaper reports after the war listed the number of dead on prison ships at 11,644, but the most careful survey, by Howard Peckham in 1974, places the number at 8,500. Still, even the most conservative estimates of 18,000 Americans aboard prison ships, with 8,500 deaths, translate to a shocking morality rate of nearly 47 percent.[43] Into the nineteenth century, New Yorkers routinely found skulls and other human remains from the prison ships washed upon their shoreline. One Brooklynite recalled the beaches "covered as thick with skulls as a cornfield ordinarily appears to be in Autumn with pumpkins."[44]

By contrast, the mortality rate for the English prisons, Forton and Mill, ran around 5 percent. Of approximately 2,500 prisoners, split nearly evenly between the prisons, about 125 men died; another 500, nearly all of them seamen, were confined in other jails in Britain and Ireland during the war.[45] Why the stark difference in mortality rates between the prisons on land and those at sea? The answer lies partly in the question, as the prisoners in ships suffered from exaggerated forms of conditions common to life at sea, including crowding, disease, poor ventilation, and want of food and clothing. The writer Philip Freneau, who spent several weeks on prison ships off of New York, accused the British of willfully killing Americans in his narrative poem "The British Prison-Ship" (1781): "ungenerous Britons, you/Conspire to murder those you can't subdue."[46] Prisoners could not make the same charge in England, where the government's Commission for Sick and Hurt Seamen helped to supervise their care by scheduling visits to the prisons, recording grievances, and forwarding petitions. In addition, the local communities surrounding the prisons provided food and other goods to alleviate the suffering of the prisoners—another sign of the unpopularity of the war against America.[47]

Despite the material differences between incarceration on land and water, the percentages of American prisoners who defected to the Royal Navy were similar. According to Paul Gilje, about one in eight prisoners (12.5 percent) in England petitioned for a royal pardon to enter the Royal Navy or to serve the Crown in some other capacity.[48] The defection rate at Mill hovered around 16 percent during the war. At Forton, where it seems the navy recruited less aggressively, the percentage did not climb above 8 percent. The defection rate on the prison ships is harder to calculate because there are fewer detailed records. The commonly accepted range, between 5 and 8 percent, does not take into account the enormous mortality rate. By taking away the dead, the defection rate on prison ships more closely resembles the figure of 12.5 percent on land.[49]

Traditionally, scholars have treated patriotism as a major reason for the relatively low defection rate on the prison ships. There is indeed strong evidence for national solidarity among the American prisoners in the face of subhuman conditions. But circumstantial factors also played a role. The mix of soldiers and sailors on the prison ships provided a lower percentage of prisoners fit for naval service (the British army took in fewer prisoners, and the navy usually insisted on sailing experience). The sailors who agreed to join British warships upon their initial capture at sea (and thus were never imprisoned) were not counted as defectors. And due to the distance of the prison ships from London, naval officers often bypassed the legal process of having prisoners petition for royal pardons before defecting. Instead, the navy simply forced prisoners in America into service, particularly during the period of active impressments in New York between 1778 and 1782.

These factors, combined with the stigma associated with defecting, explains why we have almost no accounts by Americans who voluntarily defected from prison ships. Ebenezer Fox's postwar narrative is thus particularly valuable. In spring 1781, Fox served as a cabin steward on a Massachusetts privateer that was captured by a British man-of-war while returning to Boston from the Caribbean. The British impressed a third of the crew and placed Fox and the privateer's other remaining men on the *Jersey*.[50]

Fox's narrative suggests that the conditions aboard the prison ship, which he likened to a "floating Pandemonium," provided the primary motivation for defectors. He admits "that we almost envied the lot of those who left the ship to go into the service even of our enemy." After several miserable weeks on the *Jersey*, Fox took the opportunity to enlist in the British army for service in Jamaica. He did not take the decision lightly, or at least did not want to leave that impression with readers. Fox emphasized the desperation of his conditions and a promise from the British that he would not be fighting Americans in Jamaica, as well as his intentions to desert quickly to the American service. Yet he and the other American enlistees still paused before signing their enlistment papers: "We hesitated, we stared at each other, and felt that we were about to do a deed of which we were ashamed, and which we might regret." As it turned out, within a few months of his British army service, Fox escaped to sea in a sailboat and was picked up by an American frigate on its way to France.[51]

Material conditions cannot so easily explain the decision by sailors in English land prisons to stray from their American allegiance, but some cases fit that pattern. In February 1780, the prisoner Caleb Foot explained to his wife why Americans defected from Forton: "Some others have entered on board his majesty's ships, to get clothes to cover their nakedness, which is to the shame of America."[52] More often, American prisoners in England suffered emotional despair over their slim prospects for release. In his journal at Mill, the Massachusetts seaman William Widger left a detailed record of one of his dreams. Although Lemisch has famously used the dream to frame the American prisoner experience, he and other scholars have overlooked what actually took place in it: Widger finally returns to his home of Marblehead only to discover that he has been cuckolded and his wife is pregnant with the other man's baby. The dream suggests the emasculating effects of losing one's freedom as a prisoner, regardless of material condition.[53]

Although Widger remained jailed until the end of the war, the emotional distresses of captivity that he described so vividly help to explain the large percentage of his countrymen who sought any means out of the English prisons. By one measure, 25 percent of all detainees tried to escape Mill or Forton, an option not as readily available on the prison ships.[54] Many attempted to tunnel below the prisoners but with uncertain success: Mill escapees succeeded about 8 percent of the time.[55]

That left defecting to the Royal Navy as the only reliable means of release from English prisons. Anecdotal evidence suggests that black seamen defected in higher percentages than whites. In 1778, blacks at Mill faced such abuse from their fellow prisoners for cooperating with their British captors that white and black prisoners had to be segregated in different buildings.[56] Black seafarers had the most to gain from defecting, as the Royal Navy served as one of the closest approximations of a racial meritocracy in the Atlantic world. The same emphasis on skill that rewarded impressed seamen also benefited blacks in the service. Similar professional opportunities for African Americans would emerge in the American merchant marine, due largely to gradual emancipation in the northern United States, but not until after the American Revolution.[57]

Whites who showed signs of defecting also faced potential abuse from their fellow prisoners, but not in all cases. There is evidence that the prisoners identified foremost as seamen, not as British or American. The prisoner Timothy Connor kept a songbook at Forton for two years after being captured in an American privateer in April 1777. Of fifty-six songs, only three in the book could be categorized as patriotic American tunes. The rest were traditional British songs, including a majority on topics common to sea ballads: drinking, women, forsaken love, and other trials of the sailing life.[58] Even the most patriotic of American prisoners could show empathy for their comrades who defected to the Royal Navy. In his journal entry for October 6, 1778, the staunchly American prisoner Charles Herbert described raucous celebrations by defectors the night before they departed Mill. The next morning the men joined their British warships. "As they went out, they gave us three cheers; we returned it, for in joy we parted," Herbert wrote. "Among those who went to-day were about a dozen Americans, but they were chiefly inconsiderate youths." Although Herbert could never imagine making the same choice, he tried to understand the disloyalty of his countrymen as youthful indiscretion.[59]

As the war dragged on, the temptation for American prisoners to defect increased. In May 1782, William Russell recorded in his journal at Mill how his fellow prisoners started giving up hope, even after the British government had approved their release at the end of the war: "We hear no news of our Exchange; our People are getting uneasy in the Yard, and some talk of entering British Service."[60] Russell held out, as did a fellow prisoner, the Philadelphian John Claypoole, but he too understood why others resorted to defecting. "I do not see any likely hood of our being exchanged," Claypoole wrote near the end of the war, "and it seems impossible to get out of this place with out the wretched alternative of entering into their Infernal service which however I find many are reduced to the Necessity of doing rather than stay to spend all their youthfull days in this hatefull confinement." British prisons were thus more than centers of American nationalism. They exposed the wide spectrum of loyalties, forced and voluntary, that characterized the American Revolution. As for Claypoole, he enjoyed a particularly happy American ending to his captivity. He became acquainted with another Philadelphian at Mill, Joseph Ashburn, who died before the war ended. In May 1783, Claypoole returned home and married Ashburn's widow, the famous seamstress Betsy Ross.[61]

* * *

However compromised, the decision by American prisoners to enlist in the British war effort complicates standard narratives of the Revolution that portray Atlantic seafarers as uniformly pro-American. The practice of American impressment, both of the British and of fellow Americans, further blurred lines of allegiance in the war. We now have ample records of the Continental Army and state militias resorting to different forms of involuntary service.[62] Similarly, the Continental navy and eleven state navies (all the original thirteen states except Delaware and New Jersey) secured recruits by using a range of compulsory measures, including impressment. Although the American navy impressed less than the American army or the British navy, there were greater ideological consequences. Commentators had already begun to emphasize British naval impressment in highlighting the differences between volitional citizenship in the United States and involuntary subjecthood in Britain. American naval impressment threatened a key component of the country's emerging identity.[63]

On paper, it was not obvious at the outset of the war that the Americans would have to resort to compulsory recruiting measures. While the new American republic had about thirty thousand seamen, the Continental navy at no time required more than three thousand sailors and marines. The problem came from competing for men with state navies, the Royal Navy, and, especially, American privateers. As many as three thousand privateers sailed for the American cause, with Massachusetts alone distributing more than 1,500 privateering commissions. With thousands of American sailors incarcerated in English prisons and on British prison ships, American ship captains had few men to spare. Unlike soldiers, seafarers were an inelastic resource. It required at least two years at sea for a man to acquire the skills to earn the rating of able seaman. Without the ability to "grow" enough sailors during the war, the Americans resorted to stealing them.[64]

British seamen represented the largest supply of potential recruits for American vessels. Early in the war the Marine Committee in Congress established a policy for treating British prisoners taken at sea. Much like Britain's policy, the Americans gave captives taken from Royal Navy ships and British privateers the choice of serving in the U.S. Navy or languishing in prison. The one difference was that men taken from unarmed British merchant ships could go free if they chose not to join the American side. The U.S. policy attempted to draw clear boundaries for what was often a murky situation of competing and forced loyalties among Atlantic seafarers. On more than one occasion, American ships captured British prisoners who turned out, after closer inspection, to be impressed American seamen.[65]

During the war, some Americans advocated a policy of impressing British seamen. In November 1776, a committee in Congress was unapologetic about forcing British prisoners into service to retaliate against British impressments of American sailors: "By thus executing the great and necessary law of retaliation, our Enemies may be induced to put a stop to a practice so dishonourable to human nature, and first taught the world by the british nation." Although the proposal never became law, at various times the Continental navy and state navies impressed loyalists and accepted captured army deserters into service as a form of punishment.[66] Individual American commanders also violated official policy by impressing British prisoners unwilling to serve rather than deliver them to American jails. In fall 1776, the crew of the Continental frigate *Boston*, Captain Hector McNeill commander, included thirty impressed British seamen.[67]

Most cases of British sailors on American vessels fell somewhere between impressment and voluntary enlistment. The sailor Thomas Haley represented the ambiguous position of Atlantic seafarers during the war. In September 1777, Haley was held as an American at Mill Prison and petitioned the Commissioners for Sick and Hurt Seamen to "be plac'd on board one of his Majestys Ships of War" because he had been compelled "totally against his inclination" into the American service. Yet a close reading of his petition suggests that he was never formally impressed. A self-identified Englishman, Haley served under the Virginia royal governor Lord Dunmore at the beginning of the war, until he was captured by an American privateer. He then joined the Continental navy because "he could find no other mode of subsisting honestly unless that of entring into the service of the United states of America." Haley "always entertaind hopes of quitting the American service, but never had an opportunity for effecting that purpose" and was "sorry he ever acted against the Interest of Great Britain." On one level, Haley's petition reflects the desperation of a prisoner willing to claim anything to escape his fate. On another, it highlights the common challenge for Atlantic seamen during the Revolution to navigate between the competing British and American state systems.[68]

America's most aggressive efforts at captive taking took place in European waters in response to Britain's delay in negotiating prisoner exchanges. The directive to take prisoners came from an unlikely source: Benjamin Franklin. A longtime critic of impressment, Franklin sought to ban impressment and privateering alike in treaty negotiations at the end of the war. But as minister to France, he resorted to using both practices in an effort to free the American sailors trapped in the Mill and Forton prisons.[69]

Franklin first explored other options. In February 1777, he proposed a prisoner exchange to Lord Stormont, Britain's ambassador to France. Stormont rejected the offer with a terse statement: "The Kings ambassador receives no Letters from Rebels but when they come to implore His Majesty's mercy." Franklin promptly returned the "indecent paper" to Stormont "for your Lordship's more mature consideration."[70] Later in 1777, Franklin tried to use a system of "sea paroles" to trade for American prisoners. Before releasing captured British merchant seamen, American privateers and naval officers forced the men to sign paroles. Franklin hoped to use the documents to substitute for British prisoners in exchanges. The British Admiralty, which had plenty of actual American prisoners, saw nothing to gain from the offer and refused.[71]

In 1778, with France's entry into the war, Britain's stance toward prisoner exchanges shifted. As an ally, France gave the United States a place in Europe for holding prisoners. (As a neutral, France could not keep prisoners.) Around the same time, John Paul Jones began his devastating raiding missions against the British, providing the Americans with a healthy supply of prisoners to exchange in Europe for the first time. In spring 1779, the British agreed to exchanges of one hundred men each from Mill and Forton.

The exchanges exhausted Franklin's supply of British prisoners, while hundreds of American prisoners remained in Mill and Forton. The shortage prompted an audacious plan by Franklin to commission privateers in France manned by international crews, mostly Irish but including Americans, with the express purpose of capturing British mariners for prisoner exchanges. After commissioning the first of three privateers, the *Black Prince*, in May 1799, Franklin instructed its captain, Stephen Marchant, to bring in all the prisoners possible "because they serve to relieve so many of our Country-men from their Captivity in England."[72] The privateer took the message to heart. When the *Black Prince* stopped a sloop in the English Channel that summer, its master demanded an explanation. "Damn you, come aboard. This is a press boat," Marchant answered. Like many of his contemporaries, the privateer used pressing as shorthand for taking prisoners.[73]

Despite such zeal, captive taking proved a difficult business. By one count, Franklin's privateers captured, burned, or ransomed nearly two hundred prizes in 1779 and 1780, but they brought in fewer than one hundred prisoners eligible for exchange. Captives took up space on sailing vessels and consumed valuable resources, including the manpower needed to guard them.[74] Franklin found better results with Jones, whom he had also instructed to "bring to France all the English Seamen you may happen to take Prisoners." In September 1779, Jones captured more than five hundred seamen in his victory over HMS *Serapis*. The capture led to an agreement for a third prisoner exchange with the British in early 1780, but the French and Americans botched the delivery of the British prisoners. To Jones's dismay, the French also began to trade his captives for French prisoners held by the British. Although intermittent exchanges took place in North America, the majority of American prisoners in Europe did not go free until the end of the war.[75]

By then, the Americans had sacrificed much of the moral high ground on the issue of captives. Franklin's privateering scheme, though born of worthy intentions, reduced America to the same practices long associated with Britain. In addition, Congress sponsored squalid and brutal prison ships of its own. In Martinique, William Bingham, who oversaw American privateering activity in the Caribbean, supervised one so wretched that British seamen complained of "Starving and dying each meal there." To make matters worse, Bingham refused to release any men "untill the Americans should be discharged by the English from their Prisons."[76] Americans also tightened the screws of discipline on their prison ships, claiming retaliation as justification. In September 1780, the American Board of Admiralty took reports of unruly behavior by British seamen on American prison ships as a pretext for dealing more harshly with those Britons. According to the board, "The same severe discipline which the British use with regard to our men, exercised upon their men would we believe prevent their doing mischief and suppress their refractory spirits."[77] The Americans ended the war having captured more Britons (sailors and soldiers) than the British captured Americans. Sensing its advantage, Congress rejected British offers of soldier-for-sailor trades—an idea once floated by Franklin in Europe. The Americans had come to resemble what they despised most in their enemy.[78]

* * *

Americans committed some of their worst transgressions against themselves. After taking forced military service as evidence of the pernicious character of the British monarchy in the Declaration of Independence and other writings, American revolutionaries engaged in multiple forms of impressment during the war. The most common form involved the commandeering of goods and supplies. Although Congress had limited powers of impressment, it issued recommendations to the states, which in turn passed various measures for securing goods and transports. General George Washington, always cognizant of the war for hearts and minds, impressed supplies in the least offensive manner possible. For similar reasons, the Continental navy never used impressment as its official manning policy; it had no equivalent of a separate naval recruiting division, the Impress Service, in Britain. Rather, state navies seized men, often with legal authorization, and individual Continental ship captains impressed sailors as part of their responsibility for raising men for their own ships.[79]

During the war, state assemblies passed impressment acts to respond to the manning challenges facing their respective navies. Most states targeted men by class and nationality, preferring to exploit foreigners, criminals, and idle persons for naval service rather than impress upstanding local citizens. In May and July 1777, Rhode Island authorized the impressment of "Seamen, transient foreign persons, and [those] not Inhabitants of this or any of the United States, and not enlisted into the Service of this State, or the Continent." The state took great pains to exempt state or national citizens from forced service and quickly repealed the measures after the navy's recruiting needs were met.[80]

Pennsylvania also sought ways to keep its naval vessels and privateers fully manned without offending the general populace. In April 1777, the Pennsylvania Naval Board condemned Captain John Webb of the *Experiment* galley for impressing a fisherman. "This board will by no means support the impress of any Man whatever," it claimed in ordering the man to be released.[81] Two years later, Pennsylvania responded differently when Captain James Montgomery struggled to find recruits for the *General Greene*, a privateer under the state's control. The Pennsylvania Council of Safety authorized Montgomery to impress men from the Philadelphia jail, which held a wide range of social undesirables, including deserters from the state galleys, British deserters and prisoners, and common criminals. The tactic worked. By late May, the *General Greene* shipped with a full complement of seamen.[82]

In times of necessity, states could expand the social range of men targeted for impressment. When the British harassed Virginia's coast in fall 1780, the state assembly empowered the executive to issue warrants to impress seamen. The state's impressment policy differed from Rhode Island's and Pennsylvania's by not limiting the navy to poor, imprisoned, and foreign sailors. Instead, Virginia exempted the crews of foreign vessels and sailors from neighboring states. The state also distinguished its naval impressment from the British form by limiting the period of service to nine months.[83]

The recruiting practices of individual Continental navy captains incited the most controversy during the war. Their actions threatened the sovereignty of individual states and risked alienating loyal American citizens because the captains often took the best men available, regardless of class and national standing. James Nicholson, the senior captain in the service, had experience fighting in the Royal Navy during the Seven Years' War. In spring 1777, Nicholson impressed about thirty seamen in Baltimore. The action drew the ire of Maryland's state government, particularly Governor Thomas Johnson, who implored Nicholson to release the men "instantly."[84]

Nicholson defended his impressments as standard practice for the navy. "If I had not had reason to think Congress woud not disapprove of it," he wrote, "I shoud not have done it, And I beg leave to Assure your Excellency that it is now practiced every day in Philada and has been in some of the Northern States."[85] The captain misread Congress and was ultimately forced to release some of his impressed men. However, Nicholson was not without supporters in the national government. On behalf of the Marine Committee in Congress, Robert Morris wrote to Governor Johnson and backed Nicholson's contention that impressment was common in Philadelphia. Morris further defended the practice on the grounds of necessity, the most common legal defense of impressment in Britain. Nicholson escaped serious disciplinary action over the affair and continued impressing both British and American sailors during the war.[86]

Men serving under Nicholson in the Continental navy also came under fire for impressment. In 1778, he assumed command of a small squadron charged with disturbing British commerce in North America and the Caribbean. The squadron included the frigate *Confederacy*, commanded by Seth

Harding, who was already known for using British prisoners in his crews. In fall 1779, Joseph Reed, president of the Pennsylvania Council, accused Harding of "impressing Seamen & Landsmen with many Circumstances of Hardship & Cruelty." Reed warned Congress about the possible consequences if the American navy followed the British in embracing impressment: "We cannot help observing how similar this Conduct is to that of the British Officers during our Subjection to Great Brittain and are persuaded it will have the same unhappy effects viz., an estrangement of the Affections of the People from the Authority under which they act which by an easy Progression will proceed to open Opposition to the immediate Actors and Bloodshed." Reed worried that by enforcing active participation in the war, the navy would actually spread disaffection toward the American cause. For him, impressment exemplified why America had declared its independence. He ended his grievance by identifying Harding's actions as "very derogatory to the Principles of the great Contest in which we have been engaged."[87]

Congress showed sympathy for Pennsylvania's position without completely renouncing impressment. It issued new directions that Continental commanders could not impress without the consent of the legislature or executive of the state where the impressment was being carried out.[88] The directive apparently did not change Harding's behavior, as Reed repeated Pennsylvania's grievances about the captain to Congress in 1780: "The Conduct of Capt. Harding of the *Confederacy* in impressing Seamen, stopping Vessels, searching Papers, &c., in this State without any authority or Permission from the governing powers thereof, & that after being cautioned & wrote to on the subject, cannot be longer overlook'd." Even after this second complaint, Congress failed to discipline Harding for his actions.[89]

What Congress was unable or unwilling to do, the British took care of in the spring of 1781. As the story that opened this chapter told, Harding was forced to surrender the *Confederacy* to the British, who discovered that he had manned the frigate with a number of British prisoners. Months later, James Nicholson also surrendered a vessel manned by British prisoners. In August 1781, after HMS *Iris* defeated the Continental frigate *Trumbull* under Nicholson's command, he blamed the loss on his crew of British prisoners who refused to fight. The fledgling U.S. Navy learned the hard way that it could not always count on loyal service from its forced men. The ships in the battle further reflected the dynamics of changing sides and divided loyalties in the war. The *Iris* was the former USS *Hancock*, which was armed with a twelve-pounder cannon originally intended for the *Trumbull*. "Quite possibly,

Trumbull's own guns had been used to bring about her surrender," according to the ship historian Harold Hahn. Much the same could be said about America's self-inflicted naval recruiting problems during the war.[90]

Together, these multiple cases of naval impressment contribute to growing evidence of the American Revolution as a messier—and more interesting—event than commonly thought. The Revolution's civil war at sea included not only loyalists but also forced loyalties. On the British side, the degree of resistance to naval service outpaced that of any other war in the long eighteenth century. The reasons varied, but clearly some British seamen interpreted the conflict as a civil war and resented fighting their former American countrymen. For the United States, being the anti-Britain was not enough to attract and hold the loyalty of Atlantic seafarers, who acted according to self-interest as much as national allegiance. Moreover, the Americans' use of impressment as a tactic of revenge and to man different naval vessels compromised their credibility as being different from the British. The actions suggest that the United States did not resolve fundamental questions about the proper limits of state power in the Revolution. It was only later, when facing depredations at sea by both the British and the French in the 1790s and early 1800s, that the early American republic committed fully to a voluntary navy.

The process of conforming the Revolutionary War to the larger ideals of the Revolution also took place after America's victory over Britain. At the Constitutional Convention in August 1787, Benjamin Franklin saluted the wartime patriotism of American seamen: "The late war is a glorious Testimony in favor of plebian Virtue—Military men are sensible of this Truth—I know that our Seamen prisoners in England refused all Allurements to draw them from their Allegiance—they were threatened with Halters but refused." Franklin then contrasted the supposed loyalty of American seamen with the perfidy of British tars: "This [loyalty] was not the case with the British Seamen—they entered the American Service & pointed out where they might make more marine prisoners."[91] Franklin's statement created a false dichotomy between American and British mariners and belied much of what he witnessed during the war. Franklin knew better than anyone that American prisoners defected consistently to the British, that British seafarers equaled the courage and virtue of their American counterparts, and that the United States engaged in impressment and captive taking during the war, albeit never as successfully as Britain. Jack Tar was made American after the war. During it, he was only human.

PART II

Wider Horizons
Decentering the Nationalistic Narrative

CHAPTER 6

British Union and American Revolution

Imperial Authority and the Multinational State

NED C. LANDSMAN

In the final chapter of *The Wealth of Nations* in 1776, Adam Smith famously offered his solution to the then raging American crisis. What he proposed was not necessarily his preferred solution; he suggested also the alternative for the colonies to become independent, saving Britain the costs of empire while still providing it with the natural benefits of trade. But Smith doubted that any imperial power would voluntarily agree to give away its colonial possessions, and so he proposed instead that North America be given proportional representation in the British Parliament, with the understanding that in the future, when American population and trade surpassed that of Britain, as he was certain they would, the seat of empire should naturally follow those forces and relocate across the Atlantic as well.[1]

A few quick observations about Smith's suggestion are in order. The projection that the North American colonies were destined not only to outpace Britain in growth but even to house the imperial capital had become something of a commonplace by the time Smith was writing, voiced most often and certainly most enthusiastically from Britain's provincial sector.[2] The name for such a prospect, for the full integration of Britain and its colonies, was incorporating union, the same as that for the Union of Parliaments that England and Scotland had negotiated in 1707, although Smith's notion of incorporation was a good deal more radical and thoroughgoing than anything that had been suggested at the earlier date. But Smith—perhaps because of his perspective as a Scot—was fundamentally wrong as a prognosticator, in predicting that Britain would voluntarily surrender its capital, as Scotland had in 1707. When push turned into a very large shove, it proved more willing to contract its empire than concede its primacy.

One of the puzzling aspects of the American crisis (although few have seen fit to puzzle about it) is that by the third quarter of the century the Anglo-Scottish union was widely considered to have been a major success, and nowhere more than in North America. To Americans it ranked among the foundations of Britain's liberty, power, and prosperity. Within a year of the union Boston's Benjamin Colman had celebrated the greatness of the "happy union" of "two such Great nations as ENGLAND and Scotland! And of Two such *Churches* under an equal Civil Establishment" (Figure 6.1). It was certain to be a union of "Peace," of "Interests," and of "Hearts and Affections" and would make the British "formidable abroad." To others, it seemed a perfect model of the means to stem disaffection and secure imperial harmony; Joseph Galloway described it as a "magical Charm," soothing "incessant discontent and rebellion into peace, order and just subordination."[3]

Yet as the imperial crisis unfolded, the prospect of incorporation on the model of 1707 received less and less in the way of serious consideration, even though constitutionally it might have provided the closest thing to a viable middle ground between the positions of Britain and its colonies, allowing for the simultaneous sustaining of parliamentary sovereignty and the provision of direct representation. Although the possibility was still invoked by some, including—famously—Benjamin Franklin, even well after most advocates of the American position had clearly foresworn such a solution, it became increasingly far removed from the realm of active possibility.[4] The reasons for that rejection are familiar, ranging from an increasing American distrust of Britain's ill-conceived policies to the conspiratorial fears inherent in Real Whig ideology to a growing provincial pride in the competence of their communities. Yet there had been serious objections to incorporation during the union crisis as well, and we will have to consider why such obstacles could be ignored or overcome in the one case and not in the other.

Despite the advent of the new British history, the British or Anglo-Scottish union—arguably its foundational event—remains one of the underexamined occurrences in imperial history. Indeed, while the recent tercentenary of the union produced a plethora of new books on the event itself, they were written almost entirely from a Scottish perspective by Scottish authors.[5] Its implications for British America have rarely been examined. While it is widely rec-

Figure 6.1. Title Page of Boston minister Benjamin Colman's sermon on the Anglo-Scottish Union.

ognized that the union was a boon to empire in general, and especially because it facilitated the movement of a multitude of Scots to the colonies as merchants and officials of all sorts, its ramifications for the nature of the imperial relationship and the governance of the empire have hardly been considered.[6]

This chapter will explore some of the ways that the earlier union played into the later event, which was often discussed at the time as a matter of achieving a satisfactory form of British-American union. In changing the North American colonies from dependencies of a centralizing English state to provinces of a multinational and, in important respects, multicentered United Kingdom, the union helped to disrupt ongoing efforts to unify imperial oversight in North America and instead established viable alternatives to metropolitan sources of authority in several realms.[7] The union and its implications were in fact persistent themes underlying North American discussions of empire in the eighteenth century. A comparison of the two union debates—one that succeeded and one that did not—sheds considerable light on the way empire evolved during the eighteenth century. What difference did it make, then, that the imperial crisis took place within what had become a British rather than an English empire?[8]

* * *

The Union of Parliaments was not brought about by popular demand. When Scotland's James VI succeeded to the English throne upon the death of Elizabeth in the 1603 Union of Crowns, he had something grander than just royal union in mind. Few of his mutually hostile subjects agreed. The three-kingdom wars of midcentury saw Scotland's army fight successively against both English factions before its final conquest by Cromwell. And while the Restoration reunited the crowns, the nations were governed separately, with only modest interest from either party in further incorporation.[9]

That union came undone in the wake of the Revolution of 1688. With the costs of King William's wars escalating, and the failure of Scotland's efforts to attain commercial independence through the Company of Scotland's project at Darien, Scots a bit myopically blamed the failure on a combination of English merchant opposition and royal subversion. They widely concluded that regal union inevitably favored the interests of the stronger and richer over the poorer and more peripheral nation. Thus they determined to abandon it, to the consternation of English leaders, who quite reasonably feared the possibility of a Jacobite succession in Scotland and the advent of an unfriendly power on their northern border. Following a period of mutual threats and hostile legislation from both parliaments—including the shifting of English troops to the vicinity of the Scottish border—the nations, at the queen's prompting, named commissioners to treat for a new union instead. There was little popular enthusiasm for the project, but, to many, the alternatives seemed worse.[10]

But what kind of union would it be? Scots widely preferred a federal union, by which they meant what would now be called a confederation. In that form, Scotland would keep its separate parliament, with strict limitations on the ability of the monarch to promote the interests of the larger nation at the expense of the smaller. Yet the idea of uniting with a neighbor they would be unable to control in matters of war and diplomacy held little appeal for the English negotiators, concerned as they were with the needs of the emerging "fiscal-military state." They insisted instead upon an "entire" or incorporating union, under a common parliament that the English majority would naturally dominate. Incorporation, as it emerged, did not mean annexation, however. The idea behind it was not to render Scotland a dependent kingdom, but rather to preserve outward strength by uniting the kingdoms and creating equal subjects under a new British government, with common loyalties as Britons and mutual exchange of rights.[11]

The largest obstacle to incorporation was opposition from the Scottish Kirk, the only body in that nation capable of rousing significant popular opposition, and one whose presbyterian structure could be undermined by a predominantly English union parliament. Scottish Presbyterians in fact faced a delicate task: avoiding a Catholic and Jacobite succession on the one hand, while preventing a union government from imposing English and episcopal forms on Scotland on the other. The answer was the inclusion of a series of limitations appended to the Treaty, including an act of the Scottish Parliament guaranteeing the presbyterian structure of the Kirk as an essential term of union, along with other Scottish institutions. (The English Parliament, with considerably less urgency, passed a similar act of security for their church.)[12] With that the Scottish church dropped its formal opposition to union, Scottish merchants obtained legal access to England and its trading empire in the Americas, and England secured a parliamentary majority exceeding even the large disproportion between the relative populations of the two nations. England's merchants obtained protections of their own against the inroads of aggressive Scots traders, especially in the Asian commerce.[13] While much of the Scottish populace continued to lament the sellout of national independence, that had less to do with matters of politics and policy than with culture and pride.

In reality, the union was a compromise that served interests on both sides rather than following a consistent theoretical plan. Scotland surrendered political authority to what was less a British than a slightly revamped English parliament, with a smaller Scottish representation than even its modest population would have suggested. For Scots, sovereignty and representation by themselves did not trump all other issues. In exchange, they received a substantial degree of cultural autonomy and considerable extra-political benefit. Indeed, the allocation of authority to different levels of governance anticipated certain features of what would later become federal theory. The union in effect limited the unity of governing institutions, separating the formal authority of Britain's Crown and Parliament from local and national institutions of governance such as the burghs and the churches. With two fully secured national churches, imperial Britain, unlike England or Scotland, was no longer a confessional state.[14] What made it work tolerably for many Scots was the combination of institutional protections in the union settlement with their long tradition as a diasporic population of establishing expansive and extended transnational networks in commercial, military, literary, and educational matters.[15]

What stands out about the British state after the union is not how extensive but rather how imperfect incorporation turned out to be. Rather than suppressing national differences, as the theory of incorporation implied, Britain maintained two well-secured national churches, two sets of laws and legal systems, and two sets of universities with distinct literary circles surrounding them—in Scotland's case, very prominent ones, it turned out. There were also alternative networks of merchants, military and imperial administrators, and even printers and booksellers that worked outside of, and sometimes in competition with, more favored metropolitan interests. The union in fact provided Scotland's local networks of authority with a prominence and legitimacy that was almost unique outside of the British metropolis.[16] All of those things would prove important for the North American provinces.

The biggest question going forward was whether those limitations would hold, with a large English majority in Parliament and English constitutional theory moving in the direction of full parliamentary sovereignty. The short answer was that constitutionally they could not. Within five years, a hostile Tory parliament implemented a series of measures challenging the autonomy of the Scottish church, imposing unwanted policies of toleration and church patronage, and threatening to impose a malt tax that Scots considered unconstitutional under the union. By 1713 a motion to terminate the union was narrowly defeated in the House of Lords.

In practice, constitutional conflicts proved less of a problem than some feared. The failure of the Jacobite rebellion in 1715 undermined the efforts of the High Church faction in Parliament, and thereafter the government showed little inclination to interfere with the essential presbyterianism of the Scottish church, even if it tried to curb some of the Kirk's autonomy. The Glasgow malt tax riots discouraged further intrusive taxing policies.[17] Metropolitan administrations in general found it preferable to leave it to a succession of Scots managers to control the bulk of Scottish affairs, which were rarely addressed by Parliament.[18] Thus the fact that Scotland was substantially underrepresented in the union parliament mattered less than one might expect. The sacrifice of sovereignty left Scots with a good deal of autonomy through their local institutions and was of only modest concern in a nation where rather few subjects possessed the vote anyway, where public life in general was less focused than England's on centralized institutions, and where the principal realm of popular politics continued to be ecclesiastical.[19]

* * *

To adapt the words of imperial historian J. R. Seeley, England's empire became British in a fit of absence of mind. While the granting to Scotland of access to the American trade was a significant consideration in the union negotiations, no one—then or since—seems to have given much thought to the implications of union for North America. Yet it was not long before they began to appear. The first indication began early in 1707, even before the union took effect, when the traveling Presbyterian minister Francis Makemie was arrested in New York at the instigation of the governor, Lord Cornbury, on the charge of preaching without a license. Makemie cited the Act of Toleration in his defense, which the court disputed. Toleration was a liberty granted by the English Parliament, an exemption from the operation of the penal laws. The court, in its most imperial voice, asserted that such protections applied only to England and not to the colonies, whose inhabitants could claim no such privileges beyond what their charters specifically granted, however limited those might be. There were thus few inherent restrictions on royal or imperial power.[20] Whatever liberties the Glorious Revolution had secured in Britain provided doubtful protection in the American colonies.

Makemie was still awaiting trial on May 1 of that year when the union went into effect. When he reappeared before the court he changed the basis of his plea. He now agreed that the Toleration Act did not extend beyond the bounds of England. Toleration implied a religious establishment, and Britain—unlike England—did not have one. Or, rather, it had two: an Anglican church south of the border, and a Presbyterian establishment in Scotland. Makemie belonged to a church "as nighly related and annexed unto the Crown of England, as the Church of England themselves."[21] The key point was that religious establishments within the territory of the new United Kingdom were therefore local or national rather than inherent and imperial; they reached only as far as they had explicitly been settled. Makemie won his case, the potential significance of which was recognized by New England minister Cotton Mather, who praised "that brave man, Mr. Makemie.... Without permitting the Matter to come so far as to Pleading the *Act of Toleration*, he has compelled an Acknowledgment that those Lawes aforesd are but Local ones, and have nothing to do with the Plantations."[22]

The Makemie result suggested a rather stunning fact: the union negotiators had unwittingly disestablished the imperial church. Over the next two decades a growing number of legal opinions emanating from both sides of the Atlantic confirmed the conclusion, which would become an essentially settled matter in imperial law. Presbyterians, who had been dissenters in the colonies, were dissenters no longer, except in those colonies that already had settled establishments. The most widely cited opinion was that of Britain's Lords Justices in 1725. In a case concerning the right of the Massachusetts colony to call a synod of Congregationalist ministers, they proclaimed the absence in that colony of any regular establishment of a national or colonial church. The case itself was no victory for the New Englanders, who were denied the synod and, at least in theory, their own claims to an ecclesiastical establishment. Nonetheless, it reaffirmed the absence of Anglican establishments in any colonies where they had not explicitly been created.

Nothing in those opinions precluded king and Parliament from establishing the Anglican Church in individual colonies, of course. That had happened in England's colonies before 1707 and would again in Britain's Maritime Provinces in the wake of the American Revolution, when the British government would decide that the lack of unified imperial authority had been a significant mistake. It did not happen in between. Creating an establishment outright in an existing colony is far more difficult than simply enforcing the inherent authority of an imperial church, as Cornbury had discovered. Moreover, in 1727, when the bishop of London asked a Royal Commission to reaffirm his long-standing claim to ecclesiastical supervision of the American colonies, the commission ruled that his oversight extended only to those churches "in which Divine Service according to the Rites and Liturgy of the Church of England shall have been celebrated."[23] After that, few argued for the existence of a general Anglican establishment in the colonies other than the most assertive Church of England men, and even they gradually retreated from their most aggressive claims.

As it happens, the union followed a considerable period of consolidation by the imperial state, which included an aggressive push by the Church of England and its governing allies after 1688 to attain establishment across the colonies, at least everywhere south of New England—and they would soon attempt that as well. Within a very few years before, the church had been established in Carolina and Maryland and was seeking a similar position in the southern counties of New York and Pennsylvania. The bishop of London appointed powerful commissaries in Maryland and Virginia, and the Society for the Propagation of the Gospel in Foreign Parts (SPG) began aggressive missionizing among the settler population in the northern colonies as well. There was much more. The English church at the union seemed poised to attain a dominant position in much of British America.[24]

The union made that far more difficult, owing both to the legal protections that first emerged during the Makemie case and to a new measure of security provided by potential alliance with the Church of Scotland. Thus in New York, where Anglican governors launched claims against Presbyterian ownership of their church properties, the city's Presbyterian congregation countered by granting title to its properties to the Scottish church, whose title could hardly be challenged.[25] In that and other ways, the union helped support ecclesiastical diversity in British America.

Another of those ways was the rapid growth of Presbyterianism in the mid-Atlantic region. That resulted from two forces. The first was the decision of most of the independent churches outside of the New England region to seek protection from Anglican domination by becoming Presbyterians, thereby affiliating themselves with a British church establishment. The new religious order also helped attract incoming migrants from the north of Ireland, who were disadvantaged dissenters at home but not in North America.[26] Thus the Presbyterian Church became for a time the fastest-growing communion in

British America and an important challenger to Anglican dominance. The union thus did much to disrupt a significant effort to unify secular and ecclesiastical authority in North America from a metropolitan base.

If the union precluded the creation of a universal Anglican establishment, it set off instead a long debate about the status both of the English church and of other English institutions in what were now British provinces. Ironically, in some respects the participants pushed questions about the implications of union farther in North America than they had been pursued in Britain itself. Over the next half-century such issues would underlie a variety of debates, including the legal status of New England's state churches, the autonomy and position of colonial colleges, the implications of a potential Anglican bishop in North America, and more. The issues raised sometimes anticipated concerns over authority that would emerge in the political realm.

At the heart of the debate was a question about the nature of the union itself. While the Makemie case and subsequent legal opinions had affirmed that the union transformed national churches into local institutions, other aspects of the complex settlement left open the question of whether they were equal creations. The king remained head of the English church, but not the Church of Scotland, which recognized no higher earthly authority than presbyters. Anglican bishops sat in the House of Lords, where they could act even on matters concerning the Scottish church; the Scottish church had no bishops. The English church was inextricably intertwined with the state; the Scots Kirk was decidedly and determinedly not. That situation was in fact partly paralleled in the political realm, with a Scottish Parliament that had dissolved in 1707 while that in Westminster had been enlarged and endured. Moreover, the union had joined England and the "territories thereunto belonging"—the language used in the act for securing the Church of England—to the nation that was simply labeled "Scotland." To Anglican leaders, the implication was that their church was an institution tied to the state while the Scottish Kirk was "local," a mere regional establishment, which held that status north of the border by the terms of union and nowhere else. The English church thus maintained a view of British empire that was markedly metropolitan as well as Anglocentric. The Church of England, and England itself, held pride of place in the imperial realm, in that view.

Not every Anglican endorsed such Anglocentric views, of course, either among the clergy or the laity, as we shall see. Nonetheless, church leaders in North America set out to impose their vision on the colonies. Soon after the union, Church of England men in both Carolina and New York asked officials there to bar Presbyterian preachers from their colonies for stirring up "faction and sedition." Significantly, those requests applied not to Presbyterians in general but only to Scots. The Churchmen conceded that ministers of that communion who came from England and were used to the status of dissenters might still be tolerated. Strikingly, an almost identical-sounding request came from the Episcopal commissary of Maryland's Eastern Shore, in that case asking to exclude from the colony not Presbyterian but Anglican ministers who had been trained in Scottish universities, whom he found to be "undisciplined, tainted with Presbyterian principles, and no real friends to our Episcopal Government."[27]

The commissary's point was that Episcopalians should act like churchmen and others like dissenters and neither should be permitted to disrupt existing ecclesiastical hierarchies. Yet it mattered in practice that the Scottish church ranked as a competing establishment. The Kirk's role in the colonies can be contrasted with that of the English dissenting deputies, who also formed an important overseas connection for Americans of the Reformed communions. The deputies, like the English Presbyterians in New York and Carolina cited above, acted as dissenters, preferring to use diplomatic means to achieve their ends without "endangering the quiet of the kingdom," as one of them warned British Americans.[28] The unwillingness of many Americans outside the Church of England to play the part of dissenters would long remain a source of conflict.

At about the time of the Lords Justices' opinion in the Massachusetts case, the bishop of London put forward a new argument claiming a superior status for, though not the full establishment of, the English church. He based his case on history and, somewhat ironically, the union. Citing the English act for the security of the church, the bishop contended that those colonies that had been English colonies at the union remained subordinate to the English Crown and that the act required that the place of the Church of England be secured therein. This led to an extended pamphlet debate in the colony of Connecticut, where Congregationalism had been the preferred church since the colony's beginning. The subject was the status of the English church. In 1722, a group of divinity scholars at Yale College led by the rector Timothy Cutler famously abandoned their Puritan heritage for the Church of England. Having done so, they began to claim the mantle of a national church for their communion, labeling members of the state-supported Congregational communion as dissenters. Congregational ministers led by Noah Hobart in turn invoked their own reading of the union's ramifications via the Makemie case, insisting that the Crown was no longer English but British. They equated arguments for the supremacy of the English church with claims of colonial dependency.[29]

The denial of colonial dependency by Hobart and others was both less and more significant than it sounds. The ministers were not suggesting independence from Britain or the British government, which almost no Americans at the time were even considering. This was no direct precursor to 1776. Rather they rejected the notion that they were subordinate to the English rather than the British Crown. The former had been merged into the latter, and in the coronation oaths crafted at the union British kings swore to uphold *both* churches. The deeper significance of the argument was its implication that the dependency of the colonies extended only to political matters directed by the British Parliament and British Empire, and not to those other institutions of governance, including churches, that remained local or national in scope. From those, Americans claimed full autonomy.[30]

What was perhaps most important in all of the discussions of ecclesiastical authority was how deeply the divergent views of the British state were implicated in the assumptions the participants made. That shows up most acutely in the writings of Thomas Bradbury Chandler, the Anglican missionary from New Jersey, who in 1767 published a pamphlet asking for the creation of an Anglican bishop for North America by act of Parliament. To refuse to appoint a bishop, he contended, would prejudice the liberties of what he called the "national Religion" of the British nation, a religion that stood, as he said, "in a peculiar Connection with, and Relation to, the national body." It was "happily connected and interwoven with the Civil Constitution." Without claiming an Anglican establishment in the colonies, Chandler insisted that the English church was first among equals. "If any one Denomination is intitled to a Superiority above others," he insisted, "then, the Claim of the Church of England to this Preference, is not to be disputed."[31]

Bishops, in his view, rightfully held places as civic leaders of the entire nation—in keeping with the notion of unified power envisioned within the Anglocentric state. Thus he failed to see how his opponents could object to the possibility that a bishop might hold civil office. "All that the Happiness and Safety of the Public require," Chandler wrote, was that "power be placed in the Hands of such Persons, as are possessed of the greatest Abilities, Integrity and Prudence: and it is hoped that our Bishops will always be thought to deserve this Character." In fact his opponents objected vociferously to the idea that an Anglican bishop might appropriately hold civil office. To the prospect that taxes might be required to support the bishop, he asked how anyone who would object to providing a small sum to such a purpose—the support of an American bishop—could be "considered in the Light of a good Subject, or Member of Society."[32] This the year after the repeal of the Stamp Act!

To Chandler, those seemed reasonable arguments, but they drew heated responses from the church's opponents, including some Anglicans. What caused the greatest consternation was not the prospect of a bishop per se; Chandler was careful to limit the bishop's actual powers to matters pertaining to the Church of England and to the disciplining of its clergy. The problem was the depiction of imperial authority that underlay it. Opponents rejected the very idea that there could be such a thing as a Church of England *in* America at all, as opposed to an American Episcopal Church. National churches were local matters, and English law on such matters did not apply to Britain's colonies. The further point was that the metropolitan itself could be "local" and particular, or even "provincial."[33]

For opponents of the bishop, the union provided a means of triangulation, of distancing themselves from metropolitan church authorities, in a manner that had necessary implications for aspects of the authority of Parliament also. The Churches of England and Scotland were both national churches, meaning that neither had jurisdiction through the whole of Britain nor, by extension, in British America.[34] The authority of Parliament did extend beyond England, of course, but only because the Treaty of Union had explicitly extended the Westminster body into a British parliament, through a representation that extended across the realm, although not overseas. An American bishop appointed by a British parliament had no place in such a scheme. And because the parliament that was to appoint the bishop claimed an unrestricted sovereignty, whatever limitations Chandler proposed on the bishop's authority over the laity and those outside of the church would be no more secure than limitations over politics and taxation.

It was little wonder, then, that prominent American spokesmen in the 1760s slid rather easily between opposition to parliamentary taxation and to the primacy of the English church. William Livingston, John Dickinson, Francis Alison, Charles Chauncy, and Jonathan Mayhew were just a few of those who were actively involved in both discussions. It was not just the lack of limits on authority that concerned them but also the claim that authority was fixed in institutions with an exclusively metropolitan focus. They resisted any claim of dependency beyond what was explicitly assigned to Parliament and claimed instead the status of equal subjects in other matters. Even in

Anglican strongholds such as Virginia, where the church was by law established, Anglican laymen and many clergy wanted no part of a ruling bishop who derived his authority from metropolitan hierarchies, or of any form of subordination to an English church.[35]

* * *

The union secured multiple structures of authority within the British state in several realms other than churches. Among the most important of those were the universities. The union maintained the two separate educational systems of England and Scotland and, by extension, the literary elites that surrounded them. It has been amply demonstrated that Americans in the eighteenth century developed by far their closest and most extensive academic connections with Scottish institutions, as students seeking educations abroad, in the hiring of educators, in the curricula they adopted, and more broadly in the intellectual and educational trends they assimilated.[36] There were two main reasons for that. Unlike Oxford and Cambridge, which were restricted to communicants of the Church of England, Scotland's universities functioned under Presbyterian control but were not confined to members of that church. Thus they provided North Americans with the only degree-granting alternatives to an Anglican education within the United Kingdom. Moreover, from their contributions to political economy, moral philosophy, medicine and the sciences, and what was known as practical education, the Scottish institutions established reputations as among the most progressive and enlightened in Europe.[37]

What may be most important for our purposes is that, to North Americans, those two things came to seem related. Scottish universities were widely praised for their dynamism and openness and for the host of new ideas that resulted. Oxford and Cambridge were represented, rightly or wrongly, as stagnant. Americans would craft that understanding into a prescription for their own colleges: it was the "degree of British liberty" found at those colleges, meaning their relative independence of denominational exclusions and state hierarchies, that led to enlightenment. Thus, in New York, when the Church of England sought control of what was to be a colony-chartered college, a group of opponents led by William Livingston developed an extended critique of "Party-college[s]," describing them as sites of intellectual decay. On the other side, what Livingston called religious liberty—the freedom not from state support but from state entanglement—led to prosperity, well-being, and enlightenment: to "riches, literature, and the arts." His adversaries in the English church had to rely instead only on metropolitan authority—their connection to what they termed the "established" church in an "English" colony—to support their cause.[38] Here also, the assertion of Anglican authority was entangled with the ascription of metropolitan authority and provincial dependence.

In the religiously diverse mid-Atlantic region, all of the colleges with the exception of the Dutch Reformed institution of Queen's confronted contests over denominational control. Those were also arguments about Anglican primacy. In New York the issue was an Anglican college that would be open to Protestants from across the colony but built on land donated by the Anglican Church, with a board dominated by Churchmen and headed always by a member of the Church of England. The New Jersey college, by contrast, while chartered to and dominated by Presbyterians, had no formal connection to that church but faced an Anglican challenge to its charter nonetheless. Pennsylvania created what was supposed to be a nondenominational college, with an Anglican provost and a Presbyterian deputy, although its situation devolved into ongoing conflict: Presbyterians claimed an Anglican conspiracy to dominate, and churchmen complained of the paucity of Anglicans on the staff and feared that the college was becoming a "mere Presbyterian Faction." The phrasing of their argument suggests the view that the English church held a position of primacy and entitlement.[39]

The connections to Scotland's universities and its literati, and the development of North American institutions modeled on them, contributed to new perspectives on the politics of empire. The general thrust of those views was to uphold local authority alongside metropolitan. The fact that those ideas were identified with established Scottish universities along with the growing renown of the Scots literati meant that they did not appear as the expressions of radicals or dissenters but of respected and fully sanctioned cultural authorities. Thus the rising reputation of Scottish institutions rendered North Americans less dependent on metropolitan models. Anglicization was no longer the only route to cultural status.[40]

Several perspectives associated with Scottish institutions became commonplace among North Americans. One was a popular version of the new political economy, coming together even before Smith and *The Wealth of Nations*, that formed the basis for much thinking about social development. The essential point was that it rooted political authority less in traditional claims to power and place than in the dynamic forces of population and trade. Those came to be seen as determinants of, rather than being determined by, existing political arrangements. That was implicit in Benjamin Franklin's 1751 essay on population, which was written about the same time as the famous population debates in the Edinburgh Philosophical Society, which Franklin followed.[41] Similar ideas would emerge in other writings, some offered or influenced by Franklin, which applied a mathematics of population growth to the future prospects of empire and was implicit in the growing speculation that North America would one day become Britain's imperial seat.

Confidence in provincial institutions was buttressed by the growing assimilation of the several varieties of moral sense philosophy that were becoming ubiquitous in the curriculum. It was not necessary that listeners absorb all of its intricacies; John Witherspoon's moral philosophy lectures at the College of New Jersey, for example, referred to many of the varied versions of virtue that had emerged from the pens of "late writers" or "authors of Scotland"—along with others from England and North America (Jonathan Edwards)—before concluding that "there is something true in every one of them, but that they may be easily pushed to an error by excess." Their differences were "not in fact so great as they appear," and their theories amounted to nearly the same thing "when the particulars of a virtuous life come to be enumerated."[42] That was sufficient. In addition to the fundamental consensus on a Protestant moral outlook, those theories had in common a tendency to shift the basis of ethical judgments away from traditional authorities in church and state toward the common understandings of mature and reflective communities of citizens. They shared as well an increasing emphasis on practical education, modeled on the style of sermonizing known as practical preaching, that was intended to instruct a broad portion of the citizenry in subjects that would improve their communities and their own lot in common life, from history and mathematics to technical skills and trade.[43]

None of those ideas were unique to the Scottish institutions; they were common among many groups, including English dissenters, in urban communities, within the political opposition, and among provincials broadly. Within this context, they often worked to support provincial aspirations. Nor was it lost on imperial authorities that, early in the imperial crisis, Scotland's universities were granting honorary degrees to notable Americans whose advocacy of liberty included challenges to imperial policies. Thus would Thomas Moffat in 1768 lament what he called the "too frequent profusion of honor & titles conferr'd from Scotland upon the leading preachers of sedition," in the form of the honorary degrees granted by Scottish universities to American proponents of liberty and learning—even, as it happened, from universities in which the leading figures would often turn out to be quite hostile to the extreme localism of many American claims. They managed nonetheless to offer honors to a number of the most articulate American spokesmen, who were thereby accorded the respect not of mere dissenting academies but of fully sanctioned degree-granting institutions.[44]

Similar claims might be made for other potential networks of influence. Those certainly included Scottish merchants, who took advantage of trading opportunities provided by the union—some of which they were already engaging before—to develop an extensive commerce in commodities such as tobacco and sugar. That was not always appreciated by groups such as the Chesapeake planters, who benefited from the trading opportunities the merchant houses provided but also frequently found themselves in their debt. David Hancock traced the far reaches of one largely Scots trading network that set up on the outside of the capital's main commercial sector and built an extended trade across the Atlantic and beyond. Those circles were neither exclusively nor inherently Scottish, but they were built largely of people from outside of the metropolis and beyond the sphere of the leading merchant families. With their long experience with trading diasporas, Scots merchants did much to open up new commercial opportunities. Those extended to books as well. Richard Sher has shown just how critical a role Scottish printers and booksellers played in securing the publication of the works of the Scottish Enlightenment and in making them available across the Atlantic.[45]

Another important network that developed from the union comprised the growing group of imperial officials who derived from Scotland. Together they formed several interconnected clusters of governors and military and customs officers in North America. While they differed among themselves in a number of particulars, they shared much in their outlook as well. Those officials were often hostile to the extreme localism that came to characterize much of colonial politics; Max Savelle long ago dubbed them "Tory imperialists." Yet the general thrust of their vision was more imperial than metropolitan. Imperial governance should be strictly enforced, in their view, but it should also adapt to what James Abercromby called the "wealth and strength" of the settler populations. In line with the new political economy, the implication was that power was not unalterably tied to place but would have to accommodate the natural forces of population and trade. A necessary subordination to central governing authorities was coupled with a recognition of the growing maturity and imperial contributions of those on the peripheries. Their positions were thus unionist and incorporationist, envisioning a far more perfect form of union than that which had occurred in 1707.[46]

However diverse those networks turned out to be, together they projected an implicit challenge to a metropolitan monopolization of the sites of imperial authority. Indeed, for most commercial writers the liberty of trade meant less a complete commercial freedom than opposition to the monopolistic control of the chartered trading companies. Even the large network of Scottish Episcopalians who migrated to the colonies, many of whom were Jacobites, often found their efforts to be working at cross-purposes to the Anglocentric ambitions of the most aggressive Church of England men. As North Americans approached the imperial crisis, they did so with considerable experience in aligning with nonmetropolitan sources of authority and in managing many of their own affairs.[47]

* * *

Writing in the persona of "Novanglus" on March 6, 1775, in the midst of the imperial crisis, John Adams concluded his letter with what he termed "an agreeable flight of fancy" about an imagined reversal in the imperial relationship. The time was not far off, he thought, when the colonies would have the "balance of numbers and wealth" in their favor. "If we should [then] attempt to rule [Britain] by an American parliament, without an adequate representation," he projected, Britain would certainly take up arms to resist. In that he was echoing earlier comments by Benjamin Franklin, who had remarked to Lord Kames that North America would inevitably become "a great Country, populous and mighty; and will in a less time than is generally conceiv'd be able to shake off any Shackles that may be impos'd on her, and perhaps place them on the Imposers." Moreover, adapting a projection Franklin first offered in his essay on population, Adams assumed that in twenty years the American population would equal that of Britain and in forty years would double it. Then, by rights, Crown and all must move to the colonies. For the interim, he stated, he would rest satisfied if Parliament met for a quarter of its time in North America.[48]

Adams began that very letter with a discussion of the Anglo-Scottish union. He cited it to challenge the idea that imperial authority, originally located in the English Crown, could rightfully have devolved to a British parliament through an Act of Union that had said "not one word about America."[49] To Adams, as to Franklin and others, discussion of the imperial crisis was thoroughly imbued with considerations of union, and the British union was implicated in the scope of imperial authority. The discussion was certainly provoking more wide-ranging thoughts about what union might look like than had appeared in the earlier crisis. Adams's "fancy" was a product of union in another way as well; it was rooted in the changes that nearly three-quarters of a century under British rather than English governance had produced in the provincial experience.

In fact, the course of the discussion during the imperial crisis progressed in a direction nearly opposite to that of the earlier union crisis. The union debate had begun under the Union of Crowns and progressed first to the insistence by many in Scotland on a federal union coupled with limitations on the Crown. Only later did Scots reluctantly compromise on a limited form of incorporation. By contrast, for the later debate there was at the outset vastly more popular support for the idea of union in general than there had been in 1707. That was partly owing to the widespread belief in the success of the 1707 union. Early on in the discussions there were numerous suggestions of ways to incorporate American representatives into the British Parliament. Those came from a wide range of writers of extremely diverse political sentiments, from Americans or their seeming sympathizers, such as Franklin and Thomas Pownall, to such committed imperialists as William Knox.[50]

As the crisis intensified, and as Americans began to distrust parliamentary motives, those early suggestions of incorporation began to fade from active consideration. Instead, as Alison Lacroix has noted, Americans' discussions now focused much more on the Union of Crowns than the Union of Parliaments, promoting the existence of separate parliaments under a common monarch. With a very few exceptions (including, at times, Franklin), Americans would insist instead on a federal solution without either incorporation into Parliament or the consequent sacrifice of sovereignty. That represented a challenge to metropolitan primacy and governance that those in the metropolis were no more willing to countenance in the 1770s than they had been in 1707.[51]

One major difference between the debates was that the equivalent to what had been the most pressing obstacle in the union crisis—the fate of churches and other local institutions—had essentially been settled for British America by the ramifications of the earlier union. A few of the most imperious reformers during the later crisis did advocate extending the authority of the Church of England to America, and Britain would deliberately adopt such plans in several Canadian provinces in the more tightly regulated empire after 1776.

But a half-century of contention over ecclesiastical matters had made clear that that was not going to happen in the thirteen colonies. That meant also that Britain after 1763 had little to offer in the discussions to counterbalance what would become the principal issues of sovereignty and representation. Those had not loomed so large in the original union debates, when Scotland had accepted only minimal representation in exchange for greater autonomy in other matters. Now the strictly political questions of sovereignty and representation took on an outsized focus. That was partly because American politics was vastly more participatory than Scotland's had been; it was also because parliamentary sovereignty had become fundamental in British constitutional theory and was not readily susceptible to limitations.

The widespread sense that representation and power should be proportional to "wealth and strength"—despite Thomas Whately's clever effort to deny it through the doctrine of "virtual representation"—led to another issue. If there were to be limitations embedded in any new union, on whom would they be placed? The answer had been simple in 1707; the vast disparities between England and Scotland in population and trade meant that it was the latter that was in need of protections through limitations on the former. The closer proportion between the populations of Britain and its North American provinces meant that American representatives could not simply be managed in the manner of the Scots. Moreover, the assumed stability in the relative size and strength of the two parties that underlay the earlier union was lacking in 1776. Common projections of continuous American growth made it increasingly difficult to assign the colonies a fixed number of representatives under any scheme of incorporation, as had happened in 1707, even if Americans had been willing to accept it. As the crisis progressed, they were less and less willing to do so. Still, Franklin, Adams, and others would deploy those projections aggressively to argue that it was the concept of proportionality rather than the allocation of a fixed number of representatives that had to be established were any settlement to be reached.

The prospect of union by 1776 thus implied considerable imperial reimagining and a much more thoroughgoing incorporation than had taken place in 1707. The implications of provincial growth and the new political economy collided with the doctrine of fixed sovereignty. That, of course, was not all that stood in the way of imperial reconciliation in 1776; imperial conflicts over the previous dozen years had convinced many that no level of subordination to an imperial parliament was acceptable, even if demographic facts meant that it would be for only a limited period. But for those who sincerely wanted reconciliation, projections of the future growth of North America made a solution that much more difficult to find. Thus those writers who truly sought a middle ground between Britain and the colonies in order to preserve the imperial connection were compelled to sidestep the many predictions of the future course of empire. English radical and pro-American writer John Cartwright denied outright that Americans were seeking the seat of empire. So did Franklin in his usual cagey style, avoiding or invoking it as the situation demanded. Edmund Burke ridiculed the idea of the "visionary empire" with an American seat of government that some were projecting, while Thomas Pownall called for "fixing, while it may be so fixed, the common center in Great Britain."[52] Another author proposed an "Act of Union" providing American representation at a level greater than Scotland held but less than numbers and future projections suggested.[53] Still another called for leaving authority where it was until such time as New England was capable of protecting Old England.[54] Those were all unsuccessful attempts to circumvent the structural problems that the prospect of union with a rapidly expanding provincial sector posed in the metropolis.

Among the dangers threatened by incorporation was the prospect that it might upset not only imperial relationships but domestic political structures as well. Neither for British leaders nor for their American counterparts could questions about their imperial status be wholly separated from their places at home. Within Britain, it was impossible to disentangle national distinctions from a political order that was rooted in the unchallenged sovereignty of a British parliament that was essentially continuous with its English predecessor. The union settlement had left the national diversity of the United Kingdom less evident in Parliament than in any other institution. When Scots displayed too conspicuous an unwillingness to act the part of perpetual junior partner in the political realm, especially with the rise of the Earl of Bute to political prominence in the 1760s, it provoked the most notorious outbreak of Scotophobia of the era.[55]

It is therefore not difficult to see why official Britain would have shied away from the idea of full incorporation if it left open the prospect of proportional representation in Parliament for North Americans, whose population was outpacing Britain's. And while British officials frequently suggested that Americans needed to balance their legislatures with a "middle branch" composed of American lords, or "knights and burgesses," as Thomas Pownall proposed, that would have caused still another problem in the event of incorporation. The number of Scottish lords allowed in Parliament had been strictly limited by the union, and American lords would have to have been even more severely restricted to prevent their posing a real challenge at home and abroad.[56]

Yet the continuing lack of an American peerage might have been even more troubling in the event of incorporation, posing the threat that Britain might be dominated by a society with strongly republican leanings, one that might have allied with British opposition interests. Thus would Josiah Tucker, for one, advocate that Britain declare independence from those unruly Americans, who not only would not accept a subordinate status but also might in the future lay a claim to the imperial seat, which, he noted, Hanover or Scotland or Ireland never could.[57] If we have long known that one fear that underlay Britain's new imperial policies in the years before the Revolution was that an expansive America would grasp at independence, perhaps a secondary fear was that it would not, and would choose to dominate Britain instead.

If the prospect of a complete incorporation had the potential to threaten the position of British elites, for North Americans the situation was more nearly the opposite: the denial of equal status or of entitlement to a full incorporation was what threatened the American order. That was partly a result of whiggish fears of unrestricted sovereignty; it was also a matter of authority and identity. There was in fact another kind of triangulation at work here. In the practical provincial philosophy to which many Americans subscribed, it was the very progress and maturity of their communities, and their enlightenment, that established their claim to local autonomy. It was what gave them the authority to pronounce on matters both moral and political, and to exercise that authority as full and equal subjects over themselves and others. That was what separated them also from the rude and unenlightened peoples who surrounded them—the nonsettler populations who ranked not as fellow Britons but as mere British subjects.

It is thus no coincidence that if we look at the expansive networks of imperial officials of provincial origin in British America, including temporary officeholders such as governors and revenue officers as well as those who became naturalized in North America, a common theme that emerged was a close attention both to the forms of imperial governance and to the affairs of native peoples. Those observers included governors such as Alexander Spotswood, William Keith, James Glen, Robert Hunter, and Robert Dinwiddie, scientific and medical men such as Cadwallader Colden and John Mitchell, resident imperial officials such as Archibald Kennedy, and a host of others. They hardly maintained a single position on relations with Native Americans, which ranged from relatively sympathetic to markedly hostile. What they shared was a keen interest in attending to the boundaries that separated provincial Britons from those around them, which they explored through a variety of means from negotiation and diplomacy to history, ethnography, and mapping.[58] The distinctions between provincial Britons and others who were mere British subjects was basic both to their self-image and to their claims to authority at home.

We need look no farther for such concerns than to the American Declaration of Independence, and in particular to the language of Thomas Jefferson's original draft of the Declaration. Ever since Garry Wills's otherwise problematic *Inventing America*, we have recognized the importance of the language of affection in Jefferson's draft of the Declaration—the sense of a lost kinship among peoples evoked in Jefferson's references to "our former love to them." He displayed a clear resentment at his sense of affection not reciprocated, "the last stab to agonizing affection" from those who could have been "a free and a great people together." Instead the king had made war upon them, and that sense of status and legitimate authority had been lost.[59]

Jefferson reserved his choicest language for the king's denial of a full incorporation of North Americans into that common peoplehood, revealed especially in his manner of making war, by means of others who could not at all claim the same "ties of our common kindred." The king had employed "not only soldiers of our common blood, but Scotch and foreign mercenaries"— Highlanders and Hessians—"to invade and destroy us."[60] "He has endeavored to bring on the inhabitants of our frontiers the merciless Indian savages, whose known rule of warfare is an undistinguished destruction of all ages, sexes, and conditions of existence." And while Jefferson rather disingenuously condemned the king's continuation of the slave trade as a "cruel war against human nature itself," what gave that act an especially "distinguished die" was the king's "exciting those very people to rise in arms among us." "We might have been a free and a great people together," Jefferson lamented. He clearly did not imagine that those others who had been loosed upon them could ever have been a part of *that* people, and he expressed his deepest resentment at the failure of the king, and of Britons, to mark the difference.

Yet even independence would not fully disentangle North Americans from the legacy of their involvement with the complexities of English, Scottish, and British hierarchies. In the year 1783, as the Treaty of Paris drew the American Revolution to a conclusion, the Episcopal ministers of Connecticut sent the former loyalist Samuel Seabury to England in an attempt to obtain consecration as the first bishop of what was to become the American Episcopal Church. With independence and the creation of a separate American church, American opposition to the bishop faded; the problem had never been episcopacy per se so much as an American bishop in an Anglican hierarchy. Nonetheless, Seabury waited in London for many months while the bishops debated whether they should or even could consecrate an American bishop who would not take the customary loyalty oaths to the king, which Seabury, of course, could no longer do.

Tired of waiting, Seabury took matters into his own hands. The solution lay in Scotland and the Scottish Episcopal Church. Or rather in the nonjuring or Jacobite incarnation of that church. At the Revolution of 1688, the leadership of Scotland's Episcopal Church had been overwhelmingly Jacobite and remained so—which was part of the reason that William had acceded to a Presbyterian Scottish church. Ironically, perhaps, a century later that had the consequence of freeing Scotland's Episcopalians from the constraints under which the English bishops lay. Never having sworn allegiance to the House of Hanover, and as members of a dissenting church in Scotland, Scottish bishops had no compunctions about consecrating one who had abandoned his Anglican allegiance. And so Samuel Seabury, the first bishop in the American Episcopal Church, was consecrated in Aberdeen in 1784, having first promised to do what he could to bring the practices of the American church into line with some of the distinctive forms of worship of the Scottish church. Some of those would long persist in the American church.[61] In the Seabury case, it was the very multinational character of the British state that allowed Americans (including Episcopalian Americans) finally to separate from the vestiges of an Anglican and Anglocentric ecclesiastical order.

Early American historians have never paid sufficient attention to the making of Britain, which they often either conflate with England or assume represented little more than a simple extension of English authority. But if we look beyond the level of formal politics, there was much in the creation of a United Kingdom that worked against a full concentration of metropolitan authority. The union secured separate national churches in Britain, thereby impeding the imposition of an imperial ecclesiastical establishment. The maintenance of separate laws and legal systems in the Act of Union helped insure that English law remained distinct from imperial law. In the new British world of commerce and empire, British trading interests could not be reduced to those of the metropolis; imperial reformers were not all men of the center, and enlightened learning would not be wholly dominated by metropolitan perspectives. Without always realizing what it was they were doing, provincial Americans were able to draw on those distinctions to establish far less dependent positions for their churches, communities, and societies, if not always for their polities, than had been sustainable before.

What the original union settlement did not create was a precedent to be followed. That event had been carefully negotiated to protect the essential interests of the two nations involved. Incorporation was far from complete; it left substantial asymmetries in power and in process, a product of the readily apparent differences in the goals and circumstances of the nations involved. The union solution was not easily extended to the American situation. Much of the autonomy of cultural institutions for which Scots had negotiated was already possessed by North Americans, in part as the result of the very arguments the union had provided. And where Scots and English had been able to negotiate powers and limitations on the basis of seemingly stable differences in wealth and power, the same was far more difficult during an imperial crisis in which North American growth was in many ways the most visible factor. Indeed, that growth was both the primary rationale for the official British effort to reform imperial policy and the principal obstacle to establishing a new equilibrium.

Ultimately the most viable solutions were radical ones: parliamentary incorporation to be imposed, as Franklin once thought, whether Americans agreed to it or not; a federal solution that required the sacrificing of imperial sovereignty; or a radical incorporation that might have removed Britain's imperial capital from Britain itself. Adam Smith erred in thinking British elites would prefer the last of those, with all of the social reconfiguration it would have involved. In the end, Little England still prevailed over Greater Britain, and independence for America followed.[62] Incorporation thus fell out of the conversation, to be revived in the next decade when Americans confronted their own issues of sovereignty and union, which they sought to resolve by combining a partial incorporation with federal principles.

CHAPTER 7

Revisiting the Bishop Controversy

KATHERINE CARTÉ ENGEL

In 1815, John Adams wrote, "the apprehension of Episcopacy contributed . . . as much as any other cause" to American worries about Parliament's authority.[1] Adams was, in that statement, describing the often hysterical fretting of American colonists that the Church of England might through parliamentary action install an Anglican bishop in the colonies. Fears of such an action periodically rippled through various groups of colonists across most of the eighteenth century, just as hopes for the same eventuality animated different groups of colonists. In the years before the American Revolution, the idea of an Anglican bishop was a divisive issue, and historians have long discussed it as such. They have usually described the controversy as an early phase of the coming Revolution, largely because those who advocated for a bishop, men like the future prelate of Nova Scotia Charles Inglis, almost all became loyalists, and those who fought vociferously against a bishop, like Boston minister Charles Chauncy, were vocal in support of the colonial struggle against Parliament. Yet the bishop controversy has excited little vigorous debate in recent decades. Despite obligatory repetition in both scholarly and popular histories, it has largely rested where Carl Bridenbaugh placed it in 1962, when he argued that the long contest between the authoritarian supporters of the Church of England and the devoted transatlantic community of religious dissenters nurtured an "American version of religious liberty" that was "the essential ingredient of the nascent American sense of nationality." Furthermore, he argued, the bishop controversy provides evidence that the "epoch-making mental change that we call the American Revolution occurred in a religious atmosphere."[2]

Before reassessing this argument, a few words of background. At base, the bishop controversy was a pamphlet and newspaper dispute, centered in Boston, New York, and London, across the eighteenth century but especially in the 1760s and 1770s. Those Protestants on both sides of the ocean who rejected episcopacy (that is, the office of bishop within a Christian church, especially when such a figure was allied to state power) argued against leaders of the Church of England, who saw both a practical and a theological need for an Anglican bishop for the large and growing colonial church. The former group, called dissenters, were particularly strong in New England and the middle colonies, and as a community they enjoyed historic ties to those groups in England, often descended from Puritans, who did not conform to the Church of England. For dissenters in New England, fears of a bishop were ensnarled with the related issue of the growing presence in their region of the Society for the Propagation of the Gospel in Foreign Parts (SPG), the Church of England's missionary arm. Among Anglicans, the most vocal supporters of a bishop for the colonies came from clergy serving in the middle colonies and New England, as well as their superiors in London. The majority of American Anglicans (and many of their clergy), who lived in the southern colonies, were far less sanguine about a stronger religious imperial establishment. The controversy thus was most intense in the northern colonies of British America, and it reverberated significantly in the imperial capital.

Although disputes over a potential colonial bishop began well before the Revolutionary era and were not fully concluded until open warfare settled the issue, the controversy reached its most intense point in the later 1760s, amid discussions of the Stamp Act and its repeal, colonial nonimportation and nonexportation, and the Townshend Acts. During those years, the colonists and Parliament engaged in a long process of honing their arguments and testing the waters of their relationship. On the American side, John Dickinson's *Letters from a Farmer in Pennsylvania* galvanized support for continued opposition to parliamentary taxation.[3] From a political perspective, debates about a bishop provided both sides yet more evidence of significant disagreement about the nature of the ties that bound Americans to Great Britain, as well as an occasion to deepen those disagreements as the colonies moved toward independence. Yet the bishop controversy ceased to animate voices on either side before the final crisis developed in 1774 and 1775, when the core problems of sovereignty and taxation took center stage.

The most outspoken participants were colonial dissenters, who feared that an Anglican bishop would mean the loss of religious and civil liberty. "It is not the primitive Christian Bishop they want," accused New York Presbyterian William Livingston and his cowriters in a series of columns entitled *The American Whig*. "It is the *modern, splendid, opulent, court-favoured, law-dignified, superb, magnificent, powerful* prelate" that the Church of England would install. "Such a Bishop would be one of the worst commodities . . . and must inevitably prove absolute desolation and ruin" to the colonies.[4] The public on both sides of the Atlantic watched the controversy play out during the 1760s in a series of pamphlets and newspaper articles arguing and rearguing the issue. Its participants included such prominent dissenting figures as Jonathan Mayhew, Charles Chauncy, Thomas Hollis, and Caleb Fleming.

Historians have argued for years that the debates added a religious urgency to American protests and that fears of an Anglican conspiracy convinced many Americans of all religious communities that the English government was not to be trusted.[5] Their argument has gathered its force from the idea that anger over a bishop motivated Americans to revolt, contributed a "religious atmosphere" to the contest as a whole, and formed a part of a "nascent sense of American nationality." But this line of reasoning has lost its saliency in recent years. The bishop controversy was not dramatic enough to be considered one of the war's central causes, and it was largely over before the final taxation controversies erupted. Despite Gordon Wood's assertion that the clergy were primary opinion shapers for rebelling colonists, many North Americans were only marginally, if at all, attached to formal structures of religion, and in the southern colonies, where the Church of England was legally established, many colonists and their clergy were opposed to a bishop because it would limit their flexibility in what was a locally governed establishment.[6] Moreover, recent scholars, including those in this volume, have depicted the Revolution more as a civil war than as an ideologically motivated moment of American unity, and they have tended to see a sense of American identity as resulting from, rather than predating, the war. These interpretations have left the importance of an event like the bishop controversy—the meaning of which has been lodged in its ideological power—unclear at best. Indeed, Brendan McConville's assertion that the Revolution came as an abrupt shift for a largely royalist colonial population, alongside Michael McDonnell's argument that as many as three-fifths of colonists kept the conflict at arm's length whenever they could, suggest that events like the bishop controversy must be explained as something other than a step on a proto-nationalistic path.[7]

Nonetheless, the volume of contemporary writing about a colonial bishop, both in the form of the disputants' publications and in the mentions the issue received in private correspondence, signals that it was significant to those involved, and thus it is worth reinvestigating on their terms, free from the burden placed on it by those who wished to explain incipient nationalism. What follows, therefore, does not seek to argue against John Adams when he stated that the bishop controversy was a galvanizing force for Americans; rather, it suggests that a far different significance also lies there. This examination suggests that the bishop controversy transformed the patterns of religious cooperation that had developed within the Protestant Anglophone community. Indeed, the most significant rupture caused by the bishop controversy was not between the most vocal combatants—the advocates for and against a bishop—nor was it along the deep division within the Anglican community over the advisability of a bishop.[8] Instead, it was between the North American and English dissenting communities. Despite strong historical ties and a general agreement that a bishop for the colonies was detrimental to religious liberty, American and English dissenters were not united by the bishop controversy.[9] Quite the contrary, the controversy strained the connections between the English and American wings of the dissenting network, because it challenged how that self-conscious community saw its own internal relationships. The controversy thus marked the end of an important religious imaginary that dated back to the earliest days of Puritan colonization. This version of the bishop controversy thus interprets it as part of the war's dissolution of long-standing Atlantic connections.

More important for present purposes than the issue of beginnings and endings, however, is the fact that such an approach to the religious controversy highlights that the American Revolution was a significant event in the history of religion, and specifically in the history of Protestantism.[10] Looked at in this way, the point is not to ask how the bishop controversy fits into the course of the American Revolution, but rather how the bishop controversy, as part of the American Revolution, changed the boundaries of religious communities to which both Americans and Britons believed they belonged. The Revolution forced Protestants on both sides of the Atlantic to reassess how they related to one another and to the ideal of Christian unity that they espoused. The bishop controversy, I will argue, played a key part in that process.

* * *

In order to understand how the bishop controversy altered the Anglophone Protestant community, it is first necessary to outline what constituted the Protestant community of the mid- eighteenth century. This is not a simple matter. On the one hand, the vast majority of people living in the British Atlantic empire were, by some definition, at least nominally Protestant. On the other hand, those people possessed widely varying beliefs, practices, and institutional attachments. No one claimed that he or she was, by denomination, "Protestant," yet the word appeared in any number of political contexts, as scholars have amply shown.[11] To make matters more complicated, contemporary Protestant clergy often advocated for the universalizing and normative term of "religion," rather than for their specific denominations or for Protestantism itself. To understand why the bishop controversy was disruptive to the Protestant world, then, it is necessary first to investigate the institutional Protestantism of the era and the specific meaning of religion it supported. In this endeavor, we find a powerful and state-supported system marked by a striking degree of uniformity. Looked at from the perspective of Protestantism, the bishop controversy—when seen as a dispute between Anglicans and dissenters—reinforced rather than undermined the system by which Protestants handled interdenominational dissent.

Beginning by investigating the institutional strength of Protestantism is important because it fosters more caution in what is meant by the term "religion." Although historians might associate any number of eighteenth-century practices with that term, there were, in the eighteenth century as today, intense debates over what should and what should not fall within that category. Philosopher and historian David Hume, for example, outlined a natural human progression from pantheism to monotheism, thus elevating pagan traditions to the same categorical level as that of the Scottish Presbyterians around him in Edinburgh, while orthodox Protestants, who objected to the rising tide of evangelicalism (often in addition to their objections to Hume), rejected some modes of religious expression as "fanaticism." Such diverse intellectual and cultural trends had many participants, from obscure or ostracized individuals who claimed the mantle of prophet to elite philosophers with university appointments, but in a privileged place at the center of all discussions of what might qualify as acceptable religion were the clergy of the government-recognized denominations of Protestantism, so it is with them that any discussion of institutional Protestantism must begin.[12]

Leaders of all the major denominations concurred about the outlines of what ought to constitute religion, even as they disagreed mightily about issues of theology and church governance. Anglicans, Presbyterians, Baptists, Congregationalists, German Lutherans, German Reformed, Huguenots, and even the emerging evangelical communities recognized, to a very large extent, the same institutional apparatus for religion. Congregations from Halifax and Williamsburg to Aberdeen and London met in churches for regular worship guided by clergy who upheld the authority of the Protestant Bible, believed in salvation by faith alone, and rejected the Roman Catholic Church as politically dangerous and theologically in error.[13] The fact that many in the empire, not least its many Catholics and non-Christians—not to mention a host of visionaries, prophets, and intellectuals—disputed such an understanding of religion did not significantly weaken the institutional strength of formal Protestantism in the years before the Revolution.[14]

With conformity to those structures came government recognition, either in the form of establishment or toleration. Some groups that enjoyed toleration were established elsewhere, such as so-called "foreign Protestants" in the British Empire; others, Baptists, for example, received state sponsorship nowhere but worked within formal channels and collaborated with other denominational leaders nonetheless. States depended on the networks of churches and clergy throughout their territories to inculcate moral principles in their subjects; clergy in turn enjoyed positions of state-sanctioned authority when they preached, wrote and published sermons and tracts, and coordinated for the purpose of supporting international Protestantism. Collectively, the clergy of these denominations claimed to speak for the religious welfare of the vast majority of souls in the empire, and that system marked what clergy, government leaders, and most people thought of under the categorization of "religion."

Religious leaders used terms like "religion" and "true religion" to refer to their shared institutional world and to argue for its increase. The term conjured a faith that was at once universal and unified. As Scottish minister William Dalrymple argued, cooperation and tolerance were needed for "the ends of religion and happiness," though complete unity of opinion was not.[15] For those who were "acquainted with these several parts of pure and undefiled religion, there will be little time and less inclination left for what is doubtful and contentious."[16] When divisions were put aside, unity and harmony would necessarily result. This striving for a healthy "state of religion" (another favorite phrase of the era) invoked the clerical jeremiad tradition of bemoaning the spiritual failings of the laity and of Protestant schism, but, as jeremiads had always done, it also served as a call to arms to promote religion by increasing lay piety and overcoming denominational boundaries. Both efforts, of course, also supported the influence of the Protestant clergy themselves.

Indeed, the bishop controversy can be viewed as an example of how the common effort to promote "religion" ultimately functioned to channel disputes among Protestant leaders into the reiteration of a mutual purpose, effectively unifying rather than dividing. This becomes evident through an examination of the controversy in its most obvious form, as a quarrel between dissenters who did not want a bishop in the colonies and Anglicans who did. As they disagreed, they protested their agreement on the outlines of "religion" in general and what ought to be done to support it. These were the terms used by John Ewer, bishop of Llandaff, in his controversial 1767 sermon before the Society for the Propagation of the Gospel. He touched off a firestorm in New England by arguing for strengthening the SPG and creating a colonial bishop because of the weakness of religion in Britain's colonies. "This great evil, irreligion," he wrote, "might at first have easily been prevented growing in our colonies," had proper support for the clergy been made.[17] Religion, here, was not a passive sentiment or an interior, psychological state but rather an institutional apparatus to be championed, furthered, promoted, and propagated by clergy, governments, and interested laypeople. Yet even as Ewer denied New England's "religious" status, he also reinforced the larger (and undisputed) value of "religion." Moreover, arguments about the health or weakness of "religion" deflected debate away from the deeper, and unresolvable, issue that divided Anglicans and dissenters—the scriptural basis of episcopacy—and focused it on their agreement that religion was a positive good for society.

Dissenters promoted the same version of religion. When Jonathan Mayhew wrote on the subject, he made many of the same points as Ewer but argued further that religion required an educated clergy that was willing to forgo theological or ecclesiological dispute among internal factions. He accused the Society for the Propagation of the Gospel of promoting division among Protestants by sending missionaries to places where "religion," in his terms, clearly already existed. He belabored the SPG charter's focus on those places where "for want of *learned and orthodox* ministers to instruct our said loving subjects in the principles of TRUE RELIGION," papist position might grow. Mayhew asserted that New England did possess "true religion," as it had trained orthodox clergy, and despite his anti-Anglican sensibilities, he also conceded that there could be no complaint about the SPG's operating in those places where the apparatus of religion was absent. Advancing true religion was an ideal of Protestant leaders; creating division within the Protestant fold violated that same goal.[18] Promoting the same version of religion contained disputes, like the bishop controversy, when they arose. Ewer and Mayhew disagreed passionately on ecclesiastical issues, but Anglicans and dissenters had been swiping at one another over the best means to organize Christian society for a long time, and the arguments that divided Anglicans and dissenters in the late eighteenth century lacked the venom that led those same communities to bloody civil war a century earlier in England. The bishop controversy reinforced "religion" more than it bred religious war.

Working toward the common goal of increasing "religion" also permitted a functional cooperation to develop between various Protestant denominations. A far smaller dispute confirms the assessment that relations between Anglicans and dissenters at the time of the bishop controversy were, though sometimes prickly, quite muted. In 1765, Connecticut clergyman Eleazar Wheelock sent Congregationalist minister Nathanael Whitaker and Mohegan minister Samson Occom, a former student at Wheelock's Indian school in Connecticut, to Britain to raise funds for his new college in New Hampshire. The men solicited support widely and across denominations. Scottish Presbyterians were instrumental in the effort, and the school itself was named after William Legge, 2nd Earl of Dartmouth, an evangelical Anglican. The fund's trustees, in addition to Dartmouth, also included evangelical Anglicans John Thornton and Robert Keen, who used their wealth and position to protect and further the Methodist movement within the Church of England. Lord Dartmouth, a past and future member of Lord North's cabinet in the years before the Revolution, eventually went so far as to request the support of the bishop of London for the school, in what certainly qualified as an ecumenical effort. The bishop firmly squelched such thoughts, however, saying he found it "impossible, that I could think of accepting a Trust for the erection and endowment of a College, the charter of which has never been communicated to me." He noted that the "least intimation [had not] been given to me, that a Provision is made in the charter, either that the Head of the College shall be of the Church of England, or that the Prayers made use of shall be those of our Liturgy." Moreover, the bishop scolded, he "cannot help remarking, that in the List of Trustees, . . . there are several Dissenting Ministers and not one of the Church of England. What use a Bishop of London can be to such a Trust, or with what Propriety He could accept it, I cannot see."[19]

Such minor bureaucratic rumblings were probably not long remembered by any of the participants. The dog that did not bark reminds us that the participants were well known to each other and accustomed to collaboration in the larger project of promoting religion as they knew it. Like this minor incident, the bishop controversy did little to disrupt the patterns of collaboration and frustration that characterized relations among the leaders of Protestantism's major institutions. The same is not true of the American Revolution writ large, however. The Revolution's outcome was the creation of a new national boundary in the midst of a religious community that had long considered itself one whole. To understand how that boundary came to be, a fresh look at the bishop controversy from the perspective of the dissenting community is warranted.

* * *

Dissenters understood themselves as a distinctive community within the more general category of "religion." While they advocated for the general importance of religion with those, like Anglicans, with whom they had significant differences, they shared strong bonds of affinity with fellow dissenters that they did not have with nondissenting Protestants. Dissent is perhaps best understood as, to use Charles Taylor's terms, a social imaginary, or "the ways in which [people] imagine their social existence, how they fit together with others, how things go on between them and their fellows."[20] Dissenters comprised a self-consciously transatlantic group with habits of relation, communication and shared values, all of which were reinforced through the continual circulation of participants. Yet the social imaginary of dissent was an amorphous construction, no matter how important to its members. It existed as long as its members believed and acted as if it did, and at the start of the bishop controversy, dissenters on both sides of the Atlantic assumed bonds of affinity joined them. The controversy eroded those sentiments, replacing them with feelings of betrayal and frustration, and substantially altering the habits that had linked that transatlantic community.

Dissenters traced their roots to sixteenth- and seventeenth-century English Puritanism.[21] In England, where dissent was a legal category shaped by the Act of Toleration of 1689, leaders worked through collaborative organizations, most notably the Protestant Dissenting Deputies, an advocacy group that addressed legal issues, and the Protestant Dissenting Ministers of the Three Denominations, a clerical organization. Dissenting academies educated pupils and trained ministers since nonconformists were barred from Oxford and Cambridge. Voluntary societies bridged the distance between

England and North America. The New England Company (NEC), for example, functioned as a dissenting version of the Society for the Propagation of the Gospel in Foreign Parts, as did the Presbyterian Society in Scotland for the Propagation of Christian Knowledge (SSPCK). The Society for Promoting Religious Knowledge Among the Poor (SPRKP) distributed tracts, much like the Anglican Society for Promoting Christian Knowledge. In Massachusetts and Connecticut, dissenting churches were the establishment, and ministerial associations functioned to unite various churches. Harvard, Yale, and Princeton trained clergy who moved comfortably between the various strands of dissent.[22]

Likewise, dissenting status was a recognized social marker. In 1758, Thomas Clap in Connecticut wrote to Elizabeth Scott Williams, the daughter of a prominent dissenting minister in England who had married Elisha Williams and relocated to Massachusetts. Clap used an intimate language of religious inclusivity, describing Williams's pleasant "Religious Conversation, which awakened in me all the most tender Passions of a generous Friendship; and a Strong and lively sense of Divine Things." He hoped that she would find new friends to fill the loss of her English circle: "When Persons upon some Acquaintance, find that they agree in the most important Sentiments, especially in the great things of Religion, with a peculiar agreable Turn of mind, which cannot be exprest, but only felt," then they could "lay open their whole souls."[23] Clap had evidently been inspired by a visit from Mrs. Williams, and his teaching had been reinvigorated. In addition, he had "informed [the students], from you, of sundry practices among the Dissenters in England, tending to keep a Sense of Religion, which I hope has had, and will have, some good Effect." When the young New Englander Henry Marchant took a tour of Britain in 1771 and 1772, he made a particular point of acquainting himself with dissenting circles. Ezra Stiles informed Thomas Wright in Bristol that Marchant wanted "to form an idea of the genius & piety of the Pastors & of the present state of the dissenting Interest." "He is a Congregationalist," Stiles added, "and a Friend to civil & religious Liberty."[24]

The strength of ties among dissenters was noted in British governing circles as a reason not to install a bishop in a place where it might unsettle relations or, worse, cause dissenters to rally against the government at the ballot box. In 1749 and 1750, Thomas Sherlock, bishop of London, worked concertedly for a colonial bishop, though he met with resistance from within the ministry. Horace Walpole wrote to Sherlock advising him that the plan was a poor one because the dissenters "shou'd not be provoked" into no longer supporting the government, which they might be "by the instigation and complaints of their brethren in the colonies." In this instance the Protestant Dissenting Deputies, who had the ear of the powerful Thomas Pelham-Holles, Duke of Newcastle, investigated the claims, and that body reassuringly passed along the news to its Massachusetts connections that no bishop was to be appointed.[25] Carl Bridenbaugh called the dissenting community the "first effective transatlantic and intercolonial intelligence network" and argued that dissenters used it effectively in the first phases of the conflict.[26] Alison G. Olson also pointed to the political importance of the transatlantic dissenting community during the middle decades of the eighteenth century, as well as its eventual decay.[27]

The bishop controversy was a particular challenge to dissenters because their objection to episcopacy was and always had been a definitive issue for them. As much as they concurred with the general Protestant conception of "religion," they also thought the elimination of episcopal structures was the best way to achieve that triumph of religion for which all Protestants theoretically hoped. Ezra Stiles, one of the leading spokesmen of the dissenting interest in America, articulated his vision most potently in his widely circulated sermon *Discourse on the Christian Union*. He offered an ecclesiastical solution to the problem of Christian division on earth by suggesting that all presbyterian and congregational polities could cooperate, and he took as his text Philippians 3:16: "Nevertheless, whereto we have already attained, let us walk by the same Rule, let us mind the same Thing." He explained that the apostle Paul had been "desirous to unite as many as possible with him," so "he was willing to walk *together* with his brethren the Hebrew christians *as far as they had attained*." Paul, according to Stiles, stressed unity only in essentials, "it being far better for those that agreed in essentials, to live in harmony and fellowship, than under the most specious pretexts to resolve themselves into fruitless, undeterminable controversy and alienation."[28] Stiles argued that theological division should be avoided, while fellowship among Protestants should be built on the broad territory of agreement that united them.

For Stiles, the best grounds on which to base unity was the congregational polity he embraced, which meant rejecting the corrupting office of bishop. He used geographic prevalence to make his point that the kind of bishops the Anglicans employed were both dangerous and aberrant. "And as to the present practice of the protestant world," he wrote, "the Lutheran superintendents are confessedly but *primi inter pares* [first among equals], and consequently their ordination is truly presbyterian" rather than episcopal. He went on to discuss churches in Sweden, Norway, the German territories, Switzerland, France, the Netherlands, and Scotland. "Nay," he concluded, "exclusive of the Lutherans who seem to retain a species of episcopacy, the reformed presbyterian churches comprehend double the number of souls to those of the british episcopacy." By his reckoning, "strictly speaking, the whole protestant world, except the church of England, agree in the validity of presbyterian ordination."[29]

Stiles's description of the world of episcopacy in national terms is instructive and points to the central meaning of the bishop controversy for Protestant community. Because all Protestant bishops were appointed within particular nations, opposition to episcopacy placed the relationship between dissenters and their own governments at the heart of their broader conception of Christian unity across nations, for whether one was a leader in the cause and enjoying religious liberty or one was suffering under a persecuting establishment depended on one's national church and its episcopal arrangement. This was the crux of the issue for the dissenting community. As American dissenters became more and more anxious about the prospect of an American bishop, they were calling on their English counterparts to act *politically*, as English subjects, on behalf of the American cause. In other words, the transatlantic Protestant community of dissenters depended on each group's domestic political commitments. But correspondence between dissenters on the two continents about the bishop crisis in the 1760s led to more disappointment than coordination, and the result of the bishop controversy for dissenters was the erosion of the personal networks for communication that had sustained the international language of a shared Protestant unity. Thus, even though English dissenters disproportionately objected to the North ministry's coercive strategies in 1774 and 1775, in the long decade before the Boston Tea Party, American dissenters came to believe they had been abandoned by their comrades.

The weakening of the personal relationships that supported the dissenting network became clear as early as 1764, when American leaders eagerly sought out the support of those they viewed as their compatriots in England. They found it difficult, however, to identify partners on the other side of the Atlantic. Ezra Stiles had made particular efforts to build connections, as much because he believed in the dissenting interest as because of his concerns about a bishop. He was fortunate in his choice when he wrote to Thomas Wright of Bristol that he "should be glad of a correspondence with some dissenting Ministers in your city, and address myself to you, Sir, if you shall do me the favor of a Reciprocation." Wright and Stiles exchanged letters regularly nearly until the war broke out. But Stiles was most likely disappointed in a letter he received from dissenting scholar Nathaniel Lardner in 1764. "You suppose a *Connexion* between yourselves, & *your Brethren in Europe*," chided Lardner. "But no such Unity can be effected. The Dissenters here are now too inconsiderable, & can be of no real service to you." Lardner's pessimism extended to his English brethren: "Nor are they sufficiently united among themselves," he continued. "It is well, if you are so united."[30]

American dissenters felt that they had to act to protect their religious liberties. In 1766, discussions began among leaders in the community about creating a united organization of their fellows. They envisioned one that spanned the Protestant world and could effectively oppose both the specific Anglican threat and any others that arose. As Stiles wrote to John Devotion, such an organization "of Protestant Brethren in the British Empire" would be "far more respectable than either or any of the Bodies in their Present Disconnections." He saw it growing in the future so that "in a Century, [it] would compose the bigger half of the British Empire," and would be "formidable to Episcopacy & a Bulwark against it." Stiles looked beyond the empire too: "I should be glad if the Dutch and French Calvinistic or Reformed [Churches] might be comprehended." These lofty plans could not be achieved without partners in distant places, however; Stiles and his colleagues soon had to scale the project back to a more limited cooperation between Connecticut Congregationalists and mid-Atlantic Presbyterians.[31]

The process of trying to unite dissenters into a more formal union further exposed the limits of the personal links between the English and American dissenting communities. When discussing the plan, Boston minister Charles Chauncy wrote that American dissenters "shall [immediately] open a correspondence to Awaken the dissenters in England in the name of all their Brethren in these parts of the world, engaging [their] interest and influence to serve us to the utmost of their power."[32] But again, this proved difficult to enact. Presbyterian Francis Alison of Philadelphia revealed the limits of his British connections to Stiles when he asked, "with whom you correspond in London, & what Gentleman or Minister among ye dissenters in or near that City is most likely to manage any business for us with ye ministry or nobility, if there be occasion to complain of grievances, or to ask for favors."[33] Stiles's response was not much more encouraging. Lardner, he reported, was too old and too deaf to be of much help. The others to whom he had been recommended for correspondence had not replied. He then moved into a list of names he clearly knew, but in some cases, he was even unsure if they were dissenters or churchmen. "I do not eno' know the Characters of Dr. Walker, Dr. Langford, Dr. Conder, Dr. King, Dr. Fordyce all London Ministers of some Eminence & Popularity—but none of equal Weight at Court with the late Dr. [Samuel] Chandler," Stiles wrote. He then added, "I suspect that however providence preserves a Sett of very valuable & worthy Ministers among the Dissenters, yet there are not at present among them, Men of the first Eminence in Literature, Polity, Wisdom." He suggested that Alison not be "hasty in chusing—but first gain a List of the London Minsters & their Characters, & of a few principal Gentlemen Pillars in the Cause." Clearly, Stiles, Alison, and Chauncy knew that they wanted to reach out to English dissenters, but they did not know exactly who might help them.[34]

The record from the eastern side of the Atlantic suggests that English dissenters, no matter how much they claimed allegiance to American coreligionists, had only limited political attention for their fellows' cause. English dissenters had long accustomed themselves to living with an establishment that included bishops and indeed even saw them as protectors against the petty insults of local clergy. In 1768, Nathaniel Lardner wrote to a Baptist minister in Salisbury that he had "letters from Mr. *Samuel Mather*, another from Dr. *Chauncy*: who has sent me his Sessions on the ordination of a successor to Dr. *Mayhew*, & a tract, or discourse, of 120 pages, showing that *Presbyterian ordination is scriptural and valid, with an Appendix concerning the Epistles of Ignatius*, all writ, it seems to me, in a masterly & judicious way And it affords great pleasure to see such fruits of the articles of our friends in N E."[35] Such praise on a subject so important to the Americans suggests that Lardner might be moved to support the American cause, but only a few months before, he had taken a much more discouraging tone with Stiles: "You are much alarmed by the prospect of having B[isho]ps put among you. I do not know what measures are taken for that purpose. I am apprehensive, that it will be done some time. But, perhaps, it may be deferred. We are told, that the Arch Bp says, if Bishops were sent to America, they would have no courts, have any power which could be injurious or oppressive to any, they would only perform the offices of the episcopal function: meaning, as I suppose, confirmation, ordination, & the like." Lardner emphatically rejected Stiles's concerns: "*What is the fear? What is the danger? A few persons vested with authority to ordain ministers, to confirm youth, & to visit there our clergy? Can two or three of these persons restrained to these spiritual functions, be dangerous to any in any matter?*"[36]

Stiles received a similar response from Thomas Wright, his correspondent in Bristol. The Rhode Islander had described his fears and pleaded for help, writing, "Our Brethren the Dissenters in England will do us a most essential Service by using their Influence in our Favor on this Subject." Although Wright's immediate response does not survive, in their next exchange he assured Stiles that "the Dissenters in England &c. enjoy greater liberty [than] is secured to them by the Act of Toleration." Wright followed this with a recounting of a recent victory in court (long fought for by the Dissenting Deputies) in which jurist Lord Mansfield had asserted firmly the protected status of dissenters. Stiles's English correspondents simply did not worry as he did, no matter how much they agreed with the cause in principle.[37] Even William Gordon, an English clergyman who identified so closely with American dissenters that he emigrated to the colonies shortly before the war, reassured Connecticut minister Joseph Bellamy that if a proposed bishop was only for the colonies where an episcopal establishment already existed, he could not "see that the dissenters will have any right to blame." On the other hand, he continued, "they will have cause to fear; for when once episcopacy has got a footing, there's no knowing where it will stop."[38]

Those in Boston found themselves equally disappointed when they turned to English coreligionists, who were simply not as afraid of Anglican bishops as the Americans were. In 1768, the "Congregational Pastors of the Province of Massachusetts Bay," represented by Charles Chauncy, Ebenezer Pemberton, Andrew Eliot, and Samuel Cooper, wrote to the Protestant Dissenting Deputies in London for support in protesting the imposition of a bishop. It was a logical choice, as there had long been a correspondence between the two bodies, and the Dissenting Deputies had as its primary aim the legal advocacy of dissenting issues. On the other hand, the Dissenting Deputies had not been overly eager partners in the recent past. In 1764, for example, the same body of Massachusetts ministers had written to request aid in the event of the imposition of a bishop, and though notice of the letter was entered into the minutes of the London society twice, no action on the petition was ever recorded. In their second appeal, Chauncy and his fellows laid out the case against bishops at length, then concluded by saying that the "kind and generous Assistance you have afforded us upon all occasions, encourages us to apply to you in the present critical Season." As they had done in the past, the Bostonians "trust[ed]" that the plea would "encline you to appear with Zeal and Vigour now the Attempt is renewed." The Dissenting Deputies found that the former committee of correspondence had lapsed out of existence, and its members were no longer with them, with the exception of Jasper Mauduit, the chair. A new committee had to be constituted to look into the matter; two months later, the letter was referred to that committee so that they could "enquire of such persons as they may think proper, in order to get the best information they can whether the design of introducing Bishops into America be dropt or not." One month later, the report came that there was no viable plan in motion. Although subsequent requests from Americans continued to come in to the Dissenting Deputies, the appeals met with no significant response. One 1773 request on the issue waited more than a year for an answer.[39]

Over a period of years, the disjuncture between American paranoia and British complacency wore down the relationship between the two communities. One particularly wearisome letter came to Stiles in 1772 from Philip Furneaux, another leading English dissenter, again trying to reassure Stiles that he misunderstood the situation. "I do not apprehend that the Ministry here have yet shown any disposition to the scheme of sending Bishops to America," Furneaux stated, "and I am firmly convinced have never attempted to prevail upon any of our brethren to adopt that design in any shape." Certainly, he agreed, Stiles's worries had a grounding in reason. "Some of the bishops and clergy on this side of the water, as well as the generality of the clergy, I suppose, on yours, have such a design very much at heart," Furneaux wrote, and "if it be true, that your missionaries have sent over a petition for the appointment of an American Episcopate, some attempt perhaps may be made to carry their point." Yet there was no cause to worry, as he restated directly: "I believe the ministry at present do not wish to be troubled with any such business."[40]

By the early 1770s, most of the correspondence between the American and English dissenters had dwindled or ended completely. Some key individuals, especially Thomas Hollis and Jasper Mauduit on the English side, died, and no one stepped into their places. As the political crisis deepened, the religious leaders who had led the bishop's controversy were less prominent, and thus the language and community of dissenting Protestantism was not deployed to moderate American patriotic fervor. Ezra Stiles, an individual who had invested a great deal in building international cooperation, largely stopped discussing the "dissenting interest" or trying to will it into existence between New Englanders and English dissenters. In the final years before the war, his letters to England went to more and more radical figures, such as Richard Price and Catharine Macaulay. Unmoored from the ideal of an international Protestant unity based on the principles of congregational government, Stiles began to use a language of religious liberty situated in a distinctly American context, rather than the language of international religious unity.

A final glimpse into Stiles's prewar sentiments can be seen in his correspondence of mid-April 1775, which shows the decay of the dissenting network as a bulwark of international Protestantism. Although he could hardly have known that the battles of Lexington and Concord would take place less than a week later, Stiles might have guessed from the increased military activity in Newport that communication would grow more difficult. He sent three letters with Francis Dana, who went on an errand for Massachusetts to London. One, to dissenting pamphleteer Samuel Wilton, included the declaration: "As to religious Liberty, you yourself have described my sentiments most exactly. I am a Lover of all good men of all Denominations, but will be brot under the Power of none; I inherit from my Ancestors who came out of England among the first Accessions of the last Century, an ardent inextinguishable Love of *Liberty civil & Religious*." Cutting loose from the language of Christian unity and the "interest of religion," Stiles advocated a national ideal. Lest his sentiments be vague, he added, "An ultimate [annihilation] of *religious* Liberty on the English Territories in America is the evident Tendency, if not primary Design of the Quebec Bill. Who could have thot that a [Protestant parliament] would have armed Papists [against] Protestants?" With others Stiles used even stronger language, justifying the use of force by the Americans. To Philip Furneaux, he wrote that he felt he had been forced to turn his back on his English friends: "If deserted by our Friends Brethren in G. Britain, & abandoned by the World, We confidently trust in our God that he will deliver us." Stiles expressed a nationalistic religious geography: "Our fathers fled hither for Religion & Liberty—if extracted from hence, there is no new World to flee to. God has located us here, & by this Location has commanded us to make a stand, & see the Salvation of the Ld. The Event is with the Lord of Hosts."[41]

It is a dangerous game to second-guess our sources, but Stiles presented future scholars with a tempting occasion to do just that when he crossed out the word *friends* and replaced it with *brethren*. Which word was, for him, stronger? Had he been betrayed by close family or by collegial fellow travelers? Either way, the betrayal that concerned him was of an intimate nature, and the context of his letter suggests that he was angry not just at the English political nation but also at the fellowship of dissenting clergy that he had held so dear. Its dissolution was the great casualty of the bishop controversy. Historians miss the point when they see the struggles over a bishop merely as a proxy for loyalism and patriotism. The squabble between Anglicans and dissenters that erupted over the potential of a bishop was surmountable, another in a long history of disputes within a functioning community of Protestant religious leaders. Likewise, the fear of English tyranny that may have been excited by the same issue in the American population (or at least its political leadership) cannot be seen from the controversy's participants alone, as the arguments of clergy provide little direct evidence of political action.

The foregoing investigation, however, reconfigures the question, looking at the bishop controversy not as the insertion of religion into politics but instead as the intrusion of politics into a carefully constructed world of institutional Protestantism that depended on relations among its leaders. The erosion of transatlantic religious community among the leaders of the dissenting world is evident from Stiles's complaints and from the decade of disappointment that preceded it. As leaders of the dissenting community gave up their ties to one another, they also began to relinquish their parts in a shared project of institutional Protestantism that had effectively structured official "religion" for close to a century. Over the next decade, the bishop controversy became just one of many political incidents that pushed Protestant leaders on both sides of the Atlantic to see their religious communities in national rather than broadly "Protestant" or even "religious" terms. Clergy, within and beyond the dissenting interest, began to build new partnerships within their nations. In the new United States, dissenters would be at the forefront of that effort and would help to articulate a new language of American religious nationalism that would then be transferred to the governing institutions of the United States. The bishop controversy alone did not cause this shift, of course, but as one of the "religious" events that is most frequently associated with the Revolution, it serves to remind us that the fractious and bloody creation of a new national boundary had consequences for the boundaries of the Protestant world as well.

CHAPTER 8

Empire's Vital Extremities

British Africa and the Coming of the American Revolution

BRYAN ROSENBLITHE

In a 1764 petition before the Board of Trade, the Scottish captain George Glas described the discovery of a potential colony along the Barbary Coast north of what is now Tarfaya, Morocco, as "the greatest that has been made in Commerce since the Portugueze found the Way to the East Indies by the Cape of Good Hope."[1] Almost immediately after Glas secured the territory for Britain and renamed it Port Hillsborough, a general famine in the region forced him to cast off for the Canary Islands, where Spanish authorities imprisoned him for eleven months under conditions that British officials equated with torture. Glas attributed his predicament to the Spanish "having had intelligence from London of our Discovery" and their belief that the British would use Port Hillsborough during an imminent war to "destroy their fishery and conquer the islands."[2] Anthony Bacon, a merchant, member of Parliament (MP), and partner in the scheme, lobbied the Board of Trade on Glas's behalf, leading Southern Secretary Henry Seymour Conway into a series of increasingly hostile diplomatic exchanges with Spain to secure his release.[3] Thus, Glas, his merchant backers, and Port Hillsborough insinuated themselves into a volatile cluster of Anglo-Bourbon conflicts centering on the ability to secure and exercise political control over a set of what appear in the historical record as insignificant Atlantic colonies at the same moment that Parliament was preparing to debate the repeal of the Stamp Act and the imposition of the Declaratory Act on North America.

Stories like those of Glas and the people who worked to conquer, colonize, develop, and integrate the territories ceded to Britain at the end of the Seven Years' War remain for the most part outside the historical literature on the political context from which the American Revolution emerged. From the publication in 1789 of David Ramsay's *The History of the American Revolution* to the present, historians have produced a rich and elaborate body of scholarship explaining the coming of the Revolution in terms of the activities and political and ideological commitments of patriot colonists operating on the East Coast of North America.[4] The fact that British ministers responded to colonial protests with a unanimous belief that sovereignty over the colonies remained indivisible and resided in Parliament has nourished this patriot American analytical framework, which, at the same time, has served to overemphasize the relevance of constitutional arguments about the legality of parliamentary taxation of the colonies and the effect of North American colonial protests on the making of imperial administrative policy.[5] As a result, we know surprisingly little about what motivated influential MPs to insist on asserting Parliament's authority over North America after decades of deliberate refraining from interference in colonial affairs that helped to solidify the constitutional foundations upon which the Revolution would ultimately proceed.

An account of George Glas and the British colonization of Africa during the Seven Years' War and its immediate aftermath helps to situate the Revolution's origins within the interlinked histories of British colonial expansion, political conflict, and administrative reform in the Atlantic world. Considered alongside British imperial conquests in North America, Port Hillsborough represents an extreme outlier. The few people who were aware of its existence could have measured the duration of British control over a colony—a control that amounted to little more than a signed treaty, a map, and a ship moored alongside the African coast—in days if not hours.[6] Yet as an outgrowth of the British conquest of Senegal and Gorée during the Seven Years' War and the geographic expansion of Britain's Atlantic empire at the peace of 1763, the acquisition of Port Hillsborough evinced a dramatic shift in the content and purpose of British imperialism. Like their peers throughout the Atlantic, Glas and other merchants in the African trade used the war to form alliances with MPs to gain standing within a permeable British state. Their ties to Parliament enabled them to influence the prosecution of the war and to shape the conditions of the peace. Throughout this period, they sought strategic outposts in the new African colonies to engross the trade in key commodities and to reorient African commerce on a continental scale. The conflicts they created among their fellow traders, African nations, and European imperial rivals revealed the weakness of British colonial administration in Africa during a time of massive tensions with France and Spain. The reforms that grew out of the need to impose and secure British control over these often tiny and transient spaces reveal the broader Atlantic dimensions of what John Murrin called a "crisis of political integration and centralization" that roiled the colonies and led Parliament to insist on asserting its sovereignty over North America after decades of "salutary neglect."[7]

In a meaningful way, British expansion in Africa during the eighteenth century owed to a chance encounter in 1749 at the Royal Exchange in London between the Quaker merchant Thomas Cumming and a group of Berbers tied to Trarza elites who sought to use Britain to undermine French influence over commerce at the mouth of the Senegal River. Within the African continent, Berber groups controlled the trade in gum arabic and gum senegal, vegetable resins essential in the fixing of dyes on fine calicos, and they resented French control of forts close to Portendick, a trading center north of the Senegal River where acacia trees from which the gum was harvested thrived and to which the Berbers had migrated in response to the trade.[8] Contemporaries believed the best quality gum could be found only in this area, and, as a general rule, the British textile industry depended on imported dyes, which had grown increasingly expensive and difficult to acquire from French traders by the early 1750s.[9] Indeed, many of the conquests during the war and the territories retained after it were sources of gum, indigo, logwood, archilla, and other materials used in the dying of textiles.[10] Cumming used the war with France and a promise from the Trarza emir Amar Wuld Ali Shandora of a supporting force of seven thousand troops to argue in a 1756 parliamentary petition for the capture of Fort Saint Louis in the name of the national interest. He also persuaded William Pitt, then secretary for the Southern Department, to grant him a monopoly over the gum trade in exchange for his efforts.[11]

Pitt's resignation in 1757 and the death of the emir quashed Cumming's scheme. Although Pitt quickly regained power, Cumming's lack of both a viable military ally and the capital necessary to maintain an effective monopoly forced him to ask Parliament for the assistance of the British navy and to seek the aid of an outside financier.[12] Likely through their shared interests in the African trade and gum arabic in particular, Cumming forged a financial alliance with the Manchester cotton mogul Samuel Touchet, whose activities reflected many of the mercantile, financial, and industrial possibilities of the era. Like other large-scale merchants during the period, Touchet expanded his activities to include a variety of state contracts, including military provisioning, the victualing and payrolling of troops in the Caribbean and Africa, and, in one notable case, a connivance with an agent acting on behalf of the Earl of Albemarle in Havana for an exclusive contract to supply the thousands of slaves sufficient to transform the economy of the colony within a matter of months.[13] Slaves, however, represented a secondary consideration for Touchet in his collaboration with Cumming in the trade in gum, and control over its main outlet to Europe would give Touchet a monopoly over an increasingly dear and highly sought-after commodity. Touchet coveted control over gum arabic and saw the alliance with Cumming as an opportunity to gain a tighter hold on the processing of cotton, corner the market in calico linens, and recenter the manufacture of fine textiles from India to England, a project that the interruption of Indian exports to Africa during the war made possible. Such an arrangement would furthermore redound to Touchet's slaving activities, as the brightly colored calicoes over which he sought control were critical commodities in the trade with African nations.[14]

With Touchet's support in the form of ships to assist in the invasion, the British captured Saint Louis in May 1758, and after an initial effort to seize Gorée failed, a naval force led by Augustus Keppel took the island the following December. Once it was taken, Goreé became a greater preoccupation of ministers in Whitehall than of British merchants and representatives of the Committee of Merchants Trading to Africa (CMTA) on the ground.[15] Indeed, officials had planned the operation that led to its successful capture as an adjunct to the invasion of Martinique, indicating that the operation had come to represent part of a broader shift in British war strategy toward territorial conquest. As Richard Middleton points out, because the territorial claims on Gorée and Martinique had been long settled, their capture signaled a "move from a basically defensive to a more offensive view of the war."[16] In the reckoning of military officials, the capture of Gorée would ensure the security of Fort Saint Louis. Merchants with knowledge of the French African colonies saw Gorée primarily as a slaving colony, but the governor of Fort James would later remark that in 1757 its French governor had told him, "Goree was a sinking fund to their India Company," and they used it "only as a receptacle for the slaves sent from Senegal."[17] Furthermore, it appears that ministers received intelligence before the capture of Gorée indicating that although it had "carried on a considerable Trade for slaves with the Kingdom of Damel . . . a Revolution in that Kingdom put an End to that Commerce."[18]

Internecine merchant arguments over the retention of Gorée bled into a much larger debate that began to unfold in 1759 when victories over the French in North America and the Caribbean made the prospect of British victory in the Seven Years' War appear inevitable and effectively rendered the final three years of interimperial colonial warfare a militarized negotiation over the coming of the peace. Indeed, the issues raised in the debate continued well after the peace and focused on the immediate and long-term strategic and economic value of current and potential future conquests to what all parties agreed would be a geographically reconfigured empire after the war ended. Formal peace talks began in late spring of 1761 in Augsburg, only to linger in limbo after British ministerial squabbling and French reluctance to come to terms impeded meaningful progress.[19] These halting and inconclusive efforts impelled France and Spain to resuscitate the moribund family compact, which broadened the scope of direct warfare in the Caribbean and deepened the intensity of Anglo-Bourbon jealousies throughout the Atlantic. As British conquests continued to mount throughout the dilatory peace negotiations, influential Britons could imagine a variety of scenarios in which the empire would emerge from the war with some combination if not *all* of the Bourbon Atlantic colonial possessions.

Curiously, what contemporaries referred to as the "Canada-Guadeloupe debate" appears as a footnote in the literature on the Seven Years' War, perhaps because the majority of its participants saw the retention of Britain's North American conquests and the related elimination of the French threat that had helped to provoke the war as inevitable.[20] In a letter to his son in Parliament, the Antiguan planter Samuel Martin attributed the perceived lack of ministerial resolve to retain Guadeloupe and Martinique to "the Jamaica politicks of not extending our Sugar Colonies."[21] Here Martin echoed many who believed that influential West Indian planters with seats in Parliament and influence in the City of London like the Jamaican William Beckford had foreclosed the possibility of expansion in the Caribbean to protect their monopoly over the production and price of sugar.[22] Furthermore, depending on the state of the war, the degree of ministerial unsettlement in Parliament, and the political allegiances of the writer, a number of entries into the debate used the war to impugn specific ministers for cowardice or rapaciousness. On its surface, the debate over the peace appears as a political football cloaked in the language of political economy; it was more attentive to the intrigues and vicissitudes of high ministerial politics than the disposition of the colonies that it ostensibly addressed.

Yet a few commentators looked beyond Parliament and the Western Hemisphere to stress issues related to British Africa, and their claims parallel those of influential merchants and administrators with ties to the CMTA. Perhaps because Britain's conquests in Africa were seen as tangential to the sweep of the broader conflict and its African colonies were administered by a privately chartered corporation charged with the oversight of independent traders, the specific conditions of the capture and retention of Senegal and Gorée proved susceptible to the machinations of merchants, colonial administrators, and interested MPs. Indeed, these groups appeared to exercise more influence over the final terms of the peace than their counterparts arguing for British expansion in the Caribbean.[23] From the revival of the family compact in late 1762 though the ratification of the Treaty of Paris, opinion on the value of Gorée had split into factions that divided along political, economic, and geographic lines. One group with seeming ties to Pitt deployed classic patriot arguments and alleged that the peace revealed ministerial weakness that threatened the security of the empire throughout the Atlantic. Tying Gorée to other Atlantic cessions to the Bourbons, an anonymous pamphleteer demanded, "If we cannot now keep *Martinico, Guadaloupe, Goree*, and reserve our exclusive right to the Cod-Fishery, how shall we keep *Barbadoes, Jamaica, Canada, Newfoundland, Senegal*, &c, after we have weakened ourselves and strengthened our enemy by the surrender of our present possessions?"[24] Another author writing in a similar vein concluded, "Senegal without Goree will be found to be like a coat without sleeves."[25] The Earl of Hardwicke took a more practical view and understood that the now-agreed-upon return of Gorée would provide a nettlesome distraction to his ally the Duke of Newcastle should the former first minister and his friends seek to revive an alliance with Pitt in the likely event of a change in ministries. Writing to Newcastle in November of 1762, Hardwicke observed that Pitt, now an opponent of the ministry, "will attack the Peace upon points which we, whilst of the Council, agreed to, viz. the Fishery, restoring both Martinique and Guadeloupe and Gorée."[26]

The CMTA-appointed governor of Gambia, Joseph Debat, appeared to sum up the opinion of administrators and merchants with interests on the ground in Africa when he stated, "Goree is a useless Expence to the Government," and likened its retention to "flinging so much money into the sea."[27] As Debat's missives to his connections in Africa and the CMTA in London reveal, the British officials most closely tied to African commerce believed that Gorée played a negligible role in the slave trade. "I never yet know a Vessel, that slaved of the natives but for a few number," Debat contended. "There is not Annually one hundred & fifty to two hundred sold on that Garrison."[28] One knowledgeable pamphleteer evaluated Gorée's utility in terms of Euro-African economic and military affairs and noted that the British could at any time "take *Goree*, or put what Strictures we please upon its Trade, which consists only of Slaves, and that in no competent Degree."[29] Clearly, British assessments of the relative value of its African possessions had undergone a considerable reevaluation during the course of the war. In 1758, Fort James was seen as insufficient to handle the slave traffic in the region surrounding the mouth of the Senegal River, leading Debat, among others, to call for the capture of Gorée. By 1763, Debat could recount, "At my Arrival on this fort . . . the Name of a Galam slave was not so much known in this River," but war with France had shunted the trade to the south. "What we then called Merchant trade is now termed Galam," Debat marveled, "the Trade is intirely diverted out of its proper Channel and Centers in this River."[30] In a rare public pamphlet from an African administrator, John Roberts, the governor of Cape Coast Castle, argued that if "the trade of *Gambia* and *Senegal* rivers are pursued in a proper manner, *Goree* will be of no consequence."[31]

Although the Senegal River remained under British control under the terms of the peace, the failure to address British holdings along the Gambia River in its final terms made the Treaty of Paris an object of mixed satisfaction to its merchant advocates. Certainly, the degree to which pamphleteers and MPs took note of British possessions along the Gambia River spoke to the increasing weight the region as a whole held in the reckoning of influential ministers in Whitehall. The reasons behind the lack of direct ministerial attention to the Gambia River in the negotiations remain unclear. Perhaps it owed to the lack of overt imperial combat in the area and the fact that the French presence there amounted to a single small and unarmed trading post at Albreda, which they had controlled from 1681 until British locals and their allies ran them off temporarily during the war. Nevertheless, as Peter Thomas indicates, British ministers in London "assumed" the Gambia River basin "to be a British preserve" and proved as much by thwarting aggressive French efforts to arm Albreda after the war.[32] Moreover, by asserting successfully both the need to secure Senegal and the negligible value of Gorée, groups with strong African ties advanced their interests at the peace far more than those who advocated for the retention of British conquests in the Caribbean.[33] By the end of the war, the disposition of a region whose colonization had begun with the ambitions of a single merchant spurred on by a Moroccan potentate had become an object of meaningful state attention.

Perhaps more important than the content of the debate over the coming of the peace was what remained unsaid by parties with interests in British Africa. By the end of the war, large-scale merchants and their collaborators had begun to grope toward the idea of extending British commercial settlements well to the north of Saint Louis along the coast. They sought to penetrate far more deeply into the African continent, using the Senegal River and trading forts along the Barbary Coast as points of entry.[34] The loose structure of the British state in Africa helped to shape and direct these schemes and the specific ways in which they were executed. As the alliance of Touchet and Cumming shows, merchants' efforts to use the power of the state to broaden and deepen their African interests had begun during the war. Men like Touchet enjoyed success in Britain's new colonies so long as their goals overlapped sufficiently with those of a British state that sought to win what had developed into a war of conquest and to secure what had become—far more palpably than before the war—a territorial empire. As merchants and their allies drew on the tighter alliances they had formed with the state during wartime to expand their territorial holdings in Africa after the peace, their efforts produced a backlash among rival merchants and African nations that undermined the effective authority of the CMTA on the West African Coast and led its officials to ask London for reforms to enhance its administrative powers.

The genesis of Glas's plan to found a colony opposite the Canary Islands remains unclear, but, like Cumming, he clearly sought an influential patron of substance to underwrite his colonial ambitions. In the ways he acquired influence, Glas's backer Anthony Bacon shared many similarities with Touchet and some with Glas himself.[35] Touchet and Bacon had competed directly for the privilege of victualing troops in Africa soon after the war began in 1758, with Bacon receiving a state contract after the Lords of the Treasury deemed Touchet's proposal to be "extravagant."[36] Both also sought seats in Parliament, where Touchet was returned for Shaftesbury in 1761 and Bacon took the seat at Aylesbury after the expulsion of John Wilkes in 1764. Bacon had long-held aspirations for formal public influence, and he attempted to yoke his mercantile activities with political office well before entering Parliament. A faction tied to the Earl of Granville in North Carolina attempted to have him installed as the colonial agent to Parliament, which was thwarted after a heated battle with Governor Arthur Dobbs and his associate Henry McCulloh.[37] Upon entering the House of Commons, Bacon took a quasi-formal role as a leader on debates over African issues for which he took the chair of committees of the whole.[38] Although Touchet remained far less visible than Bacon after entering the House of Commons, both men held close ties to important figures in parliamentary leadership. Touchet numbered among the retinue of Henry Fox, and Bacon enjoyed what was by all indications a genuinely warm association with George Grenville, who described him as "a merchant of very fair character and extremely well disposed in all respects."[39]

Bacon also shared with Glas a background as a successful merchant ship captain. After the death of his parents, Bacon moved as a youth to the Chesapeake, where he learned the mercantile and marine trades, taking charge of a ship owned by the eminent tobacco merchant John Hanbury, which helped him to cultivate the contacts that led to his consideration for the North Carolina agency. During the Seven Years' War, Bacon extended his mercantile activities to include the transportation of victuals to Quebec. Shortly thereafter, he began to devote his attention almost exclusively to the Caribbean and African trades, with a strong focus on the territories ceded to Britain at the peace. It is likely that their mutual ties to the Canaries during the Seven Years' War brought Glas and Bacon into contact.[40] A pamphlet presented to Parliament as a supplement to Glas's petition described him as "settled in South Barbary as an Agent for a Company of Merchants in London."[41] Although we know little about his background and upbringing, Glas was the well-educated polyglot son of an influential dissenting Presbyterian evangelical minister, and his translation from the Spanish of a historical tract on the Canaries to which he appended his own account of the social, economic, and political manners and customs of the inhabitants brought him some attention.[42] It is likely that Glas's description of an undeveloped fishery on the Barbary Coast "adjacent" to the Canaries raised the suspicions of Spanish authorities and contributed to his eventual capture.[43]

Glas's optimism about the commercial potential of the Barbary Coast matched his astonishment at the failure of the Spanish and the Moroccans to avail themselves of its full potential. "It is strange to think that the Spaniards should want to share in the Newfoundland fishery with the English," Glas observed, "when they have one much better at their own doors."[44] Glas contended that the Spanish deployed only thirty ships in the Barbary trade and remained unmolested by the Moroccans owing to their lack of navigational skill. The idea of using the site as a means to sail into the continent clearly preoccupied Glas, who heard from a Spanish fisherman of a "noble channel" running "seventy or eighty leagues inland," but closer examination revealed it as merely a bay.[45] Ultimately, Glas believed that the Catholic Church presented an insurmountable obstacle to Spanish scientific and economic development. "The English have no reason to be apprehensive of the Spaniards ever being able to bring [the fishery] to any degree of perfection," Glas scoffed. "The power of the clergy in Spain is a better security to the English against such an event, than if a fleet of one hundred sail of the line were stationed on the coast of Barbary."[46]

If we place Glas's religious chauvinism in brackets, his observations reveal how the representation of expertise in Parliament combined with the withholding of crucial recondite knowledge to create political capital that allowed for the projection of state power into areas well outside the commonly accepted boundaries of the public good. In their petitions before Parliament, Glas and Bacon used Glas's linguistic skill, geographic knowledge, and familiarity with the customs and institutions of African nations to argue for the creation of Port Hillsborough and the release of Glas after his capture. In a pamphlet submitted to Parliament as a supplement to his petition, Glas stated that while stationed in Morocco he decided to "study the Arabick Language," which enabled him to "understand the historical and geographical Accounts he received of that Country from the Natives."[47] He also claimed to have read everything "in any European Language" on the subject of Africa and its trade.[48] Similarly, although he presented himself as a disinterested observer relating information for the edification of a curious public, Glas's volume on the Canaries should be understood as part of his efforts to establish himself as an authority on Africa, its geography, commerce, and peoples, and the Canary Islands trade to which they were connected.

Certainly, by the time of his petition, Glas had undertaken multiple voyages touching on the Canaries, the Barbary Coast, and the region between the Senegal and Gambia Rivers, which suggests that his contention that Port Hillsborough sat between Goreé and the Senegal River was a willful misrepresentation.[49] As Théodore Monod demonstrates, the site of Port Hillsborough corresponded to that of the fishery described by Glas in his account of the Canaries.[50] Although it was published in the same year that he submitted his petition for monopoly control over his "discovery," Glas compiled his account in 1761, and it is possible that he and Bacon conceived the plan to found a colony during the time between its submission and eventual publication in 1764. Indeed, it appears probable that Glas and Bacon wanted the location of Port Hillsborough to remain unknown. Here, Glas's desire for secrecy resembles the terms under which Pitt agreed to support Cumming in the taking of Saint Louis. Certainly, officials with discretion over a sensitive military operation demanded secrecy, but the conditions under which Cumming executed his agreement with Pitt brought with it the desirable effect of protecting his potential monopoly from the scrutiny of merchants who ultimately thwarted the arrangement that Pitt, by all accounts, had promised but failed to fulfill.

In addition to their competition over victualing contracts, the names of Bacon and his partner Gilbert Francklyn appear on a petition contesting Cumming's and Touchet's scheme for monopolization of the gum trade. Samuel Poirier, a CMTA agent in London, summed up the opinion of the merchants of London, Bristol, and Liverpool: "an exclusive Grant will interfere very materially with the Trade to the River Gambia which has greatly increased since the Reduction of Sengall."[51] Furthermore, a petition on behalf of a group of merchants trading to the Barbary Coast alleged that Glas's pretentions to unique knowledge of the region were inaccurate. The site of Port Hillsborough was known to Europeans, and the colony would jeopardize the peace between Moroccan authorities and the British Barbary merchants. "The Emperor Claims all that part of the Country as his undoubted Right," the petitioners observed, noting that "Glas was on the coast some years past," in response to which the emperor "Ishued out orders to Seize and bring to him any European that should be caught on such clandestine Trade for this Coast."[52]

The fears of the Barbary merchants appear justified. Glas's extensive background in the gum trade and his familiarity with the Berber groups who controlled the procurement and transportation of gum into the forts on the Gambia and Senegal Rivers do suggest that he sought Port Hillsborough to siphon away trade from Fort Saint Louis and concentrate it along the Barbary Coast.[53] If true, Glas and Bacon would have reversed patterns of trade that had emerged under the influence of the French during the first two decades the eighteenth century.[54] As the Barbary merchants had predicted, a group of Berbers launched an immediate and devastating attack on Port Hillsborough, and plans to resettle the site would wait until after the reorganization of the CMTA. Moreover, the supplementary pamphlet to his petition shows that Glas and Bacon sought to use their colony as part of an ambitious plan to take control over a well-established transcontinental caravan trade that centered in Timbuktu. Glas described a pattern of trade that began in Persia and wound through Mecca into North African port towns, where caravan merchants transported East Indian and European goods to Africans in the interior who dispersed them throughout the continent.[55] "If a Settlement was made at this Port," Glas asserted of Port Hillsborough, "the Commerce of the interior Parts of Africa would of course be diverted from its old Channel, and flow into the foresaid Port."[56] In this way, Glas and Bacon sought to reorient centuries-old commercial patterns and corner the trade in East Indian and European goods within the African continent.

The eruption of conflicts among merchants in the African trade owed to the fundamental weakness inherent in the loose administrative structure of the British Empire in Africa and the incapacity of the CMTA to exercise any real authority there. Indeed, the lack of effective power over the sprawling territory under its ostensible control encouraged merchants to circumvent the CMTA and seek political allies in Parliament for the promotion of their various schemes. Established by an act of Parliament in 1750, the CMTA was conceived under free trade principles to replace the monopolistic Royal African Company. Any British subject who could pay the nominal forty-shilling fee was eligible for membership. Administrative authority within the CMTA consisted of superintending a £10,000 annual grant for the maintenance of forts, the payment of tribute to ensure friendly relations with African nations, and compensation for CMTA officials, European artificers, and the many free and enslaved Africans employed by the committee. Parliament charged CMTA officials with the task of ensuring that its British merchant members had free access along the African coast to forts that served as markets and protected British interests in the event of conflict with other European empires and African nations. Although CMTA officials were permitted to trade for their personal profit, they could not do so on their own account, nor could they engage in any activity that might "tend to lay any restraint whatsoever" on access to markets from the Port of Sallee in South Barbary to the Cape of Good Hope.[57]

In addition to its lack of jurisdiction over conflicts arising from the commerce it was charged with protecting, the CMTA proved an easy target for subversion by ambitious, well-connected merchants and their allies on the African ground. Although Port Hillsborough failed, Bacon and his agents took control of Podor, and their actions demonstrated to CMTA officials the need for fundamental changes in the structure of British administration in Senegal. Podor sat roughly seventy miles inland at the tidal limits of the Senegal River, where further passage became difficult if not impossible between December and July.[58] Very little concrete data about Podor exists in British records. That the Board of Trade neglected to include it in routine requests for demographic, economic, and strategic inventories of its African possessions indicates administrators considered it to be insignificant. Although the French Compagnie des Indes established Podor in 1748, it was most likely unoccupied when the British assumed control over it during the operation against Saint Louis.[59] Yet Podor sat at the nexus of the shifting and contested boundaries of a number of distinct sub-Saharan nations, and, like the British outposts along the Senegal River in general, it sat on the southernmost border of territory controlled by Berbers, who had consolidated their authority in the region after a series of wars beginning in the late seventeenth century.[60]

Although a precise chronology cannot be established, it is clear that Bacon and his agents assumed control of Podor by late 1763 and shortly thereafter took an adversarial stance toward British authorities in Africa. CMTA correspondence with London shows that Bacon had instructed his agents to respond to his commands alone by February of 1764. The governor of Senegal, John Barnes, reported that he sought the temporary use one of Bacon's ships to rendezvous with another vessel in the Senegal River, but its captain informed him that he was under "Positive orders not to Risque the Craft . . . Except in Mr. Bacon's Immediate Service."[61] By the middle of that April, Barnes reported complaints from other merchants that "Mr. Bacon's Agents still have some of their People at Podore" who "had form'd a scheme of Appropriating the Fort Exclusively to themselves by Paying the Customs."[62] Barnes sent news of the "unwarrantable Seizure of the Fort" at Podor to the CMTA in July, prompting him to send an agent to retake it, which proved successful only by its having "been supported by all the other Traders in the Neighbourhood."[63] A later report stating that Bacon's "Agents have demollished and Carried off, the Materials of a great part of the new Fort" shows that Bacon soon retaliated. The CMTA pursued the matter into February of the next year, but to no apparent effect.[64] At the same time, Barnes suspected that Bacon and his agents had alienated African traders by passing worthless notes in exchange for gum and slaves. The group of traders took the highly unusual step of attempting to engage directly with the surrounding African nations, perhaps in an effort to circumvent the standard (and more costly) practice of employing African intermediaries.[65] Observing that such direct engagement and trust in a European was "a little uncommon for Africans," Barnes declared, "it were a pity it should be abused."[66]

Bacon's defiant stance and the inability of CMTA administrators to control the separate merchants in general thwarted Barnes's efforts to use a war among African nations in the region to bring the area under more direct British authority. CMTA correspondence shows that customs duties had increased steadily from the end of the war and even before, a product of growing Waalo dominance over the region since the 1730s. With the outbreak of warfare between the Waalo and the Kajoor nations, Barnes floated a plan among the British merchants to restrict payment to the Brak of Waalo.[67] "All the Traders readily agreed," Barnes recounted, "except Messrs. Biggin & Bacon's Agent, who declared he had nothing to do with the Concerns of the Fort." The CMTA's inability to compel obedience made consensus critical to any agreement between it and the disparate British merchants. Bacon's refusal to cooperate "put it out of the Power of the others to Act in it."[68] Barnes understood that the CMTA's lack of real authority in the face of near-constant regional unrest and the machinations of Bacon's agents and their merchant adversaries had rendered Podor completely unstable. "The Traders have Raised such excessive Disturbances through their Violent Oppositions one against the others, to the very great Scandal of the Nation and Ruin of Trade," Barnes decried. "The consequences are greatly to be Dreaded, and several of the Poor People of the Place have already Lost their Lives."[69] Barnes concluded with what had become a recurring theme in his correspondence from the period: "it cannot be expected, that we can enforce their good Behaviour to one another having no authority for so doing."[70]

Squabbles among the separate traders dovetailed with French diplomatic and military provocations, making a situation that was already unstable potentially combustible. Shortly after the peace of 1763, the French began to rearm Gorée and use it as a base from which to militarize their remaining possessions in the region. In January of 1764, Debat informed London that "the most Christian King is become the African Merch't" and had placed his government in Africa "under military direction."[71] Moreover, French entreaties to the Ñoomi people north of the Gambia as part of an effort to resettle and arm the fort at Albreda—an object of intense CMTA concern during the peace negotiations—had rendered a valuable ally useless. "The French are settled at Albreda, notwithstanding our Opposition, and the King of Barrah's good Intentions," Debat related, noting that he "is not their Friend, but must give Way to the Opinion of his People as he's not arbitrary."[72] In addition to distributing presents among the Ñoomi, their king related that the French had attempted to enlist his aid in an assassination plot against Debat.[73] Barnes attributed the persuasiveness of the French among the Ñoomi to the presence of their clergy and asked for "a French Huguenot Clergyman" to help "Wean them in some measure from the French and from the Superstition of their

Religion."[74] The search for a qualified cleric willing to serve in a deathly climate continued well into the next year. In the shorter term, in much the way that the separate traders had thwarted CMTA efforts to leverage the Waalo and Kajoor war to their advantage, French gifts to the Ñoomi threatened British influence within the region and foreclosed what had become the standard practice in Anglo-African relations of treating directly with a nation's king. "The sweets they Obtain by having two Strings to Their Bows, makes it Impracticable to be Effected by such a Method," Debat reported.[75]

Ultimately, the inability to wield any effective influence over the merchants prevented Debat from establishing durable alliances with African nations, which made productive negotiations with the French impossible. Debat attempted to fulfill his diplomatic responsibilities, but the tenor of his correspondence with Pierre François Guillaume Poncet de la Rivière, the governor of Gorée, indicates that he thought his efforts were futile. Debat used a series of arguments steeped in examples drawn from the American colonies to alternate between ambiguous professions of affection for the French, personal insults, and direct threats should they continue to pursue their provocative agenda. Debat broached the aforementioned assassination attempt, claiming that the Ñoomi king was eager to corroborate it, only to conclude that such a move would disrespect the dignity of the French nation. "According to the Laws of our Colonies, the Evidence of a Black Man is not Valid," Debat taunted. "Was a Gentleman to accuse another on such Evidence, the Consequence in all probability wou'd be a Good Caning."[76] Debat equated French machinations to regain influence among the Ñoomi to the "Scalps and Barbarities of all kinds Committed by the Indians in N. America" and blamed both on "the Influence of your Nation."[77] Ultimately, its administrators understood that the CMTA lacked the necessary power to maintain British control over the region and sought the aid of the British military. "These people can never be bribed to good behaviour," Barnes alleged, "tho' they may be very easily overawed."[78]

In response to the incessant pleas of CMTA administrators in Africa, the Board of Trade began in April of 1764 to gather information about the French claim to Albreda. Based on Debat's accounts, the Earl of Halifax concluded after a survey of the evidence that Britain's claim to the region surrounding the Gambia River preceded that of France, the French attempt to arm Albreda was illegitimate, and the French presence in the region depended on British consent. In October, Halifax dispatched a fifty-gun ship to Gorée, which he initially tried to keep secret from French diplomats in Paris. After word reached the Conte de Guerchy of its departure, the mission became a combined military and diplomatic effort that aimed to demonstrate the threat of decisive force, while avoiding direct conflict in an attempt to contain the larger problem within the discrete territory at issue.[79] In the words of Nicholas Tracy, George Grenville and the Earl of Halifax sought to "stop French encroachment in such a way that the French Government would not feel itself challenged."[80] The strategy succeeded, resulting in the dismissal of Poncet from Gorée by the French, who disarmed their outposts along the Gambia, while the British acknowledged the legitimacy of the French trading presence in the region.[81]

As the ministry was pursuing this military and diplomatic strategy against the French, the Board of Trade appointed a committee to inquire into the effectiveness of imperial administration in Africa and to make corrective recommendations. In February of 1764, and without any apparent deliberation, Parliament had incorporated the region surrounding the Senegal and Gambia Rivers "in the same manner, and under the same Regulations, and subject to the same Rules, Orders . . . as the other Forts and Settlements on the Coast of Africa."[82] Yet by early 1765, it was apparent to all interested parties that incessant internecine merchant squabbling and the related inability to maintain stable relations with neighboring African nations had undermined Britain's strategic position in the region relative to France. In a report from February of 1765, the Board of Trade correctly attributed these issues to the distinctively tighter connection of the new settlements to the African interior. "The commerce of this District, not being confined to the sea coast," the board wrote in a report from February of 1765, "has occasioned the Establishment of several Factories within, and high up those Rivers: and this has produced in the River Senegal a Species of Settlement, that has not taken place on the other parts of the Coast."[83] In response, Parliament dissolved CMTA control over the region, brought its various territories together as the single Crown colony of Senegambia, and endowed its governor with far more personal discretion over the creation of policy and its enforcement.[84]

It was at this very moment that Halifax introduced the matter of Captain Glas into this volatile combination of disputes by presenting a copy of Anthony Bacon's memorial protesting Glas's imprisonment to the Earl of Rochford, the British emissary to Spain.[85] As in the predicament with France in Albreda, Britain had resolved a similar dispute with Spain over territorial rights along the Caribbean coast of Honduras by combining diplomacy and the demonstration of military force with the creation of a new constitutional government.[86] Similarly, Britain attempted to separate Glas's imprisonment from the wider array of Anglo-Bourbon disputes in which it was embedded. Although Halifax instructed Rochford to "immediately make proper Remonstrances to the Spanish Ministers upon this extraordinary Proceeding" and to demand that "positive orders will be immediately dispatch'd for the Releasement of His Majesty's Subject," Glas's case would wait to receive sustained ministerial attention until Henry Seymour Conway assumed the secretaryship of the Southern Department upon the Marquess of Rockingham's assuming the office of prime minister in July of 1765.[87] As late as November, Conway wrote to Rochford, "I have not chose to take up the Affair of Glass further than his personal release, because I do not wish to increase the Number of Complaints which the Spaniards give Us so much cause to make."[88] Yet Conway's missives to Rochford from the beginning of August 1765 to January of 1766 (when he learned Glas had died sailing from Teneriffe to England after his release) reveal a steadily increasing outrage toward Spain. Much as Spain suspected Glas's settlement was part of a larger British imperial strategy against Spain in Africa and the Canaries, Conway understood that "the Govr. of the Canaries did not act wholly from himself."[89]

Although it was a dispute within the British Empire, the debates in Parliament over the repeal of the Stamp Act demonstrate this tension between the desire of ministers to treat each specific instance of colonial conflict as its own discrete case and their understanding that those cases arose from and reflected a broader panorama of interimperial contest. As the work of Peter Thomas among many others has demonstrated, Parliament took the constitutional arguments advanced by the North Americans in response to the Stamp Act very seriously and responded to them with meticulous attention to their many minute details. Certainly, these arguments are critical for understanding the basis upon which North Americans made the halting, fitful, and reluctant decision to sever their allegiance to the king over the course of more than a decade. At the same time, in the words of Ian Christie, the preoccupation with the constitutional side of the imperial debate in the 1760s has served to "mask sight of the real springs of British policy."[90] Indeed, Christie described the emphasis on constitutional issues and the question of parliamentary sovereignty in the intraimperial debate as "a front line of defense for other important considerations," most important among them, that MPs "regarded the British communities on both sides of the Atlantic as belonging to one nation."[91]

It would be a mistake, however, to confine the implications of the constitutional question of sovereignty within the compass of parliamentary authority to legislate for the colonies. As Frank O'Gorman has stated, the repeal of the Stamp Act and passage of the Declaratory Act by the Rockingham administration represented "part of a thoroughgoing and ambitious overhaul of colonial and commercial affairs."[92] Indeed, the attempt to establish free ports in the Caribbean for trade with the French and Spanish colonies ranked far higher among the priorities of Rockingham, Conway, and Edmund Burke than legislation for North America.[93] Yet the success of free ports depended on relatively pacific relations with France and Spain, which required, as we have seen, political stability within Britain's Atlantic colonies. Members of Parliament in the debate over the repeal of the Stamp Act did not prefigure historians of the imperial crisis, whose analyses have tended to pay very little attention to Anglo-Bourbon relations as a factor in the initial phase of the North American rupture from Britain.[94] "If we were to be engaged in a civil war in America, a French and Spanish war would be the consequence," Conway decried in Parliament, "and this connected with an American war would be absolute ruin to this country."[95] Hans Stanley observed, "if we do not mix firmness with our lenity, [North Americans] will become more useful allies to France and Spain than to this country."[96]

Although Conway offered reluctant support for the Declaratory Act, others in the Rockingham administration understood Parliament's claim to sovereignty over the colonies as critical to the empire's survival. When Charles Yorke pointed to the inability of the colonists to defend themselves against "those gross rivals of our power in the western world," he thought not of Indian enemies to the west but of "the Bourbon league," imploring Parliament to ask of itself, "what conjuncture [France and Spain] would wish so much for as a departure from our strength of legislative power which includes the whole."[97] For Yorke, perhaps the critical minister in the passage of the Declaratory Act, the assertion of sovereignty was a means to indicate the integrity of Britain's Atlantic empire in the face of a potential Bourbon revanche by a demonstration of political control over colonial space.[98] As the example of the British struggle with its African extremities shows, the assertion of political control over North America represented not the beginning but the culmination of the first phase of the American Revolution.

CHAPTER 9

The Great Awakening, Presbyterian Education, and the Mobilization of Power in the Revolutionary Mid-Atlantic

MARK BOONSHOFT

While conducting his duties as officer of the day on February 11, 1783, Colonel Francis Barber mounted his horse and started back toward his quarters. As he rode through camp at the end of a long war, Barber was very lucky to be alive. He had suffered a severe wound at Monmouth, a less severe wound to his head at Newton, and "a slight wound in his face" from a bayonet at Yorktown.[1] More than most, Barber probably thought that the end of his service could not come soon enough. Indeed it had not; his luck ran out. Barber was killed that day "by the fell of a tree, which was cut down by a soldier of the American army, at the cantonment near Newburgh, a short time before the army was disbanded, and after the articles of peace had been signed."[2] Two days later, "He was buried with the honors of war."[3]

Though Barber rose rapidly through the ranks of the Continental Army, he was a soldier by neither training nor inclination. Barber taught at a Presbyterian academy in Elizabeth Town, New Jersey, through the mid-1770s, "until called from that employment to take . . . the field, for the defence of America."[4] His death might have been unusual, but the trajectory that brought Barber to Newburgh was not. Decades later, trustees of the First Presbyterian Church of Elizabeth Town, who supervised Barber's academy, proudly recalled that "At their country's call," the "scholars ran from their masters, and with them, to the rescue."[5] Barber and his students at the Elizabeth Town Academy were part of a much wider generational experience among young Presbyterian men. Across the mid-Atlantic, colleges and academies emerged out of the controversies of the Great Awakening to institutionalize the theological and sociological positions of denominations and denominational factions. Later, teachers and students left these schools in droves to take positions of civil and military leadership during the American Revolution. This generation of revolutionary elites represents one of the clearest links between the Great Awakening and the Revolution.

Since at least the 1966 publication of Alan Heimert's *Religion and the American Mind*, historians have debated the existence and extent of the connections between the Awakening and the Revolution.[6] In increasingly complex ways, historians have argued that the revivals were a formative experience for colonists in learning to overthrow traditional authority, which mentally prepared them for both the experience of revolution and the democratization of the early republic.[7] Critics, Jon Butler chief among them, maintain that the ostensibly antiauthoritarian revivalists often actually "strengthened rather than weakened denominational and clerical institutions." Having bolstered traditional power, Butler argues, midcentury religious change did little to bring about the Revolution, which was a fundamentally "secular event."[8]

The story of Barber, his students, and their generation reveals a middle way between these two lines of interpretation. Successful revolutions depend as much on the consolidation of new power groups as the destruction of prevailing power structures.[9] And the Awakening gave rise to a new group of essential power actors. Denominational schools and their alumni, then, highlight how the Awakening could be part of a larger transatlantic phenomenon, engender institutional stability, and still contribute to the coming of the American Revolution. Focusing in particular on Presbyterians, this chapter traces the expansion of educational infrastructure out of the mid-Atlantic Awakening, the role of denominational schools in the personal development of students and the social development of the region, and the mobilization of educational infrastructure for the revolutionary cause. The Revolution was not a religious event. Yet the trajectories of denominational schools, their students, and teachers, highlight the long-term effects of the Great Awakening on the organization of public life and political power relations in the Revolutionary era.[10]

* * *

The mid-Atlantic was growing in the eighteenth century. Due to natural increase and an influx of immigrants, as early as the 1720s, the social and religious infrastructure of the region lacked the capacity to sustain the population. Even the Presbyterian Church, which made greater strides toward organizational stability than many churches in the region, faced a looming crisis.[11] A lack of clergymen coming from overseas, coupled with the "want of a college for ye Education of young men," meant that many Presbyterian congregations did not have ministers. This created a substantial problem, especially for recently arrived immigrant groups. For them, the Presbyterian Church was "the only recognizable institution they encountered," but it strained to organize social life.[12] At least partly in response, "Mr. Will. Tennent set up a School among us," the famous "Log College," to train clergymen locally. The synod, not particularly enamored with some of Tennent's ideas, decided to create a committee to examine candidates for the ministry who lacked degrees from established universities in Britain or New England and instead trained at "private Schools" like the Log College. This plan for oversight galled Tennent and his supporters. As these disputes raged, "Mr. Whitefield came into the Country" and found a warm welcome among partisans of the Log College. This fanned the flames of the controversy, giving the synod even more cause for alarm. In 1746, the church organization officially split to reflect the divisions. The Old Side maintained control of the Synod of Philadelphia, while the New Side formed the Synod of New York. The Log College filled some open pulpits with ministers but hardly alleviated the problem of an inadequate clergy. Rather, the controversy over the school underscored the continuing difficulty the church had in providing stability for the laity in a changing world.[13]

The Log College had set the tone, and as the divisions among American Presbyterians intensified, schools remained an important instrument in the fight. In 1744 the Old Side founded an academy, the future University of Delaware, "where the Languages, Philosophy and Divinity should be taught gratis" under the direction of the Irish-born minister Francis Alison. The school respected the Synod of Philadelphia's adherence to traditional dictates on ministerial licensing.[14] As the Log College went into decline, the New Side needed new schools to fill the void. In 1746, Jonathan Dickinson—a Yale-educated, moderate New Side minister with New England Congregationalist roots—and his colleagues received a royal charter to open a school in Elizabeth Town, New Jersey. This was the foundation of the College of New Jersey.[15] Competing lineages of schools grew out of these humble beginnings. Early New Side schools trained ministers who went on to found long-standing academies in Fagg's Manor, Pennsylvania; West Nottingham,

Maryland; and Pequea, Pennsylvania. Alison moved around, taking his school from New London, Pennsylvania, to Newark, Delaware. His students widened the reach of Old Side education, opening academies at Chestnut Level, Pennsylvania, Lewes, Delaware, and keeping alive Alison's academy at different points in Newark and New Castle, Delaware. These are only some of the best known and longest running of the many academies founded by the Old and New Sides. Francis Alison also played an important role in Benjamin Franklin's nonsectarian Academy and College of Philadelphia (the future University of Pennsylvania). Other denominations also began building schools; most famously, the Dutch Reformed Church acquired a charter for Queen's College (the future Rutgers University) in 1766.[16]

Though founded for religious reasons, denominational schools proved instrumental in the development of colonial civil society across a wide range of civil and religious institutions and associations and a variety of print media. Colonists viewed the spread of education in the mid-eighteenth century as part and parcel of social development writ large.[17] Looking back on the mid-1740s, when Francis Alison first began teaching in the mid-Atlantic, the Presbyterian synod of Philadelphia recalled that "Learning was under great Discouragements, and Opportunities of Education scarce." Benjamin Franklin also thought that, to that time, "the *culture* of *minds* by the *finer arts* and *sciences*" had been "necessarily postpon'd to times of more wealth and leisure." But by 1749, as the colonies experienced social and economic growth, he argued that "those times are come."[18] Though the expansion of education evinced a more general social development in the region, education in its own right had a key role to play in this process. Through official and unofficial mechanisms, schools expanded the educated population and in turn the number of people who took part in civil society and public life. They also helped drive the development of print culture. Students needed books, schools and debating societies built libraries, and teachers took part in the burgeoning magazine culture of the eighteenth century.[19]

* * *

Despite division within and between denominations, the colleges and academies founded in the period shared a similar curriculum.[20] Heavily influenced by Scottish Enlightenment educational traditions, the schools offered what teachers believed was a range of modern and practical subjects. Most taught logic, arithmetic and other types of math, English writing and speech, natural philosophy (science), and Latin and Greek.[21] At least one student's notes on "gunnery" and "of Shooting in Mortar-Pieces" are extant.[22] The capstone was usually lectures in moral philosophy. This subject was the most open to interpretation by the teachers. Moral philosophy engaged many questions that dovetailed with religion, especially the innate habits and senses of mankind, and so lectures on the subject often reflected the theological perspectives of the teachers. Francis Alison usually gets the credit for bringing Hutchesonian ideas to the American colonies. He had a degree from Edinburgh but seems also to have studied divinity at Glasgow directly under Francis Hutcheson. Alison's moral philosophy, though filtered through his own experiences, drew heavily on Hutcheson's published writings. The College of New Jersey was relatively slow in introducing Hutchesonian moral philosophy to its curriculum. Ironically, John Witherspoon, a staunch opponent of Hutcheson in Scotland, forced the change. By the 1760s schools of all religious stripes taught a broadly similar moral philosophy derived heavily, though sometimes begrudgingly, from the work of the famed Scottish Enlightenment philosopher.[23]

The pedagogy that many instructors employed at colonial colleges and academies influenced students in different ways than did the curriculum. Despite the Calvinist cloud that hung over many of these schools, teachers relied more often on the carrot than the stick. The schools motivated students through a "Love of Credit" rather than by threat, compulsion, or the specter of retribution from "Sprits and Goblins."[24] In fact, one of the main advantages of academies over other forms of education, especially private tutoring, was that it fostered emulation. As one pamphleteer noted, "where there is a community . . . it will create an emulation, a laudable desire to excel" among students.[25] In promoting this type of pedagogy, denominational schools took part in a larger transatlantic educational culture that attempted to harness the power of emulation and ambition, which Enlightenment thinkers viewed as powerful mental tools for propelling beneficent action. In particular, historians of late eighteenth-century France have illustrated the ways in which schools and public academic prize competitions inculcated the value of emulation in a broad range of people. Putting the Enlightenment into practice, as Jeremy Caradonna has phrased it, emulation would ideally mobilize people and "reward individual energies in ways that would produce benefits for the rest of society."[26]

Not everyone in North America immediately accepted the social utility of emulation. In 1756, a pamphlet published in Germantown, Pennsylvania, bemoaned that it was "too plain to need any proof" that most colonists believed "the nature of the best education of our sons" was to "stir [students] to action from principles of *covetousness* or a desire of distinction, that they may accumulate wealth, excel others and shine in the eyes of the World." This author argued, instead, that children should "never do any thing through strife, or envy, or emulation, or vainglory. Never do any thing in order to excel other people." They should only try to please God.[27] Interestingly, much of the published criticism of using emulation and ambition in schools came from pamphlets and almanacs printed in Germantown. In opposing emulation's pedagogical value, the pamphleteer was in the minority. However, the author's particular critique probably had wider resonance than might seem at first blush. The pamphlet not so subtly alerted readers that emulation could easily lead students toward an uncontrolled desire for wealth, fame, and power. A much wider group of colonists shared the fear that the "venal" side of ambition was very difficult to control.[28]

This nefarious potential consequence of emulation was not lost on academy teachers. Hutchesonian moral philosophy, republicanism, and Calvinism, all the main streams of thought to which many of these men subscribed, cast ambition as a corrupting passion. Teachers still used emulation as a pedagogical tool for a host of reasons. Even staunch critics of ambition recognized that it had an equally problematic opposite, idleness, or as Francis Hutcheson termed it, "the love of ease."[29] Though teachers might fear ambition, their Calvinist backgrounds also made them particularly susceptible to these caricatured depictions of the innate laziness of humanity. In that light, they might find emulation more appealing. They reasoned that with their supervision and the checks that students would exert over each other, competition for distinction could "hardly ever be prostituted to mean or venal Purposes, but must be the Object of every Student's Ambition."[30] Moreover, many academy and college teachers had followed their own ambitions in ascending to noteworthy positions as both educators and clergymen. In justifying emulation as a pedagogical tool, they normalized some of their own ambitions, which frequently caused them great anxiety.

Teaching emulation and socializing students into a transatlantic Enlightenment culture, however, had unintended consequences. Francis Barber, for instance, "being designed by his parents to wear the sacred robe," attended the College of New Jersey. To the dismay of his parents certainly, but also probably his teachers, he found that "this office did not suit his taste."[31] Barber was not unusual in that way. Until the war, Barber passed his time at the

Elizabeth Town Academy. While he searched for his calling, he socialized yet another generation of students into Enlightenment culture within the walls of a religious institution. Instead of just creating ministers and reliably pious community members, the practices and pedagogy of emulation also taught young men how to distinguish themselves in secular pursuits.[32]

Students and some of their parents valued schools for the opportunities they opened at a personal level. Compared with the entrenched hierarchies of England, colonial education offered social mobility to those young men who could afford it. Over time, academy teachers came to understand the appeal of education to many colonists and designed their schools to provide a curriculum that would allow students to meet their ambitions. The schools benefited as well. Steady enrollments, even of students with little intention of entering the ministry, stabilized the operation of schools and afforded teachers the chance to carry out the goals of their denominations.

The Old Side Newark Academy was particularly adept at balancing the goals of students, and their parents for that matter, with the religious mission of the school. Francis Alison explained to Ezra Stiles, the famous Congregationalist minister and educator in Connecticut, that the students "that intend to study Divinity apply to some College" after their time in Newark. The students who chose to "study law, or Physick generally are contented with [the] Proficiency they make at this school." At Newark, then, Alison concluded, "farmers can educate their children, so as to fit [them] for almost any station in life."[33] Parents would thus find, one almanac declared, that in colonial America it was "a foolish and most absurd Piece of Thrift, for the Sake of adding 20 or 50 Pounds to a Child's Fortune, to deprive him of the Benefit of such an Education."[34] In fact, according to some prescriptive literature, parents stood to benefit from educating their children. Those parents who did, according to another almanac, would have "far better Title to his [the son's] Obedience and Duty, than [those who gave] him a large Estate without it."[35] Parents, though, found that providing their children with an advanced education was not easy.

To cater to as many people as possible, the Newark Academy actively worked to keep the cost of room and board low. In 1771, having heard that "some of the Inhabitants of Newark, had taken 18 or 20 Pounds per Ann. For the Board, &c. of Pupils," the trustees asked for and received "the fullest Assurance from the Inhabitants that they will not ask nor receive more than Fifteen Pounds per Annum for the future." Furthermore, in order to keep access to the academy as widespread as possible, the trustees maintained "that no

Student can be admitted into that Institution, whose Parents or Guardians insist upon extraordinary Attendance or Accommodations" that would presumably drive up the cost for other students, or make distinctions between them more obvious.[36] Students "could not hope for such advantages, were they obliged to educate [them] in this City [Philadelphia]." Some students still found it necessary to go to Philadelphia or elsewhere to "finish their education." Even if they did, they would have paid significantly less over the course of their education by first attending the Newark Academy.[37] Nevertheless, only a small subset of colonists could provide advanced schooling for their children. Attendance at academies and colleges was miniscule. In the 1770s, around one-third of 1 percent of white men in the colonies were college graduates.[38] Costs for academies were usually lower than for colleges. Yet very few colonists could afford an academy education, and even fewer attended.[39]

For those who could afford it, academies offered a formal and informal curriculum that taught students the skills of enlightened gentlemen. At Samuel Finley's West Nottingham Academy, students always ate meals with prominent visitors. Benjamin Rush, a student of Finley's, remembered that "The benefits derived from the news, anecdotes, and general conversations which young people are thus permitted to hear are much greater than is generally supposed." Finley also "frequently exercised his pupils in delivering and receiving letters, and in asking and receiving favors," essential skills for someone with ambitions of moving up in their profession or in politics. Rush thought this helped explain why "Many of my schoolmates filled important stations, and discharged the duties of useful professions with honor to themselves and benefit to their country."[40] In addition, through practicing emulation, students learned to harness their emotions. This helped them to strive for distinction without appearing greedy and passionate. As Nicole Eustace has argued, during the late colonial period emotion was integral to creating social distinctions. Thus the differences "between those who were subject to passion and those who had mastered it" at times served as an important determinant of status. Controlling passions could give men license to lead other men.[41]

Schools also provided students with valuable networking opportunities. The Philadelphia academy constitution provided "that the Trustees will make it their Pleasure ... to promote and establish" their students "in Business, Offices, Marriages or any other Thing."[42] Students also took much of the responsibility for themselves, actively trying to develop networks after finishing school. The famous diarist Philip Vickers Fithian created a mutual improvement society with some of his schoolmates and colleagues, which, he optimistically declared, "is most certainly of very considerable advantage to every diligent member of it." The society helped the members continue to hone their skills as rising men of the Enlightenment. They proceeded from the belief that "our personal entertainment & improvement as individuals, depends on the diligence of the Members in general."[43] Denominational education helped create a generation of men who valued personal success but believed it derived, at least in part, from group action and coordination. If schools created networks that helped cadres of students get ahead in their lives and careers, in the process these educational networks helped stitch the mid-Atlantic region together.

Networks of teachers were particularly important in cementing the connections between schools. Teachers trained with one another before venturing out and educating the next generation. The schools' very existence depended on these networks of clergymen. As Samuel Davies set off northward from Virginia to begin a transatlantic voyage to raise money for the College of New Jersey, he relied on old school friends, among others, to ease his journey and his mind, as well as to fulfill the goals of his trip. Traveling up the East Coast, he reveled in "having so many valuable Friends in various Parts!" While visiting the wife of his old teacher Samuel Blair, Davies remembered "the happy Days of my Education." When he arrived in Philadelphia, he saw an old friend from those days, John Rodgers. During his trip, Davies also met with many of the most important New Side ministers, often on church business.[44] The structure of the Presbyterian Church encouraged regional and transregional networking. Synod meetings brought together ministers, teachers, church officials, and prominent laymen from far and wide. People with connections to academies and colleges were especially involved in the synod's activities. The ministers who ran schools were often particularly prominent, and educated men were among the most influential laypeople in the church. Synod provided time to discuss church doctrine and policy and settle all the important affairs of church governance. It was also a time when friends would "expect to see you."[45] The structure of the Presbyterian Church encouraged the creation of wider formal and informal social networks, and schools were a particularly important instrument for bringing coreligionists together.[46]

Teachers and trustees continued to view colleges and academies as institutional bastions for their theological positions even as the fires of the Awakening cooled. For example, the Presbyterian reunion in 1758 did little to stop intradenominational infighting over the control of the College of New Jersey.

After Samuel Finley passed away, the latest in a line of presidents who died in short order, the Old Side angled to take control of the school by installing Francis Alison as president. The New Side, with Benjamin Rush as their chief agent in Edinburgh, convinced a reluctant John Witherspoon to come over from Scotland to take the post and fend off the Old Side power grab.[47]

Yet students quite willingly crossed denominational and factional divides. They frequently attended an academy that shared the religious affiliation of their parents. But they also attended other academies and colleges that would most help them in pursuing their career ambitions regardless of religious affiliation. For example, John Ewing attended Alison's Old Side academy in Delaware, then the New Side College of New Jersey, before working at both institutions as a teacher. He finally settled down in Philadelphia, serving as both a minister at the First Presbyterian Church and a faculty member at the Academy and College of Philadelphia. At his New Side West Nottingham Academy, Samuel Finley educated many young men who went on to attend college, some at the College of New Jersey, the lone chartered New Side college, others elsewhere. And two of his students, Edward Shippen and John Morgan, helped found the medical school at the College of Philadelphia.[48] Schools and students thus made a distinctive contribution to the construction of mid-Atlantic civil society. Students harnessed a shared educational culture to pursue their ambitions, and in the process they bridged some of the most forceful religious divides within the region. Over time, and filtered through the political culture of late colonial mid-Atlantic civil society, the consequences would prove disastrous for the British Empire. Networks of schools and alumni provided unifying organizational structures for colonists when relations with the empire soured.[49]

* * *

Early in the imperial crisis, students and teachers embroiled colleges and academies in debates about British governance in the colonies. But politicization in schools began much earlier. Whig ideals took on outsized importance in colonial politics, and Francis Hutcheson's influence amplified this tendency in academies and colleges. Hutcheson's moral philosophy emerged, in part, out of his engagement with civic republicanism. One of Hutcheson's seminal contributions was his discussion of the moral sense, an innate sense embedded in all people who felt pleasure when they pursued anything that was inherently good. In particular, he argued that a properly functioning moral sense pushed people to take actions that benefited the larger community. Moral philosophy courses, then, acquainted students with republican ideals of virtue and disinterestedness. Even though schools were not the only places where educated colonists would encounter republican ideas, they did foster political debate.[50]

Politicization, however, did not necessarily lead to revolutionary radicalism. Other circumstances usually dictated affiliations, while schools provided a place for public men to sort through their allegiances. In 1766, on the heels of the Stamp Act crisis, the College of Philadelphia held an essay competition on the topic of the "reciprocal advantages of a perpetual union" between Great Britain and the colonies. The tone of the essays submitted was measured, though some essayists did critique imperial officials for causing a disruption in an otherwise fruitful relationship.[51] The influence of the school's provost, the Anglican minister William Smith, tempered the arguments of both sides. Smith taught Hutchesonian moral philosophy to his students, and through it republican principles, but he was hardly an ardent radical. He never took as staunch a loyalist position as some, though he was at the very least ambivalent about the American Revolution.[52] Smith is an emblematic example of how the positions that educated people took during the imperial crisis largely reflected local circumstances and, in particular, their denominational and ethnic affiliations. The Anglican influence was much more welcoming to future loyalists than Presbyterian schools, which were overtly radical.[53]

At the College of New Jersey, support for resistance ran rampant and continued nearly unabated from the time of the Stamp Act on. Students focused on imperial politics in graduation orations, took part in nonimportation agreements, and even staged their own tea party.[54] The Old Side Newark Academy politicized as well, albeit much less dramatically. By 1772, one observer noted that, during their public examinations, Newark Academy students discussed "the most perplexing political topics" concerning "difficult and knotty questions, relating to the *British* constitution." Their disquisitions made him feel as though he "was within a circle of vociferous politicians at *Will's* coffee-house, instead of being surrounded with the meek disciples of wisdom, in the calm shades of academic retirement."[55] Involvement with a school often provided an extra inducement for men to take clear sides. The best data that exists is for the College of New Jersey, where over 70 percent of the living alumni in 1775 served in the military or held a civil office during the Revolution. This number does not account for those who actively supported the Revolution informally or simply did not take an overt stand.[56] This rate of revolutionary participation and allegiance stands in stark contrast to the large numbers of disaffected people described in a number of essays in this volume. Education probably dictated students' revolutionary sympathies far less than denominational affiliation and other personal and local circumstances, but education seems to have made neutrality much more difficult to maintain. Moreover, schools absolutely influenced how educated men experienced the Revolution, vaulting them into prominent public roles.

By the onset of the Revolution, much of the academy generation was ambitious to take the reins of political and military leadership, poised to do so by the status that their formal and informal education conferred on them, and embedded in larger networks of like-minded individuals. The public had begun to see these educated men as nascent elites and natural leaders, arguing that teachers "should be made Delegates in Congress, Assembly-men, Magistrates, &c." This would ensure that "patriots, heroes and lawgivers" would "ris[e] up to fill the first offices of government."[57] Academy students and teachers provided a natural link between high-level leaders and the larger mass of citizens living in communities in which academies were embedded.[58] This was not just idle talk. The academy generation transitioned very directly into the Revolutionary generation. Francis Barber's academy in Elizabeth Town provides one of the starkest examples of the mobilization of educational infrastructure and networks. A similar story played out at an academy in Somerset County, Maryland. There, "The rapid advances of the school were soon checked by the war with Britain, and the patrons engaged in a different scene. As they were the friends of literature, so were they the steady opposers of tyrannical usurpation."[59] These schools confirmed the belief that education "not only concerns the Happiness of the Individual, but the Welfare and Prosperity of Society."[60] On the biggest stage, students actively showed the utility of emulation. In joining the Revolution, students could claim to benefit their community while also raising their own status. So students and teachers harnessed the networks they formed at school and used them to help their colonies mobilize for revolution.[61]

There are very few extant lists of students or records of colonial academies, so determining who actually attended any given school is difficult. Evidentiary problems notwithstanding, New Jersey and Delaware provide clear examples of the centrality of schools to revolutionary mobilization. In these states, many newly educated men filled the ranks of the Continental Army officer corps as well as some political offices. Of the twenty-four men who served as majors, lieutenant colonels, and colonels in the New Jersey Continental line, at least one-third had a direct connection with an academy, as a student or a teacher.[62] Three attended Enoch Green's Deerfield Academy—two of the three became governor of New Jersey after the war—and one studied with William Tennent, Jr., at the Old Tennent Presbyterian Church.[63]

The central node of the New Jersey officer corps was Francis Barber's school, the Elizabeth Town Academy. The commanding officer of both the First and Third regiments for most of the war had important Elizabeth Town connections. Colonel Matthias Ogden, Barber's brother-in-law, attended Elizabeth Town during the 1760s, when the future legal educator Tapping Reeve was the teacher. Colonel Elias Dayton, who commanded the Third Regiment, was Matthias Ogden's father-in-law. Dayton's son Jonathan attended the academy when Barber was in charge. Jonathan began the war as an ensign and finished as a captain. At various times he served as the regimental paymaster.[64] This was not unusual. Academy-educated officers frequently held posts handling logistical duties and maintaining the infrastructure of the New Jersey line. William Barber, Francis's younger brother, likely studied at the grammar school in Princeton and perhaps also at his brother's academy before enrolling at the College of New Jersey. William spent the entire war in various administrative positions. Early on, Barber served as aide-de-camp to the New Jersey brigade commander General William Maxwell. Later he turned down a position as adjutant in another Continental regiment before serving as aide-de-camp to General William Alexander, Lord Stirling, and as a deputy-adjutant under the command of Marquis de Lafayette, though his service ended ignominiously with his involvement in the Newburgh Conspiracy.[65] Aaron Ogden—the namesake of the famous *Gibbons* v. *Ogden* steamboat case—had studied at the Elizabeth Town Academy when Tapping Reeve ran the school. After finishing at the College of New Jersey, Ogden returned to Elizabeth Town and taught at the academy under the supervision of Francis Barber, his brother-in-law. He had a wartime experience like William Barber's, serving as an aide-de-camp to General Maxwell and Lord Stirling, and like his good friend and schoolmate Jonathan Dayton's, serving a lengthy stint as paymaster.[66] At a slightly higher level, one of the quartermasters of the First New Jersey was Francis Barber's predecessor at Elizabeth Town, Joseph Periam.[67]

The Delaware line was much smaller, but it also felt the influence of the academy generation. Colonel David Hall commanded the Delaware line for most of the war. Hall attended an academy in Lewes, Delaware, taught by Matthew Wilson, who eventually took over Francis Alison's Newark Academy. Gunning Bedford, who served for a year as a lieutenant colonel before leaving the army for a militia commission and a seat on the Delaware state council, studied at the Academy of Philadelphia under Alison.[68] Robert Kirkwood, though only a captain, took over command of the unit after it suffered devastating losses at the Battle of Camden. He studied at the Newark Academy.[69] James Tilton, the surgeon for Kirkwood's unit, was one of Samuel Finley's students at the West Nottingham Academy and later studied at the medical school attached to the College of Philadelphia.[70]

Most of these men were new to positions of leadership. Though in many ways they looked and acted the part, their aspirations to higher elective office had been stifled during the colonial era.[71] None of the academy-educated officers from New Jersey served in the state legislature before the war. Very few of their fathers held colony-wide office either, though a fair number held lower-level local offices such as justice of the peace and sheriff. Two of the Delawareans, including David Hall, served in the colonial assembly. Yet many of the educated officers from both states who survived the war held high-level political office in the 1780s or after the ratification of the Constitution. A few peaked as state assemblymen or council members. Many served in state executive office or as representatives to the Continental Congress.[72]

A large number of the earliest national-level officeholders—delegates to the Constitutional Convention and representatives and senators to the First Congress—were educated at denominational schools. For example, Delaware sent five men to the Constitutional Convention in Philadelphia in 1787. Three had academy backgrounds. George Read studied with Alison, when he still taught in New Castle, Delaware. Read served a number of years in the Delaware assembly during the 1760s and 1770s. He also sat in the state legislature during the war and was one of Delaware's senators during the First Congress.[73] Gunning Bedford, Jr., attended the Academy of Philadelphia under Alison before graduating from the College of New Jersey in 1771. During the war, Bedford served as Delaware's attorney general and represented the state in the Continental Congress.[74] Jacob Broom was a Quaker who attended an academy in Wilmington before taking a seat in the state legislature during the 1780s.[75]

New Jersey also sent five men to Philadelphia in 1787. William Livingston was New Jersey's only delegate to the Convention with pre-Revolutionary office-holding experience. A staunch Presbyterian, Livingston graduated from Yale in 1741, a few years before the expansion of education in the mid-Atlantic really began.[76] Three of the state's delegates to the Convention, including

Jonathan Dayton, graduated from the College of New Jersey. William C. Houston attended a Presbyterian academy in Crowfield, North Carolina, before enrolling at the college. Houston stayed in Princeton after his graduation. He taught math for a time, before working as a deputy secretary to the Second Continental Congress and then as a state assemblyman in the late 1770s. New Jersey also elected him to the Continental Congress.[77] William Paterson grew up in Princeton, where he attended the academy before entering the college. He served as the state's attorney general for much of the war. Paterson was also one of New Jersey's first senators—along with Jonathan Elmer, a graduate of the medical school at the College of Philadelphia and a trustee of the College of New Jersey.[78] The state's final delegate to the Constitutional Convention, David Brearly, grew up near Princeton, in present-day Lawrenceville. It seems likely he had some schooling at the grammar school at Princeton, but it is not entirely clear.[79]

The American Revolution clearly allowed the academy generation to realize some ambitions that the social mobility of the colonial period had fostered, but that the political immobility of the period had frustrated. Even if education does not entirely explain why these men played such prominent roles in the Revolution, it seems undeniable that it was a significant factor in their collective ascent. Education mattered to these men not because it made them more like their constituents. Rather education helped them realize their political aspirations precisely because it was exclusive.[80] In this way, the academy generation's experience was not necessarily part of a wholesale and revolutionary democratization of office holding.[81] Academies and colleges taught students refinement, gentility, and a range of cultural attributes that differentiated and distinguished them from the rest of the population and in turn justified their status as leaders.[82]

* * *

As Francis Barber's friends, colleagues, and fellow soldiers mourned his death, they celebrated his valor and leadership. They remembered how "the popularity of Colonel Barber" allowed him to put down "the unfortunate mutiny of the soldiers of the Pennsylvania and New Jersey lines" in the winter of 1780–81. They recalled his conduct in battle, especially in the engagements where he suffered wounds. Yet as they tried to come to terms with just "How great the loss" of their colleague would ultimately be, they also looked to the future. Barber's death was certainly tragic. Most of all, though, it was untimely.

Barber had not reached his full potential. He was young and the war had interrupted his life even before it killed him. As his eulogist Ebenezer Elmer put it, Barber had been "Cut off in the full meridian of life, health and *usefulness!*"[83]

Elmer's eulogy paid tribute to Barber's role in making American independence possible. It also betrayed Elmer's apprehension over the nation building that lay ahead. For Elmer at least, Barber's death made these anxieties ever more acute. After the Revolution, the sudden absence of an imperial state created a crisis of infrastructure and development throughout the United States, but especially in Elmer's home state of New Jersey, where the war had proven particularly destructive. In his eulogy, Elmer foresaw the prominent role that the academy generation, Continental officers, and their allies would play in building schools, civil society, and the American state.[84] Nervous though they were, this generation had experiences to draw on. As they sought to create true national independence in a global world of nations, these Americans would embrace the lessons of their colonial past to shape their vision for the future.[85]

PART III

New Directions

CHAPTER 10

"This Is the Skin of a Whit[e] Man"

Material Memories of Violence in Sullivan's Campaign

ZARA ANISHANSLIN

Miss Buddy was likely full of anticipation as she dressed for the ball. She was among those invited to one of the most highly awaited social events of 1824: the fete at New York City's Castle Garden for the Jubilee Tour of General Lafayette, iconic hero of the American Revolution. One of the final touches to her fashionable toilette was pulling on an accessory bought especially for the ball: new elbow-length kid gloves, long, white, and supple against her skin (see Figure 10.1). After pulling the gloves up her arms and smoothing the kidskin to mold to her own, she could look down to see the decoration stamped in black ink that made her new gloves fashionable: centered on the back of each hand, a medallion portrait of Lafayette in military uniform, surrounded by the words "WELCOME LA FAYETTE THE NATIONS GUEST."[1]

Forty-five years earlier, somewhere in Iroquoia between Appletown and Albany, New York, patriot soldier Luke Swetland also held a piece of skin in his hands. Like Buddy's gloves, the parchment Luke Swetland held was made from a piece of skin that had been scraped of hair and fat before being tanned and decorated with words in ink. Like the kidskin Buddy pulled on in 1824, the skin held by Swetland in 1779 was still fresh and supple enough to be folded, wrinkled, and written on in ink. However, his feelings must have been very different from those of Buddy as she prepared for the ball. Recently fled from over a year's captivity with Seneca Indians, Swetland had only weeks

Figure 10.1. Glove (shown with tiara and fan) commemorating 1824 visit of General Lafayette, ca. 1824; leather, 21 3/4 inches; object # 1929.46. Courtesy of the New-York Historical Society.

before been stripped of his clothes and beaten by American soldiers who found him hiding in the abandoned Seneca village of cadaia, or Appletown and mistook him for an Indian or a Tory. The words in ink on the skin he held told a rather different tale from those stamped on Buddy's gloves. They read:

> This is the Skin of a Whit Man
> taken by a Ingen
> Scalped and Skined alive Belly Cut Out
> Tied to Bed of Cols and Rosted to Deth

Before signing his name, his hometown of Wyoming, and the date, he went on to detail how such "Pale skin," "if Took as Prise," was used by Indians "for Money." He added some details about the campaign itself as well, noting that he and the "brave men" of Sullivan's army, over one hundred of whom had died, had been ordered to Albany if, he added (in an allusion either grimly humorous or just plain grim), "we KEP our Skin."[2]

Two objects made of ink and skin. Both wrinkled and folded from wear or handling, both inscribed with words that told stories of patriot soldiers, both made and used in New York. They share characteristics of material, use, and origin. They seem to share little else. The one on human skin is a macabre, chilling memento of wartime violence.[3] The other on goatskin is a souvenir of an elegant ball. The one was fashioned by a common soldier in rural Iroquoia. The other was worn by a privileged young woman in Manhattan. The one bore witness to General Sullivan's scorched-earth campaign that decimated the villages and crops of the Senecas who had captured its maker;[4] it painted a vivid portrait of the mangled, tormented body of another captive. The other was a treasured token of a festive celebration of Lafayette's American tour of 1824; it was stamped with Asher Durand's serene portrait of the French general.

Yet, for all their differences, the objects served a purpose as fundamentally similar as their physical materials. Each was made to memorialize—even sacralize—patriot soldiers of the Revolution. Each was a material text, an object meant to tell a history of the past that would influence how Americans remembered the armed conflict and military violence of the war. Each served as an icon of sorts, a sacred relic to memorialize the bodies of Revolutionary War soldiers, an object that asked those wearing or seeing them to venerate soldiers as tortured martyrs or holy saints. These things narrate a history of how Americans during and after the Revolution, women and men, civilians and soldiers, used objects first to wage war and then to cope with (and at times manipulate and even falsify) memories about the violence of waging it. The memory of the Revolution was so successfully managed that the two relics of the war, both made of skin and ink, encapsulate a shift from the violence embodied in a memento made of human skin to the gentility of a fashionable object manufactured in bulk, sold in a city store, and worn against a young woman's skin to a refined entertainment.

Buddy wore the image of a Revolutionary War hero intimately against her skin, an icon of a living saint that was also a souvenir of a military history of the Revolution made devoid of death and loss. With their genteel femininity, objects like these delicate gloves erased bloody violence from the military history the general's image evoked. Swetland's note, on the other hand, was a very masculine object, one that linked his own violent history, and that of Sullivan's campaign, to the martyred body of a "whit[e] man." This note on human skin also sacralized Revolutionary military history. It did so by preserving the physical relic of a martyr's body. Rather than erasing bloody violence, it foregrounded it: recounting, memorializing, and recording it in a very visceral way.

There is no way to be certain that Swetland's skin is human skin, much less that it is, as he claimed, the "skin of a whit[e] man," or, even more specifically, that it is the "skin of a whit[e] man" killed and tortured by Native Americans. It is possible that it is all of these things, however. Given his year in captivity and subsequent time with Sullivan's campaign, Swetland had opportunity to come across such a piece of skin. Soldiers with Sullivan's campaign regularly took corporeal trophies of war like scalps, and they described both Native Americans and themselves flaying skin from legs and chests. One of the most-often-recorded incidents of flaying, in fact, happened after a battle that occurred on the same date Swetland fixed to his note. Still, lack of evidence makes corroboration of the note's story mostly speculative, and the narrative written on the note is hardly free from factual error. For example, Sullivan's campaign did not suffer anywhere near the patriot losses he records. On the contrary, it was notable for its extremely low level of casualties.

But as historical evidence, the veracity of its human origin (and its whiteness) is almost beside the point. Like the relic of a saint's body, its historical meaning depends less on the verifiable identity of the flesh and bone itself than on the story told about that flesh and on the belief in that story by those who saw or held the object. In inscribing this note on human skin, its maker created a physical relic that celebrated a dead martyr while also serving as a material text, a text whose history and rhetoric obliquely justified the racialist brutality of Sullivan's campaign. For after all, who would not sanction violence against Indians who were so savage that they would skin and roast a man alive before using his flesh for money?[5]

Writing such descriptive text on an alleged piece of tortured human skin made this object part of a larger historical narrative crafted by patriots during and after the war: a narrative that shifted the burden of blame for Revolutionary violence away from the patriots and onto Native Americans. As historians have noted, this was an integral part of the historical function the Revolution itself played in creating a national mythology. The Revolution became "the United States' creation story." In it, "the winners constructed a national mythology that simplified what had been a complex contest in Indian country, blamed Indians for the bloodletting, and justified subsequent assaults on Indian lands and cultures."[6] After the war, shifting this blame narrative to Indians was of crucial importance in places like Iroquoia, where white settlers and the American government coveted the rich land of the

Haudenosaunee for themselves. Mythologizing Indians as inhuman "savages" who fought on the wrong side in the Revolution was a convenient tool for justifying dispossession.

This is one reason this artifact illuminates the past whether it is genuine or a fake.[7] Whether created in 1779 or the nineteenth century, it could serve the same purpose. To Americans predisposed to favor expansion into Iroquoia and other Indian territory, this was an artifact that dramatically justified Sullivan's campaign and later attempts at Indian removal. To consider just one such moment: Swetland, who freely acknowledged his good treatment by the Seneca while a captive, died in 1823. Two years later, New York's canal system—which cut through Iroquoia—went into operation when the governor of New York traveled the full length of the newly completed Erie Canal. He rode on a boat named the *Seneca Chief*. The irony is obvious, and points to one reason—beyond profit to be made selling a supposed Revolutionary artifact—someone might have created a fake with Swetland's name on it. Anyone reading Swetland's captivity narrative is left with the impression that, for the most part, the Seneca were humane people who treated him well. Creating such a note also signed as Swetland's work would provide a vivid contrasting narrative, one in which natives of Iroquoia were torturing savages rather than caring family members. Swetland, conveniently dead, would not be able to refute the artifact's veracity, its negative interpretation of Native Americans, or its positive treatment of Sullivan's Army.

But Swetland's note could equally serve a useful purpose during the Revolutionary War itself, when this blame narrative served another purpose, as a way to whip up anti-British and anti-loyalist sentiment. Like their compatriots elsewhere, Sullivan's campaigners often linked Native American violence (particularly torture) to British and Tory perfidy. One minister with the campaign, recounting the sight of the skeletal remains of soldiers killed by tomahawks the year before, focused his horror on the British. "Good God!" he wondered. "Who, after such repeated instances of cruelty, can ever be totally reconciled to that government" which "has influenced the savage tribes to kill and wretchedly to torture to death, persons of each sex and every age?"[8] Loyalists were described in the same scornful terms and assigned the same blame for being cruel and vengeful. As one patriot given to sarcasm described them, the loyalists—"the virtuous and faithful allies of Great Britain"—were "dastardly reches" who did not have bravery enough to fight us" but instead "wreek their vengeance" on any outnumbered men and helpless victims they could find.[9]

Visual memory played a crucial role in crafting and managing this historical narrative of patriotism and blame. Time after time, patriots with Sullivan's campaign described in gruesome detail the mangled and dead bodies they came across. When painting pictures with words and thus memorializing the sights burned into their mind, they emphasized the visual nature of their emotional experiences, using phrases like "the most horrid sight I ever saw" and "a most Horried Spectacle to behold" to describe such moments of encounter with the material evidence of violence, torture, and death.[10]

Unsurprisingly, given the importance visual memory played in their experience and interpretation of Revolutionary-era violence, patriots used visual and material culture, as well as rhetoric and words, to record and shape the sense of the past that created this narrative of displaced ferocity. As a material text, this note allegedly written on human skin can be understood as serving the same function as print culture, a more gruesome iteration of Revolutionary-era print culture like newspapers and plays that recounted details of atrocities, which, read over and over again, created vividly imagined (if often exaggerated) historical narratives. Unlike such print culture, it is a singular text that was not replicated again and again, so it is perhaps better thought of as serving the same function as a letter or diary entry. As a material text made not of paper but of disembodied human skin, however, it also fits into other genres of visual and material culture. It is part of a larger body of representations of Indian brutality, like those expressed in displays of corporeal objects like scalps and in luridly falsified cartoons depicting subjects like Native Americans cannibalizing severed limbs.[11]

Yet Swetland's note, though part of and speaking to each, goes beyond these familiar contexts of violence in visual, print, and material culture. Although it too could be passed around from person to person across space and time, it was not familiar or often made, as were scalps and prints, nor was it easily replicated and copied. Instead, it was a distinct, and distinctly intimate and individualized, object. At an uneven, roughly twelve by eight inches, it was, like a page ripped from a journal, large enough to detail a day's events but small enough to be folded and carried in a pouch or on someone's person, or mailed in a letter. And indeed it does show physical evidence of having been folded at some point when it was still fresh enough to do so without breaking it.

It also functioned like a page from a journal, a macabre counterpart to the many paper journals soldiers on the campaign kept. But it was, of course, no ordinary journal entry. The material of the journal itself was, if anything, more important than the words recorded in it. The material on which this story was written made it a more powerful tool of visual memory and visceral materiality than any conventional journal entry. But it shared things in common with more traditional journals, including its recording of a very popular date: September 13, 1779. That date was the one recorded on this note, and it was one most of those keeping journals on the campaign wrote about in detail. Each journal writer treated it similarly. All associated it with violent military conflict, Indian and Tory perfidy, and the shared communal sight of a particularly memorable torture. Like these other journals recorded on paper, Swetland's note not only recorded events and impressions. It also served as a personal souvenir, an inscribed, tangible memento that (much like the more traditional captivity narratives he later wrote in ink on paper) allowed him to remember, share, and thus come to grips with his own complex history and experience with Revolutionary violence.

Battle trophy, relic, history, captivity narrative, call to arms, tattooed skin, and souvenir, this note on human skin is a material text rife with hybridity. It is an object caught between two cultures that each changed the other as they shared and battled for the same space. It (allegedly) had multiple makers—the anonymous Native Americans who flayed the skin off the body of the "whit[e] man" and the European American who decorated its surface, inscribing a message on it in ink and asserting his creative role in its production by signing his name on it. It was a material text that was, in its production and materials, much like a disembodied, portable tattoo. Tattoos in eighteenth-century America were physical markers that were themselves highly ambiguous. For example, they could simultaneously denote male status and honorifics to Native Americans and be seen as markers of shame by captive Anglos.[12] The tattoo-like qualities of Swetland's note not only illustrate its complexities but also heighten how much it had to do with soldiers' bodies and visual memories associated with violence done to them. The image tattooed onto Swetland's note was a textual one; words strung together to paint a visual memory. In this tattoo the story itself became visual decoration. Here, the act of writing and reading history was made into a visual and material experience.

Like this object, Luke Swetland himself was caught between worlds. He was one of the early settlers of the fertile—and disputed—valley of Wyoming in what is now the state of Pennsylvania. Along with his wife and sons, he moved to the valley in 1776, just before America declared its independence from Britain. The Wyoming Valley was disputed territory, with Pennsylvania, Connecticut, and Native Americans all laying claim to it. Swetland, who was from Connecticut's Litchfield County, was one of the Connecticut proprietors. Wyoming soon became the site of more than one dispute over its territory, as the Declaration of Independence turned it into a battleground between loyalist and patriot as well as between Connecticut and Pennsylvania. In each of these contests, of course, Native Americans also had an enormous stake and played a significant role. The contours of Swetland's life were shaped in no small part by these multiple claims to the Wyoming Valley.[13]

Not long after the Battle of Wyoming in 1778, Swetland and a neighbor began to journey along the Susquehanna River to a gristmill. Six Seneca Indians took the two men captive. Swetland's companion was "very much abused" and bloodied by their captors. His ultimate fate remains unknown. By contrast, Swetland, after an initial period of mistreatment, had a run of what was for a captive very good fortune. First he was singled out by some of his "old neighbors" among an encampment of loyalists they encountered as "an honest man," which inspired his captor to take him "to himself" and be "very tender" of him. Once they reached their destination, he was protected from running the gauntlet and adopted as an old woman's grandson. He lived among the Seneca in Cadaia, or Appletown, for just over a year. Often, he was lonely, cold, and hungry, and he did attempt to run away a few times. Yet, he later admitted that the Seneca had been "remarkably kind to" him, showed him respect, made him "many fine presents," and gave him "my liberty to do what I had a mind for." At one point when he was sick, he received the attention and care of no less a figure than Queen Catherine herself.[14]

Despite this good treatment, he yearned to get back to his white family. In late August of 1779, the approach of Sullivan's army gave him a good chance at escape. When his Indian family and the rest of their village fled to Niagara, he escaped into the woods and then returned to hide in their abandoned village. His hybrid identity was made sharply obvious by the fact that the patriot soldiers who found him were not sure what—much less who—he was. He was "entirely in Indian dress."[15] Wearing "Indian stockings" that left his "thighs naked," his integration into the Indian community was also apparent in the silver brooch he wore on a Holland shirt he characterized as one that Indian women "made for me."[16] The three riflemen who found him stripped him, leaving him naked except for his "old Indian stockings only legs," or leggings, which came up only to his thighs. They struck him with rifles and clubs, the sergeant saying "with an oath, 'You plundered this shirt,'" and "I will spare your life with a devil to it. . . . You stay here to kill white folks, do you?" before allowing him to put on "an old rag of a shirt and a coat." Driven back to the soldiers' encampment, "running and whipping" all the way, he heard other soldiers call for his death—this time as a suspected loyalist—until former acquaintances recognized him. Despite this recognition, he was kept in a liminal state, still caught between worlds. Treated as a quasi-prisoner, he was forced to guide the army on its campaign through Iroquoia before finally returning to Wyoming later that fall at the campaign's end and reuniting with his family, to his "great joy."[17] Swetland admired his adopted village's apple orchards and seemed to regret their destruction by Sullivan's army. Perhaps inspired by these orchards, upon being reunited with his white family, he moved to Connecticut and embarked on a new career for which he became locally renowned: cultivating apple orchards.[18]

In Connecticut, he also wrote a captivity narrative about his experiences. Swetland's narrative has multiple iterations. There seem to have been at least two—possibly three—manuscript versions of it. One was written not long after his return to Connecticut, one in his "later years," and one "small manuscript" written at an indeterminate time—whether in conjunction with the earlier or later one, or at some separate point, is unclear.[19] All three were published together by a descendant in the nineteenth century.[20] In the early twentieth century, another descendant combined two of the three into a single, reproduced story.[21] It is clear from reading the three different narratives that the early twentieth-century publication drew upon both the earliest one that was printed in pamphlet form and a later one printed in the nineteenth-century publication as the second of the three versions. Although the accounts do not differ in their fundamental facts, they do provide different details. The latter publication differs from the earliest account considerably, both in its ornate language and its emphasis on religion as a sustaining force in Swetland's life. Both changes would make sense in an account written later in Swetland's life, when antebellum sensibilities and his own advancing years might have inclined him toward a more florid piousness.

The convoluted creation and publication of Swetland's captivity narratives can raise conundrums for the historian researching his life. But their multiple iterations—both in manuscript form held by descendants and as publications—ensured that his story was well known at several points in time. And indeed, this is one of the reasons that Swetland's note illuminates important things about how Americans willingly shaped the memory of violence in the Revolution regardless of whether it was actually created by him in 1779, or by some other, anonymous American later. Whether it is real or a fake, attaching the name of "Luke Swetland" to it meant that it was a relic linked, very specifically, to this man with a well-known history of captivity among the Senecas in Iroquoia.

Knowing Swetland's own history means that his note must be interpreted within the context of that history as well as the history of the "whit[e] man" whose fate it recounts. In addition to creating a relic, Swetland might have crafted his note with an eye toward profit. Many members of Sullivan's campaign raided Indian tombs for relics to sell as curiosities, and Pierre Eugene du Simitière's Philadelphia museum (1782–84), which displayed such artifacts, speaks to the market possibilities these objects had. Yet Swetland had far more cause than most to be motivated by concerns beyond turning a profit. Swetland likely penned his note from motivations more complicated than the most obvious ones of profit or simple condemnation of Native American torture. He may well have written it almost as an exercise in gratitude. Safely rescued from captivity, and safe in the knowledge that he was certain to be reunited with his family, he may have looked at this memento as a material reminder that he—unlike the tortured dead man whose skin it was—had suffered no such cruel fate while captive. On the contrary, he may have felt relief that he had ended up adopted rather than tortured, and that the particular Senecas who adopted him had treated him with respect and kindness. He would have been all too aware how easily the fate of the white man whose skin he held in his hand could have been his own. The awareness could only have been a chilling one.

His note also may have been meant to serve as proof—should it be demanded again—that he was neither a loyalist nor a spy. After all, the soldiers who found him in the abandoned village of Appletown first took him for an Indian, then for a loyalist. Neither identity was an attractive one for a single man found by a patriot army on a revenge-fueled military campaign. Confirmation that he was a loyalist or a spy could easily end, as it did for other men found guilty of such charges, with his neck in a rope. Producing such a striking note condemning Indian "savagery" and praising the "brave men" of Sullivan's army would have been a memorable way to attest his own loyalty to the white patriot cause. The words written on it also would have been a way for him to keep an object that might have raised suspicion about his own implication in the very types of Native violence described on it. After all, he had lived with Indians for over a year, and he had done so as a welcome member of an Indian family. He had assimilated deeply enough to be initially mistaken for an Indian by Sullivan's men, and he made no bones about how well he was treated in his captivity narratives. Perhaps he was equally forthcoming in his conversations with soldiers and with Sullivan himself when the general interviewed him. Who but Indians kept pieces of white men's skin as trophies? The simple fact of this former adopted captive's possession of such a thing might have blurred his loyalties in the eyes of Sullivan's army. It is entirely possible that he got the piece of skin from which he crafted his note before he was with Sullivan's campaign. Although its provenance is shrouded in mystery, an archive that once held it had it filed with a note that read, "1779 Human Skin White Man English Colonist killed by Indians at Instigation of French."[22] It is possible that it was a relic left over from an earlier conflict that involved the French, such as the French and Indian War. Whether it came from the body of a man killed in the French and Indian War or in Sullivan's campaign, if Swetland wished to save this piece of skin without coming under suspicion that he might have participated in such acts of violence himself while an adopted captive, or retained affections for Indians, he might have seen the act of transcribing its anti-Indian, pro-patriot message on it as the best means to keep it without raising dangerous suspicions about his own loyalties.

His loyalties did, in fact, seem to be complex, so much so that the note also might have served as an attempt to justify Sullivan's campaign to himself as much as to posterity. Those recording his story emphasized that Swetland "appeared quite overjoyed" at his rescue.[23] Although he called his rescue "a matter of joy," Swetland also admitted to more than a little ambivalence about his time in Sullivan's army. He dwelled on how the riflemen who found him treated him "barbarously." He acknowledged that his mind was "all confused" and that he "longed to be alone, out of the noise of the army." He found his "confinement" there "a great trial."[24] Swetland's use of the word "confinement" to describe his time with Sullivan's campaign is a telling one. It evokes ideas of captivity far more than of rescue. Swetland's confusion may have stemmed in part from reconciling his desire to escape captivity with his feelings about the soldiers who rescued him. He even mentioned (with apparent satisfaction) that soon after their meeting one of the officers who mistreated him was killed by Indians. In contrast to the Seneca, who were, as he remembered, "remarkably kind" to him, the riflemen who found him treated him, as he termed it—using a word usually reserved by patriots for Tories and Indians— "barbarously."[25]

Sullivan's army also treated Swetland's Seneca captors barbarously. As is well known, Sullivan's campaign was a feat of widespread destruction, as thousands of troops burned at least forty Haudenosaunee villages and cut down, burned, or drowned acre after acre of grain, corn, orchards, and harvested provisions. As Sullivan reported to Congress, "I flatter myself that the orders with which I was intrusted are fully executed, as we have not left a single settlement or field of corn in the country of the Five Nations."[26] The campaign was waged on the orders of George Washington, who devoted an extraordinary amount of manpower and supplies to it. So devastating was this campaign that it earned Washington the nickname of "Town Destroyer" among Indians. This nickname was an apt moniker, as Washington's stated intent was to accomplish "the total destruction and devastation" of their "settlements." Washington meant Sullivan's campaign to "discourage and terrify" the native population, and advocated approaching Indians with "war whoop and fixed bayonet."[27] The campaign also was meant to capture Native American prisoners. Relatively few were actually taken, though at times Indians barely escaped, sometimes leaving so fast that the army entered to find "kettles on the fire boiling corn and beans."[28]

This was a war primarily waged on Indians' material world, one of violence against things. Orchards and crops were cut down, and houses and "Great Quantitys of Household Furniture" put to flames.[29] This violence against things was more than a pragmatic scorched-earth policy. There was also a vengeful quality to the campaign. As one man with the army put it, this was "an expedition to the westward against the Indians and Tories who had cruelly destroyed our frontiers."[30] When the army celebrated the Fourth of July on the campaign, numbers ten and eleven among the thirteen toasts the officers drank were to "Civilization or death to all American Savages" and to "the Immortal memory of those Heroes who have fallen in the defence of American liberty."[31] This vengeful component emerged most forcefully after battles or the discovery of tortured or desecrated patriot bodies. Despite their outrage at violence performed on their compatriots' bodies, patriot soldiers showed a casual disregard for the bodies of Native Americans living and dead. They scalped and flayed their skin for corporeal war trophies and also, either "through principles of Avarice or curiosity," dug up Native American graves, leaving them exposed and disturbed by removing, as one officer put it, "a good many laughable relics, as a pipe, tomahawk & beads &c."[32] Destruction of things was fueled as much by such "avarice or curiosity," or enraged emotion, as it was by systematic fulfillment of military orders.

What emerges from this complex mix of emotions was that destroying or damaging things could, and did, serve as proxy for killing or injuring people. This war fought against things was a way of indirectly hurting the bodies that could not be captured or even met on the battlefield. Destroying a house, defiling a tomb, hacking down orchards, or burning corn was not nearly as satisfying to an army bent on vengeance as capturing or killing Native Americans or loyalists would have been. But clearly it was embraced with a certain satisfaction and most certainly seen as better than nothing to men with such a motivation behind their campaign.

The army embraced the destruction of Haudenosaunee towns as a way to make manifest their Fourth of July toast of "Civilization or death to all Savages." They even described their destruction of Indian houses in terms that compared the visual sight of such destruction to Revolutionary-era celebratory spectacles like the illuminations and bonfires held by patriots in cities like Boston and Philadelphia. In mid-August, for example, the army entered a particularly large town, and, as one officer described it, "About sunrise the Genl gave orders for the Town to be illuminated—& accordingly we had a glorious Bonfire of upwards of thirty Buildings at once."[33] Destroying this town was cause as much for ritualistic celebration—the familiar spectacle of illuminations and bonfires—as it was a symbolic and actual meting out of destruction. Such parallel spectacles created a common visual memory that linked sights of urban revolutionary celebration to the campaign's acts of destruction in Iroquoia. As the destruction of houses like Thomas Moffatt's and Thomas Hutchinson's had made clear over a decade before, destroying a house was a proxy attack on the person who lived in it.[34] The violent treatment of the material world of Native Americans, of the things themselves, exemplifies how in Iroquoia as well as in Newport or Boston, things like houses could stand in for people. In a cultural construct in which things stood in for people, it was not illogical that people and their bodies, also, might become things. Swetland's note on human skin was just such a thing.

But it was not the only such thing. Scalps are among the best known, and most studied, examples of objectifying people into things, and sometimes commodifiable things at that.[35] The history narrated on Swetland's material text tied it very specifically to scalps, and to the process of physical mutilation that created scalps, as it told the reader that the "whit[e] man" whose skin was being held or seen had been "Scalped and Skined alive." Swetland's note also averred that "such pale skin" was used as "money" among Indians, which of course it was not. Paying bounties for scalps was, however, a long-running practice among European Americans in the colonies, and the Revolution was no exception; the patriot government of Pennsylvania, for example, offered such rewards.[36] But, particularly among Native Americans, scalps were far from being mere commodities. Scalps were tangible remnants of a human body that could serve as trophy, relic, material mnemonic device, or call to arms. Sullivan, for example, used scalps to justify his stance against pleas for clemency that the Oneida made on behalf of the Cayuga, saying that "in searching the houses of these pretended neutral Cayugas, a number of scalps were found, which appeared to have been lately taken, which Colonel Butler showed to the Oneidas, who said that they were then convinced of the justice of the steps I had taken."[37] In all these senses, Swetland's note, though taken from a different part of the body, functioned in similar ways to a scalp. In Sullivan's campaign, both sides took scalps with regularity. Officers' journals from the expedition are littered with casual references to scalping by patriots, scalping by loyalists, and scalping by Indians. Discussion of flayed skin is less common, but a number of witnesses recorded at least one example of patriot soldiers being flayed to produce large enough pieces of skin to create parchment like Swetland's note.

On September 13, the same date Swetland affixed to his note, a small group of riflemen went out on a scouting mission. Riflemen were the same type of troops who found Swetland hiding in Appletown, and (in his words) treated him "barbarously" (see Figure 10.2). Like Swetland's own garb in Appletown, their uniforms were a creolized amalgam of Native American and European dress. The riflemen wore hunting shirts, used "Indian stockings," "boots," or "leggings" like those Swetland was wearing when discovered, and carried tomahawks and scalping knives. Swetland himself commented on their appearance. When they found him, he hoped that "they were General Sullivan's army." He "went quick to the door," but to his "great surprise," he "saw no uniform dress, as [he] expected they all had." Instead, they "were entirely in Indian dress."[38] General Sullivan, meanwhile, characterized them as "the best troops, in my opinion, for this expedition," for they were "all marksmen, and accustomed to the Indian mode of fighting."[39]

Their famous marksmanship and "Indian mode of fighting" did this group of riflemen little good on the thirteenth of September. Surprised and overwhelmed in battle, most of them were killed, while their leader, Lieutenant Thomas Boyd, was captured along with another man, Sergeant Michael Parker. The next day, the army found the two men who had been taken captives, dead, in the middle of the large, abandoned Indian town of Genesee. The men had been tortured with what one officer described as acts "which decency will not permit me to mention." Other officers less concerned with such polite restrictions described their fates in gruesome detail. "They was both stripped naked and their heads Cut off and the flesh of Lt. Boyds head was intirely taken of[f]

"This Is the Skin of a Whit[e] Man"

Figure 10.2. Soldiers in Uniform, watercolor by Jean Baptiste Antoine de Verger, c. 1781–1784, Anne S.K. Brown Military Collection, Brown University Library. Courtesy of Brown University Library.

and his eyes punched out. . . . & Lt. Boyds privates was nearly cut of[f] & hanging down."[40] At one point Boyd's stomach was cut open, and his captors "fastened one of the intestines to the tree" to which he was tied, "unbound him, and dragged him round the tree until all were wound of his body!"[41] Another soldier observed of Boyd that "a great part of his body was skinned, leaving his ribs bare."[42] Still another noted that "the Lieut. was all skinned," and "his brother sufferer was in the like condition."[43]

Swetland's note on human skin is *his* journal entry for September 13, 1779, the date of Boyd's ill-fated battle, and an important one in most of the traditional journals written on paper by men with the campaign. Although Boyd was not "roasted over coals," this episode comes close to Swetland's description of the origins of his parchment as "Skin of a Whit[e] Man" whose "Belly" was cut out, "Scalped and Skined alive," and the coincidence of the dates makes Boyd a likely candidate for the nameless martyr sketched in the relic that is Swetland's note. It is entirely possible that Swetland—or someone else—had the chance to pick up a piece of Boyd's skin. The army quite literally stumbled across the decapitated bodies of Boyd and Parker. One soldier, "whilst hastening at a rapid step, discovered the headless corpse of Boyd. Being startled at the sudden sight, he sprang quickly forward, and the corpse of Parker was at his feet."[44] The discovery of Boyd and Parker, in other words, was a scene of confusion, followed by a burial of their bodies "with military honors" and the prolonged process of destroying the village and its crops, leaving both opportunity and time for a man to find and keep a bit of those bodies as a relic.

And keeping such a relic might have had an immediate appeal, for Boyd quickly achieved near-martyrdom status. His body was buried with military honors, toasts were drunk in his honor and memory during the campaign, and the "Torture Tree" to which he had been tied was left standing as a monument—his intestines still wound around it—while the town and surrounding crops were razed.[45] Later, in the nineteenth century, he would be celebrated as one of the "Soldiers whose blood first consecrated to freedom the soil of the Genesee Valley."[46] In the 1840s, his body was exhumed from its burial site, "partly overgrown by the roots of decayed plum-trees, within a few feet of the edge of the bank of [two] united streams," kept on view for two weeks, and reburied in Rochester in an elaborate ceremony.[47] His "mouldering relics" thus sacralized, his body and its reburial could be made to honor a martyr whose "life-blood" marked the "very limit of the great struggle for American liberty." Though he "perished nearly two hundred miles beyond the remotest western settlement," his grave was now "nearly 2000 miles east" of his "country's civilization."[48] Boyd the Revolutionary martyr became a martyr for Manifest Destiny whose body was a relic to Indian removal. If Swetland's note is a fake, this, of course, provided another moment in which it made both economic and political sense to craft it.

There is a larger Revolutionary context to the treatment of Boyd's body, however, and it highlights how important the history markedly absent from Swetland's note is for unraveling the object's meaning. Only a few weeks before the flayed body of Boyd was found, a patriot officer noted that a major had "sent out a small party" to look for "dead Indians. . . . Toward noon they found them and skinned two of them from their hips down for boot legs; one pair for the Major the other for myself."[49] A few days later, another soldier matter-of-factly noted that "this morning our trupes found two Indians and Skin thear Legs & Drest them for Leggins."[50] The ease with which this particular soldier objectified the bodies of these dead Indians is evident in his journal entry; he goes on without pause from describing the skinning and tanning of their flesh to mentioning a change in rations.

Connecting these acts of removing the fleshly equivalent of leggings from these dead bodies with Swetland's own experience in Appletown, in which riflemen stripped him naked of everything *except* his Indian leggings, hints at the symbolic importance this particular item of clothing held for the riflemen.

Figure 10.3. Marker commemorating Sullivan's Campaign, Oneida Road (County Route 60), near Newtown Battlefield State Park, Elmira, New York. Photo by Alyssa Mt. Pleasant, May 2015. Copyright Alyssa Mt. Pleasant.

These soldiers turned people into things; things that were corporeal war trophies and objects of military memory like Swetland's note. More than that, though, these leggings were objects created for wear as both personal souvenirs and military uniforms. They were a physical way to embody the visual memory of battle and Revolutionary violence. Riflemen like Boyd were prized in part for how well they had appropriated Indian fighting techniques, and they also adopted elements of Indian dress. At times, they took their appropriation of Indian clothing even further, changing their bodies as well as their clothes. Six hundred troops with the campaign "destroyed almost one whole tribe of Indians by stratagem" when an officer surprised a Seneca "castle" through disguise, "by paint[ing] his men like Indians, with cutting their hair, &c."[51] Such contexts of military appropriation made objects like these leggings especially violent statements. In wearing Indian boots made of Indian skin, these officers took their appropriation of indigenous clothing and appearance to macabre new heights. The leggings' material, and method of their construction, made them a highly symbolic statement about military violence in the American Revolution. Such leggings made a particularly pointed statement when made and worn by soldiers on Sullivan's campaign, as it was battle waged against the same people whose flayed bodies formed their material.[52]

To end, let us return to the beginning. To Miss Buddy's glove, and its erasure of military violence. In 1929, to honor the 150th anniversary of Sullivan's campaign, the state of New York commissioned stone and metal plinths to mark the army's campaign trail (see Figure 10.3). Erected on land in Iroquoia that patriots scorched, destroyed, and, not long after the Revolution, moved onto themselves, they stand as immovable sacred relics.[53] Material texts of their own, they have medallion portraits of refined generals in uniform, like the one of Lafayette on Buddy's glove. Their text gives a brief history with maps of the campaign trail and major battles, visually reinforced by a group of attacking Indians on one side and massed Continental soldiers on the other. All violence in these relics is contained in the bodies of Native Americans; just as in Swetland's note, all violence is performed by Indians. The soldiers stand at arms, dressed not in their appropriated hybrid Indian clothing as riflemen, but rather in formal regimentals. Their tomahawks and scalping knives, like their hybrid uniforms, have vanished. Their Indianness and hybridity is, like their violence, erased. In the words inscribed in the monuments, they are heroic patriots "extending westward the dominion of the United States," rather than town destroyers. They are defenders of "civilization" rather than creators—and wearers—of objects made of human skin.[54]

CHAPTER 11

Environmental History and the War of Independence

Saltpeter and the Continental Army's Shortage of Gunpowder

DAVID C. HSIUNG

Connect the words "war" and "environment" and what comes to mind? Perhaps war's effects on the environment, which we inevitably judge as negative when we consider what occurs: the loss of individual organisms, the reduction of species diversity, and the destruction of habitats. The vivid images we imagine might include the fireball at Alamogordo, New Mexico, during the first test of the atomic bomb, the forested landscapes of the Western Front shattered by artillery during the Great War, or the hundreds of oil wells that Iraqis ignited during the Persian Gulf War. The smoke from those wells blackened the skies for over four hundred thousand square miles, or an area three times greater than the current size of the states that composed the thirteen original British colonies.[1]

By reversing the order of the words, we see the many ways in which the environment almost dictated how humans waged war. Violent storms delayed and nearly canceled the D-Day landings at Normandy, France. Due in part to Vietnam's mountainous jungle terrain, Americans relied on helicopters and on defoliants such as Agent Orange. As for the War of Independence itself, nearly every reader of this volume must know of Emanuel Leutze's iconic 1851 painting, *Washington Crossing the Delaware*, with the men struggling to steer their boats through the ice-choked river.[2]

The connections between "war" and "environment" also extend beyond weather and terrain and into the realm of logistics, for military operations depend on the procurement and distribution of the environment's natural resources. During the second Gulf War, U.S. soldiers in Iraq used 1.7 million gallons of fuel a day, greater than the daily consumption of motor gasoline for the entire state of Montana. (The fuel-inefficient M1A1 Abrams battle tank, averaging 0.6 miles per gallon, gulped much of the fuel required at the war's start in 2003.) During the first year of the War of Independence, British forces in Boston spent most of their time acquiring supplies, not forts or territory, and defending against the rebels' raids on those provisioning parties, not their attacks in traditional battles.[3]

Historians have long incorporated weather, terrain, and logistics into their analyses of war, but such investigations have tended to be limited in scope. The weather during *this* campaign, the terrain for *that* battle—scholars give the environment its due in these cases but often do not consider broader perspectives, longer time frames, or deeper connections to different parts of the ecosystem. Similarly, when the study of logistics emphasizes procurement or transportation rather than the resources themselves, we miss the relationships humans formed with the environment that made those resources accessible in the first place. By incorporating environmental history into our study of war, we ground the participants in their physical world and, just as important, in their ideas about that physical world. We cannot separate those in the past from their natural world, and the ways in which those individuals thought about that world shaped their actions in critical ways.[4]

* * *

Environmental historians today generally agree that, to use Paul S. Sutter's apt phrase, "all environments are hybrid." In other words, they "see all environments as interweaving the natural and the cultural in complex ways." No "pristine" or "untouched" lands existed for humans to enter and then, in the eyes of some earlier scholars, destroy. In fact, governments, local organizations, and private individuals often created or engineered "wilderness" in places such as Yellowstone in order to attract hunters and other outdoor enthusiasts. Hybridity, Sutter argues, also runs in the other direction, for "human history and culture cannot be easily isolated from environmental forces and circumstances."

This perspective urges us to take our standard categories of analysis—the cultural, economic, political, and social spheres—and infuse them with earth and water, flora and fauna, microbes and celestial bodies. Environmental history, according to Linda Nash, "is less a coherent 'field' of study structured around key archives, topics, or questions . . . than an orientation." Although echoing social history's effort to infuse gender, class, and race into the study of the past, environmental history differs because " 'environment' is not exactly a category of analysis if only because environments are surely more than (social) categories."[5] Environmental history provides an approach that should be woven into all historical studies.

In the best of these works, the hybrid qualities of environments and of human societies have enriched our understanding of early America. Perhaps three examples will suffice. Like many of us, Brian Donahue once believed that familiar story of the colonial era, "the timeworn New England tale of rocky hill farms succumbing to hard economic reality" that then led to "nineteenth-century environmental degradation" in places such as Concord, Massachusetts. Donahue shattered this standard interpretation of economic and environmental decline with *The Great Meadow* by demonstrating that "colonial agriculture in Concord was an ecologically sustainable adaptation of English mixed husbandry to a new, challenging environment." Degradation did come by the mid-nineteenth century, due to a combination of population growth, the drive for capitalism's profits, and the resultant inability to balance the key components of the landscape: tilled fields, meadows, pastures, orchards, and managed woodlots. Only by understanding these integrated components can we grasp this central fact of life in colonial New England.[6]

A second common belief about early America, that disease wiped out the Indians, must be revised after reading the work of Pekka Hämäläinen. While many native populations did indeed suffer tremendous losses due to diseases such as smallpox, the Comanches protected themselves during the late eighteenth and early nineteenth centuries through a series of interlocking practices. They used European guns and food, expanded their empire at Spain's expense, formed economic and political alliances, adopted slaves and captives to diversify their own gene pool, and launched raids into New Mexico, Texas, and Mexico to obtain horses, thereby preserving for bison the grasslands under their control. The Comanches' intimate knowledge of the southwest borderlands environment shaped their political, economic, and social actions, and those actions, in turn, changed that environment, which led to a new round of actions. This approach enriches our understanding of the past because, as Hämäläinen convincingly argues, it reveals "the complex and unexpected ways in which transoceanic exchanges, biological encounters, and human ambition could intertwine to shape power relationships in early America." This challenges "conventional colonial histories by revealing a world where Indians benefited from Europe's biological expansion, safeguarded their homelands by displacing ecological burdens on colonial realms, and debilitated European imperialism with imperial aspirations of their own."[7]

A third staple of American history, community development on the frontier during the early republic, has also been reinvigorated by environmental history. Alan Taylor traced the life of William Cooper, his development of the vast Otsego Patent in upstate New York, and his career as a rich Federalist during a period of tumultuous political, economic, and social change. Taylor brings in the natural world when setting the scene for Cooper's activities—Otsego's glacial origins, varied soils, and mixed forests—but he goes far beyond treating the environment simply as a stage upon which humans acted. This frontier developed as it did because migrants held a complex set of beliefs about and relationships with the environment. Cooper prospered, Taylor argues, "by obliging nature to serve commerce; converting nature's waste into marketable commodities generated the profits to build substantial homes and found the public institutions of a civilized people." One of Cooper's rivals stated in 1803, "No man knows better than you the secret of subduing the Wilderness & converting forests into Cultivated fields," and Taylor reveals that secret by integrating environmental history with political, social, cultural, and economic perspectives.[8] Neither Alan Taylor nor Pekka Hämäläinen identifies himself as an environmental historian, but their orientation has illuminated our understanding of early America.

The time has now come to apply this perspective to the American Revolution. Although the literature of American environmental history has grown over the past several decades like a Lake Erie algae bloom, it has largely bypassed the Revolution's shores. Its scholarship has dealt overwhelmingly with the twentieth century, while any attention given to early America has focused predominantly on the period prior to 1760 or on locations that lay beyond the geographical boundaries usually ascribed to the Revolution.[9] Similarly, the growing scholarship on the environmental history of war has largely ignored the years 1775–83.[10] Looking at the War of Independence with an environmental perspective not only fills this historiographical gap but also brings many key topics into sharper focus.

First, consider what drove Americans to support the idea of independence. On October 17, 1775, nearly three months before the publication of *Common Sense*, British naval vessels bombarded and burned much of the town of Falmouth (now Portland, Maine). This act steeled the determination of many colonists to resist Great Britain. In a letter to the *New England Chronicle*, "A Freeman" wrote, "The savage and brutal barbarity of our enemies in burning Falmouth, is a full demonstration that there is not the least remains of virtue, wisdom, or humanity, in the British court." He predicted that "we expect soon to break off all kind of connection with Britain, and form into a Grand Republic of the American United Colonies." Why did the navy attack Falmouth and therefore drive some colonists down the road toward independence? Admiral Samuel Graves ordered the attack primarily out of frustration over the conduct of the war during the previous six months, and much of that action had centered on obtaining nature's bounty for British forces and repelling the rebels who tried to stop them.[11]

Environmental history also forces us to consider the wartime participation of those living in different, perhaps unexpected, parts of the globe. Although most of the war focused on the Atlantic world, Britain's search for specific natural resources led its leaders in the opposite direction. Ever since the 1650s, New Englanders had sent huge white pine trees—some measuring forty yards in length and forty inches in diameter—to the Royal Navy's dockyards for use as single-stick masts in the largest warships. Americans halted these shipments with the outbreak of war in April 1775, forcing Britain to turn to northern Europe and western Russia for Riga firs (so named for their main port of trade on the Baltic Sea in present-day Latvia). There they found fir trees with, in historian Robert Albion's words, the necessary combination of "cylindrical straightness, suppleness, elasticity, strength, durability, and the proper proportion of length to girth." Although New England white pines weighed 25 percent less than a Riga fir of comparable length, more resin remained in those firs after cutting, making them stronger and more durable. Britain's dependence on Riga firs reminds us that militaries consume such vast amounts of natural resources that we must calculate the effects on the original habitats. That such a calculation must include Russia forces historians of the war to include locations normally absent from their studies.[12]

Historians have long considered the role of disease in the War of Independence, with smallpox holding center stage, but no one has explained how disease works on different populations at different times as deftly as J. R. McNeill. Focusing on yellow fever and malaria, McNeill's *Mosquito Empires* takes a broad perspective—the Greater Caribbean region over three centuries—and argues that human actions fostered the growth of two mosquito species, "helping them become key actors in the geopolitical struggles of the early modern Atlantic world." The diseases conferred immunity or resistance to those who survived, so over time local populations withstood yellow fever and malaria while invading armies fell at a ghastly rate. McNeill brings these insights to bear on Britain's strategy for the American South in 1780–81. "Simply put, differential vulnerability to malaria put Cornwallis' forces at a systematic disadvantage, creating a problem for which he had no solution. Mosquitoes and malaria helped drive Cornwallis from the Carolinas and then sickened his army at Yorktown to the point where he lacked the manpower to conduct counter-siege operations properly. American resistance to the British Army had been made more effective by American resistance to malaria."[13] By understanding the *Anopheles quadrimaculatus* mosquito, its biology, and its ecological context, McNeill highlights the capacity of the physical world and nonhuman organisms to shape military planning and operations.

This chapter takes a different part of the physical world and connects it to the civilian side of military planning for the War of Independence. Historians have long asked why the Continental Army never had enough domestically produced gunpowder, but they have not considered the hybrid nature of gunpowder's crucial ingredient, saltpeter (potassium nitrate). In order to address this chronic shortage, rebel governments and newspapers published instructions on how to boost saltpeter production, instructions based on their understanding of the environment's chemical and geological properties. The ways in which Americans understood saltpeter itself stand in sharp contrast to modern chemical interpretations, but colonial methods for extracting and purifying the substance were soundly based (according to modern science). The saltpeter, even after several purification steps, did not represent "pure" or "pristine" nature but the product of this particular late eighteenth-century culture and society. The struggle to create adequate supplies of this essential compound speaks to issues of political authority and legislative power that infuse many other areas of the American Revolution. Historians have found the Continental Congress woefully unable to supply gunpowder and many other materials, but in this case, ironically, the very nature of saltpeter limited the steps Congress could take to address its shortage.

* * *

The War of Independence started on April 19, 1775. Before that day ended, the few dozen minutemen on Lexington Green were joined first by hundreds, then by thousands more who blockaded the British regulars on the peninsula of Boston. As those forces settled into a series of camps, problems related to supplies began to dog the Continentals. In early August, General George Washington stated that "Our Situation in the Article of Powder is much more alarming than I had the most distant Idea of." Initially thinking that 303½ barrels of gunpowder lay in the Continental Army's stores, Washington learned that, after correcting for a clerical error, he had only 36 barrels from Massachusetts and small amounts from the other New England colonies. This supply meant that the 17,000 soldiers under his command had no more than 3.6 ounces of powder apiece, enough for just nine rounds. According to Brigadier General John Sullivan, when Washington received this information, the general "was so Struck that he did not utter a word for half an hour."[14]

The shortage of gunpowder affected the Continental Army's ability to wage war. On June 17, 1775, the army's success at Bunker Hill ended as soon as it ran out of powder during the British army's third assault. The following February, Washington wanted "a bold & resolute Assault" against the British in Boston by crossing the ice from Dorchester and Roxbury, but in a council of war his officers talked him out of this plan. Such a direct assault would cost too many lives, and the army did not even have enough powder for a preliminary bombardment. When informing John Hancock, president of the Continental Congress, of this situation, Washington added that to arm his troops with even twenty-four rounds—the British regulars typically carried sixty—would leave him with only sixty barrels of gunpowder in reserve. "This Sir," he concluded, "Congress may be assured is a true state of Powder and will I hope bear some testimony of my Incapacity for Action in such a way as may do any essential Service."[15]

This "true state of Powder" arose because only limited supplies existed in America. Just one significant powder mill was in operation when, in October 1774, King George III cut off exports of gunpowder to America. Soon after, British soldiers and officials seized existing stores in Massachusetts and Virginia. In response, colonists from New Hampshire to Georgia raided local powder magazines and carried away, cumulatively, about 80,000 pounds of gunpowder. This supply fell well short of what the Continental Army needed at any given moment—about 200,000 pounds—especially because local militias retained some of the seized powder.[16]

Other explanations for this shortage blame Congress's inability to handle the many tasks of supplying the army while at the same time planning and financing the war, governing a new nation, and carrying out diplomatic relations. Jack N. Rakove has argued that the congressmen could not act as "both a deliberative and an executive body. Dividing their limited time and energies between two such disparate tasks merely guaranteed that neither would receive the attention it deserved." This incompetence was compounded by others' venality; according to John Ferling, "The rebels' supply system was shamefully tainted with corruption and profiteering from one end to the other, and Congress was unable, or unwilling, to do much about it." Americans did manufacture small amounts of gunpowder early in the war, but output dropped off as initial enthusiasm faded and the use of paper money (and the resultant inflation) increased, sending the costs of labor and materials sharply higher.[17] Eventually, the Continental Army received enough gunpowder from French, Dutch, and Spanish sources to wage the war to its conclusion, but supplies just trickled in before the autumn of 1775 and the flow increased only after mid-1776. Despite this influx of gunpowder, the Continental Army still experienced shortages during the summers of 1777, 1779, 1780, and 1781.[18] Therefore, during the crucial early part of the war and before regular European shipments arrived, the precarious supply of gunpowder loomed large in the thinking of both the Continental Congress and George Washington.

* * *

In the eighteenth century, gunpowder consisted of three ingredients: sulfur, which started the ignition; charcoal, the material that burned; and saltpeter (potassium nitrate, or KNO_3), the substance that, when heated, provided the oxygen that propelled the musket ball out of the muzzle. Although the ratios of these ingredients varied over time and by weapon, after the end of the sixteenth century most English cannon powder used a 1:1:6 ratio, with saltpeter composing 75 percent of the gunpowder's weight.[19] Given the general availability of sulfur and especially of charcoal, Congress focused on the production and acquisition of saltpeter.

The acuteness of the shortage forced Congress to act. In June 1775 it created a saltpeter committee that was charged to "devise ways and means to introduce the manufacture of salt petre in these colonies" and pay for any saltpeter it collected. The need for increased domestic production became more urgent when, on September 27, 1775, King George III prohibited the shipment of any saltpeter outside of Great Britain. As a result, Congress turned even more beseechingly toward the colonies. It had already asked the colonial assemblies to offer "half a dollar for each pound" of saltpeter made in their colonies before October 1.[20] In November, Congress repeated its plea that each colony "employ and set to work so many persons as they may think proper, both to work up such earth as is now fit for making salt petre, and to collect together . . . all such earth and composition of materials as are suitable to produce salt petre." It went so far as to name thirty-one prominent Virginians to oversee such activity in their home colony. Three months later, as the shortage continued, Congress asked each colony to go even further than before and "immediately establish public works in each and every county, in their respective colonies, at the expence of such colonies, for the manufacture of salt petre." The Continental Congress must have recognized the long odds of having saltpeter works established in every county, but its recommendation indicates the ongoing and desperate shortage of that compound.[21]

Because Congress could only urge and not require the colonies to act, its most important contribution to the production of saltpeter came under its own auspices. In the summer of 1775, Congress ordered the publication of a pamphlet containing several "systems or methods of making Salt-Petre, suited to different circumstances and different materials." These guidelines spurred the Committees of Safety in Massachusetts, New York, and Pennsylvania to publish their own sets of instructions. Several editors of Virginia newspapers followed suit. In relatively short order, Americans had the information experts deemed necessary for the production of saltpeter.[22] These instructions, however, described methods for making a substance that itself was poorly understood.

Theorists in the early modern period could not agree on what saltpeter was. The English philosopher and scientist Francis Bacon (1561–1626) thought of saltpeter as "the energizing 'spirit of the earth.'" The English scientist Robert Boyle (1627–91) called saltpeter "the most catholic of salts," a combination of "vegetable, animal, and even mineral" that was both "partly fixed and partly volatile." A century later William Whiting, a representative to the Massachusetts Provincial Congress, defined saltpeter as "compounded of three different materials, (viz) a nitrous acid, a volatile animal salt, and these two fixed, blended together and petrified by a vegitable or mineral alkaline salt."[23] And authorities could no more agree on how saltpeter formed than on what it was. The English medical chemist John Mayow (1643–79) argued that living rocks buried deep within the earth produced saltpeter. The French chemist Pierre Le Lorrain, abbé de Vallemont (1641–1729), explained that fires deep under the earth's surface created saltpeter and released it into the atmosphere as a gas.[24]

Early in the war, one writer in Virginia provided a brief summary of such lines of thought. "Some chymists pretend that the nitrous acid [saltpeter] is diffused through the air, and gradually deposited in such earths and stones as are qualified to receive it. Others, considering that none of it is ever obtained but from earths that have been impregnated with vegetable or animal juices, have from thence concluded those two kingdoms to be the general repositories of the nitrous acid." Still others believed that "this acid is no other than the universal or vitriolic acid [sulfuric acid, H_2SO_4], disguised indeed by a portion of the phlogiston, which is combined with it in a peculiar manner, by the means of putrefaction." In the end, the writer joined this third school of thought, arguing that saltpeter "is no other than the vitriolic acid, altered by the changes and combinations it hath undergone in its passage into and through those [vegetable and animal] substances."[25]

From our current chemical and geologic perspective, we might say that the earth does not contain living rocks, let alone rocks that create saltpeter. Saltpeter does not circulate through the atmosphere and fall like a gentle rain only on those surfaces that can attract it. Sulfuric acid does exist, but there is no such thing as phlogiston to disguise it. So we might argue that these defective eighteenth-century ideas about saltpeter help to explain the Continental Army's chronic shortages of gunpowder. Just as eighteenth-century ideas about medicine and the four humors led to treatments that harmed some patients, perhaps Americans who thought in terms of living rocks and phlogiston could not help but make impure saltpeter, less-potent saltpeter, or insufficient amounts of acceptable saltpeter.[26] Indeed, Lewis Garanger, a captain of bombardiers in the French military, asked Congress to allow him to improve the manufacture of saltpeter because, in his opinion, it was "for want of Directors sufficiently acquainted with the Theory and Practice of Chymistry" that "the Manufactories of Saltpetre have not yet fully answered the Publick expectation."[27] Given that saltpeter composes 75 percent of gunpowder by weight, inferior saltpeter would have forced gunpowder inspectors to reject the barrels before them, while insufficient quantities of acceptable saltpeter would simply have produced too few barrels in the first place.[28] David Cressy, author of the most recent and thorough study of saltpeter, argues exactly that. During the war, he says, "home-made saltpeter had high contaminations of common salt."[29]

I have found no direct evidence of impure or less-potent saltpeter, but that does not necessarily mean the end of this line of questioning. J. R. McNeill, through his masterly understanding of mosquito biology, plantation ecology, and disease vectors, demonstrates that scientific facts related to the environment can address big issues related to empires and revolutions. Perhaps the tools and insights of modern chemistry and geology can help us understand the saltpeter Americans produced and, by extension, their connections to their government and the War of Independence.

* * *

To understand saltpeter and how Americans produced it, we must return to the pamphlets and instructions that were published in 1775 and 1776. Eight principal recipes appeared, but they all followed a relatively consistent set of guidelines, although variations abounded at specific steps (see Table 11.1). They started with a quantity of soil taken from a covered place such as a stable or barn. They placed it loosely in a tub that had a drain at the bottom. Then they poured water through the soil or allowed it to stand with the soil for as long as twenty-four hours, leaching or dissolving out of the soil not just the saltpeter but other compounds as well. This solution was drained off and then sometimes boiled in order to reduce its volume, and sometimes poured through wood ashes and straw. In order to crystalize the saltpeter out of the solution, the liquid was boiled, with any resultant scum removed, and then allowed to cool in trays set in a cellar. After twenty-four hours, the first batch of saltpeter crystals was harvested. The liquid that did not crystalize, often called "the mother of nitre," was either boiled and cooled again, or mixed in with the next batch of solution.[30] To refine the saltpeter crystals, they were dissolved in water, boiled, then cooled once more in the cellar, and allowed to recrystallize. At each heating and cooling stage, impurities either floated on the surface or sank as a newly formed solid. At the end, one could "turn the kettle bottom upwards for to get your Salt petre out, which will by this time be formed in a handsome cake."[31]

Despite the eighteenth-century misunderstanding of saltpeter, or potassium nitrate, modern science validates the general process described in these eight recipes. Just about any soil in the eastern United States contains potassium but not much nitrogen, which is avidly absorbed by plants and easily leached away by water.[32] Some of the recipes wisely suggested methods for increasing the yield. For example, the Pennsylvania Committee of Safety

Table 11.1. Recipes for Making Saltpeter, 1775–76

	Congress/Brown	Rush	Graham	New York
Starting material	Soil from covered places, no dung	Soil not specified	Soil under old buildings. Not from stables, no urinous or excrementicious salts	Soil from horse stables
Additions to soil	Tobacco trash and amber. Wait two weeks, remove trash, take sweepings.			
Percolation	Warm water, then cool. Straw on bottom. Pour three gallons through one bushel of soil.	Rain, river, or pure spring water poured through.	Water in tubs, let stand for twenty-four hours, boil down to one-half of original.	Water in tub, let stand for twenty-four hours, boil for one hour.
Addition of alkali			Pour through lots of ashes (one-half barrel).	Pour through a tub of ashes.
First crystallization	Boil till reduced, cool in wet wooden trays a few hours, get crystals.	Boil in copper vessel. Scoop out common salt. Pour into copper or earthen pans. Cool in cellar, get crystals.	Boil to one-quarter of original, pour through ashes, boil to one-eighth, put in cedar cooler in cellar for twelve hours, get crystals.	Boil in kettle until it turns yellow. Put in trays and in a cool place. Get crystals.
Mother of nitre	Reboil as above		Mix in with next batch	
Refining process	Melt and boil crystals, pour on stone. Add six times the amount of water, heat and dissolve, boil, then pour off the clear liquid. Cool it to form crystals. Reheat leftover liquid.	Dissolve in pure water, boil, take out common salt, and repeat.	Put crystals in kettle, dissolve over heat, cool in cellar. Get crystals.	

	Whiting	Pennsylvania	Lynch	Virginia
Starting material	Loose covered soil from under any old building	Soil from stables or barns, with plant and animal mixed, covered, sitting for long time. Tobacco soil good. Not too much dung, urine.	Soil from old houses, dry and exposed	Turn soil into powder
Additions to soil				One-third part ashes of greenwood and quick lime (CaO)
Percolation	Pour water through the soil three times.	Cold water equal in volume with soil, sit for ten to twelve hours. Then boil to reduce by 80 percent.	Pour water through the soil in the hopper.	Pour in hot water weighing twice the soil and ashes, sit for twenty-four hours, then filter through brown paper or flannel.
Addition of alkali	Combine with a common lye liquid, then remove precipitate.	Pour two or three times through five inches of wood ashes.		
First crystallization	Boil, cool, then set in trays for twenty-four hours, get crystals.	Boil gently, scoop impurities, boil more, cool in tub, scoop out impurities. Cool in any tub twenty-four hours, get crystals	Boil until a drop coagulates on a cold substance, skim off salts, pour into trays, put in a cool place, get crystals in twenty-four hours. Reboil leftover liquid.	Boil until a drop coagulates on a cold surface, then set aside in cool place for twenty-four hours, get crystals.
Mother of nitre	Reboil as above, or mix in with next batch.	Return to boiling.	Mix with new batch.	Mix with twice the weight of hot water, boil and cool, repeat until no more crystals.
Refining process	Dissolve in water with heat, cool, get crystals. Repeat process with remaining liquid.	Heat water and crystals, take off scum. Add alum, scoop scum. More water and boiling, then cool two to three days.	Hot water to dissolve crystals, heat or set in the sun in order to evaporate, and will get crystals.	

Sources: See Appendix: Sources for Table 11.1.

recommended taking earth from the floors of animal stables, in cellars, under barns, "or any other covered place where any animal or vegetable substances mixed together with earth have been collected and have laid a long time; and it is said those places where tobacco is manufactured, &c. produce it."[33] Animal dung and urine contain nitrogen in the form of ammonia, which cannot be made into saltpeter. Fortunately, soil bacteria such as *Nitrosomona* and *Nitrobacter* oxidize ammonia (NH_3) and convert it into nitrate (NO_3^-). This conversion takes time and needs oxygen; hence the sensible committee recommendation for soils that "have lain a long time" and have therefore been well aerated. Both farm manure and tobacco are appropriate materials to add to the soil because they have high enough concentrations of nitrogen so that once the soil's microorganisms inevitably take what they need, some nitrogen will be left over to be leached out.[34]

The process of dissolving compounds by percolating water through the soil or by letting the water and soil sit together for many hours follows modern chemical explanations of solubility. The water molecule has poles with powerful opposite charges that can form strong hydrogen bonds, thus making it an excellent solvent for compounds that contain elements such as potassium (K^+), sodium (Na^+), calcium (Ca^{2+}), and chlorine (Cl^-), or salts that contain ammonium (NH_4^+) or nitrate (NO_3^-). Solubility often increases with temperature, so a recommendation such as the one Congress made with Jeremiah Brown's instructions—"the first [water] put to it [the soil] must be warmer than new milk from the cow"—would increase the likelihood of having the necessary ingredients in the solution.[35]

Four of the recipes then call for pouring the solution through a tub of wood ashes or for the addition of "a quantity of common lye drawn from ashes." Wood ashes primarily contain calcium, potassium, and magnesium. Because potassium makes up only 1.5 percent of the mass of soil solids, its infusion from the wood ashes into the solution will increase the yield of saltpeter at the end of the process. The wood ashes also produce hydroxides (OH^-) that combine with iron and aluminum, and precipitate out as insoluble salts.[36] In addition to this chemical role, the ashes may also perform the physical function of filtering impurities out of the solution. Indeed, one recipe called the vessel holding the wood ashes a "filtering tub" and another directed individuals to "filtrate it [the solution] through another tub of ashes."[37]

The process of purifying and crystallizing the saltpeter also follows the principles of solubility. Each recipe instructs the saltpeter maker to boil the solution. As the temperature rises, dramatically more saltpeter can dis-

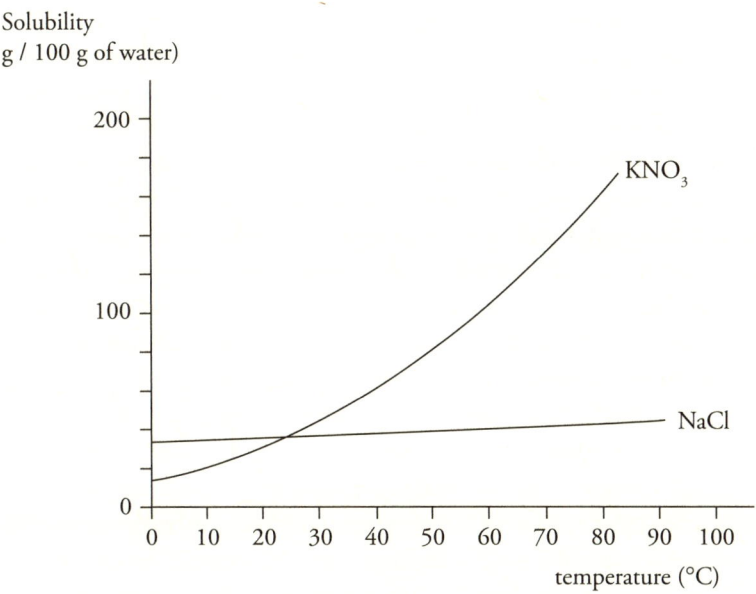

Figure 11.1. The solubility of potassium nitrate and sodium chloride at various temperatures.

solve into the solution. At 10°C, 219 grams of saltpeter can dissolve in one liter of water. At 50°C, that amount jumps to 852 grams, and at 100°C the amount is 2,460 grams. Other compounds—impurities in this case—cannot match saltpeter's solubility at these higher temperatures and therefore remain solid, readily scooped out while leaving the dissolved saltpeter undisturbed (see Figure 11.1).[38]

After the boiling step, each recipe calls for the solution to cool in trays, allowing the dissolved saltpeter to begin crystallizing. As the temperature drops further, additional molecules attach to the crystal in layer upon layer, creating a crystal lattice. These molecules have a greater attraction to other saltpeter molecules because they fit properly with the lattice. Other compounds do not attach to this lattice because of their incompatible shapes, thereby making the final crystals more pure.[39]

This process of purifying the saltpeter reminds us of that compound's hybrid character, its combination of human and physical properties. In a few exceptional locations, people could simply harvest saltpeter they found on the ground. Charles Lynch, a resident of southwestern Virginia, discovered a cave in which the ground was, in Thomas Jefferson's words, "highly impregnated [with saltpeter] to the depth of seven feet in some places" and another "piece of clear'd ground about half an acre" where the saltpeter "appears on the surface of the Earth."[40] But such naturally occurring sources of saltpeter, although welcome for being so rich and beyond the reach of British forces, were not remotely sufficient to meet the Continental Army's needs. For that, Americans had to follow printed instructions and cultivate the saltpeter, thereby creating a substance that looked "natural" but actually was more pure than what Lynch extracted from his cave or his patch along the river. Humans improved on "nature."

Those who set out to make saltpeter for the Continental Army probably did not think in terms of a crystal's lattice structure, but by modern scientific standards their empirical methods were sound. It did not matter that some believed saltpeter came out of living rocks deep within the earth or that others thought it floated on air currents above their heads. Just as some people today do not fully understand how their car's engine works but know that changing the oil regularly maintains its performance, colonists learned that if they followed the steps described in the recipes, they would have high-quality saltpeter in their trays at the end of the day. Because we do not know whether individuals followed these instructions assiduously, we cannot know how far or how well they applied the purification process. Nevertheless, the presumption that the colonists' "home-made saltpeter had high contaminations of common salt" because they misunderstood saltpeter, as David Cressy claims, cannot stand.[41] Admittedly, frauds and cheats may have "peppered" their product with such salts, but honest men and women who followed the prescribed instructions would not have been left with such impurities.

The recipes long ignored by historians compose a vital set of primary sources. Broadly speaking, they provide a window through which we can see how Americans believed the natural world worked. As such, they help us reconstruct the colonists' mind-sets. More specifically, the recipes give us a new way to approach the question of why the Continental Army lacked sufficient quantities of domestically produced gunpowder. Congress received reports of bad gunpowder, but the role saltpeter played in corrupting the ammunition remained hidden; lacking any other evidence, historians faced a dead end. The tools of modern science, however, allow us to unlock the recipes, appreciate the soundness of their empirical methods, and rule out impure saltpeter as a culprit. The orientation of environmental history, therefore, helps us see saltpeter for what it was: a compound created from the earth by human hands, and one that performed according to those humans' designs.

* * *

If pure saltpeter formed in the colonists' kettles, then the gunpowder shortage cannot be attributed to contamination during the production process. Perhaps instead these valid methods produced low yields of saltpeter, which in turn created too few barrels of gunpowder. Consider the first four stages of the process: the starting soil, the materials added to the soil, the use of water to dissolve compounds, and the addition of alkali. If at any point the amount of potassium, nitrogen, and oxygen were not maximized and fully dissolved into the solution, the final amount of saltpeter, however pure, would be low. Several of the recipes could well have shortchanged the producers' efforts in this respect.

If the soil one started with contained more nitrogen, then more saltpeter (which is potassium *nitrate*, after all) could be produced. The recipes from the Continental Congress and from the Committees of Safety of New York and Pennsylvania maximized the production of nitrates by using soils that contained decomposed animal wastes, tobacco plants, and/or tobacco juice. Yet the majority of the recipes did not urge producers to infuse the soil in this way. Benjamin Rush did not specify any particular type of soil, and Charles Lynch simply stated that one should "Dig up the floors of old houses." William Whiting allowed "earth from under any old building," which could have included barns and stables, but he did not insist on them. Dr. Graham even went so far as to give exactly the wrong advice, telling individuals to *avoid* "stables, and all other places, where the earths were impregnated with ruinous and excrementicious salts."[42] A writer in the *Pennsylvania Journal* understood how just any soil would not suffice. One had to use "the best methods of making compositions of materials the best adapted to produce saltpetre" because the soil would "be much sooner fit to yield saltpetre than the common earth we find under buildings; this not being in its nature the best adapted, nor the best situated, to collect saltpetre." This writer then described a detailed and scientifically sound process (one that called for, among other things, the regular application of urine) that would create soil rich in saltpeter. This process, however, took five or six months to complete, hardly ideal for an army desperate for gunpowder.[43]

The recipes' next step also played a critical role in attaining high yields of saltpeter. The nitrates and potassium had to dissolve out of the soil, and the Virginia recipe provided the soundest instructions: pour hot water onto the soil and let it stand for twenty-four hours. The higher temperature increased the solubility of most compounds, and a full day's soaking gave those substances every opportunity to dissolve. The other recipes did not give the nitrates and potassium as easy an opportunity to enter into the solution. The Graham, New York, and Pennsylvania recipes allowed the water and soil to sit for ten to twenty-four hours, but the water was cold. Congress's recipe used warm water, but it did "not remain long upon the earth, but in a few minutes begin to drop into the receiver [vessel]."[44] Such a percolation, lasting only a few minutes, might not have given the water enough time to dissolve all of the compounds in the soil. The recipes from Rush, Whiting, and Lynch did not even call for heated water. They simply called for cold water to be poured through the soil. Each recipe clearly followed the principles of solubility, but several of them did not give those principles much opportunity to work.

The recommendation to use wood ashes also varied from one recipe to the other. The ashes, in addition to serving as a filter, introduced extra potassium into the solution. The majority of the recipes recommended their use, but the recipes from Congress, Rush, and Lynch simply relied on the potassium extant in the soil. Those three recipes would have still yielded saltpeter (which is *potassium* nitrate), but probably in far lower quantities.[45]

When surveying all of these factors, the Pennsylvania and New York recipes gave producers the best chance to maximize their yields. The worst recipes in this regard, those by Rush and Lynch, did not specify nitrate-rich soil, allowed the least amount of time for dissolution, and added no potassium. Individuals who followed those recipes must have worked hard to attain relatively meager yields and, at the end, modest amounts of gunpowder.

* * *

Such low yields frustrated those producers, perhaps because widely circulated rhetoric described the ease with which one could generate large quantities of saltpeter. William Whiting called his recipe "an easy, simple and successful method" that was "infallible." According to John Adams, in the summer of 1775 Philadelphia residents "are very confidant, that We shall be able to furnish Salt Petre and Powder of our own Manufacture, and that very Soon." At the same time, the Committee of Safety of Cumberland County, Virginia, urged its residents to make saltpeter because "your Tobacco House and Stable Floors are Foundations from which it may be produced, with but little Trouble, in great Abundance and Perfection." Virginians read that sweeping up the dirt (and saltpeter crystals) from a sixty-foot tobacco house would result in 1,600 pounds of saltpeter a year. According to George Gilmer, Thomas Jefferson's doctor, saltpeter "may be collected [spontaneously?] in many places. It is to be collected by an easy and cheap process from all putrid subs[tances]." Given such optimism about the production of saltpeter, Gilmer spoke for many when he puzzled over why more people did not engage in this vital activity. "It is astonishing When the materials are so easily obtained, that no person should think it worth while."[46]

Many people, however, did not find the instructions so clear and simple, or the results so bountiful. On Christmas Eve in 1775, Benjamin Harrison, Jr., happened upon the man whom Virginia's congressional delegates had appointed to make saltpeter. Harrison wrote in a letter the following day, "My father writes me he wants to be dabbling in the salt-petre way, and gives me some directions how to begin such a work, but on reading them to this gent'n he finds them very erroneous." In Carlisle, Pennsylvania, during the spring of 1776, Jonathan Kearsley's significant operation had achieved little success. Working with three men for five weeks, using fourteen tubs and four boilers holding fifty gallons apiece, Kearsley reported that "the earths I have yet got are so lightly impregnated with Nitrous particles that I have as yet got but 15 lb of Salt Petre." He asked the Pennsylvania Committee of Safety "if there is Discover'd any new Method or New Materials that is in my power to procure, or fall in with, that I may in some measure be able to answer the great demand." This plea came not from a novice, but from someone whom officials in the town of Carlisle regarded as "a Gentleman who, from the knowledge he already has of the Process, and his Zeal to serve his Country, we recommend as a very suitable person, both to instruct others and to carry on the manufactory of the same."[47]

Many men in addition to Jonathan Kearsley worried about the financial costs of this work. Charles Lynch listed for Thomas Jefferson the many expenses that attended an extensive saltpeter operation in southern Virginia—"I have hands to hire, workmen to imploy, Provisions to buy, boilers &c. to purchase"—the costs of which totaled £200–300. He also believed he could "set several Places cleverly a going with five hundred Pounds." As of late November 1775, however, he found "Gentlemen here loath to risk as much cash as wou'd Make the Necessary preparations." Expenses also sank a saltpeter works started by the Committee of the City and Liberties of Philadelphia in July 1775. That October, the committee reported that operations were "now at a Stand for the Want of a sufficient Fund to carry it on."[48] The steps individuals had to take to receive payment for their saltpeter also affected their motivation to make saltpeter. Henry Wynkoop of Bucks County in Pennsylvania informed the Committee of Safety that "the mode of paying for the Saltpetre will prove discouraging to the people, as they will have to go to Philadelphia with the Officer's order before they can be paid for any small quantity of Saltpetre they may have carried in." He urged the committee to revise "such a roundabout troublesome and expensive way of getting their money." Writing from the perspective of the war's last year, Virginian Jacob Rubsamen explained that he could not develop saltpeter production in the southern parts of the state because the inhabitants could not profit financially. "Indeed, were it not that the Inhabitants of Greenbrier found they can make more money by making saltpeter than any thing else, I am fully persuaded it would have dropped in that part also."[49]

The payments these men sought were based on rates first set in the second half of 1775. Maryland followed Congress's recommendation of a half-dollar per pound of saltpeter, and eventually also offered an additional one shilling per pound for "Crude Nitre manufactured in private families" that would then be sent to a refinery for purification. Rhode Island and Virginia each offered three shillings per pound. Connecticut paid "a Premium or Bounty of *Ten Pounds* for every Hundred Pounds Weight of good and merchantable Salt Petre," a rate of two shillings per pound, but residents may have had to deliver the full hundredweight in order to receive payment. North Carolina paid £25 for every hundredweight (a rate of five shillings/pound) delivered between September 1775 and March 1776, and lowered the rate to £20 (four shillings/pound) for saltpeter delivered during the following six months. Pennsylvania started with a rate of £20 per hundredweight for the period July–September 1775, and then planned to decrease it to £15 for the following three months. In November, however, the Committee of Safety set the rate at £25 per hundredweight in an effort to generate greater production. Massachusetts provided the most generous compensation: a half-dollar per pound and, for saltpeter delivered from November 1775 to October 1776, an additional bounty of four shillings, as long as inhabitants delivered fifty pounds of saltpeter. By March 1776, Massachusetts had dropped the fifty-pound minimum and set the rate at seven shillings per pound. Perhaps this generous payment contributed to the delivery of two significant shipments to the Commissary General's stores: 2,847½ pounds in April 1776 and a remarkable 34,907¼ pounds in late May 1776.⁵⁰

The darker side of this pursuit of payments—fraud and corruption—probably tainted the production of saltpeter. It certainly showed its face in many areas throughout the war. "What an astonishing thing it is," wrote George Washington late in 1775, "that those who are employed to sign the Continental Bills should not be able, or Inclined to do it as fast as they are wanted. . . . Such a dearth of Publick Spirit, & want of Virtue; such stock jobbing, and fertility in all the low Arts to obtain advantages, of one kind or another, in this great change of Military arrangemt I never saw before." With respect to gunpowder, Kevin Phillips has suggested that when private merchant vessels, commissioned by colonial committees to acquire military supplies in the West Indies, returned to port, "not a few of the powder barrels were trundled into Yankee, Philadelphia, or Charleston warehouses in anticipation of nothing more patriotic than rising prices." Although I have found no direct evidence of this type of fraud in the production of saltpeter, it almost certainly existed. Some manufacturers might have intentionally left their saltpeter incompletely refined, counting on the extra weight of the impurities to bring in a few more shillings. If contractors during the Valley Forge winter of 1777–78 could intentionally place rocks and dirt inside casks that were supposed to contain food, then barrels holding impure saltpeter or some completely different substances would provide another explanation for gunpowder shortages.⁵¹ Circumstantial evidence must suffice for now. But there is no smoke without fire, and during the first year of the war several colonies established policies for the inspection of the saltpeter made within their borders. The Rhode Island General Assembly appointed three men "inspectors and provers of the quality" of all local saltpeter. Connecticut's General Assembly named "a suitable Number of Inspectors" who would issue "a Certificate of the Quantity and Quality of such Salt-Petre or Nitre" brought before them. New Jersey established similar regulations, stipulating that "in order that the quality of the Saltpetre may be sufficiently ascertained, the County Committees are directed to call in the aid of persons well skilled in that commodity."⁵² Certainly the causes for the bad gunpowder could be rooted in factors other than the saltpeter, but several of the colonies decided that they needed to exercise some degree of quality control over their saltpeter.

* * *

Payments and bounties did not serve as the sole motivators for saltpeter production. The Continental Congress called upon the people's revolutionary spirit when it published its recipes. Because "the safety and freedom of every community depends greatly upon having the means of defence in its own power," especially during this "present important contest for Liberty," Congress took steps so that "all persons may be encouraged to apply themselves to the manufacture of Salt-Petre." Similarly, the New York Committee of Safety's publication began with references to the "wicked practices of a corrupt Administration, and their hostile attempts to compel an obedience to several acts of the British Parliament," which led "the inhabitants of these colonies to take up arms in the defence of their lives, liberties and property." Without military stores, "the greatest unanimity, virtue and fortitude can afford us little prospect of success in the present interesting struggle."[53] Such rhetoric appeared widely at this time, not simply because patriotic fervor swept the land during the first year of the war but also because governments had limited recourse to do otherwise.

These calls for saltpeter in the name of patriotism speak to a fundamental consideration in America's conduct of the war: the critically important relationship between governments and their citizens. The Continental Congress failed to administer the war effectively in part because it could not, or would not, force Americans to act. As Max M. Edling explains, "the Revolution had been triggered by perceived abuses of a powerful imperial government beyond the control of the colonial legislatures. Americans would not tolerate the creation of a similarly powerful government in its place, especially as they were being asked to endure the sacrifices required to cast off that old imperial government."[54] The Congress held the power to conduct the war, but needed the colonies or states to provide funds and other goods. When the money, men, or supplies did not appear, Congress could do nothing but send another plea. Any attempt to levy taxes or raise duties would have been a political and legal misstep, and few in Congress even proposed doing so. Under the Articles of Confederation, each state had the right to "retain and enjoy as much of its present Laws, Rights & Customs, as it may think fit, and reserves to itself the sole and exclusive regulation and Government of its internal Police in all Matters that shall not interfere with the Articles of this Confederation."[55]

If the Continental Congress could not force the states to act, neither could the states consistently get their own citizens to abide by the laws they enacted. Many despaired that the Revolution would not realize its republican promise as corrupt officials, price-gouging farmers, hoarding traders, and military deserters symbolized a lack of virtue commonly associated with Europe. William Livingston, governor of New Jersey, listed for Henry Laurens of South Carolina some measures to aid the Continental Army, but "between the boundless Avarice of some of our Farmers & the Villainy of many of the Gentry employed in Publick Business, we are reduced to the most melancholy Situation." Individuals, families, and entire towns or counties removed themselves from the war effort. Known as the "disaffected," these individuals further tied the hands of the various governments.[56]

By understanding the "nature" of saltpeter, we have a broader sense of what government could ask—not demand—of its citizens. Saltpeter had to be coaxed from the soil; it could not be seized like a herd of livestock. Americans had to be encouraged with bounties and with appeals to patriotism to manufacture saltpeter, and jailing them for noncompliance or fining them for inaction would not have filled the barrels with gunpowder. Late in 1775, with the Continental Army desperate for 10,000 cords of wood to see it through the winter, the Massachusetts legislature did not simply rely on bounties and its powers of persuasion to get woodchoppers to enter the forests. It empowered a committee "to enter the Wood Lands of any Person or Persons within this Colony, and after apprizing the Wood thereon standing and growing, to cause the same to be cut down and carried to the Camp to supply said Army."[57] The legislature's actions generated controversy, but it could take such actions in part because the "nature" of timber enabled it to be seized and put to immediate use. Saltpeter could not be treated the same way. Even if a committee were similarly empowered to seize the crystals that formed on a cave floor, such saltpeter was far too impure to mix as gunpowder. Therefore, the chemical processes that Americans used to liberate saltpeter from the soil also limited what governments could do to acquire it.

Environmental history provides new perspectives on historical problems by opening our eyes to how people at critical moments interacted with and understood the nonhuman parts of the environment. The chemical and geological basis for the production of saltpeter reveals that Americans probably did not accidentally make an impure product. A shortage may have resulted from the use of recipes that did not fully manipulate the natural ingredients to generate the greatest yields, or from corrupt individuals who intentionally produced impure saltpeter. They would have profited from the colonial governments' bounties but, in the process, would have shortchanged the powder mills that supplied the Continental Army. The governments tried to woo their citizens not just with money but also with appeals to the Glorious Cause. These appeals apparently fell upon deaf ears. Despite the wide distribution of empirically sound recipes, Americans did not answer the call and produce enough saltpeter to meet the Continental Army's needs. If the nascent United States needed its citizens in a roiling boil, like a good saltpeter solution, then by this measure popular support for the war was tepid.

Appendix: Sources for Table 11.1

Sources for the eight saltpeter recipes listed in Table 11.1 are as follows:

- Congress/Brown: This recipe appears as the first in the Continental Congress's publication *Several Methods of Making Salt-Petre; Recommended to the Inhabitants of the United Colonies, by Their Representatives in Congress* (Philadelphia: W. and T. Bradford, 1775). The text receives no attribution, but is identical to the one published as "Mr. Jeremiah Brown's Method of Making Saltpetre, Published in Virginia by Order of the Trustees for the Improvement of Arts and Manufactures, and in England by Order of the Society for the Encouragement of Arts, Manufactures, and Commerce," *London Magazine; or, Gentleman's Monthly Intelligencer*, October 1763, 535–36. It also appears in the *Virginia Gazette* (Purdie), August 4, 1775. Brown, "an illiterate, poverty-stricken, old man" in Virginia had been working on this method since the 1750s, "whenever he could spare the time from the daily labor required to maintain his large family." See Robert Leroy Hilldrup, "A Campaign to Promote the Prosperity of Colonial Virginia," *Virginia Magazine of History and Biography*, 67 (October 1959), 425.
- Rush: Benjamin Rush, "An account of the manufactory of Salt-Petre," in *Several Methods of Making Salt-Petre* (Philadelphia: W. and T. Bradford, 1775), 12. Rush (1746–1813) was a physician and the first native-born American to be named chemistry professor, holding his position at the College of Philadelphia. See Robert B. Sullivan, "Rush, Benjamin," in John A. Garraty and Mark C. Carnes, eds., *American National Biography* (New York: Oxford University Press, 1999), 19:72–75.

- Graham: William Whiting, "Appendix," in *Several Methods of Making Salt-Petre; Recommended to the Inhabitants of the United Colonies, by the Honorable Continental Congress, and Re-published by Order of the General Assembly of the Colony of Massachusetts Bay, Together with the Resolve of Said Assembly, and an Appendix by Doctor William Whiting* (Watertown, Mass.: Benjamin Edes, 1775), 17–20. Whiting prefaced his instructions by acknowledging, "The following Method was communicated to me by a very worth Gentleman, viz Doctor GRAHAM, of Westchester County, in the Colony of New York."
- New York: The New York Committee of Safety published this method, "said to be practiced with great Success in Pennsylvania," in *Essays upon the Making of Salt-Petre and Gun-Powder* (New York: Samuel Loudon, 1776), 17–18. A pared-down version of this recipe appeared in a letter from Joseph Palmer to John Adams, June 19, 1775, in Robert J. Taylor and Gregg L. Lint, eds., *Papers of John Adams* (Cambridge, Mass.: Belknap Press, 1979), 3:28–29.
- Whiting: *Essays upon the Making of Salt-Petre and Gun-Powder*, 18–22. The New York Committee of Safety reprinted a report by William Whiting, dated December 25, 1775. Whiting served in the Massachusetts Provincial Congress and on a committee that sought improved methods for making saltpeter. He received £150 at the end of 1775 for his expenses and service. See *Journals of the House of Representatives of Massachusetts, 1775–1776*, vol. 51, pt. 2 (Boston: Massachusetts Historical Society, 1983), December 27, 1775, pp. 82–83.
- Pennsylvania: *The Process of Extracting and Refining Salt-Petre, According to the Method Practiced at the Provincial Works in Philadelphia* (Philadelphia: William and Thomas Bradford, 1776), published by the Pennsylvania Committee of Safety.
- Lynch: *Virginia Gazette* (Purdie), August 11, 1775, p. 1. Charles Lynch prefaced these instructions to Alexander Purdie, the newspaper's printer, by stating that saltpeter "may very easily be made, by observing the following directions." Lynch (1736–96) lived in Bedford County, Virginia, which became Campbell County in 1781. He represented both Bedford and Campbell in the House of Burgesses from 1769 to 1778. Brent Tarter, "Lynch, Charles," *American National Biography*, 14:164–65.

- Virginia: *Virginia Gazette* (Pinkney), July 27, 1775, p. 1. The brief instructions, taking about one-third of a newspaper column, were followed by extensive commentary on saltpeter and the extraction process. That section, titled "Observations," ran for two and two-thirds columns and nearly filled the entire page. At the time, two additional newspapers were also published under the name *Virginia Gazette*; Alexander Purdie's printed the instructions on page 2 on July 28, 1775, and John Dixon and William Hunter did so the following day, on page 3. Neither of these other two newspapers printed the lengthy "Observations."

CHAPTER 12

The Problem of Order and the Transfer of Slave Property in the Revolutionary South

MATTHEW SPOONER

In 1775 the thirteen future United States were colonies, enmeshed within one of the largest empires the world had ever seen. In 1783 those colonies were recognized by Britain as states, all conjoined into an independent republic. This was an extraordinary achievement, one that required an unprecedented degree of political, military, and economic mobilization. In every colony the changes wrought by the Revolution—an event marked by blood, loss, and strain as much as by ideas and institutions—were real and lasting. Yet in the South, where the "yelps for liberty" were loud and where armies and partisans engaged in a chaotic and protracted struggle in a countryside containing nearly half a million slaves, the changes ran deepest.

Historians have long understood that the ideological and material challenges of the Revolution marked a turning point in the development of American slavery both in the South, where the chains of bondage were drawn tighter, and in the North, where the War of Independence set slavery on a path to eventual extinction.[1] However, the overwhelming focus on the ideological contradictions between slavery and the country's revolutionary inheritance, as well as the separation between studies of slavery and studies of American history more generally, have led historians to downplay the more brutal aspects of the struggle for independence. In doing so, historians have generally remained far more impressed by continuities than discontinuities between slavery and slaveholding in the colonial era and the early republic.[2]

This chapter seeks to open new directions in our understanding of the impact of the American Revolution in the southern states by merging the histories of slavery and the War of Independence to show that the continuance of chattel slavery in the South masked deep transformations in the structure of society and the composition of the slaveholding class.³ Specifically, this chapter argues that the slave-based export economy of the prewar South created problems of control and supply that combined to create a desperate situation by 1780, one that would end in the largest transfer of property, especially slave property, that the nation would see until the Civil War. As a result, the American Revolution in the southern states allowed for the ascension of a new group of merchant planters, many of whom hailed from the underdeveloped interior, who rose in the vacuum created by war and who, in time, would work to create the mature and distinct slave society of the Old South.

The savage nature of fighting in the region, which by the end of the war resulted in a massive redistribution of land and slave property, emerged directly from the social structure of the southern colonies. The South, or rather the region that would in time come to understand itself as the South, was fractured by religion, language, and ethnicity. Yet the region remained overwhelmingly rural. Even more than in the northern colonies, where nascent industry and shipping occupied an increasingly significant amount of capital and labor and 10 percent of the population lived in cities,⁴ households in the southern colonies depended almost entirely on agricultural output.⁵

The southern colonies were also remarkably dynamic even by the standards of the eighteenth century. Driven by decreasing rates of mortality and the immigration of "a mix'd Medley from all Countries, and the off Scouring of America" from the north, each of the southern colonies experienced rapid population growth from midcentury onward.⁶ North Carolina's population soared from 70,000 in 1750 to over 180,000 in 1770 as Scotch-Irish and Germans emigrated en masse from Europe and settlers from the New England and mid-Atlantic colonies bought up the colony's cheap and abundant land.⁷ The number of South Carolinians grew from 40,000 in 1740 to 120,000 in 1770, and Georgia's population rose from little more than 6,000 in 1761 to nearly 20,000 just a decade later, an increase royal governor Sir James Wright attributed to "the great inducement people have had to come and settle in a Province, where they could get fresh and good Lands at a moderate price and plenty of good range for Cattle Horses and Hogs and where they will not be so much pent up and confined as in thick settled Countrys" to the north.⁸

Rapid growth brought upheaval and change, particularly in the backcountry (generally understood to refer to the lands above the fall line) where the greatest demographic and economic change occurred. Despite the backcountry's rapid economic development, and although the region did not lack for ambitious men aspiring to emulate planter elites of the coast, the population of the southern interior remained predominantly white throughout the colonial era. In South Carolina, where the disparity was most extreme, just 14,000 white inhabitants of the three coastal parishes of Beaufort, Charleston, and Georgetown worked more than 70,000 slaves harvesting rice and indigo, annually producing 140,000 barrels of the former before the war.[9] By contrast, only 6,500 slaves lived beyond the state's fall line in 1768 among more than 60,000 white men and women.[10] Because the greatest obstacle to the spread of slavery was the interior's lack of access to the global market, large-scale plantation agriculture had moved fully inland only in Virginia, where aspiring planters had moved away from the entailed, exhausted, and expensive land of the tidewater a generation before.[11] Yet even in the piedmont the number of slaves remained significantly lower as a total and percentage share of the population. As a result, in Virginia and elsewhere, the interests of the interior and the coast frequently and widely diverged.[12]

Despite the slow spread of slavery inland, on the eve of the Revolution the backcountry remained in its birth throes. Young and inchoate, the developing interior was fraught with tensions both between localized groups who sought to impose different visions on the region and with established interests on the coast. Eventually these tensions erupted into the so-called "Regulator" movements that engulfed North and South Carolina and reverberated throughout the southern colonies, events that—though typically described as separate phenomena—revealed the strains and upheaval experienced by backcountry inhabitants reacting to the slow yet inexorable changes brought on by economic growth and market expansion.[13] When the war finally came, the concentration of slaves along the southern coast, the South's economic dependence upon commodities for export, and the divided political loyalties and deeply held grievances within the backcountry combined to produce a crucible in which the southern states' two most pressing problems throughout the conflict—controlling internal hostile populations of slaves and loyalists, and materially sustaining the war effort—rapidly became conjoined.

Southern colonists understood very well the dangers that the fractured population posed to order within the region. From the beginning of the Revolutionary conflict, individuals and state officials within the newly formed southern states took extraordinary steps to monitor slaves and loyalists, and they repeatedly responded to real or perceived threats with swift and brutal violence. Most immediately, this meant quieting murmurs of freedom from slaves who overheard and appropriated the revolutionary rhetoric trumpeted in every town and all across the land. When Charleston authorities heard that the well-known free black boat pilot Thomas Jeremiah was holding "nightly meetings of Negroes" and informing them that "there is a great war coming soon" to "help the poor Negroes," they promptly hanged "Jerry" and burned him at the stake.[14]

Control also meant strengthening the institutional disciplinary apparatus within each state. Whereas government officials had previously been wary of damaging slave property, they now ordered patrollers to "shoot one or any number of Negroes who are armed and doth not willingly surrender their arms" and gave them "Discretionary Power, to shoot any Number of Negroes above four, who are off their Masters Plantations."[15] In the wake of Lord Dunmore's 1775 proclamation offering freedom to the slaves of rebels, Whig officials throughout the South echoed Virginia governor Patrick Henry's warning that only "An early and unremitting Attention to the Government of the SLAVES" could preserve "the publick Safety." In each colony, "Constant, and well directed Patrols" were made a first priority.[16] If slaveholders needed further urging, by 1776 state governments took the further step of offering cash bounties "For the head of every such slave making Resistance" and loosened restrictions on compensation for owners of murdered and executed slaves.[17] Slaves captured behind or attempting to reach British lines tended to be either sold to the West Indies or executed. In one extreme instance, three slaves in Dorchester, Maryland, who were captured attempting to reach Dunmore were sentenced to be "taken to the place of execution and there each of them to have their right hands cut off and to be hanged by the neck until they were dead; their heads to be severed from their bodies and their bodies to be divided each of them in four quarters and their heads and quarters to be set up in the most public places of the county."[18] Circumstances in the Revolutionary South left little room for subtlety.

Similarly, in an effort to close ranks against the enslaved population and to quiet support for the Crown in the prewar years, patriot leaders made continued and personal appeals to known British sympathizers deemed to be "men of influence" in hopes of dampening vocal enthusiasm for the mother country, particularly among recent immigrants in the backcountry. Rebel leaders made extensive tours of up-country settlements in an attempt to win support for the patriot cause. As one such leader put it, "Vigorous measures are absolutely necessary. If a dozen persons are allowed to be at large, our progress has been in vain, and we shall be involved in a civil war in spite of our teeth."[19] Patriot leaders also extended material inducements, including money and military commissions, to prominent individuals who they feared might turn Tory. South Carolina governor William Moultrie later recalled that "it was thought not only useful, but political to raise them, because the most influential gentlemen in the back country were appointed officers, which interested them" in the patriot cause.[20]

When softer tactics failed, as they often did, the same disciplinary apparatus used in the effort to quell potential slave uprisings could be employed to suppress loyalist sentiment by force. Benjamin Cleveland and William Lenoir, magistrates and ambitious landholders in backcountry North Carolina, explained the brutal killing of two suspected British sympathizers in early 1776. Acknowledging that their actions amounted to murder, the two justified themselves by explaining that they were "sensible to the great good done by extra judicially exterminating those direful wretches from amongst us which tend so much to the Annoyance of all others in the surrounding areas." The killers and their followers were quickly pardoned.[21] And in one of the most famous examples of violent intimidation, 130 armed Georgians marched to the home of recent émigré Thomas Brown in late 1775 and demanded he sign a pledge of support of the patriot cause. Brown refused. In response, the band destroyed his house, stole his livestock, and then scalped, sliced, and beat Brown within an inch of his life.[22]

Once the stakes of the conflict became clear and the promise of freedom was raised, patriot leaders could not entirely subdue the resistance of slaves or loyalist partisans as long as British forces remained nearby. After British commanders removed the bulk of their forces from the region after the failed siege of Charleston in July 1776, that surveillance and intimidation by Whig forces produced a period of uneasy calm.[23] Yet even then, slaves continued to flee plantations to hide in swamps or reach British ships within Chesapeake Bay. Groups of "banditti," including a band of rangers operating out of East Florida and led by the same Thomas Brown, launched numerous raids in Georgia and lower South Carolina, stealing slaves and livestock and burning plantations when able.[24] Privateers and British expeditionary forces harassed planters along the coast, with Virginia planter Leven Powell reporting in February 1777 that raiders had "taken about 300 Negroes from Gloucester, Lancaster and Northumberland [counties]. . . . My brother who came up from there the night past said that several people . . . have lost every slave they were possessed of."[25]

Though partisans and privateers could occasionally steal patriot slaves and devastate patriot property, their small-scale incursions could not threaten effective patriot control without the promise of British military protection. Nonetheless, the amount of energy Whig governments spent protecting property and suppressing insurgencies greatly exacerbated the second major problem faced by southern states during the war: their inability to raise the men and materiel needed to sustain a prolonged military effort. Before the British invasion of Georgia in 1778, the problem manifested itself in states' repeated failure to come close to meeting troop quotas demanded by the Continental Congress. As fighting in the North wore on in 1776 and 1777, the threat of slave or loyalist insurrection kept militias at home, either by state directive or the militiamen's own refusal to march northward. When Congress attempted to regularize troop numbers in the Continental Army by requiring states to fill quotas of troops, the results were less than encouraging. No southern state ever reached even a third of its quota despite increasingly lucrative bounties, and from 1777 to 1783, even Virginia found only 248 men willing to serve for the duration of the entire war.[26] Poor southerners, who composed the great bulk of both state troops and the Continental line, had lost what Charles Royster termed the "rage militaire" by late 1776. Anxious to grow a full harvest and provide for their families, they showed little interest in brutal campaigning several hundred miles away.[27] In response, Whig leaders made major concessions. They rewrote state constitutions to provide more equitable representation, increased allotments of food, clothing, and pay, and provided for the popular election of officers.[28] Yet even these efforts, which would powerfully affect the political development of the region, failed to raise enough troops to meet quotas or even maintain militia numbers.

Southern leaders found it even more problematic to supply those soldiers who did make it to the field. Although the former colonies had printed paper money in the past to finance their participation in imperial wars, they had normally done so by establishing sinking funds or other financial mechanisms to retire paper currency within a few years. The Revolution quickly demanded a different set of fiscal responses. After 1777, depreciation skyrocketed as state governments and the Continental Congress had little recourse but to print money continuously. Congress issued an astounding £25,000,000 worth of paper currency by the end of 1776, and the states did their best to keep pace.[29] Remarkably, the continental continued to trade roughly at par through 1778, and most state currency depreciated only to roughly three to one over the same period.[30] Rising inflation and disagreements between states as to the value of currencies made it nearly impossible to supply their respective militias in the field, let alone a Continental Army that was consuming over 900,000 pounds of flour and 800,000 pounds of fish and meat per month in 1778.[31]

Even if states had possessed the means, there was little to buy. Cut off from the British Empire and encircled by a constant and modestly effective blockade, the thirteen colonies simply could not supply either their armed forces or the general populace with essential items like salt, let alone guns, textiles, and other manufactured goods.[32] Basic manufactured items like finished metal became especially difficult to come by. Although some 257 furnaces and forges had been built in the colonies, with roughly 25 percent of them in the South,[33] they were mostly small operations and prohibited by British imperial law from producing the heavy iron needed to wage war. Their capital disappearing, states tried offering land grants and generous bounties to private interests to construct ironworks and forges, but these rarely came anywhere close to producing what was required.[34] In addition to lacking basic experience, operators of mines, forges, and other manufactories lacked manpower. It is an indication of how desperate states were for lead and iron that within a few years of the war's beginning they stopped executing captured slaves or selling them to the West Indies and began sending them west to work in places like lead mines and ironworks (often a death sentence still, though a slower one).[35] Despite these efforts, southern industry remained woefully undermanned. As an overseer in western Virginia complained in 1777, "How an iron work is to be kept in blast without hands, teams, waggons, corn, wood cutters, mine horses etc is a mistery to me. And why the 10 negro men ordered by Congress to be sent here are not sent I know not, thirty would be too few." Those few who had arrived were "so naked & barefooted that they will not long be alive," a situation that would be repeated in manufactories and plantations across the South as the war dragged on and manufactured items disappeared.[36]

To make matters worse, Whig leaders found it extremely difficult to move those foodstuffs and manufactured items that could be procured to the front lines. The basic infrastructure of the southern states, built on the cheap to support a colonial economy premised on bringing goods for export to the coast, prevented the effective movement of goods into the interior where they were now needed.[37] As a result, the problem of transport and supply fell to private interests, and speculation; corruption, and price gouging became recurrent themes throughout the war. The early historian of the Revolution David Ramsay observed in 1785 that "at no period of time were fortunes more easily or rapidly acquired" than in the lull from 1776 to the British invasion.[38] For the few who eluded roving partisans and banditti on the roads and had access to capital and political influence, Ramsay's observation certainly seemed true. The loyalist Alexander Chesney recalled in his journal that in a trade between the backcountry and Charleston he made "with care 300 per cent" on each journey, and Wade Hampton—who more than anyone illustrated the advancement one could make if lucky, ambitious, and unscrupulous enough—was clearing thousands of pounds every few months bringing food and grain to Savannah and Charleston from 1776 to 1778.[39] Elsewhere, merchants and planters alike turned to the time-honored tradition of hoarding necessary articles, especially salt and grain. The practice sparked riots in Virginia and elsewhere, provoking rebel leader Edmund Pendleton to grumble that "all honest men must be ruined by these Harpies if we can't find some way to stop the Torrent of Extortion, which appears to have no bounds."[40]

None of these issues—generating the manpower and materiel needed to supply an increasingly desperate fight; containing slaves, loyalists, and partisans from both sides; managing the war-weariness of an increasingly disillusioned and starved populace—waned as fighting continued in the North. Yet when the full force of fighting moved south with the British invasion of Georgia in late 1778, a society slowly tearing along these seams exploded into bloody and desperate civil war. In the backcountry, nascent or suppressed British sympathies reemerged emphatically as emboldened loyalists again formed militia companies and joined with British units to harass patriot forces and exact retribution for earlier treatment. The renewed presence of British troops willing to harbor slaves and utilize slave labor again sparked mass desertions of enslaved men and women from plantations and encouraged resistance among those who stayed.[41] Money turned utterly worthless, supplies ran still lower, and violence escalated as the countryside finally descended into the conflagration of plundering and murder foreshadowed in the years from 1775 to 1777.

Despite the vivid descriptions of contemporaries, historians of the American Revolution do not always convey the full scope of disorder that southerners experienced after 1778.[42] Plantations were burned, sometimes repeatedly, by each side.[43] Neighbors beheaded one another as warnings, and wounded prisoners were run through with swords.[44] Nathanael Greene, trying to make sense of what was happening in the Carolinas in 1782, came closest, perhaps, to capturing the essence of affairs when he explained to his superiors that "The whigs and tories pursue one another with the most relentless fury killing and destroying each other whenever they meet.... For want of civil government the bands of society are totally disunited, and the people, by copying the manners of the British, have become perfectly savage."[45]

The "savagery" of the Revolutionary South, which far surpassed anything seen in the North (where actions could hardly be termed civil), resulted less from the tactics employed by either side than from the intensification of the same two problems of order and supply that had undermined the war effort in the southern states from the beginning. The collapse of state governments and the presence of British troops throughout the South shattered the structures of authority that southern Whigs had erected to maintain order among slaves and loyalist insurgents. Now that military might was desperately needed to combat British soldiers and partisans, economic disruption and the loss of control over the region's primary labor force rendered patriot officials entirely incapable of raising sufficient soldiers and materiel.

Under immense pressure from the circumstances of war and from slaves themselves, both patriot leaders and British commanders turned to slave property to resolve the crisis, although they did so in different ways. British commanders found their hand forced by the actions of tens of thousands of slaves who reached their lines and who pushed them toward actions they would not otherwise have countenanced. Indeed, the British army, in attempting to quell one revolution, became itself a revolutionary force. Henry Clinton's "Philipsburg Proclamation" of 1779, which made Dunmore's plan applicable to slaves of rebels everywhere, was merely British policy catching up to facts on the ground. By 1779 slaves had already become part of the British army. The Hessian officer Johann Ewald said of Cornwallis's army that "Every soldier had his Negro, who carried his provisions and bundles. This multitude always hunted at a gallop, and behind the baggage followed well over four thousand Negroes of both sexes and all ages."[46] Though most of these slaves served officers as cooks or valets, British commanders showed little hesitation arming slaves when short of manpower. During the failed American attack on Savannah in 1779, the British armed slaves who fought ferociously alongside British regulars.[47] Perhaps most famously, British officers in Charleston organized former slaves into a legion of "Black Dragoons," who took part in larger military actions after 1781. The Dragoons also foraged among patriot plantations, carrying off "everything they could... Cattle, sheep, Hogs, horses & half the provisions" at a single plantation one night and "some twenty to thirty heads of Cattle and half as many Negroes" at another.[48]

The labor and intelligence provided by slaves was vital to the British war effort.[49] However, neither British commanders nor British policymakers could escape the quandary that slaves remained valuable property and that they had a pressing need to finance their war while maintaining the loyalty of British sympathizers, the most prominent of whom were slaveholders. Although both Dunmore's and Clinton's proclamations offered freedom only to the slaves of *rebel* owners, all sides knew that slaves did not honor the distinction. Amid the confusion of war and the massive displacement of people, slaves of loyalists could and did claim to be the slaves of rebels, provoking a budding tension between loyal planters and British commanders. In Charleston British authorities received numerous complaints about "Negroes leaving the Service of their Masters and coming to the British Army," behavior which not only hindered planters' efforts at harvest but also caused "the Negroes to contract Bad Habits, such that might be dangerous to the community hereafter . . . as well as many more mischievous effects." Other loyal planters demanded, and apparently received, rebel slaves as compensation for property destroyed or slaves plundered by rebel parties.[50] Caught between the need to assuage loyalist anger, recognition of their responsibility to slaves they continually and indiscriminately employed, and a deeper understanding of black soldiers and servants generated by continual interaction and mutual dependence, British commanders acted with trepidation. In response to complaints received in Charleston, slaves were returned only to loyalist masters who could give positive identification of their slaves and agreed "not to resent the Behaviour of the Slaves for having left his service," on risk of not having his slave returned a second time.[51]

For patriot leaders, the use of slave property was much more straightforward. Some six thousand black men did serve in American forces during the war, representing about 3 percent of total patriot enlistment.[52] Yet mobilization never threatened slavery in the South the way it did in the North, as the vast majority of black troops came from northern states, particularly Rhode Island. No southern state authorized the use of enslaved soldiers, though in every state owners used slaves as substitutes, and slaves claiming to be free could always find a recruiting officer eager enough to meet his quota that he asked few questions.[53] When local leaders and generals did suggest meeting manpower shortages by arming slaves, they were invariably rebuffed by planters and state legislatures.[54] Of course, state governments and patriot commanders did not hesitate to employ slaves on public works, though in every case they stretched themselves to compensate slaveholders both for hired time and for loss of property if a slave died in public service.[55] Slaves who remained on plantations, suffering miserably as wartime shortages left them bereft of food and clothes, received concessions from owners and overseers who realized their tenuous position and sought to prevent desertion.

Yet the overwhelming response of patriots to the problems posed by human property was to use slaves in ways that reduced them strictly to property, a course of action dictated by both the commitment to maintaining slavery and the difficulty of waging total war within a fractured and export-dependent society. In a very real sense, slave property became the imperfect solution to the logistical and material problems that had plagued the South from the beginning. The reasons were many. Perhaps most important, the war created conditions under which slaveholding became enormously profitable in areas, particularly the backcountry, where it could not flourish before. On the one hand, in their desperate need to purchase arms and supplies from abroad, state governments purchased slave-grown commodities, particularly tobacco, at hugely inflated prices in order to obtain specie or exchange for supplies directly.[56] For those in areas away from the fighting, this provided a huge incentive to increase output either by purchasing slaves or, if possible, by hiring slaves from owners desperate to remove their hands from the path of the British army.[57] Additionally, produce from the backcountry—wheat, hemp, flax, corn—that could not be sold at a distance profitably before the war became hugely important to the supply of the patriot war machine, strongly encouraging backcountry inhabitants to enter the slaveholding ranks and allowing enormous profits to those with established slave operations and also to merchants who brought backcountry produce to armies in the interior.[58]

The profits to be made in areas throughout the South made slave property increasingly desirable above all other forms of property. Inducements to slave production, coupled with the stoppage of the Atlantic slave trade and the desertion of slaves from plantations, caused demand for slave labor to skyrocket during the war. Slaves available for purchase became so scarce, and buyers so eager, that planters and merchants everywhere complained that "Negroes cannot be had in this country for any price."[59] Even as early as 1776, before depreciation had truly set in, slaves were bringing "between £700 & £800" pounds on credit or currency.[60] By the end of the war a slave could bring several times that much, even allowing for inflation.[61]

At the same time as the value of slaves continued to rise, the states continued to print paper money to compensate for their lack of specie. Consequently, the only legal tender possessed by states depreciated at a rate far faster than before the British invasion. By 1779 South Carolina's currency traded at roughly sixty-six pounds in paper money to a single pound sterling; a year later it traded at 400 to 1. In Georgia and North Carolina, where inflation was greatest, state notes traded as high as 12,000 to 1 by 1782.[62] In an interaction that illustrates both the dwindling value of currency and the increased assertiveness displayed by slaves during the war, one North Carolina planter reported with obvious alarm that a slave peddling fish in Hillsborough had refused to sell his wares without hard money and "audaciously superadded, 'Not a d—m'd Son of a B—ch in the Town shall have any without it.'"[63]

Put differently, by 1780, as currency became widely regarded as worthless even by those who might previously have been forced to accept it, and as the British invasion reduced production of salable commodities, slave property was the only form of *movable* property retaining significant (and, indeed, rapidly appreciating) value. The rising value of slaves relative to other mediums of exchange, combined with the material insufficiencies of the southern states detailed above, crystallized a context in which private interests, state governments, and the British army together effected a massive transfer of human property, one unmatched until the Emancipation Proclamation.

For state governments, the transfer of human property took three general forms. First, beginning in 1777 and especially after 1780, every southern state passed laws confiscating the property of British sympathizers. Through the confiscation acts, states came to control thousands of slaves in addition to those captured fleeing to the British or taken from enemy lines. As did British commanders, state governments compensated some patriots for property lost (or, in the case of a Richard Henderson of Georgia, "to assist his family in distress") by delivering them slaves.[64] The bulk of confiscated slaves, however, were first put under the care of state-appointed commissioners who oversaw their labor on public works or sequestered loyalist plantations and then sold them during and after the war in order to generate capital and retire increasingly sizable state debts.[65]

In the end, sales of confiscated estates failed to raise significant amounts of needed hard money or make much impact on southern states' considerable debt. They did, however, allow certain men to enrich themselves by purchasing property on long credit, worthless currency, and often with certificates and "indents," or promissory notes issued by the state in exchange for impressed goods and services rendered. Importantly, the majority of certificates and indents used to buy valuable slaves and plantations had been acquired from poorer soldiers and citizens at a huge discount. For example, the merchant John Hawrie instructed his associate in Albemarle County, Virginia, to buy up soldiers' indents with whiskey and shoe leather, though even then warning against giving more than a sixth of the indents' value.[66] It is impossible to know exactly how many certificates fell to merchants and officers in this way, or to what use they were eventually employed, but the case of Benjamin Guerard in South Carolina is instructive. Between 1781 and 1783 Guerard acquired confiscated land and slaves valued at £6,308 sterling, all in certificates, yet only £310 worth of those certificates had been originally issued to him.[67] In other words, confiscated estate sales provided men like Guerard and Hawrie with the means to transmute relatively small quantities of whiskey, food, and other necessary goods into the plantations and slaves that would form the basis for economic and political dominance in the postwar decades.

In addition to selling the slaves of loyalists at auction, states also confiscated and captured slaves under their control to pay directly for military supplies or to meet financial obligations to soldiers and politicians. Georgia, suffering from some of the bloodiest fighting and experiencing the greatest depreciation of currency, in one instance used "three hundred and twenty one pounds, fifteen shillings and six pence in negroes" to repay a debt owed for a purchase of whiskey.[68] Georgia also used confiscated slaves to compensate officials. The executive council of the state eagerly voted both itself and the governor slaves as payment in lieu of worthless currency or obligations on the state.[69] Other slaves were sold abroad, most often to French and Dutch colonies in the West Indies, in exchange for specie, which was then used to pay for supplies from foreign merchants who had wisely decided to stop accepting state money or credit. At certain points states even tried to sell slaves to other states in an attempt to obtain hard money. In 1782 South Carolina governor John Mathews wrote to Virginia governor Benjamin Harrison asking the latter to preside over a sale of 150 slaves "to be disposed of for Cash, to answer some pressing necessities of Government. The army in this State, is altogether supplied by certificates, we have no trade, consequently no money can be brought into the Country." Harrison responded that to do so would be impossible, for no hard money existed in Virginia either.[70]

Finally, by the end of war the need to raise troops and the desirability of slave property above all else led each southern state to begin offering slave bounties to recruit soldiers for the Continental line and loosely organized regiments of "state troops." Immediately after the British invasion, states had simply increased earlier forms of cash bounties. North Carolina's enlistment bounty rose from £100 in 1778 to $500 in 1780 and then an astounding £3,000 in 1781. When paper currency did not work, the state began in 1780 offering an additional 200, then 640, then up to 12,000 acres in western land in addition to clothing and a guarantee of provisions for the soldier's family.[71] Other, more drastic, measures enacted to fill military ranks similarly proved insufficient. In addition to providing land and cash bounties, South Carolina passed a vagrancy law in 1778 that ordered the immediate enlistment of "all idle men, beggars strolling or straggling persons" as privates in one of the state's six regiments. Just as increasing bounties did little, however, the vagrancy law appears to have had the ultimate effect not of filling the state's quota but of pushing vagrants out west or into neighboring provinces.[72]

As the military situation grew more desperate, and as enticements in land and currency or certificates consistently failed to generate needed soldiers, states turned to using human property as bounties, knowing it was the one form of valuable and movable property they possessed that poor farmers coveted. Slave bounties differed from state to state. Virginians taxed large planters one slave of every twenty owned to go toward enlistees, a policy that expressed lingering resentment toward the state's first families as much as it did considerations of practicality.[73] Other states initially tried to use confiscated slaves to furnish recruitment bounties, with Georgia using slaves as direct payment to purchase horses for a new regiment of future governor James Jackson's Light Dragoons.[74] When states could not meet demand, and as confiscated slaves were sold or employed in public works, certain military and political leaders in South Carolina and Georgia finally turned to a more extreme measure. Beginning with the so-called "Sumter's Law," named after Thomas Sumter, who first implemented the scheme in April 1781, soldiers were recruited on the promise of *future* plunder in slaves, from one "grown negro" for each private up to "three grown negroes and one small negro" for colonels.[75] Despite the fact that Sumter's Law essentially authorized a system of state-sanctioned plunder, a crime punishable by death in normal times, his plan was soon adopted by other men attempting to form similar regiments, including Andrew Pickens in South Carolina and James Gunn in Georgia (though many other military officials, including Nathanael Greene and Francis Marion, looked on the scheme with horror). Sumter's plan proved such a powerful inducement that, after several years of trying, he suddenly found he had little trouble filling his ranks. Even more impressive than the speed of enlistment were the facts that more than 94 percent of those who joined him had avoided prior long-term service and that his promise of plunder drew men from as far away as North Carolina.⁷⁶ Several hundred slaves were distributed among Sumter's troops during the war, and at the end of the conflict South Carolina still owed more than 570 "Grown Negroes" and 44 "small Negroes" to the men of his brigade. Importantly, the great majority of those who enlisted with Sumter, and with other regiments under similar plans, were poor farmers. The majority of them would never in their entire lifetimes have been able to accumulate the capital necessary to purchase the slaves they were now given.⁷⁷

The greatest transfer of human property during the War of Independence, however, came not through bounties or sales of confiscated estates but through the mutually enforcing relation between plunder and corruption engendered by the rising value of slaves and the disorder into which the fighting degenerated. Indeed, with the British army trapped along the coast by 1782, plundering became the prime object of the war both for many soldiers and for the bands of banditti and privateers who contemporary observers noted were increasing everywhere.⁷⁸ Although details remain hard to come by, and although we will never know exactly how many slaves were taken by whom or from where, it is clear that some of the leading figures in the early republican South enriched themselves this way. Wade Hampton, in one of his few surviving papers, wrote to his brother Richard that he had "recovered" some twenty-seven slaves from the Ball family plantation at Combahee. He also sold public horses for slaves and purchased the promissory notes of soldiers under his command as he rose from a middling trader in 1776 to the wealthiest slaveholder in South Carolina by 1800.⁷⁹ Future Georgia politician James Gunn was accused by multiple parties of similarly selling public horses for slaves and of plundering from rebel sympathizers as well as loyalists, and it is quite clear that Sumter and other officers serving in his legion kept more than their fair allotment of slaves taken from backcountry estates.⁸⁰ Many unscrupulous British officers and soldiers did the same, selling to the Caribbean many of the slaves who had come to them in hopes of obtaining their freedom.⁸¹

Along with engrossment by military officers who advanced themselves through plunder, innumerable private operators sought profit or entrance into the slaveholding ranks through similar behavior. Inhabitants of Amelia County, Virginia, petitioned the legislature for a detachment of militia to prevent further loss of slaves from "small bands . . . who have been making night time raids and seem to be ever increasing."⁸² In 1780, James Wright reported of Georgia that "this Province has been so much Distressed by the Rebellion, by Plundering Party's . . . most of the Inhabitants are dispersed and Gone, and the Number of Negroes Greatly diminished."[83] And in North Carolina residents of multiple counties complained repeatedly of "small parties of banditti . . . who take our Negroes and bring them to the southern province."[84] The situation was so bad by the end of the war that Colonel Thomas Wade of the state's Continental line wrote to General Greene and informed him that "This Country will be Ruined . . . by the Whig and Torys that form small parties under no Orders and plunder the Country."[85] For the most part it appears that these smaller bands operated independently, though often in the guise of serving one side or the other, and it is quite clear that they drew from the same ranks as the men who enlisted in military service under plans similar to Sumter's. Plunder and robbery, therefore, became a primary means of hastening the ascendancy of some and the decline of others in a Revolutionary South in which fortunes were made and lost as if overnight.

Even for those who did not directly participate in plunder, the situation proved ripe for profit. Records are sparse, but it is clear that by the end of the war the forced seizure of human property had become so frequent that numerous individuals acted as middlemen, taking slaves from "banditti" and selling them to those who asked no questions both within and outside the lower colonies. A number of slaves taken from Georgia appear to have been moved through Florida by "Chapts that Call themselves Torys that are Frequently going by with Negroes to Sell to the Spaniards, they tell the Indians anything to get liberty to pass through with their stolen property."[86] Other individuals, such as one John Kains of Virginia, facilitated the movement of stolen slaves and horses from plundered plantations in Virginia and North Carolina down into the backcountry of South Carolina.[87] The profits to be made through stealing human property appear to have been so great that even better known and more respectable men became involved. In a tantalizing set of letters, the merchant and wartime profiteer David Ross informed his business partner John Hook that, due to "our inability to receive sufficient crops" to sell in 1778 and 1779, the best profits to be had would be in a "Negro Adventure," a term that—given Ross's other interests and the state of the Atlantic slave trade—clearly refers to selling slaves taken either by privateers or smaller plundering parties operating within Virginia.[88] Another "Negro adventure" cleared some £2,000 profit for backcountry trader Richard Bennehan in North Carolina.[89] Others used slaves accumulated during the war to purchase prime land before the conflict ended. Pierce Butler of South Carolina acquired his choice plantation on "Robin's Neck," containing "a dwelling house, office, barn, 20 slave cabins, six indigo vats, machine driven pumps, and 197 cleared and fenced acres," from a fleeing loyalist for "20 prime slaves"—a deal he could only strike during the war and only for the reason that slaves could be carried away while a plantation could not.[90]

By the close of the Revolutionary period, hundreds had used the rapid transfer of slaves, land, and prestige to rise and partially displace an older elite ruined by confiscation, death, and debt.[91] At the time he died in 1822, Butler owned over one thousand slaves. David Ross became Virginia's richest citizen by 1790, and Wade Hampton the wealthiest in the entire South by the early 1800s.[92] Wartime profits allowed Bennehan to establish the Cameron family, the most powerful dynasty in antebellum North Carolina,[93] and James Jackson dominated Georgia's politics for decades.[94] For all of their considerable ambition, the leaps that these and other men made would not have been possible before the Revolution and would not be possible again once the chaos of war settled. The strain and savagery of the struggle had opened a brief window, in which land and lives melted into capital that would not again be lost or acquired so easily until the Second American Revolution of 1861. As the price of slaves and land rose over the next two decades, and as the men who had risen through the war came to dominate the region's economic and political landscape, that window closed behind them.

PART IV

Legacies: The Afterlife of the American Revolution

CHAPTER 13

The United States and the Transformation of Transatlantic Migration During the Age of Revolution and Emancipation

AARON SPENCER FOGLEMAN

Few people would disagree with the notion that migration was important to the history of early America or to that of the entire Atlantic world. Yet it has scarcely been studied in a comprehensive way during the age of revolution and emancipation, when dramatic events transformed the Americas and Atlantic relationships altogether. Understanding how transatlantic migrations changed during this era will help us better understand the larger transformations in the United States and the Atlantic world that took place at that time.[1]

The purpose of this chapter is to examine the impact of the American Revolution on migration in an Atlantic perspective and to consider different experiences of female and male migrants in the transitions. How did changes in U.S. immigration patterns resulting from the Revolution fit into larger patterns of transatlantic migration during the age of revolution and the age of emancipation? I argue that the fundamental elements in the transformation of migrations of Africans and Europeans in the United States were similar to those throughout the Americas. That is, unfree migrations (made up overwhelmingly of African slaves, but also of convicts and indentured servants) predominated before colonial independence movements, while during and after the age of revolution and the age of emancipation transatlantic migrations to the Americas of both males and females were overwhelmingly made up of free European migrants. Further, the experience or meaning of "free" migration in the United States and throughout the Atlantic world was different for women than it was for men.

But there were important differences in the U.S. experience. First, the transformation in transatlantic migration of females and males occurred earlier in the United States and was much more direct, clear, and sudden than elsewhere. Second, because of the unusual demographic circumstances in the United States, the impact of the slave trade ban (an important element in the overall transformation of transatlantic migrations) was much different in the United States than in the rest of the Americas. In fact, developments regarding slavery altogether were in many ways unique in the United States. Unlike the rest of the Americas, new immigrants arriving after the Revolutionary era entered a bifurcated republic, with slavery allowed in some areas and considered by many people to be necessary to promote their own liberty and prosperity, while in other areas the Revolution led to its prohibition. Last, the relatively larger presence of families among immigrants to British North America and the United States led to two important differences with the rest of the Americas. It meant, first, that female immigrants in British North America were relatively freer in a legal sense and, second, that the growing number of families led to a long-term feminization in the volume of U.S. migrants throughout this entire period of study that did not happen in the Americas as a whole during this era.

* * *

Like virtually all revolutions, the American Revolution was a chaotic event, filled with contradictory interests and unintended outcomes, yet it caused a great deal of change in American society, for better or worse, and a part of that change was a permanent transformation in the nature of transatlantic immigration into the United States. In order to ascertain the impact of the Revolution on immigration (or anything else, for that matter), it is important to consider not just the effects (or lack thereof) of the lofty ideological declarations by its leaders, but also everything else that was a part of the Revolution, including war, independence, forced removal of populations, disruptions in trade, new governments and constitutions, and the political maneuvers typically associated with such upheaval. The American Revolution, broadly understood to include all of these developments, was the primary factor causing the transformation from mostly unfree to overwhelmingly free transatlantic migrations.

The Revolution was important to the transformation of transatlantic immigration because it brought in new developments that permanently reversed long-developing trends in the colonial era. In the seventeenth century, almost two-thirds of migrants arrived in an unfree legal status, as slaves, convicts, prisoners, or indentured servants. In the eighteenth century, the proportion of unfree migrants rose to nearly three-fourths of the total (see Table 13.1). Although the proportion of the colonial population born across the Atlantic never reached the levels it did in the Caribbean colonies and Brazil, it was by the end of the eighteenth century much higher than in the Spanish mainland colonies. Moreover, to this day the U.S. population born abroad has never reached the level it did during the long generation before independence. This hierarchical, largely unfree immigration contributed significantly to the development of an increasingly hierarchical society in the fifty years before independence. Yet the Revolution quickly transformed immigration, so that by 1810 and especially by 1820, almost all new arrivals in the early republic were legally free. Of course, hierarchy and unfreedom remained in American society, but immigration was no longer one of its major sources, as it had been in the colonial era.[2]

The impact of the Revolution itself on the transatlantic slave trade into the early U.S. republic was complicated, yet Table 13.1 clearly shows that a transformation occurred. Although there were occasional short-term declines, the African slave trade into the British mainland colonies had been increasing throughout the eighteenth century. But the outbreak of war in 1775 abruptly and temporarily ended the trade, and two developments during the Revolutionary era led to its final demise. First, after at least two generations of natural growth in the slave population unlike anywhere else in the Americas, some planters reassessed whether transatlantic importations were even advantageous. Many planters concluded that they could make more money selling surplus slaves from their own plantations than by importing potentially troublesome Africans. Further, by the 1790s many Chesapeake planters saw the potential for selling slaves into the new southwest territories and viewed transatlantic imports as unwanted competition. For these reasons southern state legislatures began abolishing the trade. Winning independence furthered these ends because the 1783 Treaty of Paris secured open access to the southwest territories and because it removed imperial trade restrictions. Second, the elevation of liberty and equality as revolutionary ideals furthered antislavery sentiments in many states that contributed to the movement to abolish the transatlantic slave trade. Thus one state after another banned the Atlantic

Table 13.1. Estimated Immigration into the Thirteen Colonies and the United States by Condition of Servitude, 1607–1819 (to the nearest hundred)

	Unfree by Condition of Servitude								Free		Total	
	Slaves		Convicts & Prisoners		Indentured Servants							
	n	%	n	%	n	%	n	%	n	%	n	%
1607–1699	14,100	8%	2,300	1%	96,600	54%			66,300	37%	179,300	100%
1700–1775	265,800	44%	52,200	9%	111,700	19%			170,100	28%	599,800	100%
1776–1809	102,700	27%	1,000	0%	18,300	5%			253,900	68%	375,900	100%
1810–1819	5,200	4%	0	0%	5,300	4%			134,300	93%	144,800	100%
Total	387,800	30%	55,500	4%	231,900	18%			624,600	48%	1,299,800	100%

Note: Includes political exiles and kidnap victims. Adjustments were made for rounding errors.
Source: Aaron S. Fogleman, "From Slaves, Convicts, and Servants to Free Passengers: The Transformation of Immigration in the Era of the American Revolution," *Journal of American History* 85, no. 1 (June 1998): 44, with adjustments and updates.

slave trade in their territories, and they became the first states to do so in the Atlantic world. The provision in the new constitution of 1787 that prohibited the federal government from banning the trade before 1808 was a delaying action meant to pacify the delegations of Georgia and especially South Carolina, the latter of which by 1806 was the only state that still wanted the trade. Two years later, federal law banished it forever. Never again would Africa and Africans have such a direct impact on early American culture, as the system and those in it who exploited slaves shifted toward other means to continue their efforts. The way this combination of conflicting interests led to this change is a prime example of how contradictory and conflicting interests can cause historical change in revolutionary circumstances.[3]

The Revolution reversed the trend toward convict importations into British North America and the early U.S. republic as well. In the seventeenth century, English authorities transported thousands of Irish and Scot rebels, Covenanters, criminals, and others to the Caribbean colonies, but late in the century they began sending them to the mainland, especially to the Chesapeake colonies. This trend escalated with the passage of the Transportation Act of 1718, after which Britain transported 50,000 felons to the mainland, again primarily to Virginia and Maryland. After U.S. independence, it was no longer possible for British authorities to transport convicts (although they tried), so they founded a new colony in Botany Bay for this purpose, and forced convict immigration into the early republic ended.[4]

The last important form of unfree immigration into British North America and the early republic—indentured servitude—also changed dramatically primarily because of the Revolution. As with the slave and convict trades, the indentured servant trade increased in the decades before independence and then declined rapidly during and immediately after the Revolutionary era. Indentured servitude was critical to the transportation of migrants and the early settlement of the Chesapeake colonies, as it was in the English Caribbean, and it was not unimportant in New England and elsewhere on the mainland. As in the Caribbean, its importance declined in the late seventeenth century, as African slave imports increased. But unlike in the Caribbean, the practice made a comeback in the mainland colonies, now dominated by German and Irish immigrants, and it became increasingly important up to the outbreak of war in 1775, which ended almost all immigration. The practice resumed after the war ended in 1783, but only temporarily and at a lower level. Because of the disruptions of war, independence, new trade arrangements, new perceptions by some Europeans of an independent United States, and perhaps even a new view by some Americans that placing white immigrants in servitude was no longer acceptable, Americans no longer wanted indentured servants, and Europeans no longer wanted to migrate to America as servants. The trade lasted the longest among German-speaking immigrants, who were less affected by the disruptions of independence because they came from outside of the British Empire anyway, but even for them it was over by 1820, just as German immigration altogether began to increase dramatically.[5]

* * *

Table 13.2 shows that the transformation from an unfree to a free migration that took place in the United States also occurred throughout the Americas. Two factors were central to this transformation: (1) the decline of the transatlantic slave trade, and (2) the increase of free European migration, especially to North America.

The decline of the transatlantic slave trade was part of a significant but incomplete assault on slavery in the Atlantic world during the age of revolution.[6] Revolutions in this era touched off an unprecedented wave of emancipations in the Americas that occurred in a variety of ways and for different reasons. Warfare accounted for much of it, as slaves took advantage of the upheavals to free themselves by either running away or joining the armies of white leaders fighting on either side who recruited them for their respective causes.[7] Abolition movements calling for the legal end of the transatlantic trade or slavery altogether were central to these developments. Although not unheard of before this era, they expanded dramatically in the Atlantic world in the age of revolution. Humanitarian and evangelical religious sentiments also contributed toward the abolition movement, the latter especially in Protestant lands on both sides of the Atlantic, but their impact was only beginning before the age of revolution. In fact, rising humanitarian sentiment, evangelical belief, and revolutionary ideology influenced each other and the new abolition movements. This is reflected in how evangelical free blacks like Richard Allen in Philadelphia and Olaudah Equiano appropriated revolutionary ideology and appealed to the humanitarian values of their white audiences to push for abolition. Further, although a revolution never occurred in Britain, its proponents like Thomas Clarkson were crucial in the abolition movement.

A survey of developments in the Americas regarding the transatlantic slave trade and emancipation shows mixed results, but clear patterns. The slave

Table 13.2. European and African Migrations to the Americas by Category of Servitude, 1492–1870 (to the nearest hundred)

	Slaves		Convicts & Prisoners		Indentured Servants		Free		Total	
	n	%	n	%	n	%	n	%	n	%
1492–1699	1,671,600	59%	29,200	1%	281,600	10%	846,300	30%	2,828,700	100%
1700–1775	3,850,700	80%	79,800	2%	137,800	3%	772,300	16%	4,840,600	100%
1776–1830	3,843,400	87%	9,000	0%	23,600	1%	558,100	13%	4,434,100	100%
1831–1870	1,172,200	11%	19,800	0%	122,100	1%	8,995,500	87%	10,309,600	100%

Note: Adjustments were made for rounding errors. Asian immigrants are not included.
Sources: See Appendix: Methodology for Tables 13.2–13.7.

trade declined and ended in the United States, the British Empire, Haiti, the Dutch Caribbean and Guiana, the Danish West Indies (although it made a brief comeback there from 1823 to 1830), and in the former Spanish mainland colonies that gained independence. However, the effective decline of the trade in the Spanish Caribbean (Cuba and Puerto Rico), Brazil, and the rest of the French Caribbean (Martinique, Guadaloupe, and Guiana) did not occur until after 1830, primarily due to British intervention and force. The decline of the slave trade was an important part of a fundamental restructuring of Atlantic systems. As David Eltis has pointed out, the end of the slave trade was connected to the collapse of several imperial systems that had been sustained by that trade. Further, as large as the illegal trade was in the early to mid-nineteenth century, the advent of the steamship and other developments would have made the transatlantic slave trade much larger, had the U.S. Americans, British, and others not ceased to participate.[8] To put it another way, the areas for which the slave trade declined during the age of revolution had imported almost 60 percent of all African slaves taken to the Americas from 1700 to 1775 (2.3 of 3.9 million), yet from 1776 to the final end of the transatlantic trade in 1866 they only produced about 28 percent of the total (1.4 of 5.0 million).[9] Because slavery and the trade flourished economically before 1775, many million more Africans would have been forced into the Middle Passage and New World slavery had the above states not prohibited what had been for them a profitable enterprise. The interests involved in banning the trade were varied and complicated, but these events occurred during the age of revolution and were connected to its outcomes.[10]

Equally important to the transformation from unfree to free transatlantic migrations was the dramatic increase in free European migrations to the Americas. This occurred in two steps. First, unfree European migrations ended by 1830, and, second, after 1830 a dramatic increase in European transatlantic migrants altogether took place, almost all of whom were free upon arrival in the Americas.

In the colonial period, a significant minority of European migrants were indentured servants, especially in North America and the Caribbean. After dominating migration to these regions in the seventeenth century, this form of unfree migration languished in the British and French colonies in the eighteenth century, especially in the Caribbean, where planters began relying primarily on African slave labor. After emancipation, Caribbean planters and Peruvians began importing Asian indentured servants to replace lost slave labor. Peruvians imported Chinese indentured servants beginning in the 1840s, and from the 1840s to the 1870s Cuban planters imported more than 100,000 Chinese indentured servants for the same reason. In the British Caribbean, the move to import indentured servants began immediately after emancipation, and by 1870, nearly 250,000 had arrived, primarily from India, but also from China, Africa, and Madeira, while the French imported about 20,000 African and 41,000 Indian indentured servants into their Caribbean colonies by 1870. These unfree Asian immigrants were the vanguard of an important part of the cultural, economic, and political landscape of Peru and the Caribbean to this day. After emancipation, British Caribbean planters tried to revive the trade in European indentured servants as well, and by 1845 they had imported nearly 5,000, but thereafter the practice ended permanently, although it continued for Asians into the twentieth century.[11]

Another source of legally unfree European immigration in the Americas during the colonial period was that of convicts. The British transported significantly more convicts than other European imperial powers, and Britain's history of transportation was connected to developments regarding the slave trade and U.S. independence. After sending thousands of convicts, rebels, and religious dissenters to their Caribbean colonies in the mid-seventeenth century, English authorities shifted their destinations to the mainland, especially the Chesapeake colonies. As with the end of indentured servant migrations to the Caribbean at the same time, the shift in practice regarding convict transportation was connected to the rise of the slave trade. But the imprisoned population in Britain grew rapidly in the eighteenth century, so authorities transported more than 50,000 felons to the mainland before U.S. independence ended the practice and forced them to look beyond the Atlantic (namely, to Botany Bay). Spanish, Portuguese, and French authorities transported convicts to their American colonies as well, although in much smaller numbers, and independence also ended this practice. On the other hand, the French held on to their colony in Guiana, and from 1852 to 1866 transported 18,000 convicts there, for the same reasons that the British had done in the previous century.[12]

Thus by the time European transatlantic migrations dramatically increased after 1830, they were almost entirely free migrations, and the destinations for the large majority had shifted to the United States and Canada, rather than the Caribbean and Brazil. By the 1850s, Brazil, Uruguay, and Argentina became tertiary European destinations.[13]

If developments associated with the age of revolution had an impact on the increase in European migrations beginning in the 1830s, it was indirect. European economic developments associated with population growth and industrialization fueled much of the emigration in the mid-nineteenth century, and improved transportation made the movement of large numbers of migrants cheaper, safer, and faster. But a long history of successful European migrations since the colonial period and the massive westward expansion and conquest that U.S. independence made possible, along with higher wages in the growing industrial sector of the northeast, were what attracted most European immigrants to the United States in the mid-nineteenth century. Unfree migration remained numerically important for years in the Atlantic world because of the illegal slave trade and the arrival of Asian indentured servants, but the nature of the transatlantic migrations that had so fundamentally shaped Atlantic developments since 1492 had been permanently transformed.[14]

* * *

Although developments in the United States were part of the overall trends in transatlantic migrations, important differences distinguished it from other new republics in the Americas. A comparison of Tables 13.1 and 13.2 shows that, while a transformation from unfree to free transatlantic migrations took place throughout the Atlantic world, it began much earlier in the United States than elsewhere. This happened in part because the American Revolution, which did so much to end unfree immigration into the early republic, took place earlier than elsewhere. Also, the U.S. ban on the transatlantic slave trade was much more effective than bans in the rest of the Americas altogether, where they came for the most part later and were not enforced until even later. In the rest of the Americas, the slave trade ban was only effective early on in the Danish and British West Indies and in Haiti. Other new nations followed the trend as they achieved independence during the age of revolution, but often with interruptions and second thoughts. The permanent decline in the slave trade after 1830 resulted from growing British enforcement of the bans in Brazil and Cuba, the latter of which had no revolution until late in the century.

As we know, slavery ended altogether in conjunction with revolution and independence movements in a number of places in the Americas, but in other areas only the slave trade ended, and in still other areas there was virtually no movement toward emancipation. In what Ira Berlin calls "societies with slaves," like the U.S. North and the Spanish mainland colonies, significant emancipations took place, either immediately or gradually and often in conjunction with warfare. That is, men who joined armies during the wars of independence were manumitted. Their numbers were so significant in the Spanish mainland republics that they contributed toward general emancipation. However, in "slave societies" like the U.S. South, the Caribbean, and Brazil, slave systems remained secure, unless the revolution itself was forced by slaves and extended by them to neighboring colonies, as was the case with Haiti and Santo Domingo.[15]

U.S. developments regarding the end of the transatlantic slave trade were unique in how they related to the course of revolution, emancipation, and slavery altogether. By the beginning of the age of revolution, the natural growth rate of the U.S. slave population was so well established that planters no longer depended on the transatlantic trade to sustain their labor force. While planters in other slave societies in the Americas struggled to secure labor after enforcement of the trade ban took effect, and some even reverted back to the use of indentured servants, U.S. planters did not have to.

As the result of its revolution, U.S. interests and actions regarding slavery ultimately bifurcated. The northern half of the new country pursued a course of slow and painful, yet important and permanent, emancipation, while slavery flourished in the southern half, after relatively brief disruptions and questioning during the Revolutionary era. A similar bifurcation occurred in Spanish America altogether, but not within any of the new independent republics. Independence, revolution, and war ended slavery in Mexico, Colombia, Venezuela, and other societies with slaves, while the slave society in Cuba did not even revolt until much later. None of the Dutch, Danish, or French white Creoles in colonial slave societies pushed for independence in this era either, because their grievances (if any) were mild compared to the threat of a slave revolt, if they acted upon them. The Haitian revolt came from below in what had been a slave society, with no bifurcation resulting. In Brazil white Creoles found a way to achieve independence without war. Thus slavery was preserved and there was no bifurcation in the Brazilian economic, social, and political systems, as occurred in the United States.

* * *

While much has been written about the experiences of women in revolution and emancipation during this era, few historians have paid close attention to gender differences in transatlantic migrations. Jennifer Morgan has recently pointed out that much of what historians have written about the transatlantic

Table 13.3. Estimated Transatlantic European and African Migrations by Gender and Category of Servitude, 1492–1870 (in thousands)

	Slaves		Convicts & Prisoners		Indentured Servants		Free		Total	
	male	female	male	female	male	female	male	female	male	female
1492–1699	972	700	22	7	216	66	651	195	1,861	968
1700–1775	2,483	1,368	54	26	105	33	533	240	3,175	1,665
1776–1830	2,499	1,344	6	3	15	9	356	202	2,876	1,558
1831–1870	832	340	19	0	110	12	5,437	3,558	6,399	3,911
Total	6,786	3,752	102	35	445	120	6,977	4,196	14,311	8,102

Sources: See Appendix: Methodology for Tables 13.2–13.7.

Table 13.4. Percentage of Transatlantic Male and Female European and African Migrations by Category of Servitude, 1492–1870

	Slaves		Convicts & Prisoners		Indentured Servants		Free		Total	
	male	female	male	female	male	female	male	female	male	female
1492–1699	58%	42%	77%	23%	77%	23%	77%	23%	66%	34%
1700–1775	64%	36%	68%	32%	76%	24%	69%	31%	66%	34%
1776–1830	65%	35%	70%	30%	62%	38%	64%	36%	65%	35%
1831–1870	71%	29%	98%	2%	90%	10%	60%	40%	62%	38%
Total	64%	36%	74%	26%	79%	21%	62%	38%	64%	36%

Sources: Calculated from Table 13.3.

slave trade conflates the migrations of men, women, and children into the adult male experience, and this could also be said regarding the history of voluntary European migrations.[16]

To better understand possible similarities and differences in the experiences of female and male transatlantic migrants to the United States with those who went to the rest of the Americas, a quantitative overview is helpful. Tables 13.3–5 also show that, as was the case for males, the transformation from unfree to free migrations for females was the most dramatic after 1830. Nearly four million females arrived in the Americas from 1831 to 1870, over 90 percent of whom were legally free. The tables also show how the gender proportions of European and African migrations changed through various periods of Atlantic history. The tables are a work in progress, but they are complete enough

Table 13.5. Percentage Distribution of Male and Female Transatlantic European and African Migrations by Category of Servitude, 1492–1870

	Slaves		Convicts & Prisoners		Indentured Servants		Free		Total	
	male	female	male	female	male	female	male	female	male	female
1492–1699	52%	72%	1%	1%	12%	7%	35%	20%	100%	100%
1700–1775	78%	82%	2%	2%	3%	2%	17%	14%	100%	100%
1776–1830	87%	86%	0%	0%	1%	1%	12%	13%	100%	100%
1831–1870	13%	9%	0%	0%	2%	0%	85%	91%	100%	100%
Total	47%	46%	1%	0%	3%	1%	49%	52%	100%	100%

Sources: Calculated from Table 13.3. Adjustments were made for rounding errors.

to show important trends regarding the similarities and differences between male and female migrations from all major categories of servitude.

Table 13.4 shows that the overall gender composition of transatlantic migrations remained remarkably stable from 1492 to 1870 (about two-thirds male); however, Tables 13.4 and 13.5 show important differences in gender composition within categories of servitude. Over time, forced slave migrations became increasingly male, while free migrations became increasingly female (see Table 13.4). The greatest deviation in male-female trends occurred before 1700, when females were much more unfree than males (see Table 13.5). Only 20 percent of females arriving before 1700 were free and that figure declined to 14 percent during the peak period of the Atlantic system and still further to 13 percent during the age of revolution. Males also became significantly less free due to the rising slave trade, so the gender distinction in that respect vanished. In the formative period, females made up a significantly higher proportion among the African slave migrations than in all other categories (42 percent), after which a long, slow decline in the proportion of slaves who were female continued until the end of slave trade (see Table 13.4). Apparently, European men building the system found a greater need for bringing in unfree females (including convicts and servants) than migrating with free women in order to build their projects. Since many of the free females who did immigrate were children and a few were single women or widows, relatively few Atlantic migrants arrived in the Americas as free married couples before the age of revolution.[17]

The importance of gender in migration goes beyond the above comparisons because women and men who shared the same legal category experienced migration differently. The very meaning of "free" and "unfree" was different for men and women. For example, a gender bias influenced the motives of "free" European migrants for leaving their homelands. Men often emigrated to get land or higher wages or to pursue opportunity and "freedom" in other ways. "Free" women often emigrated because their husbands or fathers (or in some cases their religious or other community) desired it. Sometimes such women did not even want to go, but they had to. Although wives and mothers informed the decision, it was overwhelmingly men who decided whether the family should emigrate from Europe to America.

Even when couples migrated as part of a religious mission, a gender bias was often present. For example, a Swiss man named Jean-François Reynier joined a Moravian religious community near Frankfurt am Main to seek spiritual truth and fulfillment, and a woman named Maria Barbara Knoll left her Lutheran home to live in the same community for similar reasons, but also because she wanted to live with Moravians, who provided an attractive community life for women. Soon community leaders bound Reynier and Knoll in marriage, although they hardly knew each other, if at all, and sent them to Suriname as missionaries. Initially neither wanted to go, but religious officials chose Reynier to lead the mission because he was a pious, well-traveled, and talented doctor, and he soon accepted his role with vigor. They chose Knoll because Reynier needed a wife to do his job better and because they needed more women to work in the mission. Knoll had left her Lutheran home because she wanted to live in a Moravian community in another German territory, yet she found herself in America because the Moravians needed a missionary wife there. Not all "free" women were forced by the patriarchal bonds of matrimony to emigrate to America. Some wives were eager to go, and some unmarried women sought escape or opportunity, perhaps to flee an abusive family situation or local disgrace after the birth of an illegitimate child or to remarry or elope. But reluctant migrations in fulfillment of obedience prescribed by the marriage bond were a factor that many women and virtually no men experienced.[18]

There was no distinction among African men and women regarding the decision to emigrate, because neither wanted to go and both moved from one form of unfreedom to another, but their experiences differed by gender in other important ways. In contrast to African slavery, New World slavery was largely defined by reproduction, production, and race, which affected women differently than men. The threat of rape and other violence, as well as of familial disruption, was extreme in America. This too affected women differently and was hardly like what women typically experienced as slaves in Atlantic Africa.[19]

In fact, the meaning of the shift from legally unfree to free migrations was different for women than it was for men in ways that still need to be explored. Before the age of revolution, fewer female than male migrants were free, and even those who were free were reluctant or unwilling migrants, as explained above. After 1775, and especially after 1830, however, the percentage of females who were free was higher than the percentage of free males (see Table 13.5). The European women who arrived legally free, instead of as convicts or indentured servants, were surely in some ways better off, but the restrictions on their freedom noted above need further exploration before we can fully understand the monumental shift in the legal status of female transatlantic migrants in this era.

This leads to the question of what impact migration had on patriarchy for both European and African female migrants. It seems likely that most European women who migrated in family groups, as wives or otherwise, had little chance to alter the patriarchal controls associated with matrimony, but this view needs to be tested by examining women's voices in immigrant diaries, letters, and memoirs. For example, when Maria Barbara Knoll migrated to Suriname and then North America as a free married woman with her husband, she experienced the threat of rape and was manipulated in many ways by both her husband and other male religious leaders, but she also fought back and achieved opportunities in colonial society unavailable at home. Her life was a struggle that reveals a lot about colonial life. Knoll died in Georgia nearly forty years after leaving her family and community in the German territories, and in many ways she must have felt a great deal of satisfaction and accomplishment in her life.[20]

The position of single European women who migrated was different. Many of them emigrated to escape oppressive patriarchal controls, believing that anything could be better than what they experienced at home and hoping that long-distance migration would be a liberating experience. (In fact, women still leave home for this reason.) Also, some women signed on as indentured servants in the hopes of marrying above their station in the colonies. Sometimes women in both situations succeeded, but the risks were high. Indentured servants could and did become planters' wives in the Chesapeake colonies during the seventeenth century, but in Maryland, authorities developed and enforced a legal code that was harsh on women who did so. Elizabeth Ashbridge, originally from England, emigrated alone as an indentured servant from Ireland to New York in 1732 and was badly abused by both her ship captain and her master. Her nightmare continued after her servitude when she married a man who abused her physically and psychologically. Her situation did not improve until that husband died and she grew older and wiser. Then she returned to Ireland, where she married a better man. Historians normally stress male interests in the colonies when addressing the reasons for the male surplus in free and indentured migrations, but from the female perspective it could also mean that European women saw the downside more than the upside in transatlantic migration and did not want to go or that patriarchal restrictions prevented them from leaving even if they wanted to.[21]

The question of how transatlantic migration, including its shifting gender composition, affected patriarchy for African women is much different, because they were forced to go and because African patriarchal slave systems were much different from what European women experienced or what slave women in America experienced. The shift in the gender composition of the migrations was much less significant than the shift from unfree to free migrations, which suggests that the mass movement of peoples had little impact on patriarchy, but obviously important differences took place in the lives of women taken from Africa to America. The starting point for understanding those differences should be to more fully consider the nature of the patriarchy (or matriarchy) that shaped the lives of slave and free women in Africa. After they were taken to America, colonial conditions (including European views of race, employment in field work, and the importance of reproduction to maintaining the system in some areas) changed the nature of the patriarchy under which women lived. Transatlantic migration was a crucial factor in building and sustaining the new system in the Americas, and for African women it hardly included the possibility (however remote) of escaping such controls that was the hope of some European women.

European and African immigrant women in colonial British North America and the United States experienced the above conditions, as female migrants did in the rest of the Americas, but there were two important differences. First, Table 13.6 shows how the volume of females arriving differed. In the formative period, "U.S." (that is, British and Dutch North American) slaves were less female than those arriving in the rest of the Americas, but over time that difference diminished. Slaves imported into British North America became increasingly female and those imported into the rest of the Americas less so. This development likely reflects increasing integration of the United States into the Atlantic system. Also, Table 13.6 shows that through all periods of this study (until 1870), the percentage of females arriving in the United States increased, whereas it remained stable elsewhere in the Americas. The continued and increasing presence of families among U.S.

Table 13.6. Estimated Percentage Female of Transatlantic European and African Migrations by Category of Servitude into the United States and the Rest of the Americas, 1492–1870

	Slaves		Convicts & Prisoners		Indentured Servants		Free		Total	
	U.S. %	Other %	U.S. %	Other %	U.S. %	Other %	U.S. %	Other %	U.S. %	Other %
1492–1699	28	42	4	25	25	23	24	23	24	35
1700–1775	29	36	33	30	38	7	38	29	31	35
1776–1830	34	35	33	30	38	0	35	42	35	35
1831–1870	0	29	0	2	0	10	40	38	40	33
Total	28	36	32	22	28	17	39	32	39	35

Note: "U.S." refers to Dutch and British North America without Canada in the colonial era. "Other" refers to the rest of the Americas.
Sources: See Appendix: Methodology for Tables 13.2–13.7.

immigrants, which contrasted significantly with the overwhelmingly male character of free migrations into the Spanish colonies and Brazil, explains most of this difference. It also suggests that if there was any feminization in the volume of transatlantic migration before 1870 (or masculinization, for that matter), it occurred in specific regions like the United States and not in the Americas as a whole. Second, Table 13.7 shows that the rapid shift from legally unfree to free migrations among females occurred in the United States earlier than elsewhere in the Americas, which was also the case for male migrants. Table 13.7 also shows that while only a minority of U.S. female immigrants before 1776 were free (with all of the limitations to that concept for women), those who did arrive in this area were significantly freer than those arriving in the rest of the Americas.

In spite of these differences, perhaps the most important thing that Tables 13.6 and 13.7 show is that legal servitude of one sort or another characterized the status of most women upon arrival in the British North American colonies and United States, as it did for men. This was even more the case in the rest of the Americas, where it also took longer for this situation to change because of the persistence of the illegal slave trade and because the large free European immigrations of males and females began later. How women experienced these differences and their many limitations merits further exploration.

* * *

Table 13.7. Estimated Percentage of Female Transatlantic European and African Migrants by Category of Servitude into the United States and the Rest of the Americas, 1492–1870

	Slaves		Convicts & Prisoners		Indentured Servants		Free		Total	
	U.S.	Other	U.S.	Other	U.S.	Other	U.S.	Other	U.S.	Other
1492–1699	9%	75%	0%	1%	54%	5%	37%	19%	100%	100%
1700–1775	40%	87%	9%	1%	16%	0%	34%	12%	100%	100%
1776–1830	18%	97%	0%	0%	4%	0%	78%	3%	100%	100%
1831–1870	0%	33%	0%	0%	0%	1%	100%	65%	100%	100%
Total	4%	76%	1%	0%	2%	1%	94%	22%	100%	100%

Note: "U.S." refers to Dutch and British North America without Canada in the colonial era. "Other" refers to the rest of the Americas. Adjustments were made for rounding errors.

Sources: See Appendix: Methodology for Tables 13.2–13.7.

U.S. developments were an important part of the transformation in transatlantic migration that occurred throughout the Atlantic world, but unique demographic and political circumstances in the bifurcated early U.S. republic created a different path toward full emancipation. As David Brion Davis notes, racial slavery was central to the phenomenon of "America" as a place where liberty, opportunity, and upward mobility rested on slavery (not to mention Indian removal, which allowed westward expansion and further opportunity for some). Slavery was not an accident or an unfortunate shortcoming but rather the "dark underside of the American dream." Industrial growth, westward expansion, and democratic air (such as it was) attracted so many European migrants to the United States that they fundamentally changed the terms of all transatlantic migrations after 1830, but within a generation those migrants found themselves embroiled in a civil war that forced a resolution to the problem of slavery that the American Revolution had created in a bifurcated republic.[22]

Thus the tables and questions presented in this chapter provide the framework of a complicated story involving the United States and the rest of the Atlantic world, not a simple one. Big changes in Atlantic migration patterns, including place of origin, status, and gender, were signs of an ongoing, contrapuntal set of cultural and social changes that began during the age of revolution, of which the United States and its revolution were an important beginning. So this age must be treated as a single, long-going upheaval, lasting from the 1760s to the 1860s, whose history needs a single, organic, dramatic portrayal.

Appendix: Methodology for Tables 13.2–13.7

The construction of comprehensive tables depicting African and European migrations by gender and legal category of servitude is a large project, fraught with uncertainty and incompleteness in many areas, and it remains a work in progress. A detailed appendix with precise calculations, explanations, and documentation for the estimates in Tables 13.2–7 is beyond the scope allowable in this volume. Instead, I will explain the methodology employed below.

For estimates of forced African slave migrations, I have relied on the splendid work by the compilers of the Transatlantic Slave Trade Database available at www.slavevoyages.org, especially in the "Estimates" section. My interest is primarily in the Americas, so the data on slaves reflects disembarkations in those areas. To produce the slave gender data, I used information on gender from the database proper and applied it to the totals from the "Estimates" section using weighted averages.

Creating comprehensive estimates for free and forced European migrations to the Americas is more difficult. The best starting point is the work of David Eltis, also a key figure in the slave trade database project.[23] To make his estimates more comprehensive geographically and especially by gender, I have used the best informed estimates of specialists in the following regions: for 1492–1775, Spanish America, Brazil, French America (Canada, Louisiana, and the Caribbean), Dutch America (North America in the seventeenth century and the Caribbean), and British America (Caribbean and mainland); for 1776–1870, the United States, Canada, Brazil and other countries as they became independent, and the remaining European colonies (primarily in the Caribbean). Some of the work upon which my estimates are based is quite detailed and sound, whereas other work is impressionistic at best. In some cases, virtually no information was available, which led me to interpolate using data from neighboring geographical and chronological areas. This is hardly satisfactory, but the numbers and percentages are so small in these cases that they would not greatly affect the overall outcome, even if significant error is involved. The information provided in Tables 13.2–7 provides a more comprehensive accounting of transatlantic migration by time, place, legal status, and gender than heretofore available and with that a crucial element of what made the Atlantic world over the course of four centuries.

CHAPTER 14

First Partition

The Troubled Origins of the Mason-Dixon Line

EDWARD G. GRAY

International borders are funny things. They exist as barriers and demarcations on the land. But we only hear about them when they don't work—when they fail to keep good things in and bad things out. The U.S.-Canada border rarely makes the national news; the U.S.-Mexico border is a different story, mostly because of its failures to keep migrants and drugs out of the United States and to keep illegal weapons out of Mexico. As governments have struggled, with seeming futility, to address these failures, the line separating the United States and Mexico has changed from an abstraction into a multidimensional thing. Initially nothing more than an imagined line running down the middle of the Rio Grande and across the Sonoran Desert, it has become a fence and then a wall and now a high-security zone, with portable watchtowers, and overhead drones. All of this change, of course, is a reflection of the fundamental struggles modern states face in making borders serve their imagined purposes.[1]

Revolutionary America was a largely border-free place. There were no carefully policed and well-established borders anywhere in North America. Much like Europe at the time, the American continent was generally a place of vaguely defined jurisdictions, frontiers, and marchlands. A traveler (not constrained by subservient status as servant, apprentice, felon, slave, or Native American, the latter nominally confined to vague territorial bounds by various deeds and treaties) could move freely through the countryside, back and forth across the territorial claims of different European powers, oblivious to the geography of empire. In times of war, identity papers were often necessary, but these rarely contained declarations of citizenship or national allegiance. They were akin to letters of introduction—documents endorsed by government officials or other persons of note testifying to the good character and benevolent intent of the traveler—and they were usually needed for passing through combat zones rather than across any static international border.[2]

In Europe, the experience would have been much the same until one approached a city. Remnants of the age of siege warfare, medieval walls, and gates persisted into the eighteenth and early nineteenth centuries. A traveler approaching a city could thus expect to confront city gates and sentries demanding justification for entry. This urban security apparatus was about as close as the premodern world came to something like a modern international boarder. As Lewis Mumford observed more than four decades ago, "far more than a mere opening," the city gate "offered the first greeting to the trader, the pilgrim, or the common wayfarer; it was at once a customs house, a passport office and immigration control point, and a triumphal arch, its turrets and towers often vying . . . with those of the cathedral or town hall." In an overwhelmingly rural eighteenth-century North America, Boston had its gate and New York had its wall (of Wall Street fame), but otherwise there was very little of this kind of regulatory architecture. The sovereign limits of empires, cities, and states were rarely discernible.[3]

An absence of well-defined international borders did not mean a complete absence of political boundaries. These did exist, but they were not boundaries between distinct sovereign states. Instead, they marked the jurisdictional and territorial limits of much less well understood kinds of geopolitical entities that began their lives as English colonies and came to exist as members of a confederation of states known as the United States. Among these boundaries, one in particular acquired historical resonance its creators could scarcely have imagined. It is the boundary that separated the colonies—later states—of Maryland, Pennsylvania, and Delaware, and it still bears the name of the two British astronomers, Charles Mason and Jeremiah Dixon, who worked from 1763 to 1767 to establish its definitive location.

More than a century in the making by the time Americans declared their independence from Britain, this boundary bore little resemblance to any modern territorial limit. Much like other arbitrary divisions among Britain's American provinces—those separating Virginia from North Carolina and Pennsylvania from New York, for instance—it existed primarily as a marker of trade and tax jurisdictions.[4] In the colonial era, it had no real international significance. The territories it bounded were essentially private tracts, subject to the superior—if uncertain—legal authority of the British Crown. In the half-century after the Revolution, this state of affairs would change dramatically.

* * *

Nestled in the pastoral suburbs and gently rolling mid-Atlantic farmlands of one of the country's most prosperous regions, the Mason-Dixon Line and its innocuous stone markers hardly suggest a border of any particular significance, let alone a border as contested and fraught as the world's most contested international borders. As one passes north along I-95, from Maryland into Delaware, or south from York, along I-83 toward Baltimore, there is barely a sense of boundary crossing at all. Signs bearing the laconic welcome of state governors, perhaps a rest stop with a few extra displays of tourist brochures, or a state-line liquor and cigarette store—this is about all there is to mark one's transit across the line.

And yet, through the feverish middle decades of the nineteenth century, the territory adjoining the Mason-Dixon Line, much like the borderlands between sovereign nations at odds, became a zone of tension and conflict and a source of many of the very same kinds of anxieties and failed, futile policies that the U.S.-Mexico border has produced in our own day.

The locus of those failed nineteenth-century policies—slavery—is familiar to us. And as the many accounts of the Underground Railroad make clear, the Mason-Dixon Line was central to the experience of slavery and freedom in nineteenth-century America. It was a boundary many Americans, black and white, understood to lie between two worlds—on the one side, a place of servitude, of slavery, of grinding poverty and economic futility; on the other, opportunity, freedom, kin, and hope.

Much as is the case with the U.S.-Mexico border, so the struggles to police the Mason-Dixon Line produced alarming crises and unrest, often greeted with crude vigilantism and stopgap policy shifts.

Surely the most contentious such shift was brought by the Fugitive Slave Act of 1850, a law that ended states' abilities to prohibit the recapture or "kidnapping" of self-manumitted former slaves. In its efforts to extend the Constitution's fugitive slave clause, the act placed the control of slavery in the hands of the federal government, effectively making slavery a national institution.

Now that self-manumitted African Americans could expect to find freedom nowhere in the continental United States, some came to see the new law as in fact an assault on the line itself. As Frederick Douglass wrote, by an act of Congress, "Mason and Dixon's line has been obliterated; New York has become as Virginia; and the power to hold, hunt, and sell men, women, and children as slaves, remains no longer a mere state institution, but is now an institution of the whole United States."[5]

In fact, however, Douglass's assessment was not entirely accurate. Far from obliterating the Mason-Dixon Line, the Fugitive Slave Act secured its status as a quasi-international border. Much as has happened in other such border regions when distant federal authorities have attempted to assert control, after 1850 the regions adjoining the Mason-Dixon Line witnessed a surge of vigilantism and border violence.

On September 11, 1851, Maryland planter Edward Gorsuch and a group of slave catchers crossed into Pennsylvania near the small border town of Christiana. They had come to exercise their constitutionally guaranteed property rights. They would retrieve a group of runaway slaves and carry them back across the line and back to a life of slavery. But Gorsuch and his party were met by a large group of locals, outraged that one of their own—William Parker, an African American farmworker and self-manumitted slave—had been targeted for harboring fugitives. In the ensuing melee, Gorsuch was killed and another member of his party seriously injured.

The so-called Christiana Riots resulted in the arrest of some 141 rioters, 39 of whom were charged with treason against the United States. Although the government's case fell apart, the crisis at Christiana was indicative of a new and violent chapter in the history of the Mason-Dixon Line. However much federal authorities—or at least the pro-slavery legislators who backed the Fugitive Slave Act—may have hoped to erase the figurative Mason-Dixon Line, their actions merely accelerated trends long since under way. For decades, the Maryland-Pennsylvania borderlands, particularly at their eastern extremities, had been a locus of fear and violence; and despite old constitutional provisions for the regulation of interstate commerce and fugitive slaves, the federal government had done virtually nothing to address the problem. With the states left to legislate the issue of slavery for themselves, the nation's oldest and longest border between a slave state and a free state became a locus of conflict not long after Pennsylvania's legislature passed a law for the gradual abolition of slavery in 1780.[6]

As an increasing number of slaves sought freedom north in Pennsylvania, state authorities struggled to manage the growing problem, but to no real effect. In 1826, the Maryland State Assembly commissioned a "deputation" to visit the New Jersey, Delaware, and Pennsylvania state capitals. The delegation's charge was to extract legislation mandating the return of runaway slaves. Although Delaware pushed through a law obliging state officials to punish anyone aiding fugitive slaves, the New Jersey legislature was not in session and Pennsylvania's politicians sent the deputation home with only a watered-down version of what it hoped for. This kind of interstate diplomacy was indicative of the uncertain nature of the boundary line Mason and Dixon had drawn near the end of the colonial era: Was it governed by the rules of nations—that is, did it mark the limits of autonomous and sovereign entities, existing in a community of other such entities? Or was it largely symbolic, superseded by the overriding authority of the federal government? Slavery had very clearly pushed this pressing constitutional question toward the former principle, and by the 1830s it had turned the Pennsylvania-Maryland borderlands into a zone of surveillance much like what we now associate with modern borders between nation-states.[7]

Recalling his own 1838 flight from slavery in Baltimore to freedom in New York City, Frederick Douglass wrote, "I left my chains, and succeeded in reaching New York without the slightest interruption of any kind. How I did so,—what means I adopted,—in what direction I travelled, and by what mode of conveyance,—I must leave unexplained." To do otherwise would have put those who helped Douglass at risk. With no real certainty about where the law stood or about whose authority governed the border, and with ever-deepening division of opinion over slavery, the Underground Railroad "conductors" who helped Douglass had come to inhabit a kind of constitution-free zone, where the laws of the land and the laws of the states came together in a confused abyss.[8]

For those animated by the outrage of slavery, the consequences of this constitutional vacuum could be devastating. The Quaker abolitionist and Underground Railroad stationmaster Thomas Garrett of Wilmington, Delaware, was responsible for leading hundreds of enslaved Americans across the Mason-Dixon Line. But in 1848, a federal court presided over by Supreme Court Justice Roger B. Taney ruled against Garrett and ordered him to pay thousands to compensate Maryland slave owners. Garrett, who had been a prosperous merchant, was nearly bankrupted by the ruling. He nonetheless persisted, and in 1860 the Maryland General Assembly debated a resolution to offer a reward for his arrest.⁹

*   *   *

To summarize, then, between the Revolutionary War and the passage of the second Fugitive Slave Act in 1850, the Mason-Dixon Line emerged as the closest thing to a modern international border anywhere in North America. For contemporaries, it should be said, such an assertion would have had little meaning. The international landscape, insofar as it has come to be marked by distinct territorial demarcations, had changed very little since the time of the Revolution. Travelers still experienced little to prompt a sense of border crossing when traveling across the border between the United States and Mexico or British Canada. To speak of the borders between sovereign states as materially different from those between member states of the American federal republic would thus have meant little. The two categories of political demarcation were comparable in their general innocuousness. This is not to say that lands adjoining the Canadian or Mexican boundaries were peaceful or undisputed. Rather, it is to suggest that the level of state involvement in securing and defining these borders was nowhere near as intense as that centering on the Mason-Dixon Line.

To contemporaries, the point would only have been understood through the prism of slavery, for it was slavery and its constitutional manifestations that ultimately accounted for the strange line through the middle of America. In a lecture on the history of the Mason-Dixon Line, delivered to the Historical Society of Pennsylvania in 1854, John H. B. Latrobe attempted to capture the full redolence of the boundary between North and South. "There is, perhaps, no line, real or imagined, on the surface of the earth," he observed, "whose name has been oftener in men's mouths during the last fifty years." Mention of the Mason-Dixon Line "was always expressive of the fact that the States of the Union were divided into slaveholding and non-slaveholding—into Northern and Southern; and that those, who lived on opposite sides of the line of separation, were antagonistic in opinion upon an all-engrossing question, whose solution . . . had been supposed to threaten the integrity of the Republic." Whether the world's most admired democratic republic would survive came down to the question of whether or not it could alter what the Mason-Dixon Line had become: a borderland in its heartland. For the boundary's geographic meaning had been lost to its political significance, and "men cared little, when they referred to it, where it ran or what was its history—or whether it was limited to Pennsylvania, or extended, as has, perhaps, most generally been supposed, from the Atlantic to the Pacific." Now "it suggested the idea of negro slavery; and that, alone, was enough to give it importance and notoriety."[10]

Latrobe's assessment echoes through the historical record to the present day. Insofar as the Mason-Dixon Line figures in the story of America, it figures as a footnote to the story of the American union's nineteenth-century collapse. This is, perhaps, as it should be. The United States really only became a single, unified nation-state after the Civil War—some would say long after. So the odd incongruity: the work of two eighteenth-century British astronomers, originally known best for their observations of the transit of Venus across the sun, has become a symbol of slavery's impact on the United States.

What follows is an attempt to move beyond Latrobe and his many inheritors by lifting the Mason-Dixon Line from its mid-nineteenth-century context, and instead examining it through a lens of longer focal length, one that reaches back into the colonial era. Although the Mason-Dixon Line achieved its functional apex in the middle of the nineteenth century, the line and the problems it betrayed speak to a much deeper set of historical problems. Those problems center on the process of constitution making in the British Empire and the United States. Few chestnuts have been more resilient than the one that holds the Civil War to be the American Revolution's greatest constitutional failure. In their inability to deal with the problem of slavery, so the story goes, the founders prepared the way for the colossal constitutional failure that culminated in civil war. Insofar as something like the Mason-Dixon Line has any significance, it is symbolic: the line is primarily a metaphor for the constitutional compromises that preserved slavery.

The not-too-terribly-bold conceit of this chapter is that that chestnut rests on its own bit of received wisdom: namely, that the American Constitution—and, in turn, its failure—can be understood as an invention of the American Revolution. What I would like to do in what follows is simply ask whether or not a different view of the constituting mechanism of the American polity casts something as prosaic as a political boundary in a different light? If looked at through a constitutional process that far predated the creation of the American republic—and the Mason-Dixon Line was very much the result of such a long constitutional process—does the story of Mason and Dixon's line change?

Before going any further, it is perhaps worthwhile to be more precise about the nature of such a constitutional process. For decades, scholars have recognized a kind of constitutionalism essential to any understanding of the origins of the new United States. That constitutionalism is much less deliberate, much less immediate, and much less revolutionary than that traditionally associated with America and its written constitutions. Edmund Burke, the chief eighteenth-century theorist of this form of constitutionalism, understood it as inseparable from the political nation itself. It could be the result of no convention or constituent assembly, no electoral process or willed revision. It was indistinguishable from all that was the nation, and like the nation it was the product of history's lengthy accretions, played out in the small civilities and common associations, the mutual loves and animosities, the shared morality and collective code of being through which a people comes to define itself as a nation. "Because a nation is not an idea only of local extent, and individual momentary aggregation," Burke explained in a 1782 speech in the House of Commons, "it is a Constitution made by what is ten thousand times better than choice, it is made by the peculiar circumstances, occasions, tempers, dispositions, and moral, civil, and social habitudes of the people, which disclose themselves only in a long space of time."[11]

Understood in this light, whatever it is that *constitutes* the United States did not emerge phoenix-like from the pen of James Madison or from Independence Hall, Philadelphia, in 1787. It emerged over decades, centuries even, and it was the product of no single revolutionary reform but rather of the lengthy struggle to constitute European-style political communities on the North American continent.

The Mason-Dixon Line is best understood as an expression of this kind of constitutionalism. It began life as a constitutional problem—a dispute over the content of colonial charters. For the better part of a century, it persisted as a constitutional problem, as courts in England struggled with the competing territorial claims of proprietary entities. During the Revolutionary War, the line had little real significance. The states of Pennsylvania, Maryland, and Delaware were generally unified in their postures with respect to independence; proprietary claims had given way to the mutual ambiguities of republican sovereignty; state jurisdiction over fiscal matters was weakened and diluted by the opacity surrounding state authority to tax and control trade; much like their colonial predecessors, the states had neither the capacity nor the inclination to control the movement of free citizens; and the political order was at least as consumed with international relations at it was with intranational ones. But in the decades after the Revolution, the line reemerged as a constitutional problem, driven by the familiar problem of national sectionalism and the less familiar one of intrastate sectionalism.

Through much of this lengthy and tangled constitutional history lay an additional problem: there was simply no efficient and widely accepted method for establishing unnatural boundaries. The science of surveying remained inaccurate and deeply contentious. By the time the imperial crisis began, the astronomers Mason and Dixon had deployed science on behalf of a boundary the proprietors of Maryland and Pennsylvania could accept. But the resolution was temporary. Astronomy could not solve a problem that had festered for generations.

* * *

The history of the line began in the tumult of the English seventeenth century. Struggling against its powerful Catholic foes in Europe, wracked by religious division and civil war at home, England could barely assert its authority over its growing American claims. Its people had settled the Chesapeake colonies of Virginia and Maryland, and by the middle of the seventeenth century, as the mother country was embroiled in civil war, the Chesapeake settlements had discovered what would be their lifeblood, that smoky weed tobacco. Founded as a Catholic refuge, but primarily home to ordinary Protestants seeking to profit from the newly discovered lucre of England's Chesapeake colonies, the colony of Maryland flourished amid neglect. Its grasping population found itself growing to the east, along the intricate byways of the Chesapeake Bay. This expansion eventually carried Marylanders to the Delaware River's western shore.

As so often happened, all this colonizing quickly became intrusion. A sprawling Maryland soon found its subjects occupying lands claimed by other empire builders, in this case the minions of the governor of New Netherland, Peter Stuyvesant. Some years earlier, Stuyvesant's agents had themselves absorbed Peter Minuit's feeble Christina Colony, established on behalf of King Gustavus Adolphus of Sweden, Minuit and his colonists having taken their outpost from the local Lenni Lenape peoples.[12]

Before the collision of Maryland and New Netherland sparked an international crisis, England annexed New Netherland and England's king, Charles II, gave control of the former Dutch colony to his younger brother, James, Duke of York. Dutch efforts to reclaim the colony and the duke's disastrous tenure as King James II brought little stability to the region. Part of the problem was that the duke and his brother, much like their father, Charles I (who had granted the colony of Maryland to his loyal secretary of state, the Catholic convert George Calvert), saw in America convenient spoils.

And spoils these Stuart royals needed. Their country emerged from the middle of the seventeenth century a tottering shell of its future self. Through some clever mercantile policy, military good fortune, crafty diplomacy, and the astute management of its navy by the great Samuel Pepys, the restored monarchy persisted. But threats from within and without were ever present, and, as Charles and James looked with fear and envy upon the thriving empire of the young French king Louis XIV, the need to reward the loyal only grew. If those rewards could also serve the dictates of empire, so much the better.[13]

To this end, while still Duke of York, the future James II parceled out portions of the extensive American territories he now controlled. The colony of New Jersey, which would lie between the Delaware River and the Atlantic Ocean, would be divided between two of the duke's loyal friends, Sir George Carteret and Lord Berkeley of Stratton. Sixteen years later, seeking to repay a £16,000 family debt, King Charles II would grant the territory on the western side of the Delaware to the Quaker imperialist William Penn. And here the story of the line begins. Or really, here the story of the problem that made the line begins.

* * *

According to the patent granting Penn his colony, it would lie on the western shore of the Delaware River, between the fortieth and forty-third parallels of latitude. By design, the colony's southern boundary was to match Maryland's northern boundary, established by its 1632 charter as that "which lieth under the Fortieth Degree of North Latitude." This all seemed perfectly reasonable but for one very substantial complication. As understood by the Lords of Trade, the king's agents responsible for the Pennsylvania charter, the fortieth parallel cut through existing settlements near the small village of New Castle—formerly Dutch New Amstel, and before that, the Dutch Fort Casimir.[14]

Initially, neither the Lords of Trade nor the Duke of York were prepared to give Penn control of these settlements. It was one thing to declare foreign colonists subjects of the king of England, altogether another to give them over to the dominion of a tertiary Quaker empire builder. To accommodate this strange circumstance, the Lords of Trade ordered Pennsylvania's southern boundary to be fashioned from "a Circle drawne at twelve miles distance from New Castle Northward and Westward unto the beginning of the fortieth degree of Northern Latitude." In other words, as it headed east along the fortieth parallel, toward New Castle, Pennsylvania's southern border would turn north and then east again, leaving New Castle within the Duke of York's possessions.[15]

The problem with this provision was that it rested on the inaccuracy of another: namely, that the fortieth parallel was where the Lords of Trade presumed it to be. In fact, far from arriving somewhere in the neighborhood of New Castle, the southern boundary of Pennsylvania—as articulated in the colony's founding patent—lay twenty-five miles north of the town's center. A circle of twelve miles radius—leaving aside the question of precisely where the center of such a circle should lie—would thus never intersect the fortieth parallel. What, then, was the Crown's intention? Did it mean to place the southern boundary of Pennsylvania at the fortieth degree of latitude, or did it intend for it to lie at the latitude of New Castle?

The problem was not just that this ambiguity raised questions about the southern extent of Penn's grant; it also created questions about the northern limits of the Maryland grant. If the Lords of Trade intended for the boundary to lie at the latitude of New Castle, then Maryland's current proprietor, the third Lord Baltimore, no longer had legitimate claim to territory lying within the original bounds of his colony insofar as those bounds lay below the fortieth degree of latitude. If they presumed that the true boundary between the colonies lay at the fortieth parallel, then the Duke of York—who had long controlled the settlements in and around New Castle—had effectively annexed territory from the colony of Maryland, which his father had granted George Calvert, the first Lord Baltimore.

Clearly the Lords of Trade had no particular interest in questioning the legality of the Duke of York's American possessions, and this was just fine with William Penn. For him, the inconsistency of his colony's charter was a boon: reading it in the most favorable way possible added hundreds of square miles of territory to Pennsylvania. From the beginning, the fortieth parallel would be nothing more than a clerical error for Penn. His colony's southern boundary would lie somewhere near the latitude of New Castle. In fact, Penn's interest was less spatial than it was strategic. The viability of his experiment in Quaker empire building, he well knew, would depend on whether or not his inland colony had access to the sea. And as long as the lower Delaware River and its mouth lay in a shadowy geopolitical borderland, his colony's commercial welfare would be uncertain.

When Lord Baltimore challenged Penn's interpretation before the Lords of Trade, he encountered a brick wall of favoritism. Reverting to a combination of natural law, standing imperial practice, and realpolitik, the Lords of Trade noted that the first Lord Baltimore's initial grant included only lands inhabited by non-Christians. Since New Castle and adjoining areas along the Delaware River and the western shore of the northern Delaware Bay had been settled by Swedes, Finns, and Dutch, they were thus excluded. The Lords of Trade conveniently ignored the fact that most of these settlements had been established after the founding of the Maryland colony.

For Penn, the interpretation of the Lords of Trade had less to do with whether or not Europeans lived in the contested lands than with the fact that the Calverts never countered the colonial advance of New Netherland. In essence, foreign powers had annexed the region, and the Lords Baltimore made no reasonable counterclaim. It was a convenient position since, in effect, it secured the strategic Delaware Valley for the Duke of York. Once England took control of New Netherland, all Dutch claims—including those falling within the dominion of the Lords Baltimore—reverted to royal control. As Penn explained to one of Baltimore's agents, the principle was the same as that which governed pirate booty: "if a Shipp be taken by Piratts and kept 24 hours by them and retaken by a man of war shee shall be prize to the King and the owner looses his right to her."[16] What the king's forces take, in essence, the king rightfully owns.

In a fashion necessitated by the distance of royal courts, Penn and Baltimore initially attempted intercolonial diplomacy as a means of sorting out their border dispute. But the various meetings between their mutual agents achieved little. Penn, it turned out, had no intention of ceding his southern claims back to Baltimore. The problem, he told Baltimore, lay not with him but with the Lords of Trade. It was they who saw the advantage of access to the Delaware or Chesapeake Bays, and it was they who insisted that his colony be located accordingly. In a crafty bit of subterfuge, Penn explained to Baltimore that in his initial petition to the king, he had asked to have his colony's northern border situated five degrees north of its eventual location, thereby encompassing all of what would be upstate New York. He did this "not out of a covetous humour but only that I might reach the lake of Canada for the conveniency of an inlett to my province." In other words, Penn had initially planned a northern port for his colony, but the Lords of Trade rejected this proposal—a logical path, given the dangers of French entanglement. Alas, for his colony to be viable, Penn was left no choice but to look south for water access. The argument very conveniently reinforced the Duke of York's clams to the area as well. So valuable and strategic a water route could not be left vulnerable to the designs of foreign powers.[17]

Perhaps this was why, when Penn petitioned to acquire James's claims around New Castle, the Lords of Trade looked favorably upon him. Here was a colony builder who would in fact do the empire's bidding and secure its territory against foreign intrusion. In August of 1682, just as he was leaving England for the first time to lay claim to his American colony, Penn was thus given control of New Castle and most of the rest of what would become the Delaware colony. The grant left very little doubt about where the Crown stood with respect to Pennsylvania's southern boundary.

Once again, Baltimore protested loudly. It was one thing to accede to the claims of the king's brother; but now those claims had been granted to an expansionist neighbor. In effect, not only had Penn begun to annex the northern border of Maryland but now he had also threatened the colony's eastern shore—the peninsula between the Chesapeake and Delaware Bays. But once again, the geopolitical ignorance of England's imperial authorities played into Penn's hands. Since the full extent of New Netherland had been vague, the boundaries of the Duke of York's claims were also unclear. Beyond control of the lands adjoining New Castle and the eastern shore of the Delaware River, there was thus little territorial clarity at all about Penn's latest conquest. According to the logic of the Lords of Trade—namely, that territory not directly protected from Dutch claims effectively reverted to Crown control—much of the Delmarva Peninsula could potentially be claimed by Penn. Under this frightful scenario, Baltimore would lose his increasingly lucrative Eastern Shore.

In May of 1683, Baltimore and Penn met at New Castle to address their territorial differences. Among the solutions Penn proposed was for Baltimore to sell him the "Susquehanna River for an Inlett and Land Enough on Each Side the said River Sufficient of his Occasions."[18] In exchange, Penn would allow the fortieth parallel to stand as Maryland's northern boundary. Fearing that such a cession would simply give Penn rights to lands below the fortieth parallel under the provision that they were "Land Enough," Baltimore saw nothing to be gained and rejected the offer.

With his family's holdings steadily consumed by Penn's colonial ambition, Baltimore found himself with few options. He would have to return to England and make his case directly to the Lords of Trade. In May of 1684, he commissioned his four-year-old son, Benedict Leonard, governor of Maryland and left for the mother country. But resolution was slow in coming. For Baltimore, the delay turned out to be yet another disaster. By the time the Lords of Trade concluded their deliberations in 1685, Charles II had died and his brother James had become king of England. Now the throne was occupied by a well-known friend and ally of William Penn. Rather than rule on the legitimacy of Lord Baltimore's claims, the Lords of Trade thus simply divided the Delaware Peninsula, granting Penn control of the eastern half while leaving the remaining western portion to Maryland. Baltimore protested and would continue to do so for the rest of his life, but to no avail. Meanwhile, the problem of Pennsylvania's southern boundary festered.[19]

Penn never had any interest in the original fortieth parallel, which actually ran north of his new colonial capital at Philadelphia and which would have left his colony with no substantial deepwater port. Whether by design or by accident, his posture was made possible by the deficiencies of his colony's charter. Its contradictory provisions for a southern boundary allowed him to exploit constitutional ambiguity on behalf of territorial ambition.

Baltimore and his descendants continued to challenge Penn's southern border claims, but as British commercial interests grew more entwined with the growing Pennsylvania colony and its Philadelphia merchants, the government showed little sympathy. By the middle of the eighteenth century there was no doubt that the southern boundary of Pennsylvania would remain somewhere near where William Penn had established it decades earlier.

* * *

Until the Seven Years' War, the border issue languished in a legal morass. The fourth and fifth Lords Baltimore continued to fight for their territory, and the Penns continued to hold strong. Had circumstances in the disputed lands themselves been different, perhaps resolution would have come more quickly. With such ambiguity about who owned what, generations of colonists had grown accustomed to fending off government intrusions—taxation, militia musters, legal proceedings, and so on—by hiding behind jurisdictional ambiguity. After a time, local authorities simply abandoned the region, effectively leaving it to govern itself—perhaps one of the reasons for the area's future prosperity. Salutary neglect, it seems, was not just the province of Parliament and the Crown.

The most striking expression of this neglect involved taxes—particularly the quitrents colonial proprietors were entitled to collect from settlers. As part of testimony for a case surrounding the border brought before the Chancery Court in 1735, one deponent noted that thirty years earlier, many of the residents of Newcastle County, in what is now northern Delaware, began refusing to pay their quitrents. And they "have not, since, paid any, to any Person whatsoever, because the People were told of the different claims of the Crown, the Lord Baltimore and the Penns, and were at a loss to know their Landlord." Another deponent from Kent County in Delaware recalled that quitrents in the county were paid to the Pennsylvania proprietors until 1705, "but knows of no Quit-Rents that have been lately paid." The reason, he explained, "was because the Right to the [Delaware] counties was contested." After decades of neglect, the prospect of imposing borders and reimposing quitrents dwindled. With the people of the borderlands conditioned to minimal taxation, there was little turning back, authorities fearing that doing so would only bring "riot." A border controversy, having given way to neglect, had now become salutary. Those residing in the Pennsylvania-Maryland borderlands had come to enjoy decades of freedom from the impositions of their landlords.[20]

But of course neglect—especially of a salutary type—is rarely sustainable. As Pennsylvania expanded into the Susquehanna Valley, colonists came into conflict with the Native peoples of the area. Since the Quaker-dominated Pennsylvania government had no particular interest in military solutions to these conflicts, a culture of vigilantism emerged. Local posses—the most famous of which came to be known as the Paxton Boys—took matters into their own hands. For authorities in Maryland this was also quite a headache, as the ensuing violence had about as much respect for political boundaries as there was clarity about the nature of those boundaries in the first place. Settlers across the western reaches of the mid-Atlantic were drawn into the violence, with little regard for their putative colony of residence. As migrants continued to move into western Maryland and Pennsylvania, the question of what colonial government was responsible for whose security only grew more urgent. A series of colonial attempts to solve the problem through diplomacy and legal wrangling achieved little.[21]

With the Maryland-Pennsylvania border now the locus of unceasing ethnic violence, few continued to regard government neglect of the region as in any way salutary. But in typical fashion, the political will to achieve a solution was nowhere to be found.

Ultimately, it took war on a global scale to bring some resolution to the Maryland-Pennsylvania boundary controversy. The burden of paying for the French and Indian War, which had been particularly devastating in western Pennsylvania, would make it essential to know who lived in which province. The problem was particularly urgent for the Penn family. With its quitrent income long-since diminished, and Crown authorities demanding direct monetary contributions to the defense of its vast holdings, the family found itself facing possible financial dissolution. The problem was made all the more severe by the fact that Pennsylvania's colonial assembly, in the face of fierce objections from proprietor Thomas Penn, had passed a bill allowing it to tax Penn family lands. While the bill was not entirely successful, it did mean that the colony would now be able to tax proprietary lands. In effect, tenants would now be able to impose taxes on their lords, something utterly incompatible with the quasi-feudal principles that had informed the original terms of settlement. The Penns could no longer afford to ignore lost quitrents on their southern property. The revenue would be essential as the family struggled with the dual burdens of taxation and soaring security costs.

For the Calverts of Maryland, the situation was much less dire. Their colony spent relatively little on the war effort; its per capita wartime taxation rate was less than a third that of Pennsylvania. There was thus little legislative pressure to expand the taxation of proprietary interests. For the first time since William Penn laid claim to his American possessions, it appeared, the Calverts would have some leverage over the Penns, the latter now urgently in need of a settlement to their ancient boundary dispute. Of course, after nearly a century, there was little hope that Maryland's original northern boundary would be restored. But there was hope that the colonies would, once and for all, assert themselves in the jurisdictional marchlands adjoining the current boundary.[22]

* * *

In 1761, Thomas Penn sued Frederick Calvert, the sixth Lord Baltimore, claiming that the latter had failed to adhere to earlier agreements about the location of their shared border. The court found in favor of Penn and ordered the two proprietors to adhere to a final boundary, somewhere near the one William Penn had established almost a century earlier. To this end, Penn and Calvert turned to the astronomers Mason and Dixon for a definitive and properly located boundary. The line Mason and Dixon established, using stone monuments imported from England, would lie approximately fifteen miles south of Philadelphia and would include an anomalous circle around New Castle, Delaware.

Upon completing their heroic survey, four years after arriving in Philadelphia, Mason and Dixon put an end to the century-old colonial border conflict. But this was only a matter of semantics. Soon those colonies would be states and the conflict would be revived, in a new and very different guise. Indeed, even as Mason and Dixon finished their work, there were signs of trouble to come.

The tiny village of Baltimore, little more than a clutch of shacks before the Seven Years' War, had begun to boom after the war. Much of this growth was owing to the astonishing agricultural productivity of the Pennsylvania heartland. Bedford, Cumberland, and York counties were flourishing, their German and Scotch-Irish populations establishing some of the most productive grain- and flour-producing regions in the world. The problem with all this prosperity was that these western farmers did what any colonial farmer did: they sought the quickest and easiest path to market. And for them, that path happened to be along the Susquehanna River, south to the Chesapeake Bay and the town of Baltimore. The alternative, to carry their produce to the much more vigorous commercial center of Philadelphia, required a costly and often very dangerous crossing of the Susquehanna River. One of Pennsylvania's riverine barriers, in other words, propelled the commercial growth of Maryland's new commercial capital. By 1810, Baltimore had become the third most populous city in the United States.

The commercial expansion of Baltimore alarmed Pennsylvania authorities. As trade moved south, Philadelphia's merchants would inevitably suffer. But a perhaps more troubling problem was political. The Baltimore trade rivalry fed long-standing sectionalism within the colony—now state—of Pennsylvania. The fear was that as western Pennsylvanians, long alienated by a balance of political power that overwhelmingly favored eastern interests, tied their economic fortunes to Baltimore in Maryland, they would begin to shift their political allegiance as well. As the famed pamphleteer Thomas Paine complained to a friend in 1786, Pennsylvania's western provinces "are not affected by matters which operate within the old settled parts of the state." For "they are not only beyond the reach and circle of that commercial intercourse which takes place between all the counties on [the eastern side of] the Susquehanna and Philadelphia, but they are entirely within the circle of commerce belonging to another state, that of Baltimore."[23]

As colonies gave way to states, the most pressing problem for the new Commonwealth of Pennsylvania, then, was whether or not it would be able to create a political community contiguous with its old colonial borders. With so many of its citizens tied by commerce to Baltimore, there seemed a very real danger of political disintegration. Whatever it was that Mason and Dixon's work had designated, the commercial limits of Maryland were not established by a precisely surveyed boundary but by the Susquehanna River. In a kind of sweet revenge for the long-aggrieved Lords Baltimore, a greater Maryland had emerged, pushing its way northward, into the heart of Pennsylvania. Echoes of this colonial economic reality can be heard in the present day, as Pennsylvanians and political pundits contemplate the oddity that is "Pennsyltucky," the conservative voting bloc that lies in the farmlands between Pittsburgh and Philadelphia.

The incongruity between economic reality and geopolitical ideal persisted well into the nineteenth century. But as slavery expanded, and as Maryland's slaveholding planters found the value of their human property growing, the dynamics of this borderland began to change. From a place generally indifferent to the issue of slavery, it became one increasingly divided by it. Maryland planters, who dominated their state's politics, if not its territory, sought to protect their property. Farmers in south-central Pennsylvania sought access to cheap and ready farm labor in the form of African American freed people. The resulting divide produced the failed diplomatic maneuverings of the 1820s. But in the end, it did very little to defeat the social and economic realities of the mid-Atlantic region. Central Pennsylvania would continue to do business in Baltimore, at least until the railroads arrived in the 1840s. As a political boundary, the Mason and Dixon Line had eased the jurisdictional problems the states' colonial predecessors had struggled with—and this, of course, exacerbated political problems as westerners continued to chafe under the political dominance of an eastern establishment (a problem that led to the half-hearted measure of moving the state's capital west, first to Lancaster and then Harrisburg, both of which are east of the Susquehanna). It also left in its wake a host of constitutional issues, slavery being only one. Another was the simple reality of large republics: how does one create a political community where there is no economic community? To James Madison and other Federalists, the answer was to create a new federal government. Such an entity would, once and for all, make the tangled boundaries and barriers between colonies the stuff of a deep and buried past. The Mason-Dixon Line, vestige of imperial Britain, would vanish beneath the heavy hand of federal authority. But this never happened, and when the federal government did attempt to intervene in the 1850s, precisely the opposite occurred: the Mason-Dixon Line came to look as much like an international border as it ever would. The colonial vestige and its vexed constitutional legacy persisted, until the American union finally collapsed.

So it was that another antebellum historian wrote that the Mason-Dixon Line was an anomaly. It bounded colonies that no longer existed and it did so according to no "object, or obstacle of nature. For at neither end does it terminate, or in any part of its extended course does it touch, upon any prominent natural landmark. It is wholly, in every part, and in all its forms, an artificial, arbitrary line." And yet, this anachronism remained, "more unalterable than if nature had made it: for it limits the sovereignty of . . . States, each of whom is as tenacious of its peculiar systems of law as of its soil. It is the boundary of empire."[24]

Perhaps the persistence of the line had less to do with anachronism than the opposite. Perhaps it was precisely in its modernity that the Mason-Dixon Line came to exist so awkwardly on the land. With no natural geographic basis—far from establishing the line, the mountains and rivers that shaped human intercourse in the region defied the line—the Mason-Dixon Line is much like the most modern international boundaries of all: a partition imposed by distant powers not so much to define empire as to secure its end.

CHAPTER 15

The Power to Be Reborn

DAVID S. SHIELDS

Power. How does the American Revolution express power? What was potent about the American Revolution? How did these potencies give rise to enduring political, social, and cultural potentials? These are not new questions.

When a people seeking independence express a desire to assume a station among the powers of the earth, the question how they fulfill that ambition, how they exhibit their potency and potentialities, is a germane inquiry. Many historians have taken up these queries, conceiving power in myriad ways. In *A Struggle for Power*,[1] Theodore Draper articulated the neo-Whig interpretation, arguing that the Revolution responded to British attempts to assert control over an America that had achieved de facto independence during the colonial era. When Americans sought to retain control over their affairs, the British government deployed military force to seize power unambiguously. Power for Draper was control of the apparatus and powers of government. In *Among the Powers of the Earth*, Eliga Gould took a more circumspect view, indicating that the Revolution was a means to achieve recognition and inclusion in that community of nations and empires that had devised an international diplomatic and legal warrant for their exploitation and colonization of the world.[2] Americans' ability to conduct war under a centralized command and their effort to conform their administration to something mirroring European models of centralized governance were means to achieving a station among the powers of the earth.

The title of this volume—*The American Revolution Reborn*—suggested to me that Draper's and Gould's scholarship conceived power with a lower case *p*, a power constrained to its time and space exclusively. It is a power whose moment was the Revolutionary era. Something that is truly powerful should alter the works and lives of persons not immediately involved in the time, the place, and the circumstance of the American Revolution. True power manifests an ability to overcome the momentary character of a momentous event. It is, literally, the power to be reborn—to spread, engender, metastasize, recur.

Before I explore the consequences of this contention, let me make clear other modes of power at work in the American Revolution that were momentous but local and temporary. Having worked for a period at a military college, I was perhaps too well acquainted with the old way of speaking of power in connection with the American Revolution: firepower, the potency of unified command, and credit power—that thing William Pitt had exploited so masterfully, bankrupting and defeating France in the Seven Years' War by expanding the theater of operations to five continents, by buying vessels and underwriting troops on debt. None of these modes of power proved decisive in the American struggle.

When we look at texts from the era, "power" is a term that seems both conspicuous in presence and mutative in character. It was employed in surprisingly various ways. While it was used eight times in the Declaration of Independence to speak of the sovereign enactments of governments, its use twenty-four times in *Common Sense* ran across a range of applications from the psychological thirst of despots for dominion to the uncontrollable force of historical happenstance to entities that possess the means to act for or against the American people to government itself. Now that we are revivifying the Revolution, what modality of power at work then galvanizes attention now? Besides the force of arms, or assertion of sovereignty, or the clash of two corporate wills to power?

Let me suggest again that it was, as the title of this volume announces, the power to be reborn, to animate subsequent revolutions in other places. One of the things that interested me about this scholarly initiative was its choice of title. It didn't opt for the twenty-first century "The American Revolution Rebooted," with its sense of a mediated representational makeover. And it didn't invoke the Marxist framing of the replicative capacity of revolutions either. The title was not "The Revolution Exported." With Fidel Castro in his dotage and the retirement of the academic generation of the 1960s and 1970s, when Cuba's export of Marxist-Leninist revolution to South America excited the hopes and fears of pundits and scholars,[3] the linguistic figuration of trade in "exportable" speaks to a passé conviction that economy grounds ideology grounds political happenstance. Instead, the title went biological and reincarnational. Biology now trumps information technology and economy in its figuration of transmission over time of features in bodies politic.

Thomas Paine first articulated the power of the American Revolution to renovate nations elsewhere in *The Rights of Man*.[4] He insisted on the distinctness of that revolution from other revolutions (particularly the Glorious Revolution), citing its principled character and its universal applicability to the circumstances of other cultures in other places. Interestingly, his presentation of the universality of revolutionary principles was articulated specifically as a critical rejoinder to the arguments of Edmund Burke that rights and liberties were inherited in a national lineage. As Burke put it, "You will observe, that from the Magna Carta to the Declaration of Right, it has been the uniform policy of our constitution to claim and assert our liberties, as an entailed inheritance derived to us from our forefathers, and to be transmitted to our posterity; as an estate specially belong to the people of this kingdom without any reference whatever to any other more general or prior right."[5] What rankled Paine was the exclusivity of the heritage that Burke envisioned. Like a noble title or an ancestral estate, the forefathers' legacy was restricted and not a benefit to the world at large. In Burke's view liberty is not "reborn"; it is simply inherited. There is no sense of an atavistic reemergence—of an overthrow of death or quiescence—to reanimate a power that once was alive. In contrast, "revolution" alludes to this return of dispossessed or dead rights and liberties. What interests me is how biological metaphors permit a view in which republican ideals disseminate broadly, instead of exclusively, to reanimate communities.

A recourse to biological metaphor naturalizes political developments, making them seem outcomes of an order beyond human will. Depending on whether one views nature as a materialization of divine intention or an expression of physical laws, biological processes place political developments over and above the conscious efforts of human beings to work out their needs and interests. Political orders and disorders are informed by providence or determined by biology. Paine would have none of this, being a stalwart social contractarian. Yet then as now there is a power to biological symbolism, particularly that connected to reproduction.

In the rhetorical contests of contemporary American culture wars, a reborn American Revolution vies with the multitude of Tea Party websites hymning a divinely sanctioned "rebirth of liberty"' in a land "stupefied by dependency on government and media."[6] Announcing the Revolution's rebirth also defies those in academe who view the Revolution as a matter devoid of vitality. And doing so recalls an earlier discourse that, contra Paine, visualized the power of the American Revolution inhering in its genetic potentiality, its ability to generate political renaissance. In August of 1791, ruminating on affairs in France, the *Argus* exulted that "Liberty, that Goddess, which is destined to render happy our world, was born yesterday; She now lies smiling in her cradle."[7] In June of 1810, hailing the revolution in Colombia, the *Public Advertiser* intoned, "What an interesting spectacle does southern Colombia present, at this moment. Just risen from her chains and with her infant freedom in her arms, she hastens to announce affectionately its birth, and to claim of her dear North American sister—friendship and protection, in favour of her offspring—so dear to her and to the human race."[8]

I come from a part of the country where the biological atavism resonated strongly. Thomas Dixon named his novel *Birth of a Nation* in the same spirit that laureate Henry Timrod named his natal song for the Confederacy "Ethnogenesis." The pains of war were figured as the pangs of birth occasioned by what the Sons of Confederate Veterans still call "The Second American Revolution." Birth, blood, heritage, race, and chattel slavery's *partus sequitur ventrem*. Biology haunts what some people in my region have styled "The American Revolution Reborn."

Violence to the body and blood attend the American Revolution and its reanimations. And for that reason I do not regard the idea of the American Revolution reborn as a spiritual metaphor, harking back to being born again. Spiritual rebirth makes the flesh (the *sarx*) impertinent, since it will be renovated as the body (the *soma*), a spiritualized, immortal, post-material being. The blood that enables it has already been shed on the cross and needs not be shed again. In 2014 Thomas Fleming published *A Disease in the Public Mind*, posing the question of why the United States "is the only country in the world that fought such a horrific war to end slavery."[9] His answer was that decades of press vilification of the sections by William Lloyd Garrison and the "fire-eaters" made persons engaged in a mutual hatred answerable only in violence. Yet there is a way that the American Revolution indicated that, for independence, God ordained a cost. As Timrod said in "Ethnogenesis," the chosen people "must pass a redder sea" before securing the promised land.[10]

The Civil War was only one of a number of reborn American revolutions, and I don't want to fix on it particularly, perhaps because of my discomfort at attaching an event rather inimical to the republican animus of the American

Revolution to that patrimony. Revolutions have their genetics, and their atavistic offspring may reproduce various aspects of the original. Indeed the replication of features is the signature of their potency. The replications can be of several sorts: of ideology, of institutions of political reorganization (think of how the Glorious Revolution's extra-legislative committees of correspondence were taken up by latter revolutionists), of rhetorics of incitement, and of strategies of resistance.

Perhaps, indeed, a detection of patterns might enable prediction of features of future revolutions. Biology speaks of the heritability of features into the future. Patterns are not restricted simply to past events, but have the potential to appear in future events. One wonders whether the present embrace of the biological metaphor of rebirth might also have a "justification of the humanities" dimension to it, fundamentally renovating the ancient "past is prologue" insight that long ago calcified to cliché. Surely some graduate student this very moment is demonstrating their digital humanities skills by applying an IBM SPSS Modeler to discover patterns in historical data whose periodicity tends into the future. The more this effort seems like the gene analytics of genetic scientists, the more one can promise a knowledge that shapes what happens next. Genetic knowledge that links traits to alleles, and alleles to genes, permits the insertions of genetic material that inform the cultivars of the future. And whatever one's trepidations, moral or theological, about GMO agriculture, one cannot deny the effectuality of the genetic analytics involved and their practical consequences. Once history boasted a power of prediction. Now, other disciplines have seized that task. The more historians represent the cycles of events through times as generations, the easier to defend the proposition that knowing what came before will enable us to know much about what comes after.

Enough musing about historical genetics in general. Which of the risings in the late eighteenth and early nineteenth century should we examine for the telltale birthmark that reveals an authentic heir? Perhaps we should bracket off the Spanish American revolutions because there are dimensions to all of them that are distinctly occasioned by the Napoleonic decapitation of the Hispanic empire and the Spanish Catholic heritage. We might consider the West Florida revolution, the Texas revolutions, the War of 1812, the successful William Walker filibuster and revolution in Nicaragua.[11] But the ones that are most interesting to me are the ones least studied and least remembered: the unsuccessful revolutions in Upper and Lower Canada and the American filibuster in their support in 1837–38. As Michel Ducharme has argued, these republican rebellions looked to the American Revolution for its rhetoric, its plan of action, and its resort to violence.[12]

What interests me about this reborn American revolution was its role in making the issues of violence, slavery, and the rhetoric of liberty matters of debate in the United States. It occasioned a reconsideration of the founding crisis. It would provoke the final repudiation of revolutionary violence by the Garrisonian wing of the abolitionist movement and split the abolitionists into pacifist and political action wings. It made the abolitionists determine conclusively that liberation as an ideal had to be wrested from the tradition of military adventuring in the name of liberty that had characterized American expansion and South American independence from the 1780s onward, if it were to be attached effectively to the project of emancipation of African and African American slaves. Finally, it would prompt the most concerted attempt to demystify the American Revolution in American history.

When the British army quashed the 1837 rebellions in Upper and Lower Canada, a host of liberty-loving U.S. citizens along the northern border determined to join the remnants of the revolutionary cadre and seize Canada. When an American citizen was killed on December 29, 1837, in a Canadian militia raid against a rebel supply ship moored in U.S. waters, public opinion surged strongly in favor of the rebel cause and the various initiatives by filibusters to cross the border and wage a war on behalf of republican liberty.[13] The most vocal dissenting voice to the calls for a liberty crusade sounded in the pages of William Lloyd Garrison's abolitionist periodical, the *Liberator*. From the inception of the rebellion to the publication of the foremost of the patriot memoirs, *The Remarkable Adventures of Captain Heustis*, a decade later, writers in the *Liberator* consistently denounced the rebellion as a groundless exercise and the American filibusters as partisans of a false form of liberty. Furthermore they condemned the neo-1776 rhetoric of republican rebellion as a mask for a spirit of violence and national pride.

Let us hear the *Liberator* speak its final assessment of the Canadian episode in the review (anonymous, but written by Garrison) of the 1847 Heustis autobiography:

> The narrator . . . appears to have been animated by the strong sympathy for the oppressed peoples of Canada, and he volunteered to help them throw off their colonial yoke. We have not fault to find with his abhorrence of tyranny, nor with his desire to see it hurled in the dust; but with his retaliatory, fighting spirit, we have

no fellowship. Men of blood cannot be the true and trusty lovers of their race. Their regard for men is local, their hatred of oppression geographical, their love of liberty partial. . . . Often while they are contending for unrestricted liberty for themselves, they are oppressing others in the most brutal manner. It was so in the revolutionary war—"the times that tried men's souls," and proved them to be utterly deficient on the score of principle and consistency.[14]

Garrison goes on at length about the inappropriateness of applying American Revolutionary language to the Canadian struggles because the language is ubiquitous in the writings of the Canadian rebels. As Ducharme has indicated, the revolutionists in both Upper and Lower Canada drew their rhetoric directly from the patriots of 1776. The French Patriotes of Lower Canada and the Reform partisans of North Canada found themselves arrayed in 1837 against precisely those appointed imperial officials who were the latter-day offspring of the imperial world that emerged after 1763 to rule an extensive empire including Catholics and non-British elements. Officials from the Earl of Dalhousie to Lord Gosford found themselves at odds with local French-dominated legislatures and resorted increasingly to arms to inhibit growing restiveness. In Upper Canada the oligarchs of the Tory establishment controlled land distribution and patronage and opposed the reform initiatives of the legislatures.

The reiteration of the causes and phrases of 1776 directed at the old foe, Great Britain, excited sympathy in many patriotic Americans willing to believe that Canada at last was throwing off Toryism. The abolitionist vanguard, however, attacked the appearance of homology between the Canadian and the American Revolution: "We regard the Canadian rebellion as the movement of the most unprincipled and bloodthirsty banditti. To compare these frenzied and mad outbreaks with the calm and principled resistance of the Revolutionary fathers, would be to insult the true spirit of liberty by identifying it with the foulest revolt,—and even our Revolution ought to have been effected, as it might have been, without blood."[15] The hyperbole here was provoked by the use of violence to effect political ends. The Christian perfectionist pacificism characteristic of New England abolitionism in the early 1830s has extended to a critique of any sort of revolution wrought by arms.[16] The American Revolution itself suffered from a taint. "Their principles led them to wage war against their oppressors, and to spill human blood like water, in order to be free; Ours forbid the doing of evil that good may come."[17]

Garrison's unmuscular Christianity seemed a kind of impotency to many of his fellow Americans, even to persons in the abolitionist movement.

While the imperative to be Christlike warranted the abhorrence of war,[18] the *Liberator* also engaged in scaremongering, insisting that any violence in Canada would trigger catastrophic expansion. In abolitionist apocalyptic the probability of a war with Britain was only the first of a train of disasters leading inevitably to the implosion of the United States. Highlights of this apocalyptic include: "An alliance offensive and defensive between Great Britain and Mexico. . . . An expedition fitted out in the West Indies with an army of Free Blacks, to sympathize and take part with the two Millions of Slaves in the Southern States. . . . The Indians in the West, removed from their native soil by force, raising the tomahawk and scalping knife, and carrying fires and slaughter to the Western States on a frontier of a thousand miles . . . and finally the dissolution of the Union!"[19] The extravagance of this kind of paranoid prophecy had some influence in casting into doubt the sensibleness of abolitionist pacifism. When a troop of runaway African Americas in Upper Canada petitioned Sir Francis Head to form a force allied to the British army to quell the patriot rebellion, abolitionist sentiment split, with the *Liberator* deploring the resort to arms, while other antislavery periodicals applauded it. To frighten the proponents of war, Garrison reprinted a screed from the *Montreal Herald* calling for a Canadian invasion of the United States, with volunteer African Americans in the vanguard of the army demonstrating their appreciation of the "liberty they enjoy under the British flag" and evincing the "hatred they cherish against America."[20]

Part of the problem with the Canadian rebellion for abolitionists arose from a not-too-hidden reverence for Britain and its liberties, particularly after the 1833 abolition of slavery. "Is it true that Canada, monarchical Canada, is a refuge from the cruel and bloody despotism which is cherished in the bosom of our republic? It is true, and Americans should hang their heads in shame that it is so."[21] In August of 1837 the *Liberator* reprinted a report by an abolitionist minister, Henry Wilson, on "Colored People in Canada," painting a northern utopia in which the genius of persons of color blossomed when permitted to order their own lives: "They are a noble-minded, industrious, thriving people, unoffending in their demeanor, and more temperate in their habits than their white neighbors. . . . As a people, they are distinguished for their hospitality, mutual sympathy, and quenchless love of liberty."[22] In this picture, liberty permits the natural virtues of a race to find expression.

It was precisely this liberty that abolitionists believed in peril if the Canadian rebellion succeeded, for some simulacrum of the American Constitution (with its certification of chattel slavery) might be instituted. Should a filibuster invasion succeed in causing an annexation of Canadian territory to the United States, then the fugitives would find themselves again subject to the tainted American Constitution and the coercive power of the constitutional stipulation that fugitive slaves be returned to their owners in their home states. This prospect had particular moment in the thinking of the *Liberator* because the formation of the Republic of Texas in 1836 had brought the specter of annexation of a vast slave territory to the forefront of national consciousness.

After the admission of Arkansas as a slave state in 1836, the loss of New England's political power in Congress seemed imminent. The likelihood of the huge Texas territory being superadded as a slave region to U.S. territory promised perpetual political impotency for the North and, for abolitionists, the concretization of the slave system as a permanent feature of the American republic. The abolitionist papers viewed the Texas insurrection as a stage-managed theft of another people's sovereign territory by southern slave interests. It appeared the most recent chapter in a history of expansions commencing with Florida that were either filibuster seizures or purchases. When Joel Roberts Poinsett could not buy Texas for the United States, Sam Houston, "an intimate friend and protégé of the president," was dispatched to Texas "for the purpose of revolutionizing it."[23]

The rhetorical problem for abolitionists was that Texan fighters for independence presented themselves as sufferers under the despotism of the dictatorial Santa Ana, who had suspended the rights and protections of the Mexican constitution and instituted personal rule. The revolutionaries presented themselves as a "patriotic band, who loved liberty and hated oppression in every form . . . engaged . . . in a war for truth, life, and liberty against tyranny and oppression."[24] When the apologists for the Texan revolution made public appeals, abolitionists felt compelled to confront them, as they did in a meeting in Buffalo, with the fact that the tyranny of slavery was being upheld by the rebels. Every favorable representation of the revolution had to be supplanted with the abolitionist countertruth: "We regard the conduct of the Texans in light of a rebellion, and believe their object is to ESTABLISH AND PERPETUATE SLAVERY AND EXTEND THE SLAVE TRADE."[25] Once Texas independence was secured, the political animus of the movement shifted toward preventing its annexation to the United States.

The Canadian revolution, coming on the heels of the successful Texas revolution, offered a temptation to some New Englanders. If the South and its slave system were extending their political influence through expansion, then why not filibuster Canada and add nonslave territory to the United States as a counterweight? The *Liberator* published a brief essay written in Portland on "Texas and Canada," surmising that the newspaper editors of America had praised the Texas adventure and reviled the Canadian revolution because British gold had paid for malediction in the latter case and southern gold for praise in the former. "For our own parts, if the Union is to receive any additions, we had rather have them from the North eastern rather than the South western frontier; we would rather have the simple-hearted and virtuous Canadians admitted as fellow-citizens, than the out-laws, the cut-throats, the desperados of Texas."[26] But for the moral purists in New England this temptation to pursue a political solution through filibustering, to work liberation by arms, had to be repressed. Any addition of Canadian territory to the United States would pollute a morally pure system by putting it under the jurisdiction of a tainted polity.

"England, the mother country, has emancipated all her slaves. America the daughter sneers at her for the performance of this great deed of justice, makes it an occasion of strong national antipathy, and glories in being the greatest slaveholding country in the world." That Canadians might have suffered under a procrustean government had insufficient merit compared with the ruling truth for abolitionists: liberty for the slaves had been granted there. Any liberation that was not emancipation of the African chattel slave had lost any significance to the abolitionist vanguard. The old rhetoric of freeing Spanish subjects from the chains of monarchy and popery—the echoes of the black legend that drove the filibusters in the South and even the South American independence movement—had lost its force in abolitionist ears a decade before the Mexican War. Even the liberation discourse of the American Revolution—the founders' rhetoric renovated by the patriots of Upper and Lower Canada and by the Americans—sounded empty. Garrison in his review of the patriot captain Daniel Heustis's memoir of the attempted Canadian liberation proclaimed,

> Until the miserable slaves on the American soil are set free, we would advise Captain Heustis, and all others, not to wholly expend their stock of indignation on British misrule in Canada, but to reserve a small portion for plunderers of cradles, the defilers of

helpless women, the traders in men, in this boasted land of freedom. We wonder why Capt. H. in the plentitude of his sympathy for suffering humanity, did not try his hand at a rebellion among the slaves in the South. No cause can be more sacred than theirs; none are groaning more piteously for deliverance than themselves; no struggle for liberty can be more just.[27]

In sum, the Canadian episode provoked the abolitionist vanguard to claim the chrism of liberty exclusively for emancipation. The Great Liberator was not a Bolivar or a Heustis or a MacKenzie, but he who would be the emancipator. Much to the dismay of Garrison and his colleagues, when the emancipator did come, he wrought his liberation with arms. John Brown was his prophet and the killing fields of a civil war his harvest. He was not about the birth of a new order but a destruction of the old.

Conclusion

Beyond the Rebirth of the Revolution: Coming to Terms with Coming of Age

MICHAEL ZUCKERMAN

There is a version of the American testament that goes like this. In the beginning, the earth was almost without form and void. Savages roamed the land but did not improve it. And God said, let there be Jamestown and Plymouth, and the evening and the morning were the first day. And though it was good, it was not good enough. On the sixth day, God said, Let us make man in our own image, after our likeness. So God made the American Revolution, and created Americans in his own image, and said unto them, Be fruitful and multiply and have dominion over every living thing that moveth upon the earth. And God saw everything that he had made, and behold, it was very good.

In this version, the Revolution has been more even than the ineluctable culmination of the first chapter of our genesis. It has been the holy writ that grounds our ideas of where we come from, who we are, and what ethical obligations we bear. It has been the scripture we share that binds us together as a people. Though its tales are told as history, they function more as articles of faith. They affirm and reaffirm. The story of the audacious bravery of the minutemen at Lexington and the sanctified suffering of Washington's troops at Valley Forge is not a story for adults, who might sound its complexities and explore its ambiguities. It is a story for children, who are to learn from it their identity and their allegiance. Its tenets are not in dispute. They do not present issues of quotidian controversy or even invite questions. They specify the sacred.

If Americans embraced this version as wholeheartedly as its votaries say they should, *The American Revolution Reborn* would be an even more subversive book than it is. And it is, make no mistake, a subversive book. Even more subversive than may seem at first brush. The essays in it are written in a register Americans have rarely dared before. Some of them take direct issue with central tenets of the celebratory canon. Almost all of them challenge its assumptions of a chauvinism we all share and a divine ordination in which we all glory. They are the work of a new generation. More than that, they reflect a new sensibility that is profoundly corrosive of old verities.

They are not more subversive only because there is not more to subvert. No matter what the politicians and the schoolbooks say, Americans have never embraced the Fourth of July version of the American origin myth with the unanimity that its devotees have demanded. From the first, that cult of the founding fathers has had its adherents and its dissidents, that creed of their unsurpassed virtue its believers and its unbelievers. Just as religions proliferate sects and schools, so stories of national beginnings multiply meanings and interpretations. They are too important not to do so. Our accounts of the American Revolution, and our understanding of its significance for its heirs, have always been embattled. We have never agreed as a people about its causes, consequences, or contemporary relevance.

So *The American Revolution Reborn* participates in a civic conversation that began with the birth of the republic and has never abated. It is neither misconceived nor misbegotten. Its essays and its grander endeavor—to rethink the Revolution—are neither blasphemous nor impious. If there were holy truths in which Americans concurred, our contributors might tremble to transgress them. But the truth is that there are no such holy truths. There are only profane truths. Some of them serve sordid interests. Others reflect wishful thinking. Still others, no doubt, represent defensible differences of opinion and honest divergences in values. This collection does challenge conventional wisdom, but it does not imperil any vital accord that animates America's dearest dreams and fondest aspirations. America has no such accord. The cleavages that rend contemporary assessments of our Revolutionary heritage are already so deep that nothing in a dozen volumes such as this one could endanger the national faith. As a number of the pieces in this book argue compellingly, Americans have never had a faith in which they all concurred. Not now, not ever. Not even in the fierce crucible of the Revolution itself.

In its stead, for two centuries and more, we have had the only legacy fit for the heirs of the first of the West's great democratic revolutions: a struggle to which every generation of Americans has been condemned, to fathom the ever-shifting import of the founding. The contributors to *The American Revolution Reborn* take up that perennial task at a moment of special significance.

In a time reminiscent of the religious wars of the Reformation, Americans increasingly hunker down in sectarian silos. Blue states and red. The 99 percent and the Tea Party. Jon Stewart and Rush Limbaugh. They get their news from different newspapers and networks, and just as they inhabit different presents, they predicate different pasts. Some of them glorify the Revolution as the inspiring triumph of democracy, others as the remarkable accomplishment of a few great men, still others as God's blessing on a believing Christian people. Some hail the Spirit of '76 as a rising of common folk against the aristocratic pretensions of their self-styled betters, others as a magnificent emanation of a united nation. Most of them speak publicly to one another only to disparage the good faith and patriotism of those in other silos.

Scholars do not speak as stridently or vituperatively as ordinary Americans. They speak with, as well as to, one another, and they listen to one another besides. Paradoxically, as the rifts in popular cultural representations of the Revolution have deepened and grown more virulent, the divides in the academic discourse have flattened and grown more dessicated. This dramatic divergence can only be explained in modest measure by differing norms of civility among politicians and professors. It is also due to developments within the academy. As Patrick Spero says in his introduction to this volume, the scholastic conversation on the Revolution has grown stale in recent years. It has ceased even to engage young students of American history, let alone to animate or move them. The controversies of the past quarter-century have been very like the controversies of the quarter-century before that, and the leading controversialists are still in many cases the very same people. The only difference of any consequence is that, fifty years ago, the debates were fresh and urgent while today they are formulaic and rote. Then, a thrill of creative ferment suffused the study of the Revolution. Today, a dispiriting sense of exhaustion prevails. Those who still study the era are haunted by a dim dread that they are going through motions that were scripted long ago.

In this collection, we set ourselves to refreshing that tired conversation and returning the Revolution to its place at the symbolic heart of American history. We aspire to catalyze a renewal of Revolution studies and come collectively to new ways of thinking about the movement that made thirteen British colonies an American nation.

In that effort, we have not confined ourselves to the company of historians. Our contributors also include scholars of religion, material culture, literature, and the environment. It is no accident that the essays which we have gathered here neither point in any one direction in which we all might go nor suggest a single front on which we all might advance or about which we all might argue. Like most humanists, the authors of these pieces are reluctant to practice under a paradigm or even to work within a common frame. They glory in the scriptural assurance that in the Father's house there are many mansions. They are not by temperament team players. They resist received wisdom. They rejoice that there are more things in heaven and earth than are dreamt of in commonsense philosophy, and they are keen to have their own say about some of those things.

So, at least on first impression, *The American Revolution Reborn* offers a variety of vivifying perspectives rather than converging in a single thesis. Presenting new views from new angles of vision as it does, it was bound to end up with conceptualizations that do not add up. Indeed, many of our contributors deliberately resist synthesis even within their own essays. Denver Brunsman is merely the most explicit among them in aspiring more to muddy the waters and complicate the prevailing scholarship than to advance a grand new account of the Revolution.

In seeking more to criticize than to crystallize, our authors acknowledge that they draw—and depend—upon the work of their predecessors. Even the ones who work in other disciplines have paid their dues in the historiography. Their chapters are richer and more resonant for the conversation they take for granted with older historians.

And yet, for all that they share with those who have gone before them, our authors do not share the deep assumptions and ambitions of their elders. As they often do, first impressions mislead. These essays embody the thinking of a new generation. Despite their differences, one from another, these scholars converge in a stark disengagement from the tasks that earlier students of the Revolution took to themselves.

They disdain to strike a heroic stance. They spurn the nation-building project that has driven historical writing in the West for two centuries. They are the offspring of a new epoch, chastened, disenchanted, more loyal perhaps to the planet than to any particular parcel of it. They have little interest in defining or even exploring the distinctive character of the revolutionaries or the American people those founding fathers have long been alleged to represent. They presume that people are pretty much alike, everywhere. Except perhaps for Aaron Fogleman, they are dubious that destiny has darlings or that the fate of humankind depends or ever depended on any chosen people. Their mood is skeptical, not celebratory. Their tone is almost cranky.

Earlier writers on the Revolution saw allegiance—to the mother country as much as to the new nation—as straightforward. Our contributors see it as problematic at best. They have no trouble with the notion of a nation not yet born on the Fourth of July. Earlier writers took for granted the existence of a unique American identity in the era of independence, arguing only over whether it emerged in the generation before the Declaration or awaited the decisive break with Britain. Our contributors see it as unsettled through the war and even after the peace.

The essays in this collection are exceptionally open to ambiguity, irresolution, and the sheer capriciousness of things. They display a rare readiness to recognize that the Revolution unmade as much as it made, a rarer willingness to acknowledge the terrible toll that violence took in the war, and a still rarer ability to forgo all justifications for that violence. They blur boundaries and heighten contingency. Many of them categorically reject the parochial tropes by which we still tell the tale to our schoolchildren, as a simplistic consensus of patriots or as a scarcely less simplistic clash of rebels and Tories. Almost all of them set a complicated disorder at the core of their analyses and interpretations. The most intriguing of them insist as well on the disaffection of the masses from insurrection and loyalism alike.

Abjuring the old assumptions as they do, these essays call into question two centuries of the writing of the Revolution. They do not take for granted the primacy of public life in the experience of independence. On the contrary, they probe quotidian vicissitudes of families and communities—the ways in which the war brought unimagined devastation to some and offered sudden advancement to others—to suggest that many Americans had more powerful motives for personal conduct than politics and patriotism. And they do not accept as given the inevitability of the emergence of American nationhood. On the contrary, they examine ordinary lives—the ways in which the war unsettled allegiances and identities—to suggest that many Americans came through the conflict more confused than exalted, with loyalties more divided than defined. Just beneath the surface, then, startlingly new ways of thinking are astir in this collection. These essays are harbingers of a sensibility we have hardly had before.

It is hard to see where this new sensibility will lead. In its decentering and destabilizing of the schoolbook verities, it gives up the epic grandeur that the traditional accounts set before schoolboys and schoolgirls. In its concentration on common experience, it disdains the inspirational ideals that the old insistence on uncommon courage and self-sacrifice offered.

But it is not hard to see that this new sensibility offers possibilities that the long-regnant ones no longer do. It feeds an appetite for a renewal of our understanding of our origins that is not so remote from our current condition. That appetite is palpable in the groves of academe, and it is manifest beyond the ivory towers as well. The conference at which these essays were first presented stirred an excitement that was extraordinary for a scholarly meeting. The buzz began with the initial announcement of the program and swelled as the conference itself approached. The social media were alive with anticipation, and not just among the academic elite.

From the first, we had dreamed of a grand conclave open to all. In the end, we created a gathering fresh and tantalizing enough to provide an arena in which scholars and citizens spoke to each other.

A week before the conference opened, well over two hundred people had signed up for the conference. Since that number alone was more than our intended venues could accommodate, and since we assumed that many more were putting off registering till the proverbial last minute, we closed registration and scrambled to rearrange our meeting sites. Even as we did, the History Channel got wind of what we were doing and asked to come, tape the sessions, and interview a dozen of the luminaries in attendance for a film on the Revolution. Samuel Adams Brewing Company, in Philadelphia for a national meeting of craft brewers, offered to sponsor a lavish reception at the conclusion of the conference. And a tally of social media reaction in the weeks immediately afterward found 705 tweets and twenty-one posted photos from fifty-nine contributors. By contrast, a tally of the annual meeting of the Omohundro Institute a month later found a twitter feed of a bare handful of postings drawn from a desultory exchange among four participants.[1]

We had registrants from more than sixty colleges and universities, from all across the country (and not one but two from Japan) and all across a gamut from community colleges to elite research institutions. We had half a dozen secondary school teachers and a dozen independent scholars, one of whom impudently called himself a citizen-scholar. We had twenty-some representatives of museums, historic houses, gardens, and state and local historical societies, ranging from the Society of the Cincinnati, the Sons of the American

Revolution, and the Mount Vernon Ladies Association to the American Helicopter Museum. We had a fair number of lawyers, a nice complement of retirees, an architect, a cartographer, an investment manager, several tour guides, and an odd lot of people from the theater, the media, and digital and analytics consulting firms. We had several staffers from the National Park Service, including its regional director, others from the Smithsonian, the Library of Congress, and the NAACP, the director of the Arch Street Quaker Meeting House, and the historian of the African Episcopal Church of St. Thomas. We had counted on attracting an academic audience. We had only fantasied this thrilling expression of a far wider interest.

Despite a couple of dustups during the sessions themselves and a brief firestorm in the blogosphere a few weeks later, the most exhilarating aspect of the conference was the ease and eagerness with which so many at the meeting exchanged ideas. Once in a while, the schoolteachers and public historians asked openly what the payoff of our occasionally erudite discussions might be for their classrooms and exhibits. Once in a while, the academics expressed impatience with such questions. Far more often, participants expressed their need to learn from each other and their delight in doing so. Even if they did not know the details, they seemed to sense that the academic history of the Revolution had been disconnected from the rest of the country's history of the Revolution for far too long. Even if they did not explicitly put it that way, they seemed to realize that they were reaching out across that disheartening divide between professorial and popular interest.

Among scholars, the analytic agenda was set fifty years ago by Bernard Bailyn and a cadre of his students who argued that a peculiar constellation of ideas they called republican ideology explained better than anything else the willingness of American colonists to go to war against the most powerful military and naval force on the planet. Republican ideology, as Bailyn and his followers defined it, was as bloodless as it was arcane. It made the history of the American Revolution a history that happened primarily in the mind, not on the battlefield or in people's pursuit of their worldly lusts.

More than that—much more than that—it quarantined the Revolution from the rest of American history. In the Bailynian telling of the tale, republican ideology was a singular way of thinking that came into being at a singular moment under singular circumstances. Almost as soon as the war for independence was won, it gave way to the liberal ideology under whose aegis the rest of American history would proceed.

And that was the difficulty with the republican synthesis. Its power was also its fatal failing. By positing the swift dissolution of the Revolutionary mind-set, it could explain why, for two centuries, no one had noticed the ideas that it said sparked the rebellion. But precisely by disconnecting the foundation of the nation from all that followed, it could not explain why we had revered our Revolution through the years and supposed ourselves its inheritors. It could not catch the continuity we imputed to our past.

Bailyn's foremost student, Gordon Wood, appreciated the problem. He acknowledged the incommensurability of the Revolutionary moment and the vast expanse of American history that came after. He described the divergences between the outlook of the founders and values of their descendants as extensively and exactly as anyone ever has. But he couldn't explain at all the transition from an ideology of collective concern to an ideology of legitimate self-interest. When pressed, he could only take refuge in fatuous folderol about tectonic plates, as if idea-masses could be characterized and understood like landmasses. His desperate turn from meticulous empiricism to empty metaphor was a damning symptom of the mess that the republican synthesis made of the larger sweep of American history.[2]

Though Wood fancied himself a dispassionate student of eighteenth-century ideology with no political ax of his own to grind, the neo-progressives understood from the first that he deluded himself. The fights that they picked with him and that he picked with them, and the ferocity of those fights, made plain that the republican synthesis was profoundly partisan and that the antagonism between the contending camps was more visceral than intellectual. But the very rancor of their rivalry may instruct our effort to rethink the Revolution.

Wood and the rest of the republican school offered a deeply conservative solution to a dilemma that had long troubled the captains of American culture. Indeed, the dilemma was clear from the first, and the founders wrestled with it from the first. How were Americans to claim the Revolution yet disclaim its revolutionary implications? How were they to found the new nation on a rising against authority yet achieve a stable government? How were they to mark the Fourth of July with pageantry and parades yet not invite future insurgencies? And the dilemma has only grown more troubling with time, and American elites wrestle with it still. How are they to celebrate the rebellion that gave a puny upstart people their independence yet rejoice to be the richest, most powerful, and most counterrevolutionary country in the world? How are they to glory in the nation's incendiary origins yet assure that those antecedents carry no incendiary consequences?

The republican synthesis provided its adherents a way to deal with those dilemmas and address those questions. It allowed them to flatter themselves with a frisson of radicalism while draining the Revolution of its capacity to inspire any further radical action. The precise point of the invocation of Old Whig ideas as a configuration of thought peculiar to a provincial people on the periphery of empire in 1776 was to assure a mighty nation that commanded the globe in the late twentieth century that those ideas were played out and would never again spark a contagion of liberation.

It is not surprising that the neo-progressives resisted the republican synthesis, since it seemed so palpably to deny the relevance of revolution to our own time. But it is surprising that it fell so flat beyond the ivied halls of academe. It was scarcely even noticed, and certainly not taken up, by an establishment whose interests it could have served very effectively.

Perhaps it asked too much of Americans. Perhaps the esoteric concepts of country ideology were too intricate and exotic and too dependent on a deep encounter with history. Americans haven't much patience for history in the powerful sense that suggests that people in the past might have acted on different values and motives than we do now. Perhaps not even the elite could make any significant use of the gift the historians of republicanism offered them. Perhaps they no more than ordinary Americans were willing to make the effort necessary to appreciate the logic of the republican synthesis, or perhaps they doubted that they could sell ordinary Americans on making that effort. Perhaps that synthesis left the Spirit of '76 obscure and inaccessible. Americans may not want the founding fathers as full-throated revolutionaries, but they do want them as contemporaries, like us only better.

More likely, the explanation is much simpler. American audiences have grown up gorging their apparently insatiable appetites for violence on Hollywood's apparently boundless capacity to supply them the sadism they seem to need. The republican synthesis painted an extraordinarily antiseptic picture of the Revolution. It made a vicious and protracted war—the longest the nation ever waged before Vietnam—almost entirely about what men thought and scarcely at all about what they did. It stirred the neurons, not the blood. It offered nothing that seemed like a story to the American masses or to their media masters. And in that sense it offered nothing of a usable past to men and women who do not dwell in an ivory tower.

The failure of the republican synthesis to touch the wider world is, in retrospect, a striking testimony to the gulf between the American academy and American popular culture. For almost half a century, students of the Revolution tested and contested Bailyn's first formulations and the elaborations that ensued. Advocates and enemies alike orbited around that conceptual complex. And in all that time, scarcely any of those seething controversies percolated past the pages of the learned journals and the programs of the scholarly societies. None of the work that preoccupied the intellectuals topped the best-seller lists or turned up on airport bookshelves. Popular novels did not pick up the discoveries of the professors. Nor did Broadway musicals or movies or network television shows or mass-circulation magazines. Nor did the History Channel itself. The arguments that absorbed and the quarrels that consumed the scholars simply did not inform the treatment of the Revolution in the mass media.[3]

Politicians were as oblivious to the ideas that dominated the academy as the popular press and the entertainment industry were. Government officials are, in many ways, the teachers of the citizenry, and Fourth of July festivities are the classrooms in which they work. But neither republican nor neo-progressive interpretations of the break with Britain ever entered the oratory of Independence Day. Professional patriots did not even take their own understanding of the rebellion from the scholars, let alone distill the spirit of that scholarship and pass it along to the public.[4]

And educators who work in the actual classrooms of the nation, in its middle schools and high schools, were equally indifferent to the ferment in the Higher Learning. At the turn of the twentieth century, William Rainey Harper, the pioneering president of the University of Chicago, boldly proclaimed that "the university determines and in a large measure controls" the school system of the nation, because the university produces "the teachers or the teachers' teachers."[5] But that was then and this is now. Now, the university preoccupies itself with the clash between republican and neo-progressive—patrician and plebeian, intellectual and social—approaches to the making of America. And now, nothing of either approach, or of the clash between them, appears in the school textbooks that provide what passes for formal history for the vast majority of Americans.[6]

For the past fifty years, a semblance of the authority of the university hid the change. The title pages of the most widely adopted high school history textbooks were strewn with the names of prestigious professors at prestigious research universities: Berkeley, City University of New York, Columbia, Illinois, Princeton, Stanford, Texas A&M, UCLA, Virginia, Wisconsin, and Yale, to take a few. But the substantive history that filled the remaining pages of those formidable tomes reflected remarkably little of the actual work of the university.[7]

The luminaries whom the publishers enlisted to write the texts were certainly aware of the ascendant interpretations. It was their colleagues who wrote them and defended and disputed them. Yet the books that the professors' names graced did not even acknowledge those interpretations, let alone organize their chapters on the Revolution around them. Without exception, those chapters offered adolescent readers a military and diplomatic perspective on independence that was as inert as it was outdated.

The texts of the late twentieth and early twenty-first century all told the same hoary story of grievances, battles, and treaties. One after another, they slogged through the Sugar Act, the Stamp Act, and the rest of the regulations by which Britain tried to order its American empire between 1763 and 1776. One after another, they took their student troops on forced marches through Lexington and Concord, Trenton, Valley Forge, Saratoga, and Yorktown between 1775 and 1781. One after another, they crossed the Atlantic for the French alliance and the Treaty of Paris.

They differed only in trifling details. Lesser parliamentary affronts and lesser military engagements turned up in greater or lesser numbers and specificity from schoolbook to schoolbook. Native Americans, African Americans, women, and the occasional Jew came and went—usually segregated in sidebars or pictures—without ever disturbing the saga of combat. They were there simply to satisfy the multicultural imperative that emerged in the belated wake of the 1960s. Half a dozen appeared in one text: Laura Wolcott, Phillis Wheatley, Sybil Ludington, Salem Poor, Haym Solomon, Peter Francisco. Two or three sufficed for most.

None of the texts essayed anything beyond blank narrative. They traced the ebbs and flows of colonial resistance to metropolitan regulations without ever analyzing the philosophy that informed the protests or the social stations of the protesters. They disdained to deal with the ideas that the republican scholars discovered or with the religious, ethnic, and class cleavages that the neo-progressives emphasized. They wrote of "the Americans" as if there were no divisions among them and no real issues at stake between them. To the extent that they offered causal accounts of the break between the colonists and the mother country, they offered only antiquated and insipid fluff.

Following the century-old frontier thesis of Frederick Jackson Turner, one said that the Revolution began "when the first permanent English settlers set foot on the new continent." Following a cliché of contemporary pop psychology, another said that the eight years of brutal warfare were merely a failure of communication. Following a plausible impulse to ask "How did it all happen?" a third could muster no more of an answer than "it did." Whatever their modest differences, the histories taught in the public schools concurred in disdaining half a century of Revolutionary scholarship and indeed in presenting the past as if the accomplishments and controversies of the universities did not exist.[8]

* * *

The two rebirths of the American Revolution—that conference and this volume—provide a vivifying glimmer of a reconciliation between scholars and citizens. In these essays are the stirrings of an understanding that can resonate more widely. In them are the beginnings of a revival that can reach the big screens in our multiplexes, the smaller screens in our homes, and even the schoolrooms of our nation.

It is easy enough to dismiss such a prospect of renewal. For one thing, an understanding of the Revolution that could inform multitudes of Americans would have to have the form of a story, even of a legend. And scholars such as the contributors to this collection are, by training and choice, analysts, not storytellers or legend makers. For another, it would have to respect the country's amour propre. The Revolution has never been just an episode among episodes in the national cavalcade. It has always embodied, or at least shadowed forth, what we think we are about as a people. It has always had something of the civilly religious if not the sacred about it. And scholars such as the contributors to this collection are, by training and choice, disinclined to do such civic and spiritual work. For yet another, it would have to touch not only the truth of the past but also and much more the truth of the present, the truth of the way we live now. And scholars such as the contributors to this collection are, by training and choice, scornful of such frank presentism.

Nonetheless, a tantalizing accord runs through the contributions to this collection. Many of them remark the deep rifts that divided and the uncertain identities that afflicted Americans in the era of the Revolution. And division and diffusion are precisely the terms of our own moment, precisely the parameters of our present day. A history that pursues these themes and explores their ramifications, as so many of these essays do, could be a history of the Revolution for the twenty-first century.

The republican synthesis was not so much an expression of its time as a laggard distillation of the time of its authors. It presumed on the conception of culture in which its authors came of academic age, a conception of coherence implicit in the emphasis on consensus among historians of the 1950s and explicit in the very foundation of the American Studies movement of that day. On that notion of culture as consistent and pervasive, scholars posited a comprehensively coherent worldview—an "ideology," as Bailyn called it—held by a homogeneous people. The Bailynians took for granted that they could tap a pamphlet from Connecticut, a newspaper piece from Maryland, a letter from New Jersey, a legislative act from South Carolina, and a court decision from Pennsylvania without any more regard for the local circumstances of those expressions than a medical technician feels when drawing blood for a lab test from the left or right arm.

The republican synthesis commanded the regard it did because of its intellectual power, and its intellectual power depended in no small measure on the decades of thinking that way that had gone before. It was a culmination of a long quest for an American character conceived as a unitary entity. But, like so many culminations, it came to fullest bloom just before it withered and died. Its deepest assumptions were assumptions of the 1950s, when Americans yearned to see themselves united. Its actual appearance occurred in the late 1960s, when America splintered. It persisted because it affirmed an establishment view of the world. It came and remains under neo-progressive siege for the very same reason. And the standoff between those two scholarly camps—between those "two worlds, one dead, the other powerless to be born"—has now lasted for half a century.

The alternative that emerges in these essays refuses the predications of the republican ideologists and the neo-progressives alike. It abandons the republican assumption that the colonists shared a common culture, and it tempers the neo-progressive argument that they shared an embattled one. It asserts, as John Shy said forty years ago, that there were always more Americans who were "dubious, afraid, uncertain, indecisive," who felt "that there was nothing at stake that could justify involving themselves and their families in extreme hazard and suffering," than there were either rebels or loyalists. It goes beyond Shy, who merely said that these bystanders were "almost certainly a majority of the population," to declare flatly that there was never a majority of Americans who supported independence before independence was an accomplished fact after the Treaty of Paris ended the war.[9]

On the account that is emerging here, the polarization of "patriots" and "Tories" was merely a part—and not necessarily the largest part—of the story. The Revolution fractured the American people in ways we have barely begun to fathom. It was not a civil war so much as a seething nest of civil wars. Those wars were fought, to be sure, between Britons at home and in the colonies and between Americans who rebelled and Americans who remained loyal. But they were also fought within American communities, within American families, and within American psyches, for reasons that often had little to do with the military conflict that raged around them.

Till now, as Marjoleine Kars points out, historians have framed the Revolution so as to "privilege the anti-colonial contest over political struggles and conflicts among people in their own communities." This framing has forced the noncombatants in the war for independence into a seeming fence-sitting that masks the fact that many of them were combatants in struggles more important to them. Kars herself has shown that the men who drove the Regulator movement in North Carolina a few years earlier were "neutral" in the Revolution itself because they saw that war as a project of the very Carolinians who had crushed their own aspirations to economic and social justice. They held back from the battle against the British because they were "skeptical that their erstwhile opponents could bring them the economic democracy and independence for which they had fought" a few years before. Others have shown that others refrained from revolution, on either side, because they preferred to pursue their own salvation in religious revivals, or because they followed their consciences in pacifism, or because they were busy building the new Methodist church.[10] Those men and women, and many others for many other reasons, did not passively steer clear of the clash between the American rebels and their enemies. They actively pronounced a plague on both their houses.

In the perspective of such fragmentation, the time-hallowed tale of the Revolution takes on a very different cast. It ceases to be an ennobling example of oppressed people rising in solidarity against entrenched power. It becomes more nearly a story of a coup d'état by a determined minority, a story that begins with the violence and intimidation on which that minority relied to terrorize a "silenced majority" into acquiescence, that continues with the incessant requisitions that Continental leaders levied on poor farmers who resented those demands and depredations as nothing less than theft, and that does not end with the Peace of Paris. It illuminates the 1780s and 1790s, the years of the so-called Shays and Whiskey and Fries Rebellions and of dozens of lesser resistances to the new federal union that expressed "the sense of alienation, anti-authoritarianism, and violence" that permeated many poorer settlements in the backcountry. Even in victory, not all the winners shared the same sense of what they'd fought for and won.[11]

It hardly needs saying that such a story of fracture and fission, coercion and coup, lacks utterly the heroic dimension that our histories of the founding have had from the first. The promoters of the national project have always cherished myths of a plucky people rising against odds. The self-appointed custodians of the official culture have, generation after generation, retold the inspirational tale of an outmanned citizenry rising righteously against the mightiest military power on the planet and, somehow, prevailing.

But now the shoes are on the other feet. Now it is the United States that is the mightiest martial power on the planet. Now American expenditures on "defense" dwarf those of any other nation and exceed the combined military expenditures of the next ten nations together. Now the very grievances that drove thirteen colonies to declare their independence in 1776—an overbearing executive, a swollen peacetime army, and the rest—are the determinants of American imperial polity and economy. The United States has become the fiercest counterrevolutionary force on earth, the ancien régime, the nation that other nations regard as, by far, "the greatest threat to peace in the world today."[12]

A fair part of the American people have ceased to see the nation in the heroic terms of yesteryear. At least on the evidence of our politics, our mass media, and the survey data, we are terrified by a few terrorists and shaken to our core by their bombings. The specter of 9/11 and of al-Qaeda spurs us to an unprecedented abandonment of liberties and immunities it took our ancestors a millennium to accrue. Through seven years of sustained cultivation of fear, the Bush administration staged a deliberate assault on civic privileges and protections that had been the envy of the world. Through two more terms of the War on Terror, the Obama administration perpetuated that aggrandizement of executive privilege and expanded with drones, data-mining, and mass deportations its surveillance of a citizenry it no longer trusted.

And we did not protest, much, because we have ceased to believe, on the whole, what the rebels of 1776 believed, that people can organize themselves against the immense power of the state in movements for profound social change. We have shriveled the public life on which the American experiment was founded. We have withdrawn into our shrunken domestic spaces, and we don't even defend those against corporate and governmental intrusion. We want primarily to be unhindered in our enjoyment of our consumer choices.

We have hollowed out our founding myths. They do not fit our lives. They do not elevate our aspirations. They do not crystallize our finest feelings.

The truth is that most Americans want no part of revolution and would be embarrassed by the Spirit of '76 if they knew anything about it. Media news directors have stopped sending reporters out to the shopping malls on July 4 to ask people to sign a petition that is in fact the Declaration of Independence, because it no longer surprises us that those who trouble to read a bit of the "petition" refuse to sign it and demand to know if the reporter is a Communist. Focus groups find young adults "apathetic or cynical about politics" and unable to imagine anything for which they would willingly go to war. Asked what they think makes America unique, they first fall silent and then nod enthusiastic agreement when someone suggests cable TV. And in fact they do not go to war. In the first ten years of the twenty-first century, barely one-half of 1 percent of the American people served in the armed forces. And that was just one-fourth of the proportion that served in the Vietnam era, which was itself less than one-fourth of the proportion that served in the years of World War II.[13]

It is, as the saying goes, a free country. And it is striking how very few of the men and women most truly free devote any part of their freedom to manning America's fighting forces. Of the Congress that sent our troops into combat in Iraq in 2002, just one of the 535 representatives and senators had a son or daughter doing military duty. Of corporate CEOs, similarly negligible proportions had a child in uniform.[14]

To our shame, perhaps, we may now be able to connect and even sympathize with tales of the masses of Revolutionary Americans who kept their distance from the war as much as they could. We may now be ready to hear about the winning of our independence in ways far less elevated and valiant—but perhaps more humanly intriguing—than the ones we have always required. Indeed, if we are to connect with our founding in any way that is not farcical or fraudulent, we may well have to come to terms with the preponderant part of the American people who hoped primarily to stay out of harm's way in the Revolution. We may well have to recognize how many of our ancestors were bullied into rebellion rather than choosing it freely. We may well find that stories of trepidation and hesitation and the crassest calculation of self-interest are the stories that seem credible in the twenty-first century.

Though the conference that spawned this collection was called "The American Revolution Reborn," and though that title persists in this collection itself, rebirth is simply the wrong image for what our authors have wrought here. It reflects a hankering for infancy, childhood, youth, and innocence. It emphasizes all the aspects of immaturity that fed America's sense of exceptionalism and made the new nation a hope and a menace to the world.

The new history that is emerging in these essays represents a recognition that we are like others in a world of others. It may even afford an opening toward the evolution of a new myth, not of being born again but of growing up and of rejoining the human race.

In a global world, we could do worse.

* * *

I know very well that, in pleading that we rejoin the human race, I quit the quest for inspiration that might move the young. I can calculate as well as the next person the loss that will come of losing attachment to our most soaring ideals, ideals that still embody the last best hopes of mankind, ideals that beckon us to bend toward the better angels of our nature.

The stories that these essays tell will not lift hearts and souls as the old ones did. And something will be surrendered, something of a precious power and beauty, if we give up the grand aspirations of the old ones and their hallowed motifs of valor and self-sacrifice. Those informing impulses to equality and audacity and justice were the stars under which the American nation was born.

It is tempting to believe that the academic battles of the last half-century touched the school texts so negligibly because they touched on those ideals so lightly. It is more than a little likely that republican ideologists and neo-progressives had so little power to affect hearts because readers had so little heart for stories that merely affected minds. And it is hard not to fear that the new history of the Revolution that I envision, lurking in so many of the essays in this collection, will remain as inert and as confined to the academy as its predecessors, leaving the school-text shibboleths unscathed and ceding the schoolrooms of the nation to the smug myths of yesteryear. I worry, more than a little, about all that.

But the tales of yore were inseparable from the nineteenth-century nation-building endeavor. In their time, the primacy of politics could be taken for granted. In our time, it is stridently asserted by professors and politicians who are haunted by their awareness that that priority on nation building lost its resonance long ago. Current efforts to peddle the ancient legends instill little more than cynicism in the young. They hear the talk, but they don't see the walk, and they conclude that their elders are hypocrites, not dreamers. The chasm between our rhetoric and our reality breeds in them a civic sourness that is at least as corrosive of hope as any abnegation I ask.

And in any case, among adults, the mythical Revolution and its revelatory ideals have been powerless to impede the advance since 1945 of the national security state. Revolutionary patriotism has been powerless to prevent the rise of multinational corporations that have siphoned money and jobs from the homeland and sent them offshore without compunction. Revolutionary rhetoric has been powerless to slow the acquiescence of the American people in the maintenance of the most bloated standing peacetime army in the history of the world, the most expansive and sophisticated domestic spying and surveillance in the history of the human imagination, and more transgressions of the values of the Declaration of Independence than squadrons of scholars could ever count.

However dimly, Americans sense the dissipation of their Revolutionary—and revolutionary—dream. However uneasily, we recognize that we are not what we were. In survey after survey, ever since Ronald Reagan took office, we have told the pollsters that we think that the country is on the wrong track. And we are right. We are no longer the richest people in the world on any per capita reckoning. Our educational system is, by world standards, mediocre. We score near the bottom on every international ranking of treatment of children, quality of life, and subjective experience of happiness. We score at the top on inequality and incarceration. It is not for nothing that we do not believe the bromides of our leaders or trust any longer that the future will be better than the past or our children better off than we are.

Whatever our delusional elite would prefer, the rest of us are ready for the Revolutionary—and revolutionary—history that glimmers in these essays. Our leaders' incantatory invocation of July 4 values has not kept us or them from the abandonment of our poor to a degree that shocks Europeans and even disturbs visitors from what we used to call, condescendingly, the Third World. As I write, levels of unemployment have been higher for the past half-dozen years than at any time since the Great Depression, and the political establishment shows no discernible urgency about it. Schools are failing, roads are crumbling, the earth is warming, and the colossus inside the beltway cannot summon the will to do anything about any of that. A spirit of meanness and callousness and indifference to human suffering suffuses the land. It is rampant and righteous among the Republicans. It is scarcely less prevalent among the Democrats, who led the dismantling of welfare and regulation under Clinton and took care of Wall Street much better than Main Street under Obama. In his second presidential campaign, Clinton sent out directives to his staff never to speak of equality. In his second campaign, Obama resolutely refused to talk of poverty or the poor, confining his concern solely to the middle class.

While professing to honor our Revolutionary origins, we have become a truly savage nation. At this juncture, which has been our juncture since 1980, or 1945, it is clear that our Revolutionary values are unavailing. Some still cling to them, but their voices are drowned out by others more smug and selfish. The transformative, even transgressive time of the American Revolution is over. We are past any devotion to a singular destiny. We would lose little of consequence for the happiness of mankind if we ceased to prattle about lofty ideals that we dishonor daily by our actions. We might gain something of real moment if we settled for decency and a degree of caring for our fellows that peoples all over the planet have preserved while we have lost our way.

NOTES

ABBREVIATIONS USED IN NOTES

In citing works in the notes, short titles have generally been used. Works frequently cited have been identified by the following abbreviations:

ANB	*American National Biography Online*, http://www.anb.org
DLAR	David Library of the American Revolution, Washington Crossing, Pennsylvania
HSP	Historical Society of Pennsylvania
Franklin Papers	*The Papers of Benjamin Franklin*, ed. Leonard W. Labaree et al. (New Haven, Conn.: Yale University Press, 1959–)
JCC	*Journals of the Continental Congress, 1774–1789*, ed. Worthington C. Ford et al. (Washington, D.C., 1904–37)
PMHB	*Pennsylvania Magazine of History and Biography*
PGW	*The Papers of George Washington*, Revolutionary War Series, ed. Philander D. Chase et al. (Charlottesville: University Press of Virginia/University of Virginia Press, 1985–)
PNG	*The Papers of General Nathanael Greene*, ed. Richard K. Showman et al. (Chapel Hill: University of North Carolina Press, 1976–)
SPBL	Ezra Stiles Papers, Beinecke Library, Yale University
TNA	The National Archives of the United Kingdom, Kew, London

CHAPTER I. WAR STORIES

1. William Huntting Howell, "'Starving Memory': Antinarrating the American Revolution," in Michael A. McDonnell, Clare Corbould, Frances M. Clarke, and W. Fitzhugh Brundage, eds., *Remembering the Revolution: Memory, History, and Nation Making from Independence to the Civil War* (Amherst: University of Massachusetts Press, 2013), 93–109, esp. 93–94.

2. Michael A. McDonnell, "War and Nationhood: Founding Myths and Historical Realities," in McDonnell et al., *Remembering the Revolution*, 19–22; Howell, "'Starving Memory,'" 93–94.

3. See, for example, the organization of chapters in Francis D. Cogliano's otherwise fine textbook entitled *Revolutionary America, 1763–1815: A Political History* (New York: Routledge,

1999). For the most part, this chapter will reconsider the larger narratives told about the Revolution, which focus for the most part on white experiences. Significantly, the specialist literature on African Americans during the Revolutionary War is in important ways more sophisticated than that on white colonists because there has been less of a need to shape narratives of black freedom into a revolutionary or founding story. For a recent overview of this literature, see especially Gary B. Nash, "The African Americans' Revolution," in Edward G. Gray and Jane Kamensky, eds., *The Oxford Handbook of the American Revolution* (New York: Oxford University Press, 2013), 250–72; Nash, *The Forgotten Fifth: African Americans in the Age of Revolution* (Cambridge, Mass.: Harvard University Press, 2006); and Christopher Leslie Brown, "The Problems of Slavery," in Gray and Kamensky, *Oxford Handbook*, 427–46. As Brown notes, the history of antislavery thought in this era does not sit easily with a narrative driven by liberty or idealism. Likewise, Native American historians have had fewer difficulties seeing beyond the narrow chronology of the Revolution and the extent to which it was a new imperial war as much as it was a founding moment. See, for example, Patrick Griffin, *American Leviathan: Empire, Nation, and Revolutionary Frontier* (New York: Hill and Wang, 2007); Alan Taylor, *The Divided Ground: Indians, Settlers, and the Northern Borderland of the American Revolution* (New York: Knopf, 2006); Colin G. Calloway, *The American Revolution in Indian Country: Crisis and Diversity in Native American Communities* (New York: Cambridge University Press, 1995).

4. Arthur Shaffer, *The Politics of History: Writing the History of the American Revolution, 1783–1815* (Chicago: Precedent, 1975), quotes on 2, 50; David Ramsay, *The History of the American Revolution* (Philadelphia: R. Aitken, 1789), 1:120. Cf. Lester H. Cohen, "Creating a Usable Future: The Revolutionary Historians and the National Past," in Jack P. Greene, ed., *The American Revolution: Its Character and Limits* (New York: New York University Press, 1987), 314–17, 328; John M. Murrin, "A Roof Without Walls: The Dilemma of American National Identity," in Richard Beeman, Stephen Botein, and Edward C. Carter II, eds., *Beyond Confederation: Origins of the Constitution and American National Identity* (Chapel Hill: University of North Carolina Press, 1987), 345.

5. Charles Royster, "Founding a Nation in Blood: Military Conflict and American Nationality," in Ronald Hoffman and Peter J. Albert, eds., *Arms and Independence: The Military Character of the American Revolution* (Charlottesville: University Press of Virginia, 1984), esp. 36–49, quote on 48, from an 1815 oration; Harlow E. Sheidley, "Sectional Nationalism: The Culture and Politics of the Massachusetts Conservative Elite, 1815–1836" (Ph.D. diss., University of Connecticut, 1990), quoted in Alfred F. Young, *The Shoemaker and the Tea Party: Memory and the American Revolution* (Boston: Beacon Press, 1999), 125. For now classic takes on the remembering of the Revolution, see Michael G. Kammen, *A Season of Youth: The American Revolution and the Historical Imagination* (New York: Knopf, 1978); and Kammen, *Mystic Chords of Memory: The Transformation of Tradition in American Culture* (New York: Knopf, 1991). For studies of early American efforts to generate a sense of nationalism, see David Waldstreicher, *In the Midst of Perpetual Fetes: The Making of American Nationalism, 1776–1820* (Chapel Hill: University of North Carolina Press, 1997); Simon Newman, *Parades and the Politics of the Street: Festive Culture in the Early American Republic* (Philadelphia: University of Pennsylvania Press, 1997). But see also McDonnell, "War and Nationhood," 20–23, and passim for a critique of some of this literature, at least as it pertains to the war years. And, as Alfred F. Young and others have reminded us, this process of controlling the memory of the Revolution began even as the events were taking place. See Young, *Shoemaker and the Tea Party*, esp. 92–131. Cf. Benjamin L. Carp, "The Night the Yankees Burned Broadway: The New York

City Fire of 1776," *Early American Studies* 4 (2006): 471–511; Robert G. Parkinson, "Enemies of the People: The Revolutionary War and Race in the New American Nation" (Ph.D. diss., University of Virginia, 2005), esp. chaps. 1–5.

6. Howell, "'Starving Memory,'" 93–94. Almost all new presidents from George Washington to Barack Obama told similar stories about the Revolution (see Louisa MacDonald Hall, "'The Heirs of That First Revolution': Remembering and Forgetting America's Founding Era in Presidential Inaugural Addresses, 1789–2005" [Honors thesis, University of Sydney, 2008]; and especially Barack H. Obama, "Inaugural Address," January 20, 2009, www.bartleby.com /124/pres68.html). Near the end of his best-selling book *1776* (New York: Simon and Schuster, 2005), David McCullough quotes approvingly from Abigail Adams, Mercy Otis Warren, and Sir George Otto Trevelyan to show the consistency between the story told by the founding generation through to his own (291).

7. Allan Kulikoff, "'Such Things Ought Not to Be': The American Revolution and the First Great National Depression," in Andrew Shankman, ed., *The World of the Revolutionary American Republic: Land, Labor, and the Conflict for a Continent* (London: Routledge, 2014), 134–64; Allan Kulikoff, "The War in the Countryside," in Gray and Kamensky, *Oxford Handbook*, 216–33. At least since John Shy, historians have been asking us to take the violence of the war seriously as an historical phenomenon. Shy's essays are collected in John Shy, *A People Numerous and Armed: Reflections on the Military Struggle for American Independence* (New York: Oxford University Press, 1976). For one preliminary effort to take up this call, see Allan Kulikoff, "Revolutionary Violence and the Origins of American Democracy," *Journal of the Historical Society* 2 (2002): 229–60.

8. Timothy H. Breen, *American Insurgents, American Patriots: The Revolution of the People* (New York: Hill and Wang, 2011). For a more detailed meditation on this theme in terms of the coming of independence, see Michael A. McDonnell, "The Struggle Within: Colonial Politics on the Eve of Independence," in Gray and Kamensky, *Oxford Handbook*, 103–20. For a comparison of ideas of liberty across the British Empire and early American republic, see Trevor Burnard, "Freedom, Migration and the Negative Example of the American Revolution: The Changing Status of Unfree Labor in the Second British Empire and the New American Republic," in Eliga H. Gould and Peter S. Onuf, eds., *Empire and Nation: The American Revolution in the Atlantic World* (Baltimore: Johns Hopkins University Press, 2005), 295–314. For an example of historians' striving to reduce the causes of the Revolutionary War to a single explanatory cause that can encompass later political developments too, see Jack Rakove, "Rebel Without a Cause: A Narrow Approach to the American Revolution," in *New Republic*, November 30, 2012.

9. McDonnell, "The Struggle Within," 103–20. For mobilization and conscription, see McDonnell, *The Politics of War: Race, Class, and Conflict in Revolutionary Virginia* (Chapel Hill: University of North Carolina Press, 2007); Richard Buel, Jr., *Dear Liberty: Connecticut's Mobilization for the Revolutionary War* (Middletown, Conn.: Wesleyan University Press, 1980). Don Higginbotham, in *The War of American Independence: Military Attitudes, Policies, and Practice, 1763–1789* (New York: Macmillan, 1971), 392–93, notes the introduction of conscription in the differing states near the end of his lengthy work but does not discuss the fact further.

10. War dead figures from Shy, *A People Numerous and Armed*, 249–50; Howard H. Peckham, ed., *The Toll of Independence: Engagements and Battle Casualties of the American Revolution* (Chicago: University of Chicago Press, 1974). Edwin G. Burrows, in *Forgotten Patriots: The Untold Story of American Prisoners During the Revolutionary War* (New York: Basic Books, 2008), 200–201, asserts that Peckham was too conservative in his count of prison

deaths and estimates that as many as 18,000 Americans may have died in British prisons and prison ships around New York alone. If Burrows is right, somewhere between 32,000 and 36,000 Americans died in service, in camp, or in British prisons. Burrows also speculates that it is likely that at least some 5,300 people died while serving in loyalist forces, but admits it is at best a guess in light of the fact we have no reliable statistics on it. Along with those who fled the country, Burrows concludes that "the conflict that gave birth to the United States entailed proportionally more suffering than any other in its history" (204). For cautionary words about the need to historicize the number of deaths and their relative impact, see Nicholas Marshall, "The Great Exaggeration: Death and the Civil War," *Journal of the Civil War Era* 4 (2014), 3–27; and his distillation of it at http://hnn.us/article/155305. Cf. Frances C. Clarke, *War Stories: Suffering and Sacrifice in the Civil War North* (Chicago: University of Chicago Press, 2011), for a brilliantly rendered illumination of the meaning of death and sacrifice in the nineteenth century. Up to another twenty-five thousand may have been seriously wounded or disabled in the Revolutionary conflict. Scholars are only just beginning to take notice of their stories.

11. Sung Bok Kim, "The Limits of Politicization in the American Revolution: The Experience of Westchester County, New York," *Journal of American History* 80 (1993): 868.

12. As Michael Kammen, Sung Bok Kim, and more recently Allan Kulikoff have reminded us, American historical literature lacks "a sense of the tragic." Literature on the Revolution has often focused on the more positive outcomes of the movement for independence and the Revolutionary War. Both these events are often portrayed as a contest of ideas—loyalism versus patriotism—or as vehicles for the development of republican, democratic, and individualistic ideology or of social radicalism. Historians on the left and the right have generally ignored the destructive, the divisive, and the tragic effects of the war (see Kim, "Limits of Politicization," 868). There have been many fine studies of the war, and especially of the social dimensions of the conflict, but with few exceptions they have not altered the basic contours of the common story of the Revolution. The works are too numerous to mention, but see, for example, the collected essays in John Resch and Walter Sargent, eds., *War and Society in the American Revolution: Mobilization and Home Fronts* (DeKalb: Northern Illinois University Press, 2007); Holly A. Mayer, *Belonging to the Army: Camp Followers and Community During the American Revolution* (Columbia: University of South Carolina Press, 1996); Judith L. Van Buskirk, *Generous Enemies: Patriots and Loyalists in Revolutionary New York* (Philadelphia: University of Pennsylvania Press, 2002); Caroline Cox, *A Proper Sense of Honor: Service and Sacrifice in George Washington's Army* (Chapel Hill: University of North Carolina Press, 2004); Charles Neimeyer, *America Goes to War: A Social History of the Continental Army* (New York: New York University Press, 1997); Charles Royster, *A Revolutionary People at War: The Continental Army and American Character, 1775–1783* (Chapel Hill: University of North Carolina Press, 1979); Gregory T. Knouff, *The Soldiers' Revolution: Pennsylvanians in Arms and the Forging of Early American Identity* (University Park: Pennsylvania State University Press, 2004); Robert A. Gross, *The Minutemen and Their World* (New York: Hill and Wang, 1976); Ronald Hoffman, *A Spirit of Dissension: Economics, Politics, and the Revolution in Maryland* (Baltimore: Johns Hopkins University Press, 1973); Steven Rosswurm, *Arms, Country, and Class: The Philadelphia Militia and the "Lower Sort" During the American Revolution* (New Brunswick, N.J.: Rutgers University Press, 1989); John A. Ruddiman, *Becoming Men of Some Consequence: Youth and Military Service in the Revolutionary War* (Charlottesville, Va.: University of Virginia Press, 2014).

13. McCullough, *1776*, 35–36; Isaac J. Greenwood, ed., *The Revolutionary Services of John Greenwood of Boston and New York, 1775–1783* (New York: De Vinne Press, 1922), 5–8. Apart

from a celebrated few, the memoirs of ordinary people who lived through this period have been curiously neglected. Both Sarah J. Purcell in *Sealed with Blood: War, Sacrifice, and Memory in Revolutionary America* (Philadelphia: University of Pennsylvania Press, 2002) and Alfred F. Young in *The Shoemaker and the Tea Party* refer to the existence of the memoirs but do not engage with them much. Nor does Michael Kammen in his work *A Season of Youth*. Joseph Plumb Martin wrote the best known of these, and some, like those of Martin and Daniel Trabue, have been reprinted in modern editions: Martin, *A Narrative of a Revolutionary Soldier* (New York: Signet Classics, 2001); Chester Raymond Young, ed., *Westward into Kentucky: The Narrative of Daniel Trabue* (Lexington: University Press of Kentucky, 1981). But by and large, the bulk of these memoirs have been neglected and understudied. In part, I will argue, this is because they do not easily "confirm" the common story of the American Revolution generated first by cultural elites in the new nation. One of the clearest examples of this divergence in the storytelling of the period can be found in the published memoir of Samuel Dewees. While Dewees's account is flat and sparing, the editor saw fit to weave more well-known—and florid—accounts of glorious battles and heroic officers throughout the narrative. Only a careful reading of it reveals that Dewees is telling a very different story from the one the editor is trying to impose on the volume (John Smith Hanna, ed., *History of the Life and Services of Captain Samuel Dewees: A Native of Pennsylvania and Soldier of the Revolutionary and Last Wars* . . . [Baltimore: Robert Neilson, 1844]). For a published listing of many of the available memoirs, see J. Todd White and Charles H. Lesser, eds., *Fighters for Independence: A Guide to Sources of Biographical Information on Soldiers and Sailors of the American Revolution* (Chicago: University of Chicago Press, 1977), 64–109. My thanks to Kathie Ludwig, librarian at the David Library of the American Revolution, for her generous help in pointing out this source and tracking down other memoirs, too.

14. Greenwood, *Revolutionary Services*, 4–8. Many bound apprentices saw new opportunities to escape their masters when war came. See, for example, W. J. Rorabaugh, "'I Thought I Should Liberate Myself from the Thraldom of Others': Apprentices, Masters, and the Revolution," in Alfred F. Young, ed., *Beyond the American Revolution: Explorations in the History of American Radicalism* (DeKalb: Northern Illinois University Press, 1993).

15. Greenwood, *Revolutionary Services*, 25–42, 43, 49–83, 85–86.

16. "Journal of Simeon Lyman of Sharon, Aug. 10 to Dec. 28, 1775," in *Collections of the Connecticut Historical Society*, vol. 7 (Hartford, Conn.: Published for the Society, 1899), 128–29; John Paul Jones to Robert Morris, October 17, 1776, quoted in Michael J. Crawford, "The Privateering Debate in Revolutionary America," *Northern Mariner/Le marin du nord* 21 (2011): 226, 228. Even George Robert Twelves Hewes, celebrated for his humble origins and his role at the Boston Tea Party, also had a more modest wartime experience than his prewar role in the resistance movement might suggest. He served only about nine months in total in the militia, which was compulsory. He spent more time on board a privateer during the war, which was effectively "legalized piracy with a share of the booty for each pirate" (Jesse Lemisch, quoted in Young, *Shoemaker and the Tea Party*, 61). He might have continued privateering for longer but was bitter about being swindled out of his share of the plunder in one of these expeditions. In his reminiscences, at least, he does not seem to have even considered service in the Continental Army, and when he was drafted, he sent a substitute even though he could ill-afford it. Young, *Shoemaker and the Tea Party*, 60–61; George Robert Twelves Hewes, Revolutionary War Pension File S13367, Records of the Veterans Administration, RG15 (National Archives).

17. Young, *Westward into Kentucky*, 43, 67–68; McDonnell, *Politics of War*, 260, 358–59. Trabue recalled years later that in Chesterfield County, the Baptists and Presbyterians

supported the patriot movement, but the Anglican parson had told his father that "the people was Deluded by some of their Leaders" and warned that the "negros would also rise in Rebellion . . . if the people Did Rebel," and would "suffer much by high Fines and Taxes, etc.," in Young, *Westward into Kentucky*, 42.

18. Cox, "Public Memories, Private Lives: The Greatest Generation Remembers the Revolutionary War," in McDonnell et al., *Remembering the Revolution*," 112; Howell, " 'Starving Memory,' " 93–109; Catherine Kaplan, "Theft and Counter-Theft: Joseph Plumb Martin's Revolutionary War," *Early American Literature* 41 (2006): 515–34; John Joseph Henry, *An Accurate and Interesting Account of the Hardships and Sufferings of That Band of Heroes who Traversed the Wilderness in the Campaign Against Quebec in 1775* (Lancaster, Pa.: Printed by William Greer, 1812). Cf. Caroline Cox, "The Continental Army," in Gray and Kamensky, *Oxford Handbook*, 170. George Robert Twelves Hewes seems to have been the exception in terms of elaborating on his motives, although some of these revelations may have been prompted by his biographer. See Young, *Shoemaker and the Tea Party*, esp. 53–55. Like the Revolutionary memoirs, the Revolutionary pension records have been underused, too. In part, this is because they were often written in formulaic language, designed to convince a court and the pension board of the veracity of the applicant's claims. But it also stems from the lack of colorful detail and the kinds of stories historians hope to find in them. They have rarely been systematically analyzed for what they can tell us. For some good examples of the use of these records see Knouff, *The Soldiers' Revolution*; Judith L. Van Buskirk, "Claiming Their Due: African Americans in the Revolutionary War and Its Aftermath," in Resch and Sargent, *War and Society in the American Revolution*, 132–62; John Resch, *Suffering Soldiers: Revolutionary War Veterans, Moral Sentiment, and Political Culture in the Early Republic* (Amherst: University of Massachusetts Press, 1999).

19. John P. Becker, *The Sexagenary; or, Reminiscences of the American Revolution*, ed., Simeon DeWitt Bloodgood (Albany, N.Y.: J. Munsell, 1866; first printed in 1833), 9–12, 21, 22, 46, 55. Cf. Cox, "Public Memories, Private Lives," 117, on some veterans' desire for a public forum to reveal long-held grudges.

20. Becker, *The Sexagenary*, 102–3, 153–54, 157.

21. Ibid., 22, 73, 82, 85, 110–11.

22. Ibid., 34, 40, 58–59, 73, 82, 83, 85, 96, 100, 134–35.

23. Ibid., 102–3, 153–54, 157, 213. Becker's memoir, of course, raises questions about the genre and particularly how much of the narrative is colored and shaped by later events. While a full discussion of this issue is beyond the scope of this chapter, two particular essays might serve as useful starting points: Michael Kammen, "Some Patterns and Meanings of Memory Distortion in American History," and Michael Schudson, "Dynamics of Distortion in Collective Memory," in Daniel L. Schacter, ed., *Memory Distortion: How Minds, Brains, and Societies Reconstruct the Past* (Cambridge, Mass.: Harvard University Press, 1995), 329–45, 346–64. It is likely that had Becker met with more success in his later life (such as the individuals who populate the pages of Joyce O. Appleby's *Inheriting the Revolution: The First Generation of Americans* [Cambridge, Mass.: Belknap Press of Harvard University Press, 2000]), he might well have written a different kind of story. But part of the point here is that Becker did not meet with much success, much like thousands of others who fought and suffered during the war. What is unusual is that he and a handful of others left memoirs about their lives, giving us some insight into a group that has too often faded into obscurity precisely because they were unsuccessful. Moreover, despite his relative lack of success, Becker still did not romanticize his early days, when success was still a possibility. For some thought-provoking insights on memoirs,

autobiographies, and nostalgia, see Ben Jones, "The Uses of Nostalgia: Autobiography, Community Publishing and Working Class Neighbourhoods in Post-War England," *Cultural and Social History* 7, no. 3 (2010): 355–74.

24. Timothy H. Breen, "Samuel Thompson's War: The Career of an American Insurgent," in Alfred F. Young, Gary B. Nash, and Ray Raphael, eds., *Revolutionary Founders: Rebels, Radicals, and Reformers in the Making of the Nation* (New York: Knopf, 2011), 53–66, esp. 63; Carp, "The Night the Yankees Burned Broadway," 473–74, 481–83; Washington to John Hancock, September 22, 1776, Washington to Lund Washington, October 6, 1776, in Philander Chase and Frank E. Grizzard, Jr., eds., *The Papers of George Washington*, Revolutionary War Series, vol. 6 (Charlottesville: University Press of Virginia, 1994), 6:369, 495. Carp mounts a persuasive case that patriot arsonists were most likely behind the fire. Stories of their involvement circulated informally for years afterward.

25. See McDonnell, *Politics of War*, 169–73.

26. The same ratio of fugitives to population today would see the departure of seven million people from America's shores. The records have, of course, been used by scholars outside the United States who worked on the histories of the places loyalists ended up, most notably Canada and Sierra Leone. Two recent works that have drawn on some of these sources include Alan Taylor, *The Civil War of 1812: American Citizens, British Subjects, Irish Rebels, & Indian Allies* (New York: Vintage Books, 2011); and Maya Jasanoff, *Liberty's Exiles: American Loyalists in the Revolutionary World* (New York: Knopf, 2011). It is important to note that "Americans" kept leaving too. A further wave of refugees fled onerous new taxes at the end of the 1780s and set themselves up in Canada. Another 30,000 "Late Loyalists" then also sought out family or extended kin and cheaper land in Canada between 1792 and 1812. Taylor, *Civil War of 1812*, 8, 22, 37–38.

27. For an overview and definition of active loyalists, see especially Robert M. Calhoon, "Loyalism and Neutrality," in Jack P. Greene and J. R. Pole, eds., *A Companion to the American Revolution* (Malden, Mass.: Blackwell, 2000), 235–47. The number of loyalist combatants comes from Paul H. Smith, "The American Loyalists: Notes on Their Organization and Numerical Strength," *William and Mary Quarterly* 3rd ser. 25, no. 2 (1968), 259–77, esp. 266–67. Cf. Stephen Conway, *The War of American Independence, 1775–1783* (London: Edward Arnold, 1995), 46: and Maya Jasanoff, "The Other Side of Revolution: Loyalists in the British Empire," *William and Mary Quarterly* 3rd ser. 65, no. 2 (2008): 205–32.

28. See Elizabeth Lichtenstein Johnston, *Recollections of a Georgia Loyalist*, ed. Arthur Wentworth Eaton (New York: M. F. Mansfield, 1901), 44–46, 67, 211 (originally written in 1836 when Eliza was seventy-two). For a short biography and further details of Eliza's life in exile, see Jasanoff, *Liberty's Exiles*, xii, and passim. Edward Larkin in his chapter "Loyalism" in Gray and Kamensky, *Oxford Handbook*, 291–310, also calls for a new reading of the loyalists and looks at several important war stories told by loyalists.

29. Johnston, *Recollections of a Georgia Loyalist*.

30. Hugh Edward Egerton, ed., *The Royal Commission on the Losses and Services of American Loyalists, 1783 to 1785, Being the Notes of Mr. Daniel Parker Coke, M.P., One of the Commissioners During That Period* (Oxford: Printed for presentation to the members of the Roxburghe Club, 1915), xli–xlii. For one example of a memoir of the war and its aftermath by an African American, see "Memoirs of the Life of Boston King, a Black Preacher," in Vincent Carretta, ed., *Unchained Voices: An Anthology of Black Authors in the English-Speaking World of the Eighteenth Century* (Lexington: University Press of Kentucky, 1996), 351–68.

31. For an extended discussion of the range of activities that might be put into this category, see Michael A. McDonnell, "Resistance to the American Revolution," in Greene and Pole, *Companion to the American Revolution*, 342–51. For other works that take neutrals or the disaffected more seriously, see especially Ronald Hoffman, "The 'Disaffected' in the Revolutionary South," in Alfred F. Young, ed., *The American Revolution*, Explorations in the History of American Radicalism (DeKalb: Northern Illinois University Press, 1976), 273–318; Joseph S. Tiedemann, "A Revolution Foiled: Queens County, New York, 1775–1776," *Journal of American History* 75 (1988): 422–24; Kim, "Limits of Politicization," 868–89; Jonathan Clark, "The Problem of Allegiance in Revolutionary Poughkeepsie," in David D. Hall, John M. Murrin, and Thad W. Tate, eds., *Saints and Revolutionaries: Essays in Early American History* (New York: Norton, 1984), 292–94; Michael Kammen, "The American Revolution as a *Crise de Conscience*," in Jack P. Greene, Richard L. Bushman, and Michael Kammen, eds., *Society, Freedom, and Conscience: The American Revolution in Virginia, Massachusetts, and New York* (New York: Norton, 1976), 125–89; Aaron Sullivan, "In but Not of the Revolution: Loyalty, Liberty, and the British Occupation of Philadelphia" (Ph.D. diss., Temple University, 2014).

32. McDonnell, *Politics of War*, 446–52.

33. McCullough, *1776*, 51, 63, 65; Gregory T. Knouff, "'An Arduous Service': The Pennsylvania Backcountry Soldiers' Revolution," *Pennsylvania History* 61 (1994): 45–74; McDonnell, *Politics of War*, 378, 379.

34. Kim, "Limits of Politicization," 887.

35. McDonnell, "War and Nationhood," 19–34. John Shy long ago called attention to the need to think more carefully about the links between the war for independence and the politics of the period, but scholars of each have, by and large, remained in separate camps. Shy, *A People Numerous and Armed*, 110.

36. Murrin, "Roof Without Walls," 345. For further reflections on this issue, see McDonnell, "War and Nationhood," 31–34. For suggestions about the impact of the war and its aftermath on the delegates to the Constitutional Convention, see Shy, *A People Numerous and Armed*, 110, 132; Alfred F. Young, "The Framers of the Constitution and the 'Genius' of the People," *Radical History Review* 42 (Fall 1988), 7–47; Alfred F. Young, "Afterword: How Radical Was the American Revolution?" in Young, *Beyond the American Revolution*. The disingenuousness of the founding fathers is well documented, and many historians now recognize that the passage of the Constitution was only achieved through a number of clever subterfuges. For one convincing argument that those in favor of the Constitution were in the minority, see Lee Soltow, *Distribution of Wealth and Income in the United States in 1798* (Pittsburgh: University of Pittsburgh Press, 1989), especially chap. 10.

37. In addition to the literature cited in notes 4 and 5, above, see also Carroll Smith-Rosenberg, *This Violent Empire: The Birth of an American National Identity* (Chapel Hill: University of North Carolina Press, 2010), who notes that cultural elites in the founding era created a national sense of self by reimagining themselves in league with other white propertied males and creating and marginalizing dangerous "others" such as African Americans, Native Americans, women, and the propertyless. The desperate efforts of elites in the 1790s to celebrate the "civic texts" of the Revolution must be seen in light of the divisions among Americans over just what to remember and how. See François Furstenberg, *In the Name of the Father: Washington's Legacy, Slavery, and the Making of a Nation* (New York: Penguin, 2006).

38. For a sense of this ongoing uncertainty over the memory of the Revolution, see McDonnell et al., *Remembering the Revolution*. As Michael Kammen has noted, "by the middle of 1861 our Revolutionary tradition was a shambles, the victim of hypocritical abuse and exploitation for partisan purposes" (*A Season of Youth*, 57–58).

CHAPTER 2. THE INTIMACIES OF OCCUPATION

1. The details of the raid are best known from two accounts, Barton's own and the report on it made by British officer Frederick Mackenzie, which was compiled after visiting the Overing house the day after Prescott's capture. See William Barton, "A Narrative of the particulars relative to the capture of Major General Prescot and his aid-de-camp Major Barrington," Rhode Island Historical Society Manuscripts, MSS 9003, vol. 3, p. 13, Rhode Island Historical Society, Providence; and Frederick Mackenzie, *The Diary of Frederick Mackenzie: Giving a Daily Narrative of His Military Service as an Officer of the Regiment of Royal Welch Fusiliers During the Years 1775–1781 in Massachusetts, Rhode Island and New York*, 2 vols. (Cambridge, Mass.: Harvard University Press, 1930), 1:6

2. Ambrose Serle, *The American Journal of Ambrose Serle: Secretary to Lord Howe, 1776–1778*, ed. Edward H. Tatum (San Marino, Calif.: Huntington Library, 1940), 238.

3. *Public Advertiser*, August 22, 1777, 2.

4. Elaine Forman Crane, *A Dependent People: Newport, Rhode Island in the Revolutionary Era* (New York: Fordham University Press, 1985), 154 n. 115.

5. Maya Jasanoff, *Liberty's Exiles: American Loyalists in the Revolutionary World* (New York: Knopf, 2011); Ruma Chopra, *Unnatural Rebellion: Loyalists in New York City During the Revolution* (Charlottesville: University of Virginia Press, 2011); and Joseph S. Tiedemann, Eugene R. Fingerhut, and Robert W. Venables, eds., *The Other Loyalists: Ordinary People, Royalism, and the Revolution in the Middle Colonies, 1763–1787* (Albany: State University of New York Press, 2009). On race, slavery, and the Revolution, recent works include Jasanoff, *Liberty's Exiles*; Gary Nash, *The Forgotten Fifth: African Americans in the Age of Revolution* (Cambridge, Mass.: Harvard University Press, 2006); Cassandra Pybus, *Epic Journeys of Freedom: Runaway Slaves of the American Revolution and Their Global Quest for Liberty* (Boston: Beacon Press, 2006); Simon Schama, *Rough Crossings: Britain, the Slaves and the American Revolution* (New York: HarperCollins, 2006); Douglas R. Egerton, *Death or Liberty: African Americans and Revolutionary America* (New York: Oxford University Press, 2009); and Alan Gilbert, *Black Patriots and Loyalists: Fighting for Emancipation in the War of Independence* (Chicago: University of Chicago Press, 2012).

6. On "neutrals" or the "disaffected," see Ronald Hoffman, "The 'Disaffected' in the Revolutionary South," in Alfred F. Young, ed., *The American Revolution* (DeKalb: Northern Illinois University Press, 1976); Michael McDonnell, "Resistance to the American Revolution," in Jack P. Greene and J. R. Pole, eds., *A Companion to the American Revolution* (Malden, Mass.: Blackwell, 2000); Michael McDonnell, *The Politics of War: Race, Class & Conflict in Revolutionary Virginia* (Chapel Hill: University of North Carolina Press, 2007); and Michael McDonnell, "The Struggle Within: Colonial Politics on the Eve of Independence," in Edward G. Gray and Jane Kamensky, eds., *The Oxford Handbook on the American Revolution* (New York: Oxford University Press, 2013). Judith L. Van Buskirk, *Generous Enemies: Patriots and Loyalists in Revolutionary New York* (Philadelphia: University of Pennsylvania Press, 2002), captures the

complexities of civilian experiences and divided loyalties in an area, like Newport, where areas of British and patriot control abutted.

7. The key study of Newport in the period of the Revolution remains Crane, *Dependent People*. Recent work on the subject includes Benjamin L. Carp, *Rebels Rising: Cities and the American Revolution* (New York: Oxford University Press, 2007). Both of these studies are focused on the period before 1775, rather than the war years.

8. On the multifaceted origins and mutability of political allegiances during the war, see Chopra, *Unnatural Rebellion*, 5.

9. Unless otherwise noted, the ensuing synopsis of the military history of the war around Narragansett Bay is drawn from Paul F. Dearden, *The Rhode Island Campaign of 1778: Inauspicious Dawn of Alliance* (Providence: Rhode Island Bicentennial Foundation, 1980).

10. On Governor Wanton's journey from leading supporter of colonial rights to unhappy loyalist, see Crane, *Dependent People*, 136–37.

11. Ibid., 122.

12. Ibid., 76, 157.

13. Sidney S. Rider, ed., *The Diary of Thomas Vernon, a Loyalist . . .* , Rhode Island Historical Tracts 13 (Providence: Sidney S. Rider, 1881), v–vii.

14. Rhode Island General Assembly Papers, Revolutionary War, "Suspected Persons, 1775–1783," 10, 17, Rhode Island State Archives, Providence.

15. James Thacher, *Military Journal of the American Revolution . . .* (Hartford, Conn.: Hurlbut, Williams, 1862), 66.

16. Walter K. Schroeder, *The Hessian Occupation of Newport and Rhode Island, 1776–1779* (Westminster, Md.: Heritage Books, 2005), 5–6.

17. Christian M. McBurney, "British Treatment of Prisoners During the Occupation of Newport, 1776–1779: Disease, Starvation, and Death Stalk the Prison Ships," *Newport History: Journal of the Newport Historical Society* 79, no. 263 (Fall 2010): 28.

18. Ibid.

19. Ibid., 1–41.

20. Transcript of the diary of Mary Almy, Newport Historical Society, Newport, Rhode Island.

21. For these subsequent loyalist evacuations, see Jasanoff, *Liberty's Exiles*, 67–95.

22. On the French in Newport, see T. Cole Jones, "'Displaying the Ensigns of Harmony': The French Army in Newport, Rhode Island, 1780–1781" *New England Quarterly* 85, no. 3 (September 2012): 430–67.

23. My thinking on "microchronology" was inspired in part by recent work in political science on the "microdynamics" of civil war. See Stathis N. Kalyvas, "Promises and Pitfalls of an Emerging Research Program: The Microdynamics of Civil War," in Stathis N. Kalyvas, Ian Shapiro, and Tarek Masoud, eds., *Order, Conflict, and Violence* (Cambridge: Cambridge University Press, 2008). In her sensitive study of Revolutionary New York, Van Buskirk has rightly observed that "In order to understand the dilemmas faced by the people in this turbulent setting, it is important to imagine the place—New York and its environs during the Revolution—and to understand the experiences of Revolutionary-era Americans on the ground" (*Generous Enemies*, 4).

24. Catherine R. Williams, *Biography of Revolutionary Heroes: Containing the Life of Brigadier Gen. William Barton, and Also, of Captain Stephen Olney* (Providence, R.I.: Published by the author, 1839), 29.

25. "Memorial of Tosh Sisson to the Honble Board of War," Rhode Island Historical Society Manuscripts, MSS 9003, vol. 14, p. 317, Rhode Island Historical Society, Providence.

Sisson's name appears on a November 1779 "List of Tories &c. in Newpt," found in Rhode Island General Assembly Papers, Revolutionary War, "Suspected Persons, 1775–1783," p. 24. The term "refugees" in this context was probably particularly applied to loyalist partisan groups organized by William Franklin and others. See Chopra, *Unnatural Rebellion*, 165–74; and Jasanoff, *Liberty's Exiles*, 64.

26. On *petite guerre* and the pressure it put on British soldiers, see Stephen Conway, "'The Great Mischief Complain'd Of': Reflections on the Misconduct of British Soldiers in the Revolutionary War," *William and Mary Quarterly* 3rd. ser. 47, no. 3 (July 1990): 377.

27. Crane, *Dependent People*, 69–75.

28. Ezra Stiles, *The Literary Diary of Ezra Stiles*, ed. Franklin Bowditch Dexter, 3 vols. (New York: Charles Scribner's Sons, 1901), 2:97.

29. Mackenzie, *Diary*, 1:130.

30. Sharon Block has argued that the rape of colonial women by British soldiers was both a real feature of the Revolutionary War, like other wars across human history, and "a propaganda tool of proportions unmatched in early American history," as patriot men "proved the need for their independence from Britain through their raped women." Block, *Rape and Sexual Power in Early America* (Chapel Hill: University of North Carolina Press, 2006), 230–38.

31. Schroeder, *Hessian Occupation*, 93–94.

32. Mackenzie, *Diary*, 1:141.

33. Johann Conrad Dohla, *A Hessian Diary of the American Revolution*, ed. Bruce E. Burgoyne (Norman: University of Oklahoma Press, 1993), 80. French officers would record similar sentiments and some also formed relationships with Newport women during their time on the island. See Jones, "'Displaying the Ensigns of Harmony,'" 453–54, 464–65.

34. Stiles, *Literary Diary*, 2:96.

35. Williams, *Biography of Revolutionary Heroes*, 67.

36. Schroeder, *Hessian Occupation*, 93–94; Jasanoff, *Liberty's Exiles*, 77.

37. *Report on American Manuscripts in the Royal Institution of Great Britain*, 4 vols. (London: His Majesty's Stationery Office, 1904), 1:280. See also Don N. Hagist, "Henrietta Overing Auchmuty's Forgotten First Marriage," *Newport History: Journal of the Newport Historical Society* 83, no. 270 (Spring 2014): 30–41.

38. Clare Lyons, *Sex Among the Rabble: An Intimate History of Gender and Power in the Age of Revolution, Philadelphia, 1730–1830* (Chapel Hill: University of North Carolina Press, 2006), 187.

39. Crane, *Dependent People*, 75.

40. Ibid.; excerpt of Peebles's diary printed in "Trivia" in *William and Mary Quarterly* 3rd ser. 26, no. 3 (July 1969): 441.

41. Williams, *Biography of Revolutionary Heroes*, 133. In applying the "dance the ladies to allegiance" quip to Prescott, Williams was quoting, in slightly incorrect form, a line the poet John Trumbull had written about General John Burgoyne.

42. The brief records of the British Board of Enquiry, which vindicated Prescott's conduct, have been printed in Don N. Hagist, *General Orders, Rhode Island, December 1776–January 1778* (Westminster, Md.: Heritage Books, 2001), 129–34. A similar explanation for Prescott's choice of quarters was offered by the British sergeant Roger Lamb in his journal. Roger Lamb, *An Original and Authentic Journal of Occurrences During the Late American War from Its Commencement Until the Year 1783* (Dublin: Wilkinson & Courtney, 1809), 220.

43. Stiles, *Literary Diary*, 2:182.

44. Nicholas Cresswell, *The Journal of Nicholas Cresswell, 1774–1777* (New York: Dial Press, 1924), 258.

45. Williams, *Biography of Revolutionary Heroes*, 51.

46. For an example of this claim, see Judith A. Boss, *Newport: A Pictorial History* (Norfolk, Va.: Donning, 1981), 57.

47. "Declaration of Abel Potter Under the Pension Act of 1832," September 11, 1832, in "Pension Application File of Abel Potter," Revolutionary War Pension and Bounty-Land Warrant Application Files, Film Roll 1958, NARA microfilm publication M804, Records of the Department of Veterans Affairs, Record Group 15, National Archives, Washington, D.C. Potter's account has been published in John C. Dann, ed., *The Revolution Remembered: Eyewitness Accounts of the War for Independence* (Chicago: University of Chicago Press, 1980), 22–28. Abel Potter's name does not feature in the lists of Barton's volunteers published in nineteenth-century sources. His account also differs in some other particulars from others on the raid, including Barton's own. For instance, Potter records that the raiders took three sentries prisoner, not just one.

48. On Mary Overing and the history of the Overings' Middletown house after the Revolution, see April Lee Cummings, "Portrait of a Loyalist: Research Findings for the Nichols-Overing House," report prepared for the Newport Restoration Foundation, August 2005, 14–15. My thanks to Liz Spoden of the Newport Restoration Foundation and the NRF itself, which owns and interprets the Overing House, now part of their "Prescott Farm" site, for sharing this report and other materials on the house and the Prescott capture that the NRF has assembled.

49. *Public Advertiser*, August 19, 1777, 2.

50. James C. Gaston, "Richard Prescott and Mud Island: Epitomes of the Revolution as Seen by London's Poets," *Early American Literature* 11, no. 2 (Fall 1976): 149.

51. Stiles, *Literary Diary*, 1:653.

52. Barton, "Narrative." "Mr. Coffin" may have been one Paul Coffin, the sole person with that surname that Ezra Stiles included in a list of Newporters who remained in the town following its occupation by the British. See Stiles, *Literary Diary*, 2:133.

53. For a sampling of the multiple names for this man or men, see Williams, *Biography of Revolutionary Heroes*, 127–28; J. Lewis Diman, *The Capture of General Richard Prescott by Lt.-Col. William Barton . . .* , Rhode Island Historical Tracts 1 (Providence: Sidney S. Rider, 1877), 35–36; Thacher, *Military Journal*, 86; and Benjamin Cowell, *Spirit of '76 in Rhode Island . . .* (Boston: A. J. Wright, 1850), 150.

54. A. Van Doren Honeyman, *The Honeyman Family (Honeyman, Honyman, Hunneman, Etc.) in Scotland and America, 1548–1908* (Plainfield, N.J.: Honeyman's, 1909), 87–88.

55. Williams, *Biography of Revolutionary Heroes*, 41. For another account of Quaco's providing information on Prescott's movements, which also claims that he was the black man who broke through Prescott's door with his head, see Edward Peterson, *History of Rhode Island* (New York: John S. Taylor, 1853), 216.

56. Honeyman, *Honeyman Family*, 86.

57. John Russell Bartlett, ed., *Records of the Colony of Rhode Island and Providence Plantations in New England*, vol. 9, *1780 to 1783* (Providence: Alfred Anthony, 1864), 8:493–94, 509–10.

58. By 1810, Quaco was living in Monson, Massachusetts. Third Census of the United States, 1810, NARA microfilm publication M252, 71 rolls, Bureau of the Census, Record Group 29, National Archives, Washington, D.C.; Peterson, *History of Rhode Island*, 218; Honeyman, *Honeyman Family*, 88.

59. Williams, *Biography of Revolutionary Heroes*, 56.

60. Frank F. Swan, *General William Barton: A Biographical Sketch* (Providence, R.I.: Roger Wiliams Press, 1947), 29.

61. On Walter Graham, I am indebted to the research presented by Don N. Hagist on his blog "British Soldiers, American Revolution," http://redcoat76.blogspot.com/2009/07/deserter-walter-graham-22nd-regiment-of.html. Potter's account is in "Declaration of Abel Potter Under the Pension Act of 1832."

62. Hagist, "Henrietta Overing Auchmuty's Forgotten First Marriage," 36.

63. Some "loyalist" women stayed behind after their husbands emigrated as a deliberate strategy to protect family property; see Jasanoff, *Liberty's Exiles*, 94.

64. Alexander Fraser, *Second Report of the Bureau of Archives for the Province of Ontario . . . 1904* (Toronto: L. K. Cameron, 1905), 194–95; Peter Wilson Coldham, *American Migrations, 1765–1799: The Lives, Times, and Families of Colonial Americans Who Remained Loyal to the British Crown Before, During, and After the Revolutionary War, as Related in Their Own Words and Through Their Correspondence* (Baltimore: Genealogical Publishing, 2000), 145.

65. Edmund S. Morgan, *The Gentle Puritan: A Life of Ezra Stiles, 1727–1795* (New Haven, Conn.: Yale University Press, 1962).

CHAPTER 3. UNCOMMON CAUSE

1. John Adams to Hezekiah Niles, February 13, 1818, *The Works of John Adams*, ed. Charles Francis Adams, 10 vols. (Boston: Little, Brown, 1850–56), 10:828; John Adams to Thomas Jefferson, August 24, 1815, *The Adams-Jefferson Letters: The Complete Correspondence Between Thomas Jefferson and Abigail and John Adams*, ed. Lester J. Cappon (Chapel Hill: University of North Carolina Press, 1959), 2:455.

2. Some recent examples include Maya Jasanoff, *Liberty's Exiles: American Loyalists in the Revolutionary World* (New York: Knopf, 2011); Thomas B. Allen, *Tories: Fighting for the King in America's First Civil War* (New York: Harper, 2010); Joseph Tiedemann, Eugene R. Fingerhut, and Robert W. Venables, eds., *The Other Loyalists: Ordinary People, Royalism, and the Revolution in the Middle Colonies, 1763–1787* (Albany: State University of New York Press, 2009); Ruma Chopra, *Unnatural Rebellion: Loyalists in New York City During the Revolution* (Charlottesville: University of Virginia Press, 2011); William Pencak, "Out of Many, One: Pennsylvania's Anglican Loyalist Clergy in the American Revolution," and Douglas MacGregor, "Double Dishonor: Loyalists on the Middle Frontier," both in William Pencak, ed., *Pennsylvania's Revolution* (University Park: Pennsylvania State University Press, 2010); and the latest revision and expansion of Robert M. Calhoon et al., *Tory Insurgents: The Loyalist Perception and Other Essays* (Columbia: University of South Carolina Press, 2010). Older works of particular relevance here include Paul Hubert Smith, *Loyalists and Redcoats: A Study in British Revolutionary Policy* (Chapel Hill: University of North Carolina Press, 1964); Wallace Brown, *The King's Friends: The Composition and Motives of the American Loyalist Claimants* (Providence, R.I.: Brown University Press, 1965); and Wilbur H. Siebert, *The Loyalists of Pennsylvania* (Columbus: Ohio State University, 1920).

3. John Shy, *A People Numerous and Armed: Reflections on the Military Struggle for American Independence* (New York: Oxford University Press, 1976), 236.

4. Anne M. Ousterhout makes a compelling case for the utility of the term "disaffected" over "Loyalist" in describing much of the opposition to the Revolution in Pennsylvania. Ousterhout, *A State Divided: Opposition in Pennsylvania to the American Revolution* (New York: Greenwood Press, 1987), 5.

5. On America's strong and long-lived attachment to the Hanoverian monarchy, see Brendan McConville, *The King's Three Faces: The Rise and Fall of Royal America, 1688–1776* (Chapel Hill: University of North Carolina Press, 2006).

6. James Allen, "Diary of James Allen, Esq., of Philadelphia, Counsellor-at-Law, 1770–1778," *Pennsylvania Magazine of History and Biography* (hereafter *PMHB*) 9 (July 1985): 186.

7. James Allen, "Diary of James Allen, Esq., of Philadelphia, Counsellor-at-Law, 1770–1778 (Concluded)," *PMHB* 9 (January 1886): 427.

8. T. H. Breen, *The Marketplace of Revolution* (New York: Oxford University Press, 2004), 309.

9. Madison to William Bradford, January 20, 1775, in *The Papers of James Madison*, ed. W. T. Hutchinson and William M. E. Rachal, 3 vols. (Chicago: University of Chicago Press, 1962), 1:135.

10. Continental Association, Article 11; see "The Association," in Henry Steele Commager, ed., *Documents of American History* (New York: F. S. Crofts, 1941), 84–87.

11. Shy, *A People Numerous and Armed*, 237–39.

12. Alexander Graydon, *Memoirs of His Own Time: With Reminiscences of the Men and Events of the Revolution*, ed. John Stockton Littell (Philadelphia: Lindsay & Blakiston, 1846), 306.

13. "Resolutions Directing the Mode of Levying Taxes on Non-Associators in Pennsylvania" (November 25, 1775), in *Pennsylvania Archives*, 8th ser., 8 vols., ed. Gertrude MacKinney and Charles F. Hoban (Harrisburg: Pennsylvania Bureau of Publications, 1931–35), 8:7380–84; "Resolutions Directing the Mode of Levying Taxes on Non-Associators" (March 29, 1776), in *Pennsylvania Archives*, 8th ser., 8:7485–90; "An Ordinance for rendering the burthen of Associators and Non-Associators in the defence of this State as nearly equal as may be" (September 14, 1776), in Peter Force, ed., *American Archives*, 4th and 5th ser., 9 vols. (Washingdon, D.C., 1837–53), 5th ser., 2:42–45, available at *American Archives: Documents of the American Revolutionary Period, 1774–1776*, http://amarch.lib.niu.edu/; Steven Rosswurm, *Arms, Country, and Class: The Philadelphia Militia and the "Lower Sort" During the American Revolution, 1775–1783* (New Brunswick, N.J.: Rutgers University Press, 1987), 136.

14. "An Ordinance for punishing persons guilty of certain offences therein mentioned against the United States of America," in Force, *American Archives*, 5th ser., 2:37–38; Anne M. Ousterhout, "Controlling the Opposition in Pennsylvania During the American Revolution," *PMHB* 105, no. 1 (January 1981): 9.

15. The enabling legislation granted the council

> full power to promote and provide for the preservation of the common-wealth, by such regulations and ordinances as to them shall seem necessary, and to proceed against, seize, detain, imprison, punish, either capitally or otherwise, as the case may require, in a summary mode, either by themselves, or others, by them to be appointed for that purpose; all persons who shall disobey, or transgress the same, or the laws of this state heretofore made, for the purpose of restraining or punishing traitors, or others, who from their general conduct or conversation may be deemed inimical to the common cause of liberty, and the United States of North America.

See Samuel Hazard, ed., *The Register of Pennsylvania: Devoted to the Preservation of Every Kind of Useful Information Respecting the State*, 7 vols. (Philadelphia, 1828–31), 3:200.

16. Hazard, *Register of Pennsylvania*, 3:200; Constitution of the Commonwealth of Pennsylvania (1776), Declaration of Rights, articles 9, 10, and 12; Anne M. Ousterhout has tabulated, to the extent possible from extant records, the punishments inflicted on those accused of disloyal acts in Pennsylvania during the Revolution. See Ousterhout, "Controlling the Opposition," 18–23; Francis Jennings provides a scathing indictment of Pennsylvania's radical government, its violation of its own Declaration of Rights, and the potentially tyrannical powers of its Council of Safety; see Jennings, *The Creation of America* (Cambridge: Cambridge University Press, 2000), 180–92.

17. *Pennsylvania Archives*, 2nd ser., 19 vols., ed. John B. Linn and William H. Egle (Harrisburg: State Printer of Pennsylvania, 1874–90), 3:4 (emphasis added), 6; Robert L. Brunhouse, *The Counter-Revolution in Pennsylvania, 1776–1790* (Harrisburg: Pennsylvania Historical Commission, 1942), 40–41. The Test Act was only one of many loyalty oaths devised by Pennsylvania's revolutionary government.

18. Henry Muhlenberg, *The Journals of Henry Melchior Muhlenberg*, trans. Theodore G. Tappert and John W. Doberstein (Philadelphia: Muhlenberg Press, 1958), 3:55.

19. Brunhouse, *Counter-Revolution in Pennsylvania*, 40–41; Ousterhout, *A State Divided*, 161.

20. Unwilling to accept the people's general refusal of the test, the patriots would repeatedly revise and reinstitute the oath as the months passed. Ousterhout, *A State Divided*, 162–63, 191–94; "Proclamation of Pardon to Prisoners Under Test Laws, 1778," in *Pennsylvania Archives*, 8th ser., 7:130–31.

21. Breen, *Marketplace of Revolution*, 261–62.

22. Ibid.; Alexander Robertson, "To the Publick" (New York, June 23, 1769), *Early American Imprints* Ser. 1, no. 11445, Readex Digital Collections.

23. *Connecticut Courant*, April 3, 1775; Breen, *Marketplace of Revolution*, 327–29.

24. Commager, *Documents of American History*, 84–87.

25. T. H. Breen, *American Insurgents, American Patriots* (New York: Hill and Wang, 2010), 186, quoting the *North Carolina Gazette*, April 14, 1775.

26. James Donald Anderson, "Thomas Wharton, Exile in Virginia, 1777–1778," *Virginia Magazine of History and Biography* 89, no. 4 (October 1981): 427.

27. Ibid., 431.

28. For more focused and extensive investigations of the Virginia exiles, see Robert F. Oaks, "Philadelphians in Exile: The Problem of Loyalty During the American Revolution," *PMHB* 96 (July 1972): 298–325.

29. "Votes of the Assembly," *Pennsylvania Archives*, 8th ser., 8:7261–62 (September 29, 1775). This was the Committee of Safety created by the colonial assembly and headed by Benjamin Franklin.

30. See the address from the Committee of Privates copied in the *Pennsylvania Gazette*, October 11, 1775.

31. "An Ordinance for rendering the burthen of Associators and Non-Associators in the defence of this State as nearly equal as may be" (September 14, 1776).

32. François Furstenberg offers an insightful explanation of how Americans in the early nineteenth century overcame "the particular challenge of U.S. nationalism," which was how to "reconcile consent with stability and continuity: to find a way for future generations voluntarily to give their consent" once the Revolution was over. See Furstenberg, *In the Name of the Father: Washington's Legacy, Slavery, and the Making of a Nation* (New York: Penguin, 2006), 103.

33. Ousterhout, *A State Divided*, 134.

34. John Clark, Jr., "Letters from Major John Clark, Jr., to Gen. Washington, Written During the Occupation of Philadelphia by the British Army," in *Bulletin of the Historical Society of Pennsylvania*, vol. 1, 1845–47 (Philadelphia: Merrihew & Thompson, 1848), 25.

35. Major John Jameson to George Washington, December 31, 1777, in *The Papers of George Washington*, Revolutionary War Series, ed. Philander D. Chase et al. (Charlottesville: University Press of Virginia, 1985–),13:81–82 (hereafter *PGW*).

36. Christopher Marshall, *Extracts from the Diary of Christopher Marshall: Kept in Philadelphia and Lancaster, During the American Revolution, 1774–1781*, ed. William Duane (Albany, N.Y.: Joel Munsell, 1877), 157.

37. Brig. Gen. James Potter to Washington, January 11, 1778, *PGW* 13:202–3.

38. Col. Walter Stewart to Washington, January 18, 1778, *PGW* 13:276–77.

39. See the editors' note, *PGW* 11:189; Stephen R. Taaffe, *The Philadelphia Campaign, 1777–1778* (Lawrence: University Press of Kansas, 2003), 89, 188; General Lacey to General Washington, May 2, 1778, and Lacey to General Armstrong, May 7, 1778, both in Hazard, *Register of Pennsylvania*, 3:342–43; John Montresor, "Journal of Captain John Montresor, July 1, 1777 to July 1, 1778, Chief Engineer of the British Army (Continued)," *PMHB* 6, no. 2 (1882): 202–3; Carl Leopold Baurmeister, *Revolution in America: Confidential Letters and Journals, 1776–1784, of Adjutant General Major Baurmeister of the Hessian Forces*, trans. Bernhard A. Uhlendorf (New Brunswick, N.J.: Rutgers University Press, 1957), 168–69; John Jackson, *With the British Army in Philadelphia* (San Rafael, Calif.: Presido Press, 1979), 223–25.

40. *Journals of the Continental Congress, 1774–1789* (hereafter *JCC*), ed. Worthington C. Ford et al., 34 vols. (Washington, D.C.: U.S. Government Printing Office, 1904–37), 9:751, 784, 1013–15.

41. Washington to Brig. Gen. James Potter, January 12, 1778, *PGW* 13:209.

42. Washington to Brig. Gen. John Lacey, Jr., January 23, 1778, *PGW* 13:323–24.

43. Washington to Col. Walter Stewart, January 22, 1778, *PGW* 13:317; to Lacey, January 23, 1778, *PGW* 13:323–24; to Col. Israel Angell, February 1, 1778, *PGW* 13:433–34; and to Maj. John Jameson, February 1, 1778, *PGW* 13:437.

44. Nathanael Greene to George Washington, February 15, 1778, in *The Papers of General Nathanael Greene*, ed. Richard K. Showman et al. (Chapel Hill: University of North Carolina Press, 1976–), 2:285 (hereafter *PNG*).

45. John André, November 20, 1777, John André Manuscript, Schoff Revolutionary War Collection, William L. Clements Library, University of Michigan, Ann Arbor; Jackson also records the occasional killing of farmers by American pickets (*With the British Army in Philadelphia*, 163).

46. Washington to Brig. Gen. John Lacey, Jr., February 8, 1778, *PGW* 13:477–78.

47. "Gen. Lacey's Orders to His Scouting Party," March 19, 1778, in Hazard, *Register of Pennsylvania*, 3:308.

48. See Rosswurm, *Arms, Country, and Class*, 143–44, 145, 262.

49. See *PGW* 11:54 n. 1; *JCC*, 8:666–67; "John Hancock to Certain States," August 23, 1777, in Paul H. Smith, ed., *Letters of Delegates to Congress, 1774–1789*, 26 vols. (Washington, D.C.: Library of Congress, 1976–2000), 7:536.

50. "Return of the Militia Belonging to the State of Pennsylvania, Sept. 6th, 1777," in *Pennsylvania Archives*, 1st ser., 12 vols., ed. Samuel Hazard (Philadelphia: Joseph Severns, 1852–56), 5:595.

51. Washington to Thomas Wharton, Jr., October 17–18, 1777, *PGW* 11:539–40.

52. Major General John Armstrong to Washington, December 30, 1777, *PGW* 13:57–58; Washington to Thomas Wharton, Jr., January 1, 1778, *PGW* 13:108–9; Wharton to Washington, January 3, 1778, *PGW* 13:136–37; *PGW* 11:54 n. 1; *JCC*, 8:666–67; "John Hancock to Certain States," August 23, 1777.

53. General Lacey to Council, January 24, February 2, and February 15, 1778, in Hazard, *Register of Pennsylvania*, 3:298, 305.

54. George Adams Boyd, *Elias Boudinot: Patriot and Statesman, 1740–1821* (Princeton, N.J.: Princeton University Press, 1952), 43; *PGW* 11:315 n. 2.

55. *Pennsylvania Archives*, 1st ser., 6:390–91; Brig. Gen. John Lacey Jr., to Washington, April 20, 1778, *PGW* 14:569; Lacey to Armstrong, April 28, 1778, in Hazard, *Register of Pennsylvania*, 3:342; Washington to Thomas Wharton, Jr., February 12, 1778, *PGW* 13:519.

56. Washington to William Buchanan, February 7, 1778, *PGW* 13:465.

57. Wayne Bodle, *The Valley Forge Winter: Civilians and Soldiers in War* (University Park: Pennsylvania State University Press, 2002), 165.

58. Washington to Greene, February 12, 1778, *PGW* 13:514.

59. Greene to Washington, February 15, 1778, *PNG* 2:285.

60. Greene to Washington, February 16, 1778, *PGW* 13:557–58; the severity of Greene's measures caught the attention of at least one officer in Philadelphia. Major Baurmeister recorded that "the rebels are devastating the land and carrying off everything," that "the whole country around Valley Forge is devastated," and that revolutionaries were "always looking for [those bringing goods to Philadelphia] and maltreat those they catch." Baurmeister, *Revolution in America*, 157.

61. Greene to Washington, February 17, 1778, *PGW* 13:569–70.

62. Greene to Washington, February 15, 1778, *PNG* 2:285; Washington to Greene, February 16, 1778, *PGW* 13:556–57; Greene to Washington, February 16, 1778, *PNG* 2:286–87.

63. Joseph Reed to [not addressed], Camp Valley Forge, February 1, 1778, Joseph Reed Papers, David Library of the American Revolution (hereafter DLAR), Washington Crossing, Pa.

64. J. B. Smith [?] to Joseph Reed, February 21, 1778, Joseph Reed Papers.

65. Philadelphia, January 22, 1778, James Grant Papers, Army Career Series, Letterbook 4. Ref: MFilP/GD494/1/box 29, film 687, reel 28, DLAR.

66. "Sir William Howe's Defense (Before a Select Committee of the House of Commons) of His Conduct as Commander-in-Chief of the British Forces in the War of Independence," Henry Strachey Papers, box 2, folder 51, William L. Clements Library.

67. Brown, *The King's Friends*, 131, 138, 145–46, 137.

68. For example, see Friedrich von Muenchhausen, *At General Howe's Side, 1776–1778*, trans. Ernst Kipping (Monmouth Beach, N.J.: Philip Freneau Press, 1974), 49; memorandum sent with a letter from Major General Stirling to Washington, General Potter's Qrs [Radnor, Pa.], December 26, 1777, *PGW* 12:10–11; Potter to Washington, January 11, 1778, *PGW* 13:202–3.

69. Howe to Germain, October 21, 1777, George Sackville Germain Papers, vol. 6, William L. Clements Library.

70. Loyalist leader Joseph Galloway expected great things of the loyalists in Pennsylvania, and even General William Howe suggested that he might rally a force of five thousand from the Delaware Valley. See Joseph Galloway, "Proposal for covering and reducing the Country as the British Army shall pass through it," Sir Henry Clinton Papers, vol. 35:47, William L. Clements Library; Howe to Germain, October 21, 1777; Smith, *Loyalists and Redcoats*, 47.

71. Indeed, these groups are hardly mutually exclusive; many slaves, free blacks, and Native Americans likely entered the Revolution with very little political affection for either side.

CHAPTER 4. LOYALISM, CITIZENSHIP, AMERICAN IDENTITY

1. Rebecca Shoemaker diary, November 3, 1781, Shoemaker Family Papers, Historical Society of Pennsylvania (hereafter cited as HSP).

2. Robert Calhoon, *The Loyalists in Revolutionary America, 1780–1781* (New York: Harcourt Brace, 1965), 390–94.

3. Sarah Fatherly, *Gentlewomen and Learned Ladies: Women and Elite Formation in Eighteenth-Century Philadelphia* (Bethlehem, Pa.: Lehigh University Press, 2008), 133–37. Fatherly argues that women were essential to the crafting of a London-style elite in Philadelphia, and she also argues that Philadelphia was uniquely positioned as an Atlantic information hub during the Revolution. Women claimed political engagement as part of elite womanhood.

4. Craig W. Horle, Joseph S. Foster, and Laurie M. Wolfe, eds., *Lawmaking and Legislators in Pennsylvania: A Biographical Dictionary*, vol. 3, *1757–1775* (Philadelphia: University of Pennsylvania Press, 1991), 1284–87; introduction to Shoemaker Family Papers, HSP. Francis Rawle accidentally shot and killed himself while hunting at Point-no-Point, his country estate on the Delaware.

5. Forfeited Estate Files; Revolutionary War Legislation; and Pennsylvania State Legislature and Council of Safety Records; all in Revolutionary War Records, Pennsylvania State Archives. The Pennsylvania State Archives is hereafter cited as PSA. On the emerging definition of citizenship and identity, see Dror Wahrman, "The English Problem of Identity in the American Revolution," *American Historical Review* 106 (2001): 1236–62.

6. In Pennsylvania the confiscation of loyalist property initially targeted loyalists who participated in the British occupation in Philadelphia. The Pennsylvania legislature passed loyalist confiscation laws that targeted those individuals who were highly visible and active in the occupation. For examples, see the October 21, 1777, records in the Pennsylvania State Legislature and Council of Safety Records, Revolutionary War Records, PSA.

7. Douglas Bradburn, *The Citizenship Revolution: Politics and the Creation of the American Union, 1774–1804* (Charlottesville: University of Virginia Press, 2009), 2.

8. Ibid., 5–6.

9. Non-associators, a loosely defined category of those who refused to claim allegiance to either side in favor of neutrality, also puzzled the legislature and were often referred to in legislation as "non-jurors." Non-jurors were not as blatantly threatening to the patriots, but they were problematic because their lack of allegiance complicated their rights to citizenship. Other historians have used the term "disaffected" to refer to individuals who did not identify as patriot or loyalist during the Revolution. On the disaffected women in Philadelphia, see Judith Van Buskirk, "They Didn't Join the Band: Disaffected Women in Revolutionary Philadelphia," *Pennsylvania History* 62 (1995): 306–29.

10. Kariann Yokota, *Unbecoming British: How Revolutionary America Became a Postcolonial Nation* (New York: Oxford University Press, 2010), 9.

11. Maya Jasanoff, *Liberty's Exiles: American Loyalists in the Revolutionary World* (New York: Knopf, 2011), 6. For additional information on the loyalist diaspora, see also Keith Mason, "The American Loyalist Diaspora and the Reconfiguration of the British Atlantic World," in Eliga H. Gould and Peter S. Onuf, eds., *Empire and Nation: The American Revolution in the*

Atlantic World (Baltimore: Johns Hopkins University Press, 2005), 239–59; Jerry Bannister and Liam Riordan, eds., *The Loyal Atlantic: Remaking the British Atlantic in the Revolutionary Era* (Toronto: University of Toronto Press, 2012).

12. Jasanoff, *Liberty's Exiles*, 13, 91, 349–49. For an excellent synthesis on the loyalist Atlantic, see Jerry Bannister and Liam Riordan, "Loyalism and the British Atlantic, 1660–1840," in Bannister and Riordan, *The Loyal Atlantic*, 3–36.

13. For the Shoemakers' return to Burlington and additional information regarding their residences, see the introduction to the Shoemaker Family Papers, HSP.

14. Calhoon, *Loyalists in Revolutionary America*, 145–50.

15. Wilbur H. Siebert, *The Loyalists of Pennsylvania* (Columbus: Ohio State University, 1920), 38–55; Wallace Brown, *The King's Friends: The Composition and Motives of American Loyalist Claims* (Providence, R.I.: Brown University Press, 1965), 130–31.

16. Henry Young, "Treason and Its Punishment in Revolutionary Pennsylvania," *PMHB* 90 (1966): 289–90.

17. Ibid., 291–94. Young notes that the treason act of 1777 specified the seven offenses that constituted "treason": accepting a commission from the enemy, levying war, enlisting or persuading others to enlist in the enemy army, furnishing arms or supplies to the enemy, carrying on correspondence with the enemy, being concerned in a treasonable combination, and furnishing intelligence to the enemy. Young's article is not overly concerned with the confiscation of loyalist estates but rather with all punishments associated with treason.

18. Robert L. Brunhouse, *The Counter-Revolution in Pennsylvania, 1776–1790* (Harrisburg: Pennsylvania Historical Commission, 1942), 42–43; Brown, *The King's Friends*, 134; Lorenzo Sabine, *Biographical Sketches of Loyalists of the American Revolution* (Boston: Little, Brown, 1864), 2:301; Anne Osterhout, *A State Divided: Opposition in Pennsylvania to the American Revolution* (New York: Greenwood Press, 1987), 161.

19. Pennsylvania Council of Safety, October 21, 1777, Broadside, Revolutionary War Records, PSA.

20. Ibid. For the city of Philadelphia the commissioners were William Will, Sharp Delany, Jacob Shriner, Charles Willson Peale, Robert Smith, and Samuel Massey. For the county of Philadelphia the commissioners were William Antis, Robert Lollar, James Stroud, Daniel Hiester, and Archibald Thompson.

21. "An act for the attainder of diverse traitors," Pennsylvania Council of Safety, printed in Lancaster, by John Dunlap in 1778, Revolutionary War Records, PSA.

22. Ibid. Among them were: Joseph Galloway who had aided General Howe; John Allen who had formerly served on the committee of inspection; William Allen, a current British lieutenant colonel; James Rankin, a yeoman of York County; Jacob Duche, the previous chaplain to the Congress; Gilbert Hick, a yeoman from Bucks County; John Potts, a yeoman from Philadelphia County; Nathaniel Vernon, the former sheriff of Chester County; Christian Fouts, a lieutenant colonel; Reynold Keen, a yeoman from Berks County; John Biddle, a deputy quartermaster; and Samuel Shoemaker.

23. Ibid. For additional information on land confiscation and legislation see Anne M. Ousterhout, "Pennsylvania Land Confiscation During the Revolution," *PMHB* 102 (1978): 328–43.

24. Forfeited Estate Files; Revolutionary War Legislation; and Pennsylvania State Legislature and Council of Safety Records; all in Revolutionary War Records, PSA. On the emerging definition of citizenship, see Wahrman, "English Problem of Identity"; Bradburn, *The Citizenship Revolution*; Carroll Smith-Rosenberg, *This Violent Empire: The Birth of an American National Identity* (Chapel Hill: University of North Carolina Press, 2010). For postwar

cultural dimensions and the question of British identity in the wake of the American Revolution, see Yokota, *Unbecoming British*.

25. Confiscation of loyalist property became somewhat selective in practice. The laws dictated the confiscation of the property of notable individuals. See Pennsylvania Council of Safety Records, October 21, 1777, Revolutionary War Records, PSA, for one example.

26. Ousterhout, *A State Divided*, 161.

27. Horle, Foster, and Wolfe, *Lawmaking and Legislators in Pennsylvania*, 1284–1300.

28. Introduction to Rebecca Shoemaker's diary, Shoemaker Family Papers, HSP; introduction, Rawle Family Papers, HSP. See also Calhoon, *Loyalists in Revolutionary America*, 390–96; and Ousterhout, *A State Divided*, 171–73.

29. Introduction to Rebecca Shoemaker's diary, Shoemaker Family Papers, HSP. Other members of Shoemaker family fled to New York. Edward joined his father in New York, and Rebecca left for New York in June 1780.

30. "An act for the attainder of diverse traitors."

31. Horle, Foster, and Wolfe, *Lawmaking and Legislators in Pennsylvania*, 1292.

32. Forfeited Estate Files, Revolutionary War Records, PSA. For some information relating to Charles Peale, confiscation, and Benedict Arnold, see Benjamin Irvin, *Clothed in Robes of Sovereignty: The Continental Congress and the People Out of Doors* (New York: Oxford University Press, 2011), 251–55.

33. "Forfeited Estate Sale," *Pennsylvania Packet*, August 27, 1778.

34. For reference, see "Forfeited Estate Sale,"*Pennsylvania Packet*, June 6, 1779. Additional forfeited estates were listed in the *Pennsylvania Packet* for the following dates: July 10, 13, September 16, November 11, 1779, March 28, May 16, 1780, and January 17, 1782.

35. Philadelphia County and City Records, Forfeited Estate Sale, Revolutionary War Records, PSA; "Forfeited Estate Sale," *Pennyslvania Packet*, September 23, 1779, June 17, 1780; Revolutionary War Records, PSA. The actual revenue collected from the Shoemaker's property is difficult to discern, given the problem of payment, claims of debt, and the inability of the commissioners to record property sale transactions. For example, in September 1779 Christopher Handlman approached the Pennsylvania legislature about debts owed to him by Samuel Shoemaker. The court agreed with his claims and found the allegations of debts to be substantiated. Handlman received £89 out of the forfeited estate of Shoemaker in 1779. Moreover, the commissioners inconsistently recorded the amount of money received from the sale of property. For example, Samuel Shoemaker's property along Water Street was sold to Benjamin Davis in June 1780; however, there is no record of what it sold for and what money was collected at the time of sale. See examples in "Forfeited Estate Sale," records for September 23, 1779, June 17, 1780, October 1780, Revolutionary War Records, PSA.

36. See "Forfeited Estate Sale,"*Pennsylvania Packet*, September 23, 1779, June 17, 1780, Revolutionary War Records, PSA. The same information such as time of sale, location of sale, and terms of sale is found in all the advertisements in *Pennsylvania Packet*.

37. Introduction to the collection of Rebecca Shoemaker's letters and diaries, Shoemaker Family Papers, HSP. William Rawle remained in New York until June 15, 1781, and then sailed for England. It is unclear when exactly Edward Shoemaker arrived in New York, but he did leave with Samuel Shoemaker on November 18, 1783, for England.

38. Ibid. For information on the lives of the Shoemakers in New York, see Judith L. Van Buskirk, *Generous Enemies: Patriots and Loyalists in Revolutionary New York* (Philadelphia: University of Pennsylvania Press, 2002), 26, 162–63, 189. For additional information on New

York during the Revolution, see Ruma Chopra, *Unnatural Rebellion: Loyalists in New York City During the Revolution* (Charlottesville: University of Virginia Press, 2011).

39. Van Buskirk, *Generous Enemies*, 3–23.
40. June 7, 1780, Rebecca Shoemaker Papers, 1780–1786, HSP.
41. Rebecca Shoemaker to Anna and Peggy Rawle, June 21, 1780, Shoemaker Family Papers, HSP; Anna Rawle to Rebecca Shoemaker, June 30, 1780, Shoemaker Family Papers, HSP.
42. Peggy Rawle to Rebecca Shoemaker, February 1781, Shoemaker Family Papers, HSP.
43. Anna Rawle to Rebecca Shoemaker, March 7, 1781, Shoemaker Family Papers, HSP.
44. Anna Rawle to Rebecca Shoemaker, May 8, 1781, Shoemaker Family Papers, HSP.
45. Rebecca Shoemaker to her daughters, April 11, 1781, Rebecca Shoemaker Papers, 1780–1786, HSP; Anna Rawle to Rebecca Shoemaker, October 26, 1781, Rebecca Shoemaker Papers, 1780–1786, HSP.
46. Rebecca Shoemaker to Anna Rawle, November 3, 1781, Shoemaker Family Papers, HSP.
47. Anna Rawle to Rebecca Shoemaker, April 26, 28, 1783, Shoemaker Family Papers, HSP.
48. Rebecca Shoemaker to Anna Rawle, April 13, 1783, Shoemaker Family Papers, HSP.
49. Introduction to the collection of Rebecca Shoemaker's letters and diaries, Shoemaker Family Papers, HSP.
50. Rebecca to Samuel Shoemaker, May 12, 1784, Shoemaker Family Papers, HSP.
51. Ibid.
52. Rebecca Shoemaker to Samuel Shoemaker, June 1785, Shoemaker Family Papers, HSP.
53. "A Pennsylvania Loyalist's Interview with George III: Extract from the MS. Diary of Samuel Shoemaker," *PMHB* 2 (1878): 39. Samuel's diary details his daily life in London during his separation from Rebecca. The excerpt reprinted in *PMHB* is a selection from that diary and contains his interview with George III.
54. Samuel Shoemaker, Loyalist Claims Commission, Record series Ao 12 Roll 38, University of Delaware.
55. Sabine, *Biographical Sketches of Loyalists*, 2:302.
56. "A Pennsylvania Loyalist's Interview," 38.
57. Daniel Parker Coke, *The Royal Commission on the Losses and Services of American Loyalists, 1783–1785* (London: Oxford University Press, 1915), 382. The record does not fully state what exactly the Shoemakers received payment for and what land and goods the Claims Commission validated.
58. Ousterhout, *A State Divided*, 287.
59. Ibid., 295. Ousterhout also explores confiscation in her article "Pennsylvania Land Confiscation During the Revolution," 328–43. However, she relies on selected property claims made to the Royal Claims Commission and does not make any reference to loyalist families that returned to the United States.
60. Horle, Foster, and Wolfe, *Lawmaking and Legislators in Pennsylvania*, 1295; death notice of Samuel Shoemaker, *Poulson's American Daily Advertiser*, October 10, 1800.
61. Ousterhout, *A State Divided*, 220.

CHAPTER 5. "EXECUTIONERS OF THEIR FRIENDS AND BRETHREN"

1. *New-Jersey Gazette* (Trenton), May 9, 1781.
2. Ibid.

3. Jesse Lemisch's seminal article "Jack Tar in the Streets: Merchant Seamen in the Politics of Revolutionary America," *William and Mary Quarterly* 3rd ser. 25 (1968): 371–407, continues to influence the field. In rescuing Jack Tar from indifference and typecasting by historians, Lemisch introduced a new stereotype of Jack as reflexively American. For narratives that incorporate and build on Lemisch's work, see Gary B. Nash, *The Urban Crucible: Social Change, Political Consciousness, and the Origins of the American Revolution* (Cambridge, Mass.: Harvard University Press, 1979); Benjamin L. Carp, *Rebels Rising: Cities and the American Revolution* (New York: Oxford University Press, 2007), esp. 23–61; Marcus Rediker, "A Motley Crew of Rebels: Sailors, Slaves, and the Coming of the American Revolution," in, Ronald Hoffman and Peter J. Albert, eds., *The Transforming Hand of Revolution: Reconsidering the American Revolution as a Social Movement* (Charlottesville: University of Virginia Press, 1995), 155–98; and Peter Linebaugh and Marcus Rediker, *The Many-Headed Hydra: Sailors, Slaves, Commoners, and the Hidden History of the Revolutionary Atlantic* (Boston: Beacon Press, 2000), 211–47.

4. Paul A. Gilje, *Liberty on the Waterfront: American Maritime Culture in the Age of Revolution* (Philadelphia: University of Pennsylvania Press, 2004), 115–16.

5. Pauline Maier, *American Scripture: Making the Declaration of Independence* (New York: Knopf, 1997), 25–28; Robert G. Parkinson, "Twenty-Seven Reasons for Independence," in Christian Y. Dupont and Peter S. Onuf, eds., *Declaring Independence: The Origin and Influence of America's Founding Document* (Charlottesville: University of Virginia Library, 2008), 11–18. For the navy's use of impressment for war making, see *Preston* Log, June 17–18, 1775, and Samuel Graves to the Admiralty, Boston, November 30, 1775, in "Conduct of Vice-Admiral Graves in North America in 1774, 1775, and January 1776," Frederick L. Gay Transcripts, Massachusetts Historical Society, Boston.

6. Consider, for example, the absence of sailors in Maya Jasanoff, *Liberty's Exiles: American Loyalists in the Revolutionary World* (New York: Knopf, 2011). The theme of divided loyalties is a constant in Edward G. Gray and Jane Kamensky, eds., *The Oxford Handbook of the American Revolution* (New York: Oxford University Press, 2013), yet there is not a single essay on the sea. For important exceptions to the historiographical trend, see Paul A. Gilje, "Loyalty and Liberty: The Ambiguous Patriotism of Jack Tar in the American Revolution," *Pennsylvania History* 67 (2000): 165–93, and Gilje, *Liberty on the Waterfront*, 97–129.

7. David Starkey, "War and the Market for Seafarers in Britain, 1736–1792," in Lewis R. Fischer and Helge W. Nordvik, eds., *Shipping and Trade, 1750–1950: Essays in International Maritime Economic History* (Pontefract: Lofthouse, 1990), 29; Roland G. Usher, Jr., "Royal Navy Impressment During the American Revolution," *Mississippi Valley Historical Review* 37 (1951): 677–78, 681. The percentage for impressed seamen is likely higher because it is not clear how many ultimately accepted the king's bounty and became listed as "volunteers."

8. Nicholas Rogers, "Liberty Road: Opposition to Impressment in Britain During the American War of Independence," in Colin Howell and Richard J. Twomey, eds., *Jack Tar in History: Essays in the History of Maritime Life and Labour* (Fredericton, N.B.: Acadiensis, 1991), 55–75; Denver Brunsman, *The Evil Necessity: British Naval Impressment in the Eighteenth-Century Atlantic World* (Charlottesville: University of Virginia Press, 2013), 244–45.

9. Christopher Lloyd, *The British Seaman, 1200–1860: A Social Survey* (London: Collins, 1968), 189; Liza Picard, *Dr. Johnson's London: Life in London, 1740–1770* (London: Phoenix Press, 2000), 111.

10. Linebaugh and Rediker, *Many-Headed Hydra*, 219–20; Harcourt to Rochrord, Paris, February 20, 1771, State Papers 78/282, National Archives of the United Kingdom, Kew, London (hereafter TNA).

11. Wilkes quoted in Peter D. G. Thomas, *John Wilkes: A Friend to Liberty* (Oxford: Oxford University Press, 1996), 121; "Copy of a Memorial to the King concerning the Lord Mayor of London, and Mayor of Liverpool refusing to back the Press Warrants," December 14, 1770, Admiralty Papers 1/5117/7, TNA.

12. William Lee to Richard Henry Lee, London, July 13, 1775, in William Bell Clark et al., eds., *Naval Documents of the American Revolution*, 11 vols. (Washington, D.C.: U.S. GPO, 1964–2005), 1:1326.

13. *London Chronicle*, March 2–5, 1776, in Clark et al., *Naval Documents*, 4:941.

14. Quote from an unidentified London newspaper reprinted in *Maryland Journal*, March 25, 1777, in Clark et al., *Naval Documents*, 8:199.

15. "Extracts from Parliamentary Debates," October 31, 1776, in Clark et al., *Naval Documents*, 7:719.

16. Nicholas Rogers, *The Press Gang: Naval Impressment and Its Opponents in Georgian Britain* (London: Continuum, 2007), 45.

17. Usher, "Royal Navy Impressment," 682–83, 685; N. A. M. Rodger, *The Command of the Ocean: A Naval History of Britain, 1649–1815* (New York: Norton, 2004), 398–99; Rogers, "Liberty Road," 72.

18. For measures of the war's popularity in Britain, see James E. Bradley, *Popular Politics and the American Revolution in England: Petitions, the Crown, and Public Opinion* (Macon, Ga.: Mercer University Press, 1986).

19. Brunsman, *Evil Necessity*, 91–135. See also Dora Mae Clark, "The Impressment of Seamen in the American Colonies," in *Essays in Colonial History Presented to Charles McLean Andrews by His Students* (New Haven, Conn.: Yale University Press, 1931), 198–224.

20. "An Act for the Encouragement of the Fisheries carried on from Great Britain, Ireland, and the British Dominions in Europe, and for securing the Return of the Fishermen, Sailors, and others employed in the said Fisheries, to the Ports thereof, at the End of the Fishing Season" (15 Geo. III, cap. 31), *Statutes at Large from Magna Charta to the End of the Eleventh Parliament of Great Britain* (London, 1775), 31:56–72; Keith Mercer, "The Murder of Lieutenant Lawry: A Case Study of British Naval Impressment in Newfoundland, 1794," *Newfoundland and Labrador Studies* 21 (2006): 262–63; Keith Mercer, "Northern Exposure: Resistance to Naval Impressment in British North America, 1775–1815," *Canadian Historical Review* 91 (2010): 211–12.

21. Richard Hughes, "Proclamation," January 22, 1781, *Nova Scotia Gazette* (Halifax), January 23, 1781 (quote); Minutes of the Council, August 4, 1775, Minutes of His Majesty's Council, 1749–1867, RG 1, vol. 189, reel 15289, Public Archives of Nova Scotia, Halifax; Keith Mercer, "Sailors and Citizens: Press Gangs and Naval-Civilian Relations in Nova Scotia, 1756–1815," *Journal of the Royal Nova Scotia Historical Society* (2007): 92–92; Mercer, "Northern Exposure," 207–8.

22. Young quoted in Andrew O'Shaughnessy, *An Empire Divided: The American Revolution and the British Caribbean* (Philadelphia: University of Pennsylvania Press, 2000), 180; Brunsman, *Evil Necessity*, 119–23.

23. Minutes of the Governor's Council of West Florida, Pensacola, March 29, 1777, in Clark et al., *Naval Documents*, 8:225–26.

24. British Royal Navy, *All Gentlemen Sailors, Desirous of Rendering Themselves Useful to Their Country . . .* (Philadelphia: James Humphreys, 1777).

25. William Tryon, *By His Excellency William Tryon, Esq . . . A Proclamation* (New York, 1778). I thank Charles Foy of Eastern Illinois University for this reference.

26. British Royal Navy, *New-York, Saturday, July 15, 1780* . . . (New York, 1780).

27. For an example of impressment from government vessels, see George Rodney to William Bullen, Sandwich, Sandy Hook, November 13, 1780, Order Book of Lord George Rodney, November 22, 1779 to February 12, 1781, New-York Historical Society. For the British difficulty in maintaining supply lines, see David Syrett, *Shipping and the American War, 1775–83: A Study of British Transport Organization* (London: Athlone, 1970). For American loyalists in the British army, see Paul H. Smith, "The American Loyalists: Notes on Their Organization and Numerical Strength," *William and Mary Quarterly* 3rd. ser. 25, no. 2 (1968): 259–77.

28. *Independent Ledger* (Boston), June 29, 1778 (quote), May 22, 1780; *Pennsylvania Packet* (Philadelphia), October 1, 1778; *New-Jersey Gazette* (Trenton), November 15, 1780; *Freeman's Journal* (Philadelphia), May 16, 1781; *Connecticut Courant* (Hartford), April 16, 1782.

29. Letter by Captain Pausch, June 8, 1781, in Bruce E. Burgoyne, ed., *Enemy Views: The American Revolutionary War as Recorded by the Hessian Participants* (Bowie, Md.: Heritage Books, 1996), 480.

30. W. J. Rorabaugh, "'I Thought I Should Liberate Myself from the Thraldom of Others': Apprentices, Masters, and the Revolution," in Alfred F. Young, ed., *Beyond the American Revolution: Explorations in the History of American Radicalism* (DeKalb: Northern Illinois University Press, 1993), 189–90.

31. Jesse Lemisch, "Listening to the 'Inarticulate': William Widger's Dream and the Loyalties of American Revolutionary Seamen in British Prisons," *Journal of Social History* 3 (1969–70): 1–29; Francis D. Cogliano, *American Maritime Prisoners in the Revolutionary War: The Captivity of William Russell* (Annapolis, Md.: Naval Institute Press, 2001); Sheldon Cohen, *Yankee Sailors in British Gaols: Prisoners of War at Forton and Mill, 1777–1783* (Newark: University of Delaware Press, 1995); Edwin G. Burrows, *Forgotten Patriots: The Untold Story of American Prisoners During the Revolutionary War* (New York: Basic Books, 2008).

32. Philip Stephens to Richard Howe, London, June 23, 1776, in Clark et al., *Naval Documents*, 6:438.

33. *The Gazette of the State of South-Carolina* (Charleston), November 4, 1777, reprinted in Clark et al., *Naval Documents*, 10:398.

34. John K. Alexander, "Forton Prison During the American Revolution: A Case Study of British Prisoner of War Policy and the American Prisoner Response to That Policy," *Essex Institute Historical Collections* 103 (1967): 368.

35. Cohen, *Yankee Sailors*, 27–29, 180, 224; Burrows, *Forgotten Patriots*, 80.

36. Christopher Prince, *The Autobiography of a Yankee Mariner: Christopher Prince and the American Revolution*, ed. Michael J. Crawford (Washington, D.C.: Brassey's, 2002), 43.

37. John O. Sands, "Christopher Vail, Soldier and Seaman in the American Revolution," *Winterthur Portfolio* 11 (1976): 67 ("jelly"), 68–69 (Foster interrogation); Gilje, *Liberty on the Waterfront*, 115.

38. Jacob Nagle, *The Nagle Journal: A Diary of the Life of Jacob Nagle, Sailor, from the Year 1775 to 1841*, ed. John C. Dann (New York: Weidenfeld and Nicolson, 1988), 50.

39. Ibid., 37–70.

40. Ibid.; Denver Brunsman, "Men of War: British Sailors and the Impressment Paradox," *Journal of Early Modern History* 14 (2010): 9–44; Brunsman, *Evil Necessity*, 139–70.

41. Joshua Davis, *A Narrative of Joshua Davis, an American Citizen, Who Was Pressed and Served on Board Six Ships of the British Navy* . . . (Boston: B. True, 1811).

42. John Greenwood, *A Young Patriot in the American Revolution, 1775–1783* . . . (Tyrone, Pa.: Westvaco, 1981), 106 (quote).

43. For high estimates of prisoners and prisoner deaths, see Lemisch, "Listening to the 'Inarticulate,'" 7, 9n20; and Burrows, *Forgotten Patriots*, x–xi. I have followed Francis Cogliano in accepting Peckham's figures (*American Maritime Prisoners*, 149–50, 194 n. 32). See Howard Peckham, ed., *The Toll of Independence: Engagements and Battle Casualties of the Revolution* (Chicago: University of Chicago Press, 1974), 132.

44. "Recollections of General [Jeremiah] Johnston, Part 2," *Journal of Long Island History* 13 (1976): 24. I thank my colleague Tyler Anbinder for sharing this reference.

45. Burrows, *Forgotten Patriots*, 201; Cogliano, *American Maritime Prisoners*, 149; Alexander, "Forton Prison," 380.

46. Philip Freneau, *The Poems of Philip Freneau: Written Chiefly During the Late War* (Philadelphia: Francis Bailey, 1786), 193.

47. Cogliano, *American Maritime Prisoners*, 154–61; Cohen, *Yankee Sailors*, 77–84; Alexander, "Forton Prison," 366.

48. Gilje, *Liberty on the Waterfront*, 119.

49. Cogliano, *American Maritime Prisoners*, 116–18; Cohen, *Yankee Sailors*, 104–5, Alexander, "Forton Prison," 384; Lemisch, "Listening to the 'Inarticulate,'" 17.

50. Ebenezer Fox, *The Adventures of Ebenezer Fox, in the Revolutionary War* (Boston: Charles Fox, 1847).

51. Ibid., 94, 135, 148.

52. Caleb Foot, *Reminiscences of the Revolution: Prison Letters and Sea Journal of Caleb Foot* (Salem, Mass.: Essex Institute, 1889), 8.

53. Lemisch, "Listening to the 'Inarticulate,'" 6; William Widger, "The Diary of William Widger of Marblehead, Kept at Mill Prison, England, 1781," *Essex Institute Historical Collections* 73 (1937): 311–47.

54. Cohen, *Yankee Sailors*, 181.

55. Cogliano, *American Maritime Prisoners*, 95.

56. Charles Herbert, *A Relic of the Revolution, Containing a Full and Particular Account of the Sufferings and Privations of All the American Prisoners Captured on the High Seas, and Carried into Plymouth, England, During the Revolution of 1776* (Boston, 1847; repr., New York: New York Times and Arno Press, 1968), 117; Cogliano, *American Maritime Prisoners*, 118–19.

57. Brunsman, *Evil Necessity*, 120–22, 166; W. Jeffrey Bolster, *Black Jacks: African American Seamen in the Age of Sail* (Cambridge, Mass.: Harvard University Press, 1997).

58. Timothy Connor, *A Sailor's Songbag: An American Rebel in an English Prison, 1777–1779*, ed. George G. Carey (Amherst: University of Massachusetts Press, 1976).

59. Herbert, *Relic of the Revolution*, 172.

60. Russell quoted in Cogliano, *American Maritime Prisoners*, 113.

61. Charles Francis Jenkins, "John Claypoole's Memorandum-Book," *PMHB* 16 (1892): 186.

62. For compulsory service in the Continental Army and state militias, see Charles Royster, *A Revolutionary People at War: The Continental Army and American Character, 1775–1783* (Chapel Hill: University of North Carolina Press, 1979), 65–69, 131–35, 267–70, 303–8; Caroline Cox, *A Proper Sense of Honor: Service and Sacrifice in George Washington's Army* (Chapel Hill: University of North Carolina Press, 2004), 12–17; and Michael A. McDonnell, "Class War? Class Struggles During the American Revolution in Virginia," *William and Mary Quarterly* 3rd ser. 63 (2006): 305–44.

63. For American naval impressment, see William M. Fowler, Jr., "The Non-Volunteer Navy," U.S. Naval Institute, *Proceedings* 100 (1974): 74–78; William M. Fowler, Jr., *Rebels Under Sail: The American Navy During the Revolution* (New York: Charles Scribner's Sons, 1976),

279–89; Elizabeth Cometti, "Impressment During the American Revolution," in Vera Largent, ed., *The Walter Jackson Essays in the Social Sciences* (Chapel Hill: University of North Carolina Press, 1942), 97–109; and John W. Jackson, *The Pennsylvania Navy, 1775–1781: The Defense of the Delaware* (New Brunswick, N.J.: Rutgers University Press, 1974), 82–83, 311. For impressment and American national identity, see Denver Brunsman, "Subjects vs. Citizens: Impressment and Identity in the Anglo-American Atlantic," *Journal of the Early Republic* 30 (2010): 557–86.

64. Fowler, *Rebels Under Sail*, 225, 243–45; Cohen, *Yankee Sailors*, 25; Gardner W. Allen, *Massachusetts Privateers of the Revolution* (Boston: Massachusetts Historical Society, 1927). For able seamen, see Brunsman, *Evil Necessity*, 53–55.

65. Charles O. Paulin, ed., *Out-Letters of the Continental Marine Committee and Board of Admiralty, August 1776–September 1780*, 2 vols. (New York: Printed for Navy Historical Society by De Vinne Press, 1914), 1:167, 272; Journal of the Continental Congress, August 5, 1776, in Clark et al., *Naval Documents*, 6:63. For an example of impressed Americans taken prisoner, see John Watson to Jonathan Trumbull, Hartford, June 21, 1776, in Clark et al., *Naval Documents*, 5:659–60.

66. Journal of the Continental Congress, Philadelphia, November 2, 1776, in *JCC*, 16:919 (quote); Jackson, *Pennsylvania Navy*, 82–83; Fowler, *Rebels Under Sail*, 251.

67. Jedidiah Elderkin and Nathaniel Wales, Jr., to Jonathan Trumbull, in Clark et al., *Naval Documents*, 7:220–21; "Observations by the Late Master of the British Ship *Spiers*," in Clark et al., *Naval Documents*, 7:299.

68. Thomas Haley to the Commissioners for Sick and Hurt Seamen, Mill Prison, Plymouth, September 21, 1777, in Clark et al., *Naval Documents*, 9:652–53.

69. William Bell Clark, *Ben Franklin's Privateers: A Naval Epic of the American Revolution* (Baton Rouge: Louisiana State University Press, 1956); Catherine M. Prelinger, "Benjamin Franklin and the American Prisoners of War in England During the American Revolution," *William and Mary Quarterly* 3rd ser. 32 (1975): 276–77.

70. American Commissioners to Lord Stormont, Paris, April 3, 1777, in *The Papers of Benjamin Franklin*, 41 vols. to date, ed. Leonard W. Labaree et al. (New Haven, Conn.: Yale University Press, 1959–), 23:554 (hereafter *Franklin Papers*).

71. Prelinger, "Benjamin Franklin," 263.

72. Benjamin Franklin to Stephen Marchant, Passy, July 4, 1779, in *Franklin Papers*, 30:29. The Irish smuggler Luke Ryan used the American privateer Stephen Marchant to get a privateering commission from Franklin before later taking over the *Black Prince* (Clark, *Ben Franklin's Privateers*, 81–82).

73. Marchant quoted in Clark, *Ben Franklin's Privateers*, 49.

74. Robert H. Patton, *Patriot Pirates: The Privateer War for Freedom and Fortune in the American Revolution* (New York: Pantheon, 2008), 198.

75. Franklin's instructions to John Paul Jones, in *Franklin Papers*, 29:387; Cohen, *Yankee Sailors*, 155–59.

76. Deposition of Thomas Warner, August 19, 1777, in Clark et al., *Naval Documents*, 9:771.

77. Board of Admiralty to the Commissioners of the Navy Board of the Eastern Department, September 5, 1780, in Paulin, *Out-Letters*, 2:258.

78. Linda Colley, *Captives: Britain, Empire and the World, 1600–1850* (New York: Pantheon, 2002), 208–16; Burrows, *Forgotten Patriots*, 183–84.

79. Cometti, "Impressment"; Fowler, "Non-Volunteer Navy."

80. Cometti, "Impressment," 99–100.
81. Pennsylvania Naval Board to John Webb, Philadelphia, April 28, 1777, in Clark et al., *Naval Documents*, 8:458.
82. Jackson, *Pennsylvania Navy*, 311.
83. Cometti, "Impressment," 100.
84. Thomas Johnson to James Nicholson, Annapolis, April 24, 1777, in Clark et al., *Naval Documents*, 8:421.
85. James Nicholson to Thomas Johnson, Baltimore, April 25, 1777, in Clark et al., *Naval Documents*, 8:431.
86. Robert Morris to Thomas Johnson, Philadelphia, May 1, 1777, in Clark et al., *Naval Documents*, 8:887–88; Fowler, *Rebels Under Sail*, 288–89. For Nicholson's later impressments, see Board of Admiralty to James Nicholson, September 2, 1780, in Paulin, *Out-Letters*, 2:255–56; and Fowler, "Non-Volunteer Navy," 78. In 1797, Nicholson served as the first commander of the USS *Constitution* and the following year sailed "Old Ironsides" into the Caribbean in the Quasi-War against France.
87. Joseph Reed to Congress, October 21, 1779, in *Pennsylvania Archives*, 1st ser., 12 vols., ed. Samuel Hazard (Philadelphia: Joseph Severns, 1852–56), 7:761–62.
88. Fowler, "Non-Volunteer Navy," 78.
89. Joseph Reed to Congress [December 1780?], in *Pennsylvania Archives*, 1st ser., 8:643.
90. Harold M. Hahn, *Ships of the American Revolution and Their Models* (Annapolis, Md.: Naval Institute Press, 1988), 66. Just over a week after its triumph over the *Trumbull*, the *Iris* switched sides again. The French captured the ship and kept it until the end of the war.
91. Franklin's statement, August 7, 1787, in Max Farrand, ed., *The Records of the Federal Convention of 1787, 3 vols.* (New Haven, Conn.: Yale University Press, 1911), 2:208.

CHAPTER 6. BRITISH UNION AND AMERICAN REVOLUTION

1. Adam Smith, *An Inquiry into the Nature and Causes of the Wealth of Nations*, ed. R. H. Campbell and A. S. Skinner, 2 vols. (Oxford: Clarendon Press, 1976), book 4, chap. 7.
2. Discussions of the development of such projections include J. M. Bumsted, "'Things in the Womb of Time': Ideas of American Independence, 1633 to 1763," *William and Mary Quarterly* 3rd ser. 31 (1974): 533–64; John M. Murrin, "A Roof Without Walls: The Dilemma of American National Identity," in Richard Beeman, Stephen Botein, and Edward C. Carter II, eds., *Beyond Confederation: Origins of the Constitution and American National Identity* (Chapel Hill: University of North Carolina Press, 1987), 333–48; Ned C. Landsman, "The Provinces and the Empire: Scotland, the American Colonies, and the Development of British Provincial Identity," in Lawrence Stone, ed., *An Imperial State at War: Britain from 1689 to 1815* (London: Routledge, 1994), 258–87.
3. Colman, *A Sermon Preached Before His Excellency the Governour, and Her Majesties Council, at Boston in New-England, on July 22d. 1708: Being the Day of the Proclamation of the Happy Union of the Two Kingdoms of England and Scotland* (Boston: Bartholomew Green, 1708), 29–30; Joseph Galloway to Charles Jenkinson, ca. 1780, printed in Julian P. Boyd, *Anglo-American Union: Joseph Galloway's Plans to Preserve the British Empire, 1774–1788* (Philadelphia: University of Pennsylvania Press, 1941), 127–56, quote 136–37.
4. In 1767, Franklin wrote to his Scottish friend Lord Kames, "I am fully persuaded with you, that a consolidating Union, by a fair and equal Representation of all the Parts of this

Empire in Parliament, is the only firm Basis on which its political Grandeur and Stability can be founded. Ireland once wish'd it, but now rejects it. The Time has been when the Colonies might have been pleas'd with it; they are now indifferent about it; and, if 'tis much longer delay'd, they too will refuse it." Benjamin Franklin to Lord Kames, February 25, 1767, in *Franklin Papers*, 14:62–71, available at Founders Online, National Archives, http://founders.archives.gov/documents/Franklin/01-14-02-0032. Franklin would reiterate such ideas well after most Americans had, as he predicted, come to reject them.

5. There has been an extensive literature on the union since the tricentennial, by far the greatest part from Scottish authors. A detailed survey is Christopher A. Whatley with Derek J. Patrick, *The Scots and the Union* (Edinburgh: Edinburgh University Press, 2006); other major treatments include Allan I. Macinnes, *Union and Empire: The Making of the United Kingdom in 1707* (Cambridge: Cambridge University Press, 2007); Michael Fry, *The Union: England, Scotland, and the Treaty of 1707* (Edinburgh: Birlinn, 2006); and Stewart J. Brown and Christopher A. Whatley, eds., *The Union of 1707: New Dimensions* (Edinburgh: Edinburgh University Press, 2008; first published as a supplementary issue of *Scottish Historical Review* 87 [October 2008]); see also T. M. Devine, *Scotland and the Union, 1707–2007* (Edinburgh: Edinburgh University Press, 2008); Colin Kidd, *Union and Unionisms: Political Thought in Scotland, 1500–2000* (Cambridge: Cambridge University Press, 2008); Alvin Jackson, *The Two Unions: Ireland, Scotland, and the Survival of the United Kingdom, 1707–2007* (Oxford: Oxford University Press, 2012); as well as the works cited in notes 7–10, below. The major exception is Linda Colley, *Acts of Union and Disunion* (London: Profile Books, 2014). The discussion that follows will be based on those works unless otherwise noted.

6. Macinnes, *Union and Empire*, is the first author to give serious consideration to the role of North America in the calculations for union beyond the simple aspect of opening up the American trade, but its cultural and constitutional ramifications remain largely unexplored. On broad connections between union and empire, see John Robertson, ed., *A Union for Empire: Political Thought and the Union of 1707* (Cambridge: Cambridge University Press, 1995). There has been much more work on the involvement of Scots in empire after union, especially in regard to North America. Two comprehensive recent works are T. M. Devine, *Scotland's Empire and the Shaping of the Americas, 1600–1815* (Washington, D.C.: Smithsonian Books, 2003); and Michael Fry, *The Scottish Empire* (Edinburgh: Birlinn, 2001), which looks beyond the Americas.

7. J. G. A. Pocock, "Empire, State and Confederation: The War of American Independence as a Crisis in Multiple Monarchy," in Robertson, *Union for Empire*, 318–48, is one of the few works to address possible connections between the union and the American Revolution, albeit briefly and obliquely; see especially 338. Among those who have considered the effects of the creation of Great Britain upon imperial culture, most have followed the model of John Clive and Bernard Bailyn, "England's Cultural Provinces: Scotland and America," in *William and Mary Quarterly* 3rd ser. 11 (1954): 29–45, which focuses on seeming similarities of position between the provinces. The argument here is different: the union itself altered the nature of the imperial state in ways that had important ramifications for the governance of empire, broadly defined.

8. For a recent depiction of the extensive presence of the union as precedent in the imperial crisis see Alison L. Lacroix, *The Ideological Origins of American Federalism* (Cambridge, Mass.: Harvard University Press, 2010), esp. 24–29, 120–26. For the union's aftermath in Scotland as influence not only in that crisis but especially thereafter in the crafting of the second amendment, see David Thomas Konig, "The Second Amendment: A Missing Trans-

atlantic Context for the Historical Meaning of 'The Right of the People to Keep and Bear Arms,'" *Law and History Review* 22 (2004): 119–59; and see also the response by H. Richard Uviller and William G. Merkel, "Scottish Factors and the Origins of the Second Amendment: Some Reflections on David Thomas Konig's Rediscovery of the Caledonian Background to the American Right to Arms," in the same journal, 169–77.

Center-periphery issues in imperial development have been the particular province of Jack P. Greene; see especially *Peripheries and Center: Constitutional Development in the Extended Polities of the British Empire and the United States, 1607–1788* (Athens: University of Georgia Press, 1986) and *The Constitutional Origins of the American Revolution* (Cambridge: Cambridge University Press, 2011). Greene's *Evaluating Empire and Confronting Colonialism in Eighteenth-Century Britain* (New York: Cambridge University Press, 2013) arrived too late to be included in this discussion but has much helpful material about these questions in general.

9. Brian P. Levack, *The Formation of the British State: England, Scotland, and the Union* (Oxford: Clarendon Press, 1987), traces the long history between the Anglo-Scottish unions of 1603 (Union of Crowns) and 1707 (Union of Parliaments); and see Roger A. Mason, ed., *Scots and Britons: Scottish Political Thought and the Union of 1603* (Cambridge: Cambridge University Press, 1994).

10. The classic account of the union negotiations, emphasizing political maneuvering, is P. W. J. Riley, *The Union of England and Scotland: A Study in Anglo-Scottish Politics of the Eighteenth Century* (Manchester: Manchester University Press, 1978); see also William Ferguson, *Scotland's Relations with England: A Survey to 1707* (Edinburgh: John Donald, 1977), a much more hostile account; and Whatley, *Scots and the Union*, a more balanced treatment.

11. The union is too often equated with annexation. There was undoubtedly some truth to that in practice, but not in British law. The best reconstruction of the union debate, which fully outlines the federal option and the meaning of incorporation, is John Robertson, "An Elusive Sovereignty: The Course of the Union Debate in Scotland, 1698–1707," in Robertson, *Union for Empire*, 198–227. The principal depiction of the fiscal-military state is John Brewer, *The Sinews of Power: War, Money, and the English State, 1688–1783* (New York: Knopf, 1989); the subtitle suggests the common difficulty historians have in coming to terms with the actual workings of a British state.

12. The role of Scottish popular opinion is considered in Karin Bowie, *Scottish Public Opinion and the Anglo-Scottish Union, 1699–1707* (Woodbridge: Boydell, 2007); the role of the church, in Jeffrey Stephen, *Scottish Presbyterians and the Act of Union 1707* (Edinburgh: Edinburgh University Press, 2007).

13. Macinnes, *Union and Empire*, and Andrew Mackillop, "A Union for Empire? Scotland, the English East India Company and the British Union," in Brown and Whatley, *Union of 1707*, 116–34, both highlight the English goal of protecting their established trading interests, especially in the East India Company.

14. Lacroix, *Ideological Origins*, locates the origins of federal theory more in the precedent of Britain under the Union of Crowns than in the Union of Parliaments. The strongest argument for Britain as an ancien régime confessional state even after 1707 is J. C. D. Clark, *English Society, 1688–1832: Ideology, Social Structure and Political Practice During the Ancien Regime* (Cambridge: Cambridge University Press, 1985).

15. Scots were almost certainly the most prolific per capita exporter of prominent and educated migrants in Europe. See T. C. Smout, N .C. Landsman, and T. M. Devine, "Scottish Emigration in the Early Modern Period," in Nicholas Canny, ed., *Europeans on the Move: Studies on European Migration, 1500–1800* (Oxford: Oxford University Press, 1994), 76–112;

Landsman, "The Provinces and the Empire"; Macinnes, *Union and Empire*, chaps. 6–7; and Devine, *Scotland's Empire*.

16. For an alternative view emphasizing the integrating elements of the union and the challenge of making Britons, albeit with much interpretive nuance, see Linda Colley, *Britons: Forging the Nation, 1707–1837* (New Haven, Conn.: Yale University Press, 1992). For ruminations on union and fragmentation in both Scottish and American literatures, see Susan Manning, *Fragments of Union: Making Connections in Scottish and American Writing* (New York: Palgrave, 2002).

17. The malt tax riots had more than a little in common with the later Stamp Act riots in North America, although the de facto settlement that prevailed in Britain, like so much else connected with the union, would fail to hold in North America; see the discussion in *Gentlemen's Magazine and Historical Chronicle* 39 (1769): 39–40.

18. On Scottish "managers," see Alexander Murdoch, *The People Above: Politics and Administration in Mid-Eighteenth Century Scotland* (Edinburgh: John Donald, 1980); Roger L. Emerson, *An Enlightened Duke: The Life of Archibald Campbell (1682–1761), Earl of Ilay, 3rd Duke of Argyll* (London: Humming Earth, 2013); and Michael Fry, *The Dundas Despotism* (Edinburgh: Edinburgh University Press, 1992).

19. An important new work is Alasdair Raffe, *The Culture of Controversy: Religious Arguments in Scotland, 1660–1714* (Woodbridge: Boydell, 2012), chap. 1.

20. [Francis Makemie], *A Narrative of a New and Unusual American Imprisonment of Two Presbyterian Ministers and Prosecution of Mr. Francis Makemie* (New York, 1707), available in a modern reprint in *The Life and Writings of Francis Makemie*, ed. Boyd S. Schlenther (Philadephia: Presbyterian Historical Society, 1971), 189–244.

21. Makemie, *Narrative*, 32. For a more detailed look at the circumstances surrounding the case and its ecclesiastical ramifications, see my "The Episcopate, the British Union, and the Failure of Religious Settlement in Colonial British America," in Chris Beneke and Christopher S. Grenda, eds., *The First Prejudice: Religious Tolerance and Intolerance in Early America* (Philadelphia: University of Pennsylvania Press, 2011), 75–97.

22. Cotton Mather to Samuel Penhallow, July 8, 1707, printed in *Diary of Cotton Mather*, 2 vols. (New York: Frederick Ungar, n.d.), 1:599.

23. The original opinion of the Lords Justices is in G. Chalmers, *Opinions of Eminent Lawyers on Various Points of English Jurisprudence* (Burlington, Vt.: C. Goodrich, 1858; first published London, 1814), 44–52. It was, in fact, a mixed verdict, as its more immediate purpose was to deny the Congregationalist Church in Massachusetts the status of an established church. See also "Commission to the Bishop of London for Exercising Jurisdiction in the American Colonies," in John Remeyn Brodhead, *Documents Relative to the Colonial History of the State of New-York*, ed. F. B. O'Callaghan, 10 vols. (Albany, N.Y.: Weed, Parsons, 1856–58), 5:849–54; Arthur Lyon Cross, *The Anglican Episcopate and the American Colonies* (New York: Longmans, Green, 1902), 67–69; appendix A.5.4-6, pp. 289–94; the quote is on p. 290.

24. Landsman, "The Episcopate, the British Union, and the Failure of Religious Settlement," 82–85; and, on the British state, Brewer, *Sinews of Power*.

25. "Case of the Presbyterian Congregation at New York, 1724," Church of Scotland Ms., Scottish Record Office, Edinburgh; and *The Case of the Scotch Presbyterians of the City of New York* (New York, 1773).

26. Much of the spur to Scots-Irish migration was of course the slump in the linen trade, but ecclesiastical issues were also a significant factor. See Patrick Griffin, *The People with No Name: Ireland's Ulster Scots, America's Scots Irish, and the Creation of a British Atlantic World, 1689–1764* (Princeton, N.J.: Princeton University Press, 2001); and see Guy S. Klett, ed.,

Minutes of the Presbyterian Church in America, 1706–1788 (Philadelphia: Presbyterian Historical Society, 1976), esp. 76–77, 176.

27. Commissioner Johnston to the Secretary of the S.P.G., July 5, 1710, printed in Charles A. Briggs, *American Presbyterianism: Its Origin and Early History* (New York: Charles Scribner, 1885), lxix–lxx; see also James Anderson to the Right Reverend Mr. John Stirling, Principal of the College of Glasgow, August 1716 and August 8, 1717, in Briggs, *American Presbyterianism*, lxix–lxxvi; William Stevens Perry, comp., *Historical Collections Relating to the American Colonial Church*, 5 vols. (Hartford, Conn., 1870–78), 4:106–9; Christopher Wilkinson to Bishop Robinson, May 26, 1718, in William Wilson Manross, comp., *The Fulham Papers in the Lambeth Palace Library* (Oxford: Clarendon Press, 1965), 2:251.

28. Alison Gilbert Olson, *Making the Empire Work: London and American Interest Groups, 1690–1790* (Cambridge, Mass.: Harvard University Press, 1992), 123–24.

29. The controversy was encapsulated in a long succession of writings, including Samuel Johnson, *A Letter from a Minister of the Church of England to His Dissenting Parishioners* (New York: John Peter Zenger, 1733); James Wetmore, *A Vindication of the Professors of the Church of England in Connecticut* (Boston: Rogers and Fowle, 1747); Noah Hobart, *A Serious Address to the Members of the Episcopal Separation in New-England* (Boston: J. Bushell and J. Green, 1748); and John Beach, *A Calm and Dispassionate Vindication of the Professors of the Church of England, Against the Abusive Misrepresentations and Fallacious Argumentations of Mr. Noah Hobart* (Boston: J. Draper, 1749).

30. Hobart, *Serious Address*, 10–25.

31. Thomas Bradbury Chandler, *An Appeal to the Public, in Behalf of the Church of England in America* (New York: James Parker, 1767), 77, 117. The episcopate controversy has been discussed many times, by hostile critics such as Carl Bridenbaugh, *Mitre and Sceptre: Transatlantic Faiths, Ideas, Personalities, and Politics, 1689–1775* (New York: Oxford University Press, 1962); and by more balanced and sympathetic writers such as Donald F. M. Gerardi, "The Episcopate Controversy Reconsidered: Religious Vocation and Anglican Perceptions of Authority in Mid-Eighteenth-Century America," *Perspectives in American History* 3 (1987): 81–114. For more on these arguments, see my "The Episcopate, the British Union, and the Failure of Religious Settlement"; and Kate Engel's "Revisiting the Bishop Controversy" in this volume (chap. 7).

32. Chandler, *Appeal to the Public*, 107–8, 110, 113–14.

33. The rejection of the idea of a Church of England in America was expressed by, among others, Charles Chauncy, *The Appeal to the Public Answered, in Behalf of the Non-Episcopal Churches in America* (Boston: Kneeland and Adams, 1768), 111, 180; and see the essays in the 1768 *Pennsylvania Journal*; and "Centinel Number I," March 24, 1768, in Elizabeth Nybakken, ed., *The Centinel: Warnings of a Revolution* (Newark: University of Delaware Press, 1980), 83–90. It is striking that similar expressions of the metropolitan as local later emerged among the two Scots who sat in the Continental Congress; see John Witherspoon, "Letter Sent to Scotland for the *Scots Magazine*," in *The Works of the Reverend John Witherspoon*, 2nd ed., 4 vols. (Philadelphia: William W. Woodward, 1802), 4:281–89; and James Wilson, "Considerations on the Nature and Extent of the Legislative Authority of the British Parliament" (1774), in *Collected Works of James Wilson*, ed. Kermit L. Hall and Mark David Hall, 2 vols. (Indianapolis: Liberty Fund, 2007), 1:3–31, esp. 16–17. Wilson and Witherspoon employed the same rhetorical device in asserting that British liberty belonged not to the soil of Britain—to place—but to the people derived from that place.

34. Hobart here used the analogy of trade. Before the union, the colonies were restricted to trading with English merchants. "But since the union," he wrote, "the Colonies are *British*

Plantations. They have an equal Relation to every Part of the Kingdom of *Great-Britain,*" and goods from Glasgow were treated with the same freedom from customs duties as those from the metropolis. See Hobart, *Serious Address,* 10–11.

35. See the essays in the *Centinel* and the various essay projects involving William Livingston, including "American Whig" columns in *New York Gazette,* 1768–69. The resistance to an episcopate by Virginia Anglicans has been well examined; see especially Frederick V. Mills, Sr., *Bishops by Ballot: An Eighteenth Century Ecclesiastical Revolution* (New York: Oxford University Press, 1978); and Nancy L. Rhoden, *Revolutionary Anglicanism: The Colonial Church of England Clergy During the American Revolution* (New York: New York University Press, 1999), chap. 3. For discussions of the contribution of Scottish Presbyterian religious traditions to ideologies of resistance in North America, see Gideon Mailer, "Anglo-Scottish Union and John Witherspoon's American Revolution," *William and Mary Quarterly* 3rd ser. 67 (2010): 709–46; and the forthcoming manuscript by Mailer, *John Witherspoon's American Revolution* (Chapel Hill: University of North Carolina Press, 2016).

36. The classic works on this subject are Douglas Sloan, *The Scottish Enlightenment and the American College Ideal* (New York: Teacher's College, 1971); and Howard Miller, *The Revolutionary College: American Presbyterian Higher Education, 1707–1837* (New York: New York University Press, 1976). More recent summaries of the subject include Richard B. Sher, "Scottish-American Cultural Studies, Past and Present," in Richard B. Sher and Jeffrey R. Smitten, eds., *Scotland and America in the Age of the Enlightenment* (Edinburgh: Edinburgh University Press, 1990), 1–27; and Ned C. Landsman, *From Colonials to Provincials: American Thought and Culture, 1680–1760* (New York: Twayne, 1997).

37. On Scotland's universities, see especially Richard B. Sher, *Church and University in the Scottish Enlightenment: The Moderate Literati of Edinburgh* (Princeton, N.J.: Princeton University Press, 1985; Roger L. Emerson, *Professors, Patronage and Politics: The Aberdeen Universities in the Eighteenth Century* (Aberdeen: Aberdeen University Press, 1991); Emerson, *Academic Patronage in the Scottish Enlightenment: Glasgow, Edinburgh and St Andrews Universities* (Edinburgh: Edinburgh University Press, 2008); and Andrew Hook and Richard B. Sher, eds., *The Glasgow Enlightenment* (East Linton: Tuckwell Press, 1995). St. Andrews had no city surrounding it and did not attain the same academic reputation during the eighteenth century as did the colleges in Edinburgh, Glasgow, and Aberdeen.

38. Livingston expressed most of his opposition to the college in the 1752 *Independent Reflector, or Weekly Essays on Sundry Important Subjects More Particularly Adapted to the Province of New-York,* ed. Milton M. Klein (Cambridge, Mass.: Belknap Press, 1963), esp. 17–22, 36–39, 44, and 49–51. Anglican essays appeared in *New-York Mercury* and the *Occasional Reverberator.*

39. Archbishop of Canterbury to Jacob Duche, September 16, 1763, in Perry, *Historical Collections Relating to the American Colonial Church,* 2:389–90. On the New Jersey college charter, see the discussion in Thomas Jefferson Wertenbaker, *Princeton, 1746–1896* (Princeton, N.J.: Princeton University Press, 1946), 20–27; and the documents described therein.

40. Over the years there have been many attempts to link the distinctive ideas of the Scottish Enlightenment to Scotland's provincial position. These have been less successful for explaining the particular positions of the most profound thinkers than for the broad ethic of Enlightenment that emerged. The classic statement was Clive and Bailyn, "England's Cultural Provinces"; see also Nicholas Phillipson, "Culture and Society in the Eighteenth-Century Province: The Case of Edinburgh and the Scottish Enlightenment," in Lawrence Stone, ed., *The University and Society,* 2 vols. (Princeton, N.J.: Princeton University Press, 1975), 2:407–48; and

Roger L. Emerson, "Did the Scottish Enlightenment Emerge in an English Cultural Province?" *Lumen* 14 (1995): 1–24.

41. Franklin, "Observations Concerning the Increase of Mankind" (1751), printed in *Observations on the Late and Present Conduct of the French, with Regard to Their Encroachments upon the British Colonies in North America* (Boston: S. Kneeland, 1755), in *Franklin Papers*, 4:225–34; and see Istvan Hont, "The 'Rich Country–Poor Country' Debate in Scottish Classical Political Economy," in Istvan Hont and Michael Ignatieff, eds., *Wealth and Virtue: The Shaping of Political Economy in the Scottish Enlightenment* (Cambridge: Cambridge University Press, 1983), 271–316.

42. John Witherspoon, "Lectures on Moral Philosophy," in *The Miscellaneous Works of the Rev. John Witherspoon* (Philadelphia: William Woodward, 1803), 267–374, quotes from 286–89, 296–97, 372. For a view emphasizing Witherspoon's distance from the underlying perspectives of the new moral philosophy, see Mailer, "Anglo-Scottish Union."

43. Norman Fiering, *Moral Philosophy at Seventeenth-Century Harvard: A Discipline in Transition* (Chapel Hill: University of North Carolina Press, 1981); Landsman, *From Colonials to Provincials*, 77–82.

44. Thomas Moffat to Benjamin Franklin, November 15, 1768, in *Franklin Papers*, 20:566–70, available at Founders Online, National Archives, http://founders.archives.gov/documents/Franklin/01-20-02-0282-0016. On the politics of urban English communities, see especially Kathleen Wilson, *The Sense of the People: Politics, Culture and Imperialism in England, 1715–1785* (Cambridge: Cambridge University Press, 1998).

45. T. M. Devine, *The Tobacco Lords: A Study of the Tobacco Merchants of Glasgow and Their Trading Activities c. 1740–1790* (Edinburgh: John Donald, 1975); David Hancock, *Citizens of the World: London Merchants and the Integration of the British Atlantic Community, 1735–1785* (New York: Cambridge University Press, 1995); Douglas J. Hamilton, *Scotland, the Caribbean and the Atlantic World, 1750–1820* (Manchester: Manchester University Press, 2005); Richard B. Sher, *The Enlightenment and the Book: Scottish Authors and Their Publishers in Eighteenth-Century Britain, Ireland, and America* (Chicago: University of Chicago Press, 2006). On the complex aspects of Scottish trading networks, see Douglas Hamilton, "Transatlantic Ties: Scottish Migration Networks in the Caribbean, 1750–1800," in Angela McCarthy, ed., *A Global Clan: Scottish Migrant Networks and Identities Since the Eighteenth-Century* (London: Tauris, 2012), 48–66.

46. Max Savelle, *Seeds of Liberty: The Genesis of the American Mind* (New York: Knopf, 1948), 292–305; and see Ned C. Landsman, "The Legacy of British Union for the North American Colonies: Provincial Elites and the Problem of Imperial Union," in Robertson, *Union for Empire*, 297–317. For a different view, placing greatest emphasis on their role as imperialists, see J. Russell Snapp, "An Enlightened Empire: Scottish and Irish Imperial Reformers in the Age of the American Revolution," *Albion: A Quarterly Journal Concerned with British Studies* 33 (2001): 388–403. See also Timothy J. Shannon, *Indians and Colonists at the Crossroads of Empire: The Albany Congress of 1754* (Ithaca, N.Y.: Cornell University Press, 2000), chaps. 2–3.

47. There is a good discussion of the Scottish Episcopal Church after the Glorious Revolution in Raffe, *Culture of Controversy*, chap. 2. We badly need a study of Scots Episcopalians in America, but see Patrick Rouse, Jr., *James Blair of Virginia* (Chapel Hill: University of North Carolina Press, 1971); P. G. Scott, "James Blair and the Scottish Church: A New Source," *William and Mary Quarterly* 3rd ser. 33 (1976): 300–308; James McLachlan, "The Scottish Intellectual Migration to British North America, 1650–1770: New England and the Chesapeake," paper delivered at the conference "Scotland and the Americas, 1600–1800," John

Carter Brown Library, Brown University, Providence, R.I., June 1994; S. Charles Bolton, *Southern Anglicanism: The Church of England in Colonial South Carolina* (Westport, Conn.: Greenwood Press, 1982); Robert Lawson-Peebles, "The Problem of William Smith: An Aberdonian in Revolutionary America," in Jennifer J. Carter and Joan H. Pittock, eds., *Aberdeen and the Enlightenment* (Aberdeen: Aberdeen University Press, 1987), 52–60; Edgar Legare Pennington, *Apostle of New Jersey: John Talbot, 1645–1727* (Philadelphia: Church Historical Society, 1938). Talbot, though not a Scot, was a disciple of the Scottish Quaker-turned-Episcopalian George Keith and was both a Jacobite and a persistent foe of the British governors and English Churchmen. The most useful discussion of political economy can be found in the essays in Hont and Ignatieff, *Wealth and Virtue*.

48. "To the Inhabitants of the Colony of Massachusetts Bay, March 6, 1775," in *Novanglus and Massachusettensis; or, Political Essays, Published in the Years 1774 and 1775* (Boston: Hews & Goss, 1819), 78–94.

49. "To the Inhabitants of the Colony of Massachusetts Bay, March 13, 1775," in *Novanglus*, 96.

50. For an extended summary of many of those proposals, see Richard Koebner, *Empire* (Cambridge, Mass.: Harvard University Press, 1961), chaps. 4–5, 105–237, as well as the sources cited below. See also Greene, *Peripheries and Center*, chaps. 5–7; and John Shy, "Thomas Pownall, Henry Ellis, and the Spectrum of Possibilities, 1763–1775," in Alison Gilbert Olson and Richard Maxwell Brown, eds., *Anglo-American Political Relations, 1675–1775* (New Brunswick, N.J.: Rutgers University Press, 1970), 155–86.

51. See Lacroix, *Ideological Origins*, 120–24. The Scots Witherspoon and Wilson emerged as experts within the Continental Congress on the difference between federal and incorporating unions. See also Greene, *Peripheries and Center*, 110–14, and the discussions of the claims by such figures as Allan Ramsay, Matthew Wheelock, and others.

52. See the summary of the discussions in Koebner, *Empire*, 173–93; Thomas Pownall, *Administration of the Colonies*, 3rd ed. (London, 1766), appendix; and the texts cited below.

53. [Thomas Crowley], *A Plan of Union, by Admitting Representatives from the American Colonies, and from Ireland into the British Parliament* (Philadelphia, [1770]).

54. Review of *Thoughts on the Origins and Nature of Government, Occasioned by the Disputes Between Great Britain and Her American Colonies*, *Gentleman's Magazine, and Historical Chronicle* 39 (1769): 38–41.

55. The Scotophobia of the Wilkes era, which extended to North America, has frequently been examined; see, for one, John Brewer, "The Misfortunes of Lord Bute: A Case-Study in Eighteenth-Century Political Argument and Opinion," *Historical Journal* 16 (1973): 3–43.

56. Pownall, *Administration of the Colonies*, appendix, sect. 3, 8–9; Francis Bernard, *Select Letters on the Trade and Government of America; and the Principles of Law and Polity, Applied to the American Colonies* (London: T. Payne, 1774), 78–85.

57. Josiah Tucker, *A Series of Answers to Certain Popular Objections, Against Separating from the Rebellious Colonies, and Discarding Them Entirely* (Gloucester: R Raikes, 1776), esp. 57–59.

58. Roger L. Emerson, "The Scottish Literati and America, 1680–1800," in Ned C. Landsman, ed., *Nation and Province in the First British Empire: Scotland and the Americas, 1600–1800* (Lewisburg, Pa.: Bucknell University Press, 2001); and other works by Emerson. For the presence of Scots officials throughout the empire, see Andrew Mackillop, "Locality, Nation, and Empire: The Scots and the British Empire in Asia, c.1690–1813," in John M. MacKenzie and T. M. Devine, eds., *The Oxford History of the British Empire: Scotland and the British Em-*

pire (Oxford: Oxford University Press, 2011), 54–84; Devine, *Scotland's Empire*; and Fry, *Scottish Empire*. See also Shannon, *Indians and Colonists at the Crossroads*.

59. Garry Wills, *Inventing America: Jefferson's Declaration of Independence* (Garden City, N.Y.: Doubleday, 1978), which also includes the text of Jefferson's draft; and see Ronald Hamowy, "Jefferson and the Scottish Enlightenment: A Critique of Garry Wills's *Inventing America: Jefferson's Declaration of Independence*," *William and Mary Quarterly* 3rd ser. 36 (1979): 503–23. For Jefferson's draft, see "Jefferson's 'original Rough draught' of the Declaration of Independence," in *The Papers of Thomas Jefferson*, ed. Julian P. Boyd et al. (Princeton, N.J.: Princeton University Press, 1950–), 1:423–28, http://jeffersonpapers.princeton.edu/selected-documents/jefferson%E2%80%99s-%E2%80%9Coriginal-rough-draught%E2%80%9D-declaration-independence-0.

60. Jefferson's reference to "Scotch" mercenaries fits within his emphasis on common kindred, as Highlanders were widely considered as a separate and inferior people from Lowland Scots and other Britons, at a lower state of civilization, and not a people with whom Jefferson would have wanted to be equated.

61. Bruce E. Steiner, *Samuel Seabury, 1729–1796: A Study in the High Church Tradition* (Athens: Ohio University Press, 1972), is the principal biography of Seabury; Mills, *Bishops by Ballot*, and Rhoden, *Revolutionary Anglicanism*, are among the works that address some of the issues the American Episcopal Church confronted after the Revolution. Even after independence, it was no simple matter to disentangle the American church from the English hierarchies on which it had depended. The Episcopal Church was a dissenting communion in Scotland and a dissonant voice within the empire, with scant allegiance to the metropolitan church. Thus during the long reign of Commissary James Blair in Virginia, his enemies charged him repeatedly with "Scotticizing" and presbyterianizing the church, allowing a powerful lay vestry averse to imperial control to develop in that most Anglican of colonies. See note 27, above. See also the notes on William McLenachan and the quarrels between English and Scots Episcopalians in the mid-Atlantic in Rev. Joseph W. Dally, *Woodbridge and Vicinity: The Story of a New Jersey Township* (New Brunswick, N.J.: A. E. Gordon, 1873), http://www.archive.org/stream/woodbridgevicinio0dall/woodbridgevicinio0dall_djvu.txt.

62. For a different consideration of Greater Britain, see David Armitage, "Greater Britain: A Useful Category of Historical Analysis," *American Historical Review* 104 (1999): 427–45.

CHAPTER 7. REVISITING THE BISHOP CONTROVERSY

1. Adams to Jedidiah Morse, December 2, 1815, in *The Works of John Adams*, ed. Charles Francis Adams, 10 vols. (Boston: Little, Brown, 1850–56), 10:185.

2. Carl Bridenbaugh, *Mitre and Sceptre: Transatlantic Faiths, Ideas, Personalities, and Politics, 1689–1775* (New York: Oxford University Press, 1962), quotations xiv. For recent examples of the reiteration of this narrative of the bishop controversy, see Kevin Phillips, *1775: A Good Year for Revolution* (New York: Viking, 2012), 84–85; and Thomas P. Slaughter, *Independence: The Tangled Roots of the American Revolution* (New York: Hill and Wang, 2014), 178–82. Slaughter notably argues that the controversy ended significantly before the outbreak of war and should not be considered a *casus belli*. Other major works that deal more directly with the subject include Frederick V. Mills, Sr., *Bishops by Ballot: An Eighteenth-Century Ecclesiastical Revolution* (New York: Oxford University Press, 1978); James B. Bell, *A War of Religion: Dissenters, Anglicans, and the American Revolution* (Houndmills: Palgrave, 2008); and Kenneth R.

Elliott, *Anglican Church Policy, Eighteenth Century Conflict, and the American Episcopate* (New York: Peter Lang, 2011). J. C. D. Clark, *The Language of Liberty, 1660–1832: Political Discourse and Social Dynamics in the Anglo-American World* (Cambridge: Cambridge University Press, 1994), makes the sweeping argument that denominational rivalries played a dominant role in the development of Anglo-American political culture and includes the bishop controversy in that analysis.

3. Robert Middlekauff, *The Glorious Cause: The American Revolution, 1763–1789*, 2nd ed. (New York: Oxford University Press, 1982), 159–65.

4. "American Whig," *New York Gazette; or, The Weekly Post-Boy*, March 14, 1768.

5. For some of the most important pamphlets related to the issue of a bishop, see East Apthorp, *Considerations on the Institution and Conduct of the Society for the Propagation of the Gospel in Foreign Parts* (Boston: Green & Russell, 1763); Thomas Bradbury Chandler, *An Appeal to the Public, in Behalf of the Church of England in America* (New York: James Parker, 1767); Charles Chauncy, *A Letter to a Friend, Containing Remarks on Certain Passages in a Sermon Preached by the Right Reverend Father in God, John Lord Bishop of Landaff* (Boston: Kneeland & Adams, 1767); John Ewer, *A Sermon Preached Before the Incorporated Society for the Propagation of the Gospel* (London: E. Owen and T. Harrison, 1767); Caleb Fleming, *The Claims of the Church of England Seriously Examined: In a Letter to the Author of an Answer to Dr. Mayhew's Observations on the Charter and Conduct* (London: W. Nicholl, 1764); William Livingston, *A Letter to the Right Reverend Father in God, John, Lord Bishop of Landaff* (New York: Garrat Noel, 1768), and his "American Whig" columns published in the *New York Gazette* in 1768; Jonathan Mayhew, *Observations on the Charter and Conduct of the Society for the Propagation of the Gospel* (Boston: Richard and Samuel Draper, 1763); Thomas Secker, *An Answer to Dr. Mayhew's Observations on the Charter and Conduct of the Society for the Propagation of the Gospel in Foreign Parts* (London: John Rivington, 1764); and Secker, *Letter to the Right Honourable Horatio Walpole* (London: J. & F. Rivington, 1769). Many of these generated responses and counterresponses, as well as multiple reprintings.

6. Gordon S. Wood, "Religion and the American Revolution," in Harry S. Stout and D. G. Hart, eds., *New Directions in American Religious History* (New York: Oxford University Press, 1997), 173–205. For a strong recent assessment of the place of the clergy and sermons in the Revolutionary era, see James P. Byrd, *Sacred Scripture, Sacred War: The Bible and the American Revolution* (New York: Oxford University Press, 2013).

7. Brendan McConville, *The King's Three Faces: The Rise and Fall of Royal America* (Chapel Hill: University of North Carolina Press, 2006); Michael McDonnell, "War Stories: Remembering and Forgetting the American Revolution," in this volume. See also Maya Jasanoff, *Liberty's Exiles: American Loyalists in the Revolutionary World* (New York: Knopf, 2011).

8. As mentioned above, most colonial Anglicans did not wish to see a bishop appointed for the colonies, and even the southern clergy disagreed on the subject. Because of these internal divisions, and because of divisions over related issues such as the mode of payment of Virginia clergy, southern Anglicans were not among the controversy's major players. For Virginia's religious culture during the era, including the power wielded by lay Anglicans, see John A. Ragosta, *Wellspring of Liberty: How Virginia's Religious Dissenters Helped Win the American Revolution and Secured Religious Liberty* (New York: Oxford University Press, 2010). For more on southern Anglicans and the bishop controversy, see Rhys Isaac, *The Transformation of Virginia, 1740–1790* (Chapel Hill: University of North Carolina Press, 1982), 181–205; and Anne Y. Zimmer, *Jonathan Boucher: Loyalist in Exile* (Detroit: Wayne State University Press, 1978), 91–94.

9. For British dissenters and the American Revolution, see James E. Bradley, *Religion, Revolution, and English Radicalism: Non-conformity in Eighteenth-Century Politics and Society*

(Cambridge: Cambridge University Press, 1990); and Bradley, *Popular Politics and the American Revolution in England: Petitions, the Crown, and Public Opinion* (Macon, Ga.: Mercer University Press, 1986). See also Bartholomew P. Schiavo, "The Dissenter Connection: English Dissenters and Massachusetts Political Culture: 1630–1774" (Ph.D. diss., Brandeis University, 1976).

10. Religious historians have tended to stress continuity rather than change with regard to the American Revolution, particularly since many have focused on the significance of the rise of evangelicalism as a transnational phenomenon, a movement that certainly continued across the years of the Revolution. See, for example, W. R. Ward, *Protestant Evangelical Awakening* (Cambridge: Cambridge University Press, 1992); Mark A. Noll, *The Rise of Evangelicalism: The Age of Edwards, Whitefield, and the Wesleys* (Downers Grove, Ill.: InterVarsity Press, 2003); David Hempton, *Methodism: Empire of the Spirit* (New Haven, Conn.: Yale University Press, 2005); Frank Lambert, *Inventing the "Great Awakening"* (Princeton, N.J.: Princeton University Press, 1999); and Anna M. Lawrence, *One Family Under God: Love, Belonging, and Authority in Early Transatlantic Methodism* (Philadelphia: University of Pennsylvania Press, 2011). Scholars of Anglicanism have also emphasized longer-term continuities. Andrew Porter, "'Cultural Imperialism' and Protestant Missionary Enterprise, 1780–1914," *Journal of Imperial and Commonwealth History* 25 (September 1997): 367–91; Porter, "Church History, History of Christianity, Religious History: Some Reflections on British Missionary Enterprise Since the Late Eighteenth Century," *Church History* 71 (September 2002), 555–84; Rowan Strong, *Anglicanism and the British Empire, 1700–1850* (Oxford: Oxford University Press, 2007); Travis Glasson, *Mastering Christianity: Missionary Anglicanism and Slavery in the Atlantic World* (New York: Oxford University Press, 2011); Hilary M. Carey, *God's Empire: Religion and Colonialism in the British World, c. 1801–1908* (Cambridge: Cambridge University Press, 2011). The important exception to the rule is Carla Pestana, *Protestant Empire: Religion and the Making of the British Atlantic World* (Philadelphia: University of Pennsylvania Press, 2009).

11. Protestantism was an important concept in Anglophone political life both domestically and internationally. For the politics of the Protestant international, see Tony Claydon, *Europe and the Making of England, 1660–1760* (Cambridge: Cambridge University Press, 2007); Steven C. A. Pincus, *Protestantism and Patriotism: Ideologies and the Making of English Foreign Policy, 1650–1688* (Cambridge: Cambridge University Press, 1996); Andrew C. Thompson, *Britain, Hanover and the Protestant Interest, 1688–1756* (Woodbridge: Boydell Press, 2006); and Tony Claydon and Ian McBride, eds., *Protestantism and National Identity, c.1650–c.1850* (Cambridge: Cambridge University Press, 1998). For North American inclusion in the politics of international Protestantism, see Thomas S. Kidd, *The Protestant Interest: New England After Puritanism* (New Haven, Conn.: Yale University Press, 2004); and Mark Valeri, *Heavenly Merchandize: How Religion Shaped Commerce in Puritan America* (Princeton, N.J.: Princeton University Press, 2010), 122–34. For the links between British political identity and Protestantism, see Linda Colley, *Britons: Forging the Nation, 1707–1827* (New Haven, Conn.: Yale University Press, 1992); and Pasi Ihalainen, *Protestant Nations Redefined: Changing Perceptions of National Identity in the Rhetoric of the English, Dutch, and Swedish Public Churches, 1685–1772* (Leiden: Brill, 2005).

12. Scholars of religious studies have articulated a historical trajectory for the category of religion. See Jonathan Z. Smith, "Religion, Religions, Religious," in Mark C. Taylor, ed., *Critical Terms for Religious Studies* (Chicago: University of Chicago Press, 1998), 269–84; Tomoko Masuzawa, *The Invention of World Religions* (Chicago: University of Chicago Press, 2005); Tisa Wenger, "'We Are Guaranteed Freedom': Pueblo Indians and the Category of Religion in the 1920s," *History of Religions* 45 (November 2005): 89–113; Jordan Alexander Stein and Justine S. Murison, "Introduction: Religion and Method," *Early American Literature* 45

(Spring 2010): 1–29; Talal Asad, *Genealogies of Religion: Discipline and Reasons of Power in Christianity and Islam* (Baltimore: Johns Hopkins University Press, 1993); Hans Kippenberg, *Discovering Religious History in the Modern Age* (Princeton, N.J.: Princeton University Press, 2002); and Lynn Hunt and Margaret C. Jacob, *The Book That Changed Europe: Picart and Bernard's Religious Ceremonies of the World* (Cambridge, Mass.: Belknap Press, 2010). Identifying the history of the concept of religion also necessitates separating out what scholars such as Tisa Wenger, Pamela Klassen, and John W. Marshall have called "first order" understandings of religion (what people in the past called religion) from "second order" understandings of religion (what scholars today may identify as religion). This project examines the first order category of religion as it existed for leaders of recognized and often legally established Protestant communities during the eighteenth century. For "true" and "false" religion, see, for example, Ann Taves, *Fits, Trances, and Visions: Experiencing Religion and Explaining Experience from Wesley to James* (Princeton, N.J.: Princeton University Press, 1999).

13. Even groups who were a bit farther from the mainstream, such as the Quakers, worked within a largely comparable definition of what a religious group should look like. Jon Butler has repeatedly stressed the importance of denominational structures in the Revolutionary era. See his *Becoming America: The Revolution Before 1776* (Cambridge, Mass.: Harvard University Press, 2000), 186–204; "Enthusiasm Described and Decried: The Great Awakening as Interpretive Fiction," *Journal of American History* 69, no. 2 (1982): 305–25; and *Awash in a Sea of Faith: Christianizing the American People* (Cambridge, Mass.: Harvard University Press, 1990). For another historian of a similar view, see Mark Häberlein, "Reform, Authority and Conflict in the Churches of the Middle Colonies, 1700–1770," in David K. Adams and Cornelis A. van Minnen, eds., *Religious and Secular Reform in America: Ideas, Beliefs, and Social Change* (New York: New York University Press, 1999), 1–28. Mark Noll stresses the ecumenical impulses within evangelicalism and argues that the period between 1745 and 1770 was an era of conservative denominational growth in the British American colonies in *The Rise of Evangelicalism*. John B. Frantz discusses the aftermath of revival and denomination building among German settlers in the colonies in "The Awakening of Religion Among the German Settlers in the Middle Colonies," *William and Mary Quarterly* 33 (April 1976): 266–88. See also Michael J. Coalter, Jr., "The Radical Pietism of Count Nicholas Zinzendorf as a Conservative Influence on the Awakener, Gilbert Tennent," *Church History* 49 (March 1980): 35–46; and C. C. Goen, *Revivalism and Separatism in New England, 1740–1800* (New Haven, Conn.: Yale University Press, 1962).

14. For a nuanced analysis of these dynamics, see Susan Juster, *Doomsayers: Anglo-American Prophecy in the Age of Revolution* (Philadelphia: University of Pennsylvania Press, 2003). Juster notes that Hanoverian prophets before the 1790s "did not mount systematic attacks on the economic and political structures that sustained the church-state nexus" (7).

15. William Dalrymple, *Christian Unity Illustrated and Recommended from the Example of the Primitive Church* (Glasgow: R. and A. Foulis, 1766), 2–5.

16. Ibid., 32–33.

17. Ewer, *A Sermon Preached*, 10.

18. Mayhew, *Observations on the Charter*, 17, 6.

19. Bishop of London to William Legge, July 9, 1771, D (W) 1778-II-347, Staffordshire Record Office, Stafford, UK. For the Occom-Wheelock trip, see Leon Burr Richardson, *An Indian Preacher in England*, Dartmouth College Manuscript Series, no. 2 (Hanover, N.H.: Dartmouth College Publications, 1933).

20. Charles Taylor, *A Secular Age* (Cambridge, Mass.: Belknap Press, 2007), 171–76. For an elaboration of this idea in a somewhat similar context, see Karen Dielman, *Religious Imaginaries: The Liturgical and Poetical Practices of Elizabeth Barrett Browning, Christina Rossetti, and Adelaide Procter* (Athens: Ohio University Press, 2011).

21. Puritanism and dissent have long been studied as transatlantic movements, as in the works by J. C. D. Clark and Carl Bridenbaugh mentioned above. See, for example, Stephen Foster, *The Long Argument: English Puritanism and the Shaping of New England Culture, 1570–1700* (Chapel Hill: University of North Carolina Press, 1991); and, particularly useful in this context, Adrian Chastain Weimer, *Martyrs' Mirror: Persecution and Holiness in Early New England* (New York: Oxford University Press, 2011). For a general treatment of English dissent, see Michael R. Watts, *The Dissenters: From the Reformation to the French Revolution* (Oxford: Clarendon Press, 1978). See also John Seed, *Dissenting Histories: Religious Division and the Politics of Memory in Eighteenth-Century England* (Edinburgh: Edinburgh University Press, 2008).

22. For works on the SSPCK and NEC, particularly in an Atlantic context, see Margaret Connell Szasz, *Scottish Highlanders and Native Americans* (Norman: University of Oklahoma Press, 2007); Frederick V. Mills, Sr., "The Society in Scotland for Propagating Christian Knowledge in British North America, 1730–1775," *Church History* 63 (March 1994): 15–30; Donald E. Meek, "Scottish Highlanders, North American Indians, and the SSPCK: Some Cultural Perspectives," *Records of the Scottish Church History Society* 23 (1989): 378–96; William Kellaway, *The New England Company, 1649–1776: Missionary Society to the American Indians* (New York: Barnes & Noble, 1962). For the SPRKP, see Isabel Rivers, "The First Evangelical Tract Society," *Historical Journal* 50 (March 2007): 1–22.

23. Thomas Clap to Elizabeth [Scott] Williams, July 24, 1758, Gratz Collection, University Presidents, case 7, box 12, HSP.

24. Ezra Stiles to Thomas Wright, June 29, 1771, Correspondence folder 1016, Ezra Stiles Papers, Beinecke Library, Yale University (hereafter SPBL).

25. See Bridenbaugh, *Mitre and Sceptre,* 83–115, quotation 94. See also Robert G. Ingram, *Religion, Reform, and Modernity in the Eighteenth Century: Thomas Secker and the Church of England* (Woodbridge: Boydell Press, 2007), 209–59.

26. Bridenbaugh, *Mitre and Sceptre,* 183.

27. Alison G. Olson, "The Eighteenth Century Empire: The London Dissenters' Lobbies and the American Colonies," *Journal of American Studies* 26 (April 1992): 41–58.

28. Ezra Stiles, *Discourse on the Christian Union: The Substance of Which Was Delivered Before the Reverend Convention of the Congregational Clergy in the Colony of Rhode Island, Assembled at Bristol, April 23, 1760* (Boston: Edes and Gill, 1761), 7–8.

29. Ibid., 35–36.

30. Stiles to Thomas Wright, February 26, 1766; Nathaniel Lardner to Stiles, August 20, 1764; both in SPBL.

31. Stiles to John Devotion, June 27, 1766, SPBL. For Presbyterian-Congregational coordination, see *Minutes of the Convention of Delegates from the Synod of New York and Philadelphia and from the Associations of Connecticut* (Hartford: E. Gleason, 1843); and the discussion in Edmund S. Morgan, *The Gentle Puritan: A Life of Ezra Stiles, 1727–1795* (New York: Norton, 1962), 237–54.

32. Chauncy to Stiles, September 29, 1766, SPBL.

33. Alison to Stiles, August 20, 1766, SPBL.

34. Stiles to Alison, September 5, 1766, SPBL.
35. Lardner to John Wiche, January 21, 1768, Doctor Williams Library, London. Dr Williams's Library, London.
36. Lardner to Stiles, June 30, 1767, SPBL. Emphasis in original.
37. Wright to Stiles, March 24, 1768, SPBL.
38. Gordon to Joseph Bellamy, August 21, 1761, box 188, folder 2934, no. 81311, Case Memorial Library, Hartford Seminary, Hartford, Connecticut.
39. Minutes of the Protestant Dissenting Deputies, vols. 1 and 2, London Metropolitan Archives, London. See esp. April 18–October 10, 1764; March 9, 1768; April 1–12, 1768; January 15, February 12, March 1, 1772; January 27, 1773; October 19, 1774.
40. Furneaux to Stiles, March 2, 1772, SPBL.
41. Stiles to Wilton, April 13, 1775; Stiles to Furneaux, April 12, 1775, SPBL.

CHAPTER 8. EMPIRE'S VITAL EXTREMITIES

1. "The Memorial of George Glas," (1764), Colonial Office (CO) 388/51, The National Archives of the United Kingdom (hereafter TNA). Glas misrepresented the site for the future Port Hillsborough in his various petitions as lying between Cape Verde and the Senegal River. For a thorough and persuasive attempt to locate Port Hillsborough, see Théodore Monod, "Notes sur George Glas (1725–65) fondateur de Port Hillsborough (Sahara Marocain)," *Anuario de Estudios Atlánticos* 22 (1976): 17–55. Much work remains to be done on Africa in the Atlantic world that accounts for the actions of specific kingdoms, nations, groups, and so on. The use of the terms "African kingdoms" and "African nations" in this chapter reflects a reluctance to ascribe discrete allegiances to people and groups when they cannot be determined with precision.
2. Glas to Board of Trade, CO 388/50, fol. 138, TNA.
3. See Conway's letters to the Earl of Rochford, in Henry Seymour Conway, Diplomatic Correspondence (1765–67), vol. 8, Lewis Walpole Library, Yale University (hereafter Conway MS, LWL).
4. The literature is voluminous, but, with rare exception, historians have used North American patriots to describe the contours and chronology of the politics of the coming of the Revolution. The definitive analysis of patriot organizing in the wake of the imperial regulations of the 1760s remains Pauline Maier, *From Resistance to Revolution: Colonial Radicals and the Development of American Opposition to Britain, 1765–1776* (New York: Knopf, 1972). The rationale behind the argument remains persuasive if for no other reason than because, from the political perspective of prominent patriot colonists, it appears to be correct. That the neo-Whig interpretation represented by Maier supplanted a debate among imperial, progressive, and consensus historians that relied on a similar set of actors only serves to reinforce explanations for the coming of the Revolution that emphasize colonial or parliamentary intransigence and clearly defined demarcations between imperial center and colonial periphery. The resilience of this body of scholarship has led one prominent historian to declare that it "has largely solved the major causal problems of explaining why the Revolution occurred." See Jack N. Rakove, "An Agenda for Early American History," in Donald A. Yerxa, ed., *Recent Themes in Early American History: Historians in Conversation* (Columbia: University of South Carolina Press, 2008), 38–39. For a recent attempt to reorient this perspective, see Sarah Kinkel, "The King's Pirates? Naval Enforcement of Imperial Authority, 1740–76," *William and Mary Quarterly*

3rd ser. 71 (2014): 3–34. Also see Jack P. Greene, "'A Posture of Hostility': A Reconsideration of Some Aspects of the Origins of the American Revolution," *Proceedings of the American Antiquarian Society* 87 (1977): 27–68.

5. See P. D. G. Thomas, *British Politics and the Stamp Act Crisis: The First Phase of the American Revolution, 1763–1767* (New York: Clarendon Press, 1975).

6. The few extant accounts of Glas's early career vary in points of fact, but they are not wholly irreconcilable. For one highly readable example, see Edmund Burke, *The Annual Register . . . for the Year 1766*, 6th ed. (London, 1803), 85–88.

7. John Murrin, "A Roof Without Walls: The Dilemma of American National Identity," in Richard Beeman, Stephen Botein, and Edward C. Carter II, eds., *Beyond Confederation: Origins of the Constitution and American National Identity* (Chapel Hill: University of North Carolina Press, 1987), 338.

8. James L. A. Webb, Jr., "The Mid-Eighteenth Century Gum Arabic Trade and the British Conquest of Saint-Louis du Senegal, 1758," *Journal of Imperial and Commonwealth History* 25 (1997): 43–44. For the southward migration of the Berbers in response to the gum trade, see Boubacar Barry, *Senegambia and the Atlantic Slave Trade*, trans. Ayi Kwei Armah (Cambridge: Cambridge University Press, 1998), 57. The rendering of African names into English throughout this chapter follows Barry.

9. Joseph E. Inikori, *Africans and the Industrial Revolution in England: A Study in International Trade and Development* (New York: Cambridge University Press, 2002), 397–98.

10. Susan Fairlie, "Dyestuffs in the Eighteenth Century," *Economic History Review* n.s. 17 (1965): 488–510.

11. Webb, "Gum Arabic Trade," 44–45.

12. Ibid., 46

13. On the relationship between war and economic opportunism, see P. J. Marshall, "Empire and Opportunity in Britain, 1763–1775: The Prothero Lecture," *Transactions of the Royal Historical Society* 6th ser. 5 (1995): 111–28. Also see David Hancock's discussion of government contracting in *Citizens of the World: London Merchants in the British Atlantic Community, 1735–1785* (New York: Cambridge University Press, 1995), 221–40. For a useful summary of Touchet's background, his activities during the war, and the importance of gum to the textile industry, see Alfred P. Wadsworth and Julia De Lacy Mann, *The Cotton Industry and Industrial Lancashire, 1600–1780* (Manchester: Manchester University Press, 1931), 243–48. For evidence of Touchet's scheme to monopolize the slave trade to Guadeloupe, see Samuel Gardner, "House of Lords, John Kennion, Esq., appellant, Samuel Gardner, John Turner, Samuel Hucks, John Bindley, William Wright, and William Maskall, respondents, the Case of the Respondents" (London, 1773).

14. Wadsworth and Mann, *Cotton Industry*, 148–61.

15. See below for an explanation of the structure of the CMTA and its role in British statecraft in Africa.

16. Richard Middleton, *Bells of Victory: The Pitt-Newcastle Ministry and the Conduct of the Seven Years' War, 1757–1762* (Cambridge: Cambridge University Press, 1985), 86.

17. "Copy of a Letter from Joseph Debat Esq. Governor of James Fort Gambia to His Excellency Richard Worge Govern. of Senegal," no date, copy in CO 388/48, fol. 58, TNA.

18. First Lords of Trade, "Letter to the Rt. Honble. Mr. Secy. Pitt . . . Acquisition of the River Senegal," William Petty, 1st Marquis of Lansdowne, 2nd Earl of Shelburne Papers, 1665–1885 (Shelburne MS), fol. 19, William L. Clements Library (CL), University of Michigan, Ann Arbor. *Damel* is in fact the proper title for the ruler of the Kajoor peoples, who predominated

to the south of Saint Louis. See Philip D. Curtin, *Economic Change in Precolonial Africa: Senegambia in the Era of the Slave Trade* (Madison: University of Wisconsin Press, 1975), 38–39.

19. The fullest account of the negotiations leading to the Treaty of Paris in 1763 remains Zenab Esmat Rashed, *The Peace of Paris, 1763* (Liverpool: University Press, 1951). Also see Richard Pares, *War and Trade in the West Indies, 1739–1763* (Oxford: Clarendon Press, 1936), pp. 559–95.

20. For a bibliography of the pamphlet war treating the coming of the peace and its aftermath, see Clarence W. Alvord, *The Mississippi Valley in British Politics: A Study of the Trade, Land Speculation, and Experiments in Imperialism Culminating in the American Revolution* (Cleveland: Arthur H. Clark, 1917), 2:253–64. Jack M. Sosin's assessment of the debate as politically insignificant typifies the literature as a whole; see Sosin, *Whitehall and the Wilderness: The Middle West in British Colonial Policy, 1760–1775* (Lincoln: University of Nebraska, 1961), 7–10. More recent literature treats the pamphlet war as indicative of the views of prominent Britons on the social meanings of empire. See Paul W. Mapp, "British Culture and the Changing Character of the Mid-Eighteenth Century British Empire," in Warren R. Hofstra, ed., *Cultures in Conflict: The Seven Years' War in North America* (Lanham, Md.: Rowman & Littlefield, 2007), 23–59; Helen Dewar, "Canada or Guadeloupe? French and British Perceptions of Empire, 1760–1763," *Canadian Historical Review* 91 (2010): 637–60.

21. Samuel Martin to Samuel Martin, Jr., February 12, 1762, Add. MS 41347, fol. 123, British Library (BL), London.

22. Andrew O'Shaughnessy, "The Formation of a Commercial Lobby: The West Indian Interest, British Colonial Policy and the American Revolution," *Historical Journal* 40 (1997): 75–77; Pares, *War and Trade*, 219–21.

23. "Separate traders" was a contemporary term that distinguished the ""free trade""–oriented CMTA from the monopolistic Royal African Company.

24. *"A Review of the Arguments for an Immature Peace"* (London, 1763), 18.

25. *"The Freeborn Englishman's Unmasked Battery"* (London, 1762), 52.

26. Hardwicke to Newcastle, November 15, 1762, in Philip C. Yorke, *The Life and Correspondence of Philip Yorke, Earl of Hardwicke, Lord High Chancellor of Great Britain* (Cambridge: Cambridge University Press, 1913), 3:433.

27. Debat to Worge, CO 388/48, fol. 58, TNA.

28. Ibid., fol. 57.

29. *"Reflections on the Terms of Peace"* (London, 1763).

30. Debat to Worge, CO 388/48, fol. 57, TNA.

31. John Roberts, *"Considerations on the Present Peace, as Far as It Is Relative to the Colonies and the African Trade"* (London, 1763).

32. Peter D. G. Thomas, *George III: King and Politicians, 1760–1770* (Manchester: Manchester University Press, 2002), 114. For the British disarming of Albreda, see Nicholas Tracy, "The Gunboat Diplomacy of the Government of George Grenville, 1764–1765: The Honduras, Turks Island and Gambian Incidents," *Historical Journal* 17 (1974): 722–23.

33. As an adjunct to the tendency to treat the outcome of the debate over the peace as a foregone conclusion, historians have underestimated the breadth and depth of support for retaining large sugar islands, particularly among powerful state officials like George Grenville and Admiral Rodney. For Grenville and Caribbean expansion, see John L. Bullion, *A Great and Necessary Measure: George Grenville and the Genesis of the Stamp Act, 1763–1765* (Columbia: University of Missouri Press, 1982), 19–20; also see Rodney to Grenville, December 4, 1762, in William James Smith, ed., *The Grenville Papers: Being the Correspondence . . .* (London: J. Murray, 1852–53), 2:9–21.

NOTES TO PAGES 157–160

34. African merchants and their advocates aspired to engross the trade within the African continent from the late seventeenth century on. See William A. Pettigrew, *Freedom's Debt: The Royal African Company and the Politics of the African Slave Trade, 1672–1752* (Chapel Hill: University of North Carolina Press, 2013), 153–78.

35. The following biographical comparison of Bacon and Touchet draws on Lewis B. Namier, "Anthony Bacon, M.P., an Eighteenth-Century Merchant," *Journal of Economic and Business History* 2 (1929): 20–70; Jacob M. Price, "Bacon, Anthony (bap. 1717, d. 1786)," in *Oxford Dictionary of National Biography* (Oxford: Oxford University Press, 2004; online ed., May 2008), http://www.oxforddnb.com/view/article/50608; John R. G. Tomlinson, ed., *Additional Grenville Papers, 1763–1765* (Manchester: Manchester University Press, 1962),; and Alan J. Kidd, "'Touchet, Samuel (c.1705–1773)'," in *Oxford Dictionary of National Biography* (2004; online ed., January 2008), http://www.oxforddnb.com/view/article/57578.

36. Namier, "Bacon," 26.

37. See William L. Saunders, ed., *The Colonial Records of North Carolina, 1759–1765* (Raleigh: P. M. Hale, State Printer, 1886–90), 6:248–50, 413, 423–24, 517.

38. See, for example, *Journal of the House of Commons* 30 (1803): 245, 249, 310, 356, 382.

39. Tomlinson, *Grenville*, 78.

40. Bacon traded for the brandy used to fulfill his state contract in the Canaries; see Namier, "Bacon," 28.

41. George Glas, "A Scheme for Opening a Trade Between the Europeans and the Inhabitants of the Inland Parts of Africa," CO 388/48, TNA.

42. For a useful overview of the limited biographical literature on Glas, see Monod, "Notes sur George Glas," 3–8. Glas's father was John Glas, who founded the Glasites, or Sandemanians, a group of evangelical Presbyterians who opposed the idea of a Scottish national church.

43. George Glas, ed. and trans., *The History of the Discovery and Conquest of the Canary Islands: Translated from a Spanish Manuscript* [by Juan de Abreu de Galindo] . . . *To which is added, A Description of the Canary Islands* . . . (London: Printed for R. and J. Dodsley; and T. Durham, 1764), 293.

44. Ibid., 338.

45. Ibid., 341.

46. Ibid., 342.

47. Glas, "'Scheme for Opening a Trade'."

48. Ibid.

49. Merchants and administrators made many claims about African geography and the ease with which territory could be made to serve the good of the empire that proved more aspirational than accurate. As Charles O'Hara told Henry Seymour Conway, "the European knowledge of this Vast Continent, does not Extend beyond the Sea Shore in any place above three or four Leagues," Shelburne MS, vol. 81, fol. 101 (CL). Although hyperbolic and self-serving, O'Hara's comment reveals the fundamental lack of dependable intelligence that characterized any plan for British expansion into the African interior.

50. Monod, "Notes sur George Glas," 17–22. A petition on behalf of the Barbary merchants also indicates Glas and Bacon misled Parliament about the location of Port Hillsborough; see "The Memorial of Thomas Adams [et al.] . . . Merchants Trading to the South Barbary the Dominions of the Emperor of Morocco," May 15, 1765, CO 388/50, fol. 212, TNA.

51. Poirier to unidentified, December 12, 1762, CO 388/48, fol. 63, TNA. That the petition included nearly one hundred signatures indicates the breadth of interest in the gum trade; see

"The Memorial of the Merchants of London Trading to Africa and of the Traders & Manufacturers Concern'd in that Commerce," no date, CO 388/48, fol. 72, TNA.

52. "Memorial of Thomas Adams," fol. 212.

53. Debat's comments on Glas illustrate his reputation as a gum trader and his familiarity with the Senegal River along the coast: "As Mr. Glass has had much experience in the Gum Trade, and is well acquainted in those parts, his opinion I believe may be of Service; I suppose he is yet at Senegal" (Debat to Worge, CO 388/48, fol. 57, TNA). For Berbers in the gum trade, see Barry, *Senegambia*; James F. Searing, *West African Slavery and Atlantic Commerce: The Senegal River Valley, 1700–1800* (Cambridge: Cambridge University Press, 1993).

54. Barry, *Senegambia*, 86.

55. Glas, "A Scheme for Opening a Trade," 8–11.

56. Ibid., 10.

57. For an analysis of the institutional structure of the CMTA, see Eveline C. Martin, *The British West African Settlements, 1750–1821: A Study in Local Administration* (London: Longmans, 1927), 10–56; 23 Geo. II, clause 5, quoted from ibid., 11.

58. Curtin, *Economic Change*, 84.

59. Ibid., 109.

60. Ibid., 52; Boubacar Barry, "'Senegambia from the Sixteenth to the Eighteenth Century: Evolution of the Wolof, Sereer and Tukuloor,'" in B. A. Ogot, ed., *General History of Africa: Africa from the Sixteenth to the Eighteenth Century* (Berkeley: University of California Press, 1992), 287–88.

61. Barnes to CMTA, February 21, 1764, CO 388/48, TNA. The CMTA was able to secure the cooperation of one of Touchet's ships, but its captain's death and the refusal of his replacement to cooperate ended the temporary arrangement, despite the offer of an exorbitant fee (ibid.).

62. Barnes to CMTA, April 18, 1764, CO 388/48, TNA.

63. Barnes to CMTA, July 9, 1764, CO 388/50, fol. 31, TNA.

64. Barnes to CMTA, August 27, 1764, CO 388/50, fol. 85, TNA.

65. Ibid., fol. 86. For the central position African intermediaries occupied in the Atlantic trade during the period, see Searing, *West African Slavery*, 93–98; and George E. Brooks, Jr., "The Signares of Saint-Louis and Goreé: Women Entrepreneurs in Eighteenth Century Senegal and Goreé," in Nancy J. Hafkin and Edna Bay, eds, *Women in Africa: Studies in Social and Economic Change* (Stanford, Calif.: Stanford University Press, 1976), 19–44.

66. Barnes to CMTA, August 27, 1764, fol. 86, TNA.

67. British correspondence refers to the "Kingdom of Brack," but the term "Brak" properly indicates the ruler of the Waalo people. For the ongoing warfare between the Waalo and the Kajoor, see Barry, *Senegambia*, 86–88.

68. Barnes and Council of Senegal to the CMTA, February 7, 1765, CO 388/50, fol. 199, TNA.

69. Barnes and Council of Senegal to the CMTA, May 31, 1765, CO 388/50, fol. 311, TNA.

70. Barnes and Council of Senegal to the CMTA, February 7, 1765, fols. 187–98.

71. Joseph Debat to the CMTA, January 29, 1764, CO 388/48, TNA.

72. Ibid.

73. Joseph Debat and Council of James Fort to the CMTA, February 7, 1764, CO 388/48, TNA.

74. John Barnes to CMTA, July 9, 1764, CO 388/50, fol. 31, TNA.

75. Debat and Council of James Fort to the CMTA, February 7, 1764.

76. Ibid.
77. Debat to Poncet, March 6, 1764, CO 388/48, TNA.
78. Barnes to CMTA, July 9, 1764.
79. Tracy, ""Gunboat Diplomacy," "722.
80. Ibid., 723.
81. Ibid., 727.
82. Frederick Madden and David Fieldhouse, eds., *Imperial Reconstruction, 1763–1840: The Evolution of Alternative Systems of Government* (Westport, Conn.: Greenwood Press, 1987), 3:493.
83. Ibid., 495.
84. Although the office of governor was modeled on the American colonies, in the words of the Order in Council that published the Senegambian constitution, "as far as the differences of circumstance and situation will admit," the colony lacked a representative assembly, and the governor was both commander in chief of the military and held the power to select the chief law enforcement officer. Furthermore, the governor appointed the council (subject to royal approval), whose members he could either suspend or forbid from leaving the colony as necessary. See Martin, *West African Settlements*, 66–72.
85. Halifax to Rochford, February 19, 1765, CO 388/50, fols. 126–27, TNA.
86. The Black River colony established by British logwood merchant William Pitt (perhaps a distant relation of the British politician) in 1732, a site of episodic Anglo-Spanish skirmishes since its inception, became a source of major controversy when the Spanish governor of Yucatan informed the British that the Treaty of Paris forbade the British cutting of logwood along the Rio Nuevo and Rio Hondo in June of 1764. Like the situation in Senegambia, the settlement under Pitt's control was composed overwhelmingly of natives and experienced unsteady relations with neighboring indigenous nations and a powerful European empire. See Frank Griffith Dawson, "William Pitt's Settlement at Black River on the Mosquito Shore: A Challenge to Spain in Central America, 1732–87," *Hispanic American Historical Review* 63 (1983): 677–706; and William Shuman Sorsby, "The British Superintendency of the Mosquito Shore, 1749–1787" (Ph.D. diss., University College, London, 1969).
87. Halifax to Rochford, February 19, 1765, CO 388/50, fols. 126–27, TNA.
88. Conway to Rochford, November 8, 1755, Conway MS, LWL.
89. Ibid.
90. Ian R. Christie, "British Politics and the American Revolution," *Albion: A Quarterly Journal Concerned with British Studies* 9 (1977): 206.
91. Ibid., 207.
92. Frank O'Gorman, *The Rise of Party in England: The Rockingham Whigs, 1760–82* (London: Allen and Unwin, 1975), 154.
93. Frances Armytage, *The Free Port System in the British West Indies: A Study in Commercial Policy, 1766–1822* (London: Longmans, Green, 1953).
94. For a recent exception emphasizing international law, see Eliga H. Gould, *Among the Powers of the Earth: The American Revolution and the Making of a New World Empire* (Cambridge, Mass.: Harvard University Press, 2012).
95. R. C. Simmons and P. D. G. Thomas, eds., *Proceedings and Debates of the British Parliaments Respecting North America, 1754–1783* (Millwood, N.Y.: Kraus International, 1982–86), 2:271.
96. Ibid., 136; for a repetition of this argument by Stanley, see p. 144.
97. Ibid., 139.

98. For Yorke's insistence on combining the repeal of the Stamp Act with a Declaratory Act and his role in the writing of it, see Paul Langford, *The First Rockingham Administration, 1765–1766* (London: Oxford University Press, 1973), 151.

CHAPTER 9. THE GREAT AWAKENING, PRESBYTERIAN EDUCATION, AND THE MOBILIZATION OF POWER IN THE REVOLUTIONARY MID-ATLANTIC

1. Ebenezer Elmer, *An Elogy on Francis Barber, Esq., Lieutenant-Colonel Commandant of the Second New Jersey Regiment* (Chatham, 1783; repr., New York: For Charles F. Heartman, 1917), 12–13.

2. George Clinton Barber's Statement, Washington, D.C., June 20, 1802, in B.L.11-450, reel 136, Revolutionary War Pension and Bounty-Land-Warrant Application Files, DLAR.

3. Ebenezer Elmer, February 13, 1783, in his "Military Notes," folder 16, MG 38, Ebenezer Elmer Papers, New-Jersey Historical Society, Newark, NJ.

4. Elmer, *Elogy on Francis Barber*, 12.

5. Quote from a petition to Congress written by the trustees of the church in 1840 in Nicholas Murray, *Notes, Historical and Biographical, Concerning Elizabeth-Town, Its Eminent Men, Churches and Ministers* (Elizabeth-Town, N.J.: E. Sanderson, 1844), 105.

6. Alan Heimert, *Religion and the American Mind: From the Great Awakening to the Revolution* (Cambridge, Mass.: Harvard University Press, 1966). For a strong critique of Heimert, see Bernard Bailyn, "Religion and Revolution: Three Biographical Studies," *Perspectives in American History* 4 (1970): 83–169. William G. McLoughlin, "'Enthusiasm for Liberty': The Great Awakening as the Key to the Revolution," *Proceedings of the American Antiquarian Society* 87, no. 1 (1977): 69–96, offers trenchant support for Heimert's position. Other important studies on the topic include Richard L. Bushman, *From Puritan to Yankee: Character and the Social Order in Connecticut, 1690–1765* (Cambridge, Mass.: Harvard University Press, 1967); Nathan Hatch, "The Origins of Civil Millennialism in America: New England Clergymen, War with France, and the Revolution," *William and Mary Quarterly* 3rd ser. 31 (1974): 407–30; Harry S. Stout, "Religion, Communications, and the Ideological Origins of the American Revolution," *William and Mary Quarterly* 3rd ser. 34, no. 4 (October 1977): 519–41; Gary B. Nash, *The Urban Crucible: Social Change, Political Consciousness, and the Origins of the American Revolution* (Cambridge, Mass.: Harvard University Press, 1979), 198–232; Rhys Isaac, *The Transformation of Virginia, 1740–1790* (Chapel Hill: University of North Carolina Press, 1982); Ruth H. Bloch, *Visionary Republic: Millennial Themes in American Thought, 1756–1800* (New York: Cambridge University Press, 1985). Among Mark Noll's many works on the subject, see especially "The American Revolution and Protestant Evangelicalism," *Journal of Interdisciplinary History* 23, no. 3 (January 1993): 615–38. For a very recent perspective, see Thomas S. Kidd, *The Great Awakening: The Roots of Evangelical Christianity in Colonial America* (New Haven, Conn.: Yale University Press, 2007); and Kidd, *God of Liberty: A Religious History of the American Revolution* (New York: Basic Books, 2010). There have also been a number of useful historiographical essays on the issue; see especially John Murrin, "No Awakening, No Revolution? More Counterfactual Speculations," *Reviews in American History* 11 (1983): 161–71; Philip F. Gura, "The Role of the 'Black Regiment': Religion and the American Revolution," *New England Quarterly* 61, no. 3 (1988): 439–54; Philip Goff, "Revivals and Revolution: Historiographic Turns Since Alan Heimert's 'Religion and the American Mind,'" *Church History* 67, no. 4 (December 1998): 695–721; Allen C. Guelzo, "God's Designs: The Literature of the Colonial Revivals of Religion, 1735–1760," and Gordon S. Wood, "Religion and the American

Revolution," both in Harry Stout and D. G. Hart, eds., *New Directions in American Religious History* (New York: Oxford University Press, 1997), 141–205.

7. For instance, Patricia Bonomi argued that colonists, not just New Lights, "having taken part in dismantling of old institutions and the shaping of new ones . . . would find themselves less hesitant to do it again." Bonomi, *Under the Cope of Heaven: Religion, Society, and Politics in Colonial America* (New York: Oxford University Press, 1986), 160.

8. Jon Butler, *Awash in a Sea of Faith: Christianizing the American People* (Cambridge, Mass.: Harvard University Press, 1990), 194–224, quotes on 165 and 195; see also Butler's "Enthusiasm Described and Decried: The Great Awakening as Interpretative Fiction," *Journal of American History* 69, no. 2 (1982): 305–25, esp. 319–25; and for more on the nature of New Side institution building, see Elizabeth I. Nybakken, "New Light on the Old Side: Irish Influences on Colonial Presbyterianism," *Journal of American History* 68, no. 4 (1982): 813–32.

9. Jack P. Greene, "An Uneasy Connection: An Analysis of the Preconditions of the American Revolution," in Stephen G. Kurtz and James H. Huston, eds., *Essays on the American Revolution* (Chapel Hill: University of North Carolina Press, 1973), 35–36, 39–40.

10. My interpretation is influenced by Donald G. Mathews, "The Second Great Awakening as an Organizing Process, 1780–1830: An Hypothesis," *American Quarterly* 21, no. 1 (April 1969): 23–43.

11. Aaron Fogleman, "Migrations to the Thirteen British North American Colonies, 1700–1775: New Estimates," *Journal of Interdisciplinary History* 22, no. 4 (April 1992): 691–709; Jon Butler, *Becoming America: The Revolution Before 1776* (Cambridge, Mass.: Harvard University Press, 2000), 23–25; and Martin E. Lodge, "The Crisis of the Churches in the Middle Colonies, 1720–1750," *PMHB* 95, no. 2 (April 1971): 195–220.

12. Patrick Griffin, *The People with No Name: Ireland's Ulster Scots, America's Scots Irish, and the Creation of a British Atlantic World, 1689–1764* (Princeton, N.J.: Princeton University Press, 2001), 100.

13. Guy S. Klett, ed., *Minutes of the Presbyterian Church in America, 1706–1788* (Philadelphia: Presbyterian Historical Society, 1976), 212; Howard Miller, *The Revolutionary College: American Presbyterian Higher Education, 1707–1837* (New York: New York University Press, 1976), 17–22; Kidd, *Great Awakening*, 31–36, 60; Griffin, *People with No Name*, 125–27.

14. Klett, *Minutes*, 212. On Alison, see Elizabeth A. Ingersoll, "Francis Alison: American Philosophe, 1705–1799" (Ph.D. diss., University of Delaware, 1974).

15. Leigh Eric Schmidt, "Jonathan Dickinson and the Making of the Moderate Awakening," *American Presbyterians* 36, no. 4 (Winter 1985): 341–53; Keith Jordan Hardman, "Jonathan Dickinson and the Course of American Presbyterianism, 1717–1747" (Ph.D. diss., University of Pennsylvania, 1971), 315–16, 328–34.

16. See especially Douglas Sloan, *The Scottish Enlightenment and the American College Ideal* (New York: Teachers College Press, 1971), 55–60, and the list of schools, 281–84; Henry D. Funk, "The Influence of the Presbyterian Church in Early American History," *Journal of the Presbyterian Historical Society* 12 (1925): 167–82, and the list of academies, 184–86; and Elizabeth Nybakken, "In the Irish Tradition: Pre-Revolutionary Academies in America," *History of Education Quarterly* 37, no. 2 (July 1997): 171–78.

17. On the development of civil society and the public sphere in the colonial period, see Jack P. Greene, "Social and Cultural Capital in Colonial British America: A Case Study," *Journal of Interdisciplinary History* 29, no. 3 (January 1999): 491–509; and Jessica Choppin Roney, *Governed by a Spirit of Opposition: The Origins of American Political Practice in Colonial Philadelphia* (Baltimore: Johns Hopkins University Press, 2014). For work that focuses on the

Awakening's role in these developments, see John L. Brooke, *The Heart of the Commonwealth: Society and Political Culture in Worcester County, Massachusetts, 1713–1861* (New York: Cambridge University Press, 1989), 66–96; Frank Lambert, "'Pedlar in Divinity': George Whitefield and the Great Awakening," *Journal of American History* 77, no. 3 (December 1990): 812–37; and T. H. Breen and Timothy Hall, "Structuring Provincial Imagination: The Rhetoric and Experience of Social Change in Eighteenth-Century New England," *American Historical Review* 103 (1998): 1411–39.

18. Klett, *Minutes*, 256; *Pennsylvania Gazette* (Philadelphia), August 24, 1749.

19. Ned Landsman, *From Colonials to Provincials: American Thought and Culture, 1680–1760* (New York: Twayne, 1997), 81; Ingersoll, "Francis Alison," 85–86.

20. Landsman, *From Colonials to Provincials*, 92–93; J. David Hoeveler, *Creating the American Mind: Intellect and Politics in the Colonial Colleges* (Lanham, Md.: Rowman & Littlefield, 2004), 348; and Ned C. Landsman, "The Legacy of British Union for the North American Colonies: Provincial Elites and the Problem of Imperial Union," in John Robertson, ed., *A Union for Empire: Political Thought and the British Union of 1707* (Cambridge: Cambridge University Press, 1995), 311–12.

21. Sloan, *Scottish Enlightenment*, 61–63; Douglas Sloan, *Education in New Jersey in the Revolutionary Era* (Trenton: New Jersey Historical Commission, 1975), 11; Nybakken, "In the Irish Tradition," 172–73; and Nina Reid-Maroney, "Science and the Presbyterian Academies," in R. Albert Mohler and Darryl G. Hart, eds., *Theological Education in the Evangelical Tradition* (Grand Rapids, Mich.: Baker Books, 1996), 203–16.

22. John Ewing's math notebook, in John Ewing Papers, MS coll. 284, University of Pennsylvania Rare Book and Manuscript Library. Ewing did not serve in the military.

23. Ingersoll, "Francis Alison," 39–69; and Sloan, *Scottish Enlightenment*, 73–102. For useful discussions of how and why Witherspoon came to terms with Hutchesonian ideas, see Ned C. Landsman, "Witherspoon and the Problem of Provincial Identity in Scottish Evangelical Culture," and Peter J. Diamond, "Witherspoon, William Smith and the Scottish Philosophy in Revolutionary America," both in Richard B. Sher and Jeffrey R. Smitten, eds., *Scotland and America in the Age of the Enlightenment* (Edinburgh: Edinburgh University Press, 1990), 29–45, 115–32. Witherspoon's moral philosophy lectures have been published as John Witherspoon, *An Annotated Edition of Lectures on Moral Philosophy*, ed. Jack Scott (Newark: University of Delaware Press, 1982). Notes on Robert Smith's moral philosophy lectures, given at the New Side academy in Pequea, Pennsylvania, are available in the Robert Smith Papers, Notebooks, vol. 2, Presbyterian Historical Society, Philadelphia.

24. *Poor Roger, 1761: The American Country Almanack for the Year of Christian Account 1761* (New York: Printed and sold by James Parker, 1760).

25. *Seven Rational Sermons, on the Following Subjects, Viz. I. Against Covetousness. II. On the Vanity of This Life. III. Against Revenge. IV. Of Mirth and Grief. V. The Cruelty of Slandering Innocent, and Defenceless Women. VI. The Duty of Children. VII. Advantages of Education. Written in England, by a Lady, the Translatress of Four Select Tales from Marmontel* (Philadelphia: Printed by Robert Bell, 1777), 72.

26. John Iverson, "Introduction: Forum on Emulation in France, 1750–1800," *Eighteenth-Century Studies* 36, no. 2 (December 2003): 217–23, quote on 218; and the forum that follows, 224–48. See also Jeremy L. Caradonna, "The Monarchy of Virtue: The 'Prix de Vertu' and the Economy of Emulation in France, 1777–91," *Eighteenth-Century Studies* 41, no. 4 (July 2008): 443–58; as well as his *The Enlightenment in Practice: Academic Prize Contests and Intellectual Culture in France, 1670–1794* (Ithaca, N.Y.: Cornell University Press, 2012). For the American

colonial context, see John Fea, *The Way of Improvement Leads Home: Philip Vickers Fithian and the Rural Enlightenment in Early America* (Philadelphia: University of Pennsylvania Press, 2008), esp. 58–82; for a later period see J. M. Opal, "Exciting Emulation: Academies and the Transformation of the Rural North, 1780s–1820s," *Journal of American History* 91, no. 2 (2004): 445–70; and more generally his *Beyond the Farm: National Ambitions in Rural New England* (Philadelphia: University of Pennsylvania Press, 2008).

27. *A Patern [sic] of Christian Education, Agreable [sic] to the Precepts and Practice of Our Blessed Lord and Saviour Jesus Christ* (Germantown, Pa.: Printed by Christopher Sower, Jr., 1756), 2, 6–7, my italics. Other critical appraisals of emulation include John Tobler, *The Pennsylvania Town and Country-Man's Almanack for the Year 1754* (Germantown, Pa.: Printed and sold by C. Sower, Jr., 1753); *Christian Education Exemplified Under the Character of Paternus Instructing His Only Son* (Germantown, Pa.: Printed by Christopher Sower, Jr., 1754).

28. The line between emulation and ambition was rather porous. The *Oxford English Dictionary* (*OED*) defines the word "emulation" using the word "ambition," but "ambition" often carried a negative connotation. See *OED Online*, s.vv. "ambition, n." and "emulation, n." On the social manifestations of fears of economic ambition, see Bushman, *From Puritan to Yankee*, iv–v, 22–38, 135–43, 193, 267.

29. Francis Hutcheson, *A System of Moral Philosophy, in Three Books* (Glasgow: R. and A. Foulis, Printers to the University, 1755), 1:165.

30. *Pennsylvania Gazette*, March 11, 1755.

31. Elmer, *Elogy on Francis Barber*, 11–12.

32. The fact that they possessed a high-level formal education already differentiated them; see Jackson Turner Main, *The Social Structure of Revolutionary America* (Princeton, N.J.: Princeton University Press, 1965), 264–67.

33. Francis Alison to Ezra Stiles, Philadelphia, May 7, 1768, in Franklin Bowditch Dexter, ed., *Extracts from the Itineraries and Other Miscellanies of Ezra Stiles, D.D., LL.D., 1755–1794: With a Selection from His Correspondence* (New Haven, Conn.: Yale University Press, 1916), 433.

34. *Merry Andrew's Almanack; or, The Entertaining and Comical City and Country Register, for the Year of Our Lord 1762* (Philadelphia: Printed and sold by Andrew Steuart, 1761).

35. *The Virginia Almanack for the Year of Our Lord 1771* . . . (Williamsburg, Va.: Printed and sold by William Rind, 1770).

36. *Pennsylvania Gazette*, October 11, 1771.

37. Francis Alison to Ezra Stiles, Philadelphia, May 7, 1768, in Dexter, *Ezra Stiles*, 433.

38. See also James Kirby Martin, *Men in Rebellion: Higher Governmental Leaders and the Coming of the American Revolution* (New Brunswick, N.J.: Rutgers University Press, 1973), 128. I use the same estimate for the number of college graduates in the colonies as Martin, 3,000, but calculate the rate relative to the estimated white male population, not the total population. For estimates of the population of the North American colonies by race, see John J. McCusker and Russell R. Menard, *The Economy of British America, 1607–1789* (Chapel Hill: University of North Carolina Press, 1985), 54.

39. In a fairly generous estimate, Jackson Turner Main surmised that about 10 percent of children could afford to go to the Newark Academy. For the most part, he concluded, "Only the upper class and the urban upper middle class could acquire a formal secondary education." Main, *Social Structure*, 246.

40. George Washington Corner, ed., *The Autobiography of Benjamin Rush: His "Travels Through Life" Together with His Commonplace Book for 1789–1813* (Princeton, N.J.: Published for the American Philosophical Society by Princeton University Press, 1948), 30–33. Franklin

also thought that schools should teach letter writing; see *Idea of the English School, Sketch'd Out for the Consideration of the Trustees of the Philadelphia Academy* (Philadelphia: Printed by B. Franklin, 1751), 5.

41. Nicole Eustace, *Passion Is the Gale: Emotion, Power, and the Coming of the American Revolution* (Chapel Hill: University of North Carolina Press, 2008), quote on 197, also 190. My discussion draws, in particular, on her interpretation of anger.

42. *Constitutions of the Publick Academy, in the City of Philadelphia* (Philadelphia: Printed by Benjamin Franklin, 1749), 4.

43. "An Exercise to the Admonishing Club," Deerfield, New Jersey, March 16, 1773, in Philip Vickers Fithian Papers, vol. 2, Princeton University Library Rare Books and Special Collections. See also Fea, *Way of Improvement*, 98–99.

44. See Davies's diary entries for September 13, 1753; on Rodgers, October 3, 1753; on church business, September 11, 1753; all in George William Pilcher, ed., *The Reverend Samuel Davies Abroad: The Diary of a Journey to England and Scotland, 1753–55* (Urbana: University of Illinois Press, 1967), 12, 18, 11.

45. Oliver Reese to Fithian, Trenton, June 21, 1773, in Philip Vickers Fithian Papers, vol. 3.

46. Joseph S. Tiedemann, "Presbyterianism and the American Revolution in the Middle Colonies," *Church History* 74, no. 2 (June 2005): 337–38.

47. See Lyman Henry Butterfield, ed., *John Witherspoon Comes to America: A Documentary Account Based Largely on New Materials* (Princeton, N.J.: Princeton University Library, 1953).

48. Scott A. Mills, *History of West Nottingham Academy, 1744–1981* (Lanham: Maryland Historical Press, 1985), 23–25.

49. Joseph S. Tiedemann, "Interconnected Communities: The Middle Colonies on the Eve of the American Revolution," *Pennsylvania History* 76, no. 1 (2009): 1–41, esp. 15–16.

50. Caroline Robbins, "'When It Is That Colonies May Turn Independent': An Analysis of the Environment and Politics of Francis Hutcheson (1694–1746)," *William and Mary Quarterly* 3rd ser. 11, no. 2 (April 1954): 214–51. On republicanism, see especially Bernard Bailyn, *The Origins of American Politics* (New York: Alfred A. Knopf, 1968).

51. *Four Dissertations, on the Reciprocal Advantages of a Perpetual Union Between Great-Britain and Her American Colonies: Written for Mr. Sargent's Prize-Medal; To Which (by Desire) Is Prefixed, an Eulogium, Spoken on the Delivery of the Medal at the Public Commencement in the College of Philadelphia, May 20th, 1766* (Philadelphia: Printed by William and Thomas Bradford, 1766). For a critique of imperial policy, see, for instance, John Morgan's essay, esp. 27–28.

52. Diamond, "Witherspoon, William Smith," esp. 125–28. On Smith's unique contributions to the educational culture of the mid-Atlantic, see George W. Boudreau, "Provost Smith and His Circle: The College of Philadelphia and the Transformation of Pennsylvania," in John Pollack, ed., *"The Good Education of Youth": Worlds of Learning in the Age of Franklin* (New Castle, Del.: Oak Knoll Press, 2009), 168–87, esp. 174–84.

53. On the denominational dynamics of revolutionary affiliations, especially in the mid-Atlantic, see Kevin Phillips, *The Cousins' Wars: Religion, Politics, and the Triumph of Anglo-America* (New York: Basic Books, 1999), 161–232, esp. 164–70; J. C. D. Clark, *The Language of Liberty, 1660–1832: Political Discourse and Social Dynamics in the Anglo-American World* (Cambridge: Cambridge University Press, 1994), 335–62.

54. Sheldon S. Cohen and Larry R. Gerlach, "Princeton in the Coming of the American Revolution," *New Jersey History* 92 (Summer 1974): 69–92. John Fea traces the radicalization of a single academy, including students' participation in another tea party, in *Way of Improvement*, 42–49. A number of historians have explored the politicization of colleges; see

Howard H. Peckham, "Collegia Ante Bellum: Attitudes of College Professors and Students Toward the American Revolution," *PMHB* 95, no. 1 (January 1971): 50–72; Miller, *Revolutionary College*, 79–94; David W. Robson, *Educating Republicans: The College in the Era of the American Revolution, 1750–1800* (Westport, Conn.: Greenwood Press, 1985), 34–45, 58–93; Mark A. Noll, *Princeton and the Republic, 1768–1822: The Search for a Christian Enlightenment in the Era of Samuel Stanhope Smith* (Princeton, N.J.: Princeton University Press, 1989), 32–33, 48–54; Hoeveler, *Creating the American Mind*, 241–346.

55. *Pennsylvania Chronicle* (Philadelphia), October 31, 1772.

56. Tiedemann, "Presbyterianism and the American Revolution," 339.

57. *Norwich (Conn.) Packet*, July 27, 1779. This first appeared in the *Pennsylvania Packet* (Philadelphia), but I have not located the original.

58. For a framework for thinking about interactions between different levels of involvement in the Revolution, see Linda Grant De Pauw, "Politicizing the Politically Inert: The Problem of Leadership in the American Revolution," in William M. Fowler, Jr., and Wallace Coyle, eds., *The American Revolution: Changing Perspectives* (Boston: Northeastern University Press, 1979), 7–25.

59. *Pennsylvania Packet*, November 19, 1784. This was in a "brief history" of the school, published as part of an advertisement.

60. *Merry Andrew's Almanack . . . 1762*.

61. Benjamin Carp has told a similar but more urban story about a different civil institution, the fire company; see "Fire of Liberty: Firefighters, Urban Voluntary Culture, and the Revolutionary Movement," *William and Mary Quarterly* 3rd ser. 58, no. 4 (October 2001): 781–818.

62. Lists of officers are in Francis Bernard Heitman, *Historical Register of Officers of the Continental Army During the War of the Revolution, April 1775 to December 1783* (Washington, D.C.: Rare Book Shop Publishing, 1914); William S. Stryker, *Official Register of the Officers and Men of New Jersey in the Revolutionary War* (Trenton, N.J.: Wm. T. Nicholson, 1872).

63. For the three Deerfield students, Governors Richard Howell and Joseph Bloomfield—both majors during the war—and Colonel Silas Newcomb, see John Fea, "Rural Religion: Protestant Community and the Moral Improvement of the South Jersey Countryside, 1676–1800" (Ph.D. diss., State University of New York at Stony Brook, 1999), 452–57. Bloomfield also had an Elizabeth Town connection; his mother was an Ogden. See below. Jonathan Forman studied with Tennent and finished out the war as a lieutenant colonel, though he was a major for most of the last two years of the conflict; see Richard A. Harrison, *Princetonians, 1769–1775: A Biographical Dictionary* (Princeton, N.J.: Princeton University Press, 1980), 377–78, 328–34.

64. Harry M. Ward, "Dayton, Jonathan," *American National Biography Online* (hereafter *ANB*), February 2000; Richard A. Harrison, *Princetonians, 1776–1783*, 31–33.

65. Harrison, *Princetonians, 1776–1783*, 140–43. Grammar schools and academies differed mostly in name; see Main, *Social Structure*, 243–46.

66. Harrison, *Princetonians, 1769–1775*, 328–30.

67. Edwin Francis Hatfield, *History of Elizabeth, New Jersey: Including the Early History of Union County* (New York: Carlton & Lanahan, 1868), 520–21.

68. Gaspare Saladino, "Bedford, Gunning," *ANB*.

69. On the Delaware line, see also Michael K. Madron, *Presbyterian Patriots: The Historical Context of the Shared History and Prevalent Ideologies of Delaware's Ulster-Scots Who Took up Arms in the American Revolution* (School of Advanced Military Studies, 2009), http://www.dtic.mil/cgi-bin/GetTRDoc?AD=ADA505604.

70. Mills, *West Nottingham Academy*, 25.

71. Political immobility, though it paled in comparison to the hereditary and established hierarchies of England, was very real in colonial America. See Martin, *Men in Rebellion*, esp. 23–61. For New Jersey in particular, see Thomas L. Purvis, "'High-Born, Long-Recorded Families': Social Origins of New Jersey Assemblymen, 1703 to 1776," *William and Mary Quarterly* 3rd ser. 37, no. 4 (October 1980): 592–615; and Michael S. Adelberg, "The Transformation of Local Governance in Monmouth County, New Jersey, During the War of the American Revolution," *Journal of the Early Republic* 31, no. 3 (2011): 467–98. Brendan McConville has shown how land disputes helped rectify some of the problem of political immobility in New Jersey; see *Those Daring Disturbers of the Public Peace: The Struggle for Property and Power in Early New Jersey* (Ithaca, N.Y.: Cornell University Press, 1999), 202–5, 249–55.

72. For New Jersey, I used the list of assemblymen and councillors from 1760 to 1776 compiled in Larry R. Gerlach, *Prologue to Independence: New Jersey in the Coming of the American Revolution* (New Brunswick, N.J.: Rutgers University Press, 1976), appendix 1–2; and a copy of the New Jersey Civil List, 1664–1800, film 298, DLAR. For Delaware, I used the list of officeholders in Claudia L. Bushman, Harold Bell Hancock, and Elizabeth Moyne Homsey, eds., *Proceedings of the Assembly of the Lower Counties on Delaware, 1770–1776, of the Constitutional Convention of 1776, and of the House of Assembly of the Delaware State, 1776–1781* (Newark: University of Delaware Press, 1986), 555–83.

73. John A. Munroe, "Read, George," *ANB*. Delaware's other senator as well as the state's lone member of the House of Representatives do not seem to have received a formal education in a mid-Atlantic college or academy.

74. Harrison, *Princetonians, 1769–1775*, 131–33. Bedford may also have served in the state legislature and the Continental Army, though there is some confusion because he had a politically active cousin of the same name.

75. Dorothy Rowlett Colburn, "Broom, Jacob," *ANB*; on Delaware officeholders, see also Bushman, Hancock, and Homsey, *Proceedings*, 555–83.

76. Landsman, *From Colonials to Provincials*, 160–61.

77. James McLachlan, *Princetonians, 1748–1768: A Biographical Dictionary* (Princeton, N.J: Princeton University Press, 1976), 643–46. Douglas Sloan identifies the Crowfield Academy as a Presbyterian school; see *Scottish Enlightenment*, 283.

78. McLachlan, *Princetonians, 1748–1768*, 437–39; David J. Fowler, "Elmer, Jonathan," *ANB*. One of New Jersey's first four members of the House of Representatives studied with Alison at the Philadelphia Academy, while another graduated from Queen's College. The final two entered professions and seem to have received private educations.

79. Harry M. Ward, "Brearly, David," *ANB*.

80. Some historians have argued that, along with a quantitative change in the socioeconomic makeup of officeholders, the American Revolution precipitated a large cultural shift in conceptions of office holding. This change served to limit, at least in appearance, the social distance between ruler and ruled. For instance, Jackson Turner Main argued that during the 1780s "voters had ceased to confine themselves to an elite, but were selecting instead men like themselves." See Main, "Government by the People: The American Revolution and the Democratization of the Legislatures," *William and Mary Quarterly* 3rd ser. 23, no. 3 (July 1966): 405, also 407. Gordon Wood followed this same trend into the early republic, arguing that Americans came to think "there were no specially qualified gentlemen who stood apart from the whole society . . . all were best represented by ordinary people." Though Wood acknowledges that this did not lead to "any sudden invasion of offices by ordinary people," he argues that even edu-

cated elites "behaved as common people" when in office. Gordon S. Wood, *The Radicalism of the American Revolution* (New York: Knopf, 1992), 294–95, 304.

81. Jack P. Greene, "The American Revolution," *American Historical Review* 105, no. 1 (February 2000): 100–101.

82. Michael Braddick argues that cultural and behavioral differences provided "the unarticulated legitimization for political power" throughout the early modern British Atlantic; see "Civility and Authority," in David Armitage and Michael Braddick, *The British Atlantic World, 1500–1800*, 2nd ed. (New York: Palgrave Macmillan, 2009), 116–17.

83. Elmer, *Elogy on Francis Barber*, 8, 15, my italics.

84. On the connections between the officer corps and post-Revolutionary nationalism, see Edwin G. Burrows, "Military Experience and the Origins of Federalism and Antifederalism," in Jacob Judd and Irwin H. Polishook, eds., *Aspects of Early New York Society and Politics* (Tarrytown, N.Y.: Sleepy Hollow Restorations, 1974), 83–92; and Jackson Turner Main, *Political Parties Before the Constitution* (Chapel Hill: University of North Carolina Press, 1973), 385–87. Also helpful on the culture of the Continental officers are Charles Royster, *A Revolutionary People at War: The Continental Army and American Character, 1775–1783* (Chapel Hill: University of North Carolina Press, 1979); and Sarah Knott, "Sensibility and the American War for Independence," *American Historical Review* 109 (2004): 19–40. For the construction and eventual destruction of the conservative vision of civil society that these groups tended to promote, see John L. Brooke, "Ancient Lodges and Self-Created Societies: Voluntary Association and the Public Sphere in the Early Republic," in Ronald Hoffman and Peter J. Albert, eds., *Launching the "Extended Republic": The Federalist Era* (Charlottesville: University Press of Virginia, 1996), 273–377; and Johann N. Neem, *Creating a Nation of Joiners: Democracy and Civil Society in Early National Massachusetts* (Cambridge, Mass.: Harvard University Press, 2008).

85. For a broader view of the connections between periods, see Jack P. Greene, "Colonial History and National History: Reflections on a Continuing Problem," *William and Mary Quarterly* 3rd ser. 64, no. 2 (April 2007): 235–50, and the forum that follows.

CHAPTER 10. "THIS IS THE SKIN OF A WHIT[E] MAN"

This chapter was researched during an Andrew W. Mellon Foundation Fellowship at the Huntington Library and a Mellon Postdoctoral Fellowship at the New-York Historical Society. I am grateful to the Library Staff at the Huntington, and to Valerie Paley, Michael Ryan, and the Library Staff at the New-York Historical Society for their help. For invaluable thoughts and comments, I also thank Edward Countryman, Ann Little, Peter Mancall, Mairin Odle, Daniel K. Richter, Christina Snyder, Peter Thompson, Coll Thrush, and participants in the 2013 conferences "The In-Betweenness of Things: Materializing Mediation and Movement Between Worlds" at University College London and the British Museum, "The American Revolution Reborn: New Perspectives for the Twenty-First Century" in Philadelphia, and the American Society for Ethnohistory Annual Conference in New Orleans. A special thank you to Patrick Spero and Michael Zuckerman for their vision and support, and to Mike and the anonymous readers for the University of Pennsylvania Press for their editorial feedback.

1. The glove is an object in the collections of the New-York Historical Society, acc. no. 1929.46.

2. The note allegedly written on human skin is in the collections of the Huntington Library, no. HM 72607. Information about how the object came to the Huntington from the

Los Angeles County Medical Association is found filed with the object, as are some notes from the Conservation Department. According to the conservator's report in the object files at the Huntington, there is no way to be sure it is human skin without destroying part of it. There is no provenance information about it beyond a note provided by the Los Angeles County Medical Association that it is "1779 Human Skin White Man English Colonist killed by Indians at Instigation of French." The text quoted is found on the note itself.

General information about Swetland's capture by the Seneca, and his time with Sullivan's campaign, is found in the journals of the American military during Sullivan's campaign, many of which are collected in Frederick Cook, ed. *Journals of the Military Expedition of Major General John Sullivan Against the Six Nations of Indians in 1779, with Records of Centennial Celebrations* (Auburn, N.Y.: Knapp, Peck & Thomson, 1887); in Luke Swetland, *A Narrative of the Captivity of Luke Swetland in 1778 and 1779 Among the Seneca Indians* (Walterville, N.Y.: James J. Guernsey, 1875); and in Edward Merrifield, *The Story of the Captivity and Rescue from the Indians of Luke Swetland: An Early Settler of the Wyoming Valley and a Soldier of the American Revolution* (Scranton, Pa., 1915).

3. On the significance of removing and displaying skin and body parts during Revolutionary-era conflicts between European Americans and Native Americans in the mid-Atlantic region, see Peter Silver, *Our Savage Neighbors: How Indian War Transformed Early America* (New York: Norton, 2008); and James H. Merrell, *Into the American Woods: Negotiations on the Pennsylvania Frontier* (New York: Norton, 2000).

4. On capture and adoption in Iroquoia, see Daniel K. Richter, *The Ordeal of the Longhouse: The People of the Iroquois League in the Era of European Colonization* (Chapel Hill: University of North Carolina Press for the Omohundro Institute of Early American History and Culture, 1992); for a nuanced discussion of Indian captivity more generally, see Christina Snyder, *Slavery in Indian Country: The Changing Face of Captivity in Early America* (Cambridge, Mass.: Harvard University Press, 2010).

5. This note fits into a larger pattern of using violence to place blame during the Revolution brilliantly discussed in Silver's *Our Savage Neighbors*. See especially chapter 8, "Barbarism and the American Revolution."

6. Colin Calloway, *The American Revolution in Indian Country: Crisis and Diversity in Native American Communities* (New York: Cambridge University Press, 1995), 292–93.

7. If the note is a fake, it likely was crafted after the Revolution rather than in 1779. Although eighteenth-century spelling is notoriously poor and inconsistent, misspelling the word "Indian" as "Ingen" is somewhat odd for a 1779 document, as "Ingen," or "Injun," was a racist slang term that gained widespread popularity later, in the nineteenth century.

8. Journal of Rev. William Rogers, D.D., July 9, 1779, in Cook, *Journals*, 252.

9. Journal of Dr. Jabez Campfield, September 14, 1779, in Cook, *Journals*, 60.

10. Journals of Captain Daniel Livermore, September 13, 1779, and Major James Norris, September 14, 1779, in Cook, *Journals*, 188 and 235.

11. Silver discusses the effect of this visual and print culture on the patriot imagination in *Our Savage Neighbors*; see especially 232–53.

12. Mairin Odle captures this wide range of alternate reaction in "'The Ill Effects of It': Ambiguous Afflictions of Early American Tattoos," paper presented at the Society of Early Americanists Biennial Conference, Savannah, Georgia, March 2013.

13. See Eric Hinderaker and Peter Mancall, *At the Edge of Empire: The Backcountry in British North America* (Baltimore: Johns Hopkins University Press, 2003).

14. Swetland, *Narrative of the Captivity*, 8–9.

15. Ibid., 19.
16. Ibid., 9–10.
17. Ibid., 14.
18. Ibid., 18, 31.
19. Merrifield, *Story of the Captivity*, 14.
20. This is the 1875 publication *A Narrative of the Captivity of Luke Swetland*.
21. This is the 1915 publication by Merrifield, *The Story of the Captivity and Rescue from the Indians of Luke Swetland*.
22. Before it came to the Huntington Library, it will be remembered, it was in the collections of the Los Angeles County Medical Association, which had this note attached to it.
23. Journal of Major James Norris, September 5, 1779 in Cook, *Journals*, 233.
24. Swetland, *Narrative of the Captivity*, 19.
25. Ibid., 17.
26. Sullivan to Congress, in Thomas C. Amory, *The Military Services and Public Life of Major-General John Sullivan of the American Revolutionary Army* (Boston: Wiggin and Lunt; Albany, N.Y.: J. Munsell, 1868), 139. On Sullivan's campaign, see Calloway, *American Revolution in Indian Country*; Joseph R. Fischer, *A Well-Executed Failure: The Sullivan Campaign Against the Iroquois, July–September 1779* (Columbia: University of South Carolina Press, 1997); Max Mintz, *Seeds of Empire: The American Revolutionary Conquest of the Iroquois* (New York: New York University Press, 1999); Alan Taylor, *The Divided Ground: Indians, Settlers, and the Northern Borderland of the American Revolution* (New York: Knopf, 2006); Glenn Williams, *Year of the Hangman: George Washington's Campaign Against the Iroquois* (Yardley, Pa.: Westholme, 2005).
27. Washington to Sullivan, quoted in Gary B. Nash, *The Unknown American Revolution: The Unruly Birth of Democracy and the Struggle to Create America* (New York: Penguin, 2006), 346.
28. Journal of Lieutenant Erkuries Beatty, September 3, 1779, in Cook, *Journals*, 28.
29. Letter of Captain William Gray to "Sr.," October 28, 1778, in Cook, *Journals*, 289.
30. Journal of Dr. Jabez Campfield, May 23, 1779, in Cook, *Journals*, 52.
31. Journal of Major James Norris, July 4, 1779, in Cook, *Journals*, 226.
32. Ibid., August 11, 1779, in Cook, Journals, 229.
33. Ibid., August 12, 1779, in Cook, *Journals*, 229.
34. On destruction of houses relating to a symbolic attack on people, see Robert Blair St. George, *Conversing by Signs: Poetics of Implication in Colonial New England* (Chapel Hill: University of North Carolina Press, 1998); Benjamin L. Carp, "Changing Our Habitation: Henry Laurens, Rattray Green, and the Revolutionary Movement in Charleston's Domestic Spaces," in David S. Shields, ed., *Material Culture in Anglo-America: Regional Identity and Urbanity in the Tidewater, Lowcountry, and Caribbean* (Columbia: University of South Carolina Press, 2009), 285–309.
35. In addition to works relevant to scalping in early America previously cited, see Robert L. Hall, *An Archaeology of the Soul: North American Indian Belief and Ritual* (Urbana: University of Illinois Press, 1997); and Lawrence Keeley, *War Before Civilization: The Myth of the Peaceful Savage* (Oxford: Oxford University Press, 1996).
36. See, for example, His Excellency Joseph Reed, Esq., President, and the Supreme Executive Council of Pennsylvania, "A Proclamation," April 22, 1780 (Philadelphia: Francis Bailey, 1780), in which $2500 was offered as a bounty for Indian scalps.
37. Sullivan to Congress, in Amory, *Military Services*, 139.

38. Swetland, *Narrative of the Captivity*, 27.

39. Sullivan to Washington, April 16, 1779, in Amory, *Military Services*, 267.

40. Journal of Lieutenant Erkuries Beatty, September 14, 1779, in Cook, *Journals*, 32.

41. *Notices of Sullivan's Campaign; or, The Revolutionary Warfare in Western New-York: Embodied in the Addresses and Documents Connected with the Funeral Honors Rendered to Those Who Fell with the Gallant Boyd in the Genesee Valley, Including the Remarks of Gov. Seward at Mount Hope* (Rochester, N.Y.: William Alling, 1842), 147.

42. Journal of Lieutenant William Barton, September 14, 1779, in Cook, *Journals*, 11.

43. Journal of Lieutenant William McKendry, September 14, 1779, in Cook, *Journals*, 206. Boyd quickly became a compelling symbol of British and Tory treachery. One doctor with the expedition sarcastically described the "extreemest tortures" suffered by Boyd as inflicted by "the virtuous and faithfull allies of Great Britain." Journal of Dr. Jabez Campfield, September 14, 1779, in Cook, *Journals*, 60.

44. Recollection of "Mr. Sanborn," in *Notices of Sullivan's Campaign*, 147.

45. Apparently they were still visible there a few years later, for "If I mistake it not, it was Judge Jones who informed me that when his brother, the late captain Horatio Jones, visited the spot a few years afterwards, he found the intestines still wound around the tree." *Notices of Sullivan's Campaign*, 147.

46. Ibid., preface.

47. Ibid., 34.

48. Ibid., 102.

49. Journal of Lieutenant William Barton, August 30, 1779 in Cook, *Journals*, 8.

50. Journal of Sergeant Thomas Roberts, August 31, 1779, in Cook, *Journals*, 244.

51. Journal of Lieutenant William Barton, August 26, 1779 in Cook, *Journals*, 7.

52. Philip J. Deloria, *Playing Indian* (New Haven, Conn.: Yale University Press, 1998); Linda R. Baumgarten, "Leather Stockings and Hunting Shirts," in Ann Smart Martin and J. Ritchie Garrison, eds., *American Material Culture: The Shape of the Field* (Winterthur, Del.: Winterthur Museum, 1997), 251–76; and, for a recent work on the Indianness (real or performed) of rangers' clothing, see Christian Ayne Crouch, "'We Had Two *Real* Indians': Performance and Expertise Through Dress During War," paper given at the Society of Early Americanists Conference, Savannah, Georgia, 2013.

53. For landscapes and monuments related to Native American history, see Jean M. O'Brien, *Firsting and Lasting: Writing Indians Out of Existence in New England* (Minneapolis: University of Minnesota Press, 2010); and Christine DeLucia, "The Memory Frontier: Making Past and Place in the Northeast After King Philip's War" (Ph.D. diss., Yale University, 2012).

54. Quote is from the text on the commemorative marker erected at Lodi, New York. My gratitude to historian Alyssa Mt. Pleasant for sharing her photographs of a similar monument.

CHAPTER 11. ENVIRONMENTAL HISTORY AND THE
WAR OF INDEPENDENCE

1. William Kelleher Storey, *The First World War: A Concise Global History*, 2nd ed. (Lanham, Md.: Rowman & Littlefield, 2014), 2–3, 97; Rick Atkinson, *Crusade: The Untold Story of the Persian Gulf War* (Boston: Houghton Mifflin, 1993), 492–93. War, of course, does not always lead to such negative effects. In the middle of the seventeenth century, periods of

increased warfare in the Connecticut Valley of central Massachusetts corresponded with a decrease in the number of beaver pelts exported; people who were killing other people did not have the time to kill beavers. See Peter A. Thomas, "The Fur Trade, Indian Land and the Need to Define Adequate 'Environmental' Parameters," *Ethnohistory* 28 (Fall 1981): 363–69.

2. David M. Kennedy, *Freedom from Fear: The American People in Depression and War, 1929–1945* (New York: Oxford University Press, 1999), 717–18; George C. Herring, *America's Longest War: The United States and Vietnam, 1950–1975*, 2nd ed. (New York: Knopf, 1986), 151, 153; David Hackett Fischer, *Washington's Crossing* (New York: Oxford University Press, 2004), 1–3. While the environment can strongly influence what humans do, it does not "determine" their actions. See William Cronon, "Kennecott Journey: The Paths out of Town," in William Cronon, George Miles, and Jay Gitlin, eds., *Under an Open Sky: Rethinking America's Western Past* (New York: W. W. Norton, 1992), 28–51.

3. Robert Bryce, "Gas Pains," *Atlantic*, May 2005; Anne Flaherty, "Military Feels Fuel-Cost Gouge in Iraq," *Huffington Post*, April 3, 2008; "M1 Abrams Main Battle Tank: Specifications," GlobalSecurity.org, accessed July 25, 2014, http://www.globalsecurity.org/military/systems/ground/m1-specs.htm; David C. Hsiung, "Food, Fuel, and the New England Environment in the War for Independence, 1775–1776," *New England Quarterly* 80 (December 2007), 614–54.

4. Many recent works incorporate the environment but not the insights of environmental history. General histories of the War of Independence include John Ferling, *Almost a Miracle: The American Victory in the War of Independence* (New York: Oxford University Press, 2007); Robert Middlekauff, *The Glorious Cause: The American Revolution, 1763–1789*, 2nd ed. (New York: Oxford University Press, 2005); and Matthew H. Spring, *With Zeal and with Bayonets Only: The British Army on Campaign in North America, 1775–1783* (Norman: University of Oklahoma Press, 2008). Recent histories of specific battles and campaigns include Lawrence E. Babits and Joshua B. Howard, *Long, Obstinate, and Bloody: The Battle of Guilford Courthouse* (Chapel Hill: University of North Carolina Press, 2009); John F. Luzader, *Saratoga: A Military History of the Decisive Campaign of the American Revolution* (New York: Savas Beatie, 2010); and Fischer, *Washington's Crossing*. Landmark works on logistics include Erna Risch, *Supplying Washington's Army* (Washington, D.C.: Center of Military History, 1981); and R. Arthur Bowler, *Logistics and the Failure of the British Army in America, 1775–1783* (Princeton, N.J.: Princeton University Press, 1975).

5. Paul S. Sutter, "The World with Us: The State of American Environmental History," *Journal of American History* 100 (June 2013): 96; Linda Nash, "Furthering the Environmental Turn," *Journal of American History* 100 (June 2013): 133. For Yellowstone and "wilderness," see Karl Jacoby, *Crimes Against Nature: Squatters, Poachers, Thieves, and the Hidden History of American Conservation* (Berkeley: University of California Press, 2001); and Mark David Spence, *Dispossessing the Wilderness: Indian Removal and the Making of the National Parks* (New York: Oxford University Press, 1999).

6. Brian Donahue, *The Great Meadow: Farmers and the Land in Colonial Concord* (New Haven, Conn.: Yale University Press, 2004), quotations on xiii, xiv, and xv.

7. Pekka Hämäläinen, "The Politics of Grass: European Expansion, Ecological Change, and Indigenous Power in the Southwest Borderlands," *William and Mary Quarterly* 57 (April 2010): 173–208, quotation on p. 176. See also Pekka Hämäläinen, *The Comanche Empire* (New Haven, Conn.: Yale University Press, 2008).

8. Alan Taylor, *William Cooper's Town: Power and Persuasion on the Frontier of the Early American Republic* (New York: Knopf, 1995), 30–31, quotations on pp. 33 and 317.

9. Peter C. Mancall's wide-ranging historiographical survey "Pigs for Historians: Changes in the Land and Beyond," *William and Mary Quarterly* 67 (April 2010): 347–75, never mentions the American Revolution.

10. Richard P. Tucker and Edmund Russell, eds., *Natural Enemy, Natural Ally: Toward an Environmental History of Warfare* (Corvallis: Oregon State University Press, 2004); Peter Coates, Tim Cole, and Chris Pearson, eds., *Militarized Landscapes: From Gettysburg to Salisbury Plain* (London: Contiuum, 2010). The Civil War in particular is currently riding a scholarly wave; see Lisa M. Brady, *War upon the Land: Military Strategy and the Transformation of Southern Landscapes During the American Civil War* (Athens: University of Georgia Press, 2012); Kathryn Shively Meier, *Nature's Civil War: Common Soldiers and the Environment in 1862 Virginia* (Chapel Hill: University of North Carolina Press, 2013); and Megan Kate Nelson, *Ruin Nation: Destruction and the American Civil War* (Athens: University of Georgia Press, 2012).

11. Hsiung, "Food, Fuel, and the New England Environment," 630–35, quotations on pp. 634–35.

12. Robert Greenhalgh Albion, *Forests and Sea Power: The Timber Problem of the Royal Navy, 1652–1862* (Cambridge, Mass.: Harvard University Press, 1926), 30–31, quotation on p. 30; N.A.M. Rodger, *The Command of the Ocean: A Naval History of Britain, 1649–1815* (New York: W. W. Norton, 2005), 374–75; Jean Boudriot, *The Seventy-Four Gun Ship: A Practical Treatise on the Art of Naval Architecture*, trans. David H. Roberts (Annapolis: Naval Institute Press, 1986–88), 1:57.

13. J. R. McNeill, *Mosquito Empires: Ecology and War in the Greater Caribbean, 1620–1914* (Cambridge: Cambridge University Press, 2010), quotations on pp. 3, 233. For smallpox, see Elizabeth A. Fenn, *Pox Americana: The Great Smallpox Epidemic of 1775–82* (New York: Hill and Wang, 2001).

14. David Hackett Fischer, *Paul Revere's Ride* (New York: Oxford University Press, 1994); George Washington to John Hancock, August 4–5, 1775, in *The Papers of George Washington Digital Edition,* ed. Theodore J. Crackel (Charlottesville: University of Virginia Press, Rotunda, 2008), http://rotunda.upress.virginia.edu/founders/GEWN-03-01-02-0150 (hereafter *PGWDE*); Risch, *Supplying Washington's Army*, 340. One barrel contained 100 pounds of powder, and one round used 0.4 ounces of powder; see Richard Gridley, "Inventory of Ordnance and Stores necessary for the present Army, supposing it to consist of twenty thousand Men," October 20, 1775, in Peter Force, ed., *American Archives*, 4th and 5th ser., 9 vols. (Washington, D.C., 1837–53), 4th ser., 3:1165, available at *American Archives: Documents of the American Revolution, 1774–1776*, http://amarch.lib.niu.edu/.

15. Ferling, *Almost a Miracle*, 58; George Washington to John Hancock, February 18–21, 1776, in *PGWDE*; Edward G. Lengel, *General George Washington: A Military Life* (New York: Random House, 2005), 118–21.

16. Oswald Eve operated this one powder mill, located on Frankford Creek just north of Philadelphia; see David L. Salay, "The Production of Gunpowder in Pennsylvania During the American Revolution," *PMHB* 99 (October 1975): 423; Fischer, *Paul Revere's Ride*, 44–64; Orlando W. Stephenson, "The Supply of Gunpowder in 1776," *American Historical Review* 30 (January 1925): 271–73. Gridley, "Inventory of Ordnance and Stores," based his estimate of 200,000 pounds on an army numbering 20,000 men.

17. Middlekauff, *The Glorious Cause*, 518; Jack N. Rakove, *The Beginnings of National Politics: An Interpretive History of the Continental Congress* (New York: Knopf, 1979), 200; Ferling, *Almost a Miracle*, 569; Risch, *Supplying Washington's Army*, 343; Salay, "Production of Gunpowder in Pennsylvania," 423; Stephenson, "Supply of Gunpowder in 1776," 276.

18. Kevin Phillips, *1775: A Good Year for Revolution* (New York: Viking, 2012), 304–12. Phillips added that from April 1775 through the autumn of 1777, "roughly 90 percent of the 2.35 million pounds of powder available to the American rebels was imported or made from imported saltpeter" (313). For the later shortages, see Risch, *Supplying Washington's Army*, 344–46.

19. David Cressy, *Saltpeter: The Mother of Gunpowder* (Oxford: Oxford University Press, 2013), 10–11.

20. *JCC*, June 10 and July 28, 1775, 2:85–86, 219; Force, *American Archives*, 4th ser., 3:812.

21. *JCC*, November 10, 1775, 3:347–48; February 23, 1776, 4:170.

22. Continental Congress, *Several Methods of Making Salt-Petre; Recommended to the Inhabitants of the United Colonies, by Their Representatives in Congress* (Philadelphia: W. and T. Bradford, 1775); Massachusetts General Assembly, *Several Methods of Making Salt-Petre; Recommended to the Inhabitants of the United Colonies, by the Honorable Continental Congress, and Re-published by Order of the General Assembly of the Colony of Massachusetts Bay, Together with the Resolve of Said Assembly, and an Appendix by Doctor William Whiting* (Watertown, Mass.: Benjamin Edes, 1775); New York Committee of Safety, *Essays upon the Making of Salt-Petre and Gun-Powder* (New York: Samuel Loudon, 1776); Pennsylvania Committee of Safety, *The Process of Extracting and Refining Salt-Petre, According to the Method Practiced at the Provincial Works in Philadelphia* (Philadelphia: William and Thomas Bradford, 1776); *Virginia Gazette* (Pinkney), July 27, 1775; *Virginia Gazette* (Purdie), August 4 and 11, 1775, and January 12, 1776; and *Virginia Gazette* (Dixon and Hunter), April 27, 1776. As of the middle of 1775, residents of Williamsburg, Virginia, could read three different newspapers named *Virginia Gazette*. John Dixon and William Hunter, Jr., published the original *Virginia Gazette*, which first appeared in 1736. A second one started in 1766, and John Pinkney took over its publication in 1775. Alexander Purdie began a third *Virginia Gazette* in February 1775. The publishers each sought to use their newspapers' name to win the right to publish the official business of the colonial government. See "A History of the Virginia Gazette," *The Virginia Gazette*, accessed December 20, 2015, http://www.vagazette.com/about/va-history-front-htmlstory.html.

23. Cressy, *Saltpeter*, 13–14; Massachusetts, *Several Methods of Making Salt-Petre*, 20.

24. Carolyn Merchant, *Ecological Revolutions: Nature, Gender, and Science in New England* (Chapel Hill: University of North Carolina Press, 1989), 123, 125. Merchant argues that Vallemont's ideas, published in France in 1707 and reprinted in England in 1767, "were sufficiently widely held that they can be taken as representative of the eighteenth-century belief system. These ideas and assumptions were reflected in the scientific treatises of Harvard professors, New England divines, and the authors of farmers' almanacs." See pp. 123 and 124 n. 21.

25. *Virginia Gazette* (Pinkney), July 27, 1775, p. 1. As articulated by Georg Ernst Stahl (1660–1734), phlogiston existed in metals and in substances that could burn. Stahl published his ideas in 1723 and strongly influenced thinking into the nineteenth century. See Arthur Greenberg, *From Alchemy to Chemistry in Picture and Story* (Hoboken, N.J.: John Wiley & Sons, 2007), 239–41.

26. For the humors, see Roy Porter, *The Greatest Benefit to Mankind: A Medical History of Humanity* (New York: Norton, 1999). According to Ron Chernow, on the last day of George Washington's life, his doctors, "handicapped by the benighted state of medical knowledge," made him gargle a combination of sage tea and vinegar, placed wheat bran poultices on his legs and throat, and drained from his body about half of his blood supply. See Ron Chernow, *Washington: A Life* (New York: Penguin, 2010), 807–8, quotation on p. 808.

27. Lewis Garanger, "Reflections, Observations, and Proposals Relative to the Military Service of the United States," 1783, Papers of the Continental Congress, National Archives Microfilm Publication M247, reel 95, issue 78, vol. 10, p. 445.

28. Reports of bad gunpowder spurred Congress to pass a set of regulations in August 1776 that established a broad set of inspections. Qualified inspectors had to "examine every cask of gun powder manufactured, or to be purchased on account of the United States," in order to judge "its quickness in firing, strength, dryness, and other necessary qualities," before it could be received into the public powder magazines. Congress also recommended that the states follow suit for gunpowder made within their borders. For bad powder, see *JCC*, July 29, 1775, 2:223, and June 7, 1776, 5:425. For the regulations on inspections, see *JCC*, August 28, 1776, 5:713–14.

29. Cressy, *Saltpeter*, 164. Cressy does not support this argument with evidence.

30. "Nitre," or niter, is another name for saltpeter.

31. The eight recipes are drawn from the sources listed in note 22. The final quotation comes from Pennsylvania, *Process of Extracting and Refining Salt-Petre*, 7.

32. Duane T. Gardiner and Raymond W. Miller, *Soils in Our Environment*, 10th ed. (Upper Saddle River, N.J.: Pearson/Prentice Hall, 2004), 7–8, 87, 112, 139.

33. Pennsylvania, *Process of Extracting and Refining Salt-Petre,* 3. Similarly, the writer in the *Virginia Gazette* (Pinkney), July 27, 1775, identified the best soil when he observed, "Earths and stones that have been impregnated with animal or vegetable juice, susceptible to putrefaction, and have been long exposed to the air, but sheltered from the sun and rain, are those which yield the greatest quantity of nitre." The Virginia Committee of Safety also urged tobacco planters "to cut down and preserve all their tobacco suckers, and also to preserve the trash, stalks, and sweepings of their tobacco houses, which are found to be exceedingly useful in the production of that necessary article [saltpeter]." See *Virginia Gazette* (Purdie), October 20, 1775, supplement, p. 1.

34. Frank R. Spellman, *Chemistry for Nonchemists: Principles and Applications for Environmental Practitioners* (Lanham, Md.: Government Institutes, 2006), 230, 235; Gardiner and Miller, *Soils in Our Environment*, 137–39, 151, 153. In the Continental Congress's *Several Methods of Making Salt-Petre*, 11, Benjamin Rush reported making saltpeter from tobacco stalks. The carbon to nitrogen ratio (C:N) expresses the mass of carbon relative to the mass of nitrogen in plants and other materials. Microorganisms in the soil consume nitrogen at a 24:1 ratio. Farmyard manure has a 20:1 ratio. See USDA Natural Resources Conservation Service, "Carbon to Nitrogen Ratios in Cropping Systems," accessed February 16, 2013, http://soils.usda.gov/sqi/management/files/C_N_ratios_cropping_systems.pdf. Tobacco's ratio is 13:1; see Oregon Biodynamic Group, "Nitrogen Content and Carbon-to-Nitrogen Ratios: For Composting Waste Materials," Introductory Class On-Line, "Appendices," accessed February 16, 2013, http://www.oregonbd.org/class/ftp/CtoN%20Ratios.pdf.

35. P. A. Cox, *The Elements on Earth: Inorganic Chemistry in the Environment* (New York: Oxford University Press, 1995), 165; Theodore L. Brown, H. Eugene LeMay, Jr., and Bruce E. Bursten, *Chemistry: The Central Science*, 8th ed. (Upper Saddle River, N.J.: Prentice Hall, 2000), 110–11, 480; Continental Congress, *Several Methods of Making Salt-Petre*, 5.

36. The four recipes are William Whiting, "Appendix," in Massachusetts, *Several Methods of Making Salt-Petre*, 18 (Whiting learned of this recipe from a "Dr. Graham" of Westchester County, New York); New York, *Essays upon the Making of Salt-Petre and Gun-Powder*, 18; Pennsylvania, *Process of Extracting and Refining Salt-Petre*, 4; and New York, *Essays upon the Making of Salt-Petre and Gun-Powder*, 19 (which contains a report from Whiting, dated

December 25, 1775). See also Mahendra K. Misra, Kenneth W. Ragland, and Andrew J. Baker, "Wood Ash Composition as a Function of Furnace Temperature," *Biomass and Bioenergy* 4 (1993): 111; Gardiner and Miller, *Soils in Our Environment*, 8; Brown, LeMay, and Bursten, *Chemistry*, 110–11; personal conversation with Dr. Larry Mutti, professor of geology, Juniata College, February 13, 2013.

37. Whiting, "Appendix," 18; New York, *Essays upon the Making of Salt-Petre and Gun-Powder*, 18. The recipe in *Virginia Gazette* (Pinkney), July 27, 1775, also instructs one to "filter the liquor through brown paper, or pass it through a flannel bag."

38. Potassium Nitrate Association, "Comparison of Potassium Nitrate to Different N and K Sources," Product Features and Benefits, accessed February 18, 2013, http://www.kno3 .org/en/product-features-a-benefits/comparison-of-potassium-nitrate-to-different-n-and-k -sources; Wikipedia, "Potassium nitrate," accessed February 18, 2013, http://en.wikipedia.org /wiki/Potassium_nitrate.

39. Personal conversation with Dr. Richard Hark, H. George Foster Professor of Chemistry, Juniata College, February 24, 2011; David E. Goldberg, *Fundamentals of Chemistry*, 2nd ed., (Boston: WCB/McGraw-Hill, 1998), 331.

40. Thomas Jefferson, "Query VI, Minerals: Nitre," in *Notes on the State of Virginia* (1782), Avalon Project: Documents in Law, History, and Diplomacy, Lillian Goldman Law Library, Yale Law School, accessed August 2, 2014, http://avalon.law.yale.edu/18th_century /jeffvir.asp; Charles Lynch to Virginia's delegates in Congress, November 20, 1775, in *The Papers of Thomas Jefferson*, ed. Julian P. Boyd et al. (Princeton, N.J.: Princeton University Press, 1950–), 1:263.

41. Cressy, *Saltpeter*, 164.

42. Rush, "An account of the manufactory of Salt-Petre," in Congress, *Several Methods of Making Salt-Petre*, 12; *Virginia Gazette* (Purdie), August 11, 1775; New York, *Essays upon the Making of Salt-Petre and Gun-Powder*, 19; Whiting, "Appendix," 17. The recipe in *Virginia Gazette* (Pinkney), July 27, 1775, said vaguely, "take any quantity of nitrous earths or stones."

43. *Virginia Gazette* (Dixon and Hunter), April 27, 1776, which reprinted a *Pennsylvania Journal* article. Congress recommended another process for preparing the soil, one from the German chemist Johann Rudolph Glauber (1604–70), but this one took even more time to come to fruition: one to two years. See Congress, *Several Methods of Making Salt-Petre*, 10.

44. Congress, *Several Methods of Making Salt-Petre*, 5.

45. William Whiting stressed the importance of wood ashes or, in his recipe, a lye made from ashes. He argued that "the want of a sufficient quantity of these alkaline salts has been the sole reason why great numbers of persons have either not been able to reduce their liquor to crystals at all, or else their crystals have been small in quantity and very foul." See New York, *Essays upon the Making of Salt-Petre and Gun-Powder*, 22.

46. New York, *Essays upon the Making of Salt-Petre and Gun-Powder*, 18; John Adams to James Warren, June 27, 1775, in *Papers of John Adams*, ed. Robert J. Taylor and Gregg L. Lint (Cambridge, Mass.: Belknap Press of Harvard University Press, 1979), 3:50; Committee of Safety of Cumberland County, June 30, 1775, in H. R. McIlwaine, ed., *Proceedings of the Committees of Safety of Cumberland and Isle of Wight Counties, Virginia, 1775–1776* (Richmond: Virginia State Library, 1918), 15; *Virginia Gazette* (Pinkney), December 13, 1775, p. 1; George Gilmer to Thomas Jefferson, July 26 or 27, 1775, in *The Papers of Thomas Jefferson*, 1:237.

47. Benjamin Harrison, Jr., to Dr. Bland, December 25, 1775, in Charles Campbell, ed., *The Bland Papers: Being a Selection from the Manuscripts of Colonel Theodorick Bland, Jr., of Prince George County, Virginia* (Petersburg, Va.: Edmund and Julian C. Ruffin, 1840), 1:39–40; Jonathan

Kearsley to Committee of Safety, March 30, 1776, *Pennsylvania Archives,* 1st ser., 12 vols., ed. Samuel Hazard (Philadelphia: Joseph Severns, 1852–56), 4:727–728, 706. According to E. Wayne Carp, "overly complicated instructions for making saltpeter and small-scale, unsustained efforts by state legislatures" played a large role in America's dependency on foreign supplies of gunpowder; see E. Wayne Carp, *To Starve the Army at Pleasure: Continental Army Administration and American Political Culture, 1775–1783* (Chapel Hill: University of North Carolina Press, 1984), 23. Cressy makes the related argument that the "the work was more difficult than amateur enthusiasts envisaged" in *Saltpeter,* 163.

48. Charles Lynch to Thomas Jefferson, November 20, 1775, in *The Papers of Thomas Jefferson,* 1:261–62; Salay, "Production of Gunpowder in Pennsylvania," 426; Pennsylvania House of Representatives, October 12, 1775, in *Pennsylvania Archives,* 8th ser., 8 vols., ed. Gertrude MacKinney and Charles F. Hoban (Harrisburg: Pennsylvania Bureau of Publications, 1931–35), 8:7308. Salay attributes the troubles in Philadelphia to a "want of money and the necessary skill," but the committee makes no mention of that second failing.

49. Henry Wynkoop to Committee of Safety, January 24, 1776, in *Pennsylvania Archives,* 1st ser., 4:702–3; Jacob Rubsamen to Col. Theodorick Bland, Jr., August 2, 1782, in Campbell, *The Bland Papers,* 2:90.

50. Maryland Convention, August 14 and December 27, 1775, in Force, *American Archives,* 4th ser., 3:116; 4:723–24; Rhode Island General Assembly, August 21, 1775, in Force, *American Archives,* 4th ser., 3:232; *Virginia Gazette* (Purdie), September 8, 1775 supplement, p. 2; General Assembly of Connecticut, "An Act for Encouraging the Manufactures of Salt-Petre and Gun-Powder," December 14, 1775; *Minutes of the Provincial Congress of North Carolina,* vol. 10, September 10, 1775, p. 216, Documenting the American South, "Colonial and State Records of North Carolina," accessed February 22, 2013, http://docsouth.unc.edu/ csr/index.html/document /csr10-0089; *Minutes of the Provincial Council of Pennsylvania, From the Organization to the Termination of the Proprietary Government,* vol. 10 (Harrisburg: Theo. Fenn, 1852), 280; Force, *American Archives,* 4th ser., 3:1801; *Journals of the House of Representatives of Massachusetts, 1775,* October 31, 1775, vol. 51, pt. 1:215; March 25, 1776, pt. 3:39; April 26, 1776, pt. 3:187; article dated "Watertown, June 3," *Virginia Gazette* (Dixon and Hunter), June 22, 1776, p. 4.

51. George Washington to Lt. Col. Joseph Reed, November 28, 1775, *PGWDE*; Phillips, *1775,* 300; Ferling, *Almost a Miracle,* 280.

52. Rhode Island General Assembly, August 21, 1775, in Force, *American Archives,* 4th ser., 3:232; General Assembly of Connecticut, "An Act for encouraging the Manufactures of Salt-Petre and Gun-Powder," December 14, 1775 (New London, 1776); New Jersey Provincial Congress, March 2, 1776, in Force, *American Archives,* 4th ser., 4:1624–25.

53. Congress, *Several Methods of Making Salt-Petre,* 3–4; New York, *Essays upon the Making of Salt-Petre and Gun-Powder,* 3–4.

54. Max M. Edling, "A More Perfect Union: The Framing and Ratification of the Constitution," in Edward G. Gray and Jane Kamensky, eds., *The Oxford Handbook of the American Revolution* (New York: Oxford University Press, 2013), 391.

55. Jerrilyn Greene Marston, *King and Congress: The Transfer of Political Legitimacy, 1774–1776* (Princeton, N.J.: Princeton University Press, 1987), 300, 301 (quotation); Lucille E. Horgan, *Forged in War: The Continental Congress and the Origin of Military Supply and Acquisition Policy* (Westport, Conn.: Greenwood Press, 2002), 21.

56. Robert E. Shalhope, "Republicanism," in Jack P. Greene and J. R. Pole, eds., *A Companion to the American Revolution* (Malden, Mass.: Blackwell, 2000), 671–72; William Livingston to Henry Laurens, January 8, 1778, in *The Papers of William Livingston,* ed. Carl E.

Prince and Dennis P. Ryan (Trenton: New Jersey Historical Commission, 1980), 2:172. For an overview of the "disaffected," see Michael A. McDonnell, "Resistance to the American Revolution," in Greene and Pole, *Companion to the American Revolution*, 342–51.

57. *Massachusetts House Journals, 1775–1776*, vol. 51, pt. 2, p. 67, December 23, 1775. For a fuller treatment of the army's wood supply at this time, see Hsiung, "Food, Fuel, and the New England Environment," 645–51.

CHAPTER 12. THE PROBLEM OF ORDER AND THE TRANSFER
OF SLAVE PROPERTY IN THE REVOLUTIONARY SOUTH

1. See, most notably, David Brion Davis, *The Problem of Slavery in the Age of Revolution, 1770–1823* (New York: Oxford, 1974); Ira Berlin, *Many Thousands Gone: The First Two Centuries of Slavery in North America* (Cambridge, Mass.: Harvard University Press, 1998); William W. Freehling, *The Road to Disunion*, vol. 1, *Secessionists at Bay, 1776–1854* (New York: Oxford University Press, 1991).

2. Those works that do emphasize change tend to focus on emancipation and the ideological challenges of slavery. See, for instance, Douglas Egerton, *Death or Liberty: African Americans and Revolutionary America* (New York: Oxford University Press, 2009); Duncan MacLeod, *Slavery, Race, and the American Revolution* (Cambridge: Cambridge University Press, 1975); Donald Robinson, *Slavery in the Structure of American Politics, 1765–1820* (New York: Harcourt Brace Jovanovich, 1971).

3. This chapter follows a tradition of scholarship that emphasizes the Revolution as a transformative moment in American development, beginning with the work of Charles Beard, Carl Becker, and John Franklin Jameson and continuing more recently to scholars like Ronald Hoffman, Woody Holton, Alfred F. Young, and Michael A. McDonnell. See, among many other works, Jameson, *The American Revolution Considered as a Social Movement* (1926; repr., Princeton, N.J.: Princeton University Press, 1967); Hoffman, *A Spirit of Dissension: Economics, Politics, and the Revolution in Maryland* (Baltimore: Johns Hopkins University Press, 1973); Holton, *Forced Founders: Indians, Debtors, Slaves and the Making of the American Revolution in Virginia* (Chapel Hill: University of North Carolina Press, 1999); McDonnell, *The Politics of War: Race, Class, and Conflict in Revolutionary Virginia* (Chapel Hill: University of North Carolina Press, 2007); Alfred F. Young and Gregory H. Nobles, *Whose American Revolution Was It? Historians Interpret the Founding* (New York: New York University Press, 2011).

4. Northern seaports grew extremely rapidly in the pre-Revolutionary decades. Compare their growth to that of the South's one real city, Charleston, whose population had been eclipsed by six northern cities by 1775. See Gary Nash, *The Urban Crucible: The Northern Seaports and the Origins of the American Revolution* (Cambridge, Mass.: Harvard University Press, 1979), esp. 1–64. For the percentage of population living in cities, see the appendixes in Benjamin Carp, *Rebels Rising: Cities and the American Revolution* (New York: Oxford University Press, 2007).

5. Rhys Isaac, *The Transformation of Virginia, 1740–1790* (Chapel Hill: University of North Carolina Press, 1982).

6. The quote is from Carl Bridenbaugh, *Myths and Realities: Societies of the Colonial South* (Baton Rouge: Louisiana State University Press, 1952), 122.

7. Robert McCluer Calhoon, *The Loyalists in Revolutionary America, 1760–1781* (New York: Harcourt Brace Jovanovich, 1965), 442.

8. For South Carolina population, see Stella H. Sutherland, *Population Distribution in Colonial America* (New York: Columbia University Press, 1936). For Georgia and quotation, see "Report of Sir James Wright on the Condition of the Province of Georgia, on 20th Sept. 1773," in "Letters from Sir James Wright," *Collections of the Georgia Historical Society* 3 (1873): 158–75, 167.

9. Sutherland, *Population Distribution*, 139, 239–40.

10. Ibid.; for number of slaves, see Rachel Klein, *Unification of a Slave State: The Rise of the Planter Class in the South Carolina Backcountry, 1760–1808* (Chapel Hill: University of North Carolina Press, 1990), 20.

11. Given the enormous cost of entering the slaveholder ranks, with "prime field hands" appraised at more than the total value of many backcountry estates before the war, the cost of transporting bulky agricultural commodities from the interior to the coast remained prohibitive. Although a nascent planter class did exist above South Carolina's fall line, for example, even the largest holdings in the backcountry were dwarfed by the average holding in low-country parishes. See Klein, *Unification of a Slave State*, esp. chaps. 1 and 2.

12. For the spread of the market into the Virginia Piedmont and the role played by merchant capital from Scotland, see Jacob M. Price, "The Rise of Glasgow in the Chesapeake Trade," *William and Mary Quarterly* 3rd ser. 11 (1954): 179–99.

13. For the South Carolina Regulation, see Klein, *Unification of a Slave State*, esp. chaps. 1–2. For North Carolina Regulators, see Marjoleine Kars, *Breaking Loose Together: The Regulator Rebellion in Pre-Revolutionary North Carolina* (Chapel Hill: University of North Carolina Press, 2002).

14. Gary B. Nash, *The Unknown American Revolution: The Unruly Birth of Democracy and the Struggle to Create America* (New York: Penguin, 2006) 161; William R. Ryan, *The World of Thomas Jeremiah: Charles Town on the Eve of the American Revolution* (New York: Oxford University Press, 2010); J. William Harris, *The Hanging of Thomas Jeremiah: A Free Black Man's Encounter with Liberty* (New Haven, Conn.: Yale University Press, 2009).

15. "Proceedings of the Committee of Safety in Pitt County, July 8, 1775," in *The Colonial and State Records of North Carolina* (hereafter *CSR*), ed. William Saunders et al., 26 vols. (Raleigh, N.C.: Department of History and Archives, 1865–1908), 10:87.

16. Patrick Henry, "Circular Letter, November 20, 1775," William Augustine Washington Papers, Duke University Libraries (hereafter DUL). For the development of slave patrols, see Sally Hadden, *Slave Patrols: Law and Violence in Virginia and the Carolinas* (Cambridge, Mass.: Harvard University Press, 2001).

17. "Journal of the Commons House of Assembly," in *The Revolutionary Records of the State of Georgia* (hereafter *RRG*), ed. Allen D. Candler (Atlanta: Franklin-Turner, 1908–10), 1:292–93.

18. Dorchester County Court, quoted in Hoffman, *A Spirit of Dissension*, 185.

19. Klein, *Unification of a Slave State*, 83. William Henry Drayton to the Council of Safety, August 31, 1775, in Robert W. Gibbes, *Documentary History of the American Revolution: Consisting of Letters Chiefly in South Carolina, from Originals in Possession of the Editor* (New York: D. Appleton, 1853–55), 1:153.

20. William Moultrie, *Memoirs of the American Revolution, So Far as It Related to the States of North and South Carolina, and Georgia* (New York: David Longworth, 1802), 1:64.

21. "Petition to the North Carolina Assembly, n.d. [1776–77?]," in William Lenoir Papers, Box 31, Southern Historical Collection, University of North Carolina at Chapel Hill (hereafter SHC).

22. Maya Jasanoff, *Liberty's Exiles: American Loyalists in the Revolutionary World* (New York: Knopf, 2011), 25–27; Gary D. Olson, "Thomas Brown, Loyalist Partisan, and the Revolutionary War in Georgia," in *Georgia Historical Quarterly* 54 (1970): 1–19, 183–208.

23. After suffering the failed siege and several defeats in skirmishes, British commanders focused on subduing the Revolution in New York and Massachusetts. Sizable forces of redcoats would not enter the region again until after Burgoyne's disastrous defeat at Saratoga at the end of 1777. For the failed siege of Charleston and British strategy in the years before the invasion of Georgia in 1778, see David Lee Russell, *The American Revolution in the Southern Colonies* (Jefferson, N.C.: McFarland, 2000); David K. Wilson, *The Southern Strategy: Britain's Conquest of South Carolina and Georgia, 1775–1780* (Columbia: University of South Carolina Press, 2005).

24. In one raid in early 1778, Brown's rangers took over 2,000 head of cattle and over 200 slaves. Sylvia Frey, *Water from the Rock: Black Resistance in a Revolutionary Age* (Princeton, N.J.: Princeton University Press, 1991), 83.

25. Richard Graham to Leven Powell, February 20, 1777, Leven Powell Papers, Swem Library, College of William and Mary, Williamsburg, Va. The plundering and disorder that occurred during the war in Virginia is well covered in McDonnell, *Politics of War*.

26. McDonnell, *Politics of War*, 461.

27. Charles Royster, *A Revolutionary People at War: The Continental Army and American Character, 1775–1783* (Chapel Hill: University of North Carolina Press, 1979), esp. 221–22.

28. The narrative of these changes has been discussed with great depth and care by a number of scholars. See, in particular, McDonnell, *Politics of War*; Klein, *Unification of a Slave State*; John R. Maas, "'A Complicated Scene of Difficulties': North Carolina and the Revolutionary Settlement, 1776–1789" (Ph.D. diss., Ohio State University, 2007); Michael McDonnell and Woody Holton, "Patriot vs. Patriot: Social Conflict and the Origins of the Revolution in Virginia," *Journal of American Studies* 34, no. 2 (August, 2000): 231–56.

29. E. James Ferguson, *The Power of the Purse: A History of American Public Finance, 1776–1790* (Chapel Hill: University of North Carolina Press, 1961), 26.

30. Alan D. Watson, *Money and Monetary Problems in Early North Carolina* (Raleigh: North Carolina Department of History and Archives, 1980), 38–42; Charles Calomiris, "Institutional Failure, Monetary Scarcity, and the Depreciation of the Continental," *Journal of Economic History* 48, no. 1 (March, 1988): 47–68.

31. R. Arthur Bowler, *Logistics and the Failure of the British Army in America* (Princeton, N.J.: Princeton University Press, 1992), 70.

32. See James A. Henretta, "The War for Independence and American Economic Development," in Ronald Hoffman et al., eds., *The Economy of Early America: The Revolutionary Period, 1763–1790* (Charlottesville: University Press of Virginia, 1988), 45–87.

33. Ronald L. Lewis, *Coal, Iron, and Slaves: Industrial Slavery in Maryland and Virginia, 1715–1865* (Westport, Conn.: Greenwood Press, 1979), 9–12.

34. William Hill, *Col. William Hill's Memoirs of the Revolution*, ed. A. S. Salley, Jr. (Columbia: Historical Commission of South Carolina, 1921).

35. "Journal of the Committee of Safety," in *Calendar of Virginia State Papers and Other Manuscripts*, ed. W. P. Palmer et al. (Richmond, 1875–93), 8:77, 79, 81, 98, 113, 156, 183.

36. James Milles to Thomas Person, March 19, 1777, Person Family Papers, SHC.

37. An original and useful observation made in John Shy, "Logistical Crisis and the American Revolution: A Hypothesis," in John A. Lynn, ed., *Feeding Mars: Logistics in Western Warfare from the Middle Ages to the Present* (Boulder, Colo.: Westview Press, 1994): 161–79.

38. David Ramsay, *The History of the Revolution of South-Carolina, from a British Province to an Independent State*, 2 vols. (Trenton, N.J.: Isaac Collins, 1785), 1:177.

39. "The Journal of Alexander Chesney," ed. E. Alfred Jones, in *Ohio State University Bulletin* 26, no. 4 (October 1921): 8. Existing papers related to Hampton are extremely limited but what exists is discussed at length in Ronald Edward Bridwell, "The South's Wealthiest Planter: Wade Hampton of South Carolina" (Ph.D. diss., University of South Carolina, 1980).

40. Edmund Pendleton to Gen. William Woolford, September 13, 1777, Edmund Pendleton Letters, SHC.

41. Complaints about slaves simply refusing to work, or demanding better treatment, are numerous. For one well-documented case, see the Josiah Smith Letterbooks, SHC.

42. See, for example, Robert Middlekauff's still-standard history of the Revolution, *The Glorious Cause: The American Revolution, 1763–1789* (New York: Oxford University Press, 1985), which devotes but one chapter to the war in the South and makes little mention of plundering, looting, or beheadings. Very important exceptions to this claim exist, of course, generally among works that emphasize the Revolution as a moment of social rupture, such as McDonnell, *Politics of War*; and Nash, *Unknown American Revolution*. Other works that focus specifically on the war in the southern backcountry have emphasized the growing disorder as well. See, for instance, Jerome Nadelhaft, *Disorders of War: The Revolution in South Carolina* (Orono: University of Maine Press, 1982); John S. Pancake, *This Destructive War: The British Campaign in the Carolinas, 1780–1782* (Tuscaloosa: University of Alabama Press, 1985); Jim Piecuch, *Three Peoples, One King: Loyalists, Indians, and Slaves in the Revolutionary South, 1775–1782* (Columbia: University of South Carolina Press, 2008).

43. James Green, a North Carolina merchant, was not atypical when he petitioned the British claims commission, complaining that "Your Memorialist is a Sufferer by the continued Persecution of Ill Fortune from different Quarters. He has been pillaged by rebels as being a Loyal Subject—and despoiled by his Majesty's Loyal Subjects as if he were a Rebel!" Quoted in Christopher Crittenden, "Commerce in North Carolina, 1763–1789" (Ph.D. diss., Yale University, 1936), p. 142.

44. A loyalist named Love was lynched upon returning home after the war by neighbors who remembered him slaying wounded rebels after a skirmish. Aedanus Burke to the Governor, December 14, 1784, in Aedanus Burke Papers, South Caroliniana Library, University of South Carolina, Columbia (hereafter SCL).

45. Quoted in Nadelhaft, *Disorders of War*, 84.

46. Johann Ewald, *Diary of the American War: A Hessian Journal*, trans. Joseph P. Tustin (New Haven, Conn.: Yale University Press, 1979), 203.

47. Nearly a decade later bands of Maroons operating between Savannah and Charleston, calling themselves the King of England Soldiers, were said to be "the very fellows that fought & maintained their ground against the brave Lancers at the siege of Savannah, and they still call themselves the King of England's Soldiers." Col. James Jackson to Governor Mathews, 1787, Joseph Vallence Bevan Papers, Georgia Historical Society (hereafter GHS), Savannah.

48. Thomas Bee to Governor Mathews, December 9, 1782, Thomas Bee Papers, SCL.

49. To give a single example, slaves provided intelligence about the state of supplies in Charleston during the British siege in 1780. Additionally, an enslaved man aided in the capture of the city by leading British soldiers on a hidden path through swamps outside the city to envelop American forces. Frey, *Water from the Rock*, 108–10.

50. "Memorial of Sir James Wright to Lord Germain, Bart. Governor of the Province of Georgia and several other Gentlemen, late Inhabitants of that Province and others who have

Property therein," January 6, 1779, in "Letters from Sir James Wright," *Collections of the Georgia Historical Society* 3 (1873): 249–50.

51. Above quotes all taken from Records of the Board of Police, June 13, 1780, Microfilm, South Carolina Department of Archives and History, Columbia. In the months before the exchange with the board of police, at least four dozen slaves had been returned to loyalists by authorities in Charleston under like conditions. Reverend Jenkins Memorandum Book, May 1780, South Carolina Historical Society, Charleston.

52. Philip D. Morgan and Andrew Jackson O'Shaughnessy, "Arming Slaves in the American Revolution," in Christopher Leslie Brown and Philip D. Morgan, eds., *Arming Slaves: From Classical Times to the Modern Age* (New Haven, Conn.: Yale University Press, 2006): 180–208, 198.

53. Lorenzo J. Greene, "Some Observations on the Black Regiment of Rhode Island in the American Revolution," *Journal of Negro History* 37 (1952): 142–72. In one instance, an officer was court-martialed for waiting until after receiving his recruiting bonus before reporting his enlistment of slaves to authorities. "Records of the Court of Goochland County," in *Calendar of Virginia State Papers*, 1:582.

54. Many southerners suggested such a course of action but the two most famous were John Laurens and Nathanael Greene. For Laurens, see Frey, *Water from the Rock*, 136. For Nathanael Greene's plan, see Greene to Governor John Rutledge, December 9, 1781, in *PNG*, 10:22.

55. See, for instance, "Petition of John Calvert, Feb. 5, 1780," *Journal of the Assembly and House of Representatives*, ed. William Edwin et al. (Columbia: University of South Carolina Press, 1970), 1:270.

56. North Carolina purchased tobacco at fifty shillings sterling a hundred weight both during and after the war when the commodity had normally traded at roughly thirty-two shillings before. Papers of the Joint Standing Committee on Finance, Tobacco Subcommittee, 1/86–87, North Carolina State Archives, Raleigh (hereafter NCSA).

57. One well-documented case is Patrick Henry's hire of nineteen slaves from Georgia planter Joseph Habersham. See "Joseph Habersham and Joseph Clay Account Book," Joseph Habersham Papers, GHS; "Agreement of Hire Between Patrick Henry and Joseph Habersham," Patrick Henry Papers, Swem Library, College of William and Mary, Williamsburg, Va. Henry hired Habersham's slaves at the very high price of roughly £15 per hand per annum.

58. Wade Hampton made substantial profits supplying both patriot and loyal armies. He and his brothers supplied over 136,000 pounds of cornmeal alone to Sumter's troops in 1782–83. Bridwell, "South's Wealthiest Planter," 95–97.

59. Joseph Clay to "Dear Sir" [?], Joseph Clay Letterbooks, vol. 3, GHS.

60. William Ancrum to Marlow Pryror, 23 December, 1776, William Ancrum Letterbooks, SCL.

61. For instance, a field hand was sold at public auction in Georgia for the astounding sum of £7605. *RRG*, 2:216.

62. "Table of Depreciation," Governor's Papers, Georgia State Archives, Morrow.

63. Reverend Purcell to Governor Abner Nash, 1780, in *CSR*, 15:15–17.

64. Henderson was given two adult slaves and one young slave. Journal of the General Assembly, July 20, 1782, in *RRG*, 2:343.

65. The British did the same. Jeffrey J. Crow, "What Price Loyalism? The Case of John Cruden, Commissioner of Sequestered Estates," *North Carolina Historical Review* 58, no. 3 (July 1981): 215–33; Frey, *Water from the Rock*, 178–81.

66. John Hawrie to Bolling Clark, June 21, 1783, Clark Family Papers, DUL.

67. Another sale of slaves and land in New Bern, North Carolina, was done entirely in certificates. "Sample Returns of the Sales of Confiscated Estates and Negroes, Benjamin Sheppard, Superintendent, 1782," Loyalist Papers, NCSA. For Guerard, W. Robert Higgins, "A Financial History of the American Revolution in South Carolina" (Ph.D. diss., University of South Carolina, 1970), 215–19.

68. Journal of the General Assembly, May 17 1782, in *RRG*, 2:337.

69. Ibid., August 20, 1782.

70. John Mathews to Benjamin Harrison, March 15, 1782, in Benjamin Harrison Papers, Brock Collection, Huntington Library, San Marino, Calif.; Governor Harrison to Governor Mathews, April 30, 1782, in H. R. McIlwaine, ed., *Official Letters of the Governors of the State of Virginia*, vol. 3, *The Letters of Thomas Nelson and Benjamin Harrison* (Richmond: Virginia State Library, 1929), 199–200.

71. *CSR*, 24:338, 368–69, 420. Paul V. Lutz, "A State's Concern for the Soldiers' Welfare: How North Carolina Provided for Her Troops During the Revolution," *North Carolina Historical Review* 42 (July 1965): 315–18.

72. Walter J. Fraser, Jr., "Reflections of 'Democracy' in Revolutionary South Carolina? The Composition of Military Organizations and Relationships of the Officers and Men, 1775–1780," *South Carolina Historical Magazine* 78, no. 3 (July 1977): 202–12, 205.

73. L. Scott Philyaw, "A Slave For Every Soldier: The Strange History of Virginia's Recruitment Act," *Virginia Magazine of History and Biography* 109 (April 2001): 364–79.

74. James Stallings to Colonel James Jackson, July 24, 1782, James Stallings Letter, GHS; *RRG*, 2:306.

75. Richard Hampton to John Hampton, April 2, 1781, in Gibbes, *Documentary History*, 2:47.

76. For an excellent discussion of Sumter's regiment and the social impact that slave bounties had on the development of the South Carolina backcountry, see Justin Liles, "Thomas Sumter's Law: Slavery in the Southern Backcountry During the American Revolution" (Ph.D. diss., University of South Carolina, 2011), 104–5.

77. A number of soldiers never received their promised slaves, receiving promissory notes payable instead; many of these were, in turn, purchased by officers who eventually used them to accumulate confiscated estates and western land. Bridwell, "South's Wealthiest Planter," 206.

78. Widespread plundering led to acrimony between commanders. In 1782, General Alexander Leslie, in charge of the British garrison at Charleston, threatened Nathanael Greene to retaliate in kind if he could not get South Carolina troops to stop plundering loyalist plantations. Alexander Leslie to Nathanael Greene, April 4, 1782, Alexander Leslie Letterbooks, Microfilm, New-York Historical Society, New York.

79. Wade Hampton to Richard Hampton, January 30, 1782, Hampton Family Papers, SCL.

80. George R. Lamplugh, "The Importance of Being Truculent: James Gunn, the Chatham Militia, and Georgia Politics, 1782–1789," *Georgia Historical Quarterly* 60, no. 2 (Summer, 1996): 226–38, 228.

81. It is impossible to know how many slaves were sold by British troops, but the number was surely in the thousands. Frey, *Water from the Rock*, 209–12.

82. "Petition of the Inhabitants of Amelia County, 1781," *Calendar of Virginia State Papers*, 2:684.

83. James Wright to Lord Germain, July 17, 1780, in "Letters from Sir James Wright," *Collections of the Georgia Historical Society* 3 (1873): 308–9.

84. Petition of Jacob Alford and the Inhabitants of Anson County, January 1779, General and State Assembly Records, NCSA.

85. Thomas Wade to Nathanael Greene, April 29, 1781, in *PNG* 8:175.

86. Timothy Barnard to Major Cain, 13 April 1784, John Habersham Papers, GHS.

87. Cornet Elholm to Peter Horry, March 3, 1782; Francis Marion to Horry, March 8, 1782; Marion to Horry, March 10, 1782; all in Gibbes, *Documentary History*, 3:262, 266–68. Kains had been accused of similar practice a year earlier. He was court-martialed for "Plundering Negroes hoggs & other goods." Francis Marion Orderly Book, vol. 3, March 3, 1781, Huntington Library.

88. David Ross to John Hook, October 28, 1778; David Ross to John Hook, November 17, 1788; both in John Hook Papers, DUL. At Yorktown, General Wayne was given authority by Washington to dispose of "unclaimed Negroes or Mullattoes" after Cornwallis's surrender, a task that no doubt continued the trade in slaves at large personal profit. "After Orders, Oct 25 1781," Orderly Book of Gen. Anthony Wayne, 1781, Huntington Library.

89. "Richard Bennehan's Account with Hart, Benton, and Rochester, 1779–1781," Cameron Family Papers, SHC.

90. Pierce Butler to Morgan Brown, January 24, 1793, in *The Letters of Pierce Butler, 1790–1794: Nation Building and Enterprise in the New American Republic*, ed. Terry Lipscomb (Columbia: University of South Carolina Press, 2007), 226–28.

91. The best single study of the collapse of older planting elites concerns Virginia. Emory G. Evans, *"A Topping People": The Rise and Decline of Virginia's Old Political Elite, 1680–1790* (Charlottesville: University Press of Virginia, 2008).

92. Ross's wealth is detailed in Jackson Turner Main, "The One Hundred," *William and Mary Quarterly* 3rd ser. 11 (1954): 354–84. For Hampton, see Bridwell, "South's Wealthiest Planter."

93. Detailed in Cameron Family Papers, SHC.

94. Lilla M. Hawes, ed., "The Papers of James Jackson, 1781–1798," *Collections of the Georgia Historical Society* 11 (1955).

CHAPTER 13. THE UNITED STATES AND THE TRANSFORMATION OF TRANSATLANTIC MIGRATION DURING THE AGE OF REVOLUTION AND EMANCIPATION

1. David Eltis is one of few historians who examines European and African transatlantic migrations together over long periods of time. See David Eltis, *The Rise of African Slavery in the Americas* (Cambridge: Cambridge University Press, 2000); and David Eltis, ed., *Coerced and Free Migration: Global Perspectives* (Stanford, Calif.: Stanford University Press, 2002). Donna R. Gabaccia, long a scholar of gender and global migration in the nineteenth and twentieth centuries, is now incorporating the early modern Atlantic into her newest work; see her "Spatializing Gender and Migration: The Periodization of Atlantic Studies, 1500 to the Present," *Atlantic Studies* 11, no. 1 (April 2014): 7–27. I am addressing this point in my ongoing book project, tentatively titled "Freedom Advanced, Freedom Limited: Transatlantic Migrations in the Age of Revolution and Emancipation."

2. The above analysis summarizes my argument in Aaron S. Fogleman, "From Slaves, Convicts, and Servants to Free Passengers: The Transformation of Immigration in the Era of the American Revolution," *Journal of American History* 85, no. 1 (June 1998): 43–76. Here, I consider other factors involved that influenced changing migration patterns, but conclude that

the Revolution (with its many components) was the most important. Table 13.1 contains significant adjustments to the table presented in my previous article in two areas: the figures on slaves, based on updates in the Transatlantic Slave Trade Database, Estimates Section (www.slavevoyages.org), and the figures on indentured servants and free passengers for 1700–1775, based on more recent data regarding German-speaking immigrants in Marianne S. Wokeck, *Trade in Strangers: The Beginnings of Mass Migration to North America* (University Park: Pennsylvania State University Press, 1999), 240–76. Neither of these changes affect my overall argument.

3. Fogleman, "From Slaves, Convicts, and Servants." For individual state bans of the transatlantic slave trade, see Woody Holton, *Forced Founders: Indians, Debtors, and Slaves and the Making of the American Revolution in Virginia* (Chapel Hill: University of North Carolina Press, 1999); Hugh Thomas, *The Slave Trade: The Story of the Atlantic Slave Trade, 1440–1870* (New York: Simon & Schuster, 1997), 499–503; and Seymour Drescher, *Abolition: A History of Slavery and Antislavery* (New York: Cambridge University Press, 2009), 115–45. In recent years much has been written about the massive internal slave trade from the Chesapeake to the lower Mississippi Valley and Gulf Coast regions between the Revolution and the Civil War. For the earliest articulation of this shifting planter interest, see Allan Kulikoff, "Uprooted Peoples: Black Migrants in the Age of the American Revolution, 1790–1820," in Ira Berlin and Ronald Hoffman, eds., *Slavery and Freedom in the Age of the American Revolution* (Urbana: University of Illinois Press, 1986), 143–71.

4. A. Roger Ekirch, *Bound for America: The Transportation of British Convicts to the Colonies, 1718–1775* (Oxford: Clarendon Press, 1987); and Gwenda Morgan and Peter Rushton, *Eighteenth-Century Criminal Transportation: The Formation of the Criminal Atlantic* (New York: Palgrave Macmillan, 2004).

5. Fogleman, "From Slaves, Convicts, and Servants"; Hans-Jürgen Grabbe, *Vor der großen Flut: Die europäische Migration in die Vereinigten Staaten von Amerika, 1783–1820* (Stuttgart: Franz Steiner Verlag, 2001); Farley Grubb, *German Immigration and Servitude in America, 1709–1920* (London: Routledge, 2011), 303–71.

6. The impact of revolution on slavery continues to be debated by historians. Those who argue that revolution, including the American Revolution, was important to ending slavery in the Americas (a view that I share) include Robin Blackburn, *The American Crucible: Slavery, Emancipation and Human Rights* (London: Verso, 2013); David Brion Davis, *Inhuman Bondage: The Rise and Fall of Slavery in the New World* (New York: Oxford University Press, 2006); and Christopher Schmidt-Nowara, *Slavery, Freedom, and Abolition in Latin America* (Albuquerque: University of New Mexico Press, 2011). All of these historians stress that slavery flourished and was practically unquestioned on the eve of the age of revolution, yet ended relatively quickly thereafter (in some places more quickly than others). Blackburn argues that, beginning with 1776, revolutions influenced each other and had a cumulative effect beyond their boundaries in the assault on slavery. Davis argues that the American Revolution was important because it created the problem of slavery and a framework for ending it. Schmidt-Nowara argues that the independence movements during the 1810s and 1820s "gravely weakened" slavery in Spanish America. For a view that revolution, especially the American Revolution, had no impact on ending slavery or perhaps even strengthened it, see Drescher, *Abolition*; and Christopher Tomlins, *Freedom Bound: Law, Labor, and Civic Society in Colonizing English America, 1580–1865* (New York: Cambridge University Press, 2010).

7. See Christopher Leslie Brown and Philip D. Morgan, eds., *Arming Slaves: From Classical Times to the Modern Age* (New Haven, Conn.: Yale University Press, 2006), for numerous essays addressing this subject during the wars of independence in the Americas.

8. David Eltis, "Was Abolition of the U.S. and British Slave Trade Significant in the Broader Atlantic Context?" *William and Mary Quarterly* 3rd ser. 66, no. 4 (October 2009): 717–36.

9. All of these calculations are based on information in the Transatlantic Slave Trade Database, Estimates Section.

10. For historians who stress the importance of the American Revolution to the development of abolitionism in Britain, see, for example, Christopher Leslie Brown, *Moral Capital: Foundations of British Abolitionism* (Chapel Hill: University of North Carolina Press, 2006); and Simon Schama, *Rough Crossings: Britain, the Slaves, and the American Revolution* (New York: HarperCollins, 2006). For a view that stresses humanitarian developments within Britain, rather than U.S. influences, see Seymour Drescher, "History's Engines: British Mobilization in the Age of Revolution," *William and Mary Quarterly* 3rd ser. 64, no. 4 (October 2009): 737–56.

11. Schmidt-Nowara, *Slavery, Freedom, and Abolition*, 113–14 and 126 on Peru and Cuba; David Northrup, "Freedom and Indentured Labor in the French Caribbean, 1848–1900," in Eltis, *Coerced and Free Migration*, table 1 (210); Walton Look Lai, *Indentured Labor, Caribbean Sugar: Chinese and Indian Migrants to the British West Indies, 1838–1918* (Baltimore: Johns Hopkins University Press, 1993), tables 5 and 6 (276); David Northrup, *Indentured Labor in the Age of Imperialism, 1834–1922* (New York: Cambridge University Press, 1995), table A.2, 159–61. Chinese immigrants who began arriving in California with the gold rush were voluntary, free immigrants upon arrival. See Ronald Takaki, *A Different Mirror: A History of Multicultural America* (Boston: Little, Brown, 1993), 192–93.

12. Ekirch, *Bound for America*; Morgan and Rushton, *Eighteenth-Century Criminal Transportation*; Schmidt-Nowara, *Slavery, Freedom, and Abolition*, 20; and in Eltis, *Coerced and Free Migration*, see both David Eltis, "Free and Coerced Migrations from the Old World to the New," 33–74, here 74: and Colin Forster, "Convicts: Unwilling Migrants from Britain and France," 259–91, here 282–84.

13. For European immigration in South America, see Walter F. Wilcox, *International Statistics*, vol. 1, *Statistics of Migrations, National Tables* (Cambridge, Mass.: National Bureau of Economic Research, 1929), 539, 549–50, and 566.

14. There is a long list of works that examine European immigration to the United States during the nineteenth century and its causes. For a recent survey, see James M. Bergquist, *Daily Life in Immigrant America, 1820–1870: How the First Great Wave of Immigrants Made Their Way in America* (Chicago: Ivan R. Dee, 2008).

15. For the distinction between societies with slaves and slave societies, see Ira Berlin, *Many Thousands Gone: The First Two Centuries of Slavery in North America* (Cambridge, Mass.: Harvard University Press, 1998), 7–13. See Brown and Morgan, *Arming Slaves*, especially Christopher Leslie Brown, "The Arming of Slaves in Comparative Perspective," 330–53, who provides a thought-provoking comparison of developments in Africa and the Americas.

16. Jennifer L. Morgan, *Laboring Women: Reproduction and Gender in New World Slavery* (Philadelphia: University of Pennsylvania Press, 2004). Joan R. Gundersen, *To Be Useful to the World: Women in Revolutionary America, 1740–1790*, rev. ed. (Chapel Hill: University of North Carolina Press, 2006), 17–43, describes some of the different experiences women had in mobility of all sorts, to include overseas immigration. For global perspectives that include the Atlantic region, see Gabaccia, "Spatializing Gender and Migration."

17. See Morgan, *Laboring Women*, table 1, p. 58; and Eltis, *Rise of African Slavery*, 105–10, and 85–113 for a discussion of the relative absence of European women in transatlantic migrations.

18. For Reynier and Knoll, see Aaron Spencer Fogleman, *Two Troubled Souls: An Eighteenth-Century Couple's Spiritual Journey in the Atlantic World* (Chapel Hill: University of North Carolina Press, 2013). For a thorough discussion of the variety of ways German-speaking women experienced the decision to emigrate to Pennsylvania in the eighteenth century differently than men, see Christine Hucho, *Weiblich und Fremd: Deutschsprachige Einwanderinnen im Pennsylvania des 18. Jahrhunderts* (Frankfurt: Peter Lang, 2002), 66–82. In his study of male and female experiences on the Overland Trail in the United States during the mid-nineteenth century, John Mack Faragher notes that the decision to migrate was made by males dreaming of economic improvement, adventure, and identification. Although migration itself was a family matter, and women were great sources of strength to the traveling parties, they frequently participated only reluctantly in the decision to leave their homes, and they did so because they had accepted the obedient role that marriage imposed. Thus migration in many ways advanced patriarchy and transferred sexual roles to a new environment without changing them. There were important differences, but the length and difficulties of the overland migrations Faragher describes, as well as the permanent change they led to, were not unlike the experiences of European transatlantic migrants. See his *Women and Men on the Overland Trail*, 2nd ed. (New Haven, Conn.: Yale University Press, 2001), esp. 163–78 and 183–87. In her work on early Spanish migrations to the Americas, in which husbands often preceded their wives and children, Ida Altman presents a different view. There were exceptions, she notes, but in her reading of indirect evidence and inferences she concludes that women participated in the decision to emigrate, without coercion or reluctance. See Ida Altman, *Transatlantic Ties in the Spanish Empire: Brihuega, Spain and Puebla, Mexico, 1560–1620* (Stanford, Calif.: Stanford University Press, 2000), 152–54.

19. Morgan, *Laboring Women*. For gender roles in free and forced migrations to the Chesapeake, see Lorena S. Walsh, "The Differential Cultural Impact of Free and Coerced Migration to Colonial America," in Eltis, *Coerced and Free Migration*, 117–51, esp. 135–40.

20. Fogleman, *Two Troubled Souls*.

21. Lois Green Carr and Lorena S. Walsh, "The Planter's Wife: The Experience of White Women in Seventeenth-Century Maryland," *William and Mary Quarterly* 3rd ser. 34, no. 4 (October 1977): 542–71; Mary Beth Norton, "Gender, Crime, and Community in Seventeenth-Century Maryland," in James A. Henretta, Michael Kammen, and Stanley N. Katz, eds., *The Transformation of Early American History: Society, Authority, and Ideology* (New York: Knopf, 1991), 123–50; "Some Account of the Fore Part of the Life of Elizabeth Ashbridge (1755)," in William L. Andrews et al., eds., *Journeys in New Worlds: Early American Women's Narratives* (Madison: University of Wisconsin Press, 1990), 147–70.

22. Davis, *Inhuman Bondage*, 102.

23. See especially the tables in Eltis, *Rise of African Slavery*, 9 and 95; and Eltis, "Free and Coerced Migrations," 62–63.

CHAPTER 14. FIRST PARTITION

1. A study of the U.S.-Mexico border that has particularly influenced what follows is Rachel St. John, *Line in the Sand: A History of the Western U.S.-Mexico Border* (Princeton, N.J.: Princeton University Press, 2011). I have also benefited from Samuel Truett's *Fugitive Landscapes: The Forgotten History of the U.S.-Mexico Borderlands* (New Haven, Conn.: Yale University Press, 2006); and Wendy Brown, *Walled States, Waning Sovereignty* (New York: Zone Books, 2014).

2. On identity papers in early America, John Michael Huffman, "Americans on Paper: Identity and Identification in the American Revolution" (Ph.D. diss., Harvard University, 2013). See also Craig Robertson, *The Passport in America: The History of a Document* (New York: Oxford University Press, 2010); and John Torpey, *The Invention of the Passport: Surveillance, Citizenship, and the State* (Cambridge: Cambridge University Press, 2000).

3. Yair Mintzker, *The Defortification of the German City, 1689–1866* (Cambridge: Cambridge University Press, 2012); and Lewis Mumford, *The City in History* (1961; Harmondsworth: Penguin, 1973), 350.

4. Colonial boundary controversies were, it seems, endless. See, for example, John E. Potter, "The Pennsylvania and Virginia Boundary Controversy," *PMHB* 38 (1914): 407–26; Maj. H. W. Clarke, *Report of the Regent's Boundary Commission upon the New York and Pennsylvania Boundary . . .* (Albany, N.Y.: Weed, Parsons, 1886), 40–67; Marvin Lucian Skaggs, *North Carolina Boundary Disputes Involving Her Southern Line* (Chapel Hill: University of North Carolina Press, 1941); and Louis De Vorsey, Jr., *The Georgia–South Carolina Boundary: A Problem in Historical Geography* (Athens: University of Georgia Press, 1982). Also, Kevin Joel Berland, *The Dividing Line Histories of William Byrd III of Westover* (Chapel Hill: University of North Carolina Press, 2013).

5. "The Internal Slave Trade," July 5, 1852, excerpted in *The Complete Autobiographies of Frederick Douglass* (Radford, Va.: Wilder, 2008), 264. More generally on the Fugitive Slave Act, see Don E. Fehrenbacher and Ward McAfee, *The Slaveholding Republic: An Account of the United States Government's Relations to Slavery* (New York: Oxford University Press, 2001), chaps. 7–8.

6. The definitive treatment of the Christiana Riots is Thomas P. Slaughter, *Bloody Dawn: The Christiana Riot and Racial Violence in the Antebellum North* (New York: Oxford University Press, 1991). On the lengthy constitutional problem presented by slavery, see, for example, David Waldstreicher, *Slavery's Constitution: From Revolution to Ratification* (New York: Hill and Wang, 2009); George William Van Cleve, *A Slaveholder's Union: Slavery, Politics, and the Constitution in the Early American Republic* (Chicago: University of Chicago Press, 2010); Fehrenbacher and McAfee, *The Slaveholding Republic*; Don E. Fehrenbacher, *Slavery, Law, and Politics: The Dred Scott Case in Historical Perspective* (New York: Oxford University Press, 1981); Michael Vorenberg, *Final Freedom: The Civil War, the Abolition of Slavery, and the Thirteenth Amendment* (Cambridge: Cambridge University Press, 2004). Also relevant is Peter B. Knupfer, *The Union as It Is: Constitutional Unionism and Sectional Compromise, 1787–1861* (Chapel Hill: University of North Carolina Press, 1991).

7. Stanley Harrold, *Border War: Fighting over Slavery Before the Civil War* (Chapel Hill: University of North Carolina Press, 2010), 74–76, and more generally on interstate diplomacy across the Mason-Dixon Line, chap. 4.

8. *Narrative of the Life of Frederick Douglass, an American Slave*, ed. John W. Blassingame et al. (New Haven, Conn.: Yale University Press, 2001), 74.

9. Patience Essah, *A House Divided: Slavery and Emancipation in Delaware, 1638–1865* (Charlottesville: University Press of Virginia, 1996), 54–65; and Wilbur H. Siebert, *The Underground Railroad from Slavery to Freedom* (New York: Macmillan, 1898), 53.

10. *The History of Mason and Dixon's Line; Contained in an Address Delivered by John H. B. Latrobe, of Maryland, Before the Historical Society of Pennsylvania* (Philadelphia: Lippincott, Grambo, 1855), 5–7.

11. Edmund Burke, "Speech on a Motion Made in the House of Commons, the 7th of May 1782, for a Committee to Inquire into the State of the Representation of the Commons in

Parliament," in *On Empire, Liberty, and Reform: Speeches and Letters*, ed. David Bromwich (New Haven, Conn.: Yale University Press, 2000), 274. My own perspective on this subject has been influenced by scholars who have emphasized America's plural constitutional traditions. See, for example, Daniel J. Hulsebosch, *Constituting Empire: New York and the Transformation of Constitutionalism in the Atlantic World, 1664–1830* (Chapel Hill: University of North Carolina Press, 2005); Mary Sarah Bilder, *The Transatlantic Constitution: Colonial Legal Culture and the Empire* (Cambridge, Mass.: Harvard University Press, 2004); Jack P. Greene, *The Constitutional Origins of the American Revolution* (Cambridge: Cambridge University Press, 2011); Christian G. Fritz, *American Sovereigns: The People and America's Constitutional Tradition Before the Civil War* (Cambridge: Cambridge University Press, 2008); Larry D. Kramer, *The People Themselves: Popular Constitutionalism and Judicial Review* (New York: Oxford University Press, 2005); Pauline Maier, *Ratification: The People Debate the Constitution, 1787–1788* (New York: Simon and Schuster, 2011); Akhil Reed Amar, *America's Unwritten Constitution: The Precedents and Principles We Live By* (New York: Basic Books, 2012).

12. On the settlement of the lower Delaware, see Bernard Bailyn, *The Barbarous Years: The Peopling of British North America; The Conflict of Civilizations, 1600–1675* (New York: Knopf, 2013), chaps. 8–10.

13. On James's French orientation, in particular, see Steve Pincus, *1688: The First Modern Revolution* (New Haven, Conn.: Yale University Press, 2009), esp. part 2. Also see Owen Stanwood, *The Empire Reformed: English America in the Age of the Glorious Revolution* (Philadelphia: University of Pennsylvania Press, 2011).

14. "The Charter of Maryland: 1632," *The Avalon Project: Documents in Law, History and Diplomacy*, http://avalon.law.yale.edu/17th_century/ma01.asp.

15. "Charter for the Province of Pennsylvania—1681," *Avalon Project*, http://avalon.law.yale.edu/17th_century/pa01.asp.

16. "Report of a conference between Col Talbot and William Penn . . . ," in Clayton Colman Hall, ed., *Narratives of Early Maryland, 1633–1684* (New York: Charles Scribner's Sons, 1910), 442.

17. "A Conference held between the right Honorble the Lord Baltemore Proprietor of Maryland and William Pen Esqre Proprietary of Pensilvania," in Hall, *Narratives*, 426.

18. "The sume and substance of what was argued and spoken by Charles Lord Baltemore and William Penn Esqr at their Private Conference . . . ," in Hall, *Narratives*, 436.

19. On the early phases of the boundary controversy, Aubrey C. Land, *Colonial Maryland: A History* (Millwood, N.Y.: KTO Press, 1981), 80–82; John A. Munroe, *Colonial Delaware: A History* (Millwood, N.Y.: KTO Press, 1978), 79–93; and Charles McLean Andrews, *Colonial Self-Government, 1652–1689* (New York: Harper and Brothers, 1904), chap. 11. For a particularly definitive treatment that covers later chapters in the controversy, see Edward Bennett Mathews, "History of the Boundary Dispute Between the Baltimores and Penns Resulting in the Original Mason and Dixon Line," part 3 of *Report on the Resurvey of the Maryland-Pennsylvania Boundary Part of the Mason and Dixon Line* (Harrisburg, Pa.: State Printer, 1909).

20. William H. Egle, ed., *Pennsylvania Archives*, 2nd ser., vol. 16, *The Breviate: In the Boundary Dispute Between Pennsylvania and Maryland* (Harrisburg: E. K. Meyers, 1890), 743–44, 655.

21. On the Pennsylvania backcountry, see Kevin Kenny, *Peaceable Kingdom Lost: The Paxton Boys and the Destruction of William Penn's Holy Experiment* (New York: Oxford University Press, 2009); James H. Merrell, *Into the American Woods: Negotiators on the Pennsylva-

nia Frontier (New York: Norton, 2000); Jane T. Merritt, *At the Crossroads: Indians and Empires on a Mid-Atlantic Frontier, 1700–1763* (Chapel Hill: University of North Carolina Press, 2003); Peter Silver, *Our Savage Neighbors: How Indian War Transformed Early America* (New York: W. W. Norton & Co., 2008).

22. Alvin Rabushka, *Taxation in Colonial America* (Princeton, N.J.: Princeton University Press, 2008), 648–50; 679–86.

23. Paine to Daniel Clymer, Esq., September 1786, in *The Complete Writings of Thomas Paine*, ed. Philip Foner (New York: Citadel Press, 1945), 2:1256. More generally, see James Weston Livingood, *The Philadelphia-Baltimore Trade Rivalry, 1780–1860* (Harrisburg: Pennsylvania Historical and Museum Commission, 1947).

24. James Veech, *Mason and Dixon's Line: A History* (Pittsburgh: W. S. Haven, 1857), 6.

CHAPTER 15. THE POWER TO BE REBORN

1. Theodore Draper, *A Struggle for Power: The American Revolution* (New York: Times Books, 1996).

2. Eliga H. Gould, *Among the Powers of the Earth: The American Revolution and the Making of a New World Empire* (Cambridge, Mass.: Harvard University Press, 2012).

3. Thomas C. Wright, *Latin America in the Era of the Cuban Revolution*, 2nd ed. (New York: Praeger, 2000).

4. Jack Fruchtman, *The Political Philosophy of Thomas Paine* (Baltimore: Johns Hopkins University Press, 2010), 34.

5. Edmund Burke, *Reflections on the Revolution in France* (London, 1790), 47.

6. See http://www.libertyreborn.com; https://www.facebook.com/pages/The-New-Liberty-Tree-Rebirth-of-America/1122813754908̀43; https://www.oilgasandmining.com/read/editorial/100-taxation-without-representation-or-tea-party-reborn; https://www.hillsdaleforliberty.com/civicrm/contribute/transact?reset=1&id=208&custom_1=1402-11754&custom_2=LP174H.

7. From the *Argus*, "The Echo, No. IV—Truth No. 1," *American Mercury*, (Albany, N.Y.) August 5, 1791, p. 1.

8. "Voice of South Columbian Liberty," *American Watchmen*, June 23, 1810, p. 3.

9. Thomas Fleming, *A Disease in the Public Mind: A New Understanding of Why We Fought the Civil War* (New York: Da Capo Press, 2014), xii–iv.

10. Henry Timrod, "Ethnogenesis," in *The Poems of Henry Timrod* (New York: E. G. Hale & Son, 1872), 103.

11. I have treated all of these in "'We Declare You Independent Whether You Wish It or Not!' The Print Culture of Early Filibusterism," *Proceedings of the American Antiquarian Society* 116, part 2 (2006): 233–60.

12. Michel Ducharme, "Closing the Last Chapter of the Atlantic Revolution: The 1837–38 Rebellions in Upper and Lower Canada," *Proceedings of the American Antiquarian Society* 116, part 2 (2006): 413–30.

13. Sam Watson, "United States Army Officers Fight the 'Patriot War': Responses to Filibustering on the Canadian Frontier, 1837–39," *Journal of the Early Republic* 18 (Fall 1998): 486–87.

14. "The Canadian Rebellion," *Liberator*, April 16, 1847, p. 62.

15. Rev. Cyrus P. Grosvenor, "Canadian Affairs," *Liberator*, December 7, 1838, p. 196. Republished from the *Christian Reflector* (Worcester, Mass.).

16. John Demos, "The Antislavery Movement and the Problem of 'Violent Means,'" *New England Quarterly* 37, no. 4 (December 1964): 501–26.

17. *Liberator*, December 14, 1833, p. 195.

18. The Christology of the abolitionist non-resistors neglected episodes such as whipping and smashing of the tables of the money changers in the Temple.

19. *Liberator*, January 5, 1838, p. 4. Reprint of a handbill entitled "Prophecy" circulating in New York.

20. "Anti-Republican Hatred," *Liberator*, March 30, 1838, p. 51

21. Philanthropist, "The Contrast," *Liberator*, September 28, 1938, p. 154.

22. H. Wilson, "Colored People in Canada," *Liberator*, August 25, 1837, p. 140.

23. David Lee Child, "Slavery: Texas," *Liberator*, April 23, 1836, p. 1. Reprint from the *Quarterly Anti-Slavery Magazine*.

24. "Texas," *Liberator*, April 23, 1836, p. 66.

25. Ibid.

26. "Texas and Canada," *Liberator*, August 11, 1837, p. 130.

27. "The Canadian Rebellion," *Liberator*, April 16, 1847, p. 62.

CONCLUSION

1. Andrew Schocket, "The American Revolution Reborn," *Eventifier*, http://eventifier.com/event/revreborn13.

2. Gordon Wood, "Equality and Social Conflict in the American Revolution," *William and Mary Quarterly* 3rd ser. 51 (1994): 703–16.

3. A lone exception: the barroom quarrel over Wood's scholarship in *Good Will Hunting*.

4. Again, a solitary exception: Newt Gingrich's occasional—and effusive—reference to Wood. See Christopher Tomlins, "Review Essay—The Consumption of History in the Legal Academy: Science and Synthesis, Perils and Prospects," *Journal of Legal Education* 61 (2011): 139–65, 145n36.

5. William Rainey Harper, *The Trend in Higher Education* (Chicago: University of Chicago Press, 1905), 25.

6. On the dominance of those two approaches, see the recent reconnaissance of the historiography in Edward Gray and Jane Kamensky, "Introduction: American Revolutions," in Edward Gray and Jane Kamensky, eds., *The Oxford Handbook of the American Revolution* (New York: Oxford University Press, 2013), 1–11.

7. For lists of the most widely adopted middle school and high school texts in American history, see James Loewen, *Lies My Teacher Told Me: Everything Your American History Teacher Got Wrong*, 2nd ed. (New York: Simon and Schuster, 2007), 435–36; and American Textbook Council (ATC), "Widely Adopted History Textbooks," http://www.historytextbooks.org/adopted.htm, 1–3. The best collection of such texts is at the Gottesman Libraries at Teachers College, Columbia University. I was able to see nine of Loewen's eighteen and four of ATC's eight there. The others were variously not in the collection, checked out, or otherwise unavailable. The ones listed by Loewen that I did not see are Peck, Jantzen, and Rosen; Green, Becker, and Coviello; Bauer; Kownslar and Frizzle; Roden et al.; Appleby, Brinkley, and McPherson; Kennedy, Cohen, and Bailey; Danzer et al.; and Boyer. The ones listed by ATC that I did not see are: Appleby; Appleby; Ayers; and Danzer. I am grateful to Allen Foresta at

the Gottesman Libraries for invaluable assistance in tracking down these textbooks and making them available to me.

8. Thomas Bailey and David Kennedy, *The American Pageant: A History of the Republic*, 7th ed. (Lexington, Mass.: D. C. Heath, 1983), 81; Lewis Todd and Merle Curti, *Triumph of the American Nation*, 9th ed. (Orlando, Fla.: Harcourt Brace Jovanovich, 1986), 120; James West Davidson and Mark Lytle, *The United States: A History of the Republic*, 3rd ed., annotated teacher's ed. (Englewood Cliffs, N.J.: Prentice Hall, 1986), 135–36.

9. John Shy, *A People Numerous and Armed: Reflections on the Military Struggle for American Independence* (New York: Oxford University Press, 1976), 13, 215.

10. Marjoleine Kars, "Opting Out," *Common-place: The Interactive Journal of Early American Life* 14, no. 3 (Spring 2014). See, among many, Kars, *Breaking Loose Together: The Regulator Rebellion in Pre-Revolutionary North Carolina* (Chapel Hill: University of North Carolina Press, 2002); J. M. Bumsted, *Henry Alline, 1748–1784* (Toronto: University of Toronto Press, 1971); Jan Stieverman, "Defining the Limits of Liberty: Pennsylvania's Peace Churches During the Revolution," in Jan Stieverman and Oliver Scheiding, eds., *A Peculiar Mixture: German Language Cultures and Identities in Eighteenth-Century North America* (University Park: Pennsylvania State University Press, 2013); Francis Fox, *Sweet Land of Liberty: The Ordeal of the American Revolution in Northampton County, Pennsylvania* (University Park: Pennsylvania State University Press, 2000); Dee Andrews, *The Methodists and Revolutionary America, 1760–1800: The Shaping of an Evangelical Culture* (Princeton, N.J.: Princeton University Press, 2000).

11. Kars, "Opting Out"; and Patrick Griffin, *American Leviathan: Empire, Nation, and Revolutionary Frontier* (New York: Hill and Wang, 2007), 222–23. See, more generally, Allan Kulikoff, *From British Peasants to Colonial American Farmers* (Chapel Hill: University of North Carolina Press, 2000); and Terry Bouton, *Taming Democracy: "The People," the Founders, and the Troubled End of the American Revolution* (New York: Oxford University Press, 2007).

12. WIN/Gallup International polls results reported in Eric Brown, "In Gallup Poll, the Biggest Threat to World Peace Is . . . America?" *International Business Times*, January 2, 2014.

13. Drew Silver, "Most Members of Congress Have Little Direct Military Experience," www.pewresearch.org/fact-tank/2013/09/04.

14. Nick Palmisciano, "You Are the 0.45%," RangerUp.com, November 3, 2011.

CONTRIBUTORS

Zara Anishanslin is assistant professor of history and art history at the University of Delaware. Her first book, *Portrait of a Woman in Silk: Hidden Histories of the British Atlantic World* is forthcoming from Yale University Press in 2016. Her new project is a material history of the American Revolution.

Mark Boonshoft received his PhD (2015) from Ohio State University and is now a postdoctoral research fellow at the New York Public Library, where he works on the Early American Manuscripts Project. He is the author of "The Litchfield Network: Education, Social Capital, and the Rise and Fall of a Political Dynasty, 1784–1833," which appeared in the *Journal of the Early Republic* in 2014.

Denver Brunsman is associate professor of history at George Washington University. He is the author of *The Evil Necessity: British Naval Impressment in the Eighteenth-Century Atlantic World* (2013) and coeditor (with David J. Silverman) of *The American Revolution Reader* (2013).

Katherine Carté Engel teaches history at Southern Methodist University. She is the author of *Religion and Profit: Moravians in Early America* (2009), and she has published articles in *Church History* and *Early American Studies*. Her current book project, *The Cause of True Religion: International Protestantism and the American Revolution*, chronicles how that conflict transformed Protestantism and the Protestant community in the Atlantic world between 1763 and 1792.

Aaron Spencer Fogleman is presidential research professor at Northern Illinois University, where he has taught early American and Atlantic history since 2002. His books include *Two Troubled Souls: An Eighteenth-Century Couple's Spiritual Journey in the Atlantic World* (2013), *Jesus Is Female: Moravians and Radical Religion in Early America* (2007), and *Hopeful Journeys: German Immigration, Settlement, and Political Culture in Colonial America, 1717–1775* (1996). He has published articles in the *Journal of American History*, *William & Mary Quarterly*, *Historische Anthropologie*, *Atlantic Studies*, and elsewhere. His current book project, tentatively entitled *Freedom Advanced, Freedom Limited: Transatlantic Migrations in the Age of Revolution and Emancipation*, is a comprehensive study of forced and free migrations from Africa and Europe to the Americas.

Travis Glasson, associate professor of history at Temple University, is the author of *Mastering Christianity: Missionary Anglicanism and Slavery in the Atlantic World* (2012). His other publications include articles in the *William and Mary Quarterly* and the *Journal of British Studies*. His current project examines neutrality, disaffection, and divided loyalties around the British Empire during the American Revolution.

Edward G. Gray is professor of history and chair of the department of history at Florida State University. His most recent book is *Tom Paine's Iron Bridge: Building a United States*.

David C. Hsiung, the Charles R. and Shirley A. Knox Professor of History at Juniata College, in Huntingdon, Pennsylvania, is the author of *Two Worlds in the Tennessee Mountains: Exploring the Origins of Appalachian Stereotypes* (1997). His article, "Food, Fuel, and the New England Environment in the War for Independence, 1775–1776," in the *New England Quarterly* (December 2007) won the 2008 Theodore C. Blegen Award from the Forest History Society.

Ned C. Landsman is professor of history at Stony Brook University. His latest work is the chapter on Scotland for the *Oxford Bibliography of the Atlantic World* in *Oxford Bibliographies Online*. He is working on a study of the Anglo-Scottish Union of 1707 and the North American colonies.

Michael A. McDonnell is associate professor of history at the University of Sydney, Australia. He is the author of *The Politics of War: Race, Class, and Conflict in Revolutionary Virginia* (2007), winner of the 2008 NSW Premier's

History Prize, and *Masters of Empire: Great Lakes Indians and the Making of America* (2015), and coeditor of *Remembering the Revolution: Memory, History, and Nation-Making from Independence to the Civil War* (2013). His work was included in the *Best American History Essays 2008*, published by the Organization of American Historians (OAH), and he won the Lester Cappon Prize for the best article published in *William and Mary Quarterly* in 2006. He has received numerous research scholarships and grants in the United States and Australia and has served as a distinguished lecturer for the OAH.

Kimberly Nath is a PhD candidate in American history at the University of Delaware. She is currently completing her dissertation, titled "The British are Coming, Again: The Flight, Return, and Reintegration of Mid-Atlantic Loyalists, 1776–1800."

Bryan Rosenblithe is a PhD candidate in early American and British Atlantic history at Columbia University. He is completing his dissertation, "Peripheral Interests: British Expansion and the Tropical Underpinnings of Imperial Reform, 1758–1773."

David S. Shields is the Carolina Distinguished Professor at the University of South Carolina and the chair of the Carolina Gold Rice Foundation. He publishes monographs in the fields of early American literature and culture, the history of photography, and food studies, most recently *Still: American Silent Motion Picture Photography*, which won the Ray and Pat Browne Award for Best Single Work in American Popular Culture for 2013, and *Southern Provisions: The Creation and Revival of a Cuisine* (2015). The summer 2015 special issue of the *Journal of the Early Republic* is devoted to the five collaborative lectures on the Republican Court that he delivered between 1994 and 2005 with Fredrika Teute.

Patrick Spero is librarian and director of the American Philosophical Society. Previously, he taught history at Williams College. He is a specialist in revolutionary America. He has published numerous articles and review essays on early American history and is the author of *A Frontier Country: The Wars and Politics of Early America* (2016).

Matthew Spooner is a visiting scholar at Harvard University's Hutchins Center and the Margaret Henry Dabney Penick Postdoctoral Fellow in Early

American History at the Smithsonian Institution. He has published on topics including revolutionary violence, the founding of Liberia, Christianity in the slave South, and slavery in the Age of Revolutions. His forthcoming book, *Origins of the Old South: The American Revolution and the Remaking of Southern Slavery*, examines the reconstitution of slave society in the southern United States during the first decades of the early republic.

Aaron Sullivan received his PhD from Temple University in 2014. His research explores political disaffection during the American Revolution and the British occupation of Philadelphia.

Michael Zuckerman is professor emeritus of history at the University of Pennsylvania. His first book, *Peaceable Kingdoms*, helped initiate the (no-longer-) New Social History. His subsequent writings—four more books and over one hundred articles—range widely over such areas as American character, popular culture, and the history of childhood and the family. He has presented papers and lectures on five continents and published in Brazil, China, France, Great Britain, Italy, Japan, the Netherlands, Poland, and Russia.

INDEX

A
abolitionists, 256, 294–99
Adams, John, 48–49, 64, 124–25, 133, 222
Africa. *See also* British Africa: migrations to Americas by category of servitude, 257, 262; migrations to Americas by gender, 262; patriarchy in, 266
African Americans. *See also* slaves: in Canadian rebellions, 296; in merchant marine, 96; in Newport occupation, 42–44; as Pennsylvania farm labor, 287
African colonies, 152, 153, 158–59, 163–65
Alison, Francis, 144–45, 170–71, 177
allegiance: authors' views of, 304; oaths of, 34, 53–54, 72–73
Allen, Stephen, 88–89
Allen, William, 88–89
Almy, Mary, 35
Altman, Ida, 390n18
American colonies. *See also individual colonies*: British impressment in, 86–88; churches in, 114–20, 125–26 (*see also* bishop controversy); diversity across and within, 13; free and unfree migration to, 256–60; jurisdictional ambiguity in, 283–85; as part of multicentered United Kingdom, 107–8, 110, 113, 127 (*see also* imperial authority); political boundaries of, 271; in Revolutionary South (*see* southern colonies); slave trade in, 258; transatlantic migration to, 266, 267
American identity, 51, 69–70, 74, 80–81, 134. *See also* citizenship
Anglo-Scottish union, 108–25, 131; ecclesiastical authority, 114–20; governors and military and customs officers, 123–25; implications for North America, 113; limitations of, 112–13; success of, 108; trading opportunities, 123; universities in, 120–23
Argentina, migration to, 259
Ashbridge, Elizabeth, 265–66

B
Bacon, Anthony, 150, 157–63
Bailyn, Bernard, 306
Baltimore, Lord (Charles Calvert), 280–83
Baltimore, Lord (Frederick Calvert), 285–86
Baltimore, Maryland, 286–87
Barber, Francis, 168–69, 173–74, 182–83
Barber, William, 180
Barnes, John, 162–63
Barton, William, 29–30, 34, 36, 37, 42, 44, 327n1
Baurmeister, Carl Leopold, 335n60
Becker, John P., 18–20, 324–25n23
Bedford, Gunning, 181
Bingham, William, 100
bishop controversy, 132–49, 354n8; background of, 133–35; central meaning of, for Protestants, 143; dissenters in, 133–35, 138–48; as intrusion of politics into Protestantism, 149; and Protestant community of mid-eighteenth century, 136–40
Block, Sharon, 329n30
Bonomi, Patricia, 365n7
borders, 270–72. *See also* Mason-Dixon Line
Boyd, Thomas, 200–202
Bradburn, Douglas, 70
Brazil, 258–61, 267
Britain: Anglo-Scottish union, 108–25; colonies' subordination to, 118; convicts transported to North America by, 255; creation of United Kingdom, 130–31; as multinational state, 110 (*see also* imperial authority); search for natural resources by, 209; slave trade in empire, 258

British Africa, 150–67; Bacon in, 157–63; Canada-Guadeloupe debate, 154–55; and colonial conflict as interimperial contests, 166–67; French claims in, 163–65; Glas' imprisonment and, 165–66; Glas' plan for, 150–51, 157–61; merchant agreements and, 152–57; and parliamentary sovereignty, 166, 167; peace terms, 154–57; Seven Years' War, 151–52, 154
British identity, 70–71
British Parliament: assertion of authority of, 151, 152; authority of, 119, 124, 132; CMTA and, 161, 165; Glas' petition to, 159; merchant agreements, 152–56; and Seven Years' War, 151–52; treatment of colonial conflicts in, 166, 167
Brown, Jeremiah, 218, 228
Brown, Thomas, 235
Bruce, Andrew, 39
Burke, Edmund, 277, 291
burning of towns, 20–21
Burrows, Edwin G., 321–22n10
Butler, Pierce, 246–47

C
Calvert, Charles (Lord Baltimore), 280–83
Calvert family, 285
Calvert, Frederick (Lord Baltimore), 285–86
Canada: loyalists moving to, 71; migration to, 259; Upper and Lower Canada rebellions, 293–99; U.S. border with, 270, 274
Caribbean colonies, 154, 165–67, 255, 258–59
Carp, E. Wayne, 379–80n47
Chandler, Thomas Bradbury, 118–19
Charles II, king of England, 278, 279, 283
Chauncey, Charles, 144, 146
Chernow, Ron, 377n26
Chesapeake colonies, 255, 259, 265, 278
Christie, Ian, 166
citizenship, 68–81; and confiscation of loyalist property, 68–77, 80; defining, 69–70, 80–81; establishing, 70–71; and exile of loyalists, 76–80; oaths of allegiance, 53, 72–73; and treason, 72–74, 80
civil war: Revolution as, 13, 25, 30–31; at sea, 83–84, 104 (*see also* naval impressment)
Civil War, 276; as reborn revolution, 292–93
Clap, Thomas, 141
Claypoole, John, 96–97
Cleveland, Benjamin, 235

Colombia, 261, 292
Connecticut, 117–18, 141, 193–94
Connor, Timothy, 96
constitutionalism, 277–78
Constitution of the United States, 27; and Civil War, 276; as invention of Revolution, 276
Continental Congresses, 26, 59, 181–82, 236–37
convict importations, 251–55, 257, 259, 262, 263, 267, 268
Conway, Henry Seymour, 150, 166, 167
Cooper, William, 208
corporeal reminders of war, 187–93
Cuba, 258–61, 290
Cumming, Thomas, 152–53, 160

D
Dartmouth, Lord (William Legge), 139
Davies, Samuel, 176
Davis, Benjamin, 338n35
Davis, David Brion, 388n6
Davis, Joshua, 92
Dayton, Jonathan, 180–82
deaths during the Revolution, 13–14, 60–61, 321–22n10
Debat, Joseph, 155–56, 164, 3622n53
Declaration of Independence, 83, 129, 290
Delaware, 179–81, 274, 277, 281–84; Mason-Dixon Line, 277, 281–84
denominational schools, 168–83; benefits of, 173–75; curriculum of, 171–72, 174, 175; growth of, 169–71; networks formed at, 175–77; pedagogy of, 172–73; and politicization in advanced education, 177–79; revolutionary leaders from, 179–82
Dewees, Samuel, 322–23n13
Dickinson, John, 133, 170
disaffection, 48–67; causes of, 50; "excommunication" for, 55–56; forms of, 50; motives underlying, 31; "neutrality" vs., 50; and occupation of Philadelphia, 58–66; patriot label of, 24, 25; punishments for, 19–20, 52–56; and saltpeter production, 227; tests of, 51–55; threat from, 50, 56–58, 66
Dixon, Jeremiah, 286
Donahue, Brian, 207
Douglass, Frederick, 273, 274
Dunmore, Lord (John Murray), 234

INDEX

E
Edling, Max M., 226
Eltis, David, 387n1
England. *See also* Britain: seventeenth-century tumult in, 278, 279; slave trade by, 153–54, 156
Enlightenment culture, 171–74, 176
environmental history, 205–30; and composition of saltpeter, 213–15; defining, 206–7; effect of, on Revolutionary War, 208–10; and financial incentives for saltpeter production, 223–25; and low yields of saltpeter, 221–23; and myths about early America, 207–8; and political incentives for saltpeter production, 226–27; saltpeter recipes, 215–21, 228–30; and supply of gunpowder, 210–13; and treatment of resources by American government, 227–28; and war, 205–6
Eve, Oswald, 376n16
Ewald, Johann, 48, 239
Ewer, John, 138
Ewing, John, 177

F
Faragher, John Mack, 390n18
Fatherly, Sarah, 336n3
Fea, John, 368–69n54
Finley, Samuel, 175
Fithian, Philip Vickers, 175–76
Fleming, Thomas, 292
Foster, J., 91
Fox, Ebenezer, 94–95
France: claims in Africa, 153, 163–65; French fleet, 35, 36; and prisoner exchanges, 99–101; revolution in, 292
Franklin, Benjamin, 99–100, 104, 124, 171, 345–46n4
free migrations, 251–54, 258–59. *See also* transatlantic migration; gender differences in, 262–66; to US and other Americas, 266–68
French colonies, 258, 259
Furneaux, Philip, 147
Furstenberg, François, 333n32

G
Gabaccia, Donna R., 387n1
Galloway, Joseph, 335n70
Garrett, Thomas, 274–75
Garrison, William Lloyd, 294–96, 298–99
gender: citizenship and, 71; overland migrations, 390n18; transatlantic migration differences by, 261–68
George III, king of England, 79, 83, 211–13
Georgia: banditti raids, 235–36; British invasion, 238; currency, 242; end of slave trade, 255; human property trade, 243–46; population, 232
Gilmer, George, 223
Glas, George, 150, 157–61, 165–66, 358n1, 362n53
Glauber, Johann Rudolph, 379n43
Gorsuch, Edward, 273
Graham, Walter, 44–45
Grant, James, 64
Graves, Samuel, 209
Graydon, Alexander, 52
Greene, Nathanael, 62–63, 238–39, 335n60, 386n78
Green, James, 384n43
Greenwood, John, 15–17, 92–93
Guerard, Benjamin, 243
Guiana, 258, 259
Gunn, James, 245
gunpowder, 210–13, 378n28. *See also* saltpeter

H
Hahn, Harold, 103–4
Haiti, 258, 260, 261
Haley, Thomas, 98–99
Halifax, Earl of (Sir Francis Wood), 164–66
Hall, David, 180–81
Hämäläinen, Pekka, 207–8
Hampton, Wade, 238, 245, 385n58
Handlman, Christopher, 338n35
Harding, Seth, 82, 102–3
Hardwicke, Earl of (Philip Yorke), 155
Harper, William Rainey, 309
Harrison, Benjamin, 243
Hawrie, John, 243
Henry, Patrick, 234, 385n57
Heustis, Daniel, 298–99
Hewes, George Robert Twelves, 323n16, 324n18
histories of the Revolution, 10–11, 300–318, 322n12. *See also* war stories; acceptance of, 300–301; and attachment to ideals, 316–17; authority of the university, 309–10; conference presenting essays, 305–6; and current attitudes of Americans, 314–15; and current division and

histories of the Revolution (continued)
diffusion, 311–12; framing in, 313; and gulf between academy and popular culture, 309, 311; neo-progressive, 307–9, 312; presented in these essays, 2–6, 312–14, 316; republican synthesis, 306–9, 312; in textbooks, 309–10
Hobart, Noah, 117–18, 349–50n34
Honeyman, James, 42, 43
Honeyman, Quaco, 42–44
Houston, William C., 182
Howe, Robert, 21
Howe, Sir William, 59, 64–65, 72, 335n70
Hutcheson, Francis, 172, 177

I
idealism, 2
ideals, 1, 316–17
imperial authority: Anglo-Scottish union, 108–25; and creation of Britain, 130–31; factors in American incorporation, 126–29; Smith on, 107–8
impressment: by Continental Army and militias, 97; of goods and supplies, 101; by loyalists or British, 22; by patriots, 19, 20; by states, 101–2
indentured servants: transatlantic migration by, 251–59, 262, 263, 265–68

J
Jamaica, 71
James, Duke of York, 278–79
James II, king of England, 278–79, 283
James VI, king of England, 110
Jefferson, Thomas, 83, 129, 219–20, 353n60
Jeremiah, Thomas "Jerry," 234
Jones, John Paul, 16, 100
Juster, Susan, 356n14

K
Kains, John, 387n87
Kammen, Michael, 327n38
Kearsley, Jonathan, 223
Knoll, Maria Barbara, 264, 265

L
Lacey, John, Jr., 60–61
Lardner, Nathaniel, 144, 145
Latrobe, John H. B., 275–76
legitimacy of revolutionary governments, 55–57

Lemisch, Jesse, 340n3
Lenoir, William, 235
Leonard, James, 88–89
Leslie, Alexander, 386n78
liberty, 291–92; and Canadian rebellions, 294–97; and specter of terrorism, 314
Lichtenstein, Elizabeth, 22–23
Livingstone, William, 120–21, 133–34, 227
localism, 26–27, 123
loyalists, 49; British impressment of, 88–89; citizenship and, 70–72, 80; confiscated property of, 68–77, 80, 338n35; deaths among, 14; diaspora of, 71; exile of, 76–80; linking Native American violence to, 191; motives of, 31; in Pennsylvania, 65; percent of colonists as, 22; slaves of, 240; states' attempts to control, 233–35, 239; Stiles' ratings of, 45–46
loyalty oaths, 33, 55
Luttrell, Temple, 85
Lynch, Charles, 219–20, 223, 229
Lyons, Clare, 39

M
Mackenzie, Frederick, 38, 327n1
Main, Jackson Turner, 367n39, 370–71n80
Makemie, Francis, 113–14
Marchant, Stephen, 99–100
Martinique, 153, 154, 258
Maryland: Baltimore, 286–87; conflict with Native peoples, 284; Fugitive Slave Act, 273–75; jurisdictional ambiguity, 283–85, 287; Mason-Dixon Line, 277, 278, 279–83, 285–87; slavery in, 287; tobacco exports, 278; unfree migrations to, 255, 265
Mason, Charles, 286
Mason-Dixon Line, 270–88; and actual location of borders, 279–83; as constitution-free zone, 274; continuing disagreement about, 283–85; emergence of, 278–79; as expression of constitutionalism, 277–78; finalization of, 285–86; and Fugitive Slave Act, 272–75; historical significance of, 275–76, 287–88; and nature of borders, 270–72
Massachusetts, 20, 141, 207, 209, 383n23
material relics of war, 187–89
Mather, Cotton, 114
Mayhew, Jonathan, 138
McCullough, David, 15, 321n6
McNeill, J. R., 209–10

meanings of war for diverse participants, 14, 24–25
memoirs, 323n13, 324–25n23; of non-veteran citizens, 18–21; of those who left United States, 21–24; of veterans, 15–18
Merchant, Carolyn, 377n24
Mexico: end of slavery in, 261; U.S. border with, 270, 274
migration, 251. *See also* transatlantic migration; free and unfree, 251–54; overland, 390n18
Montgomery, James, 101–2
moral philosophy, 122, 172, 177–78
Morris, Robert, 16, 102

N
Nagle, Jacob, 91–92
nationalism, 1, 11, 27, 134, 135
national mythology, 290–92
Native Americans: attention to affairs of, 128–29; deaths among, 14; justifying dispossession of, 190–91, 202; losses due to diseases, 207–8; mid-Atlantic conflicts with, 284; scalping by, 199–200; and Sullivan's campaign, 193–94, 197–99, 202–4; violence by, 190–91, 196, 197, 200, 201
naval impressment, 82–104; by Americans, 82–84, 97–103, 104; of Americans, 82–84, 89, 97; by British, 82–89, 104; British recruiting practices, 102–3; British treatment of captives, 89–90; as "civil war at sea," 83–84, 104; defection of Americans to Royal Navy, 90–97
neo-progressives, 307–9, 312
neutrality of populace. *See also* disaffection: disaffection vs., 50; motives underlying, 31; non-associators/non-jurors, 336n9
Newfoundland, 86–87, 158–59
New Jersey, 121, 179–83, 274, 279
New Netherland, 278–79, 281, 282
Newport occupation, 29–47; capture of Prescott, 29–30, 34, 39–42; end of, 35–36; experiences of African Americans in, 42–44; experiences of Newport women during, 37–42; population decrease during, 33; rebel dominance preceding, 31–34; as refuge for other New England loyalists, 37; and Revolution as a civil war, 30–31; Stiles' diary of, 45–47; and Test Act, 33

New York, 120–21, 383n23
New York City, 20–21, 88, 271
Nicholson, James, 102, 103
North Carolina: currency, 242; disorder and destruction, 238–39; enlistment bounty, 243–44; human property trade, 246; population, 232; "Regulator" movement, 233

O
oaths of allegiance, 34, 53–54, 72–73
Obama, Barack, 321n6
Odle, Mairin, 372n12
office holding, 370n80
O'Hara, Charles, 361n49
Ousterhout, Anne M., 333n16, 339n59
Overing family, 40–41, 44–46
Overing, Henrietta, 39
Overing, Henry, 33, 45, 46
Overing, Mary, 41, 45–46

P
Paine, Thomas, 286–87, 291
Parker, Michael, 200–202
Paterson, William, 182
patriots, 358n4. *See also* revolutionaries; categorization by, 24; deaths among, 13–14; near-failures of, 13; troop quotas for, 236–38; use of slave property by, 240–42
Pennsylvania: citizenship requirements in, 68–81; collapse of state militia, 61–62; college established in, 121; commerce ties to Baltimore, 286–87; conflict with Native peoples, 284; foraging expedition/methods in, 62–64; Fugitive Slave Act and, 273–74; impressment in, 101–2; jurisdictional ambiguity, 283–85, 287; Mason-Dixon Line, 277–83, 285–87; militia participation in, 51, 52, 56, 61; occupation of Philadelphia, 58–66, 68, 72; penalties for perceived dissent in, 52–56; revolutionary leadership of, 52; shifting political affections in, 63–65; Wyoming Valley dispute, 193, 194
Penn, Thomas, 285–86
Penn, William, 279–83
Peru, 258–59
Philadelphia, Pennsylvania: loyalist life and British occupation, 68–81; rights of citizenship in, 68–76; trade, 58–66, 286

Pitt, William, 160, 363n86
Portuguese colonies, 259
Potter, Abel, 41, 44–45, 330n47
Potter, James, 41
Powell, Leven, 235–36
power: to be reborn, 290; conceptions of, 289–90; revolutions and, 169, 289–91
Prescott, Richard, 29–30, 34, 37, 39–42
Prince, Christopher, 90–91
prisoners: classification as rebels vs., 90; defection of, 89–97; escape attempts by, 95; impressment of, 82, 89–93; taken at sea, 98–101; transatlantic migration by, 251–54, 255, 257, 259, 262, 263, 267, 268; treatment of, 14, 34, 89–94, 100
privateering/pirating, 16, 37, 88, 91–93, 97, 99–100, 235, 323n16
Protestantism. *See also* denominational schools: and bishop controversy (*see* bishop controversy); cooperation within, 139–40, 144; dissenting status in, 140–49; Great Awakening, 169; in mid-eighteenth century, 136–40; nation-centric, 149
Puerto Rico, 258

R
Ramsay, David, 11, 238
Rawle, Anna, 76–78
Rawle, Francis, 336n4
Rawle, Peggy, 76–78
Rawle, William, 78, 338n37
Read, George, 181
rebirth, 290, 292, 293, 311, 316. *See also* revolutions
Reed, Joseph, 64, 103
refugees, 14, 23, 35, 325n26
religion, 136–40, 256. *See also* Protestantism
religious liberty, 132–34
republican ideology, 306–9, 312
revolutionaries, 49, 50. *See also* patriots; from denominational schools, 179–82; and need for universal consent, 56–57; in Pennsylvania leadership, 52
revolution(s), 289–99; American Revolution (*see individual topics*); Americans' readiness for, 317; biological metaphors for, 291–93; Canadian, 293–99; Civil War as, 292–93; and liberty, 291–92; patterns predicting, 293; and power, 169, 289–91; slave trade/slavery and, 256, 258, 260, 261; Texan, 297–98

Reynier, Jean-François, 264
Rhode Island, 32; impressment in, 101; independence, 33; Newport occupation, 29–47
Roberts, John, 156
Ross, David, 246
Rush, Benjamin, 175, 228, 378n34
Russell, William, 96

S
saltpeter, 212–30, 379n43, 379n44; composition of, 213–15; incentives for producing, 223–27; recipes for, 215–21, 228–30, 378n33, 378n34
Schmidt-Nowara, Christopher, 388n6
scholarship on the Revolution, 3–4, 302–3, 306, 312. *See also* histories of the Revolution
schools: and Great Awakening (*See* denominational schools); Scottish universities, 120–23
Scotland, 110–11, 353n61. *See also* Anglo-Scottish union
Scottish universities, 120–23
Seabury, Samuel, 130
Shaffer, Arthur, 10–11
Sherlock, Thomas, 141–42
Shoemaker, Edward, 338n37
Shoemaker family, 68–71, 75–80, 338n29
Shoemaker, Rebecca, 68, 69, 75–80
Shoemaker, Samuel, 69, 73–75, 78–80, 338n35, 338n37, 339n53
Shy, John, 49, 312, 321n7, 326n35
Sisson, Jack, 29–30, 42
Sisson, Tosh, 36–37
skin, articles made from, 187–93, 198, 200–204, 371–72n2
Slaughter, Thomas P., 353–54n2
slavery, 231–32; and Canadian rebellions, 294–99; end of, 260; and end of slave trade, 260–61; Fugitive Slave Act, 272–75; impact of revolutions on, 388n6; and Mason Dixon Line, 287; reasons for fighting war over, 292; significance of Mason-Dixon Line for, 275–76; as solution to logistical/material problems, 241; and Texas rebellion, 297–98; transatlantic migration and, 252; United States divided by, 261
slaves: in Caribbean colonies, 258; demand for, 241; intelligence from, 240, 384n49; as

medium of trade, 242–47; in military forces, 238–41, 261; in mines/ironworks, 237; in Newport occupation, 42–44; states' attempts to control, 233–35, 239; stealing of, 235–36; transatlantic migration by, 251–55, 257, 262–64, 266–68

slave trade: continuation of slavery after end of, 260–61; end of, 253, 255, 256, 258, 260–61; by England, 153–54, 156; transatlantic migration and, 252–56

Smith, Adam, 107

Smith, William, 178

South Carolina: banditti raids, 235–36; currency, 242; disorder and destruction, 238–39; end of slave trade, 255; enlistment law, 244; human property trade, 244–46; population, 232, 233; "Regulator" movement, 233

southern colonies, 231–47; currency problems in, 241–42; disorder and destruction in, 238–39; harrassment by British forces, 235–36; inland vs. coastal regions in, 233–35; slaves in military forces, 239–41; social structure of, 232–33; supply of men and materials for troops, 236–38; transfer of human property in, 242–47

Spanish colonies, 158–59, 165–67, 258–61, 267

Stahl, Georg Ernst, 377n25

Stiles, Ezra, 40, 45, 46, 141–49

stories, 9; of the American Revolution, 300–301, 311 (see also war stories); founding stories, 9, 14; in textbooks, 309–10

Stormont, Lord (David Murray), 99

Sullivan, John, 198, 211

Sullivan's Campaign, 187–204; and blame for violence, 191–92; destruction of property in, 197–99; and Indians in national mythology, 190–91; physical mutilation committed during, 199–204; and Luke Swetland, 193–97

Sumter, Thomas, 244, 245

Swetland, Luke, 187–89, 193–97, 200

T

Talbot, John, 351–52n47

Taylor, Alan, 208

Tennent, William, 170

Texan revolution, 297–98

Touchet, Samuel, 152–53, 157–58

Trabue, Daniel, 17, 323–24n17

transatlantic migration, 251–69; to the Americas and Caribbean, 256–60; and ban of slave trade, 260–61; convict importations in, 255; free vs. unfree, 252–54; gender differences in, 261–68; indentured servitude in, 255–56; in mid-nineteenth century, 259–60; slave trade in, 253–56

treason, 72–74, 80, 90, 337n17

U

unfree migrations, 251–54, 258–60. See also transatlantic migration; gender differences in, 262–66; to US and other Americas, 266–68

United States: acceptance of Revolution stories in, 300–301; armed forces, 315; ban on slave trade, 259, 260; belief in power of the state in, 314–15; borders, 270, 274 (see also Mason-Dixon Line); and Canadian rebellions, 294–99; constitutionalism in origin of, 277–78; current attitudes toward revolution, 315; current conditions, 317–18; current sectarian silos, 302; gulf between academy and popular culture, 309; as present counterrevolutionary force in world, 314; readiness for revolution in, 317–18; "societies with slaves" vs. "slave societies" in, 260–61; transatlantic migrations to, 256, 259–61, 266–68

Uruguay, 259

V

Vail, Christopher, 91

Van Buskirk, Judith, 328n23

Venezuela: end of slavery in, 261

Virginia: burning of Norfolk, 21; convict importations, 255; established church, 120; plantation agriculture, 233; tobacco exports, 278; trade in human property, 245, 246; troops from, 236

W

Wallace, James, 32–33

Walpole, Horace, 141–42

war stories, 9–28. See also histories of the Revolution; experiences of diverse participants, 14, 24–25; founding stories, 9, 14, 300–301; historians' telling of, 9–11; meanings of war for diverse participants,

war stories (continued)
  14, 24–25; as means of forgetting the past, 27–28; in memoirs of those who left United States, 21–24; in memoirs of those who stayed in United States, 15–21; more comprehensive/inclusive approach to, 12–14
Washington, George, 21, 59–63, 101, 198, 211, 225, 377n26
Wayne, Anthony, 387n88
Webster, Daniel, 1–2
West Indies, 86, 87, 154–55, 258, 260
Wheelock, Eleazar, 139
Whiting, William, 222, 229, 379n45
Widger, William, 95
Williams, Catherine, 42–43
Witherspoon, John, 172
Wood, Gordon, 307, 370–71n80
Wright, Edward, 24
Wright, James, 245–46
Wright, Sir James, 232
Wright, Thomas, 146

Y

Young, Henry, 337n17

ACKNOWLEDGMENTS

For a long weekend in May 2013, over three hundred people descended on the American Philosophical Society in Philadelphia for the first major conference on the American Revolution in over a decade. The aim of the conference was to reinvigorate the study of the Revolution. By all accounts, it was a smashing success. Scholars and the public spent a long weekend grappling with some of the thorniest issues surrounding the study of the struggle for independence. That conference also served as the genesis of this book. Each of the chapters that comprise this book began as a shorter paper or, in some cases, a provocative, almost off-the-cuff remark at that conference.

Without the support of the many people who helped that conference come to be, the scholarship that the conference has encouraged would not have happened. They all deserve special thanks. First and foremost, Frank Fox gave us the idea to host the conference, and he provided the seed money that brought together a group of scholars and institutions focused on a common purpose: to get people talking about the American Revolution again.

With Frank's support, we began assembling a group of scholars whose expertise would help us discover how to create a compelling conference that could revive a field. We sought a group of leading thinkers whose individual and collective expertise would represent a wide range of approaches to doing history. The people we invited to join us were Kathleen DuVal, Woody Holton, Benjamin Irvin, Brendan McConville, Andrew O'Shaughnessy, and Rosemarie Zagarri. This committee showed a dedication to the cause and a commitment of time that were rare in our busy world. They engaged with us and with each other in long e-mail conversations, several conference calls, and, twice, afternoon-long meetings in person to plan the conference. They reviewed proposals, created panels, identified people to serve as commentators on sessions, and themselves chaired and commented on panels at the conference. Their work made the conference a triumph.

One of the defining features of the conference was its structure. Rather than having presenters read or talk at length about their work, we precirculated condensed versions of their papers and gave our authors a still-shorter time—just eight minutes—to talk about their most provocative findings. That left the better part of each session for audience response. Then, after each such session, we convened a set of senior scholars who commented on the papers and the ensuing discussion and provided further perspectives on the issues they thought the session had raised. Their incisive contributions helped make the conference a success by encouraging wide-ranging conversations that continued in the corridors, during receptions, and on social media. We thank them all: Kathleen Brown, Linda Colley, Edward Countryman, Annette Gordon-Reed, Ed Gray, Christine Heyrman, Li Jianming, Jane Kamensky, Marjoleine Kars, Margaretta Lovell, Barbara Oberg, Marcus Rediker, Thomas Slaughter, Claudio Saunt, David Shields, Alan Taylor, Peter Thompson, Laurel Thatcher Ulrich, and David Waldstreicher.

When it came to putting the conference together, we received a remarkable level of institutional support. The American Philosophical Society, the David Library of the American Revolution, the McNeil Center for Early American Studies, and the Museum of the American Revolution all provided matching funds to enable the conference to realize its potential. The University of Pennsylvania and Williams College also provided generous support.

The success of the events of the conference itself was due to many other friends who helped make everything run smoothly. Boston Beer Company and Bob Pagano, vice president of Brand Development, helped lubricate the informal conversations that wove through the receptions and were often as productive as the questions and answers during formal conference sessions. HISTORY provided free videotaping of the conference. The Library Company of Philadelphia generously hosted a special reception for participants on Friday night. The facilities staff at the American Philosophical Society ensured that everything ran smoothly during the panels. Amy Baxter-Bellamy and Barbara Natello, along with Alicia DeMaio and Emily Merrill, helped staff the conference. The University of Pennsylvania, the McNeil Center, and the Museum of the American Revolution all provided space for parts of the conference. Nicole Scalessa designed the program and website, which were critical to getting word of the conference out.

We also owe a debt of gratitude to a number of people who helped us turn a bunch of short conference papers into this collection. Bob Lockhart at the University of Pennsylvania Press was supportive of the project from the very beginning. He attended the conference, advised us on revising portions for publication, and pushed us across the finish line. Three outside reviewers saved us from making many errors, and their honest criticism forced us to rethink our entire endeavor. They showed us that this book could be more than merely the proceedings of the conference. Their feedback pushed us to think about the project anew, realize its real significance, and point this book toward the fulfillment of Frank Fox's vision.